LEEDS UNITED

The Complete European Record

LEEDS UNITED

The Complete European Record

Martin Jarred and Martin Macdonald

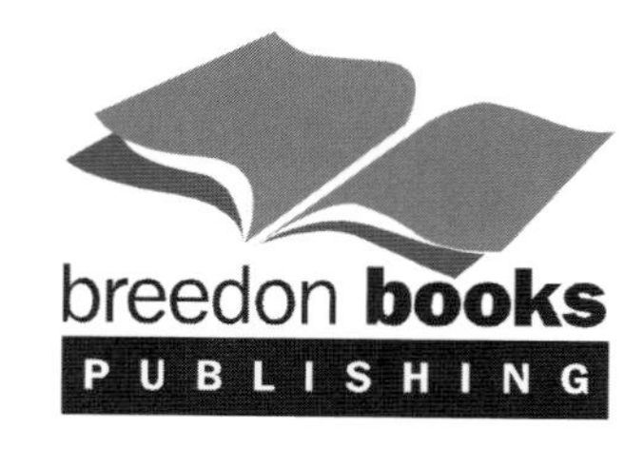

First published in Great Britain in 2003 by
The Breedon Books Publishing Company Limited
Breedon House, 3 The Parker Centre,
Derby, DE21 4SZ.

ISBN 1 85983 373 X

Printed and bound by Butler & Tanner, Frome, Somerset, England.

Cover printing by Lawrence-Allen Colour Printers, Weston-super-Mare, Somerset, England.

Contents

LUFC

Acknowledgements

The authors wish to acknowledge the following:

Association of Football Statisticians (and numerous members), Jenny Jarred, Leeds United FC (for pictures), Isobel Macdonald, UEFA, Rec. Sport Soccer Statistics Foundation, York and County Press, York Reference Library, Yorkshire Post Newspapers (for pictures),

LUFC

Foreword

ELLAND Road has witnessed some fantastic European nights.

Lifting the Fairs Cup in 1971, the European Cup semi-final victory over Barcelona four years later, the heroic comeback against Stuttgart in the Howard Wilkinson era and the 2000/01 squad of David O'Leary which upset all the odds in the Champions League are just some of the highlights.

On the continent there have been equally amazing performances as United became the first British club to lift the Fairs Cup in 1969 when holding Ferecvaros in Budapest, shook mega-rich Lazio in the Olympic Stadium and rang rings round Anderlecht in the Champions League.

Then there are the low points ... the nightmare in Istanbul where two Leeds fans lost their lives, the violence in the aftermath of the 1975 European Cup final defeat in Paris and the Cup Winners' Cup final robbery in Salonika.

They are all here in *Leeds United: A Complete European Record.*

We have put together brief match reports of each competitive game United have play in Europe together with match line-ups of both United and the opposition.

Research has taken many, many years but the advent of the Internet has enabled us to track down missing information so we have been able to plug nearly all the gaps. The website of the Rec.Sport Soccer Statistics Foundation has been a valuable source of information.

The book has been compiled using many different sources which we believe is the most comprehensive and accurate record of Leeds United's campaigns for European honours.

Between us we have attended most of the home games and details have been taken from our own notes as well as programmes, contemporary newspaper and magazine reports, opposition clubs and their supporters

Inevitably there have been difficulties – particularly in presenting the team line-ups.

When United first played in Europe in the glittering Don Revie era, team line-ups were recorded at the time in the following order – goalkeeper, full backs, half-backs and forwards. Shirt numbers in those days reflected the position of the player wearing it.

Gradually, as tactics and formations changed, wing-halves and inside forwards became midfielders, centre-halves were known as central defenders and centre forwards called strikers

Managers would adopt different formations 4-4-2, 5-3-1 etc for different matches. In some cases several different systems were used in the same match.

However, the team that took the field only wore shirts from 1 to 11. United line-ups in this book are in shirt number order until the advent of squad numbers in 1994. Since that year we have given line-ups in this order – goalkeeper, full-backs, central defenders, midfielders, forwards.

We hope that you enjoy reading *Leeds United: A Complete European Record* which we hope should solve a few arguements in the pub.

Hopefully, it will not be too long before United are taking on the cream of Europe once more.

Martin Jarred
Malcolm MacDonald

LUFC

Euro newcomers

JUST before eight o'clock on a miserable, wet dank September night in 1965, Billy Bremner set Leeds United's European bandwagon rolling.

The little Scottish firebrand powered in a shot of wicked trajectory which curved, bent, dipped, swerved and finally went through the grasp of Torino goalkeeper Lido Vieri into the net. Elland Road exploded. Leeds had created their first milestone on a fascinating journey which was to take them to all corners of the continent in search of glory.

Three years earlier the very thought of European football being played at Elland Road was laughable.

The early months under new manager Don Revie, the former England inside forward, were not happy ones as Leeds faced up to the prospect of relegation into Division Three for the first time in the club's history. Only a 3-0 win at Newcastle on the final day of the 1961-62 season guaranteed hard-up Leeds's survival.

With little cash at his disposal, Revie pinned his faith in a burgeoning youth policy and within two years was able to reap the dividends as his young side swept to the Division Two title.

Predications that Leeds would struggle on their return to the top flight in 1964-65 proved false. They showed a will-to-win, magnificent teamwork, fitness and skill, which, allied to Revie's tactical know-how made them a formidable force. Often criticised for a rugged approach, Leeds were hardly the most popular side outside the West Riding but Revie had moulded them into a side to be feared.

It was a remarkable transformation and European football the following season was guaranteed long before the end of the 1964-65 campaign. But in which competition would Leeds make their European bow?

United had a place in the Inter-Cities Fairs Cup in the bag, but they were gunning for a League and FA Cup double. If they could pip arch-rivals Manchester United to the title they would go into the European Cup. But the men from Old Trafford snatched the League championship on goal average.

Five days after seeing the title go to Sir Matt Busby's men, Leeds lost 2-1 in extra-time to Liverpool at rain-lashed Wembley and with it went a place in the European Cup Winners Cup.

That left the Fairs Cup – a competition which Leeds were to dominate for the next few years.

The tournament began in 1955 with the tongue-twisting title of the International Industries Fairs Inter-Cities Cup. It was originally intended for representative sides from cities who annually held trade fairs.

The first competition involved a dozen teams and took three years to complete, Barcelona beating London in a final over two legs.

The idea of entering representative sides from each city soon gave way to the entry of club teams and in 1958 Chelsea represented London and Birmingham City flew the flag for Birmingham.

Barcelona retained their title, beating Birmingham in the final. City were also beaten finalists in 1960-61, losing to Roma.

The competition was growing in stature year by year with an increasing number of clubs taking part. Spanish sides dominated with Valencia winning in 1962 and 1963 but were denied a hat-trick by their fellow countrymen, Real Zaragoza in 1964.

Ferencvaros, the Hungarian side, eliminated Manchester United in the 1965 semi-final, then pulled off a surprise 1-0 win in the final over Italian giants Juventus in Turin.

These top club sides had become well versed in the art of European football over the years, but were about to be joined by an unknown quantity in the shape of Leeds United.

Revie's team were a surprise at home, never mind abroad, but the rookies were to prove quick learners. Title runners-up Leeds and third-placed Chelsea were England's representatives in the 1965-66 Inter-Cities Fairs Cup.

CONSOLATION: Billy Bremner lashes in United's goal against Liverpool in the 1965 FA Cup final at Wembley, but the men from Anfield went on to win the trophy, leaving Championship runners-up Leeds with a place in the Inter-Cities Fairs Cup.

Revie's tactical flanker

MASTER TACTICIAN: Leeds United boss Don Revie.

NO manager paid greater attention to small detail than Leeds supremo Don Revie who even removed the players' billiard table from the Elland Road ground in preference to a table tennis table because he felt it would improve their footwork.

Armed with information from master-spy Maurice Lindley's trip to Italy, this United team stepped out on the rain-lashed Elland Road pitch well prepared for their tough Fairs Cup debut against Torino –

1 Gary Sprake, 2 Paul Reaney, 3 Paul Madeley, 4 Billy Bremner, 5 Jack Charlton, 6 Norman Hunter, 7 Alan Peacock, 8 Bobby Collins, 9 Terry Cooper, 10 Peter Lorimer, 11 Johnny Giles.

The quick-thinking Revie had tried to pull a last-ditch tactical flanker on his opposite number Nereo Rocco, one of the most respected coaches in Italian football.

Five minutes before the kick-off he announced five numerical changes in the United attack to confuse the Italians.

In fact, England international Peacock, despite wearing No 7 played in his usual centre forward's role, former Manchester United man Giles played on the right wing and Cooper on the left wing, leaving the veteran Collins and fellow Scot, 18-year-old Lorimer, in the inside forward berths.

Venables and Graham hammer Roma

Terry Venables

FUTURE Leeds United bosses Terry Venables and George Graham were the goal heroes as Chelsea beat Italian big guns Roma 4-1 in a tough battle at Stamford Bridge.

England international Venables scored a hat-trick with fellow midfielder Graham getting the other goal. Graham's fellow Scot, full-back Eddie McCreadie, was sent off for the Pensioners in an uncompromising match.

First round, first leg

AC Milan 1 (Fortunato), Strasbourg 0
Antwerp 1 (Vandevelde), Glentoran 0
Bordeaux 0, Sporting Lisbon 4 (Figueiredo 2, Oliveira Duarte, Fernando Peres)
Daring Brussels 1 (Randoux), AIK Stockholm 3 (B Carlsson, Nilden, Backman)
Chelsea 4 (Venables 3, Graham), Roma 1 (Barison)
Hibernian 2 (Scott, McNamee), Valencia 0
Leeds United 2 (Bremner, Peacock), Torino 1 (Orlando)
Liege 1 (Demerteau), Dynamo Zagreb 0
Malmo 0, TSV Munich 3 (Rebele, Brunnemeier, Groser)
Nuremberg 1 (Greif), Everton 1 (Harris)
PAOK Salonika 2 (Koudas, Muratidis), SK Vienna 1 (Rafreider)
Red Star Belgrade 0, Fiorentina 4 (Bertini 2, Harnn, Nuti)
Spartak Brno 2 (Chaloupka, Vojta), Lokomotiv Plovdiv 0
Stade Francais 0, Porto 0
Union Luxembourg 0, Cologne 4 (Krallthausen 2, Thielen, Löhr)
Utrecht 0, Barcelona 0

Byes: ***Aris Salonika, Barreriro, Basle, BK Copenhagen, Dunfermline Athletic, Espanyol, Goztepe Izmir, Hanover, Hearts, Lokomotiv Leipzig, Real Zaragoza, Red Flag Brasov, Servette, Shamrock Rovers, Ujpest Doza, Valerengen.***

Plan pays off but tie remains in the balance

Brilliant United off to flying start

MATCHWINNER: Alan Peacock nods in the winner against Torino to get United's Euro campaign off to a winning start.

DON Revie's tactical smokescreen appeared to work in the opening minutes as United forced three corners and a familiar European pattern was soon established – the home team on all-out attack and the away side defending in depth.

Torino, without the injured skipper Giorgio Ferrini in midfield, struggled to get hold on the ball in the early stages as Leeds piled forward from all angles.

All-action Billy Bremner ended 25 minutes of stubborn resistance as he cut in from the left and unleashed a vicious bender which the under-seige keeper could only tip into his own net.

Chances came and went but Leeds added a second just after the interval when Lido Vieri, under pressure from Terry Cooper, palmed a cross from the indefatigible Bremner, to Johnny Giles who headed the ball back into the middle for Alan Peacock to nod it into an empty net.

Peacock, who had been chosen to lead England's attack against Wales

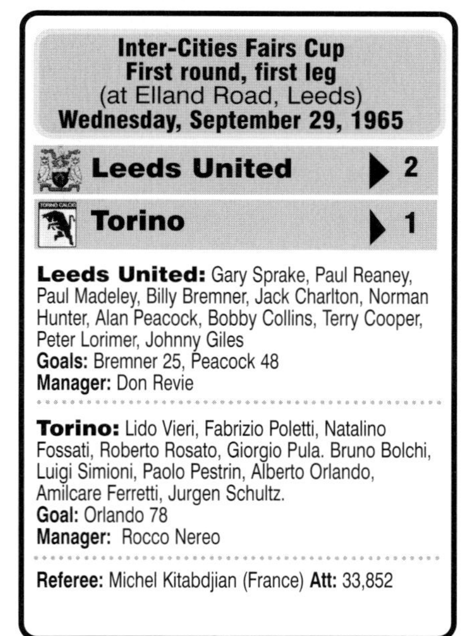

Inter-Cities Fairs Cup
First round, first leg
(at Elland Road, Leeds)
Wednesday, September 29, 1965

Leeds United	2
Torino	1

Leeds United: Gary Sprake, Paul Reaney, Paul Madeley, Billy Bremner, Jack Charlton, Norman Hunter, Alan Peacock, Bobby Collins, Terry Cooper, Peter Lorimer, Johnny Giles
Goals: Bremner 25, Peacock 48
Manager: Don Revie

Torino: Lido Vieri, Fabrizio Poletti, Natalino Fossati, Roberto Rosato, Giorgio Pula. Bruno Bolchi, Luigi Simioni, Paolo Pestrin, Alberto Orlando, Amilcare Ferretti, Jurgen Schultz.
Goal: Orlando 78
Manager: Rocco Nereo

Referee: Michel Kitabdjian (France) **Att:** 33,852

the following Saturday, had the 33,852 crowd on its feet again with a close range shot, but French referee Michel Kitabdjian ruled the effort had not crossed the line. Kitabdjian was to cross United's path in even more controversial circumstances in the European Cup final 10 years later, but on this occasion kept a firm grip on a high-speed game dishing out bookings for Bremner and Italians Bruno Bolchi and Amilcare Ferretti.

Leeds were 2-0 up and pressing for a killer third when Torino scored with a rapid counter-attack 12 minutes from the end. Cooper, who was still finding his way into the first team as a left winger, lost the ball in a tackle to Fabrizio Poletti, who quickly pumped the ball forward. Alberto Orlando was on the ball in an instant, squeezing a shot past Gary Sprake and the lunging Paul Reaney on the line.

The 2-1 scoreline flattered Torino and Revie purred: "The team has never played better since I became manager at Elland Road. They were splendid in their skill and determination."

Torino's players returned to their Queen's Hotel base in City Square knowing their goal had given them a good chance of pulling back the deficit on home soil.

Collins tragedy

...but United defy the odds

First round, second leg

ROMA were banned from the Fairs Cup for three years after their fans stoned the Chelsea bus with the players on board outside the Flaminio Stadium.

Chelsea drew 0-0 to go through and were joined by Everton who beat Nuremburg with a Jimmy Gabriel goal at Goodison Park.

Scottish side Hibernian went out on a play-off against Valencia – later to face Leeds.

AIK Stockholm 0, Daring Brussels 0 *AIK win 3-1 on agg*
Barcelona 7 (Verges, Zaldúa 4, Vicente, Pereda), Utrecht 1 (van der Linden) *Barcelona won 7-1 on agg*
Cologne 13 (Thielen 4, Lohr 3, Overath 2, Neumann 2, Weber, Muller), Union Luxembourg 0. *Cologne won 17-0 on agg*
Dynamo Zagreb 2 (Vaha, Azimovic), Liege 0. *Zagreb won 2-1 on agg*
Everton 1 (Gabriel), Nuremburg 0 *Everton won 2-1 on agg*
Fiorentina 3 (Hamrin, Pirovano, Brugnera), Red Star Belgrade 1 (Milosevic). *Fiorentina won 7-1 on agg*
Glentoran 3 (Thompson 2, Hamilton), Antwerp 3 (Segers, van Moer, Vandevelde) *Antwerp won 4-3 on agg*
Lokomotiv Plovdiv 1 (Kanchev), Spartak Brno 0 *Spartak Brno won 2-1 on agg*
Porto 1 (Manuel Antonio), Stade Francais 0. *Porto won 1-0 on agg*
Valencia 2 (Waldo, Sanchez Lage), Hibernian 0. *Play off: Valencia 3 (Munoz 2, Guillot), Hibernian 0*
Roma 0, Chelsea 0 *Chelsea won 4-1 on agg*
SK Vienna 6 (Hot 4, Gayer 2), PAOK Salonika 0. *SK Vienna won 7-2 on agg*
Sporting Lisbon 6 (Lourenco 2, Fernando Peres, Oliveira Duarte, Figueiredo, Ferreira Pinto), Bordeaux 1 (Abossolo) *Sporting Lisbon won 10-1 on agg*
Strasbourg 2 (Hauss pen, Fanas), AC Milan 1 (Bemgm) *Agg 2-2. Play-off: AC Milan 1 (Augelillo), Strasbourg 1 (Szczpaniak) AC Milan won on draw of lots*
TSV Munich 4 (Brunnemeier, Heiss, Groser, Rebele), Malmo 0. *Munich won 7-0 on agg*

UNITED had learned a lesson about concentration in that first leg against Torino and were soon to learn another in Italy – that continental opposition can be uncompromising.

Revie opted to field the same Leeds side which had performed so well at Elland Road, but his meticulous preparations were thwarted. The United party and fans who had paid £26 for the round trip air excursion to Turin were delayed at Leeds/Bradford Airport by fog for five hours. The patience United showed in their long airport wait was also put to the test by some sharp Italian tackling.

Shortly after half-time a challenge by Fabrizio Poletti left little Bobby Collins prostrate on the pitch. The inspirational 34-year-old Scot's thigh-bone had been shattered. The experience, passing skills and leadership of the veteran Collins, a £25,000 snip from Everton, had help lift United out of the Second Division and earned him the 1965 Footballer of the Year award. Such an appalling injury cast doubts over the long-term future of Collins' career, but United faced a short-term problem. The age of the substitute had not yet arrived so Leeds had to play the last 40 minutes with 10 men.

CAPTAIN COURAGEOUS: Skipper and Footballer of the Year Bobby Collins, who broke a thighbone in Turin.

As Collins was whisked away wrapped in Revie's raincoat to the Maria Vittoria Hospital in Turin, United's defence closed ranks to keep Torino out. Jack Charlton and Norman Hunter were superb as the Torino attackers simply bounced off them. An early miss from just three yards by Orlando was as close as Torino got as United turned in an epic defensive performance.

Proud Revie said: "They all worked like Trojans to make up for having lost Bobby. The way they tackled the job proved beyond all doubt what tremendous professionals they were."

Supreme skill was also shown by surgeon Professor Carlo Re who pieced Collins' thigh back together in an hour-long operation. Doctors declared that he would be able to play again, but it would be a long, hard, lonely road on the journey to full fitness.

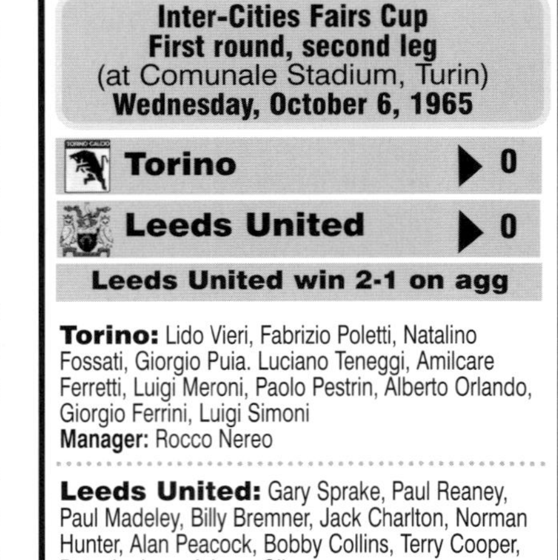

Inter-Cities Fairs Cup
First round, second leg
(at Comunale Stadium, Turin)
Wednesday, October 6, 1965

Torino	**0**
Leeds United	**0**

Leeds United win 2-1 on agg

Torino: Lido Vieri, Fabrizio Poletti, Natalino Fossati, Giorgio Puia. Luciano Teneggi, Amilcare Ferretti, Luigi Meroni, Paolo Pestrin, Alberto Orlando, Giorgio Ferrini, Luigi Simoni
Manager: Rocco Nereo

Leeds United: Gary Sprake, Paul Reaney, Paul Madeley, Billy Bremner, Jack Charlton, Norman Hunter, Alan Peacock, Bobby Collins, Terry Cooper, Peter Lorimer, Johnny Giles
Manager: Don Revie

Referee: Piet Roomer (Holland) **Att:** 26,000

Inter-Cities Fairs Cup
Second round, first leg
(at Zentral Stadium, Leipzig)
Wednesday, November 24, 1965

Locomotiv Leipzig 1

Leeds United 2

Lokomotiv Leipzig: Horst Weigang, Michael Faber, Peter Giessner, Claus Pfeufer, Hans-Jurgen Naumann, Manfred Geisler, Dieter Englehardt, Rainer Trolitzsch, Henning Frenzel, Arno Zerbe, Wolfram Lowe.
Goal: Frenzel 83
Manager: Gunter Konzack

Leeds United: Gary Sprake, Paul Reaney, Willie Bell, Billy Bremner, Jack Charlton, Norman Hunter, Jim Storrie, Paul Madeley, Peter Lorimer, Johnny Giles,Mike O'Grady
Goals: Lorimer 80, Bremner 81
Manager: Don Revie

Referee: Anton Buchelli (Switzerland) **Att:** 8,000

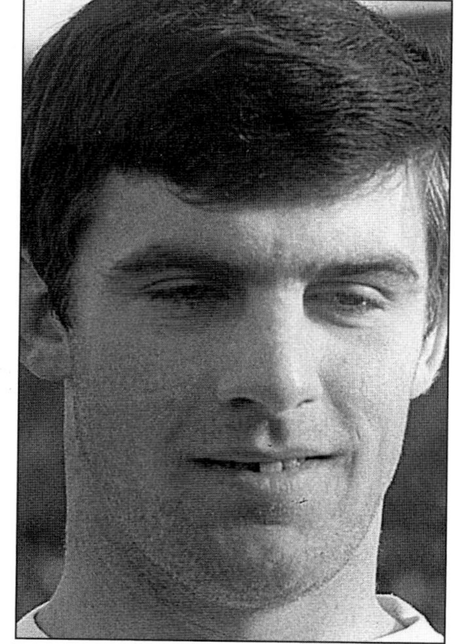

DOUBLE SCOTS: Billy Bremner (left) and Peter Lorimer (right), who were on target in the victory in bitterly cold Leipzig.

United keep cool

THE atmosphere had been red hot in Turin but in Leipzig it was ice cold. United's second round East German opponents' were struggling to get their snow-covered pitch ready as the bitter temparatures sent the mercury below freezing point.

Leipzig warmed up with a special match against a local club, Thveringe, while Don Revie took one look at the Germans' pitch and declared: "In the conditions I will be glad of a draw."

The Arctic weather was braved by only 8,000 souls and many of them had returned frost-bitten to their homes before the match warmed up with a flurry of goals in the final minutes.

Swiss referee Marcel Buchell gave the game the go-ahead and Leeds stepped gingerly onto the icy pitch with a much changed side to the one which got past Torino. With Bobby Collins out for virtually the rest of the season, Revie brought in Willie Bell at left back and switched Paul Madeley to midfield. Alan Peacock was out with hamstring trouble so experienced Scot Jim Storrie was brought into the attack. Finally, Terry Cooper's place on the left wing went to Mike O'Grady, Revie's new signing from Huddersfield.

Bremner and Lorimer turn up heat on Germans

United's line-up carried no out and out centre forward, but after five minutes of cat and mouse, little Billy Bremner was switched from his usual wing half position to lead the front line, nipping in and out of the burly German defenders like a little terrier.

It seemed the match would end goal-less, but it burst into life in the last 10 minutes. Youngster Peter Lorimer collected O'Grady's cross 10 minutes from the end and clubbed home a 15-yard shot.

From the re-start, United stole possession and full back Klaus Pfeufer miscued the ball on the slippery surface and the ball looped into the air. Lorimer calmly headed the ball back for Bremner to head the ball over defender Michael Faber on the line.

The rapid one-two had Leipzig on the ropes, but they produced a counter punch of their own within a minute as Henning Frenzel escaped the attention of Jack Charlton for the only time to shoot past Gary Sprake.

SCOTTISH side Dunfermline Athletic turned on the style to thrash Bold Klub Copenhagen 5-0 at East End Park.

Hearts also recorded a 1-0 home victory over Norwegian side Valerengen, but there was little joy for Everton, who were whipped 3-0 in Hungary by Ujpest Doza.

England's other representatives, Chelsea, went down 1-0 in Austria to SK Vienna.

Irish outfit Shamrock Rovers pulled off one of their greatest results, holding Spanish side Real Zaragoza 1-1 in Ireland.

Second Round, first leg

AIK Stockholm 2 (B Carlsson, Eriksson), Servette 1 (Schindelholz)
Antwerp 2 (van der Wee, Segers), Barcelona 1 (Rife)
Aris Salonika 2 (Fillipou 2), Cologne 1 (Sturm)
Barreriro 2 (Oliveira, Abelroado pen), AC Milan 0
Basle 1 (Hausser), Valencia 3 (Waldo 2, Munoz)
Dunfermline 5 (Fleming, Robertson, Paton 2, Callaghan), BK Copenhagen 0
Dynamo Zagreb 2 (Bubanj 2), Red Flag Brasov 2 (Goran, Neftanaila)
Fiorentina 2 (De Sisti, Hamrin), Spartak Brno 0
Goztepe Izmir 2 (Cengiz, Ertan), TSV Munich 1 (Konietzka)
Hannover 5 (Rodekamp, Siemensmayer 2, Bandura, Nix), Porto 0
Hearts 1 (Wallace), Valerengen 0
Lokomotive Leipzig 1 (Frenzel), Leeds United 2 (Lorimer, Bremner)
Shamrock Rovers 1 (Tuohy), Real Zaragoza 1 (Reija)
SK Vienna 1 (Gayer pen), Chelsea 0
Sporting Lisbon 2 (Duarte, Lourenco), Espanyol 1 (Miralles)
Ujpest Doza 3 (Solymosi, Bene, Kuharszki), Everton 0

Pitching in for victory

MATCHWINNER: Leipzig goalkeeper Horst Weingang flies through the air to punch the ball clear at snow-covered Elland Road.

UNITED returned to West Yorkshire to discover that the block of cold air which had Europe in its icy grip had taken hold of Elland Road.

United were forced to call off their big League clash with Manchester United because the Elland Road pitch was frozen and the race was on to get the pitch fit.

As Leeds went into cold storage for the weekend, Leipzig had a confidence -boosting 3-1 win over East German Cup winners Magdeburg to go top of their League.

Although Leipzig trailed 2-1 after the first leg they knew a single goal win would force a play-off in a neutral country as the 'away goals count double' rule had yet to be introduced.

United's main goal was simply to get the game on. Under the command of United director Bob Roberts, a local building contractor, 80 volunteers cleared snow and ice from the pitch and terraces while burning braziers helped soften the pitch. The fans who rushed to United's aid were rewarded with fish-and-chip suppers but they almost saw their side digest a rare home defeat.

The Germans, who had been training at the near-by Elland Road dog track, saw their crisp first-time passing and neat ball skills having United floundering on the slippery surface with Wolfram Loewe hitting a post early on.

Although the Leipzig build-up was brilliant, their finishing was weak and Leeds were able to escape with a goalless draw and a 2-1 aggregate victory.

United had few chances themselves with Lorimer missing the best opportunity – a header from an O'Grady cross. It proved to be Alan Peacock's last European outing for Leeds. Blighted by cartilage trouble, he went to Plymouth Argyle in October 1967.

The match had another footnote. After the game there were complaints from the German camp that some of United's players had nails sticking out of their boot studs – a charge strenuously denied by Revie who branded it "diabolically rude" of their visitors to make such an accusation.

The complaint was made by forward Rainer Trolitzch to the referee at half-time after he and several of his team-mates pick up cuts and abrasions. But referee Adriaan Boogaerts made no approach to the United dressing room, revealed Revie, who said the explanation was that the German injuries had been caused by ice on the pitch.

Inter-Cities Fairs Cup
Second round, second leg
(at Elland Road, Leeds)
Wednesday, December 1, 1965

Leeds United 0
Locomotiv Leipzig 0
Leeds United win 2-1 on agg

Leeds United: Gary Sprake, Paul Reaney, Willie Bell, Billy Bremner, Jack Charlton, Norman Hunter, Jim Storrie, Peter Lorimer, Alan Peacock, Johnny Giles, Mike O'Grady
Manager: Don Revie

Locomotiv Leipzig: Horst Weingang, Michael Faber, Peter Giessner, Claus Pfeufer, Hans-Jurgen Naumann, Manfred Geisler, Dieter Englehardt, Rainer Trolitzsch, Henning Frenzel, Arno Zerbe, Wolfram Lowe
Manager: Gunter Konzack

Referee: Adriaan Bogaerts (Holland) **Att:** 32,111

Milan scrape through

ITALIAN giants AC Milan overturned a 2-0 deficit in the San Siro to force a play-off against Portuguese side Setubal which they won with a goal by Lodetti.

First-half goals by Bert Murray and Peter Osgood gave Chelsea a 2-0 win over Weiner SK to edge in to the third round 2-1 on aggregate, while Everton went out to Ujpest Doza, from Hungary.

Second round, second leg

AC Milan 2 (Sormani pen, Angelillo), Barreriro 0 *Agg score 2-2. Play-off AC Milan 1 (Lodetti), CUF Setubal 0 in Milan*

Barcelona 2 (Rifé, Zaballa), Antwerp 0 *Barcelona won 3-2 on agg*

Chelsea 2 (Murray, Osgood) SK Vienna 0 *Chelsea won 2-1 on agg*

Cologne 2 (Thielen 2), Aris Salonika 0 *Cologne win 3-2 on agg*

Copenhagen 2 (Petersen, Andersen), Dunfermline 4 (Edwards, Paton, Fleming, Ferguson) *Dunfermline won 9-2 on agg*

Espaynol 4 (Rodilla 2, Miralles, José Maria), Sporting Lisbon 3 (Lourenco, Figueiredo, Duarte) *Agg score 5-5 .*
Play-off: Espanyol 2 (Rodilla 2), Sporting Lisbon 1 (Lourenco) in Barcelona

Everton 2 (Harris, Nosko og), Ujpest Doza 1 (Kuharszki) *Ujpest Doza win 4-2 on agg*

Leeds United 0, Lokomotiv Leipzig 0 *Leeds won on 2-1 on agg*

Porto 2 (Manuel Antonio, Custodio Pinto), Hannover 1 (Bena 43) *Hannover win 6-2 on agg*

Real Zaragoza 2 (Santos, Canario), Shamrock Rovers 1 (Fullam) Real *Zaragosa win 3-2 on agg*

Red Flag Brashov 1(Hasoti), Dynamo Zagreb 0 *Reg Flag Brasov won 2-1 on agg*

Servette 4 (Nemeth, Daina, Makay, G Bjorn), AIK Stockholm 1 (Erikisson) *Servette win 5-3 on agg*

Spartak Brno 4 (Hradsky 2, Lichtnegl 2), Fiorentina 0 *Spartak Brno won 4-2 on agg*

TSV Munich 9 (Rebele 3, Konietzka 3, Luttrop, Heiss, Radenkovic), Goztepe Izmir 1 (Ertan Oznur) *TSV Munich win 10-3 on agg*

Valencia 5 (Waldo 2, Urtiaga, Muñoz, Guillot), Basle 1 (Benthaus) *Valencia win 8-2 on agg*

Valerengen 1 (Knudsen), Hearts 3 (Kerrigan 2, Traynor) *Hearts win 4-1 on agg*

LEEDS UNITED 1965/66: This United squad was the first to represent Leeds in Europe. Back row, from left to right: Billy Bremner, Willie Bell, Paul Madeley, Gary Sprake, Paul Reaney, Norman Hunter, Jimmy Greenhoff. Front row, from left to right: Don Weston, Terry Cooper, Johnny Giles, Jim Storrie, Alan Peacock, Bobby Collins, Jack Charlton and Albert Johanneson.

United we stand

IF a football popularity contest was held in 1966 then Leeds United would have finished somewhere near the bottom. Their critics, particularly the London-based press were quick to label them methodical and ruthless.

But as far as Elland Road fans were concerned, Don Revie's mixture of youth and experience was delivering rare, and overdue, success.

United had little to shout about since their formation in 1920 with just a Division Two Championship to their name in 1923-24 and three other promotions from that division.

But Revie had built a team to last and after sweeping to the Second Division title in 1963-64 they came desperately close to the Championship and FA Cup double the following season.

Veteran Scottish international Bobby Collins was an inspirational leader and it was around his midfield pocket general that Revie's well-oiled football machine revolved. The defence was particularly formidable with young Welsh international goalkeeper Gary Sprake well protected by the outstanding half-back line of Billy Bremner, Jack Charlton and Norman Hunter, who figured in all 11 Fairs Cup matches United played in their maiden Euro campaign. Club stalwart Charlton, awesome in the air, developed into one of England finest post-War centre halves and was joined in the 1966 World Cup squad by the young Hunter, whose tackling was outstanding.

Bremner, another who had shot up through the youth ranks, was maturing from a Scottish firebrand into one of the most complete players of the era.

Reliability was the name of right back Paul Reaney, who was usually partnered by either Willie Bell, a Scottish international, or Leeds-born Paul Madeley, who was rapidly developing a reputation for his ability to play in a variety of positions.

Johnny Giles, a £35,000 steal from Manchester United, was one of the few men Revie had paid money for. Initially a winger, he later assumed Collins' midfield mantle after the Scot failed fully to recover from his shattering thigh injury in Torino.

At £53,000, centre forward Alan Peacock was the most expensive player in the squad. Although he scored on a regular basis since his arrival from Middlesbrough he did suffer badly from injuries.

That paved the way for Revie to introduce more youngsters in attack like Peter Lorimer, Jimmy Greenhoff and young wingers Terry Cooper and Eddie Gray before the £30,000 purchase of Huddersfield winger Mike O'Grady, a Leeds-born player.

There was also flying South African winger Albert Johanneson and Jim Storrie whose goals had done much to lift United out of Division Two.

Inter-Cities Fairs Cup
Third round, first leg
(at Elland Road, Leeds)
Wednesday, February 2, 1966

	**Leeds United**	
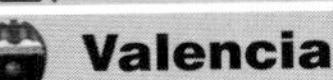	**Valencia**	

Leeds United: Gary Sprake, Paul Reaney, Willie Bell, Billy Bremner, Jack Charlton, Norman Hunter, Jim Storrie, Peter Lorimer, Rod Belfitt, Johnny Giles, Mike O'Grady
Goal: Lorimer 65
Manager: Don Revie

Valencia: Rivero 'Nito', Alberto Arnal, Francisco Vidagany, 'Roberto' Gil Esteve, Manuel Mestre, Francisco Garcia 'Paquito', Vicente Guillot, Jose Palau, Valentin Garcia Pascual 'Toto', Jose Maria Sanchez Lage, Juan Munoz
Goal: Munoz 17
Manager: Sabino Berinaga

Referee: Leo Horn (Holland) **Att:** 34,414

Off! Off!

Mass brawl leads to madness on night

THE Leipzig spat paled into insignificance after United's third round opponents, the Spanish side Valencia, had finished playing at Elland Road.

The opening third round game was dubbed 'The Battle of Elland Road' as the game resembled a bull-fight rather than a football match.

Police had to separate fighting players, three men were sent off and the referee took the sides off for 11 minutes to cool down.

It was one of European football's blackest nights. Valencia's pedigree in the Inter Cities Fairs Cup was impressive. Winners in 1962 and 1963, beaten finalists in 1964, they seemed hell-bent of lifting the trophy for a third time.

On the way to meeting United they had eliminated Scottish side Hibernian after a third meeting in Basle and were renowned for their tough defence.

United's hopes of puncturing that defence had been dashed by the absence of Alan Peacock with twisted knee ligaments, so Revie drafted in 19-year-old Rod Belfitt, a former draughtsman, for his first taste of European football.

It was to prove an unpalatable experience for the Doncaster-born youngster as he took a tremendous hammering from the Spanish defence.

The tone of the match was set in the opening minute when United's iron-man defender Norman Hunter brought down Sanchez-Lage. From that moment the Spaniards seemed to want to take retribution and the catalogue of fouls, shirt-pulling and niggle mounted as Dutch referee Leo Horn took a lenient view.

Little football was played and Valencia cashed in on an uncharacteristic error in United's back-line after

MAYHEM: Jack Charlton is restrained by referee Leo Van Horn after being kicked by Valencia defender Vidagany.

San Siro late show by Graham lifts Chelsea

GEORGE Graham's late headed goal gave Chelsea a lifeline as they lost 2-1 against AC Milan in the San Siro.

The Italians had fielded weakened sides in the early rounds and had received plenty of criticism from their own supporters for failing to take the Fairs Cup tournament seriously.

They only got past moderate French side Strasbourg on the toss of a coin and needed an extra match to see off Portuguese side Setubal in the first two rounds.

But they were deadly serious against the Londoners. Despite missing a penalty, Milan went 2-0 up with five minutes left with a goal from Gianni Rivera, the golden boy of Italian football, and it looked black for Chelsea, but Graham's goal changed the complexion of the tie.

Dunfermline and Hearts continued to battle on for Scotland.

Hearts were held 3-3 at Tynecastle by slick Spanish side Real Zaragoza, whose star-studded forward line twinkled, while Dunfermline defeated Czech outfit Spartak Brno through Bert Paton and an Alex Ferguson penalty.

Third round, first leg

AC Milan 2 (Amarildo, Rivera), Chelsea 1 (Graham)
Cologne 3 (Lohr 2, Sturm), Ujpest Dozsa 2 (Gorocs, Solymosi)
Dunfermline 2 (Paton, Ferguson pen), Spartak Brno 0
Espanyol 3 (Amas 3), Red Flag Brashov 1 (Zaharia)
Hannover 2 (Siemensmeyer 2), Barcelona 1 (Zaldua)
Hearts 3 (Anderson, Wallace, Kerrigan), Real Zaragoza 3 (Lapetra 2, Enderiz)
Leeds United 1 (Lorimer), Valencia 1 (Munoz)
Servette 1 (Daina), TSV Munich1 (Konietzka)

Off!

red card of shame

17 minutes to take the lead. Hunter and Paul Reaney dithered over a harmless ball and Juan Munoz darted between the pair to round Gary Sprake with ease.

Valencia withdrew in to their shell to build a wall of nine red shirts in their own area to keep United out at any cost. Trouble was never far from the surface.

Mike O'Grady's cross-shot scraped the woodwork, Nito saved superbly from Peter Lorimer and Jim Storrie saw a header cleared off the line. United's patience was wearing thin at their inability to crack the tough Spanish defence when young Lorimer grabbed the equaliser after 66 minutes, volleying in after a neat run and centre from Johnny Giles.

Tension on the pitch finally snapped with 15 minutes to go. Charlton challenged Nito for the ball at the Elland Road Scratching Shed end and the keeper lashed out at the centre half. Immediately a posse of Valencia players surrounded Big Jack, who was kicked by Francisco Vidagany.

That sparked a mass brawl which referee Horn could not stop. About a dozen police officers and officials ran onto the field to pull apart the fighting players and the only way Horn could restore order was to take off the teams.

The cooling off period lasted 11 minutes and when the teams re-emerged each were a man short – Charlton and Vidagany having been sent off. The atmosphere remained highly-charged and it was no surprise that Sanchez-Lage was ordered off with eight minutes left after bringing down Storrie.

RED CARD: Jack Charlton became the first Leeds player to be sent off in Europe with his dismissal against Valencia.

War of words breaks out

AS soon as the whistle sounded the end of the battle, the war of words began.

Leeds boss Don Revie snapped: "If this is European football I nearly think we are better off out of it. Charlton would have to be a saint not to retaliate."

Valencia manager, Sabino Berinaga, the former Real Madrid inside forward, lay the blame at United's door. "Leeds started it with that first minute foul by Hunter. They then lost their heads when we scored first".

About the only thing the clubs did agree on was the weak display of the referee whom they felt shold have acted much earlier to nip the trouble in the bud.

Charlton, who ran at least 30 yards to boot Vidagany up the backside after the Spaniard had kicked the irate Geordie defender, was later fined £50 and severely censured by the FA.

But Charlton was able to play in the return leg at the Mestalla Stadium where United knew they would have to produce something out of the ordinary in a white-hot atmosphere to progress to the quarter-finals.

Coming of age

O'Grady's winner shatters Spaniards

AT 1-1 the odds were firmly on Valencia to go through and United morale was none too high after just being knocked out of the FA Cup by Chelsea.

Despite that shattering defeat at Stamford Bridge, Don Revie reckoned his men had given one of their best-ever displays and opted to field the same side in Valencia. At Chelsea, play-anywhere star Paul Madeley had worn the No 9 shirt but had been used very successfully to blot out Chelsea's new rising star forward Peter Osgood.

Revie, knowing his side was likely to come under intense pressure in Spain, stuck to the same formation. Chelsea, who were also going well in the Fairs Cup.

There was immense speculation that the game in Valencia would be another savage encounter, but Leeds remained cool, calm and collected as they heeded Revie's pre-match words of wisdom. "I will not give any special pep talk to my boys. I will merely tell then to go out and play like they did at Chelsea. My only reference to a fortnight ago will be to tell them to keep it out of their minds."

Leeds, sporting yellow jerseys and blue shorts, followed Revie's instructions to the letter, turning in a magnificent rearguard action. Charlton overpowered the threat of star Brazilian forward Waldo and although Valencia had the lion's share of possession found the Leeds defence in superb form with Welsh international keeper Gary Sprake an unbeatable last line of defence.

UNBEATABLE: Gary Sprake plucks the ball out of the air despite the presence of Valencia's Brazilian striker Waldo.

The game turned United's way after a series of incidents about 20 minutes from the end. Valencia were beoming more and more anxious as time began to slip away and suffered twice in a minute as Vicente Guillot grazed the bar from 10 yards then slapped a shot against a post.

As Valencia were still cursing their luck, United fashioned a killer goal that had 'Made in Leeds' stamped all over it. Leeds-born Madeley broke the Valencia offside trap and Mike O'Grady, another local lad, powered past two defenders and shot past Nito. The 'keeper and left back Toto were convinced O'Grady was offside and raced up to one of the linesmen to grab his flag out of his hand. Swiss referee Othmar Huber waved away their protests and deep down, Valencia, without a win in their last 10 Spanish League games, knew they were heading out of Europe.

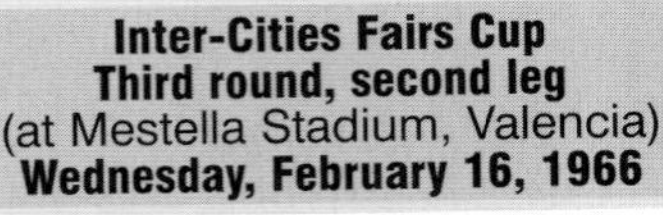

Inter-Cities Fairs Cup
Third round, second leg
(at Mestella Stadium, Valencia)
Wednesday, February 16, 1966

Valencia

0

Leeds United

1

Leeds United win 2-1 on agg

Valencia: Rivero 'Nito', Garcia Verdugo, Valentin Garcia Pascal 'Toto', 'Roberto' Gil Esteve, Manuel Mestre, Francisco Garcia 'Paquito', Manuel Poliario, Jose Maria Sanchez Lage, 'Waldo' Machado da Silva, Vicente Huillot, Juan Munoz
Manager: Sabino Berinaga

Leeds United: Gary Sprake, Paul Reaney, Willie Bell, Billy Bremner, Jack Charlton, Norman Hunter, Jim Storrie, Peter Lorimer, Paul Madeley, Johnny Giles, Mike O'Grady
Goal: O'Grady 75
Manager: Don Revie

Referee: Othmar Huber (Switzerland) **Att:** 45,000

Pensioners' progress

CHELSEA went through on the toss of a coin after a third game failed to resolve their tie with AC Milan.

Their 2-1 victory at Stamford Bridge ensured the tie finished 3-3 on aggregate. Chelsea appeared to be on the way to victory in the third game in Italy until Milan equalised with a controversial last-gasp equaliser by Fortunato.

It was one of four ties decided by play-offs, one of them seeing Hearts go out to Real Zaragoza.

Zaragoza were joined by Barcelona and Espanyol as Spain's three representatives in the last eight.

Rapidly maturing United were drawn with Hungarian side Ujpest Doza.

Third Round, second leg

Barcelona 1 (Fuste), Hannover 0 *Agg score 2-2. Play-off Hannover 1 (Bandura), Barcelona 1 (Pujol) in Hannover. Barcelona won on lots*

Chelsea 2 (Graham, Osgood), AC Milan 1 (Sormani) *Agg score 3-3. Play-off: AC Milan 1 (Fortunato), Chelsea 1 (Bridges) in Milan. Chelsea won on lots*

Real Zaragoza 2 (Santos, Marcelino), Hearts 2 (Anderson, Wallace) *Agg score 5-5. Play-off Real Zaragoza 1 (Marcelino), Hearts 0 in Zaragoza*

Red Flag Brashov 4 (Ivanescu 2 , Pescaru, Goran), Espanyol 2 (Martinez, José Maria) *Agg score 5-5. Play-off Espanyol 1 (Re), Red Flag Brashov 0 in Brashov*

Spartak Brno 0, Dunfermline 0 *Dunfermline win 2-0 on agg*

TSV Munich 4 (Konietzka, Grosser, Brunnenmeier 2), Servette 1 (Georgy) *TSV Munich win 5-2 on agg*

Valencia 0, Leeds United 1 (O'Grady) *Leeds won 2-1 on agg*

Ujpest Dozsa 4 (A Dunai, Bene 2, Kuharszki), Cologne 0 *Ujpest Doza won 6-3 on agg*

DOG COLLARED: A bobble-hatted fan (left) attempts to catch the runaway pooch which proved too nippy for United defender Jack Charlton (right).

United's tails up

United put bite on dogged Hungarians

WHAT was expected to be a close encounter against the Hungarians turned out to be a one-sided affair as United rose to the occasion in Europe to turn on a blistering attacking display.

Ujpest sank 4-1 in the mud, three of United's goals coming in a spell-binding eight-minute period before the interval.

Several of the Hungarian players were to catch the eye in the magnificent balmy summer of England's 1966 World Cup, but on a rain-lashed March night in Leeds they simply could not live with United. Pools of water stood on the pitch, but the United players just seemed to skim over them. Leeds were literally walking on water.

Just six minutes had gone when left winger Terry Cooper swept the ball into the net after Willie Bell's low drive had been parried by Anatal Szentmihalyi.

Leeds poured forward. Jim Storrie had a header disallowed for offside, while Johnny Giles and Billy Bremner directed operations from midfield.

United were attacking down every conceivable avenue and the only ally Ujpest could find came in the shape of a small black dog which trotted on to the muddy field. The game was stopped for 10 minutes by referee Gerhard Schulenburg as around 50 officials tried to catch the elusive mutt. The pantomime finally ended when the fugitive pooch leapt onto a concrete wall and disappeared into the boys' pen.

Would the dog break United's momentum? No. Leeds were straining at the leash. For the remainder of the first half they treated the ball like a dog with a bone – no one else was going to get a piece of it.

Ujpest hardly saw the ball as United produced a magical goal-scoring spell. On 35 minutes Bell headed in Lorimer's centre, Storrie back-headed the third after a sparkling piece of wing trickery by O'Grady, who cut through the defence for Bremner to walk in United's fourth goal.

It was scintillating stuff, but Ujpest reshaped their side after the break with Ferenc Bene, tipped by many to be the new Puskas, switching to the wing to provide more width and balance.

It helped take the sting out of United's play and Ujpest were rewarded for their persistence with a late goal, prodded in by Antal Dunai after Sprake could not hold a fierce shot from Erno Solymosi.

Inter-Cities Fairs Cup
Quarter-final, first leg
(at Elland Road, Leeds)
Wednesday, March 2, 1966

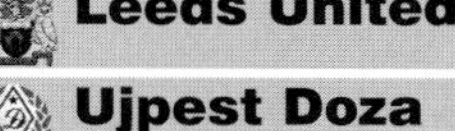

Leeds United 4

Ujpest Doza 1

Leeds United: Gary Sprake, Paul Reaney, Willie Bell, Billy Bremner, Jack Charlton, Norman Hunter, Mike O'Grady, Peter Lorimer, Jim Storrie, Johnny Giles, Terry Cooper
Goals: Cooper 7, Bell 35, Storrie 42, Bremner 43
Manager: Don Revie

Ujpest Doza: Antal Szentmihalyi, Beno Kaposzta, Kalman Sovari, Erno Solymosi, Matyas Csordas, Erno Nosko, Bela Kuharszki, Janos Gorocs, Ferenc Bene, Antal Dunai, Sandor Zambo
Goal: Dunai 74
Manager: Sandor Balogh

Referee: Gerhard Schulenburg (West Germany)
Att: 40,462

Barcelona edge home

ALFREDO Di Stefano, the legendary Real Madrid maestro turned out at centre forward for Espanyol in the all-Spanish quarter-final at Barcelona.

The match at the Nou Camp Stadium was won 1-0 by Barca thanks to a goal by Benitez.

Two opportunist goals by Bobby Tambling gave Chelsea a 2-2 draw at TSV Munich, who had lost to West Ham in the final of the Cup Winners Cup the previous year.

Quarter-final, first leg

Barcelona 1 (Benitez), Espanyol 0
Dunfermline 1 (Paton), Real Zaragoza 0
Leeds United 4 (Cooper, Bell, Storrie, Bremner), Ujpest Doza 1 (A Dunai)
TSV Munich 2 (Kohlars, Konietzka) Chelsea 2 (Tambling 2)

Semi-finals here we come as...

United hold firm

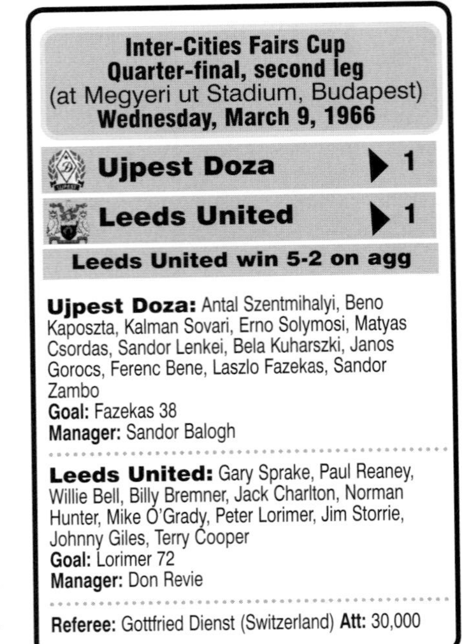

Inter-Cities Fairs Cup
Quarter-final, second leg
(at Megyeri ut Stadium, Budapest)
Wednesday, March 9, 1966

Ujpest Doza	**1**
Leeds United	**1**

Leeds United win 5-2 on agg

Ujpest Doza: Antal Szentmihalyi, Beno Kaposzta, Kalman Sovari, Erno Solymosi, Matyas Csordas, Sandor Lenkei, Bela Kuharszki, Janos Gorocs, Ferenc Bene, Laszlo Fazekas, Sandor Zambo
Goal: Fazekas 38
Manager: Sandor Balogh

Leeds United: Gary Sprake, Paul Reaney, Willie Bell, Billy Bremner, Jack Charlton, Norman Hunter, Mike O'Grady, Peter Lorimer, Jim Storrie, Johnny Giles, Terry Cooper
Goal: Lorimer 72
Manager: Don Revie

Referee: Gottfried Dienst (Switzerland) **Att:** 30,000

THE 4-1 home victory meant United were almost as good as through but they were given a rough ride in Budapest where their defence was given a thorough examination by Ujpest's crafty attackers.

Having already played 40 games during the season, Don Revie took a 'softly, softly' approach to the game, light walks by the banks of the Danube replacing the fiendish training sessions devised by Les Cocker.

United packed their defence around the towering figure of Jack Charlton who had another marvellous match. He repelled raid after raid as Ujpest attacked frantically from the first whistle, prompting Revie to compare the hosts with the Mighty Magyars of 1953.

United's massed defence was on the rack but prevented Ujpest from grabbing an early goal and held on until the 38th minute when Gary Sprake could only knock down Erno Solymosi's rasping free kick and Laszlo Fazekas rolled in the loose ball.

It was vital that United did not conceded another before half time and it needed a brilliant save by Sprake to prevent Ferenc Bene making it 2-0 on the night and cutting United's aggregate lead to a single goal.

Leeds were gradually edging along the tightrope towards the semi-finals but needed Paul Reaney to pull off a miraculous double goal-line clearance after Fazekas hit the bar.

Leeds gained further breathing space when Sandor Zambo went down in the area, but appeals for a penalty were turned down. The tremendous effort the Hungarian team were putting in began to tell in the final quarter as they began to fade.

United, quick to sense that Ujpest minds and limbs were beginning to tire, broke out of defence with deadly venom to equalise after 73 minutes. Mike O'Grady, in a rich vein of form for his club, fed Peter Lorimer, who showing remarkable coolness for a 19-year-old dummied his way past defender Matyas Csordas and cracked in the equaliser which ended Ujpest's brave fight.

United's 5-2 aggregate win captured the imagination of the Leeds public who were enjoying their first sample of European soccer. On their arrival, United received a 'Beatles-style' reception as about a thousand fans flocked to Leeds/Bradford Airport to welcome home their heroes. Roads were so clogged up to the airport entrance that United's coach had to make its getaway to Elland Road via a back route.

IN GOOD HANDS: Goalkeeper Gary Sprake, who had a fine game in Budapest, clutches the ball.

Brave Scots out

DUNFERMLINE'S great European adventure ended in glorious failure at Real Zaragoza, going out 4-3 on aggregate after extra-time in Spain.

Peter Osgood's goal against TSV Munich ensured Chelsea would join Leeds in the semi-finals

Quarter-final, second leg

Ujpest Doza 1 (Fazekas), Leeds United 1 (Lorimer) *Leeds won 5-2 on agg*

Chelsea 1 (Osgood), TSV Munich 0 *Chelsea won 3-2 on agg*

Espanyol 0, Barcelona 1 (Vidal) *Barcelona won 2-0 on agg*

Real Zaragoza 4 (Villa 2, Santos, Marcelino), Dunfermline 2 (Ferguson, Lunn) *Zaragoza won 4-3 on agg after extra-time.*

England's standard bearers

IT was England v Spain in the semi-finals. United met Real Zaragosa and Chelsea were paired with mighty Barcelona.

The prospect of an all-English final between two of the Football League's big rivals was something to savour, but the flag of St George was about to be lowered.

While United went down in Zaragoza, ultra-defensive Chelsea crashed 2-0 to Barcelona in another rugged game the Nou Camp Stadium to goals by Jose Maria Fuste and Jose Antonio Zaldua, the second coming a minute from the end.

Semi-final, first leg

Real Zaragoza 1 (Lapetra), Leeds United 0
Barcelona 2 (Fuste, Zaldua), Chelsea 0

DEBUT DUO: Eddie Gray (left) and Jimmy Greenhoff, who, along with Albert Johanneson, were given their European debuts in the semi-final in Zaragoza.

Spain reigns

THE first leg of the Fairs Cup semi-final was played in the La Romerada Stadium and Don Revie gave plenty of thought to his line-up as the United party touched down at a U.S. airfield on the outskirts of Zaragoza.

On board the chartered aircraft was United's midfield general Bobby Collins, who was back in training after his terrible injury in Turin. But he was still not considered fit enough by Revie to return. However European debuts went to three players – Albert Johannesson, Jimmy Greenhoff and Eddie Gray – as Revie reshaped his attack.

Johannesson, a greyhound of a winger from South Africa, had struggled to find his form after the FA Cup final defeat against Liverpool. He was always a nervous character and seemed to freeze on the big day and took months to return to his peak. He came in for young Terry Cooper on the left wing, while on the opposite flank Barnsley-born Jimmy Greenhoff took over from the injured Mike O'Grady.

The third newcomer, 18-year-old Eddie Gray, who had only made his League debut three months earlier, came in for another Scottish youngster, Peter Lorimer, who was showing signs of tiredness in recent weeks.

Although Revie's side looked inexperienced in attack, the defence looked formidable with the Bremner-Charlton-Hunter axis at half back acknowledge as one of the best in Europe. United's game against Valencia had been a bruising affair and Zaragosa proved to be in the same mould as trainer Les Cocker was on the pitch three times in the opening 10 minutes to tend to Jim Storrie, Willie Bell and Johnny Giles. Zaragoza whose attack were known throughout Spain as 'The Famous Five" found Jack Charlton a towering obstacle while Gary Sprake's safe handing kept scares to a minimum.

Marcelino smacked one shot against a post, but the goal came with the hour approaching when Billy Bremner handled a goal-bound header from Isasi. Sprake almost saved Carlos Lapetra's penalty as he pushed the shot against an upright before it crossed the line.

After that Leeds soaked up pressure and the match seemed to be drifting aimlessly towards its conclusion when Giles and Jose Luis Violetta were sent off five minutes from time after a dust-up.

Both players retired to their respective dug-outs, only to be pursued by French referee Marcel Bois, who shooed them away down the tunnel.

United would have settled for a 1-0 defeat before the kick off and Revie was confident his men would overturn the deficit at Elland Road the following week.

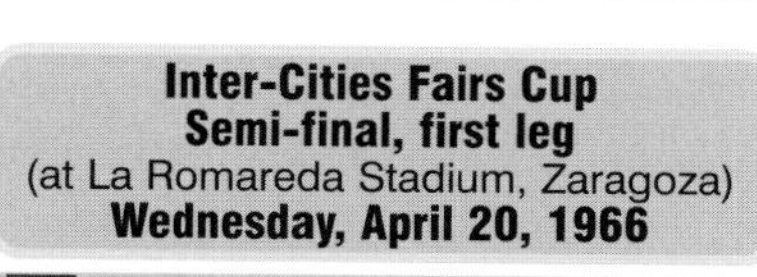

Inter-Cities Fairs Cup
Semi-final, first leg
(at La Romareda Stadium, Zaragoza)
Wednesday, April 20, 1966

Real Zaragoza	**1**
Leeds United	**0**

Real Zaragoza: Enrique Yarza, Jose Ramon Irusquieta, Santiago 'Isasi' Salazar, Antonio 'Pais' Castroagudin, Francisco Santamaria, Jose Luis Violetta, Darcy Silveira dos Santos 'Canario', 'Santos' Brito, 'Marcelino' Martinez Cao, Juan Manuel Villa, Carlos Lapetra
Goal: Lapetra pen 59
Manager: Fernando Daucik

Leeds United: Gary Sprake, Paul Reaney, Willie Bell, Billy Bremner, Jack Charlton, Norman Hunter, Jimmy Greenhoff, Eddie Gray, Jim Storrie, Johnny Giles. Albert Johanneson
Manager: Don Revie

Referee: Marcel Bois (France) **Att:** 35,000

OPENING GOAL: Jack Charlton's header fell to Albert Johanneson (above) who was able to stab the ball past Zaragoza goalkeeper Jose Maria Goicoechea.

Over the blue moon

YORKSHIRE grit against Spanish skills provided a clash of styles in the semi-final at Elland Road.

Zaragoza dominated the opening 20 minutes and should have wrapped the tie up but for three missed chances by Santos.

But the pendulum swing towards Leeds when Norman Hunter's pass picked out Willie Bell, who laid the ball square from the left for Johnny Giles to lob the ball into the box. Jack Charlton, a constant menance to Zaragosa in the air, headed down and Albert Johannesson, virtually on the line, kicked the ball in.

The complexion of the match changed. Bremner and Jim Storrie's running began to worry the Spaniards, Bell headed against a post then just failed by a bootlace to touch in another Charlton header.

With time on their side, United were looking a good bet for a second goal and a place in the final.

But Elland Road's 45,008 crowd was stunned into silence midway through the second half when Canario sent a superb half volley flying past Gary Sprake.

Zaragoza and their star-studded attack were now in the driving seat, but their spell at the wheel lasted just three minutes as Charlton did what he had threatened to do all night – score with a header.

Big Jack spent most of the rest of the game causing havoc in Zaragosa's box, but the well-drilled Spanish defence hung on. Indeed, had Sprake not made a great smothering save to deny Carlos Lapetra at the death, then United's dreams of reaching a European final at the first attempt would have lay in ruins.

The game had finished 2-2 on aggregate and the teams tossed a coloured disc – red on one side, blue on the other – to determine which club would stage the third game. Charlton correctly called blue and Don Revie leapt into his big skipper's arms with delight, knowing his skipper had earned Leeds a vital edge.

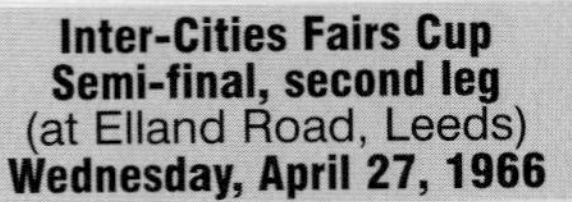

Inter-Cities Fairs Cup
Semi-final, second leg
(at Elland Road, Leeds)
Wednesday, April 27, 1966

Leeds United ▶ 2

Real Zaragoza ▶ 1

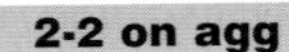

2-2 on agg

Leeds United: Gary Sprake, Paul Reaney, Willie Bell, Billy Bremner, Jack Charlton, Norman Hunter, Jimmy Greenhoff, Eddie Gray, Jim Storrie, Johnny Giles, Albert Johanneson
Goals: Johanneson 22, Charlton 65
Manager: Don Revie

Real Zaragoza: Jose Maria Goicoechea, Jose Irusquieta, Sanatiago 'Isasi' Salazar, Antonio 'Pais' Castrogudin, Francisco Santamaria, Jose Luis Violettta, Darcy Silveira Dos Santos 'Canario'. Santos Brito, 'Marcelino' Martinez Cao, Juan Manuel Villa, Carlos Lapetra
Goal: Canario 62
Manager: Fernando Daucik

Referee: Piet Roomer (Holland) **Att:** 45,008

Extra-time at the double

BOTH Fairs Cup semi-finals went in to an extra match.

While United were battling with Zaragoza in a tight game at Elland Road, Chelsea managed to pull back a 2-0 deficit against Barcelona at Stamford Bridge.

The Blues were helped by the 40th minute dismissal of Eladio and took the tie to a play-off thanks to two own-goals in the last 20 minutes.

Semi-final, second leg

Leeds United 2 (Johanneson, Charlton), Real Zaragosa 1 (Canario) *Agg 2-2.*

Chelsea 2 (Torres og, Reina og), Barcelona 0 *Agg 2-2*

Replay wrangle

England's friendly puts back play-off date

INTERNATIONAL DUO: United defenders Norman Hunter and Jack Charlton were required for England duty by Alf Ramsey.

ORIGINALLY United's Fairs Cup semi-final play-off match was scheduled for Tuesday, May 3 – six days after the Elland Road clash.

But that date was scrapped because England manager Alf Ramsey wanted Jack Charlton and Norman Hunter to play against Yugoslavia the following night at Wembley.

With the World Cup just weeks away it was regarded as an important match by the FA.

United immediately told the Fairs Cup Committee, which discussed the matter in Switzerland, and after getting agreement from Zaragoza, the match was to be played on Wednesday, May 11.

Ironically, when Ramsey had named the original 22 for the Yugoslavia match he had omitted Liverpool's candidates because they were due to play Borussia Dortmund in the European Cup Winners' Cup Final at Hampden Park the day after the England international.

Both Hunter and Charlton played against the Slavs at Wembley in front of 55,000 – England winning with goals from Big Jack's brother, Bobby, and Jimmy Greaves in a team skippered by Blackpool full-back Jimmy Armfield, who was later to manage the Leeds team to the European Cup final.

Chelsea's play-off with Barcelona was put back even further, a fortnight after the third United v Zaragoza match. That was scheduled to be played in Spain as Tommy Docherty's side had lost the flip of a disc to decide who would stage their play-off.

United's play-off against Zaragoza came four days after Revie's men notched up their fourth successive League victory with a 1-0 victory at Burnley, courtesy of an Alex Elder own-goal.

Although they were to lose at Newcastle and drew their final match at Old Trafford against Manchester United, Leeds finished runners-up to Liverpool and knew they would be playing in the Fairs Cup again next season.

But would they resume in the competition as holders? The third confrontation against the talented Spaniards from Zaragoza would soon provide the answer.

Zaragoza the

Stunning Spaniards

Inter-Cities Fairs Cup
Semi-final, play-off
(at Elland Road, Leeds)
Wednesday, May 11, 1966

Leeds United		1
Real Zaragoza		3

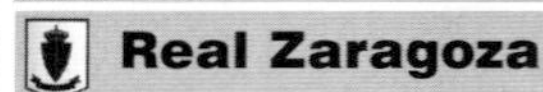

Zaragoza qualify for final

Leeds United: Gary Sprake, Paul Reaney, Willie Bell, Billy Bremner, Jack Charlton, Norman Hunter, Jimmy Greenhoff, Peter Lorimer, Jim Storrie, Johnny Giles, Mike O'Grady
Goal: Charlton 79
Manager: Don Revie

Real Zaragoza: Enrique Yarza, Jose Irusquieta, Severino Reija, Antonio 'Pais' Castrogudin, Francisco Santamaria, Jose Luis Violetta, Darcy Silveira Dos Santos 'Canario', Santos Brito, 'Marcelino' Martinez Cao, Juan Manuel Villa, Carlos Lapetra
Goals: Marcelino 1, Villa 5, Santos 14
Manager: Fernando Daucik

Referee: Hans Carlsson (Sweden) **Att:** 43,046

HOPES of an all-English Fairs Cup final were blown away by a Spanish one-two.

Inside the first quarter of an hour at Elland Road, the brilliant Zaragoza attack tore United's normally iron defence to shreds. It was the night the "Magnificent Five" as Zaragosa's front men were known, lived up to their awesome reputation.

Meanwhile, Chelsea, succumbed to Barcelona as the English fleet were sunk by the Spanish Armarda.

United fans were stunned after just 54 seconds when Juan Manuel Villa prised open United's back-line and his pass across the face of the goal was rammed in by for Marcelino to score.

It was a sweet moment for the 25-year-old Spanish international centre forward who had been sent off in a 4-1 Spanish Cup win at Sabadell at the weekend.

Leeds barely had time to digest that bodyblow when the outstanding Villa, fed by Santos Brito down the middle of the pitch rattled in the second after only six minutes.

The third came eight minutes later when Santos Brito galloped through unchallenged to fire in from outside the penalty area.

The quick-fire start meant you could hear a pin drop inside the ground as United's dreams had been shattered in a matter of minutes.

CAUGHT COLD: Just 54 seconds are on the clock as Marcelino sweeps the ball in to the Leeds net despite the attentions of Gary Spra

real deal

race into Fairs final

United's troubles grew when the injured Jimmy Greenhoff went off for prolonged attention and finally withdrew from the contest 20 minutes from the end. By that time defender Willie Bell and Jim Storrie had both hit the woodwork, but Zaragosa's opening burst had enabled them to sit back and hit back on the counter.

United, typically, never gave up and ten minutes from the end Charlton's low shot squeezed past the 35-year-old Yarza in goal.

But it was a mere consolation as United were unable to hold the sheer brilliance of the Zaragoza forwards early on.

"We gave it all we had but it was nowhere near good enough," admitted Revie.

For United it had been a great European campaign – the first of many. It had been a marvellous journey covering 11 matches which had seen them tested by some of the finest sides on the continent.

United's fans too had taken European football to their hearts with 228,895 supporters clicking through the turnstiles, giving an average gate of over 38,000. There had even been plans to show the semi-final first leg in Zaragoza on closed circuit television at Elland Road but a land line was not available in France so the proposal was scrapped.

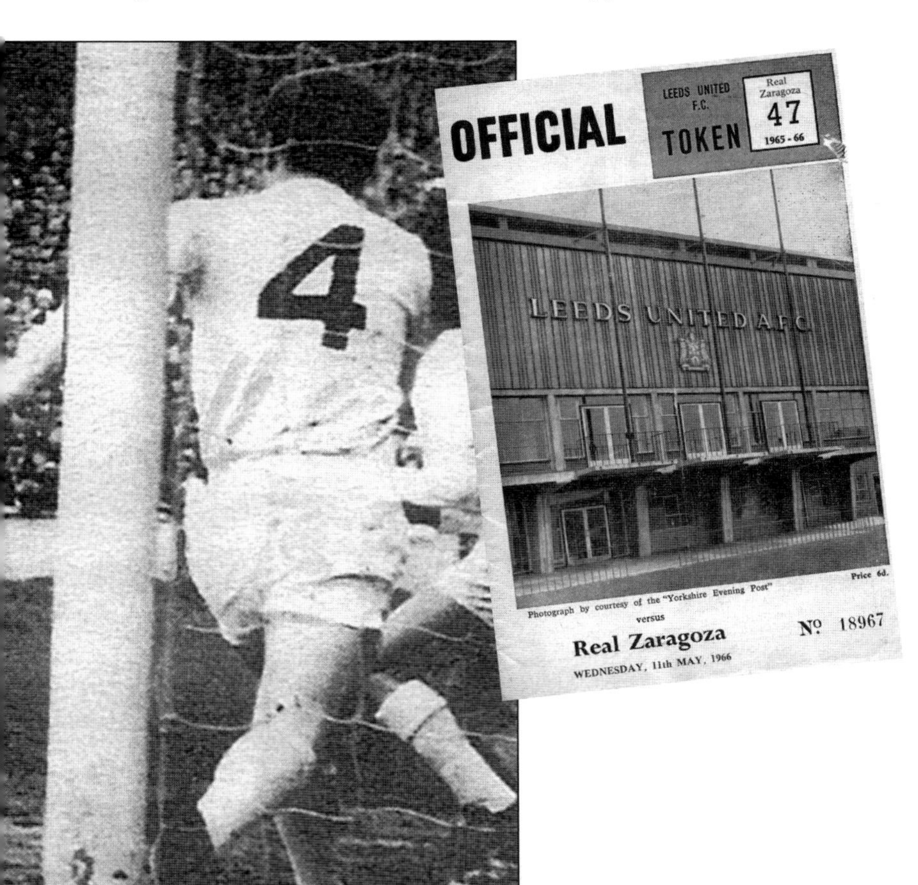

k Charlton, Billy Bremner and Paul Reaney.

Brilliant Barcelona

WHILE United were suffering at the hands of Zaragoza, Chelsea were mauled 5-0 by Barcelona.

Despite a super display by goalkeeper Peter Bonetti, the Londoners were never in the hunt after Fuente had fired the Catalans in to a seventh minute lead.

The Spanish Federation managed to put the final back until after the World Cup and the all-Spanish affair proved to be a dramatic one.

Canario scored the only goal of the first leg to give Zaragoza a 1-0 advantage to take back to the Romareda Stadium.

Zaragosa were now odds on to lift the trophy but Barcelona had other ideas in a gripping second leg.

Marcelino put away two headers for Zaragoza, but he was upstaged as Barca roared back to grab a 3-2 lead after 90 minutes to force extra-time with goals by Pujol and Zaballa.

Then with 30 seconds reamining Pujol, a late replacement, completed his hat-trick as Barcelona completed their third Fairs Cup victory, becoming the first side to come back from a first leg deficit at home to win the competition.

Semi-final play-offs

Leeds United 1 (Charlton), Real Zaragosa 3 (Marcelino, Villa, Santos) in Leeds

Barcelona 5 (Fuste 2, Rife 2, Zaballa), Chelsea 0 in Barcelona

Final, first leg

(Nou Camp Stadium, Barcelona)
September 14, 1966
Barcelona 0, Real Zaragoza 1

Barcelona: Sadurni, Benitez, Gallego, Eladio, Montesinos, Torres, Zaballa, Muller, Zaldúa, Fuste, Vidal.
Manager: Roque Olsen
Real Zaragoza: Yarza, Irusquieta, Severino Reija, País, Santamaria, Jose Violeta, Canario, Eleuterio Santos, Marcelino Martinez, Villa, Lapetra. **Goal:** Canario 40
Manager: Ferdinand Daucik
Referee: Istvan Zsolt (Hungary)
Attendance: 50,000

Final, second leg

(Romareda Stadium, Zaragoza)
September 21, 1966
Real Zaragoza 2, Barcelona 4
(after extra-time)
Barcelona won 4-3 on aggregate

Real Zaragoza: Yarza, Irusquieta, Severino Reija, Pais, Santamaria, Jose Violeta, Canario, Eleuterio Santos, Marcelino, Villa, Lapetra.
Goals: Villa 20, Marcelino 50,
Manager: Ferdinand Daucik
Barcelona: Sadurni, Poncho, Gallego, Eladio, Montesinos,Torres, Zaballa, Mas, Zaldua, Fuste, Pujol. **Goals:** Pujol 2, 100, Zaballa 79, Torres 85
Manager: Roque Olsen
Leading scorers: 7 – Konietzka (TSV Munich), Thielen (Cologne), 6 – Lohr (Cologne), Zaldúa (Barcelona), 5 – Lourenco (Sporting Lisbon), Marcelino (Real Zaragoza), Munoz (Valencia), Waldo (Valencia)

Revie boys get a break

UNITED'S failure to win the Fairs Cup meant they had to rely on qualification for Europe via their 1965-66 League placing. This was never really in doubt as they finished runners-up behind Liverpool, who went into the European Cup.

Joining United in the Fairs Cup were Burnley, who had finished third on goal average, and League Cup winners West Bromwich Albion.

Leeds gained a bye into the second round when the draw was made in Zurich on October 3, 1966.

Once again the competition had an entry of 48 clubs and Don Revie's side was certainly one to avoid. They had established themselves quickly in Europe after reaching the semi-finals of the Fairs Cup at the first attempt.

Jack Charlton, in particular, had made a name for himself on the world stage in the summer.

He was a member of the England side that beat West Germany 4-2 on that marvellous Wembley afternoon on July 30, 1966 when England became champions of the world.

A fortnight after that never-to-be forgotten day and United's stars were back in training.

Once again Bobby Collins, at the age of 35, was to skipper the side and led United out on their 1966/67 opening day 3-1 defeat to the season at Tottenham. But he suffered ligament damage in the 2-1 win over West Brom a few days later. Charlton had seemed the natural choice as skipper in the absence of the injured Collins but he did not want to lead the side as he had a superstition about being the last man to run out on the pitch.

Charlton reluctantly took on the role of skipper again, but made it clear to Revie that he did not really want the job. Revie later solved the leadership dilemma in spectacular fashion.

While United and West Brom received byes in to the second round, England's other Fairs Cup representatives, Burnley were not so lucky.

HONOURED: Jimmy Adamson with his 1961/62 Footballer of the Year trophy.

The Lancashire club were paired with Stuttgart and did well to draw 1-1 in Germany, Northern Ireland striker Willie Irvine getting the Clarets goal. They completed the job at Turf Moor with a 2-0 win.

Making a big impresion on the Clarets' coaching staff was Jimmy Adamson, the former Burnley stalwart, who later took Leeds briefly in to Europe. Adamson, Footballer of the Year in 1962/63, played for Burnley when they reached the European Cup quarter-finals in 1961.

First round, first leg

Aris Salonika 0, Juventus 2 (Del Sol, Menichelli)
Djurgaarden 1 (P Persson, Lokomotiv Leipzig 3 (Frenzel, Lowe, Berger)
Drumcondra 0, Eintracht Frankfurt 2 (Lotz 2)
Dynamo Pitesti 2 (C Radu, Naghi), Seville 0
Frigg Oslo 1 (Petterssen), Dunfermline 3 (Ferguson, Fleming 2)
Goztepe Izmir 1 (Ceyhan), Bologna 2 (Vastola, Nielsen)
Nice 2 (Santos, Loubet), Orgryte 2 (A Simonsson, Hansson)
Nuremberg 1 (Strehl), Valencia 2 (Claramunt, Waldo)
Olympic Lubiana 3 (Franceskin, Kokot, Arslanagic), Ferencvaros 3 (Albert 2, Rakosi)
Porto 2 (Custodio Pinto, Pavao), Bordeaux 1 (Rustichelli)
Red Star Belgrade 5 (Djajic 2, Mihajovic, Ostojic 2), Atletico Bilbao 0
Spartak Brno 2 (Lichtnegl, Bubnik), Dynamo Zagreb 0
SK Vienna 1 (Knoll), Napoli 2 (Cane, Orlando)
Stuttgart 1 (Weiss), Burnley 1 (Irvine)
Union Luxemborg 0, Antwerp 1 (Van Moer)
Utrecht 2 (Stocker og, Wery), Basle 1 (Odermatt)

First round, second leg

Antwerp 1 (Janssen), Union Luxembourg 0 *Antwerp win 2-0 on agg*
Athletico Bilbao 2 (Estefano 2), Red Star Belgrade 0 *Red Star Belgrade win 5-2 on agg*
Basle 2 (Firgerio 2), Utrecht 2 (Wery, Van Der Linden) *Utrecht win 4-3 on agg*
Bologna 3 (Pace 2, Haller pen), Goztepe Izmir (Gundogon) *Bologna win 5-2 on agg*
Bordeaux 2 (Peri, Texier), Porto 1 (Djalma) *Agg 3-3 – Bordeaux win on toss of a coin*
Burnley 2 (Coates, Lochhead), Stuttgart 0 *Burnley win 3-1 on agg*
Dunfermiline 3 (Delaney 2, Callaghan), Frigg Oslo 1 (Ballgrund) *Dunfermline win 6-2 on agg*
Dynamo Zagreb 2 (Zambata, Jukic), Spartak Brno 0 *Zagreb won on toss of coin*
Eintracht Frankfurt 6 (Kraus 2, Lotz, McGrath og, Huberts, Solz), Drumcondra 1 (Whelan) *Frankfurt win 8-1 on agg*
Ferencvaros 3 (Albert, Rakosi, Varga), Olympic Lubiana 0 *Ferencvaros win 6-3 on agg*
Juventus 5 (Menichelli, Favalli 2, De Paoli, Gon), Aris Salonika 0 *Juventus win 7-0 on agg*
Lokomotiv Leipzig 2 (Trolitzsch, Karlsson og), Djurgaarden 1 (Wiestahl) *Leipzig win 5-2 on agg*
Orgryte 2 (Simonsson, Hansson), Nice 1 (Barrionuevo) *Orgryte won 4-3 on agg*
Seville 2 (Dieguez, Cabrai), Dynamo Pitesti 2 (Prepurgel, Naghi) *Pitesti win 4-2 on agg*
Valencia 2 (Ansola, Waldo pen), Nuremburg 0 *Valencia win 4-1 on agg*

Byes: *Barcelona, BK Odense, Benfica, Dundee United, DWS Amsterdam, Hvidovre, IF Copenhagen, Kilmarnock, La Gantoise, Lausanne, Leeds United, Liege, Spartak Plovdiv, Sparta Prague, Toulouse, West Bromwich Albion, Vitoria Setubal*

The 'Dam busters

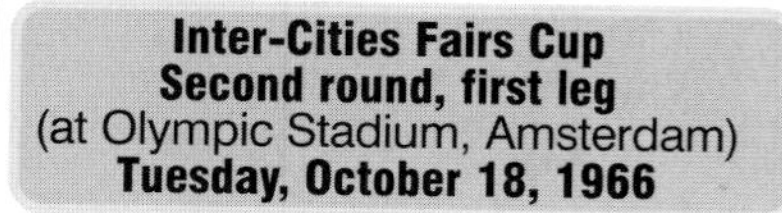

Inter-Cities Fairs Cup
Second round, first leg
(at Olympic Stadium, Amsterdam)
Tuesday, October 18, 1966

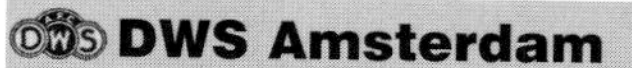

DWS Amsterdam  **1**

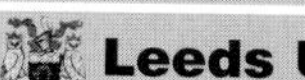

Leeds United  **3**

DWS Amsterdam: Jan Jongbloed, Jan Der Zander, Theo Cornwall, Andre Pijlman, Anton Adam, Jos Vonhof, Piet Boogaard, Frans Geurtsen, Pim Waaijenburg, Piet Kruiver, Rob Rensenbrink
Goal: Boogaard 90
Manager: Laszlo Zalai

Leeds United: Gary Sprake, Paul Reaney, Willie Bell, Billy Bremner, Jack Charlton, Norman Hunter, Mike O'Grady, Jimmy Greenhoff, Paul Madeley, Johnny Giles, Albert Johanneson
Goals: Bremner 11, Johanneson 27, Greenhoff 46
Manager: Don Revie

Referee: Anton Buchelli (Switzerland)
Att: 7,000

UNITED were paired with Dutch side DWS Amsterdam which posed some adminstration difficulties.
Leeds were actually first out of the hat, but DWS shared the 63,000 capacity Olympic Stadium in the Dutch capital and would have difficulty in staging the second leg because of other commitments at the stadium.

United's assistant manager Maurice Lindley and assistant secretary Peter Crowther flew to Amsterdam on October 8 and the clubs agreed to switch the legs around.

Ten days later United marched out at an eerie Olympic Stadium occupied by just 7,000 fans.

United boss Don Revie was extremely confident. "Last season we learned a lot on the field and off the field about football and how it should be presented," he said.

But there was still a hitch as Billy Bremner could not find his passport, drove to the passport office in Liverpool to get another, then went on to Manchester's Ringway Airport to catch a flight on his own to join up with the rest of the squad in Amsterdam.

DWS NEWS: The programme from United's trip to Amsterdam.

Dutch treat as United cruise home

Bremner's arrival meant that Revie could field the same side which had beaten Arsenal 3-1 in a League game on Saturday.

The only difference was on the substitutes' bench where goalkeepers were the only replacements allowed in Fairs Cup ties, so 18-year-old David Harvey found himself in the squad as cover for Gary Sprake.

In the event, Harvey was not called into action – and neither was Sprake really as the injury-hit Dutch side were totally outclassed as United cruised to a 3-1 win.

DWS, the 1964 Dutch champions, hardly lived up to their motto – "Strong by Willpower" – and fell behind after 12 minutes.

Mike O'Grady, was obstructed 20 yards from the DWS goal, Johnny Giles tapped the ball to Bremner, whose shot was deflected past 'keeper Jan Joengbloed.

Bremner was at the hub of all United's good moves and his long pass found fellow Scot Willie Bell raiding down the right and his centre was missed by Joengbloed, leaving Albert Johanneson to nod the ball over the line.

Any hope the Dutch had of getting back into the game vanished shortly after the interval when their defence failed to pick up Jimmy Greenhoff as the young blond-haired forward ghosted in to head Giles' centre into the net.

Such was Leeds' control that they eased off long before the end – although it cost them a goal late on. Paul Reaney, who had cleared the ball off the United line, sold Greenhoff short with a pass and Piet Boogard was able to score a late consolation goal.

Baggies bag draw

Second round, first leg

WEST Brom had also been drawn against Dutch opposition in their first crack at European football and opened with a 1-1 draw in Utrecht.

Burnley cruised to a 3-1 win in Switzerland over Lausanne. But the biggest shock of the night was Dundee United's 2-1 win over holders Barcelona – just weeks after the Catalan giants had won the trophy.

Antwerp 0, Kilmarnock 1 (McInally)
Barcelona 1 (Fuste), Dundee United 2 (Hainey, Seemann pen)
BK Odense 1 Haastrup), Napoli 4 (Sivori 2, Altafini, Cane)
DWS Amsterdam 1 (Boogaard), Leeds United 3 (Bremner, Johannesson, Greenhoff)
Dunfermline 4 (Delaney, Edwards, Ferguson 2), Dynamo Zagreb 2 (Gucmirtl, Zambata)
Eintracht Frankfurt 5 (Lotz, Huberts, Schamer, Soltz, Bronnert), Hvidovre 1 (Hansen)
Juventus 3 (Castano, Favalli, Del Sol), Vitoria Setubal 1 (Carlos Manuel)
La Gantoise 1 (Lippens), Bordeaux 0
Lausanne 1 (Armbruster), Burnley 3 (Coates, Harris, Lochhead)
Lokomotiv Leipzig 0, Liege 0
Orgryte 0, Ferencvaros 0
Sparta Prague 2 (Masek, Pospichal), Bologna 2 (Turra, Haller pen)
Spartak Plovdiv 1 (Dishkov), Benfica 1 (Eusebio)
Toulouse 3 (Dorsmi 2, Soukhane), Dynamo Pitesti 0
Utrecht 1 (Van Der Linden), West Bromwich Albion 1 (Hope)
Valencia 1 (Ansola), Red Star Belgrade 0

Poor DWS are swept aside by hat-trick

Prince Albert

UNITED completed the DWS job with a 5-1 victory at Elland Road eight days later, Albert Johanneson scoring the first European hat-trick by a United player.

Lack of goals had been concerning Revie, who had inquired about Aston Villa's big centre forward Tony Hateley, but had been put off by the £125,000 price tag – Hateley eventually joined Chelsea for £100,000.

The transfer speculation certainly whipped young Peter Lorimer into action as he hammered in five goals in an 8-0 reserve team win over Derby – but it was not enough to earn him a place against DWS.

The men from Holland, fresh from a 4-4 draw with NAC Breda, replaced Joengbloed in goal with 19-year-old Piet Schrijvers, but he could do little to prevent United from racking up a 8-2 aggregate scoreline.

Revie had announced to the press that his men were going all-out for goals against a side weaken by injury.

After a sloppy opening, United went ahead after 20 minutes when neat passing by Norman Hunter and Paul Madeley paved the way for Johanneson to fire in his opening goal.

Twelve minutes later the South African flier cracked in a right foot shot and it became 3-0 before the interval with a penalty after Bremner had been brought down.

The Dutch, after putting together some good football in the opening period, collapsed in rather feeble fashion.

With United leading 6-1 on aggregate, United fans got in the party mood and playfully booed their own penalty taker, Johnny Giles, as they wanted to see the popular Johanneson complete his hat-trick. Unfazed, Giles scored easily.

Johanneson was enjoying some of his best football at Leeds and DWS simply culd not cope with his speed.

ON THE BALL: DWS Amsterdam Piet Schrijvers vainly appeals for offside as Paul Madeley's header nestles in the net.

Inter-Cities Fairs Cup
Second round, second leg
(at Elland Road, Leeds)
Wednesday, October 26, 1966

Leeds United	**5**
DWS Amsterdam	**1**

Leeds United win 8-2 on agg

Leeds United: Gary Sprake, Paul Reaney, Willie Bell, Billy Bremner, Jack Charlton, Norman Hunter, Jim Storrie, Paul Madeley, Jimmy Greenhoff, Johnny Giles, Albert Johanneson
Goals: Johanneson 20, 33, 75, Giles pen 41, Madeley 65
Manager: Don Revie

DWS Amsterdam: Piet Schrijvers, Jan Der Zander, Theo Cornwall, Andre Pijlman, Jan Van De Weijer, Jos Vonhof, Gerard Hoogenbirk, Frans Geurtsen, Pim Waaijenburg, Piet Kruiver, Rob Rensenbrink
Goal: Geurtsen 55
Manager: Laszlo Zalai

Referee: Kurt Handwerker (West Germany)
Att: 27,096

Frans Geurtsen pulled a goal back for DWS, but Madeley, looking suspiciously offside, headed in United fourth and 15 minutes from the end United fans got their wish when Johanneson completed his treble with a shot which deflected off full back Theo Cornwall past Schrijvers.

But for young Schrijvers United would have won by a bigger margin and it was no surprise that the big blond goalkeeper went on to join Dutch giants Ajax and established himself as Holland's No 1 in the 1978 World Cup squad.

Ironically he was injured in the second phase and lost his place to Joengbloed, then with JAC Roda. Joengbloed went on to play in the final against Argentina at the age of 37. He finished up on the losing side for the second successive tournament, having kept goal in the 1974 final against West Germany.

All that was well in the future, of more concern to United and their officials was the potentially explosive tie they had drawn in the Fairs Cup third round – Valencia.

hero Johanneson

ON THE BALL: Flying South African-born winger Albert Johanneson became the first United player to net a hat-trick in Europe.

England's treble tops

ALBERT Johanesson was not the only player from an English club to score a hat-trick against a Dutch side in the Fairs Cup second round.

Tony Brown grabbed a treble as West Brom thumped DOS Utrecht 5-1 with the other two goals coming from John Kaye and Leeds-born Clive Clark.

Andy Lochhead made hit a treble hat-trick for Football League clubs by scoring three times in the 5-0 demolition of Lausanne.

But the British highlight of the night was at Dundee United where the Scots beat Barcelona 2-0 to complete a magnificent 3-1 aggregate victory over the Fairs Cup holders.

But there was agony for Dunfermline, who went out on the away goals rule as Dynamo Zagreb wiped out a first leg deficit of 4-2 by winning 2-0 at home.

Second round, second leg

Benfica 3 (Dimov og, Eusebio, Torres), Spartak Plovdiv 0 *Benfica win 4-1 on aggregate*

Bologna 2 (Haller 2), Sparta Prague 1 (Jurkanin) *Bologna win 4-3 on aggregate*

Bordeaux 0, La Gantoise 0 *La Gantoise win 1-0 on aggregate*

Burnley 5 (Lochhead 3, O'Neill, Irvine), Lausanne 0 *Burnley win 8-1 on aggregate*

Dundee United 2 (Mitchell, Hainey), Barcelona 0 *Dundee United win 4-1 on aggreate*

Dynamo Pitesti 5 (Radu 2, David, Dobrin, Turcan), Toulouse 1 (Dorsini) *Pitesti win 5-4 on aggregate*

Dynamo Zagreb 2 (Zambata 2), Dunfermline 0 *4-4 on aggregate, Zagreb win on away goals*

Ferencvaros 7 (Albert 4, Nemeth 2, Szoke), Orgryte 1 (Magnusson) *Ferencvaros win 7-1 on aggregate*

Hvidore 2 (Larssen, Olsen), Eintracht Frankfurt 2 (Bronnert, Schamer) *Frankfurt win 7-3 on aggregate*

Kilmarnock 7 (McInally 2, Queen 2, McLean 2, Watson), Antwerp 2 (Beyers, Van De Weide) *Kilmarnock win 8-2 on aggregate*

Leeds United 5 (Johannesson 3, Giles, Madeley), DWS Amsterdam 1 (Geurtsen) *Leeds win 8-2 on aggregate*

Lokomotiv Leipzig 2 (Lowe 2), Liege 1 (Genscjik) *Leipzig win 2-1 on aggregate*

Napoli 2 (Braca, Altafini), BK Odense 1 (Haastrup) *Napoli win 6-2 on aggregate*

Red Star Belgrade 1 (Ostojic), Valencia 2 (Waldo 2) *alencia win 3-1 on aggregate*

Vitoria Setubal 0, Juventus 2 (Bon, De Poali) *Juventus win 5-1 on aggregate*

West Bromwich Albion 5 (Brown 3 -1 pen, Clark, Kaye), Utrecht 2 (De Vroet, De Kuyper) *West Brom win 6-3 on aggregate*

Football League Cup date finally hammered out

A FEW hours before the kick-off against DWS, Football League secretary Alan Hardaker announced that United's Football League Cup tie with West Ham would be played at Upton Park on Monday, November 7.

The match had turned in to a protracted wrangle between the two clubs, the League and the FA.

Various dates originally put forward for the game co-incided with England squad training ahead of a game against Czechoslovakia at Wembley.

United stars Jack Charlton, Norman Hunter and Paul Reaney, together with Hammers' famous trio of Bobby Moore, Geoff Hurst and Martin Peters were all in Sir Alf Ramsey's national squad.

When the League Cup tie did go ahead Leeds crashed to a 7-0 defeat!

SPANISH SLIDE: Valencia goalkeeper Jose Pesudo bravely plunges at the feet of United winger Terry Cooper. Shortly before the interval the Spanish 'keeper was forced off through injury.

Inter-Cities Fairs Cup
Third round, first leg
(at Elland Road, Leeds)
Wednesday, January 18, 1967

Leeds United	1
Valencia	1

Leeds United: Gary Sprake, Paul Reaney, Paul Madeley, Billy Bremner, Jack Charlton, Norman Hunter, Johnny Giles, Eddie Gray, Jimmy Greenhoff, Bobby Collins, Terry Cooper
Goal: Greenhoff 11
Manager: Don Revie

Valencia: Jose Pesudo (Angel Aberlardo 43), Juan Cruz Sol, Francisco Vidagany, 'Roberto' Gil Esteve, Manuel Mestre, Francisco 'Paquito', Jose Claramunt, 'Waldo' Machado Da Silva, Fernando Ansola, Manuel Polinario, Vicent Guillot
Goal: Claramunt 37
Manager: Edmundo Suarez

Referee: Hans-Joachim Weyland (West Germany)
Att: 40,644

Peace and quiet this time round

THE ill-tempered Valencia match the previous season had sparked a brawl, but both clubs played down the prospect of a repeat of the fisticuffs.

Valencia, second in the Spanish League behind Real Madrid, were shaping up well under their new coach Edmundo Suarez.

In contrast, Don Revie's team were scratching around for their best form and went into the game without injured duo Mike O'Grady and Willie Bell and flu victim Albert Johanneson.

Revie banked on experience which meant a welcome return to European action for veteran midfielder Bobby Collins. His guile would be needed to crack open a Valencia defence which had earned top marks from master spy Maurice Lindley, who had flown to the Canaries to see them force a 0-0 draw with Las Palmas in a domestic game.

Giles, out since late November was also back, but playing on the right wing to accommodate Collins.

The Spaniards were not used to the cold January air in Yorkshire and trained at Elland Road in gloves but were confident that Brazilian-born striker Waldo could add to his 19 goals in only his 18th match of the season.

Despite all the hype about it being a grudge match, the game only contained 16 fouls and there was much good football to be admired.

Valencia were quickly into the stride and Sprake needed to be at his acrobatic best to tip a header from Fernando Ansola over the bar. But after only 11 minutes United grabbed the lead when Jimmy Greenhoff drilled in a shot past goalkeeper Pesudo. The Spaniards didn't panic and slowly wrestled control of the match away from Leeds, deserving their 37th minute equaliser when Jose Claramunt whipped the ball in from the edge of the six-yard box.

Pesudo tipped an Eddie Gray header over the bar, but needed treatment for an injury and minutes later the trainer was on the pitch again after another Leeds attack to attended to Pesudo and defender Sol.

Play was delayed for five minutes and as referee Hans-Joachim Weyland resumed play Pesudo twice sat down on his line. The Leeds crowd, suspecting time wasting, bayed for blood, but their suspicions were unfounded as Pesudo limped off and replacement goalkeeper Angel Abelardo came on for the last two minutes of the half.

The goalkeeper, the only substitute permissable under Fairs Cup rules, proved a great replacement, twice denying Bremner. But at the other end Sprake had to be at his best to block efforts by Ansola and Polinario.

Burnley's Italian job

BURNLEY recorded a great 3-0 home win over Napoli of Italy, but West Brom's hopes of making the quarter-finals were dented as they also faced Italian opposition, losing 3-0 at Bologna.

Third round, first leg

Bologna 3 (Turra, Neilsen, Haller), West Bromwich Albion 0
Burnley 3 (Coates, Latcham, Lochhead), Napoli 0
Dynamo Pitesti 0, Dynamo Zagreb 1 (Zambata)
Eintracht Frankfurt 4 (Lotz, Abbe 2, Huberts), Ferencvaros 1 (Albert)
Juventus 3 (Cinesinho 2, Menichelli), Dundee United 0
Kilmarnock 1 (Murray), La Gantoise 0
Leeds United 1 (Greenhoff), Valencia 1 (Claramunt)
Lokomotiv Leipzig 3 (Jacinto og, Frenzel 2), Benfica 1 (Jose Augusto)

Express delivery

Father Giles celebrates in great style

THE Spanish, slight pre-match favourites, were now seen as home bankers to progress to the quarter finals after their draw at Elland Road.

That view gained credence in the build up to the return leg as United's plans were disrupted by a series of injuries.

Alan Peacock was out with a broken leg, Paul Reaney had a calf muscle injury and was joined on the sick list by Mike O'Grady (groin strain), Terry Cooper (knee ligament damage), Jimmy Greenhoff and Albert Johanneson (thigh strains) and reserve forward Rod Johnson (broken nose).

However, Billy Bremner was cleared to play despite being handed a 14-day ban (the fourth suspension of his career) and a £100 fine after being sent off at Nottingham Forest.

Revie had no option to turn to the younger members of his squad for the Valencia game and brought in Terry Hibbitt, 19, for his first start. The likes of Eddie Gray, 19, Peter Lorimer, 20, and Rod Belfitt, 21, were also still feeling their way into the first team.

"The team will fight to the last and we might pull it off," mused Revie as he prepared his young troops for battle.

Valencia, despite losing their unbeaten home record when going down 2-0 to Atletico Madrid the previous Sunday, were confident of putting United's rookies out of Europe. Perhaps they were over confident.

Ten minutes before the teams went out a telegram arrived in the Leeds dressing-room announcing that Johnny Giles' wife, Ann, had given birth to a daughter. Eight minutes into the game father Giles delivered for Leeds. Capitalising on an error by full back Toto he had a free run on goal and shot past Jose Pesudo for United's first away goal since Christmas Eve.

The stunned Spaniards almost let in another a minute later, but Manuel Mestre got in a vital tackle as Belfitt was poised to strike.

Valencia poured forward in search of an equaliser, but everything in the air was won by Jack Charlton and behind him Gary Sprake made four world class saves.

The Leeds midfield continually fell back to help out their defence, so posession was almost exclusively at the feet of the Spanish and inevitably chances were created.

FATHER FIGURE: Johnny Giles, who celebrated the birth of his daughter with a goal in Valencia.

Fortunately for Leeds, Brazilian centre forward Waldo had an off night, missing three opporunities, the worst being a close range header and a shot from six yards out. United always looked dangerous on the counter attack and Hibbitt had a shot cleared off the line by Pasquito.

Then three minutes from the end United sealed a superb victory with a breakaway goal. Paul Madeley powered up the right wing, his shot was blocked but Giles quickly whipped in a centre which Lorimer flicked home to guarantee United's place in the last eight.

Revie beamed: "They were all magnificent. I am a very proud man."

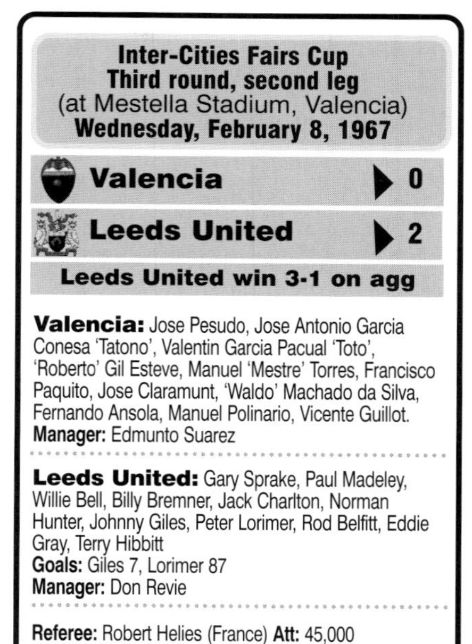

Inter-Cities Fairs Cup
Third round, second leg
(at Mestella Stadium, Valencia)
Wednesday, February 8, 1967

Valencia	**0**
Leeds United	**2**

Leeds United win 3-1 on agg

Valencia: Jose Pesudo, Jose Antonio Garcia Conesa 'Tatono', Valentin Garcia Pacual 'Toto', 'Roberto' Gil Esteve, Manuel 'Mestre' Torres, Francisco Paquito, Jose Claramunt, 'Waldo' Machado da Silva, Fernando Ansola, Manuel Polinario, Vicente Guillot.
Manager: Edmunto Suarez

Leeds United: Gary Sprake, Paul Madeley, Willie Bell, Billy Bremner, Jack Charlton, Norman Hunter, Johnny Giles, Peter Lorimer, Rod Belfitt, Eddie Gray, Terry Hibbitt
Goals: Giles 7, Lorimer 87
Manager: Don Revie

Referee: Robert Helies (France) **Att:** 45,000

Bottle of Clarets

BURNLEY survived ugly scenes in the San Paolo Stadium in Naples to book their place in the quarter-finals.

Trailing 3-0 from the first leg, the Italians reverted to roughouse tactics late in the game. While several Napoli players and fans became involved in ugly scenes, the Clarets kept their heads to hold on to a 0-0 draw and a 3-0 aggregate victory.

West Brom were no match for Bologna and tumbled out 6-1 on aggregate.

Dundee United, conquerors of Barcelona, could not repeat the feat against Juventus, going out 3-1, but did enjoy a 1-0 home victory over the Italians.

Valencia's departure at the hands of Leeds left Spain without any representatives in the Fairs Cup.

Third round, second leg

Benfica 2 (Eusebio 2), Lokomotiv Leipzig 1 (Frenzel) *Leipzig win 4-3 on agg*
Dundee United 1 (Dossing), Juventus 0 *Juventus win 3-1 on agg*
Dynamo Zagreb 0, Dynamo Pitesti 0 *Zagreb win 1-0 on agg*
Ferencvaros 2 (Rakosi, Novak pen), Eintracht Frankfurt 1 (Huberts) *Frankfurt win 5-3 on agg*
La Gantoise 1 (Ghellinck), Kilmarnock 2 (McInally, McLean) *Kilmarnock win 3-1 on agg*
Napoli 0, Burnley 0 *Burnley win 3-0 on agg*
Valencia 0, Leeds United 2 (Giles, Lorimer) *Leeds win 3-1 on agg*
West Bromwich Albion 1 (Fairfax), Bologna 3 (Neilsen 2, Bulgarelli) *Bologna win 6-1 on agg*

United stuck in

Reserves on stand-by

THE unexpected victory over Valencia plunged United headlong into fixture chaos. Not only were they in hot pursuit of League leaders Manchester United, but were locked in a marathon battle with Sunderland in the FA Cup.

Revie's men had drawn 1-1 at Roker Park and extra-time produced the same result at Elland Road on Wednesday, March 15 in front of a club record crowd of 57,892. A third game against Sunderland would have to be played the following week, but that would clash with the European tie against Bologna in Italy. The Sunderland replay was pencilled in for Monday, March 20 at Boothferry Park, home of Hull City, two days before the Fairs Cup tie. Leeds asked the Italians for the first leg Fairs Cup tie to be put back, but Bologna, already knocked out of the Italian Cup and out of the running in their league, needed to qualify for Europe via the Fairs Cup again, so rejected the idea. United appealed to the Fairs Cup Committee on the basis that the FA ruled that their own competition took preference over European tournaments. They were confident because both legs of the European tie were not scheduled to be completed by April 21 and suggested that the sides meet in Italy on April 5.

UP FOR THE CUP: Rod Belfitt gives United the lead in the FA Cup tie fifth round replay against Sunderland at Hull's Boothferry Park. It was a controversial encounter which was to have a knock-on effect for the Fairs Cup trip to Bologna.

FINE SAVES: Gary Sprake, who was in top form in Bologna.

Revie's relief as Leeds keep

DON Revie and his men didn't have time to ponder the prospects of a sixth round home tie with Manchester City after the dramatic victory over Sunderland.

They sped away from Hull City's Boothferry Park to a hotel in Bridlington, rose at 5am the following day to take a plane from Brough to Luton where they were flown 900 miles, by chartered aircraft, to Forli, 40 miles from Bologna.

The whole journey lasted eight hours and United skipped the pre-match cocktail party as they were worn out and the players went back to bed after lunch. The actual preparation, or lack of it, for the game proved more exciting than the match itself.

Terry Cooper, the winger whom Revie was converting into a left back, had not recovered from a bruised toe injury, so Willie Bell retained his place in the defence while the versatile Paul Madeley came in for forward Jimmy Greenhoff.

With goalkeeper Gary Sprake in first class form, Bologna were frustrated until just after the hour when Danish international

a fixture pile-up

to travel to Bologna

But Bologna secretary Vittori Ugolini flatly refused because Bologna wanted a free week to prepare for domestic games against Inter Milan on April 9 and Juventus on April 16.

He also pointed out that it was Leeds who had orginally suggested March 22 as the first leg date and asked the European authorities to stick to that date.

Louis Carniglia, the Bologna coach, snapped: "Leeds seem to think that just by sending a telegram saying they do not want to play they can send all our plans up in smoke. If they do not want to play on Wednesday (March 22) we will put the match off for 24 hours to Thursday. They can send their reserves or whoever they wish, but we insist this match must be played next week as agreed."

Putting the match back a day was little use to Leeds who were faced with three Easter holiday games to come over the follwing weekend.

The Fairs Cup Committee sided with Bologna, but Leeds faced a further complication – the FA had ruled that should the FA Cup tie with Sunderland be drawn again the third replay should be played on March 22.

In other words, Leeds could be faced with playing two games on the same night in different countries.

Revie was prepared for all eventualities and took two teams to Hull for the Sunderland replay on the Monday night and declared that if a third replay of the FA Cup was necessary that fixture would be fulfilled by the first team and the second team squad would be despatched to Bologna.

"We certainly would not scratch, not after going all that way in the Fairs Cup and you never know with our reserves we might still have a second chance in the second leg at Elland Road", declared the Leeds boss.

He chose Gary Sprake, Paul Reaney, Willie Bell, Billy Bremner, Jack Charlton, Norman Hunter, Paul Madeley, Rod Belfitt, Mick Bates, Johnny Giles, Jimmy Greenhoff, Terry Cooper, Terry Hibbitt, Albert Johanneson and David Harvey for the FA Cup tie.

Of the reserve squad on stand-by to fly to Italy, only Alan Peacock, who was recovering from a leg injury, was widely known. The rest were reserves and juniors – Derek Edmonds, Bobby Sibbald, Ian Kerray, James Craggs, Jimmy Lumsden, Paul Mundell, Nigel Davey, Maurice Parkin, Dennis Hawkins, Willie Waddell, Pegram, David Walls and Steve Briggs.

Everything hinged on the outcome of the Sunderland match and it looked as though a draw was in prospect when Alan Gauden wiped out Belfitt's early goal with 11 minutes left.

With extra-time just minutes away Leeds snatched a controversial winner when Greenhoff went down in a challenge by Cec Irwin. Sunderland protested that Greenhoff was both offside and had 'dived' to earn Leeds a spotkick.

Giles ignored the protests and slotted in the winning kick, but the match ended in uproar as Sunderland pair George Mulhall and George Herd were ordered off by referee Ken Stokes, there was a mini-invasion by around 40 Sunderland fans and United trainer Les Cocker was hit on the head with a bottle on the final whistle.

It was a bitter end to a fierce contest, but United had little time to dwell on the result as they faced the prospect of tackling Bologna before returning to face Blackpool on Good Friday – three games in five days.

he tie alive

Harald Neilsen scored the only goal of the game. Francesio Turra charged down Jack Charlton's headed clearance onto Helmut Haller's back and Nielsen poked the ball home.

Haller hit the bar with virtually the last kick of the match. Had that gone in then Leeds would have struggled to regain the initiative back in Yorkshire, but at 1-0 Revie knew his men were still in business.

"Considering the hard cup tie with Sunderland, the travel and lack of sleep, I thought the players did magnificently," he said.

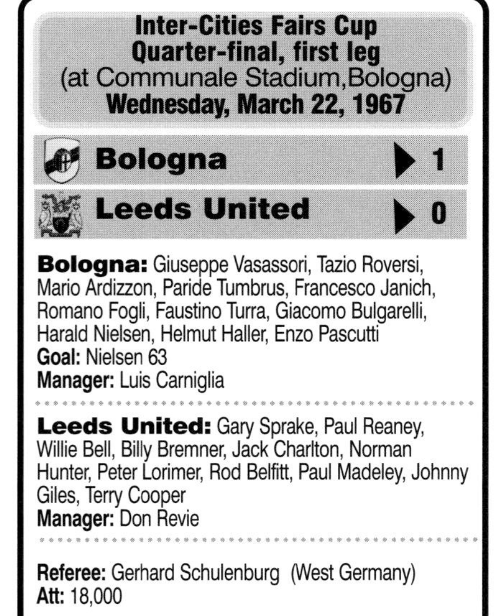

Inter-Cities Fairs Cup
Quarter-final, first leg
(at Communale Stadium,Bologna)
Wednesday, March 22, 1967

Bologna	**1**
Leeds United	**0**

Bologna: Giuseppe Vasassori, Tazio Roversi, Mario Ardizzon, Paride Tumbrus, Francesco Janich, Romano Fogli, Faustino Turra, Giacomo Bulgarelli, Harald Nielsen, Helmut Haller, Enzo Pascutti
Goal: Nielsen 63
Manager: Luis Carniglia

Leeds United: Gary Sprake, Paul Reaney, Willie Bell, Billy Bremner, Jack Charlton, Norman Hunter, Peter Lorimer, Rod Belfitt, Paul Madeley, Johnny Giles, Terry Cooper
Manager: Don Revie

Referee: Gerhard Schulenburg (West Germany)
Att: 18,000

No quarter given

BRITAIN supplied three of the eight quarter-finalists for the 1967 Fairs Cup.

Apart from United, Burnley were still in the hunt and were well satisfied with their first leg 1-1 draw in Germany against Eintracht Frankfurt. Included in the Burnley side that night was Dave Merrington, later to have a spell as assistant manager at Leeds in the Jimmy Adamson era.

Scottish side Kilmarnock, like Leeds, lost 1-0 away, going down in East Germany to Lokomotiv Leipzig.

Quarter-final, first leg

Bologna 1 (Nielsen), Leeds United 0
Eintracht Frankfurt 1 (Freidrich), Burnley 1 (Miller)
Juventus 2 (Zigom, Stacchini), Dynamo Zagreb 2 (Jukic 2)
Lokomotiv Leipzig 1 (Berger), Kilmarnock 0

UP FOR IT: United forward Rod Belfitt is beaten to the ball as Bologna's Mario Ardizzon comes flying in to intercept a dangerous cross.

Penalty king Giles keeps cool

Johnny on the spot !

THE second leg against Bologna in West Yorkshire was a tight affair settle by the toss of coloured disc – a method of victory unacceptable to all parties.

It led to an increase in the campaign to introduce penalty shoot-outs to settle ties.

Ironically United won the game 1-0 with a ninth minute penalty awarded by German referee Erwin Vetter when Jimmy Greenhoff went down under a challenge by Francesco Janich. Johnny Giles calmly put the ball to the left hand corner as goalkeeper Guiseppe Vavassori guessed correctly but could not stop Giles's kick.

That put Leeds in the driving seat but they were unable to break down a tough Italian defence in a gusty wind which swept dust up from a bone dry Elland Road pitch. Giles almost made it 2-0 with a fierce cross-shot but at the other end Gary Sprake made a great reflex save to deny Giacomo Bulgarelli and Billy Bremner, who played despite a grumbling appendix, headed an effort by Marino Perani off the line.

In a frantic finish, Terry Cooper shot over from 10 yards and Willie Bell, playing at centre half for broken toe victim Jack Charlton, came periously close to putting through his own net.

The Fairs Cup had come into line with the European Cup and Cup Winners' Cup competitions in 1966-67 and it was decided that away goals would count double after 90 minutes of the second leg if the scores were level.

With the aggregate scores level at 1-1 the match went into extra-time, but the deadlock was not broken so the match was decided by the toss of a disc, thus eliminating the need for a third match.

MR COOL: Johnny Giles calmly places his penalty to the right of Bologna's Guiseppe Vavassori to level the Fairs Cup quarter-final tie with the Italians.

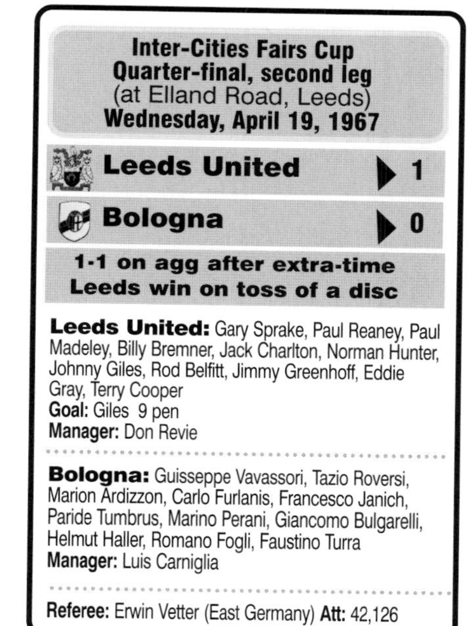

PAUSE FOR THOUGHT: Billy Bremner (right) gathers his thoughts before the toss up. Above, he's mobbed by team-mates after Giacomo Bulgarelli called incorrectly.

It's all white on the night

Billy's turn as United's spin doctor

THE tension was unbearable as the two sides awaited the toss to decide who would go through to the semi-final.

Captains Billy Bremner and Giacomo Bulgarelli made their way to the centre circle where referee Erwin Vetter span the red and white disc.

Bulgarelli called red, but it came down on white to put Leeds through.

Bremner immediately leaped into the arms of Don Revie while the 42,126 crowd, a figure which had taken attendances at Elland Road beyond the 1 million mark in a season for the first time in the club's history, went wild.

Bremner had only recently suceeded Jack Charlton, who was absent with a toe injury, as skipper but had immediately brought Leeds luck.

Revie recognised that it was an unsatisfactory way for his men to go through to the semi-finals, even though the disc-winning toss was worth an estimated £15,000 to Leeds.

"I think it was a terrible way for Bologna to go out," said the Leeds boss, "I think it would be a good idea to decide a tie like this in a series of penalties, the first team to miss being the loser."

It was the second time that Bologna had lost a game in such a fashion and their coach Luis Carniglia moaned: "Rather than have a toss up, matches like this ought to be decided on a neutral ground.

"United are a very good English team although they have not much imagination. I thought the penalty was invented by the referee."

Inter-Cities Fairs Cup
Quarter-final, second leg
(at Elland Road, Leeds)
Wednesday, April 19, 1967

Leeds United	**1**
Bologna	**0**

1-1 on agg after extra-time
Leeds win on toss of a disc

Leeds United: Gary Sprake, Paul Reaney, Paul Madeley, Billy Bremner, Jack Charlton, Norman Hunter, Johnny Giles, Rod Belfitt, Jimmy Greenhoff, Eddie Gray, Terry Cooper
Goal: Giles 9 pen
Manager: Don Revie

Bologna: Guisseppe Vavassori, Tazio Roversi, Marion Ardizzon, Carlo Furlanis, Francesco Janich, Paride Tumbrus, Marino Perani, Giancomo Bulgarelli, Helmut Haller, Romano Fogli, Faustino Turra
Manager: Luis Carniglia

Referee: Erwin Vetter (East Germany) **Att:** 42,126

Killie derail Loco

BURNLEY'S run ended when they crashed out at home to Eintracht Frankfurt, but Kilmarnock overturned a first leg deficit to beat Locomotiv Leipzig 2-0 with goals from Jim McFadzean and Brian McIlroy to set up a semi-final show-down with United

Quarter final, second leg

Burnley 1 (Miller), Eintracht Frankfurt 2 (Lotz, Huberts) *Frankfurt win 3-2 on agg*

Dynamo Zagreb 3 (Novak, Mesic, Belin), Juventus 0 *Zagreb win 5-2 on agg*

Kilmarnock 2 (McFadzean, McIlroy), Lokomotiv Leipzig 0 *Kilmarnock win 2-1 on agg*

Leeds United 1 (Giles pen), Bologna 0 *1-1 on agg aet, Leeds win on toss of disc*

Hot Rod does the trick for United

EXACTLY a month after the Bologna match, Leeds entertained Scottish side Kilmarnock in the semi-final in front of another 40,000-plus gate.

Leeds had ensured qualification for the next Fairs Cup campaign with a 2-0 win at Sunderland on Saturday, May 13 and wrapped up the season on Monday with a 1-0 victory at Sheffield Wednesday.

That Roker Park triumph was soured by a bizarre accident to Jimmy Greenhoff who injured himself when leaping for joy when Eddie Gray found the net. Ironically Gray's 'goal' was disallowed.

Rod Belfitt came on as substitute in that match and retained his place for the game at Hillsborough and Revie had little hesitation in handing him the No 9 shirt against Kilmarnock in the Fairs Cup semi-final at Elland Road on a Friday night.

SIGNED, SEALED AND DELIVERED: United centre forward Rod Belfitt heads in his second goal.

Leeds had done their usual efficient job by having chief coach Syd Owen watch Killie in action against Celtic earlier in the week. Apart from their good showing in the League, Leeds had a couple of other reasons to celebrate. Jack Charlton had been named as Player of the Year and up and coming utility player Paul Madeley was selected for the FA tour of Canada along with Norman Hunter.

Killie were shattered by a hat-trick from reserve striker Belfitt who fired in a treble inside half an hour as United stormed to a 4-2 victory.

Just 63 seconds were on referee Jan Dorpmans' stopwatch when goalkeeper Bobby Ferguson and Jackie McGrory left the ball to each other and Belfitt was able to loop in a header. Three minutes later Mike O'Grady's cross was flicked in by Belfitt's diving header.

United had Kilmarnock by the throat but instead of pressing for more goals allowed the Scots to get back into the game and Brian McIlroy nipped in between Madeley and Bell to turn a centre past Sprake after 21 minutes.

But after surviving a couple more scares, Belfitt struck again when he slid through the mud to knock in Gray's cross.

Three minutes later provider Gray saw a backpass stick on the tacky surface and McIlroy nipped in for his second goal. United regained their two-goal cushion on 39 minutes when a centre destined for Belfitt's head was handled by McGrory and Giles beat Ferguson from the penalty spot.

After the flood of first half goals, both sides predictably tightened up their defences after the interval and United were satisfied with their 4-2 advantage.

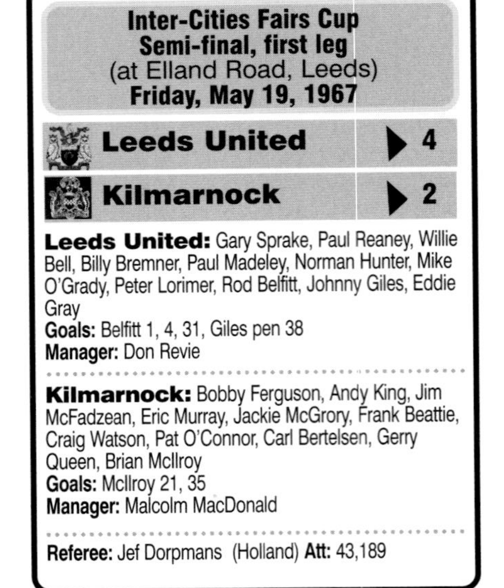

Inter-Cities Fairs Cup
Semi-final, first leg
(at Elland Road, Leeds)
Friday, May 19, 1967

Leeds United	4
Kilmarnock	2

Leeds United: Gary Sprake, Paul Reaney, Willie Bell, Billy Bremner, Paul Madeley, Norman Hunter, Mike O'Grady, Peter Lorimer, Rod Belfitt, Johnny Giles, Eddie Gray
Goals: Belfitt 1, 4, 31, Giles pen 38
Manager: Don Revie

Kilmarnock: Bobby Ferguson, Andy King, Jim McFadzean, Eric Murray, Jackie McGrory, Frank Beattie, Craig Watson, Pat O'Connor, Carl Bertelsen, Gerry Queen, Brian McIlroy
Goals: McIlroy 21, 35
Manager: Malcolm MacDonald

Referee: Jef Dorpmans (Holland) **Att:** 43,189

Frankfurt in command

THE odds were firmly stacked on a Leeds v Eintracht Frankfurt final after the semi-final first legs.

The Germans built up a 3-0 advantage over Dynamo Zagreb thanks to goals by Jurgen Grabowski, Walter Bechtold and Wolfgang Solz.

Semi-final, first leg
Leeds United 4 (Belfitt 3, Giles), Kilmarnock 2 (McIlroy 2)
Eintracht Frankfurt 3 (Grabowski pen, Bechtold, Solz), Dynamo Zagreb 0

Inter-Cities Fairs Cup
Semi-final, second leg
(at Rugby Park, Kilmarnock)
Wednesday, May 24, 1967

Kilmarnock	**0**
Leeds United	**0**

Leeds United win 4-2 on agg

Kilmarnock: Bobby Ferguson, Andy King, Jim McFadzean, Eric Murray, Jackie McGrory, Frank Beattie, Tommy McLean, Jackie McInally, Carl Bertelsen, Gerry Queen, Brian McIlroy
Manager: Malcolm MacDonald

Leeds United: Gary Sprake, Paul Reaney, Willie Bell, Billy Bremner, Paul Madeley, Norman Hunter, Peter Lorimer, Eddie Gray, Rod Belfitt, Johnny Giles, Terry Cooper
Manager: Don Revie

Referee: Vital Loraux (Belgium) **Att:** 28,000

PRESSURE POINT: United goalkeeper Gary Sprake comes under pressure from Kilmarnock's Danish centre forward Carl Bertelsen.

Defence kills off Kilmarnock

FIVE days after their free-scoring semi-final opener, United and Kilmarnock met again at Rugby Park with Don Revie opted for 'what we have, we hold' policy.

He offered a big clue to United's away tactics immediately after the first leg 4-2 victory.

"I don't think our defence will play as badly again," declared Revie, who knew that Rod Belfitt's hat-trick had got United's defence out of jail.

Skipper Billy Bremner, who was marked out of the first leg, played very deep in the return and Belfitt was left to forage up front on his own.

It was United's 61st game of the campaign and was a disappointing match in which fouls were common, marking was tight and tackles ferocious.

For all their possession, Kilmarnock only really extended Gary Sprake just before half time when a Brian McIlroy shot came off the Leeds net-minder's chest. United, rarely threatened but made the most of what little ball they got with Paul Madeley heading against the bar and a thunderous Terry Cooper shot coming off Bobby Ferguson's foot.

Kilmarnock, who had eliminated Royal Antwerp, Gantoise and Locomotiv Leipzig on the way to the semi-final, kept probing without suggesting they could break down United's cast-iron defence.

Indeed it was Leeds who almost broke the 0-0 deadlock near the end when Peter Lorimer's 25-yard shot fizzed past a post.

The goalless draw guaranteed United's place in the final, while Kilmarnock missed out on a Scottish European treble.

The night after Kilmarnock's exit at the hands of United, Celtic became the first British winners of the European Cup with a 2-1 victory over Inter Milan in Lisbon.

The following week Rangers went down 1-0 after extra-time to Bayern Munich in the Cup Winners Cup final in Nuremburg.

Zagreb hit back

ALTHOUGH United booked their place in the Fairs Cup final, the identity of their opponents was unknown.

The other semi-finalists Eintracht Frankfurt and Dynamo Zagreb were not scheduled to play out their duel until June.

Zagreb produced a sensational comeback in Yugoslavia. Trailing 3-0 from the first leg, they triumphed 4-0 to go through to their second Fairs Cup final, having been defeated over two legs by Valencia in 1963.

Semi-final, second leg

Kilmarnock 0, Leeds United 0 *Leeds win 4-2 on aggregate*

Dynamo Zagreb 4 (Zambata, Novak, Gucmirtl, Belin), Eintracht Frankfurt 0 aet *Zagreb win 4-3 on aggregate*

DYNAMO ZAGREB 1966/67. Back row, from left to right: Mladen Ramljak, Slaven Zambata, Zlatko Skoric, Branko Gracanini, Filip Blaskovic, Daniel Piric. Front row: Rudolf Belin, Krasnadar Rora, Marijan Cercek, Marijan Brncic, Josip Gucmirtl.

Dynamic Dynamo

THE first leg of the Fairs Cup final was held on 30 August in the Dynamo Stadium in Zagreb where Spartak Brno, Dunfermline, Dinamo Ploesti and Juventus, along with Frankfurt, had perished en route to the final without scoring a goal.

Clearly the Yuogoslavs were a formidable unit on their home turf and United went into the game under strength and, for once, a little upre-pared.

It was just three games into United's domestic season and they had started badly, being held 1-1 by Sunderland, losing 1-0 at Manchester United and 2-0 at Wolves.

With injuries ruling out Johnny Giles, Willie Bell, Paul Madeley and Albert Johannesson, manager Don Revie handed a European baptism to Doncaster-born midfielder Mick Bates.

United normally went into a match of such magnitude armed with tactical information from Syd Owen, but his plans to see Dynamo in action against Partizan Belgrade were destroyed when the flight from London was cancelled.

The die was seemingly cast and when United arrived in Zagreb then found themselves playing in stifling 80 degrees-plus heat.

Inter-Cities Fairs Cup
Final, first leg
(at Maksimir Stadium, Zagreb)
Wednesday, August 30, 1967

Dynamo Zagreb	**2**
Leeds United	**0**

Dynamo Zagreb: Zlatko Skoric, Branko Gracanin, Marian Brncic, Rudolf Belin, Mladen Ramljak, Filip Blaskovic, Marijan Cerek, Daniel Piric, Slaven Zambata, Josip Cucmirtl, Krasnadar Rora
Goals: Cerek 39, Rora 59
Manager: Branco Zebec

Leeds United: Gary Sprake, Paul Reaney, Terry Cooper, Billy Bremner, Jack Charlton, Norman Hunter, Mick Bates, Peter Lorimer, Rod Belfitt, Eddie Gray, Mike O'Grady
Manager: Don Revie

Referee: Adolfo Bueno Perales (Spain) **Att:** 40,000

Revie's men simply melted away in the humidity in a dull uninspiring game in which United sorely missed the creativity of Giles, who had taken over the role of midfield orchestrator from Bobby Collins so adroitly

Short-sleeved Leeds went to defend and were doing so fairly successfully until the 39th minute when Marijan Cercek, an 18-year-old reserve winger, headed in a cross, although Leeds claimed Jack Charlton would have won the ball in the air but was pushed as he went for the ball.

Charlton and Gary Sprake performed heroics in the United defence as Dynamo came forward at every oportunity and it came as no surprise when Slaven Zambata, the game's outstanding performer, created the opportunity for Krasnadar Rora to crack in a spectacular half volley on the run just before the hour.

Zambata, along with goalkeeper Zlatko Skoric and full-back Rudolf Belin were the only survivors from the

LEEDS UNITED 1966/67: Back row, from left to right: Norman Hunter, Alan Peacock, Jack Charlton, Paul Madeley, Eddie Gray, Rod Belfitt. Middle row: Don Revie (manager), Willie Bell, Mike O'Grady, David Harvey, Gary Sprake, Albert Johanneson, Rod Johnson, Jimmy Greenhoff. Front row: Paul Reaney, Bobby Collins, Johnny Giles, Billy Bremner, Jim Storrie, Peter Lorimer, Terry Cooper.

generate lead

Dynamo side that had been beaten in the 1963 final by Valencia.

Long before the end the home fans were burning newspapers on the terraces to celebrate their 2-0 win and the smoke which drifted into the Zagreb night sky was like a funeral pyre of United's hopes of European glory.

Revie remained upbeat. "I am quite certain we can do it," he said, but the words had a hollow ring to them.

United, who had conceded two goals on foreign soil for the first time, were out of form and would need to pull off something extra special the following week if they were to lift their first pieces of European silverware.

SNUFFED OUT: Zagreb goalkeper Zlatko Skoric thwarts Jack Charlton (5), Rod Belfitt, Norman Hunter and Mike O'Grady in this Leeds raid in the first leg of the 1967 Fairs Cup final.

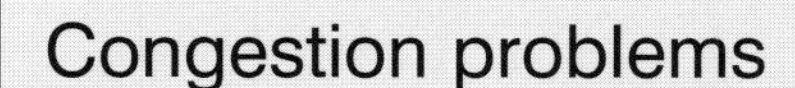

Congestion problems

BECAUSE the Fairs Cup final of 1966/67 had been held over to the start of the following season, United were immediately plunged in to fixture chaos.

Even before the 1967 final had been finished, the draw for the first round of the 1967/68 campaign had been announced.

United were paired with minnows Spora Luxembourg.

The dates United agreed with the club from the tiny European Duchy were outside the first round deadline date of September 30 scheduled by the Fairs Cup management committee. So United and Spora had to get special dispensation from the committee to play the ties in October.

Hopes of playing Spora in consecutive weeks were dashed as United expected to play in the third round of the League Cup.

Final hurdle just

United can't breach

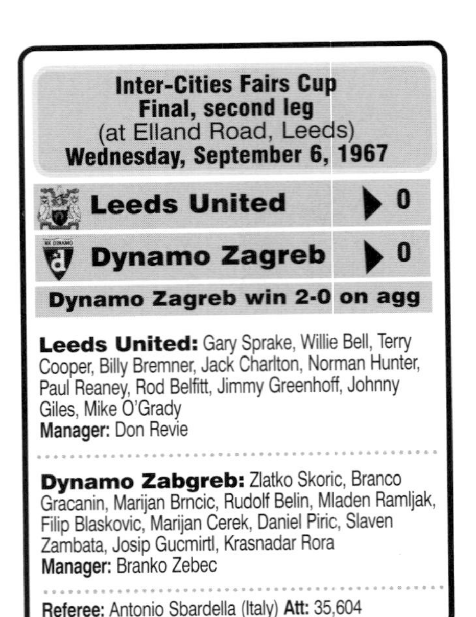

Inter-Cities Fairs Cup
Final, second leg
(at Elland Road, Leeds)
Wednesday, September 6, 1967

Leeds United	**0**
Dynamo Zagreb	**0**

Dynamo Zagreb win 2-0 on agg

Leeds United: Gary Sprake, Willie Bell, Terry Cooper, Billy Bremner, Jack Charlton, Norman Hunter, Paul Reaney, Rod Belfitt, Jimmy Greenhoff, Johnny Giles, Mike O'Grady
Manager: Don Revie

Dynamo Zabgreb: Zlatko Skoric, Branco Gracanin, Marijan Brncic, Rudolf Belin, Mladen Ramljak, Filip Blaskovic, Marijan Cerek, Daniel Piric, Slaven Zambata, Josip Gucmirtl, Krasnadar Rora
Manager: Branko Zebec

Referee: Antonio Sbardella (Italy) **Att:** 35,604

THE Fairs Cup management committee ruled that should Leeds win 2-0 then the cup would be shared for six months each – but there was little likelihood of that against the well organised Yugoslavs.

Despite a 2-0 home win over Fulham three days after the trip to the continent, Don Revie knew he had a problem in attack and on Monday – just two days before the second leg of the final – gave injury-hit Alan Peacock an outing in a reserve game at Preston.

But clearly Peacock was not fully match fit and Revie retreated to the Yorkshire Dales with his squad to plan his strategy. Dynamo, meanwhile, were being entertained at Harewood House, home of Lord Harewood, United's president.

Revie's answer to find goals was to bring in Willie Bell at right back and play Paul Reaney as an orthodox right winger. It didn't work, but it was not for the lack of trying.

Reaney supplied a stream of centres as United bombarded a 10-man defence in which international goalkeeper Zlatko Skoric pulled off several elastic saves.

Charlton, who spent as much time in the opposition penalty box as his own, added his height to the attack and both he and Belfitt had efforts disallowed. Jimmy Greenhoff shaved a post with a header early on, Charlton and Billy Bremner had efforts cleared off the line and as the minutes ticked away fears that United would over-commit themselves were beginning to grow.

SUPER SKORIC: Goalkeeper Zlatko Skoric gave a brilliant display at Elland Road. Above, he denies Jimmy Greenhoff and Rod Belfitt. Right, he tips a header over the bar under pressure from Belfitt.

too high Zagreb wall

With Slaven Zambata again looking a class act in midfield, Leeds were almost caught by a lightning counter attack which saw Daniel Piric rattle Sprake's bar with a tremendous shot

In the end United simply didn't have guile, or the luck, to punch through an extremely well organised side who held out for the 0-0 draw to receive the prophy from FIFA president Sir Stanley Rous.

Revie was generous in his tribute to the victors, the first Yugoslavian side to win the competition, and his own side.

"Our men gave everything. I have never seen a side play itself out as they did, far beyond duty. Zagreb are a fine all-round team and deserved to take the cup. But they had the little bits of fortune that were going at times."

United had to content themselves with record receipts of £20,177, which no doubt helped towards the club record £100,000 fee which Revie paid a fortnight later for Sheffield United's Mick Jones to beef up his attack.

Morris takes over from chairman Harry

MASTER TACTICIAN: New chairman Albert Morris congratulates the winning Zagreb squad.

JUST before the second leg of the final against Zagreb, United chairman Harry Reynolds announced he was stepping down because of ill health.

Reynolds, a self-made millionaire, ran an engineering company and was the man who appointed Don Revie as United's manager.

He joiined the board in 1955 and was appointed chairman on December 11 1965, standing down because of severe arthritis. The role was taken on by Albert Morris, the club's finance chairman, who had been a director since November 1961.

Both Reynolds and Morris had been instrumental in turning round a financially ailing club in to one of the most successful in the country.

Harry Reynolds.

Record romp for United hot-shots

Spora sunk by goal blitz

UNITED could not have been handed an easier draw had Don Revie chosen it himself as Leeds set off on their third Fairs Cup campaign.

Just a month after suffering the disappointment of defeat in the final against Zagreb, United found themselves facing Spora, the amateurs from Luxembourg.

Revie didn't even bother having Spora watched. United opted to save the air fare to spy on a club which had failed to progress beyond the first round of any European competition in which they had taken part since 1956.

After 14 minutes of a one-sided encounter at the Muncipal Stadium in was obvious they were not going any further in the 1967/68 tournament either.

Jimmy Greenhoff swung his boot at the ball and missed, but Peter Lorimer was on hand to thump the ball in.

United were up and running and finished 9-0 winners to set a new club record score, beating the 8-0 by which Leicester City were hammered in 1934. Lorimer added the second goal from the penalty spot after Rene Schmitt handled, then completed a 15-minute hat-trick with a deflected shot that went in off a post.

Billy Bremner lobbed over goalkeeper Friedhelm Jesse to close a half in which goalkeeper David Harvey, making his European debut because Gary Sprake had a back strain, handled the ball just twice.

Although Spora made two changes at the interval, making use of the new substitutes' ruling which had been introduced. Previously, only a substitute goalkeeper had been allowed.

But despite Spora's changes in personnel United rolled on, Lorimer knocking in his fourth from close range after 55 minutes then Greenhoff added a couple – a tap in and deflected shot.

Paul Madeley's header made it 8-0 and the final goal was nodded in by Mick Jones for his first goal for the club since his record £100,000 switch from Sheffield United.

WHIPPING BOYS: Spora's team which was put to the sword by United. Back row, from left to right: Joseph Krier, Arthur Schmitz, Harald Werwie, Mathias Ewen, Friedhelm Jesse, Francois Hostert, Peter Scholtes, Janos Gerdov (manager). Front row: Jean Kremer, Rene Schmitt, Pierrot Hut, Carlo Devillet, Emile Meyer, Gaston Bauer.

Inter-Cities Fairs Cup
First round, first leg
(at Municipal Stadium, Luxembourg)
Tuesday, October 3, 1967

Spora Luxembourg 0

Leeds United 9

Spora Luxembourg: Freidhelm Jesse, Arthur Schmitz, Rene Schmitt, Pierrot Hut, Mathias Ewen, Jean Kremer (Gaston Bauer HT), Carlo Devillet (Harald Werwie HT), Peter Scholtes, Joseph Krier, Emile Meyer, Francois Hostert
Manager: Janos Gerdov

Leeds United: David Harvey, Paul Reaney, Paul Madeley, Billy Bremner, Jack Charlton, Norman Hunter, Jimmy Greenhoff, Peter Lorimer, Mick Jones, Eddie Gray, Terry Cooper
Goals: Lorimer 13, 24 pen, 29, 54, Bremner 45, Greenhoff 69, 77, Madeley 80, Jones 81
Manager: Don Revie

Referee: Helmut Fritz (West Germany) **Att:** 2,500

Hateley at the double

TONY Hateley, whose son Mark was to have a brief spell on loan with United, was the toast of Anfield.

His two goals gave Liverpool a flying start to their Fairs Cup campaign in a 2-0 victory in Sweden over Malmo.

England's other representatives, Nottingham Forest won 1-0 in Germany over Eintracht Frankfurt, Joe Baker grabbing the goal.

Holders Dynamo Zagreb hammered Petrolul Ploesti, of Rumania, 5-1.

First round, first leg

Antwerp 1 (Frankel), Goztepe Izmir 2 (Zemzem 2)
Bologna 2 (Clerici, Pace), Lyn Oslo 0
Bruges 0, Sporting Lisbon 0
Cologne 2 (Ruhl, Lohr), Slavia Prague 0
DWS Amsterdam 2 (Rensenbrink, Van Der Berg), Dundee 1 (G McLean)
Dynamo Dresden 1 (Riedel), Rangers 1 (Ferguson)
Dynamo Pitesti 3 (Fercan, Dobrin, Kraus), Ferencvaros 1 (Albert)
Dynamo Zagreb 5 (Jukic 2, Kia 2, Zambata), Petrolul Ploesti 0
Eintracht Frankfurt 0, Nottingham Forest 1 (Baker)
FC Zurich 3 (Winiger 2, Kuhn), Barcelona 1 (Zaldua)
Frem 0, Athletico Bilbao 1 (Arroyo)
Hibernian 3 (Cormack 2, Stevenson), Porto 0
Lokomotive Leipzig 5 (Lowe 2, Zerbe 2, Faber), Linfield (Pavis)
Malmo 0, Liverpool 2 (Hateley 2)
Napoli 4 (Girado, Laszig og, Altafini 2), Hannover 0
Nice 0, Fioerntina 1 (Maraschi)
Partizan Belgrade 5 (Hasanagic 3, Kovacevic, Raaovic), Lokomotiv Plovdiv 1 (Ilev)
POAK Salonika 0, Liege 2 (Mardaga, Banovic)
St Patricks 1 (Hennessy), Bordeaux 3 (Chorda pen, Masse, Couecou)
Servette 2 (Bjorn, Heun), TSV Munich 2 (Lex pen, Grosser)
Spora Luxembourg 0, Leeds United 9 (Lorimer 4, Greenhoff 2, Bremner, Jones, Madeley)
Utrecht 3 (Van Veen, Wery, van Wliet), Real Zaragoza 2 (Villa 2)
Vienna SK 2 (Laitner, Calleja og), Atletico Madrid 5 (Garate 5, Luis Aragones)
Vojvodina 1 (Dakic), Barreiro 0

In the lap of luxury

Revie's boys on easy street

UNITED returned from the Principality with just one aim in mind – to net another nine goals to set a European aggregate victory record.

It had been established two years earlier when Cologne beat Union Luxembourg 4-0 and 13-0 to post a 17-0 aggregate victory.

But in Leeds, Hungarian-born coach Janos Gerdov opted the pack his defence and charitable United fell a couple of goals short of the record on a muddy pitch lashed by wind and rain. This time it took Leeds 10 minutes to get the scoreboard ticking, Albert Johannesson slipping the ball in after goalkeeper Friedhelm Jesse missed Greenhoff's cross.

Within a couple of minutes Gerdov sent on substitute John Hilbert, but didn't bring anyone off and Spora actually played with 12 men for a few moments until a linesman attracted Irish referee Peter Coates of the mathematical blunder. Much to the amusement of the Leeds crowd, who were already cheering the opposition, Dominique Da Fonseca came off to restore numerical parity.

REMINDER: Don Revie.

Johanneson added another goal from a Jimmy Greenhoff cross, but Leeds went in a half-time well behind the required scoring rate to beat Cologne's record.

Manager Don Revie must have reminded his men of their target as they moved up several gears after the interval, Greenhoff's header crowning a fine sweeping move to make it 3-0.

With nearly an hour gone Terry Cooper netted the fourth then further goals by Peter Lorimer and Greenhoff in quick succession gave Leeds some hope of hitting their target with 20 minutes left.

But all they could muster was Johanneson's hat-trick goal on 80 minutes and finished the match 7-0 winners for an aggregate score of 16-0.

United's second round opponents would certainly not be such a piece of cake.

The draw pitched them in with Partizan Belgrade, keen Yugoslavian rivals of Dynamo Zagreb, who had beaten United in the final about three months earlier.

Inter-Cities Fairs Cup
First round, second leg
(at Elland Road, Leeds)
Wednesday, October 17, 1967

Leeds United 7

Spora Luxembourg 0

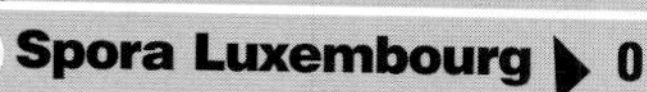

Leeds United win 16-0 on agg

Leeds United: Gary Sprake, Paul Reaney, Terry Cooper, Paul Madeley (Mick Bates HT), Jack Charlton, Norman Hunter, Jimmy Greenhoff, Peter Lorimer, Rod Belfitt, Terry Hibbitt, Albert Johanneson
Goals: Johanneson 10, 34, 80, Greenhoff 51, 69, Cooper 59, Lorimer 67
Manager: Don Revie

Spora Luxemburg: Freidhelm Jesse, Arthur Schmitz, Pierrot Hut, Rene Schmitt, Mathias Ewen, Domenique Da Fonseca (John Hilbert 12), Carlo Devilet, Peter Scholtes, Joseph Krier, Emile Meyer, Francois Hostert (Jean Kremer HT)
Manager: Janos Gerdov

Referee: Peter Coates (Republic of Ireland) **Att:** 15,196

Scottish trio join United, Liverpool and Nottingham Forest in second round

UNITED, Liverpool and Nottingham Forest were joined in the second round by a trio of Scottish clubs.

Rangers edged out Dynamo Dresden with goals by Andy Penman and John Greig. Dundee beat DWS Amsterdan 3-0 at Dens Park to wipe out the Dutch side's first leg lead, Jim McLean scoring two of the goals.

Hibernian snatched a vital penalty at Porto to squeeze through on aggregate – Joe Davis being the scorer from the spot.

First round, second leg

Athletico Bilbao 3 (Arraiz, Uriarte, Arieta), Frem 2 (Nielsen, Pnntzlau) *Bilbao win 4-2 on agg*
Athletico Madrid 2 (Cardona 2), SK Vienna 1 (Schmidt) *Athletico Madrid win 7-3 on agg*
Barcelona 1 (Zaldua), FC Zurich 0 *Zurich win 3-2 on agg*
Barreiro 1 (Fernando Silva), Vojvodina 3 (Trivic 2, Rakic) *Vojvodina win 4-1 on agg*
Bordeaux 6 (Calleja, Ruiter, Duhayot 2, Wojciak 2), St Patrick's 3 (Campbell 2, Ryan) *Bordeaux win 9-4 on agg*
Dundee 3 (Wilson, J McLean 2), DWS Amsterdam 0 *Dundee win 4-2 on agg*
Ferencvaros 4 (Albert 2, Novak, Varga), Dynamo Pitesti 0 *Ferencvaros win 5-3 on aggregate*
Fiorentina 4 (De Sisti, Brugnera 2, Bertini), Nice 0 *Fiorentina win 5-0 on agg*
Goztepe Izmir 0, Antwerp 0 *Izmir win 2-1 on agg*
Hanover 96 1 (Straschitz), Napoli 1 (Banson) *Napoli win 5-1 on agg*
Leeds United 7 (Johannesson 3, Greenhoff 2, Cooper, Lorimer), Spora Luxenbourg 0 *Leeds win 16-0 on agg*
Liege 3 (Andries 2, Mardaga), POAK Salonika 2 (Afendouhdis, Makris) *Liege win 5-2 on agg*
Linfield 1 (Hamilton), Lokomotiv Leipzig 0 *Leipzig win 5-2 on agg*
Liverpool 2 (Yeats, Hunt), Malmo 1 (Szepanski) *Liverpool win 4-1 on agg*
Lokomotiv Plovdiv 1 (Vasillev), Partizan Belgrade 1 (Petrovic) *Partizan win 6-2 on agg*
Lyn Oslo 0, Bologna 0 *Bologna win 2-0 on agg*
Nottingham Forest 4 (Baker 2, Chapman, Lyons), Eintracht Frankfurt 0 *Forest win 5-0 on agg*
Petrolul Ploesti 2 (Dridea, Grozea), Dynamo Zagreb 0 *Zagreb win 5-2 on agg*
Porto 3 (Valdir 2, Custodio Pinto), Hibernian 1 (Davis pen) *Hibernian win 4-3 on agg*
Rangers 2 (Penman, Greig), Dynamo Dresden 1 (Kreische) *Rangers win 3-2 on agg*
Real Zaragoza 3 (Bustillo 3), Utrecht 1 (Maiwald) *Zaragoza win 5-4 on agg*
Slavia Prague 2 (Tesar, Lala), Cologne 2 (Lohr, Ruhl) *Cologne win 4-2 on agg*
Sporting Lisbon 2 (Lourenco 2), Bruges 1 (Lambert) *Sporting win 2-1 on agg*
TSV Munich 4 (Kuppers, Grosser pen, Brundl, Peter), Servette 0 *TSV Munich win 6-2 on agg*

Partizan fighters no match for United

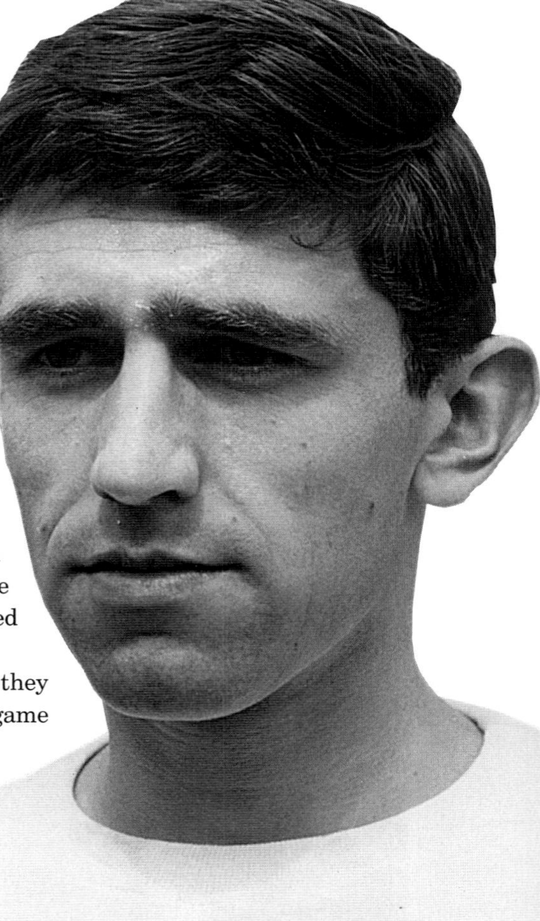

MR RELIABLE: United reserve forward Rod Belfitt continued his good form in Europe with a goal in Belgrade.

THE match at Partizan Belgarde was one of the most fierce encounters on United's continental travels.

Leeds had built up a reputation of being a tough, uncompromising team, but even their physical strength was put to the test in Yugoslav capital.

Partizan's Milan Vukelic had been sent off the previous Sunday and started the match on the sub's bench but by the time he came on for the injured Boroa Djordjevic after 27 minutes, Leeds were already ahead.

Eddie Gray had been hacked down and Lorimer's blistering 25-yard free kick was too hot to handle for Ivan Curkovic who could only help the youngster's shot into his own net.

Two minutes later Partizan won a free kick in a similar position but Josip Pirajer's drive was kept out by David Harvey's superb diving save. Harvey was playing because Gary Sprake was ruled out with a bruised arm. Sprake didn't pass a fitness test but Jack Charlton did play after recovering from a neck injury and had a crucial role in United's second goal.

Rising high, he headed a corner from the left against a post and Rod Belfitt netted the rebound.

Leeds were looking comfortable when the trouble that had been bubbling throughout the match exploded in the 83rd minute when substitute Mick Bates and Milan Damjanovic clashed. Kicks were exchanged and Bates was ordered off.

Partizan immediately sensed they could get something out of the game and swept forward forcing Harvey to tip away a Ljuan Prekazi shot and holding on to a Idriz Hosic header. But the pressure finally told three minutes from the end when Blagoje Paunovic headed in to keep the tie alive.

Liverpool run riot at Anfield

BRILLIANT Liverpoo ran riot as they hammered hapless German side TSV Munich1860 8-0 at Anfield.

England men Roger Hunt and Ian Callaghan scored two apiece to make the second leg a formality. Six of the goals came in an amazing 25-minute spell either side of half-time.

It was a different story at the City Ground as Nottingham Forest struggled to a 2-1 win over Swiss outfit FC Zurich, Ian Storey-Moore hitting the winner from the penalty spot

Rangers built up a healthy 3-0 lead against Cologne, Alex Ferguson scoring twice.

Alex Stuart was also on target a couple of times as Dundee defeated Belgian side Liege 3-1.

Hibernian, however, faced a stiff task after losing 4-1 in Italy against Napoli.

Holders Dynamo Zagreb were also in Italy, earning a 0-0 draw in Bologna, both sides United had played the previous season.

Second round, first leg

Atletico Madrid 2 (Garate, Cardona), Goztepe Izmir 0
Bologna 0, Dynamo Zagreb 0
Bordeaux 1 (Abossolo), Athletico Bilbao 3 (Rojo, Arieta, Unarte)
Dundee 3 (Stuart 2, Wilson), Liege 1 (Sillon)
Liverpool 8 (St John, Hateley, Smith pen, Hunt 2, Thompson, Callaghan 2), TSV Munich 0
Napoli 4 (Cane 3, Altafini), Hibernian 1 (Stein)
Nottingham Forest 2 (Newton, Storey-Moore), FC Zurich 1 (Kunzli)
Partizan Belgrade 1 (Paunovic), Leeds United 2 (Lorimer, Belfitt)
Rangers 3 (Ferguson 2, Henderson), Cologne 0
Real Zaragoza 2 (Marcelino 2), Ferencvaros 1 (Szoke)
Sporting Lisbon 2 (Laurenco, Peres pen), Fiorentina 1 (Magli)
Vojvodina 0, Lokomotiv Leipzig 0

Inter-Cities Fairs Cup
Second round, first leg
(at JNA Stadium, Belgrade)
Wednesday, November 29, 1967

Partizan Belgrade 1

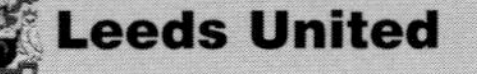

Leeds United 2

Partizan Belgrade: Ivan Curkovic, Milos Radakovic, Milan Damjanoic, Bora Djordjevic (Milan Vukelic 27), Blagoje Paunovic, Ljobomir Mihailovic, Mane Bajic, Ljuan Pekazi, Mustafa Hasanagic, Idriz Hosic, Josip Prmajer
Goal: Paunovic 87
Manager: Stjepan Bobek

Leeds United: David Harvey, Paul Reaney, Terry Cooper, Billy Bremner, Jack Charlton, Norman Hunter, Jimmy Greenhoff, Peter Lorimer, Paul Madeley, Rod Belfitt. Eddie Gray (Mick Bates HT)
Goals: Lorimer 24, Belfitt 53
Manager: Don Revie

Referee: Dogan Babacan (Turkey) **Att:** 8,000

Inter-Cities Fairs Cup
Second round, second leg
(at Elland Road, Leeds)
Wednesday, December 6, 1967

Leeds United	1
Partizan Belgrade	1

Leeds United win 3-2 on agg

Leeds United: Gary Sprake, Paul Reaney, Terry Cooper, Billy Bremner, Jack Charlton, Norman Hunter, Jimmy Greenhoff, Peter Lorimer, Paul Madeley, Eddie Gray, Terry Hibbitt (Albert Johanneson HT)
Goal: Lorimer 29
Manager: Don Revie

Partizan Belgrade: Ivan Curkovic, Milos Radakovic, Milan Damjanoic, Bora Djordjevic (Milan Vukelic 27), Blagoje Paunovic, Ljobomir Mihailovic, Mane Bajic, Ljuan Pekazi, Mustafa Hasanagic, Idriz Hosic, Josip Prmajer
Goal: Petrovic 59
Manager: Stjepan Bobek

Referee: Othmar Huber (Switzerland) **Att:** 34,258

Brilliant Hibernian stun Napoli

HIBERNIAN took the honours for Britain with a sensational 5-0 home win over Napoli, who had held a 4-1 first leg lead.

The Easter Road men spread the goals around with Bobby Duncan, Pat Quinn, Peter Cormack, Pat Stanton and Colin Stein on target.

United were to meet Hibs in the next round.

Willie Henderson's goal in extra-time proved vital as Rangers squeezed through in Cologne.

Individual star of the night was George McLean who scored all Dundee's goals as they thrashed Liege 4-1 in Belgium.

Christian Winiger's goal gave Swiss side FC Zurich a 1-0 win over Nottingham Forest, who went out on the away goals count double ruling which had been introduced in the Fairs Cup this season. Holders Dynamo Zagreb went out at Bologna.

Second round, second leg

Athletico Bilbao 1 (Arroyo), Bordeaux 0 *Bilbao win 4-1 on agg*
Cologne 3 (Overath, Ruhl, Weber), Rangers 1 (Henderson) aet *Rangers win 4-3 on agg*
Dynamo Zagreb 1 (Belin), Bologna 2 (Haller, Pace) *Bologna win 2-1 on agg*
FC Zurich 1 (Winiger), Nottingham Forest 0 *2-2 on agg, Zurich win on away goals*
Ferencvaros 3 (Katona, Varga, Novak), Real Zaragoza 0 *Ferencvaros win 4-2 on agg*
Fiorentina 1 (Maraschi), Sporting Lisbon 1 (Peres) *Sporting win 3-2 on agg*
Goztepe Izmir 3 (Gundogon 2, Aksel), Atletico Madrid 0 *Izmir win 3-2 on agg*
Hibernian 5 (Duncan, Quinn, Cormack, Stanton, Stein), Napoli 0 *Hibernian win 6-4 on agg*
Leeds United 1 (Lorimer), Partizan Belgrade 1 (Petrovic) *Leeds win 3-2 on agg*
Liege 1 (Lojenue), Dundee 4 (G McLean 4) *Dundee win 7-2 on agg*
Lokomotiv Leipzig 0, Vojvodina 2 (Savic, Djordjic) *Vojvodina win 2-0 on agg*
TSV Munich 2 (Kohlars 2), Liverpool 1 (Callaghan) *Liverpool win 9-2 on agg*

Saved by flag of convenience

MICK Bates' dismissal meant he was unavailable for the return leg with Partizan, but United welcomed back Welsh international Gary Sprake in goal.

England drew 2-2 with Russia at Wembley on the same night, but United's England players were released from international duty to face Belgrade.

Leeds began at high speed, but Jimmy Greenhoff was out of touch in front of goal, while Terry Hibbitt's shot on the run skimmed the angle of bar and post.

On the half hour Leeds got their reward with a scruffy goal. Norman Hunter carried the ball upfield where he was fouled by Partizan skipper Milan Vukelic who grabbed hold off Swiss referee Othmar Huber to protest, receiving a booking for his trouble.

Billy Bremner hosited the free kick into the area, Jack Charlton's challenge prompted 'keeper Ivan Curkovic to miscue his punch and Peter Lorimer scrambled the ball in. With a 3-1 aggregate lead in their pocket, United seemed to take their foot off the gas and were punished around the hour mark when Mikan Petrovic rifled in a low cross-shot.

Leeds had an uncomfortable finish to the match as Partizan took control and a linesman's flag saved United ten minutes from the end when Idriz Hosic ran through and scored, only to be pulled up for offside.

It had not been United's greatest display of the season but had done enough and shortly afterwards were able to announce a £64,714 profit – the third successive year the club had made a surplus.

United's successful run to the Fairs Cup final against Dynamo Zagreb had helped with the finances but the Elland Road directors opted to shelve plans to develop the Geldard End until more cash was in the coffers.

HOT SHOT: United's young Scot Peter Lorimer was among the goals in 1967/68 and his strike at home to Partizan Belgrade proved crucial.

Shaken by Shanks

Bill's brother makes cautious United struggle

CAUGHT COLD: Just four minutes were on the clock when Eddie Gray rifled the ball home to give United the lead against Hibernian on a cold Elland Road night.

IN the third round Don Revie found himself in opposition to a familiar name – Shankly.

Bob Shankly, brother of Liverpool legend Bill was manager of Hibernian and had masterminded a remarkable comeback by the Edinburgh club in the second round.

Trailing 4-1 to Naples after the first leg, Hibs won 5-0 at Easter Road to set up an all-British clash with Leeds, whose recent performances had been listless. That dip in form prompted Revie to bring back injured pair Mick Jones, out injured since September, and Johnny Giles, who had not played for eight weeks because of injury.

He could not have wished for a better start on a cold night. After four minutes goalkeeper Willie Wilson sent a poor goalkick straight to Jimmy Greenhoff, who beat skipper Joe Davis and crossed for Eddie Gray to shoot. The ball struck John Madsen and span back to Gray, who made no mistake at the second attempt.

Despite the worst possible start, Hibs settled down to run midfield where the skilful Peter Cormack outmanouvred Billy Bremner and only excellent defensive work by Norman Hunter kept the Scottish side at bay.

Colin Stein thought he had equalised in the 21st minute when he challenged Gary Sprake on the goal-line. The Welsh 'keeper grabbed the ball and when he bounced it to clear Stein prodded the ball into the net. Irish referee Jack Russell immediately gave the goal, but then disallowed it after seeing a linesman's flag and ruled that Stein had put the ball into the net through dangerous play. It was to be the centre forward's last meaningful contribution as he went off injured minutes later.

Leeds also had a goal disallowed just after the hour when Peter Lorimer netted Jones's pass from an offside position.

In a frantic finish, Wilson made a point blank save from Jones and at the other end Sprake foiled Alex Scott in a rare Hibernian raid.

Hesitant United had struggled to find their rythmn on a bone hard Elland Road surface but the pitch didn't stop Cormack putting on a super show and it was no real surprise to United followers that he was to go on to make a big impression in English football with Nottingham Forest and Liverpool, playing under Bill Shankly at the latter.

Oddly, the attendance of 31,522 was virtually the same as when Hibs were the opposition when United played under floodlights for the first time. The switch-on of the £7,000 lights on November 9, 1953 was celebrated in style with a 4-1 victory with two goals each from John Charles and manager Raich Carter.

Inter-Cities Fairs Cup
Third round, first leg
(at Elland Road, Leeds)
Wednesday, December 20, 1967

 **Leeds United** 

Hibernian 

Leeds United: Gary Sprake, Paul Reaney (Paul Madeley HT), Terry Cooper, Billy Bremner, Jack Charlton, Norman Hunter, Jimmy Greenhoff, Peter Lorimer, Mick Jones, Eddie Gray, Johnny Giles
Goal: Gray 4
Manager: Don Revie

Hibernian: Willie Wilson, Bobby Duncan, Joe Davis, Pat Stanton, John Madsen, Alan McGraw, Alex Scott, Pat Quinn, Colin Stein (Jimmy O'Rourke 30), Peter Cormack, Eric Stevenson
Manager: Bob Shankly

Referee: Jack Russell (Northern Ireland)
Att: 31,522

Clubs missing in action

NO less than four sides received byes through to the quarter-finals and were not obliged to play in the third round.

While Hibernian tackled United, fellow Scottish clubs Rangers and Dundee walked straight through to the last eight along with Bologna and Atletico Bilbao.

It meant that only four third round ties went ahead with United's deadly rivals, Liverpool, losing to a 44th minute goal against Ferencvaros by Sandor Katona in Hungary.

Third round, first leg

FC Zurich 3 (Winiger, Mayer, Neumann), Sporting Lisbon 0
Ferencvaros 1 (Katona), Liverpool 0
Leeds United 1 (Gray), Hibernian 0
Vojvodina 1 (Savic), Goztepe Izmir 0

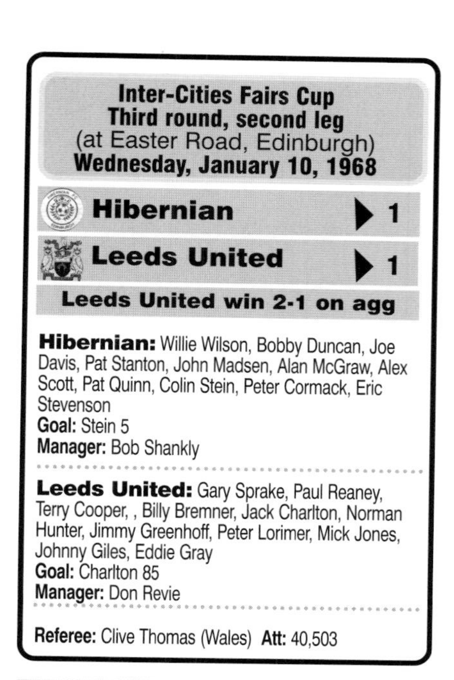

Inter-Cities Fairs Cup
Third round, second leg
(at Easter Road, Edinburgh)
Wednesday, January 10, 1968

Hibernian	1
Leeds United	1

Leeds United win 2-1 on agg

Hibernian: Willie Wilson, Bobby Duncan, Joe Davis, Pat Stanton, John Madsen, Alan McGraw, Alex Scott, Pat Quinn, Colin Stein, Peter Cormack, Eric Stevenson
Goal: Stein 5
Manager: Bob Shankly

Leeds United: Gary Sprake, Paul Reaney, Terry Cooper, , Billy Bremner, Jack Charlton, Norman Hunter, Jimmy Greenhoff, Peter Lorimer, Mick Jones, Johnny Giles, Eddie Gray
Goal: Charlton 85
Manager: Don Revie

Referee: Clive Thomas (Wales) **Att:** 40,503

IN THE NICK OF TIME: Jack Charlton leaps to head the ball past Hibs goalie Willie Wilson to send United in to the Fairs Cup quarter-finals.

United quell Easter Road uprising

UNITED'S slender 1-0 margin was wiped out within five minutes of the second leg when Colin Stein, leading marksman in the Scottish League, chipped over the advancing Gary Sprake.

Suddenly Leeds faced an uphill battle on a frozen Easter Road pitch with around 40,000 passionate Hibernian fans roaring on the home side.

With Liverpool already out, Leeds were the last English side in the competition, but their pre-match preparations were hit when they opted to go the 191 miles to Edinburgh by rail and arrived two and a half hours late.

After Stein's early goal, Leeds had to rely on guts and effort rather than skills and flair on the icy surface.

Hibs always looked dangerous on the break and Sprake, clad in tracksuit bottoms, did well to save from Pat Quinn, while Stein missed two presentable chances. Leeds hung on and snatched the crucial equaliser five minutes from the end to pinch a 2-1 aggregate victory.

As in the first leg it stemmed from a misjudgement by goalkeeper Willie Wilson, who under pressure from Peter Lorimer, carried the ball too many steps and Welsh ref Clive Thomas awarded a free-kick. Johnny Giles duly lobbed the ball into the area where the ever dependable Jack Charlton headed in United's 50th – and one of the most crucial – Fairs Cup goal in three seasons.

The draw, made in Zurich the following day, handed United a return trip to Scotland, this time to face Rangers.

Liverpool crash out to slick Ferencvaros

HOPES of an all-English Fairs Cup final ended when Liverpool went out of the competition at the hands of Ferencvaros.

The Hungarian side played some brilliant football at Anfield and merited their 1-0 victory which stunned a near 48,000 crowd.

The Reds had been confident of clawing back the 1-0 deficit from the first leg, but were outplayed by the slick passing side from Budapest.

Laszlo Branikovits scored after 9 minutes and the super confident Ferencvaros side, Fairs Cup winners in 1965, played some wonderfully creative football.

The Kop recognising their side had met their match applauded the Hungarians off the pitch at the final whistle.

Clearly Ferencvaros were a side to avoid while FC Zurich, conquerers of Nottingham Forest, could afford to lose 1-0 in Portugal to progress 3-1 on aggregate at the expense of Sporting Lisbon.

The other tie saw Yugoslavian outfit Vojvodina complete a 2-0 aggregate victory with a 1-0 win in Turkey against Goztepe Izmir.

Third round, second leg

Goztepe Izmir 0, Vojvodina 1 (Travic) *Vojvodina win 2-0 on agg*
Hibernian 1 (Stein), Leeds United 1 (Charlton) *Leeds win 2-1 on agg*
Liverpool 0, Ferencvaros 1 (Branikovits) *Ferencvaros win 2-0 on agg*
Sporting Lisbon 1 (Carlitos), FC Zurich 0 *Zurich win 3-1 on agg*

Byes: *Athletico Bilbao, Bologna, Dundee, Rangers*

UP FOR THE CUP: Billy Bremner is hoisted aloft with the League Cup after United beat Arsenal 1-0 at Wembley with a Terry Cooper goal. It was United's first piece of senior silverware and the victory guaranteed them a place in the 1968/69 Fairs Cup. Just three weeks after that League Cup triumph United were lining up against Rangers with a Fairs Cup semi-final spot at stake.

Beaming United

SUCH was the interest in the Rangers match that it was beamed back to Elland Road and shown on five 40ft by 30ft screens.

While 60,000 fans squeezed into Ibrox, a further 21,000 saw the first closed circuit TV game shown at Leeds.

The kick-off was scheduled for 8.30pm so the extra hour of darkness would give a better flood-lit picture and a crowd limit of 38,000 was set.

It was a bold venture by Leeds, but they didn't hit the break-even attendance of 24,000.

As satisfied Leeds made their way back to Yorkshire their manager stayed in Scotland to see Dundee beat FC Zurich 1-0 at Dens Park with a goal by centre half Jim Easton, his first goal for the Tayside club.

Leeds boss Don Revie mused: "I have a hunch we will meet one of them in the semi-finals." Prophetic words indeed. But first Leeds had some unfinished business with Rangers to attend to as they knew David White's side were still capable of winning at Elland Road.

Goals by Hungarian international Florian Albert and Dezso Novak gave Ferencvaros a 2-1 home win over Spanish side Athletico Bilbao while Bologna and Vojvodina fought out a goal-less draw in Italy.

Quarter final, first leg

Bologna 0, Vojvodina 0
Dundee 1 (Easton), FC Zurich 0
Ferencvaros 2 (Albert, Novak), Athletico Bilbao 1 (Argoitia)
Rangers 0, Leeds United 0

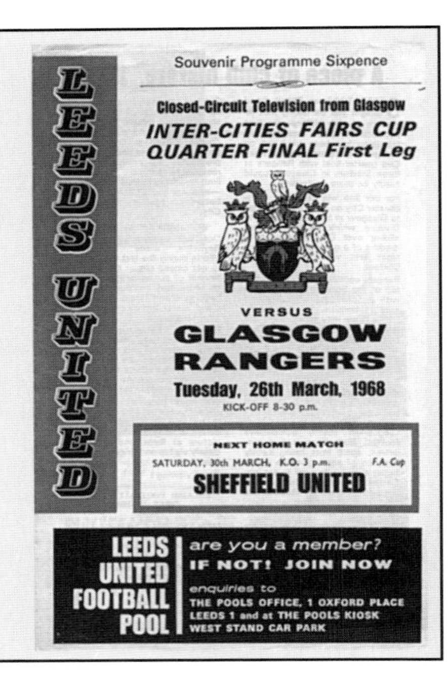

Cast iron defence shuts out Rangers

UNITED crossed the border in good heart as their 1-0 victory over Arsenal in the League Cup final at Wembley three weeks earlier had given them their first major honour and a guaranteed passport to Europe.

But they had no intention of relaxing against Rangers at Ibrox as both sides went into the tie at the peak of their form and treated the match like a cup final.

Leeds flew up to Scotland and stayed at Kilmalcolm Hydro in Renfrewshire, a base recommended by former Leeds player Eric Smith, who was coach at Morton.

MAN MARKER: League Cup final matchwinner Terry Cooper, who shackled Rangers dangerman Willie Henderson.

Rangers set up camp at Largs on the Ayrshire coast immediately after their 3-1 win at Hibernian, their 27th game unbeaten in the Scottish League, cemented their place at the top.

On the same day United had also moved to the head of the table in England after beating Manchester City 2-0 with goals by Jack Charlton and Johnny Giles so the tussle at Ibrox was billed as a mouth-watering affair.

In the event, the match didn't offer too much for fans either side of the border to cheer as United gave a typically well-organised defensive display to force a 0-0 draw and extend their own unbeaten run to 23 games.

Inter Cities Fairs Cup
Quarter-final, first leg
(at Ibrox Stadium, Glasgow)
Tuesday, March 26, 1968

Rangers	**0**
Leeds United	**0**

Rangers: Erik Sorensen, Kai Johansen, Willie Mathieson, John Greig, Ronnie McKinnon, David Smith, Willie Henderson, Alex Smith, Alex Ferguson, Willie Johnston, Orjan Persson
Manager: David White

Leeds United: Gary Sprake, Paul Reaney, Terry Cooper, Billy Bremner, Jack Charlton, Norman Hunter, Jimmy Greenhoff (Rod Belfitt 3), Peter Lorimer, Mick Jones, Johnny Giles, Paul Madeley
Manager: Don Revie

Referee: Gottfried Dienst (Switzerland) **Att:** 60,000

Key to the match was Terry Cooper's tight marking job on flying winger Willie Henderson. Cooper's goal against Arsenal at Wembley had seen United lift the League Cup but on this occasion it was his defensive qualities which shone through.

Charlton won everying in the air but it was Big Jack's miskick on a surface sodden by nine hours of Glaswegian rain, which presented Rangers with a rare chance, but both Henderson and Alex Smith were so surprised that Paul Reaney was able to nip in and snuff out the danger.

Willie Johnston then rapped a shot against Gary Sprake's legs from only six yards, but that was all Rangers were able to muster against a superb Leeds defence.

United almost pinched victory near the end when Rod Belfitt, who had come on for ankle strain victim Jimmy Greenhoff after only three minutes, forced Danish goalkeeper Erik Sorensen into a fine save.

Leeds skipper Billy Bremner was in no doubt about the value of the result. "Just wonderful. As good as a win.", was his verdict.

Mark of respect

BOTH United and Rangers wore black armbands at Elland Road to mark the passing of Leeds chairman Albert Morris.

He had only been chairman a matter of months and died on April 7 1968 in Leeds General Infirmary two days before the second leg.

A director of Morris Wallpapers Ltd, he had served on the United board since November 1961.

Vice-chairman, Percy Woodward, stepped up to become United's new man at the helm and was to oversee some of the club's greatest achievements.

A former Lord Mayor of Leeds, he ran a packing case manufacturers and merchants in the city and had been vice-chairman for 20 years.

His son, Brian, had been a part-time professional at Elland Road after the War and played first team football for both York City and Hereford United.

TOP MAN: Percy Woodward.

COOL IT: Rangers skipper John Greig (left) leads the pleas to Gers fans to behave after bottles were thrown on to the pitch and referee Kurt Tschencher feared he may have to abandon the game.

United and Giles show

ALTHOUGH the match was screened in Scotland, an estimated 15,000 Rangers fans were at Elland Road, boosting the attendance mark beyond 50,000 for a European home tie for the first time.

Even though Gary Sprake was serving a suspension after being sent off in an FA Cup tie against Bristol City, Rangers knew the odds were stacked against them.

United were unbeaten at home in 14 matches and had just set up a club record run of 26 games stretching back to a 2-0 loss at Liverpool on 9 December 1967. They were impressive statistics and it was soon clear they were to be improved in a fast, furious game which saw Johnny Giles at his imperious best for Leeds in midfield.

The little Irishman stroked United ahead from the penalty spot after 27 minutes after a handling offence and a push on Billy Bremner by Alex Ferguson – the man who was to go on to have extraordinary success as Manchester United manager.

No joy for Fergie at Elland Road

WEARING the number nine shirt for Rangers was rumbustious centre forward Alex Ferguson, later to earn fame and fortune, as well as a knighthood, with Manchester United.

He actually conceded the penalty which saw Johnny Giles give United the lead and didn't enjoy the best of spells at Ibrox after his £65,000 move from Dunfermline. He later played for Falkirk and Ayr before managerial spells at East Stirling, where he also played, St Mirren and Aberdeen paved the way for his enormous success at Old Trafford.

STRIKER: Alex Ferguson.

MR COOL: Johnny Giles calmly despatches his penalty past the despairing dive of Rangers' Danish goal-keeping star Erik Sorensen to put United ahead.

brilliant their bottle

Six minutes later United rubber-stamped their semi-final place with Giles again at the centre of things. His free-kick picked out Jimmy Greenhoff whose miscued shot fell kindly to Peter Lorimer who steered the ball home.

The Scottish giants, who had been runners-up in the European Cup Winners Cup the previous season, probably knew they were a beaten side with just a third of the game gone.

Rangers could not cope with Leeds' speed of movement and non-stop running and a Lorimer shot against a post and a Jack Charlton back-header which grazed the bar almost saw United double their lead.

For some Rangers followers it was too much to swallow and mid-way through the second half referee Kurt Tschenscher halted the game and asked Rangers skipper John Greig to appeal to Rangers' fans to stop throwing bottles on to the pitch or he would abandon the game. Order was restored and United eased to a 2-0 win and Revie's hunch proved correct – in the semi-final United were drawn against Dundee, 2-1 aggregate victors over Zurich.

Many dazed Rangers fans who had marched down the Headrow in Leeds City Centre in huge numbers at tea-time confident of victory headed home with their tails between their legs.

However, United's own hopes of a cup treble were still on the cards. With the League Cup already in the Elland Road trophy cabinet, United were through to both the semi-finals of the Fairs Cup and were also on course for FA Cup glory.

Four days after the Ibrox game, a Paul Madeley goal against Yorkshire rivals Sheffield United at Elland Road had fired Leeds through to the semi-finals of the FA Cup and the possibility of a remarkable cup treble.

Dundee's delight

WHILE Rangers slid out against Leeds, battling Dundee made it through to a semi-final showdown with Don Revie's boys. Sammy Wilson's goal at FC Zurich sealed a 2-0 aggregate victory over the Swiss side to set up an all British semi-final match.

The battle for a place in the last four saw Hungarian outfit Ferencvaros, whose progress had been impressive, face Bologna, the Italian side United had eliminated from the Fairs Cup on the toss of a coin in the previous season's quarter-final.

The Hungarians won 2-1 in Spain against Athletico Bilbao with goals by Laszlo Branikovits and Mate Fenyvesi to complete a 4-2 aggregate victory.

A tough, well-organised Bologna looked strong in winning 2-0 in Yugoslavia against Vojvodina.

Quarter final, second leg

Athletico Bilbao 1 (Betzuen), Ferencvaros 2 (Branikovits, Fenyvesi) *Ferencvaros win 4-2 on agg*

FC Zurich 0, Dundee 1 (Wilson) *Dundee win 2-0 on agg*

Leeds United 2 (Giles, Lorimer), Rangers 0 *Leeds win 2-0 on agg*

Vojvodina 0, Bologna 2 (Pace, Clarici) *Bologna win 2-0 on agg*

Inter-Cities Fairs Cup
Quarter-final, second leg
(at Elland Road, Leeds)
Tuesday, April 9, 1968

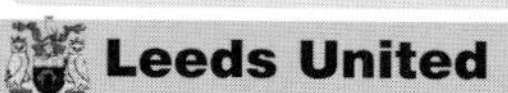
Leeds United  **2**

Rangers  **0**

Leeds United win 2-0 on agg

Leeds United: David Harvey, Paul Reaney, Terry Cooper, Billy Bremner, Jack Charlton, Norman Hunter, Jimmy Greenhoff, Paul Madeley, Mick Jones, Johnny Giles, Peter Lorimer
Goals: Giles 25 pen, Lorimer 31
Manager: Don Revie

Rangers: Erik Sorensen, Kai Johansen, Willie Mathieson, John Greig, Ronnie McKinnon, David Smith, Willie Henderson, Alex Willoughby (Andy Penman 68), Alex Ferguson, Willie Johnston, Orjan Persson.
Manager: David White

Referee: Kurt Tschenscher (West Germany)
Att: 50,498

Madeley's header gives United edge

HAVING disposed of Rangers in such impressive fashion, Dundee were not expected to give United much trouble, but Don Revie's men went into the semi-final just four days after missing out on a place in the FA Cup final.

The 1-0 defeat against Everton at Villa Park not only cost Leeds a place at Wembley but stripped them of the injured Gary Sprake (shoulder) and Mick Jones (right leg) for the trip to Dens Park.

United were billeted near Carnoustie golf course where Revie formulated his tactics to scupper a Dundee side who were enjoying their first-ever bid for Fairs Cup glory.

United bossed the match, despite the threat of 34-goal striker George McLean, who kept Sprake's replacement, David Harvey, on his toes.

Billy Bremner had a quite outstanding match and the overlapping runs of Paul Reaney were a constant menace to Bobby Ancell's team.

Shots by Peter Lorimer and Paul Madeley early on went close before Harvey had to punch a McLean effort away at the expense of a corner.

Lorimer and Bremner then cut Dundee open but Alistair Donaldson saved brilliantly to deny Eddie Gray.

Fittingly, Bremner had a big say in United taking a deserved 26th minute lead when he beat David Swan on the right and his cross was headed in by Madeley.

The Leeds-born Madeley was dubbed 'Mr Versatile' for his ability to slot in to any outfield berth and during the 1967/68 campaign played in nine different positions.

Dundee, whose fighting spirit got them past FC Zurich in the previous round, levelled ten minutes later when a free-kick 25 yards out was lofted into the area and Alec Kinninmonth's goal-bound header was headed off the line, only to go straight to Bobby Wilson, who nodded into the empty net.

After that Leeds adopted a more cautious approach and although rarely threatened themselves, kept Dundee at arm's length. The only real scare coming six minutes from the end when George Stewart's lob landed on top of Harvey's net.

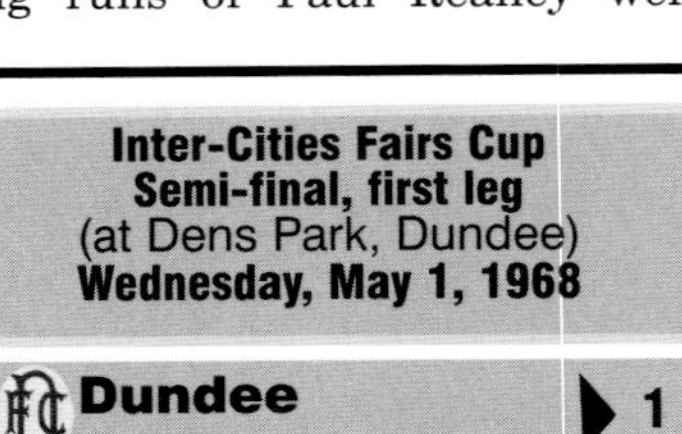

Inter-Cities Fairs Cup
Semi-final, first leg
(at Dens Park, Dundee)
Wednesday, May 1, 1968

Dundee	1
Leeds United	1

Dundee: Alistair Donaldson, Bobby Wilson, Dave Swan, Steve Murray, Jim Easton, George Stewart, Billy Campbell, Jim McLean, Sammy Wilson, George McLean, Alec Kinninmonth
Goal: B Wilson 36
Manager: Bobby Ancell

Leeds United: David Harvey, Paul Reaney, Terry Cooper, Billy Bremner, Jack Charlton, Norman Hunter, Jimmy Greenhoff, Peter Lorimer, Paul Madeley, Johnny Giles, Eddie Gray
Goal: Madeley 27
Manager: Don Revie

Referee: Gerhard Schulenburg (West Germany)
Att: 30,000

Thriller in Budapest

Ferencvaros gained a 3-2 first leg advantage over Bologna to set up a fascinating re-match in Italy.

Semi-final, first leg
Dundee 1 (Wilson), Leeds United 1 (Madeley)
Ferencvaros 3 (Branikovits 2, Varga), Bologna 2 (Clerici, Perani)

MR VERSATILE: Paul Madeley, standing in for the injured Mick Jones at centre forward, headed United in front at Dundee.

Fixture pile up means extra-time looming again

DUNDEE wanted to play the second leg on Tuesday, May 7 – a date to which United objected as both Jack Charlton and Norman Hunter were required for England's European Nations Cup quarter-final in Spain the following day.

That international meant that United had already put back their League game against Arsenal from May 7 to Tuesday, May 14. United came up with the idea of playing on Saturday, May 18, two hours after the FA Cup final between Everton and West Brom.

Eventually the two clubs and the other semi-finalists, Bologna and Ferencvaros, were summoned to the Fairs Cup Management Committee's annual general meeting in Zurich on Monday, May 13, to sort the mess out. The organisers were anxious to avoid a repeat of the previous year when the final was put back to the start of the following season but soon realised they would not get the 1967/68 final played by the first week of June because of international demands.

The Committee eventually bowed to the inevitable and ruled that the final, once again, would be staged at the start of the following season.

VACANT PLOT: There's a huge yawning gap behind Alistair Donaldson's goal where the Spion Kop once stood as Leeds United put pressure on the Dundee defence.

Ghosting through

United Kop place in final

RARELY can a match of such importance have been played out in such an eerie atmosphere

Elland Road was under going major structural changes with the roofing of the old Spion Kop which would temporarily cut the stadium capacity from 52,000 to 33,000.

Talks were held with Sheffield Wednesday about the use of Hillsbrough should United be obliged to play the final before the start of the 1968/69 season. That became immaterial once the Management Committee agreed to hold the final over – and there was also the little matter of getting past Dundee.

Eventually the clubs settled on Wednesday, May 15, for the second leg, played at Elland Road with the Kop shut because of building work.

The state of the ground and the poor turnout made for an odd atmosphere and seemed to affect United's first half performance as Dundee dominated, suprising United with the quality of their approach work.

The Scots made the most of a strong wind at their backs and Gary Sprake did well to save a deflected free-kick from George McLean, who also knocked a good chance over the bar. Terry Cooper got in the way of a Billy Campbell shot and Jim McLean tested Sprake as United were forced onto the back foot.

It needed a tactical switch by Don Revie to get United back on track, moving Billy Bremner into a more advanced position. Immediately, the pendulum of pressure swung towards the visitors' goal as United chances started to mount.

Johnny Giles was a yard wide with a shot, then a dipping 30-yard volley from Norman Hunter went close. Bremner, much more involved as an attacking force, then fed Giles whose shot came off a post into the grateful arms of 'keeper Alistair Donaldson.

Two minutes later a Peter Lorimer header span from Donaldson's grasp, but he just managed to grab it again as the ball span against a post.

With ten minutes left Dundee's resistance was broken when Eddie Gray drove home a thumping shot from a Jimmy Greenhoff corner to seal a second successive Fairs Cup final appearance for United.

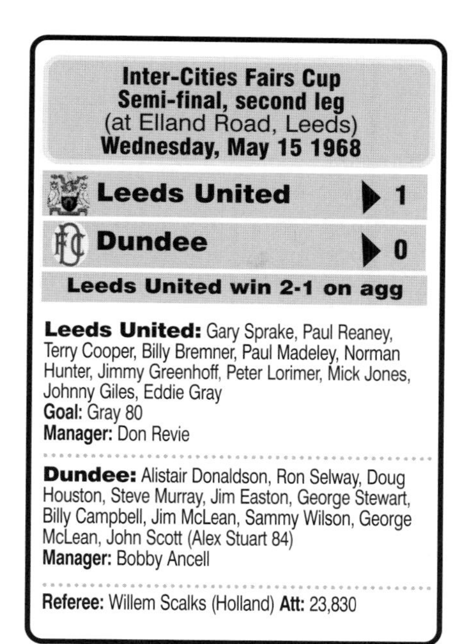

Inter-Cities Fairs Cup
Semi-final, second leg
(at Elland Road, Leeds)
Wednesday, May 15 1968

Leeds United	**1**
Dundee	**0**

Leeds United win 2-1 on agg

Leeds United: Gary Sprake, Paul Reaney, Terry Cooper, Billy Bremner, Paul Madeley, Norman Hunter, Jimmy Greenhoff, Peter Lorimer, Mick Jones, Johnny Giles, Eddie Gray
Goal: Gray 80
Manager: Don Revie

Dundee: Alistair Donaldson, Ron Selway, Doug Houston, Steve Murray, Jim Easton, George Stewart, Billy Campbell, Jim McLean, Sammy Wilson, George McLean, John Scott (Alex Stuart 84)
Manager: Bobby Ancell

Referee: Willem Scalks (Holland) **Att:** 23,830

Ferencvaros through

BOLOGNA pushed Ferencvaros hard in Italy but the Hungarians hug on for a 2-2 draw to clinch a 5-4 aggregate victory.

With Liverpool's scalp already under their belts, Ferencvaros were clearly a side which would test United to the limit in the final.

Semi-final second leg

Bologna 2 (Perani, Tentorio), Ferencvaros 2 (Varga, Havasi) *Ferencvaros win 5-4 on agg*

Leeds United 1 (Gray), Dundee 0 *Leeds win 2-1 on agg*

Jones nudges

THE decision to play the 1967 final at the start of the following season backfired on United from a financial point of view.

The first leg at Elland Road against Ferencvaros, the 1965 Fairs Cup winners, was an anti-climax.

Fewer than 26,000 turned up for a game staged in the middle of the annual Leeds holidays and was being screened live on television, the BBC outbidding ITV for coverage rights to show the first televised live game at Elland Road.

While Syd Owen watched Ferencvaros locked in a goal-less draw with MTK Budapest in the Hungarian League, United warmed up for their 1968/69 season with a 2-1 win over Celtic in a high-profile friendly at Celtic Park in front of 75,110.

But the Elland Road crowd for the Ferencvaros clash was only a third of that massive Celtic attendance, the increase in ticket prices putting many Yorkshire fans off, despite the chance to stand on the Kop for the first time with a £200,000 roof over their heads.

In a dour match, littered with fouls and stoppages, Leeds pinched a 1-0 advantage to take to Hungary.

Inter-Cities Fairs Cup
Final, first leg
(at Elland Road, Leeds)
Wednesday, August 7, 1968

Leeds United	**1**
Ferencvaros	**0**

Leeds United: Gary Sprake, Paul Reaney, Terry Cooper, Billy Bremner, Jack Charlton, Norman Hunter, Peter Lorimer, Paul Madeley, Mick Jones (Rod Belfitt 70), Johnny Giles (Jimmy Greenhoff 65), Eddie Gray
Goal: Jones 41
Manager: Don Revie

Ferencvaros: Istvan Geczi, Dezso Novak, Miklos Pancsics, Sandor Havasi, Istvan Juhasz, Lajos Szucs, Istvan Szoke, Zoltan Varga, Florian Albert, Gyula Rakosi, Mate Fenyvesi (Laszlo Branikovits 65)
Manager: Karoly Lakat

Referee: Rudolf Scheurer (Switzerland)
Att: 25,268

Ferencvaros packed their defence with even star centre forward Florian Albert, who earned many admirers during the 1966 World Cup, playing in a withdrawn role as Leeds, kitted out unfamiliar blue shirts and yellow shorts, found it difficult to pick their way through a congested midfield to provide chances up front.

MISSING FANS: Although the Lowfields Road stand looks packed, a disappointing crowd of less than 26,000 turned up to see the first leg of the delayed Fairs Cup final aganst Ferencvaros at Elland Road.

Jack Charlton puts the all-white defence of the visitors under aerial pressure.

Leeds had an early scare when Albert fed Istvan Szoke, who wasted the chance when well placed.

However, United should have taken the lead when goalkeeper Istvan Geczi miscued a free kick straight to Mick Jones, who set up a glorious opportunity for Peter Lorimer only for the 'keeper to make amends by forcing the ball out for a corner. The next chance fell to the Magyars, but Szoke was unable to convert Mate Fenyvesi's cross and Leeds escaped.

United made the visitors pay a heavy price for that escape. Five minutes from half-time Leeds won a corner at the Elland Road end, Lorimer curled it in from the right and Jack Charlton headed the ball down and Jones forced the ball in from no more than a yard for a priceless lead.

The Hungarians protested that Charlton had fouled Geczi, but referee Rudolf Scheurer allowed the goal to stand. After that ill-feeling crept into the game as the tackles flew in and Ferencvaros frustrated Leeds with time-wasting tactics.

Revie's men were unable to build on their advantage and Ferencvaros missed a great opening when Szoke blazed wide.

Leeds lost Giles, who had double vision, with Jimmy Greenhoff coming on, and scorer Jones also had to leave the field after he chased a long ball into Geczi's box and collided with the goalkeeper.

A poor match drifted to a close with Greenhoff, who was transferred to Birmingham City for £100,000 shortly afterwards, shooting weakly from close range and Gyula Rakosi's effort lacked power enabling Gary Sprake to make a leaping save to his left.

The draw for the 1968/69 competition had already been made with United, who finished fourth in the League behind champions Manchester City, paired with Belgian side Standard Liege.

United nearer to Fairs glory

MATCH WINNER: Mick Jones forces the ball over the line to give United a priceless 1-0 advantage to take to Budapest.

Rival managers at loggerheads

THE stop-start match prompted as many arguements off the field as on it.

Ferencvaros coach Dr Karoly Lakat complained: "It was more of a fight than a game of football. Leeds were more rugged."

Don Revie countered: "They started it – pushing, jersey-pulling, handball and obstruction."

Lakat, a former Ferencvaros player of 12 years, reponded: "Leeds are a very good side, but one goal is not going to be good enough in Budapest."

The same thought was going through the minds of the Leeds supporters – would Mick Jones' goal be sufficient to bring United their first European trophy?

Glory, glory Leeds United

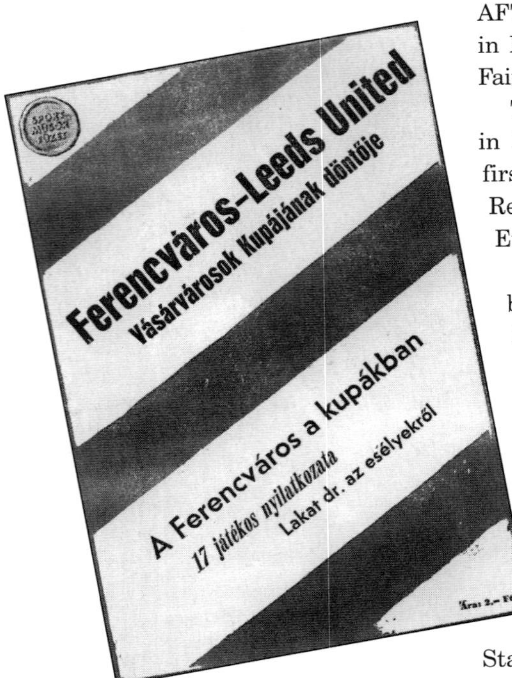

AFTER a night of unremitting tension in Budapest, United finally lifted the Fairs Cup.

The 0-0 draw against Ferencvaros in Hungary meant that Mick Jones' first leg goal was good enough for Don Revie's boys to lift their first piece of European silverware.

It was a sweet moment after being losing finalists and semi-finalists the previous two seasons.

Although Ferencvaros thought one goal would not be enough for Leeds to defend, they overlooked the fact that United had only once conceded more than one goal on continental soil.

In a tense battle by the banks of the Danube, United held firm in the giant Nep Stadium to force the 0-0 draw that saw them become the first British club to win the Fairs Cup in its 10-year history. United had built a reputation for hard-line football with the emphasis on defence, but in Budapest all sections of the English media saluted a tremendous display.

It was virtual non-stop Ferencvaros pressure from start to finish but United weathered the storm and always looked capable of scoring on the break.

Gary Sprake had one of his best-ever games for Leeds, Jack Charlton won everything in the air and Terry Cooper, Paul Hunter and Paul Madeley were everywhere tackling and harrying the Hungarians.

Ferencvaros failed to get the ball out wide and their centrally-based attacks were repelled by the mighty Charlton and Co. It took the Magyars 20 minutes to get a sniff at goal, but Gyula Rakosi's shot was cleared by a spectacular overhead kick by Cooper, who then bravely deflected a goal-bound Florian Albert shot wide.

The pressure was intense, but on the half hour United almost grabbed a crucial away goal, Mick Jones' header coming back off the Ferencvaros bar.

That encouraged Leeds to nudge forward and four minutes later Mike O'Grady, making his first European start since the previous season's final against Dynamo Zagreb, fired in a shot which struck the bewildered goal-keeper Istvan Geczi before going to safety.

But those were rare raids from a Leeds side, lacking the injured Johnny Giles (knee), which defended in depth with great skill and some slices of luck.

United regrouped at half-time knowing the job was nearly done but knew a single mistake could see their tentative hold on the trophy slip away.

BEATEN FINALISTS: Ferencvaros, who gave United's defence a through examination in Budapest. Back row, from left to right: Dr Karoly Lakat (manager), Istvan Szoke, Zoltan Varga, Florian Albert, Gyula Rakosi, Sandor Katona. Middle row: Janos Karaba, Istvan Juhasz, Sandor Matrai, Lajos Szucs, Miklos Pancsis, Mate Fenyvesi. Front row: Laszlo Horvath, Istvan Geczi, Bela Takas, Ratkai.

CELEBRATION TIME: United boss Don Revie (top left) and Les Cocker celebrate with their squad after a nerve-wracking night in Budapest.

Sprake's handling had to be at its best to hold a cross-shot from Szoke soon after the restart as the game settled back into a familiar pattern – Ferencvaros attack, Leeds defence.

Rakosi went close after Zoltan Varga's curling cross eluded the United defence but the minutes were ticking away and Leeds were edging ever-closer to glory.

With 25 minutes left Revie replaced Terry Hibbitt with Mick Bates, who immediately got behind the ball in defence.

The final few minutes were played exclusively in and around the United box and the home side came within a whisker of levelling the tie when Varga's overhead kick eluded a clutch of in-rushing forwards.

Then Albert showed his dribbling skills by weaving through United's defence, but Sprake had read the danger and raced out to smother the ball at Albert's feet.

Tension on the pitch was matched by the tension in the dug-out.

Revie recalled: "When we got into those final few minutes my heart almost stopped beating. Every minute as the final whistle grew nearer seemed like an hour."

Eventually German referee Gerhardt Schulenberg put Revie and his men out of their misery by blowing for time to trigger scenes of great joy among the United party.

Fittingly it was an Englishman, Sir Stanley Rous, president of the Fairs Cup Committee, who presented the trophy to jubilant United skipper Billy Bremner.

After lifting the League Cup earlier in the year, United were at long last winning trophies after so many near misses. They now had the respect of the whole of Europe.

Inter-Cities Fairs Cup
Final, second leg
(at Nep Stadium, Budapest)
Wednesday, September 11 1968

Ferencvaros	**0**
Leeds United	**0**

Leeds United win 1-0 on agg

Ferencvaros: Istvan Geczi, Dezso Novak, Miklos Pancsics, Sandor Havasi, Istvan Juhasz, Lajos Szucs, Istvan Szoke (Janos Karaba 60), Zoltan Varga, Florian Albert, Gyula Rakosi, Sandor Katona
Manager: Karoly Lakat

Leeds United: Gary Sprake, Paul Reaney, Terry Cooper, Billy Bremner, Jack Charlton, Norman Hunter, Mike O'Grady, Peter Lorimer Mick Jones, Paul Madeley, Terry Hibbitt (Mick Bates 62)
Manager: Don Revie

Referee: Gerhard Schulenburg (West Germany)
Att: 75,000

Hot shot Lorimer

UNITED'S Peter Lorimer finished as leading scorer in the competition with eight goals – one more than Dundee's George McLean.

Lorimer's goals came against Spora (5), Partizan Belgrade (2) and Rangers.

United resume

JUST seven days after that never-to-be forgotten night in Budapest, United began the defence of their trophy.

They started as they left off – with a 0-0 away draw.

This time Belgian side Standard Liege were the ones to be blunted by United's near-impregnable defence.

Standard, fresh from a 3-0 league win over Daring of Brussels, felt that United would not be able to repeat their defensive supershow in the Sclessin Stadium.

The Belgians boasted nine men over six-foot tall and were confident that they would cause United aerial problems.

But Leeds, fielding the side which triumphed in Hungary, set the pace with Terry Cooper going close after a fine solo run.

Gradually Liege took control through Leon Semmeling's speed and skill down the right preventing Cooper from making much more progress as an attacker and pressure mounted around the United goal. But Gary Sprake, who was not without his critics, was once again in brilliant form despite having treatment on a damaged ankle before the match. The Welsh star confidently pulled down a 35-yard rocket shot from Wilfrid van Moer, then did well to keep out an Erwin Kostedde shot after Antal Nagy had clipped the bar with an inswinging corner.

United also hit the woodwork when Mick Jones clipped the ball

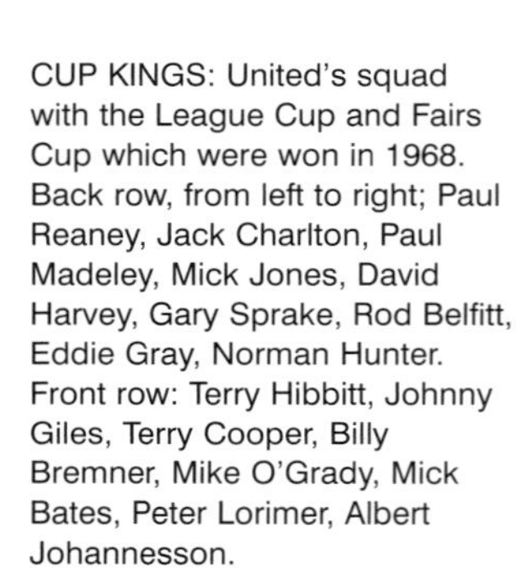

CUP KINGS: United's squad with the League Cup and Fairs Cup which were won in 1968. Back row, from left to right; Paul Reaney, Jack Charlton, Paul Madeley, Mick Jones, David Harvey, Gary Sprake, Rod Belfitt, Eddie Gray, Norman Hunter. Front row: Terry Hibbitt, Johnny Giles, Terry Cooper, Billy Bremner, Mike O'Grady, Mick Bates, Peter Lorimer, Albert Johannesson.

Geordies get off to a flying start bu

SCORER: Bryan Robson.

NEWCASTLE United made a remarkable European debut, thrashing classy Dutch side Feyenoord 4-0 at St James' Park.

Jim Scott opened the scoring with a sixth minute effort .

Bryan 'Pop' Robson added the second and Tommy Gibb made it 3-0 before half-time, Wyn Davies completing the scoring 20 minutes from the end.

Robson later played for his native Sunderland and West Ham and had a spell as Carlisle's manager. He was also a noted coach and was recruited by David O'Leary to look after the Leeds Under-19 Academy side.

In his playing days, Robson was regarded as one of the best uncapped strikers in the country, and was to have a major influence in Newcastle's exciting Fairs Cup campaign of 1968/69. The Magpies had only qualified for Europe through sheer luck. They had finished tenth in the League but because of the Fairs Cup ruling that only one club from each city could enter they found themselves in the hat with a group of other Euro-hopefuls and were fortunate enough to be drawn out of a hat to enter.

Also among the goals were Chelsea, now managed by Dave Sexton. They put five past Scottish outfit Morton, but Liverpool lost 2-1 in Spain to Athletico Bilbao where Roger Hunt's second-half goal gave the Merseysiders some hope for the second leg.

Rangers, knocked out by Leeds in 1967/68, gained a 2-0 home advantage over Yugoslavian representatives Vojvodina with one of the goals coming from the penalty spot by skipper John Greig.

normal service

over the advancing goalkeeper Jean Nicolai only to see it come back off a post

Sprake smothered the ball at Nagy's feet and just after half-time Kostedde hit the woodwork before Paul Reaney headed a Semmeling centre off the line. As United's attacks became more sporadic they contented themselves to play the ball around in midfield and a lively match eventually petered out into rather a tame draw as United extended their unbeaten start to the season to 13 games.

Inter-Cities Fairs Cup
First round, first leg
(at Sclessin Stadium, Liege)
Wednesday, September 18, 1968

Standard Liege 0
Leeds United 0

Standard Liege: Jean Nicolai, Jacques Beurlet, Jean Thissen, Nicolas Dewalque, Leon Jack, Louis Pilot, Leon Semmeling, Henri Depireaux, Erwin Kostedde, Wilfrid Van Moer, Antal Nagy
Manager: Rene Hauss

Leeds United: Gary Sprake, Paul Reaney, Terry Cooper, Billy Bremner, Jack Charlton, Norman Hunter, Mike O'Grady, Peter Lorimer, Mick Jones, Paul Madeley, Terry Hibbitt
Manager: Don Revie

Referee: Gerhard Kunze (West Germany) **Att:** 35,000

IN SAFE HANDS: Leeds United boss Don Revie and members of his backroom staff with the Fairs Cup. From left to right: Syd Owen (coach), Maurice Lindley (assistant manager), Revie, Les Cocker (trainer), Bob English (physiotherapist) and Cyril Partridge (youth team manager).

Revie's brilliant backroom boys

UNITED boss Don Revie reckoned he had the best backroom staff in the business.

His assistant was Maurice Lindley, an Everton player for 17 years, who had managerial experience with Swindon and Crewe. His European scouting missions with coach Syd Owen, the former Luton defender, provided valuable information on opponents.

Whipping United in to shape was Les Cocker, a former Accrington forward, who joined the Elland Road set-up in 1960 when he arrived with Owen from Luton where he had been assistant trainer-coach.

Shankly's Liverpool lose in Bilbao

First round, first leg

Aris Salonika 1 (Alexiadis), Hibernians Paola 0
Athletic Bilbao 2 (Estefano, Ornaza), Liverpool 1 (Hunt)
Atletico Madrid 2 (Luis Aragonés, Barriocana), Waregem 1 (Bettens)
Beerschot 1 (Houben), DWS Amsterdam 1 (van der Vall pen)
Bologna 4 (Turra, Cresci, Pace, Savoldi), Basle 1 (Konrad)
Chelsea 5 (Osgood, Birchenall, Cooke, Boyle, Hollins), Morton 0
Daring Brussels 2 (Randoux, Coppens), Panathinaikos 1 (Gonios)
Dynamo Zagreb 1 (Zambata), Fiorentina 1 (Pirovana)
Goztepe Izmir 2 (Halil Gundogon 2), Marseilles 0
Hannover 3 (Siesensmeyer, Heynckes, Skoblar), Odense 2 (Richter , Hansen)
Hansa Rostock 3 (Drews, Decker 2), Nice 0
Lausanne 0, Juventus 2 (Zigoni, Leonciri)
Legia Warsaw 6 (Pieszko 2, Blaut, Deyna, Zimijewski, Gadocha), TSV Munich 0
Leixoes 1 (Horacio), Arges Pitesti 1 (Nutu)
Lyon 1 (Guy), Coimbra 0
Metz 1 (Hausser) SV Hamburg 4 (Dorfel, Seeler, Krämer, Honig)
Napoli 3 (Altafini, Salvi 2,) 3, Grasshoppers 1 (Rugg)
Newcastle United 4 (Scott, Robson, Gibb, Davies), Feyenoord 0
Olimpia Lubiana 0, Hibernian 3 (Stevenson, Stein, Marinello)
Rapid Bucharest 3 (Nasturescu 2, Neagu), OFK Belgrade 1 (Stepanovic)
Rangers 2 (Greig pen, Jardine), Vojvodina 0
Skeid Oslo 1 (Mathisen), AIK Solna (K Andersson) 1
Slavia Sofia 0, Aberdeen 0
Sporting Lisbon 4 (Lourenco 2, Goncalves, Ernesto), Valencia 0
Standard Liege 0, Leeds United 0
Trakia Plovdiv 3 (Dermendzhiev, Popov, Glushev), Real Zaragoza 1 (Tejedor)
Utrecht 1 (Van Veen), Dundalk 1 (Stokes)
SK Vienna 1 (Buzek), Slavia Prague 0
Vitoria Setubal 3 (Tomé, Carneo, Figueiredo), Linfield 0
Wacker Innsbruck 2 (Aust, Lotz og,) Eintracht Frankfurt 2 (Abbe, Grabwowski pen)

Lokomotiv Leipzig walkover BK Copenhagen (withdrew)
Ujpest Doza walkover Union Luxembourg (withdrew)

Standard

Inter-Cities Fairs Cup
First round, second leg
(at Elland Road, Leeds)
Wednesday, October 23 1968

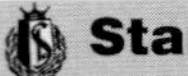

Leeds United	3
Standard Liege	2

Leeds United win 3-2 on agg

Leeds United: Gary Sprake, Paul Reaney, Terry Cooper (Mick Bates HT), Billy Bremner, Jack Charlton, Norman Hunter, Mike O'Grady, Peter Lorimer Mick Jones, Paul Madeley, Terry Hibbitt (Eddie Gray 65)
Goals: Charlton 52, Lorimer 75, Bremner 89
Manager: Don Revie

Standard Liege: Jean Nicolai, Daniel Blaise, Jean Thissen, Nicolas Dewalque, Leon Jeck, Louis Pilot, Leon Semmeling, Wilfrid Van Moer, Erwin Kostedde, Henri Depiraux, Milan Galic
Goals: Kostedde 41, Galic 51
Manager: Rene Hauss

Referee: Gunnar Michaelsen (Denmark) **Att:** 24,178

COLOUR CLASH: United skipper Billy Bremner and a Standard opponent look bemused as both sides went on the pitch in an all white strip.

ON paper the return leg against Standard Liege looked a formality for Leeds, but Don Revie's men struggled for form in the month between the two European matches.

They lost three of their five games including a shock exit in the League Cup to Crystal Palace and a crushing 5-1 League defeat at Burnley. Things were not going smoothly – even though United remained top of the First Division – and the sense of uncertainty at Elland Road grew as a remarkable tie against Liege unfolded.

It began with a touch of comedy as both sides took to the field in white jerseys, prompting a touchline discussion between referee Gunnar Michaelsen, from Denmark, and officials of the two clubs.

Standard, who played in red in the first game, rejected an offer to play in blue and it was the home side, Leeds, who left the field and returned in blue.

The match started 18 minutes late and the colour clash didn't endear Liege to the Leeds crowd, who booed the Belgians.

But the terraces fell silent as Liege moved into a 2-0 lead against an off-key United, who had hardly been able to muster a shot at goal.

Four minutes before half-time Jack Charlton's pass was picked off by the classy Wilfrid Van Moer, who slipped in a pass for Erwin Kostedde to squeeze between Paul Reaney and Norman Hunter to score at the second attempt.

Ten minutes after the interval Milan Galic had ample time and space to score Liege's second and United now needed to score three times otherwise they would be out of the competition.

United were desperate for a quick goal and got it – within a minute of Galic's goal Charlton forced Peter Lorimer's cross over the line.

United were now committed to all out attack and Liege almost capitalised as Henri Depireaux hit a post and Reaney headed another effort off the line.

Those escapes proved vital as substitute Eddie Gray came on to run at the Liege defence and was immediately fouled, Peter Lorimer scoring from the twice-taken free-kick.

With around 15 minutes left United needed to score again or would be out on the away goals count double ruling.

The minutes ticked away and spirited United bombarded the Liege defence who were just one minute away from eliminating the holders when United won a corner.

Lorimer bent in the flag-kick, Charlton flicked the ball on and Billy

SHOCK LEAD: The Belgians surprised United with the quality of their attacking play and things looked bleak for United when Erwin Kostedde put the visitors 1-0 up by shooting past Gary Sprake after the Welsh goalkeeper had blocked his initial effort.

fireworks

Bremner completes amazing fightback

Bremner, who had spent most of the second half as an attacker, forced the ball over the line to complete the great escape.

For goal hero Bremner it was the icing on the cake. It was his first match in a Leeds shirt since captaining Scotland for the first time.

The Stirling-born midfielder led his country out the previous week in Copenhagen where the Scots beat Denmark 1-0.

Human dynamo Bremner was developing in to one of the best midfield men in Europe and his partnership with Johnny Giles, the master of passing the ball. They dovetailed perfectly and the combination was the envy of many a club, both at home and on the continent.

United could not afford to be anything but at their best against their next opponents – Napoli, one of Italy's most fearsome sides.

BILLY'S A HERO: Skipper Billy Bremner celebrates his dramatic last-gasp winner.

Luckless Liverpool spun out at Anfield

LIVERPOOL went out at the first hurdle against Athletico Bilbao in dramatic circumstances at Anfield.

Trailing 2-1 from the first leg in Spain, the Reds looked down and out when Jose Maria Argoitia scored after 32 minutes.

But Bill Shankly's side forced extra-time with goals by Chris Lawler and Emlyn Hughes in the last 12 minutes.

The extra period failed to find another goal for either side and the Merseysiders went out on the spin of a disc.

Newcastle were brought down to earth win a 2-0 defeat in Holland but still went through against Feyenoord 4-2 on aggregate.

Chelsea had too much firepower for Morton but there was better news for Scotland's other sides with Hibernian easing past Olimpia Lubiana and Rangers hanging on to squeeze past Vodjovina 2-1 in aggregate.

First round, second leg

Aberdeen 2 (Robb, Taylor), Slavia Sofia 0 *Aberdeen win 2-0 on agg*

AIK Solna 2 (Lundblad, Ohlsson) 2, Skeid Oslo 1 (Sojberg) *Solna win 3-2 on agg*

Arges Pitesti 0, Leixoes 0 *1-1 on agg. Arges Pitesti win on away goals*

Basle 1 (Hauser), Bologna 2 (Pace, Savoldi) *Bologna win 6-2 on agg*

Coimbra 1 (Manuel Antonio), Lyon 0. *1-1 on agg. Lyon won on lots*

Dundalk 2 (Stokes, Morrisey), Utrecht 1 (Nieuwenhuys) aet *Dundalk win 3-2 on agg*

DWS Amsterdam 2 (Pijlman, Rensenbrink), Beerschot 1 (Houben) *DWS win 3-2 on agg*

Eintract Frankfurt 3 (Kalb, Nickel 2), Wacker Innsbruck 0 *Frankfurt win 5-2 on agg*

Feyenoord 2 (Kindvall, Van Der Heide), Newcastle 0 *Newcastle win 4-2 on agg*

Fiorentina 2 (Amarildo, Maraschi), Dynamo Zagreb 1 (Novak) *Fiorentina win 3-2 on agg*

Grasshoppers 1 (Grahn), Napoli 0 *Napoli win 3-2 on agg*

Hamburg 3 (Honig, Kramer, Seeler), Metz 2 (Hitz, Niesser) *Hamburg win 7-3 on agg*

Hibernian 2 (Davis 2 pens), Olimpia Lubiana 1 (Popivoda) *Hibernian win 5-1 on agg*

Leeds United 3 (Charlton, Lorimer, Bremner), Standard Liege 2 (Kostedde, Galic) *Leeds United win 3-2 on agg*

Linfield 1 (Scott), Vitoria Setubal 3 (Vítor Batista, Figueiredo, Arcanjo) *Vitoria Setubal win 6-1 on agg*

Liverpool 2 (Lawler, Hughes) Athletico Bilbao 1 (Argoitia) *3-3 on agg. Bilbao win on toss of disc*

Hibernians Paola 0, Aris Salonika 6 (K Papaioannou 3, Siropoulos, Alexiadis, Grimbelakos) *Salonika win 7 -0 on agg*

Juventus 2 (Benetti, Del Sol), Lausanne 0 *Juventus win 4-0 on agg*

Marseilles 2 (Joseph, Gueniche), Goztepe Izmir 0 *2-2 on agg. Goztepe Izmir win on toss of disc*

Morton 3 (Thorup, Mason, Taylor), Chelsea 4 (Baldwin, Birchenall, Houseman, Tambling) *Chelsea win 9-3 on agg*

Nice 2 (Goyvaerts pen, Robin), Hansa Rostock 1 (Drews) *Hansa Rostock win 4-2 on agg*

OFK Belgrade 6 (Santrac 4, Turudija), Rapid Bucharest 1 (Codreanu) *Belgrade win 7-4 on agg*

Panathinaikos 2 (Rokidis, Frantzis), Daring Brussels 0 *Panathinaikos win 3-2 on agg*

Real Zaragoza 2 (Bustillo 2), Trakia Plovdiv 0 *Agg 3-3 Real Zaragoza win on away goals*

Slavia Prague 5 (Nepomucky 2, Tesar, Zigler, Kopecky), SK Vienna 0 *Slavia Prague win 5-1 on agg*

TSV Munich 2 (Patzke pen, Schutz 40), Legia Warsaw 3 (Blaut, Pieszk, Brychczy) *Legia Warsaw won 9-2 on agg*

Valencia 4 (Claramunt, Blayet 2, Soi), Sporting Lisbon 1 (Chico Fana) *Sporting Lisbon win 5-4 on agg*

Vojvodina 1 (Nikezic), Rangers 0 *Rangers win 2-1 on agg*

Waregem 1 (Bettens), Atletico Madrid 0 *2-2 on agg. Waregem win on away goals*

Jack in the box pops up

HEAD MASTER: Jack Charlton nods in United's second against Napoli.

NAPOLI had a reputation of being a hard side, but their strongarm tactics could not prevent United from building a 2-0 first leg lead at Elland Road thanks to a couple of Jack Charlton headers.

The Italians, who knocked out Swiss side Grasshoppers in the previous round, were not in the best of form. They had lost 2-1 at Bologna in Serie A on the Sunday before the Leeds game and were in dispute with their star forward Enrique Sivori over his lack of fitness.

But Naples coach Guiseppe Chiapelle knew he would need Sivori against a side as powerful as Leeds. The talented Sivori, capped by both Argentina and Italy, did play at Elland Road, but was rarely seen as Leeds dominated. As early as the second minute, Mick Jones, wearing the unfamiliar No 8 shirt, crashed in a shot which was well saved by Dino Zoff.

Jones and his co-attacker Rod Belfitt ran the Napoli defence ragged, while Mike O'Grady was a source of menace on the right wing.

Despite all his craft and graft it was not to be Jones' night. He had two goals disallowed and claimed he was punched in an off-the-ball incident as the Italians tried unsuccessfully to wind up the England forward. But while Jones appeared to be singled out for the rough stuff, Napoli fatally took their eye off Charlton, who headed in a 23rd minute Billy Bremner free kick, then a Johnny Giles inswinging corner two minutes later.

Despite ricking his back in training before the game, Bremner was inspirational in midfield as United battled in vain for the third goal which would effectively kill of the Neapolitans.

"If we lose our lead in Naples we will deserve to be beaten," said Don Revie, who feared more tough tactics by the Italians were in store in the return leg – both on and off the field.

Inter-Cities Fairs Cup
Second round, first leg
(at Elland Road, Leeds)
Wednesday, November 13, 1968

Leeds United	**2**
Napoli	**0**

Leeds United: Gary Sprake, Paul Reaney, Paul Madeley, Billy Bremner, Jack Charlton, Norman Hunter, Mike O'Grady, Mick Jones, Rod Belfitt, Johnny Giles, Peter Lorimer
Goals: Charlton 23, 25
Manager: Don Revie

Napoli: Dino Zoff, Stelio Nardin, Dino Panzanto, Amedeo Stenti, Aristide Guarneri, Mario Zurlini, Jose Altafini, Antonio Juliano, Harald Nielsen (Claudio Sala 76), Omar Sivori, Paolo Barison
Manager: Guiseppe Chiapella

Referee: Paul Schiller (Austria) **Att:** 26,967

Scots leave opponents reeling

WILLIE Henderson and Alex Ferguson each scored twice as Rangers thrashed Irish part-timers Dundalk 6-1 at Ibrox.

It was a great night for Scotland as Hibernian beat Lokomotiv Leipzig 3-1 with a Joe McBride hat-trick while Aberdeen edged out crack Spanish side Real Zaragoza.

Chelsea were frustratingly held 0-0 at Stamford Bridge by DWS Amsterdam, while Newcastle were denied victory in Portugal by Jose Morais 89th minute goal for Sporting Lisbon.

Second Round, first leg

Aberdeen 2 (Forest, J Smith), Real Zaragoza 1 (Tejedor)
Aris Salonika 1 (Konstantinidis), Ujpest Doza 2 (Bene, A Dunai)
Chelsea 0, DWS Amsterdam 0
Goztepe Izmir 3 (Aksel 2, Ertan), Arges Pitesti 0
Hamburg 4 (Schultz, Fock, Kramer 2 – 1 pen), Slavia Prague 1 (Tesar)
Hansa Rostock 3 (Kostmann, Barthels, Herqessell), Fiorentina 2 (Marasciu, Rizzo)
Hibernian 3 (McBride 3), Lokomotive Leipzig 1 (Fritsch)
Juventus 0, Eintracht Frankfurt 0
Leeds United 2 (Charlton 2), Napoli 0
OFK Belgrade 1 (Santrac), Bologna 0
Panathinaikos 0, Athletic Bilbao 0
Rangers 6 (Henderson 2, Greig, Ferguson 2, Brennan og), Dundalk 1 (Murray)
Sporting Lisbon 1 (Joao Morais), Newcastle United 1 (Scott)
Vitoria Setubal 5 (Tome 3, Carrico, Petitia), Lyon 0
Waregem 1 (Lambert pen), Legia Warzaw 0

Red letter day

Skipper Billy calls it right

UNITED progressed to the third round after a tense, and often brutal, night in Naples.

The Italians levelled the tie in the the 85,000 capacity San Paolo Stadium, only for Billy Bremner to win for Leeds on the toss of a coin after extra-time.

Napoli had no less than 50,000 season ticket holders, but the support proved fickle when times were hard and a 2-0 defeat at Vincenza three days before the Leeds match left them near the bottom of Serie A with just one League win under their belt.

Fans were so disgusted with recent performances that they launched a campaign to boycott the Leeds tie and pre-match ticket sales were just 200.

When the game started at 9.15pm there were just 15,000 spectators in the vast bowl but the diehards saw a thrilling fightback by their side.

Mick Jones and Eddie Gray both missed early chances to make the tie academic, but Claudio Sala knocked Leeds out of their stride by shooting past Gary Sprake after 14 minutes.

From then on it was a question of hanging on for United as Napoli laced their considerable skills with nastiness. United players complained of being poked in the eyes and Bremner appeared to be hit in the face as he got up from one tackle.

As the match was drawing to close the small crowd grew more hostile and a broken bottle thrown from the crowd over the 8ft wide moat into the Leeds goalmouth gashed Sprake's hand.

With trainer Les Cocker laid low by a stomach bug, it was left to United's medical officer to attend to the big Welsh 'keeper. It was felt that it would be too risky for Sprake to continue, so with eight minutes left on came David Harvey. One of the first things the young goalkeeper had to do was pick the ball out of the back of the net. Sala was brought down by Jack Charlton as Napoli won a disputed penalty which Antonio Juliano converted to take the game into extra-time.

In the additional half hour United stood firm with Charlton and Norman Hunter rocks of reliabilty to ensure that the match would be determined by the toss of a disc.

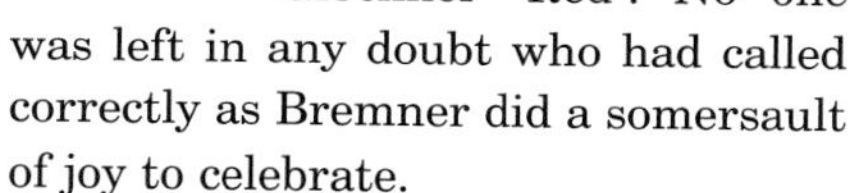

CHANCE: Mick Jones.

Leeds skipper Bremner was given the right to call by counterpart Juliano and told referee Rudi Glockner 'Red'. No one was left in any doubt who had called correctly as Bremner did a somersault of joy to celebrate.

United had suffered only their fourth defeat in 39 European ties but they had gone through, although Revie was fuming about the home side's brutal tactics.

"I hope we never have to play in Naples again," he blazed. "They were far worse than anything I expected. It was quite our worst experience in the Fairs Cup."

Inter-Cities Fairs Cup
Second round, second leg
(at San Paolo Stadium, Naples)
Wednesday, November 27 1968

Napoli	**2**
Leeds United	**0**

2-2 on agg after extra-time
Leeds win on toss of a disc

Napoli: Dino Zoff, Stelio Nardin, Luigi Pogliana (Romano Micelli HT), Mario Zurlini, Dino Panzanato, Ottavio Bianchi, Egido Salvi, Antonio Juliano, Claudio Sala, Omar Sivori (Vicenzo Montefusco HT), Paolo Barison
Goals: Sala 14, Juliano 84 pen
Manager: Guiseppe Chiapella

Leeds United: Gary Sprake (David Harvey 82), Paul Reaney, Terry Cooper, Billy Bremner, Jack Charlton, Norman Hunter, Mike O'Grady, Paul Madeley (Rod Belfitt 61), Mick Jones, Johnny Giles, Eddie Gray
Manager: Don Revie

Referee: Rudi Glockner (East Germany) **Att:** 15,000

Robson winner for Newcastle

NEWCASTLE'S adventure continued with a 10th minute Bryan Robson goal eliminating Sporting Lisbon at St James' Park.

Chelsea, however, embarrassingly failed to score in Amsterdam and were knocked out, like Naples, on the spin of a disc.

Scottish sides Rangers and Hibernian both progressed with ease but Aberdeen went out at Real Zaragoza.

Second Round, second leg

AIK Solna 4 (Ohlsson 3, Grip), Hannover 96 2 (Anders, Siesenmeyer)
Arges Pitesti (Prepurgel, Derebasio, Jercan) 3, Goztepe Izmir 2 (Zemzem, Ertan) *Goztepe Izmir win 5-2 on agg*
Athletico Bilbao 1 (Rojo) Panathinaikos 0 *Athletico Bilbao win 1-0 on agg*
Bologna 1 (Muiesan), OFK Belgrade 1 (Santrac) *OFK Belgrade win 2-1 on agg*
Dundalk 0, Rangers 3 (Mathieson, Stein 2) *Rangers win 9-1 on agg*
DWS Amsterdam 0, Chelsea 0 *0-0 on agg. DWS win on spin of a disc*
Eintracht Frankfurt 1 (Bechtold), Juventus 0 aet *Eintract Frankfurt win 1-0 on agg*
Fiorentina 2 (Rizzo, Merlo), Hansa Rostock 1 (Kostmann 26) *4-4 on agg Fiorentina win on away goals*
Hannover 5 (Skoblar 2, Heynckes 3), AIK Solna 2 (Nilsson, Lundblad) *Hannover win 7-6 on agg*
Lyon 1 (Felix), Vitoria Setubal 2 (Figueiredo, Arcanjo) *Vitoria Setubal win 7-1 on agg*
Legia Warsaw 2 (Deyna, Gadocha), Waregem 0 *Legia Warsaw win 2-1 on agg*
Locomotiv Leipzig 0, Hibernian 1 (Grant) *Hibernian win 4-1 on agg*
Napoli 2 (Sala, Juliano), Leeds United 0 *2-2 on agg Leeds United win on spin of a disc*
Newcastle United 1 (Robson), Sporting Lisbon 0 *Newcastle United win 2-1 on agg*
Real Zaragoza (Marcelino, Tejedor, Villa) 3, Aberdeen 0 *Real Zaragoza win 4-2 on agg*
Slavia Prague 3 (Kopecky, Vesely, Lukac), Hamburg 1 (Honig) *Hamburg win 5-4 on agg*
Ujpest Doza (A Dunai 4, E Dunai, Bene, Kuharszki, Solymosi, Nagy), Aris Salonika 1 (Siropoulos) *Ujpest Doza win 11-2 on agg*

Five live for Revie's men

UP AND RUNNING: Just four minutes are on the clock and Mike O'Grady fires United ahead against Hannover.

UNITED turned on the style to cruise past German outfit Hannover 96 at Elland Road.

The visitors, coached by Zlatco Cajkovski, who won 60 caps for Yugoslavia, were swept aside by a fantastic display by the Whites.

Prompted by Billy Bremner and Johnny Giles, United attacked from start to finish and but for some remarkable saves by Horst Podlasly Leeds would have hit double figures.

Just four minutes had gone when Norman Hunter exchanged passes with Giles and his cross from the left was turned in by Mike O'Grady.

Half an hour later Hunter surged forward and slammed a right foot drive from 30 yards past Podlasly.

But United's 2-0 interval lead could so easily have been bigger but Peter Lorimer and Mick Jones, who went into the match without a goal in his last 14 games, both had shots cleared off the line.

Peter Loof came on for Hannover captain Hans Siemesmeyer at the break but immediately presented United with a third goal. He hit a clearance straight to Giles who fed Lorimer and the Scottish forward smashed in an angled drive.

Just after an hour Bremner was brought down on the edge of the box, Giles chipped in the free kick and Jack Charlton's header made it 4-0.

Lorimer, who had a heart-to-heart with manager Revie the previous month after failing to hold down a regular place, drove in the fifth just a couple of minutes later.

Leeds continued to pour forward with Paul Madeley's overlapping runs down the left a feature of the game, but thanks to Podlasly's elasticity, Hannover managed to stem the tide of goals and near the end netted a consolation when Hans-Josef Hellingrath lobbed the ball over goalkeeper Gary Sprake.

Inter-Cities Fairs Cup
Third round, first leg
(at Elland Road, Leeds)
Wednesday, December 13, 1968

Leeds United	**5**
Hannover 96	**1**

Leeds United: Gary Sprake, Paul Reaney, Paul Madeley, Billy Bremner, Jack Charlton, Norman Hunter, Mike O'Grady (Terry Hibbitt 64), Peter Lorimer, Mick Jones, Johnny Giles, Eddie Gray
Goals: O'Grady 4, Hunter 34, Lorimer 51, 63, Charlton 61
Manager: Don Revie

Hannover 96: Horst Podlasly, Hans-Josef Hellingrath, Klaus Bohnsack, Peter Anders, Christian Breuer, Rainer Stiller, Rainer Zobel, Josef Heynckes, Jurgen Bandura, Jospit Skoblar, Hans Siemensmeyer (Peter Loof HT)
Goal: Hellingrath 86
Manager: Zlatko Cajkovski

Referee: Adolfo Bueno Perales (Spain) **Att:** 25,162

Battling Magpies still flying

NEWCASTLE United's exciting campaign continued with a thrilling match in Real Zaragoza.

Although they lost 3-2 in Spain, the Magpies scored vital away goals with strikes from Bryan Robson and Wyn Davies, who netted with a great diving header.

Rangers took control of their tie against DWS Amsterdam, conquerers of Chelsea, with a 2-0 win in Holland courtesy of goals from Willie Johnston and Willie Henderson.

Hibernian, like Leeds, were in action against German opposition, going down 1-0 in Hamburg to a Heinz Honig goal.

Third round, first leg

Athletico Bilbao 1 (Unarte), Eintracht Frankfurt 0
DWS Amsterdam 0, Rangers 2 (Johnston, Henderson)
Hamburg 1 (Honig), Hibernian 0
Leeds United 5 (Lorimer 2, O'Grady, Hunter, Charlton), Hannover 1 (Hellingrath)
Legia Warsaw 0, Ujpest Doza 1 (A Dunai)
OFK Belgrade 3 (Santrac 3), Goztepe Izmir 1 (Zemzem)
Real Zaragoza 3 (Santos, Bustillo, Planas), Newcastle United 2 (Robson, Davies)
Vitoria Setubal 3 (Jose Maria 2, Arcanjo), Fiorentina 0

TAKING THE MICK: United striker Mick Jones slots home Norman Hunter's cross to put United 2-0 up in Hannover.

Inter-Cities Fairs Cup
Third round, second leg
(at Niedersachsen Stadium, Hannover)
Tuesday, February 4 1969

Hannover 96	**1**
Leeds United	**2**

Leeds United win 7-2 on agg

Hannover 96: Bernd Helmschrot, Hans-Josef Hellingrath, Peter Loof, Peter Anders, Christian Breuer, Rainer Stiller, Rainer Zobel (Winfried Wottka 61), Claus Bruner, Jurgen Bandura, Joseph Heynckes, Bernd Kettler (Kurt Ritter 21)
Goal: Heynckes 87
Manager: Zlatko Cajkovski

Leeds United: Gary Sprake, Paul Reaney, Terry Cooper, Billy Bremner, Jack Charlton, Norman Hunter, Mike O'Grady, Peter Lorimer, Mick Jones, Rod Belfitt, Eddie Gray
Goals: Belfitt 5, Jones 16
Manager: Don Revie

Referee: Jef Dorpmans (Holland) **Att:** 15,000

Tonic for the troops

SEVEN weeks after the first leg against Hannover, United flew out to Germany and simply started in the same vein they had at Elland Road.

United left Johnny Giles (thigh) and Paul Madeley (ankle) behind for the two-hour flight from Yeadon and landed in a snowstorm. Milder weather quickly followed and the pitch was in perfect condition and the 15,000 crowd was swelled by a large contingent of British soldiers who were soon booming out "Ilkla Moor bah't 'at".

Bernd Helschrot, in for first leg goalkeeping hero Horst Podlasly, had already fumbled a long free-kick from Jack Charlton when he spilled a fifth minute shot from Mike O'Grady to leave Rod Belfitt with an easy goal. United put the tie completely beyond Hannover's reach when Helschrot failed to cut out Norman Hunter's low cross and Mick Jones converted. That gave United a 7-1 aggregate lead and they held onto it with ease but the Germans became more frustrated and the tackles started to fly in thick and fast. The match turned nasty when Christian Breuer fouled Billy Bremner and a police guard was called to man the moat surrounding the pitch.

Within minutes United found themselves a man down when Terry Cooper was sent off after a foul on sub Winfried Wottka, who certainly made the most of the challenge.

Manager Don Revie complained: "I thought it was a harsh decision especially considering what Hannover had been doing. I thought their players got upset when they were making no impression on us."

United's sense of grievance was not helped by another foul on Bremner, just after the Cooper incident, which earned Jurgen Bandura a booking rather than a red card.

The spiky ending took the gloss off the best goal of the night – a thumping free-kick from the edge of the box by Josef Heynckes. But United, 7-2 aggregate winners, marched into the quarter-finals.

Zaragoza can't crack Newcastle

NEWCASTLE produced another thrilling display in front of just over 56,000 at St James' Park to edge out Real Zaragoza. Bryan Robson's 30 yarder after just two minutes got the Magpies on level aggregate terms and Tommy Gibb's diving header nudged them in front.

The Spaniards hit back through Armando Martin to set up a tense second half but the Geordies held on to a 2-1 victory to go through on the away goals rule.

Third round, second leg

Eintracht Frankfurt 1 (Lotz), Athletico Bilbao 1 (Igartua) *Athletico Bilbao win 2-1 on agg*

Fiorentina 2 (Amarildo, Rogora), Vitoria Setubal 1 (Mancin og) *Vitoria Setubal win 4-2 on agg*

Goztepe Izmir 2 (Gundogon, Ertan), OFK Belgrade 0 *3-3 on agg. Goztepe Izmir win on away goals*

Hannover 1 (Heynckes), Leeds United 2 (Belfitt, Jones) *Leeds United win 7-2 on agg*

Hibernian 2 (McBride 2), Hamburg 1 (Seeler) *2-2 on agg. Hamburg win on away goals*

Newcastle United 2 (Robson, Gibb), Real Zaragoza 1 *4-4 on agg, Newcastle United win on away goals*

Rangers 2 (Smith, Stein), DWS Amsterdam 1 (Geurtsen) *Rangers win 4-1 on agg*

Ujpest Doza 2 (A Dunai, Solymosi pen), Legia Warsaw 2 (Stachurski, Zmijewski) *Ujpest Doza win 3-2 on agg*

IN THE SWING OF THINGS: United goalkeeper Gary Sprake is left sat on the deck as Ujpest's Laszlo Fazekas swings on the bar to celebrate Antal Dunai's winner at Elland Road.

Hungarian pests

Ovation for skilful Ujpest at Elland Road

FEW in the United camp expected Hungarian side Ujpest Doza to cause United much trouble.

After all they had been whipped 4-1 on their prevous visit to Elland Road in 1966 in the same stage of the Fairs Cup.

But almost three years to the day after that impressive United performance the tables were turned as the Magyars gave a stunning display and richly deserved their 1-0 victory.

The surprise result turned on two key incidents.

Ten minutes into the second half an Eddie Gray cross was handled by defender Erno Nosko, but Antal Szentmitalyi, Doza's 6ft 2in goalkeeper dived low to his right to keep out Johnny Giles' penalty kick.

It was a rare miss by the normally deadly Irishman and United were to pay a high price as the winner came on 72 minutes when Ferenc Bene fed a short pass to Albert Dunai, who hooked a powerful 25 yard shot into Gary Sprake's top right hand corner.

United, clad in blue, began well with Gray pulling a left-foot shot wide, Paul Madeley heading against the bar and Rod Belfitt, preferred to Peter Lorimer, shooting over the bar after Szentmihalyi did well to parry a hard shot by Giles.

But it was not all one-way traffic as Jack Charlton was forced to head against his own bar and Madeley had to head over to relieve the pressure in the same attack.

Ujpest were lightning quick on the break and at the final whistle received a standing ovation from an appreciative Elland road crowd.

"They are an excellent side, good all-round and very fast on the break from defence into attack," said an admiring Don Revie, who would take his side to Hungary for their 47th European match for the first time going into an away leg in arrears.

Inter-Cities Fairs Cup
Quarter final, first leg
(at Elland Road, Leeds)
Wednesday, March 5, 1969

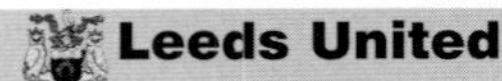

Leeds United 0

Ujpest Doza 1

Leeds United: Gary Sprake, Paul Reaney, Paul Madeley, Billy Bremner, Jack Charlton, Norman Hunter, Mike O'Grady, Rod Belfitt (Peter Lorimer 60), Mick Jones, Johnny Giles, Eddie Gray
Manager: Don Revie

Ujpest Doza: Antal Szentmihalyi, Beno Kaposzta, Erno Solymosi, Istvan Bankuti, Ede Dunai, Erno Nosko, Laszlo Fazekas, Janos Gorocs, Ferenc Bene, Antal Dunai, Sandor Zambo
Goal: A Dunai 72
Manager: Lajos Baroti

Referee: Robert Helies (France) **Att:** 30,906

Best of British

WHILE United went down at home to Ujpest Doza, Britain's two other Fairs Cup representatives hit top form.

Rampant Newcastle hammered Vitoria Setubal 5-1 at St James' Park, while at Ibrox, Rangers fans saw their heroes shatter Athletico Bilbao 4-1.

Quarter- final, first leg

Leeds United 0, Ujpest Doza 1 (A Dunai)
Newcastle United 5 (Robson 2, Davies, Foggon, Gibb), Vitoria Setubal 1 (Jose Maria)
Rangers 4 (Ferguson, Penman, Persson, Stein), Athletico Bilbao 1 (Clemente)

Catching a cold

Bene give United a headache

UJPEST Doza proved their victory in Yorkshire was no fluke as they became the first side to beat United in both legs with a 2-0 win in Budapest.

It was to prove too difficult a task for a flu-hit United to claw back that one-goal deficit, especially as they went into the game without the bed-ridden Jack Charlton, Mike O'Grady and Paul Reaney, while Norman Hunter, Billy Bremner, Terry Cooper, Paul Madeley and Mick Jones were also suffering from sore throats and flu-like symptoms.

Don Revie pulled a surprise by playing Bremner at right-back in place of Reaney, while Mick Bates, despite wearing No 2, came into midfield.

United began well as Jones dived in and almost connected with crosses from both flanks. They were still in the tie at the interval and almost drew level when Giles' brilliant volley skimmed passed an upright.

But the killer blow came midway through the second half when Madeley brought down the lively Ferenc Bene in the box.

Referee Heinz Siebert gave the decision from the centre circle with United protesting there had been no contact between the players. The protests led to bookings for Bremner and Giles, but Erno Solymosi kept his cool and sent Gary Sprake the wrong way from the spot.

Revie's response was to push Bremner into midfield at the expense of Lorimer, who was replaced by young Welsh utility player Terry Yorath, who came on for his European debut and slotted into the right-back postiion.

Just over 10 minutes from the end dangerman Bene, was picked out in the box by Janos Gorocs and cracked a low drive past Sprake.

Six months earlier United had beaten a Hungarian side, Ferencvaros to win the cup, and had now relinquished it to another top-notch Magyar outfit.

Flu in the United camp spread to such an extent that their League game at Liverpool the following Saturday was postponed.

STAR TURN: Hungarian international forward Ferenc Bene, who scored one and made one as United crashed to Ujpest Doza.

Inter-Cities Fairs Cup
Quarter-final, second leg
(at Megyeri Stadium, Budapest)
Wednesday, March 19, 1969

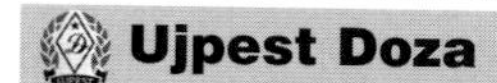

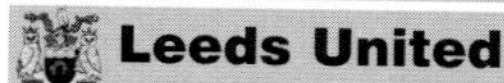

Ujpest Doza win 3-0 on agg

Ujpest Doza: Antal Szentmihalyi, Beno Kaposzta, Erno Solymosi, Istvan Bankuti, Ede Dunai, Erno Nosko, Laszlo Fazekas, Janos Gorocs, Ferenc Bene, Antal Dunai, Sandor Zambo
Goals: Solymosi 63 pen, Bene 75
Manager: Lajos Baroti

Leeds United: Gary Sprake, Mick Bates, Terry Cooper, Billy Bremner, Paul Madeley, Norman Hunter, Peter Lorimer (Terry Yorath 70), Rod Belfitt, Mick Jones (Terry Hibbitt 85), Johnny Giles, Eddie Gray
Manager: Don Revie

Referee: Heinz Siebert (West Germany) **Att:** 40,000

Newcastle and Rangers to meet in all-British semi-final

BOTH Newcastle and Rangers came through tough second legs to set up a blockbusting all-British semi-final.

The pair were grateful to their big first leg leads. The Geordies,having won 5-1 in a snowstorm on Tyneside, lost 3-1 to Vitoria Setubal in Portugal where Wyn Davies' goal just before half-time helped ease the pressure.

Rangers were under the cosh in Spain where they lost 2-0 to Athletico Bilbao but went through 4-3 on aggregate.

Ujpest Doza, who eliminated Don Revie's team in emphatic fashion, were drawn with Goztepe Izmir in their semi-final.

The Turkish club had made it through to the last four when SV Hamburg withdrew from the competition at the quarter-final stage.

Quarter-final, first leg

Athletico Bilbao 2 (Estofano, Ibanez), Rangers 0 *Rangers win 4-3 on agg*

Ujpest Doza 2 ((Solymosi, Bene), Leeds United 0 *Ujpest Doza win 3-1 on agg*

Vitoria Setubal 3 (Figueiredo, Petita, Jacinto João), Newcastle United 1 (Davies) *Newcastle United win 6-4 on agg*

Goztepe Izmir walkover Hamburg (with-drew)

Newcastle shock winners

NEWCASTLE were shock winners of the 1969 Fairs Cup after out-gunning the highly fancied Hungarians Ujpest Doza.

The Magyars, who had looked so impressive in knocking out Don Revie's aces, took their hot form in to the semi-finals where star international forward Ferenc Bene was in sensational form. He scored twice in the away leg in Turkey and then netted a hat-trick in the the 4-0 thumping of Goztepe Izmir in Budapest.

Newcastle's passage was harder, holding Rangers to a 0-0 draw in Scotland before winning a fierce encounter on Tyneside 2-0.

Second half goals by Jim Scott and Jackie Sinclair proved decisive. But it sparked an ugly pitch invasion by 'Gers fans, prompting the game to be held up for 17 minutes.

In the final, two goals by skipper Bobby Moncur – his first in competitive football – and one from Scott gave Newcastle a 3-0 lead.

Ujpest hit back in humid Budapest with two first-half goals before Moncur's left-foot shot triggered a Geordie revival and they romped home 6-2 on aggregate.

Semi-final, first leg

Goztepe Izmir 1 (Caglayan), Ujpest Doza 4 (Bene 2, A Dunai 2)
Rangers 0, Newcastle United 0

Semi-final, second leg

Newcastle United 2 (Scott, Sinclair), Rangers 0 *Newcastle United win 2-0 on agg*
Ujpest Doza 4 (Bene 3, Nagy), Goztepe Izmir 0 *Ujpest Doza win 8-1 on agg*

Final, first leg

(St James' Park, Newcastle)
May 29, 1969
Newcastle United 3, Ujpest Doza 0

Newcastle United: McFaul, Craig, Clark, Gibb, Burton, Moncur, Scott, B Robson, Davies, Arentoft, Sinclair (Foggon 75)
Goals: Moncur 69, 72, Scott 83
Manager: Joe Harvey
Ujpest Doza: Szentimihayi, Kaposzta, Solymosi, Bankuti, E Dunai, Nosko, Fazekas, Gorocs, Bene, A Dunai, Zambo
Manager: Lajos Baroti
Referee: Joseph Hannet (Belgium)
Attendance: 59,500

Final, second leg

(Nep Stadium, Budapest)
June 11, 1969
Ujpest Doza 2, Newcastle United 3
Newcastle United won 6-2 on agg

Ujpest Doza: Szentimihayi, Kaposzta, Solymosi, Bankuti, E Dunai, Nosko, Fazekas, Gorocs, Bene, A Dunai, Zambo.
Goals: Bene 28, Gorocs 31
Manager: Lajos Baroti
Newcastle United: McFaul,Craig, Clark, Gibb, Burton, Moncur, Scott (Foggon 76), B Robson, Davies, Arentoft, Sinclair.
Goals: Moncur 46, Arentoft 50, Scott 75
Manager: Joe Harvey
Referee: Joseph Heymann (Switzerland)
Attendance: 18,000

Leading scorers: 9 – A Dunai (Ujpest Doza), Bene (Ujpest Doza), Santrac (OFK), 6 – B Robson (Newcastle United), 5 – Scott (Newcastle United)

TOP OF THE CLASS: Leeds United, League champions 1968/69. Back row (left to right): Paul Reaney, Norman Hunter, Allan Clarke, Mike O'Grady, David Harvey, Gary Sprake, Paul Madeley, Eddie Gray, Rod Belfitt, Jack Charlton. Front row: Mick Jones, Terry Cooper, Terry Hibbitt, Billy Bremner, Johnny Giles, Mick Bates, Peter Lorimer.

Champions! Champions!

AFTER knocking on the door for so many seasons, United were finally crowned League champions for the first time in their history in 1968/69.

Their quarter-final defeat against Ujpest Doza, coupled with early FA Cup and Football League Cup exits paved the way for United to have a clear run at the title.

It meant that they would enter the European Cup in 1969/70 and tackle the continent's best sides. Don Revie's team were regarded as one of the best equipped English sides to enter Europe's premier competition after four successive campaigns in the Fairs Cup.

United's title success was based on a cast iron defence which was in typically defiant mood at Liverpool where United drew 0-0 on April 28 and were hailed by the Kop as 'Champions! Champions!'.

Victory two nights later at home to Nottingham Forest meant United had amassed a record 67 points, beating the previous best set by Arsenal (1930-31) and Tottenham (1960-61).

Other records to fall to United were the most home points (39), most wins (27), most home wins (18), fewest defeats (2 – both away, another record).

United were unbeaten at Elland Road, equalling the feat they achieved in their 1963-64 Division Two championship season.

It had been a fantastic season and it was no surprise when the outstanding Revie was named Manager of the Year.

Division One 1968/69

	P	W	D	L	F	A	Pts
LEEDS UNITED	42	27	13	2	66	26	67
Liverpool	42	25	11	6	63	24	61
Everton	42	21	15	6	77	36	57
Arsenal	42	22	12	8	56	27	56
Chelsea	42	20	10	12	73	53	50
Tottenham Hotspur	42	14	17	11	61	51	45
Southampton	42	16	13	13	57	48	45
West Ham United	42	13	18	11	66	50	44
Newcastle United	42	15	14	13	61	55	44
West Bromwich Alb	42	16	11	15	64	67	43
Manchester United	42	15	12	15	57	53	42
Ipswich Town	42	15	11	16	59	60	41
Manchester City	42	15	10	17	64	55	40
Burnley	42	15	9	18	55	82	39
Sheffield Wed	42	10	16	16	41	54	36
Wolverhampton W	42	10	15	17	41	58	35
Sunderland	42	11	12	19	43	67	34
Nottingham Forest	42	10	13	19	45	57	33
Stoke City	42	9	15	18	40	63	33
Coventry City	42	10	11	21	46	64	31
Leicester City	42	9	12	21	39	68	30
Queens Park Rgrs	42	4	10	28	39	95	18

Ten out of ten

DON Revie made it perfectly plain that his men would be hell-bent on European Cup glory.

He said: "Of all the competitions open to us this season, this is the one we would like to win more than anything."

They certainly hit the ground running, slaughtering Norwegian part-timers Lyn Oslo 10-0 at Elland Road to equal the ten-goal European victories of Manchester United and Ipswich over Anderlecht and Floriana respectively.

The Oslo rout started after only 35 seconds, which at that time was reckoned to be the fastest-ever goal in the competition. Transfer-listed Mike O'Grady despatched a left foot drive past goalkeeper Sven Olsen.

Olsen had only got to the ground 35 minutes before the kick-off. He had not been able to travel with the rest of the Lyn party because of a family bereavement. His arrival at Heathrow was delayed and his onward flight to Leeds/Bradford Airport was delayed and eventually cancelled because of poor weather.

He dashed across London to catch a 3.50pm train and was met at Leeds Station by a taxi and a police escort whisked him through to Elland Road.

But the nightmare was only just starting for the 24-year-old Norwegian international. He had hardly time to reflect on being beaten by O'Grady when Mick Jones scored with a header and the Leeds centre-forward shot United 3-0 up after only nine minutes.

HORIZONTAL HOLD: Lyn Oslo goalkeeper Sven Olsen flies through the air to punch the ball away from danger as Mick Jones closes in.

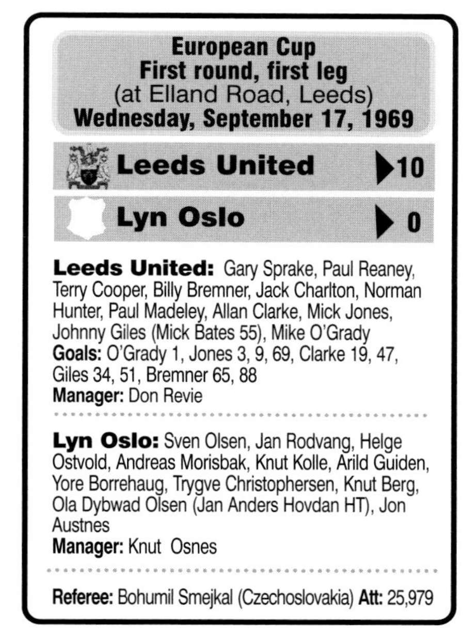

European Cup
First round, first leg
(at Elland Road, Leeds)
Wednesday, September 17, 1969

Leeds United 10
Lyn Oslo 0

Leeds United: Gary Sprake, Paul Reaney, Terry Cooper, Billy Bremner, Jack Charlton, Norman Hunter, Paul Madeley, Allan Clarke, Mick Jones, Johnny Giles (Mick Bates 55), Mike O'Grady
Goals: O'Grady 1, Jones 3, 9, 69, Clarke 19, 47, Giles 34, 51, Bremner 65, 88
Manager: Don Revie

Lyn Oslo: Sven Olsen, Jan Rodvang, Helge Ostvold, Andreas Morisbak, Knut Kolle, Arild Guiden, Yore Borrehaug, Trygve Christophersen, Knut Berg, Ola Dybwad Olsen (Jan Anders Hovdan HT), Jon Austnes
Manager: Knut Osnes

Referee: Bohumil Smejkal (Czechoslovakia) **Att:** 25,979

Ten minutes later Allan Clarke, United's new £165,000 striker from Leicester City, dribbled round three men and planted a left foot shot into the net and before half-time Johnny Giles' 30-yard drive soared past Olsen.

Leeds moved into a 6-0 lead when Billy Bremner centred for Clarke to head in two minutes after the interval. Then a short free-kick routine saw Giles send a drive fizzing past Olsen.

Jones completed his hat-trick with a 25-yarder via an upright and when Bremner's long range effort made it 9-0 a dozen goals seemed on the cards as there were still 25 minutes left. But United managed just one more score with another shot from distance by Bremner deflecting past Olsen.

Prati double as holders Milan cruise home

EUROPEAN Cup holders AC Milan made a flying start to their defence of the trophy with a 5-0 thumping of Luxembourg minnows Avenir Beggen in Italy.

Pierino Prati, who had scored a hat-trick in the 1969 final when Milan beat Ajax Amsterdam 4-1, netted twice in the first round opener.

Scotland's standard-bearers, Celtic, who had become the first British side to win the European Cup in 1967, drew 0-0 in Basle.

Preliminary round, first leg

Turku Palloseura 0, KB Copenhagen 1 (Skouborg)

Preliminary round, second leg

KB Copenhagen 3 (Skouborg 2, Brage, Praest), Turku Palloseura 0
KB Copenhagen won 4-0 on agg

First round, first leg

AC Milan 5 (Prati 2, Rivera pen, Rognoni, Combin), Avenir Beggen 0
Basle 0, Celtic 0
Bayern Munich 2 (Brenninger, Roth), St Etienne 0
Benfica 2 (Eusebio 2), KB Copenhagen 0
CSKA Sofia 2 (Zhekov 2), Ferencvaros 1 (Rakosi)
FK Austria 1, Dynamo Kiev 2
Fiorentina 1 (Maraschi), Oesters 0
KR Reykjavik 2 (Baldvinsson, Bjornsson), Feyenoord 12 (Geels 4, Kindvall 3, Romejin, Van Duivenbode, Wery, Van Hanegem 2) – played in Rotterdam,
Galatasaray 2 (Gokmen 2), Waterford 0
Hibernians 2 (Cassar, Bonello), Spartak Trnava 2 (Adamec, Martinkovic)
Leeds United 10 (O'Grady, Jones 3, Clarke 2, Giles 2, Bremner 2), Lyn Oslo 0
Olympiakos Nicosia 0, Real Madrid 8 (Amancio, Gento 2, Grosso, Fleitas 2, Grande, Pirri) – played in Madrid
Red Star Belgrade 8 (Karasi 3, Lazarevic, Klenkovski, Acimovic, Dlajic 2), Linfield 0
Standard Liege 3 (Depireux 3), Nendori Tirana 0
UT Arad 1 (Domide), Legia Warsaw 2 Zimijewski, Gadocha)
Vorwaerts Berlin 2 (Piepenburg 2), Panathinaikos 0

Revie has plenty in reserve

DOUBLING UP: Terry Hibbitt, who netted twice in Oslo.

LYN OSLO'S main concern for the second leg was that Leeds field a strong so the locals at the Ullevall Stadium could see as many stars as possible.

Allan Clarke (ankle) and Jack Charlton (hamstring) were ruled out and Revie didn't risk either Johnny Giles or Norman Hunter, the latter missing a European tie for the first time.

In came the likes of Terry Hibbitt, Mick Bates and Rod Belfitt, although Chris Galvin, originally selected for the squad, didn't go as he was injured in a five-a-side practice match.

Despite a relatively weakened side, United again proved far too strong for a side who were battling against relegation.

It took United just six minutes to get on the scoresheet when Belfitt steered in a Hibbitt cross for his first goal of the season.

Before half-time Hibbitt netted his first European goal with a snapshot and on the half-hour Peter Lorimer dribbled round the Lyn defence and saw his blocked shot roll to Mick Jones who tapped it over the line.

Hibbitt drove in his second on 54 minutes and United's fifth, thumped in from ten yards by Lorimer bettered Ipswich's British record 14-0 aggregate mauling of Maltese side Floriana in 1962.

Before the end Billy Bremner opened up the Lyn defence yet again and Belfitt collected his second goal to complete a 6-0 win and 16-0 aggregate rout – just two goals short of equalling Benfica's 18-0 record aggregate triumph over Aris, of Luxembourg.

With steadier finishing United could have eased past that record, but Don Revie was more than delighted with his side's gentle introduction to European Cup football. However, he knew that the draw in Geneva the following day would hand United with much tougher opponents.

European Cup
First round, second leg
(at Ulleval Stadium, Oslo)
Wedneday, October 1, 1969

Lyn Oslo	**0**
Leeds United	**6**

Leeds United win 16-0 on agg

Lyn Oslo: Sven Olsen, Jan Rodvang, Helege Ostvold, Tore Borrehaug, Knut Knolle, Trygve Christophersen, Andreas Morisbak, Jan Anders Hovdan, Knut Berg, Ola Dybwad Olsen, Sven Birkeland
Manager: Knut Osnes

Leeds United: Gary Sprake, Paul Reaney, Terry Cooper, Billy Bremner, Paul Madeley, Eddie Gray, Peter Lorimer, Rod Belfitt, Mick Jones, Mick Bates, Terry Hibbitt
Manager: Don Revie
Goals: Belfitt 6, 72, Hibbitt 21, 54, Jones 30, Lorimer 68

Referee: Antoine Queudeville (Luxembourg) **Att:** 7,595

Heavy artillery pound Euro minnows

UNITED were not the only side to stroll in to the second round.

AC Milan, Feyenoord, Red Star Belgrade, Legia Warsaw and Real Madrid all cruised through to the second round after disposing of weak opposition by aggregate scores in double figures.

Goals by Harry Hood, in the first minute, and Tommy Gemmell, took Celtic past Basle.

First round, second leg

Avenir Beggen 0, AC Milan 3 (Combin, Sormani, Rivera) *AC Milan win 11-0 on agg*

Celtic 2 (Hood, Gemmell), Basle 0 *Celtic win 2-0 on agg*

Dynamo Kiev 3 (Muntjan, Byshovets, Puzach), Austria Vienna 1 (Pants) *Dynamo Kiev win 5-2 on agg*

Ferencvaros 4 (Szoke 2 – 1 pen, Branikovics, Rakosi), CSKA Sofia (Marashliev) *Ferencvaros win 5-3 on agg*

Feyenoord 4 (Geels 2, Kindvall, Wery), KR Reykjavik 0 *Feyenoord win 16-0 on agg*

KB Copenhagen 2 (Skouborg 2 – 1pen), Benfica 3 (Eusebio 2, Duamantino) *Benfica win 5-1 on agg*

Linfield 2 (McGraw 2), Red Star Belgrade 4 (Antonijevic 4) *Red Star Belgrade win 12-2 on agg*

Legia Warsaw 8 (Blaut, Gadocha 2, Brychczy, Stachurski, Deyna, Zimijewski, Pieszko pen), UT Arad 0 *Legia Warsaw win 10-1 on agg*

Lyn Oslo 0, Leeds United 6 (Belfitt 3, Jones, Hibbitt, Lorimer) *Leeds United win 16-0 on agg*

Nentori Tirana 1 (Kazanxhi), Standard Liege 1 (Galic) *Standard Liege win 4-1 on agg*

Panathanilkos 1 (Antoniadis), Vorwarts Berlin 1 (Laslop) *Vorwarts Berlin win 3-1 on agg*

Real Madrid 6 (de Diego 2, Planelies, Grande, Avaramides og, Fleitas), Olympiakos Nicosia 1 (Kettenis) *Real Madrid win 14-1 on agg*

St Etienne 3 (Revelli 2, Keita), Bayern Munich 0 *St Etienne win 3-2 on agg*

Spartak Trnava 4 (Hrusecky, Adamec 2, Azzoppardi og), Hibernians 0 *Spartak Trnava win 6-2 on agg*

Muddy marvels

United swamp Magyars

OPEN GOAL: Mick Jones ploughs through the mud to score against Ferencvaros.

THE second round draw certainly rased a few eyebrows as United were paired with Ferencvaros, the Hungarian side they had beaten in the final of the Fairs Cup in 1968.

Once again United had home advantage first and made it pay in a breathtaking first half in which the Magyars floundered on a muddy pitch.

The visitors' star forward Florian Albert was missing after being badly injured in an international against Denmark four months earlier. Zoltan Varga, another Hungarian international forward, and inside-forward Gyula Rakosi were also ruled out – and United made the most of the absence of such quality players.

As against Lyn, Leeds made the perfect start. Just two minutes had elapsed when Billy Bremner, showing no ill effects from flu which had threatened his place in the starting line-up, backheeled the ball to Giles, who curled a shot round goalkeeper Istvan Geczi from 12 yards.

United took inspiration from that flying start and played some superb football, their pin-point passes skidding from feet to feet over the tacky surface. Ferencvaros were left chasing shadows and after 20 minutes Jones followed up to score from close range after Lorimer's shot was blocked.

With Paul Reaney's overlapping runs down the right causing chaos, it was no surprise when United surged into a 3-0 lead on 34 minutes as Lorimer and Giles opened up the Ferencvaros defence for Jones to round Geczi.

Referee Tofik Bakhramov, better known as 'the Russian linesman' from the 1966 World Cup Final, denied both Norman Hunter and Jack Charlton further goals because of offside, but Revie was in raptures after the game.

"I have never seen a United side play better against anybody in my eight years with them. They were splendid," he said. Bookies also took note of United's demolition job and installed Leeds as 3-1 favourites to win the European Cup.

European Cup
Second round, first leg
(at Elland Road, Leeds)
Wednesday, November 12, 1969

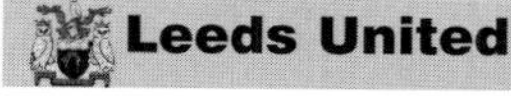

Leeds United	**3**
Ferencvaros	**0**

Leeds United: Gary Sprake, Paul Reaney, Paul Madeley, Billy Bremner, Jack Charlton, Norman Hunter, Peter Lorimer, Mick Bates, Mick Jones, Johnny Giles, Eddie Gray
Goals: Giles 2, Jones 21, 35
Manager: Don Revie

Ferencvaros: Istvan Geczi, Deszo Novak, Miklos Pancsics, Laszlo Balint (Miklos Nemeth 56), Arpad Horvath, Istvan Megyesi, Istvan Szoke, Stvan Juhasz, Laszlo Branikovits, Lajos Scucs, Sandor Katona
Manager: Karoly Lakat

Referee: Tofik Bakhramov (Soviet Union) **Att:** 37,291

Great night for classy Celtic

SUPER Celtic turned on the style at Parkhead to beat highly-rated Benfica 3-0. Goals by Tommy Gemmell and Willie Wallace inside quarter of an hour put the Hoops in control and Harry Hood's goal 20 minutes from time sealed a great night for the Scots. Apart from the matches involving the British sides, the rest of the games were tight affairs.

One of the biggest surprises came in Belgium where Real Madrid lost to Erwin Kostedde's goal for Standard Liege.

Dutch side Feyenoord gave themselves a chance by restricting AC Milan to a 1-0 victory at the San Siro, French forward Nestor Combin getting the only goal.

The other Italian side in the competition, Fiorentina, came away from Dynamo Kiev with a splendid 2-1 victory.

Legia Warsaw came from behind to defeat French side St Etienne 2-1, Kazimierz Deyna, who later played in England for Manchester City, scoring a late winner for the Polish outfit.

Second round, first leg
AC Milan 1 (Combin), Feyenoord 0
Celtic 3 (Gemmell, Wallace, Hood), Benfica 0
Dynamo Kiev 1 (Serebriannikov), Fiorentina 2 (Chiarugi, Maraschi)
Leeds United 3 (Giles, Jones 2), Ferencvaros 0
Legia Warsaw 2 (Pieszko, Deyna), St Etienne 1 (Revelli)
Spartak Trnava 1 (Kabat), Galatasaray 0
Standard Liege 1 (Kostedde), Real Madrid 0
Vorwarts Berlin 2 (Frassdorf, Begerad), Red Star Belgrade 1 (Antonijevic)

Hungarian waltz for smart United

IF Ferencvaros found the going tough in Leeds, then it was even tougher in their own Nep Stadium where a dominant United doubled their aggregate victory.

Crippled by injuries and poor form, Ferencvaros were given no hope by their own fans of overturning the big first leg deficit.

Less than 5,500 people bothered to turn up on a rain-lashed night and the game in the huge stadium was played out in stunned silence.

Leeds, in all red, took an instant grip in midfield through Billy Bremner, Johnny Giles and Paul Madeley, and didn't really look in any danger.

Indeed goalkeeper Istvan Geczi received a taste of things to come when a shot by Mick Jones hit him on the head and cannoned onto the bar, then post.

That was an incredible let-off for the home side, but Jones got his deserved reward after 35 minutes when Peter Lorimer's cross eluded Geczi and the big Leeds front-runner was able to scramble the ball in off defender Deszo Novak.

Ferencvaros could only offer token resistance and although Istvan Szoke shot against the bar, Leeds finished the stronger with Jones driving home his eighth goal of the competition four minutes from the end and Lorimer capped another memorable Euro-night with a 25-yard drive.

Boss Don Revie had also been able to blood teenager Chris Galvin, who had yet to make his League debut. He had won an England Youth call-up the previous week, celebrated his 18th birthday a couple of days before the game in Budapest and crowned a great few days by coming on for the last ten minutes as a replacement for Eddie Gray.

DEBUT DAY: Forward Chris Galvin, who made his European debut by coming on for Eddie Gray in Budapest.

Celtic tie turns on its head

CELTIC needed a huge slice of luck to get past Portuguese champions Benfica.

Holding a 3-0 lead it seemed plain sailing for Jock Stein's side but two goals inside five minutes from Eusebio and Jaime Graca put Benfica back in the tie just before half time.

The Scots looked as though they were about to hold on to their goal advantage when Costa Diamantino scored in the final minute to take the tie in to extra-time.

There was no additional score in the extra period and Celtic succeeded on the spin of a disc.

Standard Liege put on a brave display to win 3-2 in Real Madrid to complete a surprise 4-2 aggregate victory.

Another big name, AC Milan, also tumbled out. Tired after their physical battle against Argentinian side Estudiantes in the World Club Championship, Milan struggled in Rotterdam where Feyenoord drew level inside eight minutes through Wim Jansen and snatched victory near the end through Wim Van Hanegem.

Second round, second leg

Benfica 3 (Eusebio, Graca, Diamantino), Celtic 0 *3-3 on agg. Celtic win on toss of a disc*

Fiorentina 0, Dynamo Kiev 0 *Fiorentina win 2-1 on agg*

Ferencvaros 0, Leeds United 3 (Jones 2, Lorimer) *Leeds United win 6-0 on agg*

Feyenoord 2 (Jansen, Van Hanegem), AC Milan 0 *Feyenoord win 2-1 on agg*

Galatatsaray 1 (Ergun), Spartak Trnava 0 *1-1 on agg, Galatasaray win on toss of a disc*

Real Madrid 2 (Valazquez, Genton pen), Standard Liege 3 (Pilot, Depireux, Galic) *Standard Liege win 4-2 on agg*

Red Star Belgrade 3 (Karasi 2, Acimovic), Vorwarts Berlin 2 (Begerad 2) *4-4 on agg. Vorwarts win on away goals rule*

St Etienne 0, Legia Warsaw 1 (Deyna) *Legia Warsaw win 3-1 on agg*

European Cup
Second round, second leg
(at Nep Stadium, Budapest)
Wednesday, November 26, 1969

Ferencvaros	**0**
Leeds United	**3**

Leeds United win 6-0 on agg

Ferencvaros: Istvan Geczi, Deszo Novak, Laszlo Balint, Istvan Megyesi, Istvan Juhasz, Lajos Scucs, Istvan Szoke, Laszlo Branikovits, Arpad Horvath (Laszlo Vajda 61), Mikos Nemeth, Sandor Katona
Manager: Karoly Lakat

Leeds United: Gary Sprake, Paul Reaney, Terry Cooper, Billy Bremner, Jack Charlton, Norman Hunter, Peter Lorimer, Paul Madeley, Mick Jones, Johnny Giles, Eddie Gray (Chris Galvin 80)
Goals: Jones 36, 81, Lorimer 88
Manager: Don Revie

Referee: Jose Maria Ortiz De Mendibil (Spain)
Att: 5,400

LE NUMERO : 10 FRANCS — COUPE D'EUROPE — 4 MARS 1970

STANDARD SPORT

FIAT

S.A. Turin-Motor

FIAT

AUTO-SERAING

LEEDS UNITED

LEEDS
CANDIDAT CHAMPION
DU MONDE DES CLUBS

Si les supporters du Standard arrivent ce soir dans leur forme " Coupe d'Europe "

L'Enfer sera plus terrible que jamais

Prochain match à Sclessin : STANDARD - F. C. BRUGES le 15 mars

AUSTIN Ets SODIA

Fryns & Bastin

RESTAURANT «BORGIA»

MAKING THE NEWS: Standard Liege's newspaper-style programme for the European Cup quarter-final in Belgium.

United lay siege to Liege

UNITED'S' passage into the last eight had been smooth, but getting into Standard's Sclessin Stadium was more problematical.

Because they did not recognise United's party, gatemen refused the players' entry to the ground and for 10 uncomfortable minutes they were jostled by supporters before getting inside to safety.

The Belgian club's authoritites were probably more concerned with getting the match on than getting United in.

Torrential rain had left the pitch extremely heavy and a helicopter was brought in to hover over the pitch to dry it out. United made light of these difficulties as they played with supreme authority and control.

Paul Madeley marked midfield dangerman Wilfried Van Moer out of the game and consequently Gary Sprake only had a couple of routine saves to make. His opposite number, Christian Piot, was far busier, producing a one-handed save to deny Peter Lorimer a seventh minute opener.

Both Lorimer and Mick Jones wasted other chances while Johnny Giles shot over from near the penalty spot. Just as it looked as though United's fine work was to bring no reward, Allan Clarke, who had shaken off a knee injury to link up with Jones, found space on the left. The former Leicester City striker laid the ball back for Terry Cooper to loft it in towards the far post. Defender Leon Jeck missed it and Lorimer was able to thump the ball in cleanly.

Standard skipper Leon Semmelling, who had faced Cooper the previous week in Brussels when England strolled to a 3-1 win, was full of admiration for United's performance.

"We thought we were playing against 15 men. Every time we got the ball there appeared to be three of four men on top of us."

BOUNCING BACK: Allan Clarke returned to the United line-up after missing the previous three European Cup games.

European Cup
Quarter-final, first leg
(at Sclessin Stadium, Liege)
Wednesday, March 4, 1970

Standard Liege 0

Leeds United 1

Standard Liege: Christian Piot, Jacques Beurlet, Jean Thissen, Nicolas Dewelque, Leon Jeck, Wilfried Van Moer, Leon Semmeling, Louis Pilot, Milan Galic, Henri Depireux, Sylvester Tacac
Manager: Rene Hauss

Leeds United: Gary Sprake, Paul Reaney, Terry Cooper, Billy Bremner, Jack Charlton, Norman Hunter, Peter Lorimer, Allan Clarke, Mick Jones, Johnny Giles, Paul Madeley
Goal: Lorimer 70
Manager: Don Revie

Referee: Antonio Saldanha Ribeiro (Portugal)
Att: 38,000

Celtic are simply cock-a-Hoops

MAGNIFICENT Celtic turned on a dazzling display at Parkhead to sink Italian champions Fiorentina.

Bertie Auld fired in the opener with Willie Wallace capping a great night for the Scots with the third after Carpenetti put through his own-goal.

Quarter final, first leg

Celtic 3 (Auld, Carpenetti og, Wallace), Fiorentina 0
Galatasaray 1 (Ayhan), Legia Warsaw 1 (Brychzy)
Standard Liege 0, Leeds United 1 (Lorimer)
Vorwarts Berlin 1 (Piepenburg), Feyenoord 0

MR COOL:
Standard Liege goalkeeper Christian Piot has no chance as Johnny Giles beats him from the penalty spot to seal United's passage in to the semi-finals of the European Cup.

Standard bearers

Treble chasers on course

AS the 1969-70 season reached its climax, United had captured the footballing public's imagination.

They were still on for an unprecedented treble – European Cup, League Championship and FA Cup.

The second leg of their European tie against Standard Liege attracted 48,775 to Elland Road, the biggest crowd to see United take on continental opposition. The receipts of £25,000 were also a record.

At the weekend United had slugged out a 0-0 draw with deadly rivals Manchester United in the FA Cup semi-final, while Standard had beaten Brugge 2-0 to virtually guarantee retaining the Belgian title.

The FA Cup tie against the men from Old Trafford seemed to have taken some of the sting out of Leeds' play and there was an early let off when Paul Madeley and Jack Charlton collided, but winger Sandor Takac put the opportunity into the side-netting. Liege's confidence lifted in the bitterly cold cross-wind and a quarter of the match had blown away before United began to play with some purpose. Terry Cooper's seering thrusts from left back started to create gaps in the Standard defence and goalkeeper Christian Piot needed to be at his acrobatic best to keep out headers by Allan Clarke and Mick Jones.

United clearly needed the cushion of a goal but it did not come until 11 minutes from time when Jones was pushed in the box by a combination of Leon Jeck and Jean Thissen, leaving Johnny Giles to convert his ninth penalty of the season and keep dreams of the treble alive.

European Cup
Quarter-final, second leg
(at Elland Road, Leeds)
Wednesday, March 18, 1970

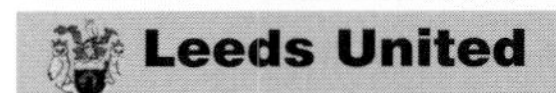

Leeds United 1

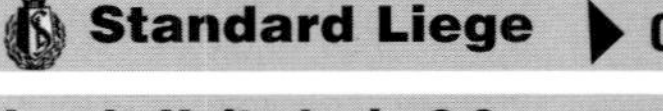

Standard Liege 0

Leeds United win 2-0 on agg

Leeds United: Gary Sprake, Paul Reaney, Terry Cooper, Billy Bremner, Jack Charlton, Norman Hunter, Peter Lorimer, Allan Clarke, Mick Jones, Johnny Giles, Paul Madeley
Goals: Giles 79 pen
Manager: Don Revie

Standard Liege: Christian Piot, Jacques Beurlet, Jean Thissen, Nicolas Dewalque, Leon Jeck, Louis Pilot, Leon Semmeling, Wilfried Van Moer, Milan Galic, Henri Depireux, Sylvester Tacac
Manager: Karoly Lakat

Referee: Concetto Lo Bello (Italy) **Att:** 48,775

Stein's Celtic safely through

CELTIC made it through to the semi-finals with a disciplined display in Italy.

Defending their 3-0 first leg lead, Jock Stein's side were punctured just once by Fiorentina by Chiarugi's 37th minute goal.

Feyenoord continued their impressive progress by overturning a 1-0 deficit against Vorwarts Berlin with goals by Ove Kindvall and Henk Wery in Amsterdam.

Quarter final, second leg

Feyenoord 2 (Kindvall, Wery), Vorwarts Berlin 0 *Feyenoord win 2-1 on agg*

Fiorentina 1 (Chiarugi), Celtic 0 *Celtic win 3-1 on agg*

Leeds United 1 (Giles pen), Standard Liege 0 *Leeds United win 2-0 on agg*

Legia Warsaw 2 (Brychczy 2), Galatasaray 0 *Legia Warsaw win 3-1 on agg*

Ticket frenzy for Battle of Britain

TWO days after their triumph over Standard Liege, the semi-final draw took place and United were paired with Glasgow giants, Celtic, in a tie that was instantly dubbed the "Battle of Britain".

GOLD DUST: A ticket for the United v Celtic first leg game at Elland Road.

The semi-final matches gripped the public's imagination. It was a genuine heavyweight showdown between Jock Stein's Scottish masters and Revie's footballing machine which was still in with a chance of the treble.

Of the 50,000 tickets for the first leg at Elland Road, large numbers made their way to Glasgow, even though the Parkhead club officially only received 6,000.

Tickets valued at £2 were going for three times that much on the Scottish black market but the odds on United getting through were lengthening along with their fixture list. They had been involved in an almighty struggle with Everton for the title but a shock 3-1 home reverse at the hands of unfancied Southampton just 10 days after beating Liege at Elland Road virtually saw the Championship Trophy move across the Pennines to Merseyside.

Revie virtually conceded defeat on Easter Monday by fielding a reserve side at Derby County, two days before the first Celtic clash, and a 4-1 defeat all but condemned United to finishing behind Everton.

Matches were coming thick and fast and Revie fielded his reserves at the Baseball Ground as his men were "physically and mentally drained". The FA did not really accept his explanation and United were later fined £5,000 for failing to put out their strongest side.

Even though Revie's men had come through three gruelling FA Cup ties with Manchester United to book an FA Cup final place against Chelsea, it was clear that they were not in tip-top condition as they went into the biggest game in the club's history against Celtic. Astonishingly, had United required a third FA Cup replay against Manchester United it would have taken place at Huddersfield the night after the first leg against Celtic.

MEXICO BOUND: United's Terry Cooper (left) and Norman Hunter.

World Cup wizards

UNITED'S arrival as a major footballing force was reflected on the international scene.

Shortly before the Celtic game England manager Sir Alf Ramsey named five Leeds players in his 28-man squad for the World Cup in Mexico.

Four defenders – Jack Charlton, Norman Hunter, Terry Cooper and Paul Reaney were named for the trip along with striker Allan Clarke.

Mick Jones was named among the 12 reserves but his exclusion from the squad along with Paul Madeley was a disappointment to their club boss Don Revie, whose trainer Les Cocker was also in the England party.

Sir Alf's men were scheduled to fly out to South America to begin the defence of their trophy on May 4, even though the European Cup final was scheduled for May 6 in Milan.

UNITED faced a staggering nine games in 22 days – a punishing schedule which ultimately led Don Revie to controversially fielding his reserves at Derby on Easter Monday.

		March		
Sat 14	Manchester United	FA Cup semi-final	D	0-0
Wed 18	Standard Liege (H)	European Cup quarter-final 2nd leg	W	1-0
Sat 21	Wolverhampton W (A)	Division One	W	2-1
Mon 23	Manchester United	FA Cup semi-final replay	D	0-0
Thurs 26	Manchester United	FA Cup semi-final 2nd replay	W	1-0
Sat 28	Southampton (H)	Division One	L	1-3
Mon 30	Derby County (A)	Division One	L	1-4
		April		
Wed 1	Celtic (H)	European Cup semi-final 1st leg	L	0-1
Sat 4	Burnley (H)	Division One	W	2-1

United simply

MISCUE: Both Mick Jones and George Connelly, Celtic's matchwinner swing and miss the ball.

MATCH OF THE DAY: The first leg programme.

NIGHT SHIFT: Celtic goalkeeper Evan Williams clears his lines despite the efforts of United's Allan Clarke to charge the ball down.

run out of gas

Celtic in the driving seat

SUPER Celtic cashed in on United's heavy schedule of games to take a huge stride towards their second European Cup final in four years with a 1-0 victory at Elland Road.

It was United's 57th game of an arduous season and they were without one of their key men, Norman Hunter, who had not played since the Liege game at Elland Road because of a knee injury.

His number six shirt was filled by Paul Madeley, but barely a minute into the game, when Madeley failed to clear properly, Bobby Murdoch immediately fed George Connolly, whose shot deflected past the wrong-footed Gary Sprake – the first goal United had let in in 540 minutes of European Cup football.

It was a devastating, morale-sapping blow from which United were never able to recover.

Pre-match predictions that Terry Cooper's attacking skills would cut the Scots open proved false as the England full back was given a tortuous night by the dazzling ball skills of Jimmy Johnstone.

Don Revie had set his team a 2-0 target to take to Glasgow, but it was Celtic who looked more likely to achieve that scoreline.

In the first minute of the second half Connolly turned in Johnstone's pass from the by-line, but was ruled offside.

United almost made the most of that escape when Eddie Gray weaved his way into the penalty area and smacked a shot against the Celtic bar, but roared on by a massive away following, Celtic, inspired by Johnstone's wing wizardry, deservedly hung on to their advantage.

United boss Revie acknowledged: "Celtic were the better side on the night, but we are still not out of it."

To rub salt into United's wounds they trooped off to hear that Everton had just beaten West Brom 2-0 to take their title.

The agony increased the following night when United drew 2-2 in a meaningless League encounter at West Ham in which right back Paul Reaney broke his leg and was unable to take his place in England's Mexico World Cup squad.

United were desperate for a break, but it didn't come in the FA Cup final against Chelsea. Despite a virtuoso display by Eddie Gray, United were unable to kill off a dogged Chelsea, the opening Wembley encounter finishing 2-2 after extra-time.

United's marathon season continued four days after the FA Cup final with the European Cup return leg in Glasgow.

Revie somehow had to instill some self belief in his side that they could be come the first team to come from 1-0 down after a home semi-final to go through.

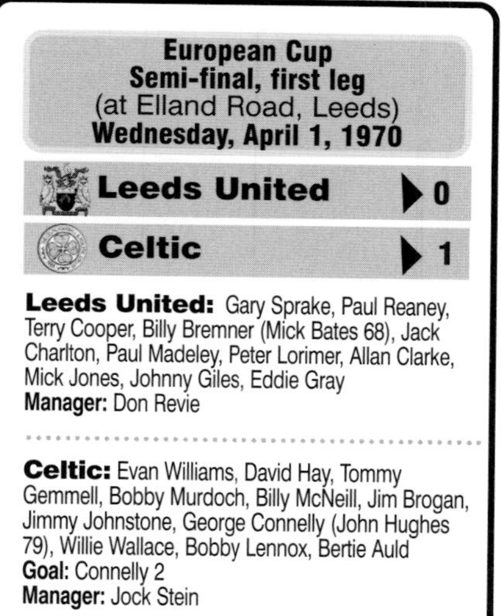

European Cup
Semi-final, first leg
(at Elland Road, Leeds)
Wednesday, April 1, 1970

Leeds United	**0**
Celtic	**1**

Leeds United: Gary Sprake, Paul Reaney, Terry Cooper, Billy Bremner (Mick Bates 68), Jack Charlton, Paul Madeley, Peter Lorimer, Allan Clarke, Mick Jones, Johnny Giles, Eddie Gray
Manager: Don Revie

Celtic: Evan Williams, David Hay, Tommy Gemmell, Bobby Murdoch, Billy McNeill, Jim Brogan, Jimmy Johnstone, George Connelly (John Hughes 79), Willie Wallace, Bobby Lennox, Bertie Auld
Goal: Connelly 2
Manager: Jock Stein

Referee: Michel Kitaddjian (France) **Att:** 45,505

Poles held at home

GEORGE Connelly's goal at Elland Road was the only one in either semi-final.

Dutch side Feyenoord put up the shutters in Poland where they held Legia Warsaw to a 0-0 draw.

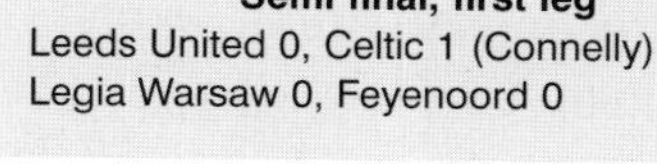

Semi final, first leg
Leeds United 0, Celtic 1 (Connelly)
Legia Warsaw 0, Feyenoord 0

NO WAY THROUGH: Jack Charlton flicks a header towards the Celtic goal.

Hampden roar

HEADS WE LOSE: United had plenty of players back but could not prevent Bobby Murdoch from making it 2-1.

Celtic prove

TO cater for the massive demand for tickets, Celtic switched the game to Hampden Park and a staggering 136,505 went through the turnstiles – the biggest attendance for any European Cup tie.

Predictably Celtic tore into United, but were rocked after only 14 minutes when Billy Bremner collected Norman Hunter's short pass and sent a 25-yard shot twisting into the roof of goalkeeper Evan Williams' net.

However, Celtic were not knocked out of their stride and the pressure mounted on United's goal with Paul Madeley and Terry Cooper making desperate clearances.

United got through to half-time with their advantage intact, but it dissolved within minutes of the restart. Bertie Auld took a quick 47th minute corner and John Hughes glanced in in equaliser. United had to score again, but were having difficulty in getting the ball out of their own half and fate dealt the Yorkshire side another blow when Gary Sprake was carried off with a knee injury after a collision with Hughes.

David Harvey came on as his replacement and his

LEVEL HEADED: A diving John Hughes (left) nods Celtic ahead on aggregate in the titanic clash at Hampden Park.

at full volume

too powerful

first touch was to fish the ball out of the net after Bobby Murdoch crashed a shot past him from 15 yards. The noise which greeted the winner was deafening and Celtic never looked like surrendering their 3-1 aggregate advantage.

The Glasgow game, played just four days after United's epic 2-2 FA Cup final draw with Chelsea at Wembley over 120 minutes, signalled the end of United's European Cup hopes. Their bold, but fruitless, efforts to land an amazing treble ended in further tears when they lost 2-1 to Chelsea after extra-time in their FA Cup final replay at Manchester's Old Trafford.

Failure to retain their league crown or win the European or FA Cups meant that United would return to the Fairs Cup competition in 1970-71.

European Cup
Semi-final, second leg
(at Hampden Park, Glasgow)
Wednesday, April 15, 1970

Celtic	**2**
Leeds United	**1**

Celtic win 3-1 on agg

Celtic: Evan Williams, David Hay, Tommy Gemmell, Bobby Murdoch, Billy McNeill, Jim Brogan, Jimmy Johnstone, George Connelly, John Hughes, Bertie Auld, Bobby Lennox
Goals: Hughes 47, Murdoch 53
Manager: Jock Stein

Leeds United: Gary Sprake (David Harvey 51), Paul Madeley, Terry Cooper, Billy Bremner, Jack Charlton, Norman Hunter, Peter Lorimer (Mick Bates 71), Allan Clarke, Mick Jones, Johnny Giles, Eddie Gray
Goal: Bremner 14
Manager: Don Revie

Referee: Gerhard Schulenburg (West Germany)
Att: 136,505

LOOK BACK IN ANGUISH: Another view of Hughes' goal with all United eyes are on the ball.

Dutch masters lift Cup

CELTIC went into the final against Feyenoord as firm favourites and everything was going to plan when Tommy Gemmell lashed in a trademark free-kick.

But within minutes skipper Rinus Israel headed the equaliser and Celtic were under severe pressure in the second half as the Dutch dominated a disappointing final.

The Scots hung on until deep in to extra-time when Swedish striker Ove Kindvall got away to break Celtic's resistance.

Semi-final, second leg

Celtic 2 (Hughes, Murdoch), Leeds United 1 (Bremner)
Celtic win 3-1 on agg
Feyenoord 2 (Van Hanegem, Hasil), Legia Warsaw 0
Feyenoord win 2-0 on agg

Final
(San Siro Stadium, Milan)
May 6, 1970
Celtic 1, Feyenoord 2

Celtic: Williams, Hay, Gemmell, Murdoch, McNeill, Brogan, Johnstone, Hughes, Wallace, Lennox, Auld (Connelly 77)
Goal: Gemmell 29
Manager: Jock Stein
Feyenoord: Pieters-Graafland, Romeijn (Haak 107), Israel, Laseroms, Van Duivenbode, Hasil, Jansen, Van Hanegem, Moulijn, Wery, Kindvall
Goals: Israel 31, Kindvall 117
Manager: Ernst Happel (Austria)
Referee: Concetto Lo Bello (Italy)
Attendance: 53,187

Leading scorers – 8 Jones (Leeds United), 6 – Geels (Feyenoord), Kindvall (Feyenoord), 5 – Eusebio (Benfica), Karasi, Antonijevic (Red Star Belgrade), Skouborg (BK Copenhagen)

Lorimer to the rescue

UNITED kicked off their Fairs Cup campaign with a trip to Norway to face the amateurs of Sarpsborg – their 50th tie in Europe.

The town of 18,000 welcomed United with open arms but there was local disappointment that Don Revie arrived without a full-strength team. World Cup players Norman Hunter and Allan Clarke were rested, Jack Charlton and Johnny Giles (both ankle injuries) and the emerging young Welsh player Terry Yorath (knee ligaments) were left behind in Yorkshire with long-term injury victim Paul Reaney.

David Kennedy, United's 19-year-old reserve centre half, was given his European debut against stubborn opposition.

Leeds were simply dreadful in the first half and little better in the second against a team which had just one class performer – Egil Olsen – the Norwegian international centre forward who went on to manage the national side before trying his hand in the English Premiership with Wimbledon.

Olsen, fresh from Norway's 4-2 defeat against Sweden at the weekend, gave young Kennedy a testing time, but despite their lethargy, United were always in control, forcing 16 corners as the home side were content to pack their defence.

Mick Jones did produce a fine clutching save from goalkeeper Kolbjorn Nilsen in the second half, then had a goal disallowed for offside.

As Sarpsborg faded United made their superior fitness tell late in the game. A Peter Lorimer chip rebounded off a defender onto a post and away for a corner but he did break the deadlock 13 minutes from the end with his first goal of the season, drilling home a low hard drive from just outside the area. It was a well worked goal out of keeping with a slack display.

FACE-SAVER: Peter Lorimer, whose goal spared United's blushes.

European Fairs Cup
First round, first leg
(at Sarpsborg Stadium, Sarpsborg)
Tuesday, September 15, 1970

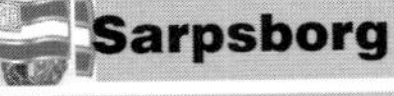 **Sarpsborg** 0

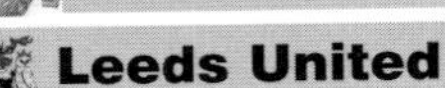 **Leeds United** 1

Sarpsborg: Kolbjorn Nilsen, Ingar Loken, Bjorn Woodruff, Sigmund Johansen, Per Anker Holt, Age Gjerlaugsen, Dag Navestad, Terje Andresen (Age Johansen 70), Egil Olsen, Knut Spydevold, Kai Kjonnigsen
Manager: Bjorn Spydevold

Leeds United: Gary Sprake, Paul Madeley, Terry Cooper, Billy Bremner, David Kennedy, Eddie Gray, Peter Lorimer, Rod Belfitt, Mick Jones, Mick Bates, Terry Hibbitt
Goal: Lorimer 76
Manager: Don Revie

Referee: Preben Christophersen (Denmark) **Att:** 8,769

Coventry hot-shot O'Rourke in Sky Blue heaven

THE Fairs Cup had dropped the Inter-Cities bit of its title in 1969/70 and was now known as the European Fairs Cup.

Euro newcomers Coventry City made a fairytale start to their campaign, beating Trakia Plovdiv 4-1 in Bulgaria with John O'Rourke getting a hat-trick.

Arsenal, the holders, were denied victory in Rome by two late Georgio Chinaglia goals for Lazio. They had followed United and Newcastle in winning the competition by lifting the trophy in 1970, coming from 3-0 down at one stage against Anderlecht to beat the Belgians 4-3 on aggregate.

First round, first leg

AB Copenhagen 7 (Hansen 2, Carlsen 2, Neilsen, Petersen, Sultana og), Sliema Wanderers 0
AEK Athens 0, Twente Enschede 1 (Van Der Kerkhof)
Bayern Munich 1 (Beckenbauer), Rangers 0
Coleraine 1 (Mullan), Kilmarnock 1 (Mathie)
Cologne 5 (Parits, Thielen, Rupp 2, Lex), Sedan 1 (Pierron)
Cork Hibernian 0, Valencia 3 (Claramunt 2, Barrachina)
CUF Barreiro 2 (Serafim, Campera), Dynamo Zagreb 0
Dundee United 3 (I Reid, Markland, A Reid), Grasshoppers 2 (Grahn, Meier)
Dynamo Bucharest 5, (Dumitrache 3, Popescu 2), PAOK Salonika 0
Hadjuk Split 3 (Jerkovic, Pavlica, Jovanic), Slavia Sofia 0
Hibernian 6 (McBride 3, Duncan 2, Blair), Malmo 0
Ilves 4 (Nupponen 2, Lundberg, Nuoranen), Sturm Graz 2 (Kaiser, Laine og)
Inter Milan 1 (Celia), Newcastle United 1 (Davies)
Juventus 7 (Pablowski og, Bettega 2, Anastasi 4), Rumelange 0
Katowice 0, Barcelona 1 (Rexach) in Chorzow
La Gantoise 0, Hamburg 1 (Nogly)
Lausanne 0, Vitoria Setubal 2 (Jacinto Joao, Vitor Baptista)
Lazio 2 (Chinaglia 2 – 1 pen), Arsenal 2 (Radford 2)
Liverpool 1 (Graham), Ferencvaros 0
Norkopping 2 (Olsen, Hansen), Hertha Berlin 4 (Brungs 2, Gayer, Steffenhayen)
Partizan Belgrade 0, Dynamo Dresden 0
Ruch Chorzow 1 (Faber), Fiorentina 1 (Vitali)
Sarpsborg 0, Leeds United 1 (Lorimer)
Seville 1 (Eloy), Eskisehirsport 0
Sparta Prague 2 (Migas, Gogh), Atletico Bilbao 0
Sparta Rotterdam 6 (Venneker, Kowalik, Koudijzer, Heijrman 2 – 1 pen, Walbeek), Akranes 0
Spartak Trnava 2 (Doblas, Masny), Marseille 0
Trakia Plovdiv 1 (Radkov), Coventry City 4 (O'Rourke 3, Martin)
Universitatea Craiova 2 (Taralunga, Stenmbeanu), Pecsi Doza 1 (Mate)
SK Vienna 0, Beveren 2 (Rogiers, Janssens)
Vitoria Guimaraes 3 (Bernando 2, Peres), Angouleme 0
Zeleznicar 3 (Osim, Sprecko, Mujkic), Anderlecht 4 (Puis 2, Van Binst, Mulder)

Sarpsborg stroll

MOST of United's big guns were back for the second leg against Sarpsborg, but they were not firing on all cylinders.

United went into the Elland Road encounter with just three goals in seven games and were largely unconvincing in a first half which saw them ensnared in Sarpsborg's well-oiled offside trap which saw three goals disallowed. The only effort to stand in a drab opening half came when Jack Charlton walked the ball into the net after miscuing his original effort.

European Fairs Cup
First round, second leg
(at Elland Road, Leeds)
Wednesday, September 29, 1970

Leeds United	**5**
Sarpsborg	**0**

Leeds United win 6-0 on agg

Leeds United: Gary Sprake, Paul Madeley, Terry Cooper (Paul Reaney HT), Billy Bremner, Jack Charlton, Norman Hunter, Peter Lorimer, Allan Clarke, Rod Belfitt, Mick Bates, Eddie Gray
Goals: Charlton 22, 61, Bremner 71, 88, Lorimer 90
Manager: Don Revie

Sarpsborg: Kolbojorn Nilsen, Ingar Loken, Finn Johansen (Per Anker Holt , Bjorn Woodroff, Age Gjerlaugsen, Sigmund Johansen, Kai Kjonnigsen (Arne Melby), Terje Andresen, Egil Olsen, Knut Spydevold, Dag Navestad
Manager: Bjorn Spydevold

Referee: Mario Gomes Alves (Portugal) **Att:** 19,283

The sparse crowd were warmed after the interval by the arrival of substitute Paul Reaney for his first game since breaking his leg five months earlier and United finally rewarded their fans with a late flurry which saw them stroll to a 5-0 win. On the hour Charlton notched his second with a fierce angled drive then Billy Bremner marked his 50th European appearance with a couple of strikes – a 25-yard shot, then a header – while Peter Lorimer tapped in the fifth in injury time.

TOP MAN: Billy Bremner, pictured with his 1970 Player of the Year award, was on target twice against Sarpsborg.

Inter 'keeper Vieri off as Magpies storm through

NEWCASTLE United put on a superb display to knock out star-studded Inter Milan at St James' Park.

Building on their 1-1 draw in the San Siro, the Geordies went in front with a 29th minute header by Bobby Moncur and after Italian goalkeeper Lido Vieri was sent off for punching the Belgian referee, Wyn Davies sealed the Magpies' passage into the second round with a diving header.

First round, second leg

Akranes 0, Sparta Rotterdam 9 (Klijnjan 3, Kristensen, Kowalik 3, Van Der Veen, Venneker) *Sparta Rotterdam win 15-0 on agg*

Anderlecht 5 (Ejderstedt 2, Puis 2, Van Himst), Zeljeznicar 4 (Bukal 2, Spreco 2) *Anderlecht win 9-7 on agg*

Angouleme 3 (Castellan 2, Gallice), Vitoria Guimaraes 1 (Ademir Belo) *Vitoria Guimaraes win 4-3 on agg*

Arsenal 2 (Radford, Armstrong), Lazio 0 *Arsenal win 4-2 on agg*

Atletico Bilbao 1 (Uriarte), Sparta Prague 1 (Chovanec) *Sparta Prague win 3-1 on agg*

Barcelona 3 (Pujol, Marti-Filosia, Rexach), Katowice 2 (Rother, Nowak pen) *Barcelona win 4-2 on agg*

Beveren 3 (Rogiers, Van Der Linden, Janssens), SK Vienna 0 *Beveren win 5-0 on agg*

Coventry City 2 (Joicey, Blockley), Trakia Plovdiv 0 *Coventry City win 6-1 on agg*

Dynamo Dresden 6 (Kreische 4, Sammer, Sachse), Partizan Belgrade 0 *Dynamo Dresden win 6-0*

Dynamo Zagreb 6 (Novak 4, Lalic 2), CUF Barreiro 1 (Campora) *Dynamo Zagreb win 6-2 on agg*

Eskisehirsport 3 (Heper 3), Seville 1 (Acosta) *Eskisehirsport win 3-2 on agg*

Ferencvaros 1 (Mucha), Liverpool 1 (Hughes) *Liverpool win 2-1 on agg*

Fiorentina 2 (Chiargui, Mariani), Ruch Chorzow 0 *Fiorentina win 3-1 on agg*

Grasshoppers 0, Dundee United 0 *Dundee United win 3-2 on agg*

Hamburg 7 (Dorfel 4, Honig, Zaczyk pen, Volkert), La Gantoise 1 (Benedito) *Hamburg win 8-1 on agg*

Hertha Berlin 4 (Hoor, Brungs 2, Gergely), Norkopping 1 (Rasmussen) *Hertha Berlin win 8-3 on agg*

Kilmarnock 2 (McLean, Morrison), Coleraine 3 (Dickson 3) *Coleraine win 4-3 on agg*

Leeds United 5 (Charlton 2, Bremner 2, Lorimer), Sarpsborg 0 *Leeds United win 6-0 on agg*

Malmo 2 (Larsson, Jonsson), Hibernian 3 (Duncan, McEwan, Stanton) *Hibernian win 9-2 on agg*

Marseille 2 (Couecou, Skoblar), Spartak Trnava 0 *2-2 on agg aet. Spartak Trnava win 4-3 on pens*

Newcastle United 2 (Davies, Moncur), Inter Milan 0 *Newcastle United win 3-1 on agg*

PAOK Salonika 1 (Kudas), Dynamo Bucharest 0 *Dynamo Bucharest win 5-1 on agg*

Pesci Doza 3 (Kocsis 2, Mate), Universitatea Craiova 0 Pesci Doza win 4-2 on agg

Rangers 1 (Stein), Bayern Munich 1 (Muller) *Bayern Munich win 2-1 on agg*

Rumelange 0, Juventus 4 (Novellini 3, Landini) *Juventus win 11-0 on agg*

Sedan 1 (Dellamore pen), Cologne 0 *Cologne win 5-2 on agg*

Slavia Sofia 1 (Davidov), Hadjuk Split 0 *Hadjuk Split win 3-1 on agg*

Sliema Wanderers 2 (Cani, Jessen og), BK Copenhagen 3 (Nielsen 2, Hansen) *BK Copenhagen win 10-2 on agg*

Sturm Graz 3 (Albrecht, Murlasits, Kaiser), Ilves 0 *Sturm Graz win 7-2 on agg*

Twente Enschede 3 (Pahlplatz 2, Van Der Kerkhof), AEK Athens 0 *Twente Enschede win 4-0 on agg*

Valencia 3 (Sergio 2, Jara), Cork Hibernian 1 (Wigginton) *Valencia win 6-1 on agg*

Vitoria Setubal 2 (Jose Maria, Vitor Baptista), Lausanne 1 (Dufour) *Vitoria Setubal win 4-1 on agg*

Struggle to break down iron curtain

DON Revie's team selection against Dynamo Dresden was clouded by a stomach bug which swept through the United camp.

Revie was among those affected and missed the game in which his assistant Maurice Lindley handed a European debut to Nigel Davey, a local-born right back, who had limited League experience.

Revie's illness also delayed the signing from Scottish club Morton of 18-year-old Joe Jordan, who was to emerge as a European star in his own right in years to come.

Predictably the East Germans went to Elland Road and erected a human wall round their goal in which the 6ft 4in Klaus Sammer was the largest brick.

With Allan Clarke going through a thin time in front of goal, United needed to be patient to find a way past goalkeeper Manfred Kallenbach and his defenders.

Terry Cooper and Norman Hunter hit top form for United, but it was a struggle up front where the only goal came in the 56th minute. Rod Belfitt, in for fractured cheekbone victim Johnny Giles, saw a header beat Kallenbach, but it was palmed over the bar by Hans-Jurgen Dorner.

Peter Lorimer, who had seen a rare header saved by Kallenbach's feet, despatched the penalty in the absence of Giles.

United were unable to get that elusive second goal and were almost caught out at the end when both Hans-Juergen Kreishe and 18-year-old Frank Richter shaved a coat of paint off the posts.

A tough return leg was in prospect against an experiended, well-organised Dresden outfit.

ON TARGET: United's Peter Lorimer breaks Dresden's resistence at Elland Road by slotting a 56th minute penalty past Manfred Kallenbach.

Bayern swamp poor Coventry

COVENTRY'S European dream was spectacularly shattered in Munich where Bayern stormed to a 6-1 win, World Cup star Gerd Muller getting a couple of goals.

Liverpool cruised to a 3-0 win at Anfield over Dynamo Bucharest – all the goals coming in the second half.

Second round, second leg

Barcelona 1 (Marcial), Juventus 2 (Haller, Bettega)
Bayern Munich 6 (Schneider 2, Schwarzenbeck, G Muller 2, Roth), Coventry City 1 (Hunt)
BK Copenhagen 1 (Nielsen), Anderlecht 3 (Mulder, Ejderstedt, Yde og)
Dynamo Zagreb 4 (Lalic 2, Cercek, Schultz og), Hamburg 0
Eskishirsport 3 (Gundogon, Haper 2), Twente Enschede 2 (Pahplatz, Van Der Kerkhof)
Fiorentina 1 (Mariani), Cologne 2 (Flohe 2)
Hertha Berlin 1 (Horr), Spartak Trnava 0
Hibernian 2 (Duncan, Stanton), Vitoria Guimaraes 0
Leeds United 1 (Lorimer pen), Dynamo Dresden 0
Liverpool 3 (Lindsay, Lawler, Hughes), Dynamo Bucharest 0
Newcastle United 2 (Moncur, Davies), Inter Milan 0
Sparta Prague 3 (Jurkanin 2, Vrana), Dundee United 1 (Traynor)
Sparta Rotterdam 2 (Klijnjan 2), Coleraine 0
Sturm Graz 1 (Zamul), Arsenal 0
Valencia 0, Beveren 1 (De Raeymaeker)
Vitoria Setubal 2 (Jose Maria, Jacinto Joao), Hadjuk Split 0

European Fairs Cup
Second round, first leg
(at Elland Road, Leeds)
Wednesday, October 21, 1970

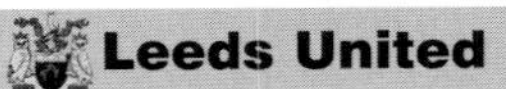

Leeds United 1

Dynamo Dresden 0

Leeds United: David Harvey, Nigel Davey, Terry Cooper, Billy Bremner, Jack Charlton, Norman Hunter, Peter Lorimer, Allan Clarke, Mick Jones, Rod Belfitt, Paul Madeley
Goals: Lorimer 56 pen
Manager: Don Revie

Dynamo Dresden: Manfred Kallenbach, Frank Ganzera, Hans-Jurgen Dorner, Klaus Sammer, Joachim Kern, Wolfgang Haustein, Uwe Zeigler, Hans-Jurgen Kreische, Meinhard Hemp, Gert Heidler, Frank Richter
Manager: Walter Fritzsh

Referee: Alfred Delacourt (Belgium) **Att:** 21,292

RED CARD: Mick Bates.

Gunners blast back

FUTURE Leeds United manager George Graham was in the Arsenal team which wiped out a 1-0 deficit against Sturm Graz by winning 2-0 at Highbury.

But while Liverpool went through easily in Bucharest, Coventry and Newcastle went out, the Magpies losing on penalties to Pesci Doza after extra-time in Hungary

Second round, second leg

Anderlecht 4 (Nordahl 2, Elizeu, Van Himst), BK Copenhagen 0 *Anderlecht win 7-1 on agg*
Arsenal 2 (Kennedy, Storey pen), Sturm Graz 0 *Arsenal win 2-1 on agg*
Beveren 1 (De Raeymeacker), Valencia 1 (Forment) *Beveren win 2-1 on agg*
Coleraine 1 (Jennings), Sparta Rotterdam 2 (Koudijze, Kristensen) *Sparta Rotterdam win 4-1 on agg*
Cologne 1 (Biscup pen), Fiorentina 0 *Cologne win 3-1 on agg*
Coventry City 2 (Martin, O'Rourke), Bayern Munich 1 (Hoeness) *Bayern Munich win 7-3 on agg*
Dundee United 1 (Gordon), Sparta Prague 0 *Sparta Prague win 3-2 on agg*
Dynamo Bucharest 1 (Salceanu), Liverpool 1 (Boersma) *Liverpool win 4-1 on agg*
Dynamo Dresden 2 (Hemp, Kriesche), Leeds United 1 (Jones) *2-2 on agg Leeds United win on away goals*
Hadjuk Split 2 (Nadoveza, Hlevnjak), Vitoria Setubal 1 (Jose Maria) *Vitoria Setubal win 3-2 on agg*
Hamburg 1 (Honig), Dynamo Zagreb 0 *Dynamo Zagreb win 4-1 on agg*
Juventus 2 (Bettega, Capello), Barcelona 1 (Pujol) *Juventus win 4-2 on agg*
Pesci Doza 2 (Moncur og, Mate pen), Newcastle United 0 *Agg 2-2 after extra-time. Pesci Doza win 3-0 on penalties*
Spartak Trnava 3 (Kuna, Wild og, Bozik), Hertha Berlin 1 (Gayer) *Spartak Trnava win 3-2 on agg*
Twente Enschede 6 (Jeuring 3, Van Der Kerkhof, Streuer, Nagy), Eskishirsport 1 (Heper) *Twente Enschede win 8-4 on agg*
Vitoria Gimaraes 2 (Goncalves, Belo), Hibernian 1 (Graham) *Hibernian win 3-2 on agg*

Rough ride in Dresden

UNITED only just scraped through on the aways goals ruling after an explosive night in Dresden.

Things started to go wrong for United even before the arrived in Germany.

Their flight was due to leave Leeds/Bradford Airport at 10am, but because of delays they travelled to Manchester and got up in the air four hours late, landing at Templehof Airport in Berlin shortly before 5pm.

The United party then boarded a coach for the drive to Dresden, but just outside the approach to the city the rear near side tyre burst and the journey was completed – 12 hours behind schedule – in a fleet of taxis.

Interest among home fans was high and all 35,000 tickets had been snapped up within three hours of going on sale.

It was not long before they were cheering a home goal. Dieter Reidel swept through the middle, sent a pass out to the right where Uwe Zeigler whipped the ball in for Meinhard Hemp to shoot past Gary Sprake, who slipped in sawdust in the goalmouth and the ball bobbled into the net.

United netted a crucial away goal just after half an hour when Jack Charlton chested Peter Lorimer's cross into the path of Mick Jones who crashed in the equaliser.

Dresden, roared on by the crowd, were giving United plenty to deal with, but Norman Hunter was at his brilliant best at the back.

Just when United seemed to have got the measure of the home side, the game erupted 10 minutes after the interval when Charlton and home forward Frank Richter both went down in the Leeds box and the Dresden player stayed down while the German fans howled for a penalty. Bottles from the crowd were hurled into the penalty area and skipper Klaus Sammer ran to the touchline to appeal for calm.

Dresden continued to look dangerous and just after an hour Hans-Jurgen Kreische headed his side into a 2-1 lead, levelling the aggregate scores in the process.

United's away goal was still their trump card but all hell broke loose eight minutes from time after Allan Clarke, who had already been booked, brought down substiute Gert Heidler just outside the Leeds box.

Fighting broke out among some of the players and after he restored order Austrian referee Ferdinand Marschall sent off United's Mick Bates and Eduard Geyer, one of Dresden's subs.

From the free kick Sprake did well to push the ball away for the expense of a corner and United were relieved to hear the final whistle.

But the trouble didn't stop as angry spectators ran onto the pitch and one tried to attack Charlton, before being restrained by fellow supporters.

European Fairs Cup
Second round, second leg
(at Rudolf Harbig Stadium, Dresden)
Wednesday, November 4, 1970

Dynamo Dresden 2
Leeds United 1

Agg 2-2 Leeds United win on away goals

Dynamo Dresden: Manfred Kallenbach, Frank Ganzera, Hans-Jurgen Dorner, Klaus Sammer, Wolfgang Haustein, Uwe Zeiglerm, Meinhard Hemp, Hans-Jurgen Kreishe, Dieter Riedel (Eduard Geyer 77), Frank Richter, Rainer Sacse (Gerd Heidler HT)
Goals: Hemp 15, Kreische 63
Manager: Walter Fritzsch

Leeds United: Gary Sprake, Nigel Davey, Paul Madeley, Billy Bremner, Jack Charlton, Norman Hunter, Peter Lorimer, Allan Clarke, Mick Jones, Johnny Giles, Mick Bates
Goal: Jones 32
Manager: Don Revie

Referee: Ferdinand Marschall (Austria) **Att:** 35,000

Brought to book

THE day after United's thumping of Sparta Prague, Jack Charlton was admonished by the FA for comments he made on television the previous month.

He revealed he kept names in a little black book and how he would 'do' two players in the book.

Charlton said that the remarks were light-hearted in manner, but the FA took a dim view and had told England team boss Sir Alf Ramsey not to pick Charlton until they had dealt with the matter – a hollow threat as his international career had ended at the 1970 World Cup where he figured in just one game.

HEADS WE WIN: Jack Charlton gets in a spectacular header on Sparta Prague's goal.

Six-shooters blast Sparta

European Fairs Cup
Third round, first leg
(at Elland Road, Leeds)
Wednesday, December 2, 1970

Leeds United	**6**
Sparta Prague	**0**

Leeds United: Gary Sprake, Paul Madeley, Terry Cooper, Billy Bremner, Jack Charlton, Norman Hunter, Peter Lorimer, Allan Clarke, Rod Belfitt (Paul Reaney 21), Johnny Giles, Eddie Gray
Goals: Clarke 19, Chovanec og 24, Bremner 26, Gray 28, 36, Charlton 54
Manager: Don Revie

Sparta Prague: Antonin Kramerius, Pavel Melichar, Vaclav Migas, Eduard Kessel, Oldrich Urban, Frantisek Chovanec, Bohumil Veseley (Tibor Semndak 72), Frantisek Gogh, Vaclav Masek (Petr Ulicny HT), Josef Jurjanin, Vaclav Vrana
Manager: Karel Kolsky

Referee: Koen Brouwer (Holland) **Att:** 25,843

UNITED turned on a super show as they demolished Sparta Prague of Czechoslovakia 6-0 to make the away leg a formality.

"It was a privilege to watch," purred Don Revie after seeing his side cut apart one of the competition's highly-rated teams who had put out Bilbao in the first round.

Mick Jones was out injured, Mick Bates was suspended following his red card in Dresden and Terry Yorath was also missing as he was on Welsh Under 23 international duty against England. But United didn't need the trio as they powered into a 5-0 interval lead and only a heroic goalkeeping display by Antonin Kramerius kept the final score below double figures. It took United until the 19th minute to register their first goal, Rod Belfitt flicking the ball on for Allan Clarke to net Leeds' 50th goal of the season.

Belfitt got injured in the process and went off to have three stitches inserted into a head wound, allowing Paul Reaney to come on, Paul Madeley moving to midfield and Billy Bremner switching to attack.

Rather than weaken Revie's line-up it strengthened it as four more goals flew past Kramerius in a magical 12-minute spell.

Reaney's first touch was a cross from the right which Frantisek Chovanec headed into his own net, then Bremner collected Johnny Giles' pass to fire into the corner of the Sparta net.

Eddie Gray sidefooted home number four then headed in a Peter Lorimer cross, but the only score in the second half came when Lorimer's deep far post centre was headed in at the far post by Charlton.

Lorimer and the big Leeds centre half also hit the woodwork and Bremner had a goal disallowed on a night of unremitting attack.

Title rivals Arsenal thump Beveren

ARSENAL, second in the League behind United, made their second leg a formality as they sank Belgian outfit Beveren 4-0 at Highbury, Ray Kennedy scoring twice. Liverpool completed an outstanding night for English clubs as John Toshack's goal gave them a 1-0 victory against Hibernian at Easter Road.

Third round, first leg

Anderlecht 2 (Ejderstedt, Mulder), Vitoria Setubal 1 (Vagner)
Arsenal 4 (Kennedy 2, Graham, Sammels), Beveren 0
Bayern Munich 2 (Schneider, Muller), Sparta Rotterdam 1 (Heijerman)
Dynamo Zagreb 2 (Gucmirtl 2), Twente Enschede 2 (Pahlplatz, Van Der Kerkhof)
Hibernian 0, Liverpool 1 (Toshack)
Leeds United 6 (Gray 2, Clarke, Chovanec og, Bremner, Charlton), Sparta Prague 0
Pesci Doza 0, Juventus 1 (Causio)
Spartak Trnava 0, Cologne 1 (Dobia og)

Czechs bounced

United stroll to easy victory in Prague

NO WAY THROUGH: United's Paul Madeley and sub Terry Yorath close down Vaclav Masek.

UNITED were amazed to find that goalkeeper Antonin Kramerius, the one Sparta player to return to Prague with his reputation intact, was axed for the academic second leg.

Although their side had no hope of going through, news of United's brilliance had filtered through to the Czech capital and all 30,000 tickets were sold out inside two hours.

United, able to rest several players, didn't dissappoint and had built up a 9-0 aggregate lead by half-time, drawing generous applause from the locals.

Vladimir Brabec, Kramerius' replacement in goal, misjudged Eddie Gray's shot and allowed the ball to bounce gently over his head as he dived for the ball.

European Fairs Cup
Third round, second leg
(at Letna Stadium, Prague)
Wednesday, December 9, 1970

Sparta Prague	**2**
Leeds United	**3**

Leeds United win 9-2 on agg

Sparta Prague: Vladimir Brabec, Pavel Melichar, Vaclav Migas, Eduard Kessel, Oldrich Urban, Frantisek Chovanec, Bohumil Veseley, Jaroslav Barton, Vaclav Masek, Josef Jurkanin, Vaclav Vrana
Goals: Barton 66, Urban 82
Manager: Karel Kolsky

Leeds United: Gary Sprake (David Harvey HT), Paul Reaney, Terry Cooper, Billy Bremner, Paul Madeley, Norman Hunter (Terry Yorath HT), Peter Lorimer, Allan Clarke, Rod Belfitt, Mick Bates, Eddie Gray
Goals: Gray 12, Clarke 32, Belfitt 34
Manager: Don Revie

Referee: Aureilio Angonese (Itay) **Att:** 30,000

United had the freedom of the Letna Stadium and just after half-an hour Clarke drifted into the box past a group of static defenders to tap in the second goal.

Two minutes later United pieced together another scoring move. Terry Cooper took Billy Bremner's pass down the right and crossed for Rod Belfitt, proving an excellent deputy for the injured Mick Jones, to score with a low hard shot into the corner.

Such was United's dominance that Revie was able to withdraw Gary Sprake, who had been a virtual spectator, and Norman Hunter and send on David Harvey and Terry Yorath.

Carelessness crept into the United play and Sparta were able to silence the ironic jeers of their own fans with a couple of goals in the final third of the game.

After Cooper did well to block a drive from Vaclav Migas, Jaroslav Barton squeezed the ball past Harvey from 30 yards and minutes from the end Oldrich Urban completed the scoring.

England trio marching on

UNITED were joined in the quarter-finals by Liverpool and Arsenal. The Merseysiders, facing a Hibernian side who had sacked manager Willie McFarlane on the eve of the first leg, wrapped up a 3-0 aggregate victory with goals by Steve Heighway and Phil Boersma at Anfield.

Arsenal had little difficulty in shutting out Sturm Graz in Austria.

World Cup star Gerd Muller grabbed a hat-trick in Rotterdam as Bayern Munich swept in to the last eight while two goals by Pietro Anastasi gave Juventus a 2-0 win in Turin over Pesci Doza to go through 3-0 on aggregate.

Third round, second leg

Beveren 0, Arsenal 0 *Arsenal win 4-0 on agg*

Cologne 3 (Biscup pen, Hemmersbach, Rupp), Spartak Trnava 0 *Cologne win 4-0 on agg*

Juventus 2 (Anastasi 2), Pesci Doza 0 *Juventus win 3-0 on agg*

Liverpool 2 (Heighway, Boersma), Hibernian 0 *Liverpool win 3-0 on agg*

Sparta Prague 2 (Barton, Urban), Leeds United 3 (Gray, Clarke, Belfitt) *Leeds United win 9-2 on agg*

Sparta Rotterdam 1 (Knatensen), Bayern Munich 3 (Muller 3) *Bayern Munich win 5-2 on agg*

Twente Enschede 1 (Jeuring), Dynamo Zagreb 0 *Twente Enschede win 3-2 on agg*

Vitoria Setubal 3 (Guereiro 2, Vitor Baptista), Anderlecht 1 (Desanghere) *Vitoria Setubal win 4-3 on agg*

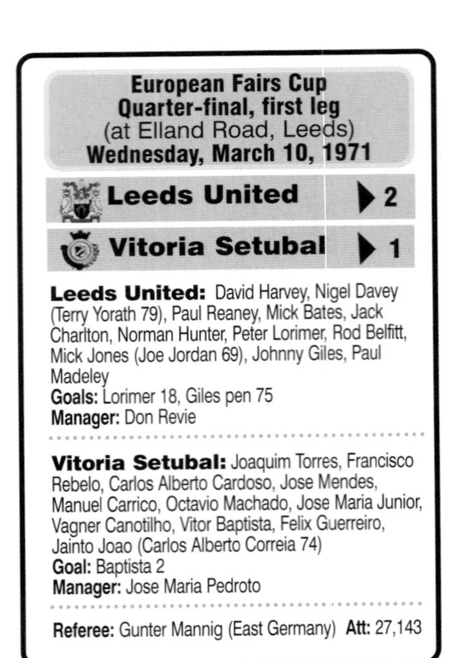

European Fairs Cup
Quarter-final, first leg
(at Elland Road, Leeds)
Wednesday, March 10, 1971

Leeds United	**2**
Vitoria Setubal	**1**

Leeds United: David Harvey, Nigel Davey (Terry Yorath 79), Paul Reaney, Mick Bates, Jack Charlton, Norman Hunter, Peter Lorimer, Rod Belfitt, Mick Jones (Joe Jordan 69), Johnny Giles, Paul Madeley
Goals: Lorimer 18, Giles pen 75
Manager: Don Revie

Vitoria Setubal: Joaquim Torres, Francisco Rebelo, Carlos Alberto Cardoso, Jose Mendes, Manuel Carrico, Octavio Machado, Jose Maria Junior, Vagner Canotilho, Vitor Baptista, Felix Guerreiro, Jainto Joao (Carlos Alberto Correia 74)
Goal: Baptista 2
Manager: Jose Maria Pedroto

Referee: Gunter Mannig (East Germany) **Att:** 27,143

CATCH ME IF YOU CAN: Furious Setubal players chase referee Gunter Mannig after he awarded United a late penalty converted by Johnny Giles.

Penalty storm

Setubal's spot-kick fury

AFTER a three-month break from the competition, United resumed their Fairs Cup campaign with a controversial clash with Portuguese side Vitoria Setubal at Elland Road.

United's flu-hit squad, minus Billy Bremner, Allan Clarke and Terry Cooper found themselves behind after 90 seconds through Vitor Batista.

But United didn't panic and racked up chances, only to find goalkeeper Joaquim Torres in inspirational form.

It needed a Peter Lorimer special – a crunching 22-yard drive to level the scores on 18 minutes. United kept chipping away but the brilliant Torres saved superbly from Mick Jones (twice) and substitute Joe Jordan, who came on for his European debut.

Then all hell broke loose in the 75th minute. East German referee Gunter Mannig gave handball in the box against Carlos Cardoso and found himself chased, pushed and jostled by the Setubal players.

Manager Jose-Maria Pedroto and other members of the Setubal entourage were out of the dug-out in protest. "The penalty did not exisit," stormed Pedroto afterwards, "But I did not agree with the way my players reacted."

Missiles were thrown at the Setubal bench and police had to move in to calm things on and off the pitch.

Eventually when order was restored Johnny Giles kept his cool and squeezed the ball past Torres, even though the 'keeper got his hand to the Irishman's spot-kick.

United almost increased their lead with a last-minute Madeley header, but all the talk after the game was about the penalty rather than the slender margin of United's victory.

Good Evans

YOUNG striker Alun Evans made a sensational comeback for Liverpool.

Playing his first game in four months after injury he netted a hat-trick as the Reds thrashed Bayern Munich 3-0 at Anfield.

Peter Storey netted Arsenal's winner against Cologne at Highbury after Karl-Heinz Thielen equalised Frank McLintock's 25th minute opener just before half-time.

Juventus took control of their tie with Dutch side Twente Enschede with a 2-0 home win.

Quarter-final first leg

Arsenal 2 (McLintock, Storey), Cologne 1 (Thielen)
Juventus 2 (Haller, Novellini), Twente Enschede 0
Leeds United 2 (Lorimer, Giles pen), Vitoria Setubal 1 (Baptista)
Liverpool 3 (Evans 3), Bayern Munich 0

MATCH WINNER: Johnny Giles slots the ball past Joaquim Torres from the spot.

United Set fair

Portuguese tamed

European Fairs Cup
Quarter-final, second leg
(at Bonfim, Stadium, Setubal)
Wednesday, March 24, 1971

Vitoria Setubal 1

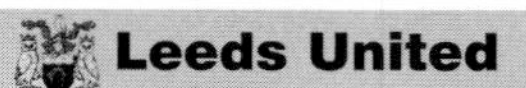

Leeds United 1

Leeds United win 3-2 on agg

Vitoria Setubal: Joaquim Torres, Joaquim Da Conceicao (Joaquim Arcanjo 26), Carlos Alberto Cardoso, Jose Mendes, Francisco Rebelo, Octavio Machado (Mateus Luis Santos 70), Jose Maria Junior, Vagner Canotilho, Vitor Baptista, Feliz Guerreiro, Jacinto Joao
Goal: Baptista 83
Manager: Jose Maria Pedroto

Leeds United: David Harvey (Gary Sprake 82), Paul Reaney, Terry Cooper, Mick Bates, Jack Charlton, Norman Hunter, Peter Lorimer, Allan Clarke, Mick Jones, Johnny Giles, Paul Madeley
Goal: Lorimer 18
Manager: Don Revie

Referee: Roland Marendaz (Switzerland) **Att:** 30,000

UNITED set up camp at the fishing resort of Sesimbra for the return leg in Portugal to prepare for what would be their 50th match of the season.

Don Revie's men went into the game in upbeat mood as a profit of £172,000 had been announced the day prior to the match.

He backed his men to do the job by attacking. "We have too many players possessing flair to sit back. We are prepared to pit our skills against theirs."

The key moment of the match – and the tie – came after just 18 minutes. The dangerous Vitor Baptista powered towards goal but failed to see the unmarked Jacinto Joao in support. A simple pass would have put Joao in a great goal-scoring position, but United were able to snuff out Baptista and regain possession.

Immediately United moved upfield and the ball arrived at the feet of Peter Lorimer, who scored for the seventh successive match by driving the ball through the legs of Joaquim Torres from close range.

Setubal, now needing to score three times to rescue the tie, visibly wilted and almost fell further behind when an Allan Clarke header hit the underside of the bar.

INJURED: David Harvey.

A perfect night was spoiled near the end when David Harvey damaged knee ligaments in a slick Setubal move which required Norman Hunter to kick the ball off the line.

Welsh star Gary Sprake came on for Harvey and was immediately beaten from close range by Baptista to set up a nervous ending which saw Sprake produce a dazzling late save to deny Baptista another goal which would have taken the game into extra-time.

But United hung on, and deservedly so for Mick Bates and Johnny Giles had dictated matters in midfield throughout, while Clarke and Mick Jones were a constant menace up front.

United's jubilant party were 22,000 feet in the air flying back to Yorkshire when news of the semi-final draw came through – a mouth-watering clash with domestic rivals Liverpool.

Liverpool to tackle Leeds in semis

LIVERPOOL enjoyed a comfortable passage in to the Fairs Cup semi-finals with a 1-1 draw at Bayern Munich giving them a 4-1 aggregate victory.

Utilty player Ian Ross gave the Reds a 1-0 advantage in Germany on 74 minutes but Bayern managed an equaliser shortly afterwards.

Four days later Bill Shankly's men made it through to the FA Cup final by beating Everton 2-1. Their opponents at Wembley would be Arsenal, who were still doggedly chasing Leeds in the race for the Championship.

However, Arsenal didn't make it though to the last four of the Fairs Cup as they lost 1-0 to an early Werner Biskup penalty in Cologne, going out on the away goals ruling.

The goal they conceded to the Germans at Highbury came when Bob Wilson let the ball go straight in to his goal from a corner.

While Leeds would line up against Liverpool in an all-English semi-final, Cologne would take on Juventus, who were pegged back at Twente Enschede before two extra-time goals by Pietro Anatstasi saw them home,

Quarter-final, second leg

Bayern Munich 1 (Schneider), Liverpool 1 (Ross) *Liverpool win 4-1 on agg*

Cologne 1 (Biskup pen), Arsenal 0 *2-2 on agg. Cologne win on away goals*

Twente Enschede 2 (Pahlplatz, Droost), Juventus 2 (Anastasi 2) *Juventus win 4-2 on agg after extra-time*

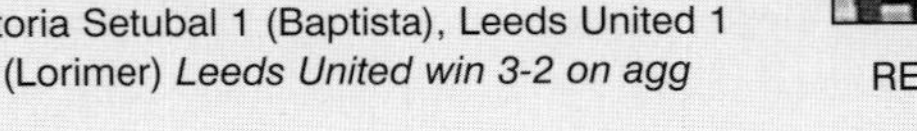

Vitoria Setubal 1 (Baptista), Leeds United 1 (Lorimer) *Leeds United win 3-2 on agg*

REVIE'S RIVAL: Liverpool's charismatic manager Bill Shankly.

Billy's smash and grab

KOP THAT: Leeds skipper Billy Bremner celebrates his goal with Jack Charlton.

ONE of Don Revie's biggest-ever gambles in Europe paid off as United snatched a priceless 1-0 semi-final first leg win at Liverpool.

The only goal came from inspirational skipper Billy Bremner in his first senior game for three months. Just hours before the match he had figured in a friendly against Bradford and that was enough for Revie to put him in the side.

But with Rod Belfitt (groin strain) joining Peter Lorimer (pulled hamstring) on the injured list, Revie played the little man at Anfield – and sprung a further surprise by playing him up front alongside Allan Clarke and Mick Jones.

Predictably Liverpool, attacking the Kop end, made all the early running. Larry Lloyd hooked a shot just over the bar and Gary Sprake was forced to field a Steve Heighway header as the home pressure mounted.

United's only chance of the first half came when Bremner and Johnny Giles fashioned an opening for Paul Madeley, whose shot was turned over the bar by goalie Ray Clemence.

Soon after the interval United had a great escape. Sprake dropped a cross from John Toshack and the ball landed at Alun Evans' feet, four yards out, but he screwed his shot against a post.

It was a costly miss as United stole the lead on 67 minutes. Giles curled in a free-kick from the left, it eluded all the big men stationed in the area, but Bremner, free in space flung himself forward to head the ball into the net under the noses of the stunned Kop. It was United's 100th goal of the season.

The rest of the game was one-way traffic towards the Leeds goal as Liverpool stepped up the pressure. Toshack had a shot blocked on the line and then Sprake clutched a header from his Welsh international colleague.

Towards the end Emlyn Hughes was put through and seemed certain to equalise, but the England man seemed to get his legs in a tangle and the chance was lost. Somehow United, playing their 50th Fairs Cup tie, had hung on to become the first side to win at Anfield that season.

European Fairs Cup
Semi-final, first leg
(at Anfield, Liverpool)
Wednesday, April 14, 1971

Liverpool	**0**
Leeds United	**1**

Liverpool: Ray Clemence, Chris Lawler, Alec Lindsay, Tommy Smith, Larry Lloyd, Emlyn Hughes, Ian Callaghan (Bobby Graham 68), Alun Evans (Peter Thompson 69), Steve Heighway, John Toshack, Brian Hall
Manager: Bill Shankly

Leeds United: Gary Sprake, Paul Reaney (Nigel Davey 83), Terry Cooper, Billy Bremner, Jack Charlton, Norman Hunter, Mick Bates, Allan Clarke, Mick Jones, Johnny Giles, Paul Madeley
Goal: Bremner 67
Manager: Don Revie

Referee: Jef Dorpmans (Holland) **Att:** 52,877

Juventus to face United

UNITED'S opponents in the Fairs Cup final would be Juventus, whose developing young team were becoming the talk of Italy.

They had led for most of the match in Cologne until Thielen's 87th minute goal wiped out Roberto Bettega's first-half strike. The Germans were never really in the second leg in Turin after Fabio Capello scored inside two minutes, Pietro Anastasi securing a 2-0 home win and 3-1 semi-final aggregate victory.

Although United were through to the Fairs Cup final their hopes of representing England in the European Cup the following season had been shattered by Arsenal.

The Gunners gradually reeled in United's big lead at the top of the table – even though Leeds beat them 1-0 at Elland Road two days before United's second leg Fairs Cup clash with Liverpool.

But Arsenal, who had already beaten Liverpool in the FA Cup final, completed the 'Double' by beating Tottenham at White Hart Lane on May 3.

Semi-final first leg
Cologne 1 (Thielen), Juventus 1 (Bettega)
Liverpool 0, Leeds United 1 (Bremner)

Semi-final second leg
Juventus 2 (Capello, Anastasi), Cologne 0
Juventus win 3-1 on agg
Leeds United 0, Liverpool 0
Leeds United win 1-0 on agg

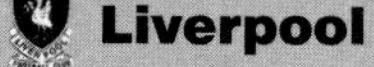

Leeds United	0
Liverpool	0

Leeds United win 1-0 on agg

Leeds United: Gary Sprake, Paul Madeley, Terry Cooper, Billy Bremner, Jack Charlton, Norman Hunter, Mick Bates, Allan Clarke (Paul Reaney HT), Mick Jones (Joe Jordan 53), Johnny Giles, Eddie Gray
Manager: Don Revie

Liverpool: Ray Clemence, Chris Lawler, Ron Yeats, Tommy Smith, Larry Lloyd, Emlyn Hughes, Ian Callaghan, Peter Thompson, Steve Heighway, John Toshack, Brian Hall
Manager: Bill Shankly

Referee: Tom Wharton (Scotland) **Att:** 40,462

TAKING THE MICK: United midfielder skipper Mick Bates skips past Ron Yeats.

Cast iron defence

Liverpool kept at bay

UNITED sealed their passage to their third European final in five years with a hard-fought 0-0 draw with old rivals Liverpool at Elland Road.

With Billy Bremner's header in the bank, United knew they could afford to be fairly conservative, but were the first to show when Mick Bates' dipping shot went narrowly past a post.

The men from Merseyside responded when Chris Lawler slung a pass out to Steve Heighway on the left. The leggy forward cut in at speed and forced Gary Sprake to save at full stretch at the expense of a corner.

United responded when Eddie Gray danced down the left and his cross was headed against the bar by Mick Jones before the Liverpool defenders scrambled the ball clear.

Heighway, the biggest threat to United's security, almost restored parity when he rapped in a terrific volley which whistled inches past Sprake's far post.

With Allan Clarke failing to resume after the break through injury and Jones limping off shortly after the restart, United had lost their two top strikers and at that stage opted to protect the lead they had gained at Anfield.

Liverpool forced the issue in the closing stages, but United's defence looked solid. The only scares came when Emlyn Hughes almost forced his way through, Sprake comfortably collected an Ian Callaghan shot and a goal-bound shot by Brian Hall was blocked.

The Elland Road crowd sensed long before the end that the Reds were not going to break United down and roared their approval when referee Tom Wharton blew for time.

What a washout

Downpour washes out Turin final

SPLASH HITS: United striker Allan Clarke retrieves the ball from a puddle.

TORRENTIAL rain turned United's first leg of the Fairs Cup final against Juventus in to a farce.

A six-hour cloudburst over Turin turned the Comunale Stadium pitch into a lake, forcing Dutch referee Leo Van Ravens to abandon the match.

Six minutes into the second half he brought an end to the watersports. The game should probably have not even started but there were 46,501 in the ground, many huddled under umbrellas.

The supporters, who had paid around 150 million lire to watch, were the biggest losers on the night as they did not get a refund because the match was not abandoned until after half-time.

Leeds skipper Billy Bremner, sensing a 0-0 draw was very much on the cards waved his arms in protest at Van Ravens' decision – but it was undoubtably the right one.

Incidents had been few and far between although both sides hit the woodwork – Franco Causio thumping a shot against an upright and Johnny Giles striking the bar with a 25-yard drive.

The most significant action came in the 20th minute when Eddie Gray suffered a reoccurence of a dislocated shoulder he had suffered when playing for Scotland against Wales a fortnight earlier.

Gray was sent home while the two clubs and UEFA decided how to get the match on.

Juventus, standing fourth in the Serie A, agreed that if the match was washed out again then they would play both legs of the final in Leeds.

Fortunately, there was no need for that generous cessation from Juventus as the weather did improve and the match was able to go ahead two days later.

SPLASH-HAPPY: United striker Mick Jones attempts to pass the ball on the sodden surface of the Comunale Stadium in Turin.

European Fairs Cup Final, first leg
(at Comunale Stadium, Turin)
Wednesday, May 26, 1971

Juventus	**0**
Leeds United	**0**

Match abandoned after 51 mins

Juventus: Massimo Piloni, Luciano Spinosi, Gianpietro Marchetti, Guiseppe Furino, Francesco Morini, Sandro Salvadore, Helmut Haller, Franco Causio, Pietro Anastasi, Fabio Capello, Roberto Bettega
Manager: Cestmir Yycpalek

Leeds United: Gary Sprake, Paul Madeley, Terry Cooper, Billy Bremner, Jack Charlton, Norman Hunter, Peter Lorimer, Allan Clarke, Mick Jones, Johnny Giles, Eddie Gray (Terry Yorath 21)
Manager: Don Revie

Referee: Laurens Van Raven (Holland) **Att:** 46,501

THE ITALIAN JOB: Juventus goalkeeper Massimo Piloni is left on his knees after failing to deal with a Johnny Giles cross and Mick Bates is on hand to hammer United's second equalier in to the roof of the net.

Final goals made in Yorkshire

Bates and Madeley strikes give United edge over Juve

European Fairs Cup Final, first leg
(at Comunale Stadium, Turin)
Friday, May 28, 1971

Juventus	2
Leeds United	2

Juventus: Massimo Piloni, Luciano Spinosi, Gianpietro Marchetti, Guiseppe Furino, Francesco Morini, Sandro Salvadore, Helmut Haller, Franco Causio, Pietro Anastasi (Adriano Novellini 73), Fabio Capello, Roberto Bettega
Goals: Bettega 27, Capello 55
Manager: Cestmir Yycpalek

Leeds United: Gary Sprake, Paul Reaney Terry Cooper, Billy Bremner, Jack Charlton, Norman Hunter, Peter Lorimer, Allan Clarke, Mick Jones (Mick Bates 73), Johnny Giles, Paul Madeley
Goals: Madeley 48, Bates 77
Manager: Don Revie

Referee: Lauren Van Ravens (Holland) **Att:** 45,000

FITTINGLY goals by Yorkshire-born Paul Madeley and Mick Bates gave United the edge against Juventus.

Twice behind, United hit back to force a draw with strikes by Leeds-born Madeley and Doncaster's Bates.

True Yorkshire grit had given United two priceless away goals and the Fairs Cup final odds were shifting towards Don Revie's team.

Leeds didn't find room in their line-up for Terry Yorath, who had replaced Eddie Gray in the first attempt to play. Paul Reaney was recalled instead.

United showed no sign of nerves and began the match on top but fell behind against the run of play. Terry Cooper lost the ball to German star Helmut Haller, who quickly switched it to Pietro Anastasi. The ball was moved on to Roberto Causio and his low hard centre across the Leeds box saw Roberto Bettega wriggle inside Reaney to put Juve ahead.

United refused to panic and deservedly drew level when Peter Lorimer fed Madeley, who strode into space and belted in a 20-yard shot which deflected past Massimo Piloni off Sandro Salvadore for the equaliser. It was United's first-ever goal on Italian soil in four games.

Six minutes after the break some devastating Juventus approach play by their much-vaunted £1 million attack was crowned when Fabio Capello crashed a ferocious shot past Gary Sprake from 20 yards.

Back in front, the Italians threatened to take complete control, but Revie's tactical switch paid dividends when he pushed Billy Bremner into attack and sent on Mick Bates to join Johnny Giles in midfield.

Within four minutes of his arrival Bates was on the spot to punish a Piloni error. The goalkeeper fluffed a Giles cross from the left and the ball dropped to the Leeds substitute who fired the ball into the roof of the net.

Suddenly the balance of power switched to Leeds with Giles masterminding several dangerous counter attacks and could have snatched a winner but with the match all-square and two away goals in the bag, United returned home in good spirits.

Triumphant United enjoy

White

'THEY SHALL NOT PASS: United's Norman Hunter (right) and Paul Reaney shut out Pietro Anastasi, Juventus' scorer.

FLAMING June had arrived by the time Elland Road hosted the second leg of the final against Juventus six days later.

Fittingly, short-shirted Leeds made a start as bright as the Yorkshire sunshine with a goal inside 12 minutes.

Surging towards the Kop, Leeds looked to have missed an early chance to go ahead when Peter Lorimer fluffed a shooting chance from a Billy Bremner free-kick but Allan Clarke, ever alert in the box, hit a shot low past goalkeeper Roberto Tancredi.

It was a miserable start for the Italians, who had been forced to field their reserve 'keeper after Massimo Piloni was injured in training.

But their expensively assembled side stunned the home fans with an equaliser seven minutes later.

Franco Causio intercepted a spare midfield pass by Paul Madeley and the ball was swept on to Giuseppe Furino, whose magnificent ball sliced open the

BEATEN FINALISTS: Juventus, who gave United a run for their money in the 1971 European Fairs Cup final. Back row, from left to right: Sandro Salvadore, Gianpietro Marchetti, Gianluigi Roveta, Antonello Cuccureddu, Massimo Piloni, Roberto Tancredi, Ferioli, Landini, Roberto Bettega, Francesco Morini, Luciana Spinosi, Helmut Haller. Front row: Giuseppe Zaniboni, Savoldi, Montorsi, Adriano Novellini, Pietro Anastasi, Luigi Danova, Giuseppe Furino, Franco Causio, Fabio Capello.

place in the sun

Heat

Leeds defence and £440,000 forward Pietro Anastasi completed a fine move with a precise finish.

After that it was nip and tuck with Juventus showing plenty of imagination in midfield but with Terry Cooper posing a constant threat down the left, United always carried that extra edge in attack.

Tancredi made a great save from a Mick Jones header just before half-time and at the other end Gary Sprake had to be alert to deny Roberto Bettega.

Madeley was carried off after 56 minutes to receive stitches in a head wound and was replaced by Mick Bates, his fellow scoring hero of the first leg.

Although Leeds did the bulk of the attacking there was always the fear that Juventus may strike with one of their lightning counter-punches. Tension mounted as the minutes ticked away but Leeds were still in the driving seat with the away goals counting double ruling in their favour.

Defenders Jack Charlton and Norman Hunter kept Juventus at arm's length while another good save from a Jones header stopped United from going 2-1 ahead.

But United lasted the pace in the heat and when referee Rudi Glockner blew for full-time Leeds fans were able to celebrate in style.

"I'm very, very proud," beamed Revie whose side had edged out Italian opposition for the third time in four matches via the rule book.

"Although we had to rely upon the rule which says away goals count double, let no-one mistake the fact that Leeds took the trophy on merit.", added Revie, whose side would defend the trophy the next season after finishing second in the League.

European Fairs Cup Final, second leg
(at Elland Road, Leeds)
Thursday, June 3, 1971

Leeds United	**1**
Juventus	**1**

2-2 on agg Leeds United win on away goals

Leeds United: Gary Sprake, Paul Reaney, Terry Cooper, Billy Bremner, Jack Charlton, Norman Hunter, Peter Lorimer, Allan Clarke, Mick Jones, Johnny Giles, Paul Madeley (Mick Bates 56)
Goal: Clarke 12
Manager: Don Revie

Juventus: Roberto Tancredi, Luciano Spinosi, Gian Pietro Marchetti, Guiseppe Furino, Francesco Morini, Sandro Salvadore, Helmut Haller, Franco Causio, Pietro Anastasi, Fabio Capello, Roberto Bettega
Goal: Anastasi 19
Manager: Cestmir Vycpalek

Referee: Rudi Glockner (East Germany) **Att:** 42,483

IT'S OURS AGAIN: United skipper Billy Bremner shows off the Fairs Cup as he and Johnny Giles take a well earned breather in the dressing room.

ON THE UP: Jack Charlton causes chaos in the Juventus defence at Elland Road.

Rookies in charge

Belgians can't match youngsters

HOLDERS United began the defence of the Fairs Cup, now known as the UEFA Cup, with a routine 2-0 win in Belgium over SK Lierse.

Flemish football wasn't noted from its strength in depth and only two years earlier Manchester City had thrashed Lierse 8-0 in Europe.

It was a tie Leeds, in their seventh successive European campaign, were expected to win in comfort and Don Revie opted not to risk any of his senior players who were carrying injuries.

Paul Madeley, Jack Charlton, Terry Cooper and Mick Jones were all out, so reserve centre half John Faulkner was handed his European debut.

DEBUT: John Faulkner.

Faulkner had been signed from Isthmian League amateurs Sutton United after starring against Leeds in the FA Cup the previous year.

United's resources were further depleted when Allan Clarke was injured in training, so 19-year-old Chris Galvin was drafted into the starting line-up.

The youngster gave United the lead after 26 minutes of cat-and-mouse play when he expertly turned in Peter Lorimer's cross.

Although United were in control, they did not have things all their own way on a bumpy pitch with the dangerous Peter Ressel bringing a fine clawing save from Gary Sprake.

United found they had to be composed under pressure but took a firm grip on the tie midway through the second period when Peter Lorimer perfectly executed a waist-high volley.

UEFA Cup
First round, first leg
(at Lisper Stadium, Lierse)
Wednesday, September 15, 1971

Lierse 0

Leeds United 2

Lierse: Carl Engelen, Roger Dierckx, Tomas Krivitz, Ronny Michielsen, Rene Golen, Frans Vermeyen, Corneel De Ceulaer, Dimitri Davidovic (Walter Mertens 62), Frans Janssens, Andre Denul, Peter Ressel
Manager: Frans De Munck

Leeds United: Gary Sprake, Paul Reaney, Terry Yorath, Billy Bremner, John Faulkner, Norman Hunter, Peter Lorimer, Chris Galvin, Rod Belfitt, Johnny Giles, Mick Bates
Goals: Galvin 26, Lorimer 57
Manager: Don Revie

Referee: Joaquim Fernandes De Campos (Portugal)
Att: 17,000

United seemed content to rest on their two clinically-taken goals but the Belgians played some progressive football and United were happy not to concede.

With a two-goal advantage to take to Elland Road there seemed only one side that could possibly progress to the second round – Leeds.

Gilzean leads Tottenham goal glut in Iceland

BALD-HEADED Scot Alan Gilzean scored a hat-trick as Tottenham Hotspur strolled to a 6-1 victory in Iceland against Keflavik.

Southampton came from behind at The Dell with two goals in five second-half minutes from Tommy Jenkins and Mick Channon, the England man's winner coming from the penalty spot.

Wolves completed a clean sweep of English victories as they thumped Portugese side Coimbra 3-0 at Molineux with goals by defender John McAlle (28 minutes), John Richards (62) and Northern Ireland striker Derek Dougan (80).

Included in the Wolverhampton side was Mike O'Grady, who had joined the Midlanders from Leeds in September 1969 for £80,000.

First round, first leg

AC Milan 4 (Villa 2, Maghermi, Golin), Morphou 0
Arad 4 (Both, Kun, Brosovschi, Domide), Salzburg 1 (Ritter)
Atletico Madrid 2 (Bacerra, Irureta) Panionios 1 (Lagos)
Basle 1 (Hasler), Real Madrid 2 (Aguilar, Santillana)
Bologna 1 (Perani), Anderlecht 1 (Van Himst)
Carl Zeiss Jena 3 (Ducke pen, Vogel 2 – 1 pen), Lokomotiv Plovdiv
Celta Vigo 0, Aberdeen 2 (Harper, Forrest)
Chemie Halle 0, PSV Eindhoven 0
Den Haag 5 (Kila 2, Roggeven, Couperlis, Mansveld pen), Aris Bonnevoie 0
Dundee 4 (Bryce 2, Wallace, Lambie), AB Copenhagen 2 (Carlsen 2)
Dynamo Zagreb 6 (Miljkovic 2, Rora, Lahc, Vabec 2), Botev 1
Fenerbache 1 (Mumcuoglu), Ferencvaros 1 (Ku)
Glentoran 0, Eintracht Brunswick 1 (Brundl)
Keflavik 1 (Juliusson), Tottenham Hotspur 6 (Gilzean 3, Coates, Mullery 2)
Hamburg 2 (Zaczyk 2), St Johnstone 1 (Pearson)
Hertha Berlin 3 (Hermandung, Varga, Steffenhagen), Elfsborg 1 (Rokaas)
Lierse 0, Leeds United 2 (Galvin, Lorimer)
Lugano 1 (Luttrop pen), Legia Warsaw 3 (Cmikiewicz, Stachurski, Nowak)
Marsa 0, Juventus 6 (Haller 2, Causio, Novellini, Capello, Cuccureddu)
Napoli 1 (Lupesco og), Rapid Bucharest 0
OFK Belgrade 4 (Zec, Turudija, Santrac, Meananovic), Djurgardens 1 (Renburg)
Porto 0, Nantes 2 (Marcos 2)
Rosenborg 3 (Morkved, Hansen, Meink), HJK Helsinki 0
Rapid Vienna walkover Vilaznia (withdrew)
Southampton 2 (Jenkins, Channon), Athletic Bilbao 1 (Arieta)
Spartak Moscow 2 (Silagadze pen, Yegorovich), Kosice 0
St Etienne 1 (Sarramagna), Cologne 1 (Simmet)
Vasas 1 (Menczel), Shelbourne 0
Vitoria Setubal 1 (Torres), Nimes 0
Wolverhampton Wanderers 3 (McAlle, Richards, Dougan), Coimbra 0
Zaglibie 1 (Galas), Union Templice 0
Zeljeznicar 3 (Spreco, Katalinski, Bukal), Brugges 0

HOLDERS AGAIN: The United squad at the start of the 1971/72 season with the Fairs Cup – a trophy they were ultimately to hand over to Barcelona. Back row, from left to right: Rod Belfitt, Norman Hunter, Gary Sprake, David Harvey, Joe Jordan, Terry Yorath. Middle row: John Faulkner, Chris Galvin, Mick Jones, Paul Madeley, Allan Clarke, Jack Charlton. Front row: Paul Reaney, Mick Bates, Peter Lorimer, Johnny Giles, Billy Bremner, Nigel Davey, Terry Cooper.

United lose play-off to keep hold of Fairs Cup

Barca's keepsake

IN between the Lierse legs, United jetted out to Spain to fight for the right to keep the Fairs Cup.

The competition had been replaced by the UEFA Cup and Europe's football mandarins decreed that a match between the last winners of the Fairs Cup (United) and the first (Barcelona) should be held to determine who should keep the trophy permanently.

It was probably more of an inconvenience to Don Revie as his troops already had a busy schedule and it was no surprise to see the squad head to Barca without six internationals – Allan Clarke, Paul Madeley, Terry Cooper, Mick Jones, Terry Yorath, Eddie Gray as well as Mick Bates. That gave several of the fringe players, like Chris Galvin and Nigel Davey, an opportunity to shine in the imposing Nou Camp Stadium and gain some vital European experience.

There was also the matter of United receiving 30 per cent of the gate receipts from the match, which was part of a festival to celebrate the opening of a multi-sports centre in the Catalan city.

Revie was still able to field a strong side and any team containing Billy Bremner was bound to be competitive. In fact, referee Istvan Zsolt had to dish out words of warning to Johnny Giles and Marcial Pina Morales in the opening 15 minutes after some rough exchanges on a pitch made sodden by heavy rainfall.

United matched their illustrious hosts but fell behind on 50 minutes when Teofilio Duenas cracked a shot against the bar and poked the rebound over the line.

Scottish striker Joe Jordan, making his first United start, equalised when goalkeeper Salvador Sadurni could not hold a Peter Lorimer free-kick and he tucked in the loose ball.

When Irish midfield star Johnny Giles hit the bar with a lob it seemed as though United were on the verge of taking control, but Barca finished strongly and won the match six minutes from time with a blistering shot by Duenas, who was then denied a hat-trick when Paul Reaney cleared another effort from the striker off the line.

Barcelona, who won the Fairs Cup in 1958, 1960 and 1966 now had it for keeps, while United boarded the plane home empty-handed.

Fairs Cup
Play-off for possession of trophy
(at Nou Camp Stadium, Barcelona)
Wednesday, September 22, 1971

Barcelona	**2**
Leeds United	**1**

Barcelona: Salvador Sadurni, Joaquin Rife, Eladio Silvetre Graells, Antonio Torres, Francisco Gallego, Enrique Costas, Carlos Rexach, Juan Carlos, Teofilio Duenas, Marcial Pina Morales, Juan Asensi (Jose Maria Fuste 81)
Goals: Duenas 51, 84
Manager: Rinus Michels

Leeds United: Gary Sprake, Paul Reaney, Nigel Davey, Billy Bremner, Jack Charlton, Norman Hunter, Peter Lorimer, Joe Jordan, Rod Belfitt, Johnny Giles, Chris Galvin
Goal: Jordan 53
Manager: Don Revie

Referee: Istvan Zsolt (Hungary) **Att:** 35,000

Horror show

United crushed by Belgians' 'miracle'

A NIGHT TO FORGET: The programme from the Lierse disaster night at Elland Road.

THIS was one of European football's biggest-ever shocks.

United were humbled in front of their own fans by the unlikely lads from Lierse.

"It was sensational. Miracles do happen," exclaimed a stunned Lierse coach Frank de Munck after his side overturned United's first leg advantage with an amazing 4-0 win at shell-shocked Elland Road.

For once the United camp, so noted for their meticulous approach to matches, dropped their guard and the unfancied Belgians delivered a stunning knockout blow.

Revie fielded a relatively inexperienced side including teenage Euro debutants John Shaw and striker Jimmy Mann.

But even without eight internationals on the field they still should have been far too strong for a Lierse squad which only contained seven full-time professionals.

The Leeds public, sensing a dead tie, also gave the match a miss, only just over 18,000 turning out for what began as a training excercise.

In the opening half-hour Leeds were content to tread water while the nervous Belgians seemed as though they were on a damage limitation excercise.

Then the tie was turned on its head in the space of six staggering minutes.

First, Frans Vermeyen had a shot blocked and Frans Janssens roared in to blast a shot through a ruck of defenders, clipping Paul Reaney on its way past Shaw.

Hopes that the goal would stir Leeds proved unfounded as United momentarily stopped in midfield as Paul Madeley appeared to be obstructed and Peter Ressel raced away to slip the ball past the exposed Shaw.

From the kick-off, Lierse regained possession and attacked Unted's confused ranks once again and snatched the lead with a catastrophic goal. Poor Shaw, 17, let Ressel's routine cross slip through his hands and Janssens, virtually stood on the goal-line, had the easiest of tap-ins to give his side a shock 3-2 aggregate lead.

Revie made drastic changes at half-time, bringing on Gary Sprake in goal and replacing Mann with the experienced Norman Hunter.

Knowing Leeds had to score twice in the second half to rescue the tie, Lierse packed their defence as United began an all-out assault on their goal.

The pressure mounted minute by minute but the closest Leeds got to a goal came when Peter Lorimer shot against the bar after 65 minutes.

Both United's attacks and the Lierse defending grew more and more desperate but United were punished again ten minutes from time when they overcommitted themselves and were caught on the break, the impressive Ressel providing an expert finish for a truly amazing victory.

Philosophical Revie said: "We have no excuses... Shaw is very upset but he will learn from this experience and show what we all know – that he is a very good goalkeeper."

UEFA Cup
First round, second leg
(at Elland Road, Leeds)
Wednesday, September 29, 1971

Leeds United	**0**
Lierse	**4**

Lierse win 4-2 on agg

Leeds United: John Shaw (Gary Sprake HT), Paul Reaney, Terry Cooper, Terry Yorath, John Faulkner, Paul Madeley, Peter Lorimer, Jimmy Mann (Norman Hunter HT), Rod Belfitt, Mick Bates, Chris Galvin
Manager: Don Revie

Lierse: Carl Engelen, Roger Dierckx, Tomas Krivitz, Ronny Michielsen, Rene Golen, Frans Vermeyen, Corneel De Ceulaer, Dimitri Davidovic, Frans Janssens, Andre Denul, Peter Ressel
Goals: Reaney og 31, Ressel 35, 80, Janssens 37
Manager: Frans De Munck

Referee: Gerhard Kunze (East Germany)
Att: 18,680

Lierse continue to upset all the odds

UNITED'S conquerers Lierse continued to amaze by reaching the quarter-finals.

As against Leeds they looked dead and buried when they lost 4-1 in Norway to Rosenborg.

But an Andre Denul hat-trick at home got the Belgians through on away goals.

In the third round they came from behind to put out PSV Eindhoven. They lost 1-0 in Holland but swept to a comprehensive 4-0 win at the Lisper Stadium to go through to the quarter-finals against mighty AC Milan.

Also in the last eight were Tottenham and Wolverhampton Wanderers. who had made steady progress.

Spurs squeezed past Nantes before outclassing Rapid Bucharest while Wolves thrashed Den Haag and Karl Zeiss Jena.

First round, second leg

AB Copenhagen 0, Dundee 1 (Duncan) *Dundee win 5-2 on agg*

Anderlecht 0, Bologna 2 (Savoldi, Rizzo) *Bologna win 3-1 on agg*

Athletic Bilbao 2 (Ortunondo, Arieta), Southampton 0 *Athletic Bilbao win 3-2 on agg*

Bonnevoie 2 (Mousel, Da Silva), Den Haag 2 (Mansveld, Roggeveen) *Den Haag win 7-2 on agg*

Botev 1 (Tashkov), Dynamo Zagreb 2 (Renic, Sensen) *Dynamo Zagreb win 8-2 on agg*

Brugges 3 (Rijnders, Carteus 2), Zeljeznicar 1 (Derakovic) *Zeljeznicar win 4-3 on agg*

Coimbra 1 (Antonio), Wolverhampton Wanderers 4 (Dougan 3, McAlle) *Wolverhampton Wanderers win 7-1 on agg*

Cologne 2 (Simmet, Glowacz), St Etienne 1 (Reveiil)

Djurgaarden 2 (Renberg, Sjoberg), OFK Belgrade 2 (Zec, Yurenck og) *OFK Belgrade win 6-3 on agg*

Eintracht Brunswick 6 (Brundl 5 – 1 pen, Gerwien), Glentoran 1 (McCaffrey) *Eintracht Brunswick win 7-1 on agg*

Elsborg 1 (Sund), Hertha Berlin 4 (Horr 2, Steffenhagen, Gutzeit) *Hertha Berlin win 7-2 on agg*

Ferencvaros 3 (Bratikovits 3), Fenebache 1 (Sukru) *Ferencvaros win 4-2 on agg*

HJK Helsinki 0, Rosenborg 1 (Morkved) *Rosenborg win 4-0 on agg*

Juventus 5 (Novellini 3, Haller, Furmo), Marsa 0 *Juventus win 11-0 on agg*

Kosice 2 (Swallen, Halasz), Spartak Moscow 1 (Stovcik og) *Spartak Moscow win 3-2 on agg*

Leeds United 0, Lierse 4 (Reaney og, Ressel 2, Janssens) *Lierse win 4-2 on agg*

Legia Warsaw 0, Lugano 0 *Legia Warsaw win 3-1 on agg*

Lokomotive Plovdiv 3 (Ankov, Bonev 2), Carl Zeiss Jena 1 (Scheitler) *Carl Zeiss Jena win 4-3 on agg*

Morphou 0, AC Milan 3 (Villa 2, Rivera) in Trieste *AC Milan win 7-0 on agg*

Nantes 1 (Maas), Porto 1 (De Michele og) *Porto win 3-1 on agg*

Nimes 2 (Octavio og, Adams), Vitoria Setubal 1 (Torres) *2-2 on agg. Vitoria Setubal win on away goals*

Panios 1 (Intzoglu pen), Atletico Madrid 0 *2-2 on agg. Panionios win on away goals*

PSV Eindhoven walkover Chemie Halle *PSV Eindhoven qualify for next round*

Rapid Bucharest 2 (Dimitru, Ene), Napoli 0 *Rapid Bucharest win 2-1 on agg*

Real Madrid 2 (Aguilar, Santillana), Basle 1 (Siegenthaler) *Real Madrid win 4-2 on agg*

Salzburg 3 (Hirnschrodt, Kibler, Stadier), Arad 1 (Domide) *Arad win 5-4 on agg*

Shelbourne 1 (Murray), Vasas 1 (Torok) *Vasas win 2-1 on agg*

St Johnstone 3 (Hall, Pearson, Whitelaw), Hamburg 0 *St Johnstone win 4-2 on agg*

Tottenham Hotspur 9 (Chivers 3, Perryman, Coates, Knowles, Gilzean 2, Holder), Keflavik 0 *Tottenham Hotspur win 15-1 on agg*

Union Templice 2 (Strahl, Smetana), Zageblie 3 (Kiawtkowski 2, Augusthniak) *Zageblie win 4-2 on agg*

Second round, first leg

AC Milan 4 (Prati 2, Benetti, Biasiolo), Hertha Berlin 2 (Steffenhagen, Beer)

Cologne 2 (Scheerman, Lohr), Dundee 1 (Kinninmonth)

Den Haag 1 (Hestad pen), Wolverhampton Wanderers 3 (Dougan, McAlliog, Hibbitt)

Dynamo Zagreb 2 (Kafka 2), Rapid Vienna 2 (Hof, Jagodic)

Eintracht Brunswick 2 (Brundle 2), Athletic Bilbao 1 (Arieta)

Ferencvaros 6 (Albert 3, Ku, Meyyesi, Branikovits), Panionios 0

Juventus 2 (Anastasi, Murray og), Aberdeen 0

Nantes 0, Tottenham Hotspur 0

OFK Belgrade 1 (Santrac), Carl Zeiss Jena 1 (Scheltler)

Rapid Bucharest 4 (Ene 2, Neagu 2), Legia Warsaw 0

Real Madrid 3 (Anzarda, Aguilar, Amancio) pen), PSV Eindhoven 1 (Hoekema)

Rosenborg 4 (Christiansen 2, Hansen, Loraas), Lierse 1 (Davidovic)

Spartak Moscow 0, Vitoria Setbual 0

St Johnstone 2 (Connelly pen, Pearson), Vasas 0

Zaglibie 1 (Kwiatkowski), Arad 1 (Brosovschi)

Zeljeznicar 1 (Bukal pen), Bologna 1 (Perani)

Second round, first leg

Aberdeen 1 (Harper), Juventus 1 (Anastasi) *Juventus win 3-1 on agg*

Arad 2 (Domide, Kun), Zaglibie 1 (Pawowski) aet *Arad win 3-2 on agg*

Athletic Bilbao 2 (Uriarte, Rojo), Eintracht Brunswick 2 (Erler, Brundl) *Eintracht Brunswick win 4-3 on agg*

Bologna 2 (Fedele 2), Zeljeznicar 2 (Jankovic 2) *3-3 on agg Zeljeznicar win on away goals*

Carl Zeiss Jena 4 (Mitrovic og, Scheltler 2, Stein), OFK Belgrade 0 *Carl Zeiss Jena win 5-1 on agg*

Dundee 4 (Duncan 3, Wilson), Cologne 2 (Simmet, Flohe) *Dundee win 5-4 on agg*

Hertha Berlin 2 (Hoor 2 – 1 pen), AC Milan 1 (Bigon) *AC Milan win 5-4 on agg*

Legia Warsaw 2 (Nowak, Blaut), Rapid Bucharest 0 *Rapid Bucharest win 4-2 on agg*

Lierse 3 (Denul 3), Rosenborg 0 *4-4 on agg. Lierse win on away goals*

Panionios v Ferencvaros not played, Panionios disqualified *Ferencvaros qualify for third round*

PSV Eindhoven 2 (Mulders, Hoekema), Real Madrid 0 *3-3 on agg. PSV Eindhoven win on away goals*

Rapid Vienna 0, Dynamo Zagreb 0 *2-2 on agg. Dynamo Zagreb win on away goals*

Tottenham Hotspur 1 (Peters), Nantes 0 *Tottenham Hotspur win 1-0 on agg*

Vasas 1 (Puskas), St Johnstone 0 *St Johnstone win 2-1 on agg*

Vitoria Setubal 4 (Machado, Torres 2, Joao), Spartak Moscow 0 *Vitoria Setubal win 4-0 on agg*

Wolverhampton Wanderers 4 (Dougan, Weimar og, Mansveld og, Van Den Buch og), De Haag 0 *Wolverhampton Wanderers win 7-1 on agg*

Third round, first leg

AC Milan 3 (Rivera, Stewart og, Benetti), Dundee 0

Arad 3 (Domide, Sima, Kun), Vitoria Setubal 0

Carl Zeiss Jena 0, Wolverhampton Wanderers 1 (Richards)

Eintracht Brunswick 1 (Erler), Ferencvaros 1 (Ku)

PSV Eindhoven 1 (Mulders), Lierse 0

Rapid Vienna 0, Juventus 1 (Bettega)

St Johnstone 1 (Connolly), Zeljeznicar 0

Tottenham Hotspur 3 (Peters, Chivers 2), Rapid Bucharest 0

Third round second leg

Dundee 2 (Wallace, Duncan), AC Milan 0 *AC Milan win 3-2 on agg*

Ferencvaros 5 (Juhasz, Balint 2, Branikovits 2), Eintracht Brunswick 2 (Brundle, Erler) *Ferencvaros win 6-3 on agg*

Juventus 4 (Bettega 3, Causio pen), Rapid Vienna 1 (Lorenz) *Juventus win 5-1 on agg*

Lierse 4 (Janssens 2, Vermeyen, Denul), PSV Eindhoven 0 *Lierse win 4-1 on agg*

Rapid Bucharest 0, Tottenham Hotspur 2 (Pearce, Chivers) *Tottenham Hotspur win 5-0 on agg*

Vitoria Setubal 1 (Jose Maria), Arad 0 *Arad win 3-1 on agg*

Wolverhampton Wanderers 3 (Hibbitt, Dougan 2) *Wolverhampton Wanderers win 4-0 on agg*

Zeljeznicar 5 (Jankovic, Bukal, Spreco), St Johnstone 1 (Rooney) *Zeljeznicar win 5-2 on agg*

Tottenham keep the flag of St George flying

DESPITE United's early exit from the competition, England were able to win it for an amazing fifth successive year.

Tottenham followed United (twice), Newcastle and Arsenal on to the winners' rostrum by beating Wolves in an all-English final.

Spurs beat ultra defensive AC Milan at White Hart Lane in the semi-finals with a couple of long range Steve Perryman goals while Alan Mullery, recalled from a loan spell at Fulham, scored a crucial early goal in the San Siro.

Free-scoring Wolves were beaten 2-1 at home in the final by a couple of Martin Chivers goals, the winner coming three minutes from the end.

The sides drew 1-1 in a tough battle in the return leg. Kenny Hibbitt, brother of Terry Hibbitt, the former Leeds player who had left Elland Road for Newcastle in August 1971, was in both Wolves' line-ups.

Quarter-final, first leg

AC Milan 2 (Rivera pen, Bignon), Lierse 0
Arad 0, Tottenham Hotspur 2 (Morgan, England)
Ferencvaros 1 (Albert), Zeljeznicar 2 (Bukal, Spreco)
Juventus 1 (Anastasi), Wolverhampton Wanderers 1 (McCalliog)

Quarter-final, second leg

Tottenham Hotspur 1 (Gilzean), Arad 1 (Domide) *Tottenham Hotspur win 3-1 on agg*
Lierse 1 (Vermeyen pen), AC Milan 1 *AC Milan win 3-1 on agg*
Wolverhampton Wanderers 2 (Hegan, Dougan), Juventus 1 (Haller) *Wolverhampton Wanderers win 3-2 on agg*
Zeljeznicar 1 (Bratic), Ferencvaros 2 (Ku, Branikovits) *2-2 on agg aet. Ferencvaros win 5-4 on penalties*

Semi-final, first leg

Ferencvaros 2 (Szoke, Albert), Wolverhampton Wanderers 2 (Richards, Munro)
Tottenham Hotspur 2 (Perryman 2), AC Milan 1 (Bennetti)

Semi-final second leg

Wolverhampton Wanderers 2 (Daley, Munro), Ferencvaros 1 (Ku)
Wolverhampton Wanderers win 4-3 on agg
AC Milan 1 (Rivera pen), Tottenham Hostpur 1 (Mullery)
Tottenham Hotspur win 3-2 on agg

Final, first leg

(Molineux Stadium, Wolverhampton)
May 3, 1972
Wolverhampton Wanderers 1,
Tottenham Hotspur 2
Wolverhampton Wanderers: Parkes, Shaw, Taylor, Hegan, Munro, McAlle, McCalliog, Hibbitt, Richards, Dougan, Wagstaffe
Goal: McCalliog
Manager: Bill McGarry
Tottenham Hotspur: Jennings, Kinnear, Knowles, England, Mullery, Beal, Gilzean, Perryman, Chivers, Peters, Coates (Pratt 68)
Goals: Chivers 56, 87
Manager: Bill Nicholson
Referee: Tofik Bakhramov (Russia)
Attendance: 38,562

Final, second leg

(White Hart Lane, London)
May 17, 1972
Tottenham Hotspur 1,
Wolverhampton Wanderers 1
Tottenham Hotspur win 3-2 on agg
Tottenham Hotspur: Jennings, Kinnear, Knowles, England, Mullery, Beal, Gilzean, Perryman, Chivers, Peters, Coates
Goals: Mullery 29
Manager: Bill Nicholson
Wolverhampton Wanderers: Parkes, Shaw, Taylor, Hegan, Munro, McAlle, McCalliog, Hibbitt (Bailey 55), Richards, Dougan (Curran 84), Wagstaffe
Goal: Wagstaffe 40
Manager: Bill McGarry
Referee: Laurens van Ravens (Holland)
Attendance: 54,303

Leading scorers: 10 – Brundl (Eintracht Brunswick), 8 – Chivers (Tottenham Hotspur), Dougan (Wolverhampton Wanderers), 7 – Branikovits (Ferencvaros)

Wolves shatter United's dreams of the Double

UNITED'S shock early exit from the UEFA Cup left them to concentrate on making an all-out assault on the League Championship and FA Cup double.

Matters came to a head at the end of another epic season in which United had played some magnificent football including televised demolitions of Manchester United (5-1) and Southampton (7-0) in successive League matches.

Playing with great freedom of expression, United were winning friends with their exciting brand of football which swept them along Wembley Way to the FA Cup final against Arsenal.

There Allan Clarke's diving header gave Don Revie's team their one – and to date, only – FA Cup triumph.

That guaranteed them a crack at the European Cup Winners Cup the following season but two days after that Wembley triumph they lost their final League game – played two days later at the FA's insistence – at Wolves and with it went the League title, leaving Brian Clough's Derby County, who had already finished their fixtures as League champions and England's representatives in the European Cup.

It's no Turkey trot for United

JOE Jordan's growing reputation was enhanced with a vital goal in Turkey.

The youngster, standing in for the injured Mick Jones, struck a vital away goal for United as they drew 1-1 at Ankaragucu.

It was a satisfactory result for United who gave European debuts to their two summer signings from West Yorkshire neighbours Huddersfield Town, Trevor Cherry and Roy Ellam.

The defenders had been brought in as Jack Charlton, now 37, was growing ever closer to retirement after two decades service at Elland Road.

It was new territory for United, their first trip to Turkey in what was a high-profile game for the locals.

They had beaten Izmir in the Turkish Cup final and excitement was at fever pitch for Ankaragucu's first-ever European tie.

The big match build-up continued as United's players received bouquets before the kick-off and they tossed the flowers high over the wire fence surrounding the playing area as a gesture of goodwill.

The match was played at a leisurely pace on a bumpy uneven surface but Leeds generally controlled matters and should have taken the lead when Jordan beat goalkeeper Aydin Tohumcu in the air and the ball fell to Peter Lorimer who side-footed his shot over the bar.

NEW FACE: Roy Ellam, a United recruit from Huddersfield who made his European debut in Ankara.

But United did achieve the breakthrough just before the interval when Johnny Giles swung in a corner to the back post where Trevor Cherry headed the ball on for Jordan to slam in a volley.

The stage was set for United to build on their one-goal lead but they received a rude awakening shortly after half-time when Coscun appeared to stumble in the area before Norman Hunter was able to get in a tackle. Romanian referee Kevorc Ghemigean pointed to the spot and Mujdat Yalman fired the penalty past David Harvey, who had ousted Gary Sprake from the No 1 jersey the previous season.

The Turks had a flurry of attacks after that but it was United who almost regained the lead three minutes from time, Lorimer, shooting on the turn, striking a post.

European Cup Winners' Cup
First round, first leg
(at May 19 Stadium, Ankara)
Wednesday, September 13, 1972

Ankaragucu 1

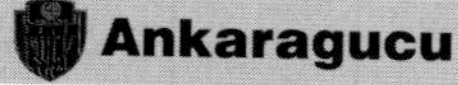

Leeds United 1

Ankaragucu: Adin Tohumcu, Remzi Hotlar (Mehmet Aktan 50), Ismail Dilber, Erman Toroglu, Mujdat Yalman, Zafter Gonculer, Metin Yilmaz, Selcuk Yalcintas, Melih Atacan, S Coscun, Koskal Mesci
Goal: Yalman pen 49
Manager: Ziya Taner

Leeds United: David Harvey, Paul Reaney, Trevor Cherry, Billy Bremner, Roy Ellam, Norman Hunter, Peter Lorimer, Chris Galvin (Terry Yorath 44), Joe Jordan, Johnny Giles, Paul Madeley
Goal: Jordan 43
Manager: Don Revie

Referee: Kevorc Ghemigean (Romania) **Att:** 20,000

Wrexham's Welsh dragons breathing fire

MINNOWS Wrexham were the Welsh Cup standard-bearers and the Third Division side put on a great display in Switzerland to draw 1-1 with experienced Euro campaigners FC Zurich.

Billy Ashcroft scored the all-important away goal for Wrexham, whose side included a youthful Micky Thomas, who was to have a brief spell with Leeds a decade later.

First round, first leg

Ankaragucu 1 (Yalman pen), Leeds United 1 (Jordan)
Bastia 0, Atletico Madrid 0
Carl Zeiss Jena 6 (Vogel 3, Stein 3), Mikkeli 1 (Kaarianen)
Floriana 1 (Arpa), Ferencvaros 0
Fremad 1 (Ryde), Besa 1 (Merhori)
Pesporikos 1 (Dufy), Cork Hibernians 2 (Lawson pen, Sheehan)
Red Boys Differange 1 (Klien), AC Milan 4 (Prati 2, Golin, Chiarugi)
Schalke 2 (Russmann, Fischer), Slavia Sofia 1 (Georgiev)
Sporting Lisbon 2 (Fraguito, Manaca), Hibernian (Duncan)
FC Zurich 1 (Kunzli), Wrexham 1 (Kinsey)
Hadjuk Split 1 (Nadoveza), Fredrikstad 0
Rapid Bucharest 3 (Stelian 2, Angulescu), Landskrona 0
Rapid Vienna 0, PAOK Salonika 0
Spartak Moscow 1 (Bulgakov), Den Haag 0
Standard Liege 1 (Dewalque), Sparta Prague 0
Vikingur Reykjavik 0, Legia Warsaw 2 (Biaas, Balcerczak)

Jones ends Turks' delight

European Cup Winners' Cup First round, second leg (at Elland Road, Leeds) Wednesday, September 27, 1972	
Leeds United	1
Ankaragucu	0
Leeds United win 2-1 on agg	

Leeds United: David Harvey, Paul Reaney, Trevor Cherry, Billy Bremner, Roy Ellam, Norman Hunter, Peter Lorimer, Allan Clarke, Mick Jones, Johnny Giles, Mick Bates
Goal: Jones 69
Manager: Don Revie

Ankaragucu: Aydin Tohumcu, Remzi Hotlar, Ismail Dilber, Erman Toroglu, Mujdat Yalman, Mehmet Aktan, Selcuk Yalcintas, Metin Yilmaz (Zafter Gonculer 9), Behzat, S Coscun, Koksal Mesci
Manager: Ziya Taner

Referee: Klaus Ohmsen (West Germany)
Att: 22,411

HEAD BOY: Mick Jones heads United's winner.

TURKEY side Ankaragucu were expected to be ready for plucking at Elland Road.

But the visitors, playing outside their own country for the first time, continually frustrated United whose only reward was a Mick Jones header midway through the second half.

That was enough to put United through 2-1 on aggregate, but there were given a real battle by a physical Turkish side.

Ankaragucu coach Taher Ziya deployed 6ft 3in Ismail Dilber behind a packed defence with only one man up front. Coupled with a rigid offside plan, Ankaragucu were able to keep chances down to a minimum.

Johnny Giles had a couple of headers well saved by skipper Aydin Tohumcu and Peter Lorimer's 16-yard drive flashed over the bar.

But these were rare chances as United stuggled to breakdown the firm rearguard and were further frustrated on the hour when Jones put the ball in the net after working a sweet one-two with Allan Clarke, only to be flagged for offside. Just when United were looking as though they were running out of ideas, Lorimer played a short corner to Billy Bremner, who whipped the ball in for Jones to ram home a firm header.

That guaranteed United's passage into the next round but they could not get the second goal manager Revie wanted so he could give 17-year-old substitute Frank Gray, brother of Eddie, his first taste of European football.

Wrexham roll over Swiss at Racecourse

LITTLE Wrexham completed a major shock when they sent FC Zurich tumbling at their Racecourse Ground.
The Welsh side looked in deep trouble when Rosario Martinelli scored with a diving header just after half-time.
Micky Thomas then supplied the cross for Billy Ashcroft to head in the equaliser and Mel Sutton then headed in the winner on 73 minutes to complete a 3-2 aggregate win.
Jim O'Rourke scored a hat-trick as Hibernian thrashed Sporting Lisbon 6-1 at their Easter Road ground in Edinburgh to overturn a 2-1 first leg deficit.

First round, second leg

AC Milan 3 (Chiarugi 2, Benetti), Red Boys Differange 0 *AC MIlan win 7-1 on agg*
Atletico Madrid 2 (Salcedo, Luis Aragones), Bastia 1 (Felix) *Atletico Madrid win 2-1 on agg*
Besa 0, Fremad 0 *1-1 on agg. Besa win on away goal*
Cork Hibernians 4 (Wallace, Lawson 2, Dennehy), Pezoporikos 1 (Miller) *Cork Hibernians win 6-2 on agg*
Den Haag 0, Spartak Moscow 0 *Spartak Moscow win 1-0 on agg*
Ferencvaros 6 (Ku 2, Branikovits 2, Szoke, Mucha), Floriana 0 *Ferencvaros win 6-1 on agg*
Fredrikstad 0, Hadjuk Split 1 (Nadoveza) *Hadjuk Split win 2-0 on agg*
Hibernian 6 (O'Rourke 3, Gordon 2, Manaca og), Sporting Lisbon 1 (Yazalde) *Hibernian win 7-3 on agg*
Landkrona 1 (Lindgren), Rapid Bucharest 0 *Rapid Bucharest win 3-1 on agg*
Leeds United 1 (Jones), Ankaraguku 0 *Leeds United win 2-1 on agg*
Legia Warsaw 9 (Biaas 2 – 1 pen, Pieszko 3, Stachurski, Deyna 2, Czmikkeli pen), Vikingur Reykjavik 0 *Legia Warsaw win 11-0 on agg*
Mikkeli 3 (Kangaskorpi, Vanhanen, Toivola), Carl Zeiss Jena 2 (Vogel, Schgneiter) *Carl Zeiss Jena win 8-4 on agg*
PAOK Salonika 2 (Aslanidis pen Sarafis), Rapid Vienna 2 (Gallos, Krankl) *2-2 on agg Rapid Vienna win on away goals*
Slavia Sofia 1 (Mikhailov), Schalke 3 (Braun, Scheer, Lutkebohmert) *Schalke win 5-2 on agg*
Sparta Prague 4 (Kara 3, Urban), Standard Liege 2 (Takac, Henroty) *Sparta Prague win 4-3 on agg*
Wrexham 2 (Ashcroft, Sutton), FC Zurich 1 (Martinelli) *Wrexham win 3-2 on agg*

Focused United in control

SNIFFER: Allan Clarke, who came close to breaking the deadlock in Jena.

UNITED negotiated another tough test behind the Iron Curtain by forcing a 0-0 draw against Carl Zeiss Jena in East Germany.

Indeed, with a bit more luck in front of goal they could have been celebrating a handsome victory.

Three times they hit the woodwork as Jena found the attacking spearhead of Peter Lorimer, Allan Clarke and Joe Jordan difficult to contain.

The home side had only lost one European tie at home – to Wolves the previous season in the UEFA Cup – and several of their players had won bronze medals at the Munich Olympics earlier in the year with their national side.

Jena, based at the world-famous Carl Zeiss lens factory, soon showed their eye for goal with Lothar Kurbjuweit crashing a long range shot against a post after earlier being denied by a good save by David Harvey, who also took a difficult cross well under pressure.

But after absorbing this early pressure United gradually got the measure of their opponents with Lorimer shaking an upright with a 22-yard shot, the ball bouncing back to Clarke whose effort to knock in the rebound was blocked by goalkeeper Wolfgang Blochwitz.

The game was being played at a relatively leisurely pace but Paul Madeley was getting up a full head of steam for Leeds at right- back.

He made several powerful runs down the right with his graceful stride eating up the yards to supplement United's attack.

But he was always on hand to do his defensive duties, clearing an Eberhard Vogel header off the line as Jena forced their first corner after half an hour.

United moved up a gear after the break and nearly made the breakthrough in the 53rd minute when Jordan hit the underside of the bar.

Another chance came and went when Clarke backheaded a free-kick into Jordan's path but the young Scot saw the ball bounce clear after hitting the woodwork again.

Jena responded with a spell of pressure, forcing Trevor Cherry to clear off the line, but the Leeds left-back almost gifted the home side victory quarter of an hour from the end when his mistake let in Dieter Scheitler, who fired inches wide.

European Cup Winners' Cup
First round, second leg
(at Ernst Abbe Sportsfield, Jena)
Wednesday, October 25, 1972

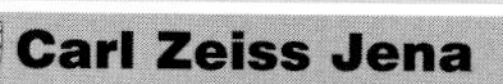

Carl Zeiss Jena 0

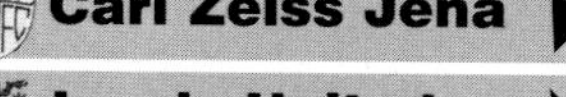

Leeds United 0

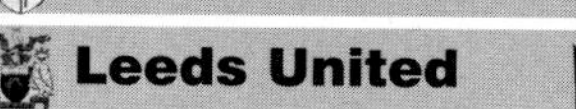

Carl Zeiss Jena: Wolfgang Blochwitz, Gerhard Hoppe, Michael Strempel, Konrad Weise (Peter Rock HT), Lothar Kurbjuweit, Harald Irmscher, Martin Goebel, Rainer Schlutter, Peter Ducke, Dieter Scheitler, Eberhard Vogel (Norbert Schumann 74)
Manager: Hans Meyer

Leeds United: David Harvey, Paul Madeley Trevor Cherry, Billy Bremner, Jack Charlton, Norman Hunter, Peter Lorimer, Allan Clarke, Joe Jordan, Mick Bates, Eddie Gray
Manager: Don Revie

Referee: Leo Van Der Kroft (Holland) **Att:** 18,000

Rampant O'Rourke

JIM O'Rourke scored his second successive Cup Winners Cup hat-trick as classy Hibernian turned on the style to crush Albanian side Besa 7-1.

Wrexham continued their adventure by beating Hadjuk Split from Yugoslavia 3-1 at The Racecourse, Brian Tinnion scoring twice.

Second round, first leg

Atletico Madrid 3 (Aragones pen, Overjero, Becerra), Spartak Moscow 4 (Redin 2, Piskarev, Bulgakov)
Carl Zeis Jena 0, Leeds United 0
Cork Hibernians 0, Schalke 0
Ferencvaros 2 (Ku, Mucha), Sparta Prague 0
Hibernian 7 (Cropley, O'Rourke 3, Duncan 2, Brownlie), Besa 1 (Kariqi)
Legia Warsaw 1 (Deyna), AC Milan 1 (Golin)
Rapid Vienna 1 (Gallos), Rapid Bucharest 1 (Neagu)
Wrexham 3 (Tinnion, Smallman, Mulinic og), Hadjuk Split 1 (Jovanic)

Cherry picks off East Germans

DEBUT GOAL: Mick Bates takes evasive action as Trevor Cherry blasts in United's opener against Jena – it was Cherry's first goal in European competition.

European Cup Winners' Cup
Second round, second leg
(at Elland Road, Leeds)
Wednesday, September 29, 1972

Leeds United	**2**
Carl Zeiss Jena	**0**

Leeds United win 2-0 on agg

Leeds United: David Harvey, Paul Reaney, Trevor Cherry, Billy Bremner, Jack Charlton, Norman Hunter, Peter Lorimer, Allan Clarke, Mick Jones, Mick Bates (Johnny Giles 79), Terry Yorath
Goals: Cherry 55, Jones 64
Manager: Don Revie

Carl Zeiss Jena: Wolfgang Blochwitz, Gerhard Hoppe, Peter Rock, Konrad Weise, Lothar Kurbjuweit, Michael Strempel, Rainer Schlutter, Martin Goebel, Peter Ducke (Dieter Scheitler 70) Harald Irmscher, Eberhard Vogel
Manager: Hans Meyer

Referee: Concetto Lo Bello (Italy) **Att:** 26,885

TREVOR Cherry's first European goal set patient United on their way to a 2-0 home victory over Carl Zeiss Jena.

The man-marking Germans had stuck doggedly to their task until the 55th minute when Peter Lorimer chipped the ball into the middle from a corner which was only half cleared to Cherry, whose left foot despatched the ball into the left hand corner of the net.

Lorimer, the provider, was the one Leeds player who had looked capable of breaking through the Jena rearguard.

He gave his marker Lothar Kurbjuweit a real roundaround with his power-packed shooting a potent weapon.

Goalkeeper Wolfgang Blochwitz had made a stunning save to deny the Scot on the stroke of half-time but Lorimer gained his revenge after 64 minutes with another key role in United's second goal. Billy Bremner was fouled by Rainer Schlutter outside the box and Lorimer stepped up to blast in a free-kick which was too hot for Blochwitz to handle and Jones was on hand to head an easy goal to wrap up the tie. Blochwitz said of Lorimer – "He's the most dangerous marksman I have played against."

That observation was backed up by a delighted Don Revie, who purred: "When Peter's on song there isn't a goalkeeper in the world who can stop him." Lorimer's explosive shooting and tricky dribbling blew the Germans' game-plan wide apart but even after they fell behind the visitors still only kept one man, Peter Ducke, in attack, preferring to pack their midfield.

But with Paul Reaney keeping a close eye on Eberhard Vogel there was virtually no supply to the isolated Ducke and David Harvey was a virtual spectator throughout the game.

To add to a good night's work for Leeds, Johnny Giles, who didn't make the starting line-up because of a knee injury, came on for the last ten minutes to give United more options and United went into their four-month European break on a high.

BEATER BLOCKER: Jena goalkeeper Wolfgang Blochwitz clears in spectacular style from Mick Jones.

Wrexham dream over

WREXHAM'S giant-killing came to an end in Split where they went out in cruel fashion.

They lost 2-0 in Yugoslavia to go down on the away goals ruling but the Welsh camp were unhappy with the referee's performance in front of a volatile crowd.

Second round, second leg

AC Milan 2 (Zignoli, Chiarugi), Legia Warsaw 1 (Pieszko) aet *AC Milan win 3-2 on agg*
Besa 1 (Pagria), Hibernian 1 (Gordon) *Hibernian win 8-2 on agg*
Hadjuk Split 2 (Nadoveza 2), Wrexham 0 *3-3 on agg. Hadjuk Split win on away goals*
Leeds United 2 (Cherry, Jones), Carl Zeiss Jena 0 *Leeds United win 2-0 on agg*
Rapid Bucharest 3 (Krankl og, Boc, Petreanu), Rapid Vienna 1 (Hof) *Rapid Bucharest win 4-2 on agg*
Schalke 3 (Ehmke, Braun, Kremers pen), Cork Hibernians 0 *Schalke win 3-0 on agg*
Sparta Prague 4 (Barton 2, Urban 2), Ferencvaros 1 (Mucha) *Sparta Prague win 4-3 on agg*
Spartak Moscow 1 (Khusainov), Atletico Madrid 2 (Salcedo 2) *5-5 on agg Spartak Moscow win on away goals*

United in good Nick

UNITED turned on a five-star show to demolish Rapid Bucharest at Elland Road to virtually book their place in the Cup Winners' Cup semi-finals.

The Romanians simply didn't have the answer to United's speed and skill as they were swept aside by a tidal wave of attacking play.

Spurs boss Nicholson's advice pays big dividends

Don Revie had enlisted the help of veteran Tottenham manager Bill Nicholson in his preparations for the game. Spurs had whipped Rapid 5-0 the previous season in the same competition and Nicholson sent Revie a dossier on how to play the men from Bucharest.

Whatever gems on information the report contained it certainly did the trick as United matched the London club's comprehensive scoreline.

Rapid seemed to employ dubious tactics from the outset, announcing that they would only play in all white. That cut no ice with United, who, as the home side, wore their own colours and Rapid reluctantly agreed to play in red.

When the match started Rapid's Alexandru Grigorias and Marin Florin only seemed content to clatter into Leeds players, but United rode above the strong-arm stuff to take a 15th minute lead. Johnny Giles had already gone close from 12 yards when goalkeeper Necula Radacanu made a mess of a punched clearance and the little Irishman collected the ball and chipped it over the stricken goalkeeper.

Ten minutes later Norman Hunter launched an attack from his own half and the ball was played forward by Giles to Joe Jordan who headed it on for Allan Clarke to score with ease.

United were carving Rapid open at will and the third goal arrived before half-time, Clarke's pass releasing Peter Lorimer, who converted from ten yards. Lormer added his second soon after the interval with a trademark thunderbolt from 20 yards.

Just after an hour Jordan got the goal his excellent all-round play deserved after Clarke's clever footwork confused the Rapid defence. After that Leeds eased up a bit knowing that their passage through to the last four was virtually assured.

European Cup Winners' Cup
Quarter-final, first leg
(at Elland Road, Leeds)
Wednesday, March 7, 1973

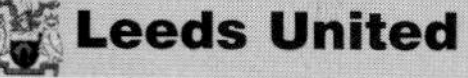

Leeds United ▶ 5

Rapid Bucharest ▶ 0

Leeds United: David Harvey, Paul Reaney Trevor Cherry, Billy Bremner, Gordon McQueen (Terry Yorath 83), Norman Hunter, Peter Lorimer, Allan Clarke, Joe Jordan, Johnny Giles, Paul Madeley
Goals: Giles 15, Clarke 26, Lorimer 33, 56, Jordan 65 **Manager:** Don Revie

Dynamo Bucharest: Necula Raducanu, Ion Pop, Alexandru Grigoras, Gheorghe Codrea, Marin Stelian, Constantin Musat, Constantin Nasturescu (Ion Naom 74), Mircea Savu, Alexandru Neagu, Marin Florin, Dumitru Dumitriu
Manager: Bazil Marian

Referee: Bohumil Smejkal (Czechoslovakia)
Att: 25,702

UP AND RUNNING: Midfield maestro Johnny Giles netted United's opener against Rapid Bucharest.

Treble chance for attack-minded Hibs

HIBERNIAN forward Alan Gordon netted a hat-trick as Hibernian continued their free-scoring European form. His treble came as the Easter Road side beat Hadjuk Split 4-2 and was the third Hibs hat-trick of the campaign after Jim O'Rourke's efforts against Sporting Lisbon and Besa.

Quarter-final, first leg
Hibernian 4 (Gordon 3, Duncan), Hadjuk Split 2 (Hievnjak 2)
Leeds United 5 (Giles, Clarke, Lorimer 2, Jordan), Rapid Bucharest 0
Schalke 2 (Ehmke, Russmann), Sparta Prague 1 (Barton)
Spartak Moscow 0, AC Milan (Benetti)

Rapid thaw

Hot United melt Bucharest hearts

UNITED'S growing reputation and popularity in Europe was confirmed after their 3-1 victory in Bucharest.

They were cheered off the snow-covered Republic Stadium pitch and the Leeds coach was applauded heartily by the Romanian public as it made its way back to the airport.

At home United had been labelled a dour side in the 1960s, but throughout the 1972/73 campaign they had played some splendid attacking football. That shift in emphasis was underscored in Bucharest where they gave another dazzling display of football to gift- wrap a place in the semi-finals.

They were masters from the first minute when Mick Bates tore onto Eddie Gray's pass to fire United 6-0 ahead on aggregate. The fates were less kind to Bates a few minutes later when he was carried off with damaged ankle ligaments but United strolled across the snowy surface almost as though it was a training excercise.

Mick Jones was a constant threat each time the ball came anywhere near him the Rapid defence deteriorated into near panic. He had already been denied twice by goalkeeper Necula Radacanu and had a goal disallowed before heading in Paul Madeley's 23rd minute cross from the right to make it 2-0.

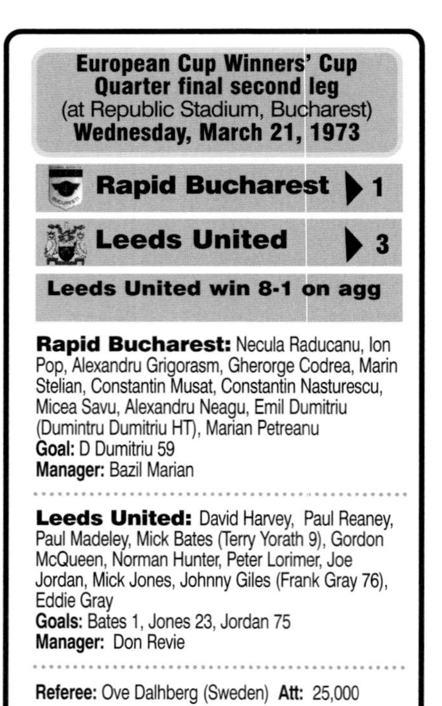

European Cup Winners' Cup
Quarter final second leg
(at Republic Stadium, Bucharest)
Wednesday, March 21, 1973

Rapid Bucharest 1

Leeds United 3

Leeds United win 8-1 on agg

Rapid Bucharest: Necula Raducanu, Ion Pop, Alexandru Grigorasm, Gherorge Codrea, Marin Stelian, Constantin Musat, Constantin Nasturescu, Micea Savu, Alexandru Neagu, Emil Dumitriu (Dumintru Dumitriu HT), Marian Petreanu
Goal: D Dumitriu 59
Manager: Bazil Marian

Leeds United: David Harvey, Paul Reaney, Paul Madeley, Mick Bates (Terry Yorath 9), Gordon McQueen, Norman Hunter, Peter Lorimer, Joe Jordan, Mick Jones, Johnny Giles (Frank Gray 76), Eddie Gray
Goals: Bates 1, Jones 23, Jordan 75
Manager: Don Revie

Referee: Ove Dalhberg (Sweden) **Att:** 25,000

Rapid could not cope with United's movement and slick passing on the slippery surface and although substitute Dumitru Dumitriu pulled a goal back, Don Revie's team made sure they had the last word with one of the most peculiar goals they have ever scored in Europe.

Jordan headed the ball on towards goal from 40 yards out. Raducanu came out for what looked like a routine gather, but spotted the lurking Jones lurking nearby, took his eye off the ball and allowed it to trickle over the line.

As the sides left the pitch at the end, United were given a generous ovation while the hapless Rapid's players were pelted with snowballs as the locals demonstrated their anger after an 8-1 aggregate thrashing.

HAIRY MOMENTS: Mick Jones'created havoc in Bucharest – perhaps the Romanians were terrified of his big, bushy sideburns.

Split personality

YUGOSLAVIAN outfit Hadjuk Split overturned a 4-2 first leg deficit to knock out Hibernian on the away goals rule and book a place against United in the semi-finals. AC Milan and Sparta Prague would meet in the other semi-final.

Quarter-final, second leg

AC Milan 1 (Bignon), Spartak Moscow 1 (Piskarev) *AC Milan win 2-1 on agg*

Hadjuk Split 3 (Boskovic, Hievnjak, Blackley og), Hibernian 0 *Hadjuk Split win 5-4 on agg*

Rapid Bucharest 1 (Dumitriu), Leeds United 3 (Bates, Jones 2) *Leeds United win 8-1 on agg*

Sparta Prague 3 (Jurkanin, Kara, Barton), Schalke 0 *Sparta Prague win 4-2 on agg*

GREAT SCOTS: United boss Don Revie gradually started introducing new young players to his squad in 1973/74 including Gordon McQueen (left) and Frank Gray, pictured above with older brother Eddie (right). United had a remarkable contingent of Scots on their books at the time.

Revie revolution

United boss remodels squad

UNITED'S reputation as a vibrant attacking force had spread well beyond Britain.

The reception they earned in Bucharest proved that – and a glance at the United line-up showed that boss Don Revie had quietly freshed up his squad.

The Romanian romp had seen the introduction of another talented Scot, Gordon McQueen.

Centre half Jack Charlton was nearly at the end of his long and distinguished playing career at Elland Road. The home win over Carl Zeiss Jena was his 56th – and last – European outing in a Leeds shirt and at the end of the season announced his retirement, at the age of 37, and began a successful career in management with Middesbrough.

Big Jack's imminent departure left a big hole in the United defence for Revie to plug. Initially he tried Roy Ellam who had joined United at the start of the season from Huddersfield with Trevor Cherry. While Cherry slotted in smartly at left-back for Terry Cooper, who had broken his leg at Stoke towards the end of the 1971/72 season, Ellam struggled to make much of an impression.

Versatile Paul Madeley could, of course, be used in central defence, but he was too valuable in other positions. Welsh international Terry Yorath could also fill in alongside Norman Hunter, but Revie was looking further ahead and had paid £30,000 to St Mirren for 20-year-old McQueen, a 6ft-plus giant centre-back.

Four days after his League debut against Derby, McQueen played in his first European game, the 5-0 romp over Rapid Bucharest. The second leg in Bucharest also saw the European bow of 17-year-old Frank Gray, Eddie's kid brother, while a third Scot, striker Joe Jordan continued on his learning curve as cover for Mick Jones and Allan Clarke.

Revie had carefully nurtured the young talent and had skilfully planted them in the side to gain valuable European experience.

The two Grays, McQueen, Jordan, Billy Bremner, Peter Lorimer – and even Yorkshireman David Harvey, whose grandmother was born north of the border, all played international football for Scotland.

TARTAN TERROR: Joe Jordan gets in the ball for United.

Doing the Splits

Goal hero Clarke sees red

MASTER TACTICIAN: Allan Clarke hammers in the only goal of the first leg against Hadjuk Split at Elland Road – but was later ordered off and would miss the second leg and the final.

UNITED were feared throughout Europe and many foreign coaches believed the only way to beat them over two legs was to frustrate them at Elland Road.

That was certainly the case in an ill-tempered semi-final with Yugoslavian side Hadjuk Spilt.

United, having reached the FA Cup final against Sunderland, were on course for a cup double.

Split coach Zebec Branco sent his side out with strict orders to defend in depth and they carried out his instructions to the letter with skipper Dragan Holcer organising the backline from his role as sweeper.

United found chances hard to create but it needed a superb Holcer tackle to keep out Peter Lorimer, who also missed an opportunity from seven yards when Wilson Dzoni miskicked.

The priceless breakthrough came on 21 minutes when Allan Clarke collected the ball from Johnny Giles, drifted past Holcer, into the box, beat Mario Boljat and clipped a superb left-foot shot beyond Radomir Vukcevic in the Hadjuk goal.

It was Clarke's 24th goal of the season, United's 100th of the campaign and he thought he had got another a minute later but was ruled offside.

The goal didn't change Split's defensive posture and they sought to break the game up at every opportunity. Several of their players went to ground very easily and feigned injury – a ploy designed to break United's concentration.

It appeared to work as the crowd's frustration transmitted itself to the United players while Split issued a firm reminder that they too could play football when Ivica Hlvevnjak's run set up Jurica Jerkovic, whose hard drive was tipped over the bar by David Harvey.

The war of attrition continued in the second half and United sent on Joe Jordan after the hour mark for midfielder Mick Bates to add some firepower to the attack.

Within minutes the game turned nasty with Mick Jones and Ivan Buljan cautioned after a clash just outside the penalty area.

Tackles were flying in from all angles and one of the chief targets – Clarke – snapped when he was hacked down. The Leeds striker retaliated against Boljat and was ordered off by Hungarian referee Gyula Emsberger, who said later: "I sent Clarke off because he kicked a Yugoslav player twice on the thigh."

The hostilities didn't cease there and Leeds fans roared for Ivan Surjak to be sent off when he brought down Terry Yorath, but Emsberger settled for a booking.

Clarke had become the fifth Leeds player sent off in 71 European ties and although United were down to ten men they continued to dictate proceedings but at the final whistle it was Split who were celebrating. They were confident of overturning United's slender advantage, particularly as hot-shot Clarke would be suspended from the second leg.

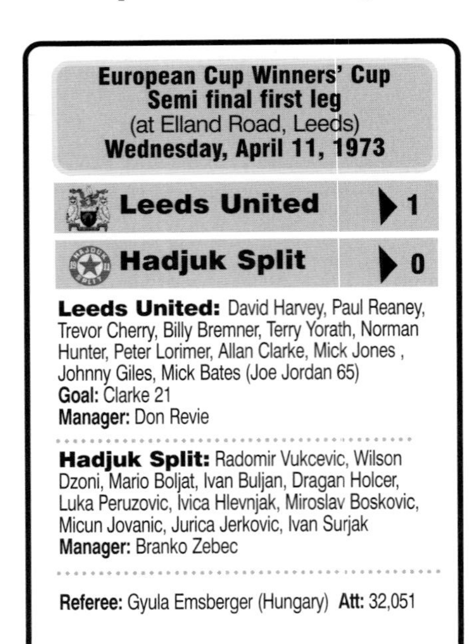

European Cup Winners' Cup
Semi final first leg
(at Elland Road, Leeds)
Wednesday, April 11, 1973

Leeds United	1
Hadjuk Split	0

Leeds United: David Harvey, Paul Reaney, Trevor Cherry, Billy Bremner, Terry Yorath, Norman Hunter, Peter Lorimer, Allan Clarke, Mick Jones , Johnny Giles, Mick Bates (Joe Jordan 65)
Goal: Clarke 21
Manager: Don Revie

Hadjuk Split: Radomir Vukcevic, Wilson Dzoni, Mario Boljat, Ivan Buljan, Dragan Holcer, Luka Peruzovic, Ivica Hlevnjak, Miroslav Boskovic, Micun Jovanic, Jurica Jerkovic, Ivan Surjak
Manager: Branko Zebec

Referee: Gyula Emsberger (Hungary) **Att:** 32,051

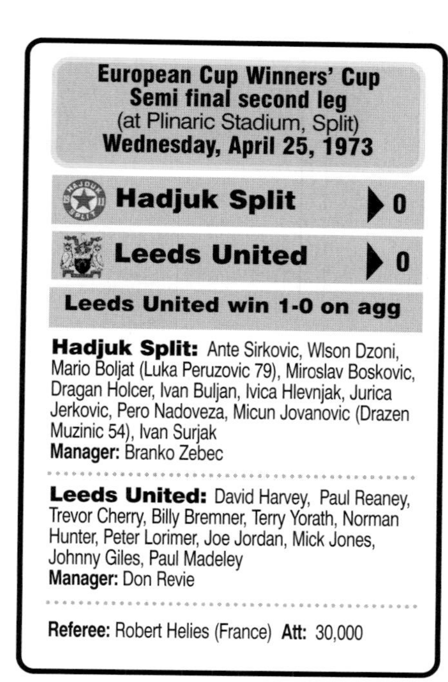

European Cup Winners' Cup
Semi final second leg
(at Plinaric Stadium, Split)
Wednesday, April 25, 1973

Hadjuk Split	**0**
Leeds United	**0**

Leeds United win 1-0 on agg

Hadjuk Split: Ante Sirkovic, Wlson Dzoni, Mario Boljat (Luka Peruzovic 79), Miroslav Boskovic, Dragan Holcer, Ivan Buljan, Ivica Hlevnjak, Jurica Jerkovic, Pero Nadoveza, Micun Jovanovic (Drazen Muzinic 54), Ivan Surjak
Manager: Branko Zebec

Leeds United: David Harvey, Paul Reaney, Trevor Cherry, Billy Bremner, Terry Yorath, Norman Hunter, Peter Lorimer, Joe Jordan, Mick Jones, Johnny Giles, Paul Madeley
Manager: Don Revie

Referee: Robert Helies (France) **Att:** 30,000

MR METICULOUS: United boss Don Revie makes plans for the future.

Split second

UNITED had little room to manouvre in the Adriatic port of Split.

They took a narrow lead to the Plinaric Stadium and had these words of advice frm Don Revie ringing in their ears – "The main thing is to be patient and wait for the breaks."

As Leeds were holed up in their hotel, convoys of cars containing banner-waving Split fans roared past with horns blaring in an effort to disrupt United players' sleep.

Terry Yorath probably didn't get much sleep anyway. His wife, Christine, had given birth to a baby girl – Gabrielle, who went on to be an ITV football presenter over two decades later – as Yorath was en route to Yugoslavia.

Although Paul Madeley was handed the No 11 shirt, he operated in defence next to Norman Hunter, with Yorath slotting into midfield as a ball-winner.

For once, United put their adventurous streak on hold and turned in a display which Revie ranked alongside the Ferencvarous Fairs Cup-winning night. For all their pre-match confidence, Split simply couldn't find a way

Slavs can't get past patient United

past Madeley and Hunter. United really only had two big danger moments. The first came early on when Micun Jovanic stabbed in a shot which David Harvey did well to block with his arm. Then with time ticking away Ivan Surjek headed wide when it looked easier to score. After that chance, 15 minutes from the end, Split's confidence waned and United finished the stronger.

Peter Lormer had clubbed the bar with a seering volley in the first half and twice came close in the dying minutes when Mick Jones was denied by goalkeeper Ante Sirkovic and Trevor Cherry dived in within inches of getting his head to another cross.

At the death, Johnny Giles powered home a shot but referee Robert Helies had blown for time a split second earlier, so the goal, which United didn't need, was ruled out.

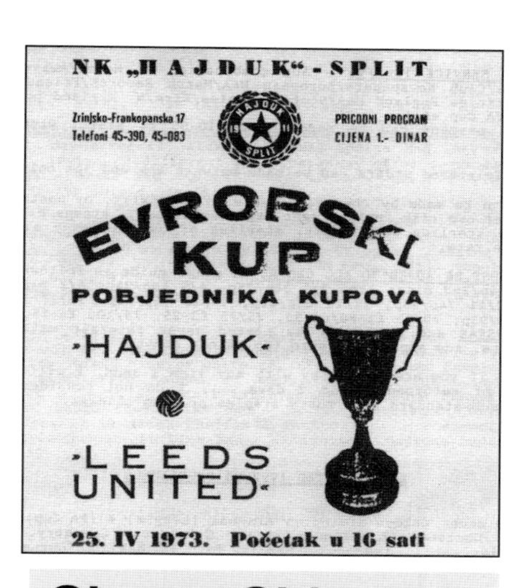

Classy Chiarugi

AC Milan's cast-iron defence ensured their place in the final against United. They had only conceded four goals in their eight Cup Winners' Cup games and Sparta Prague were unable to break the Italians down in the semi-finals, Luciano Chiargui scoring in both legs.

Semi final, first leg
AC Milan 1 (Chiarugi), Sparta Prague 0
Leeds United 1 (Clarke), Hadjuk Split 0

Semi final, second leg
Hadjuk Split 0, Leeds United 0 *Leeds United win 1-0 on agg*
Sparta Prague 0, AC Milan 1 (Chiarugi) *AC Milan win 2-0 on agg*

Last act of a

United mugged by Milan in Salonika

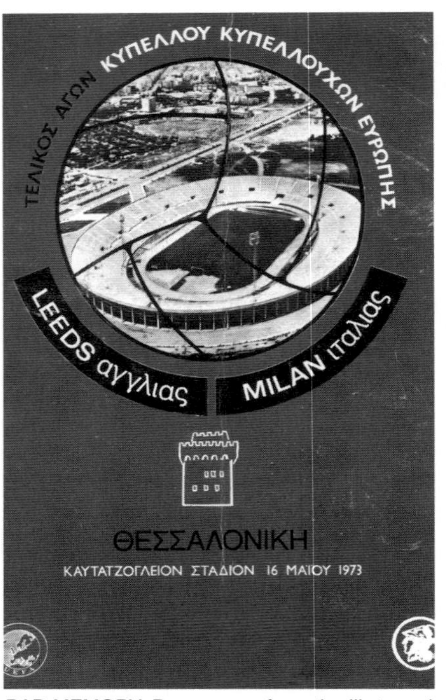

BAD MEMORY: Programme from the ill-starred 1973 Cup Winners Cup final against AC Milan in Salonica.

FOR once United went into a major final unprepared.

After their shock FA Cup final defeat at the hands of Second Division Sunderland stories persisted that Don Revie had been offered a king's ransom to manage Everton.

It was against this uncertain backdrop that United travelled to Greece to take on AC Milan in Salonika. United were without the suspended Billy Bremner (ruled out as a result of a booking in the semi-final second leg) and Allan Clarke as well as the injured midfield fulcrum, Johnny Giles and wizard of the dribble Eddie Gray.

Few observers gave United a chance against one of Italy's most powerful and lira-rich clubs.

Acting skipper Paul Reaney led out a United side which included Eddie's brother, Frank, who was starting his first European match.

Thunder rumbled and lightning

flashed around the Stadio Kaftantzoglio, but United were unprepared for the storm which was about to be unleashed on the pitch.

Just four minutes had gone when Greek referee Hristos Michas controversially awarded a free-kick against United midfielder Paul Madeley for an innoccuous challenge on Alberto Bignon outside the Leeds box. Luciano

CUP WINNERS: AC Milan, Back row, from left to right: Karl Heinz Schnellinger, William Vecchi, Pierino Prati, Albertino Bignon, Gianni Rivera, Romeo Bennetti. Front row: Angelo Anquilletti, Graziano Gori, Ricardo Sogliano, Guiseppe Sabatini, Luciano Chiarugi.

European Cup Winners' Cup Final
(at Kaftantzoglio Stadium, Salonika)
Wednesday, May 16, 1973

Leeds United	**0**
AC Milan	**1**

Leeds United: David Harvey, Paul Reaney Trevor Cherry, Mick Bates, Paul Madeley, Norman Hunter, Peter Lorimer, Joe Jordan, Mick Jones, Frank Gray, (Gordon McQueen 54), Terry Yorath
Manager: Don Revie

AC Milan: William Vecchi, Guiseppi Sabadini, Giulio Zignoli, Angelo Anquiletti, Maurizio Turone, Roberto Rosato (Dario Dolci 59), Roberto Sogliano, Romeo Benetti, Alberto Bignon, Gianni Rivera, Luciano Chiarugi
Goal: Chiarugi 4
Manager: Nereo Rocco

Referee: Christos Michas (Greece) **Att:** 40,154

Greek tragedy

HEART-BREAKER: Luciano Chiarugi blasts in the controversial fourth-minute free-kick which enabled AC Milan to win the Cup Winners Cup on a stormy night in Salonika.

Chiarugi stepped up and drove in a shot which clipped off Madeley in the defensive wall and into the corner of the net beyond the grasp of David Harvey.

The goal was greeted with a chorus of boos from the locals whose wrath increased with every passing moment.

To their astonishment their Greek referee appeared to give every decision to the Italians while wild challenges on Leeds players went unpunished.

A goal up, Milan packed their defence and used every possible tactic to keep Leeds off the scoresheet.

A Mick Bates short free kick to Peter Lorimer was knocked into the box where Norman Hunter's header was saved by William Vecchi, Bates and Terry Yorath, moving up from the back, both went close with long range efforts.

Michas turned a blind eye to three strong United penalty claims – the first when Mick Jones was brought down when following up a Joe Jordan shot. Then Romeo Bennetti clearly handled a Reaney cross and finally, Reaney himself was floored in the area when leading an attacking raid.

It all became too much for Norman Hunter, who, striding through midfield, was hacked down from behind in the final minute by Gianni Rivera, Hunter retaliated, tangled with Riccardo Sogliano and the pair were sent off, while the pertetrator of the incident Rivera was allowed to stay on the field.

Angry Greek fans, who had been looking forward to the game for months, were furious with the dislay of referee Michas and the crude tactics of Milan, whose coach was stoned and spat upon as it left the ground after one of European football's darkest nights.

The United camp were bitter about the injustice of it all while the Greeks felt embarrased by the whole episode with people telephoning local newspapers to brand the performance of Michas a disgrace.

WEMBLEY WIZARDS: United's 1972-73 squad with the FA Cup which earned them entry to the UEFA Cup Winners Cup. Back row, from left to right: Paul Reaney, Roy Ellam, Chris Galvin, Joe Jordan, David Harvey, Gary Sprake, Jack Charlton, Mick Jones, Norman Hunter, Paul Madeley. Front row: Peter Lorimer, Allan Clarke, Trevor Cherry, Billy Bremner, Johnny Giles, Mick Bates, Eddie Gray, Terry Yorath.

UEFA ban for Michas

but Salonika result stands

GREEK referee Christos Michas performance in the Cup Winners Cup final was so bad that he was suspended by his own Federation and UEFA.

But the latter drew the line at launching an inquiry as to why he had been so inept, thus adding fuel to the suspicion that United had somehow been stitched up.

Leeds, so often saddled with a hard, uncompromising, label at home, were regarded as the moral victors.

"We played so well and got nothing for it," sighed Revie, who added "We outplayed them in every department. If someone says we deserved three penalties that would be the understatement of the year."

Leeds had not only lost the final but were also still in danger of losing Revie to Everton and the Leeds boss announced that he would not make a decision until after the AC Milan match. Everyone connected with Elland Road breathed a huge sigh of relief when he announced that he would be staying following a counter-offer by the Leeds board.

Later that summer he also rejected an offer – ironically given the circumstances in Salonika – to manage the Greek national team

It had been another hugely frustrating season for the Whites with the sickening defeat in Greece being the final blow.

Despite playing some brilliant football, United finished third behind champions Liverpool and runners-up Arsenal, while hopes of a return to the Cup Winners Cup ended in spectacular fashion at Wembley. United were bankers to retain the trophy but were stunned when Sunderland became the first Second Division club to win the famous trophy for 42 years thanks to Ian Porterfield's 32nd minute goal.

The controversial Milan defeat meant the only avenue open to United for the 1973-74 season would be the UEFA Cup. With the 'one city, one club' restriction applying to the UEFA Cup, United, Ipswich, Tottenham and Wolves were all nominated by the Football League.

So it was 'business as usual' when United kicked off their 1973/74 season – with one major change. The club adopted a new 'smiley' logo as the club badge to replace the old Leeds coat of arms logo it had used for several decades.

Now the team aimed to put the smile back on their fans' faces.

IN DISGRACE: Greek referee Christos Michas.

Young Graham scores a

RISING star Arthur Graham was on the scoresheet as Aberdeen sank Irish club Finn Harps 4-1 at Pittodrie.

Graham, later to have a productive spell with Leeds, had shot to prominence by winning a Scottish Cup medal with the Dons in 1970 when he was just 17.

Wolves virtually booked their place in the second round with a 2-0 win in Portual against Beleneses where John Richards and Derek Dougan were on target.

Tottenham were even more impressive on their travels rolling over Swiss club Grasshoppers 5-1 with Martin Chivers and Alan Gilzean scoring two each.

Ipswich, under the astute management of Bobby Robson, made a winning return to European football.

Benito Rubinan's second half own-goal gave them a famous win over Real Madrid – 11 years after their last European tie.

First round, first leg

Aberdeen 4 (Miller, Jarvie 2, Graham), Finn Harps 1 (Harkin)
Admira Vienna 1 (Svojanovsky), Inter Milan 0
Ards 3 (Cathcart, McAvoy, McAteer), Standard Liege 2 (Bukal 2)
Beleneses 0, Wolverhampton Wanderers 2 (Richards, Dougan)
BK Copenhagen 2 (Nielsen, Thorn), Solna 1 (Zetterlund)

Odd's act of god

Norwegian amateurs end United's winning sequence

EUROPEAN success had always been high on Revie's agenda but there seemed to be a softening of that attitude in 1973-74.

Don Revie made regaining the title they had fought so hard to win in 1968-69 their main priority. They certainly made the perfect start wining their first seven games in the First Division.

They fully expected to extend that run when they travelled to Norway to take on with the relatively unknown club Stromsgodset, whose amateur side included a 5ft 7in postman goalkeeper, office workers, a draughtsman, mechanic and lumberjack.

Gary Sprake.

With United banking a 16-0 aggregate win over Norwegian opposition in Lyn Oslo just three years earlier it was the perfect opportunity for Revie rest players.

In addition to the suspended Norman Hunter, United were missing David Harvey, Paul Reaney, Peter Lorimer, Billy Bremner, Johnny Giles and Joe Jordan for the trip. Despite the absent stars, the game had attracted so much interest that it was switched from Stromsgodset's base in the industrial town of Drammen to the Ullevaal Stadium in Oslo.

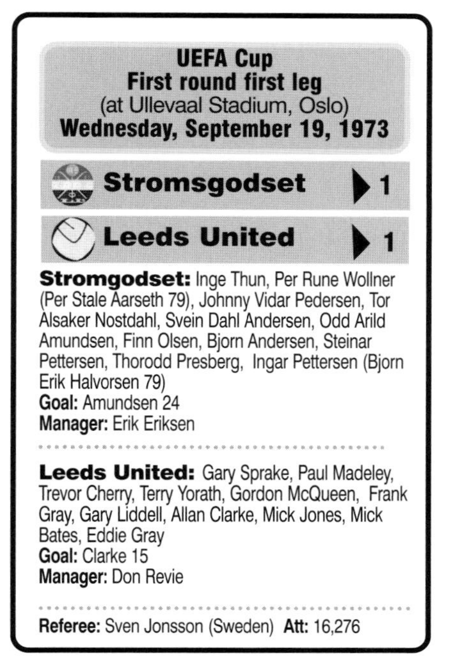

UEFA Cup
First round first leg
(at Ullevaal Stadium, Oslo)
Wednesday, September 19, 1973

Stromsgodset 1

Leeds United 1

Stromgodset: Inge Thun, Per Rune Wollner (Per Stale Aarseth 79), Johnny Vidar Pedersen, Tor Alsaker Nostdahl, Svein Dahl Andersen, Odd Arild Amundsen, Finn Olsen, Bjorn Andersen, Steinar Pettersen, Thorodd Presberg, Ingar Pettersen (Bjorn Erik Halvorsen 79)
Goal: Amundsen 24
Manager: Erik Eriksen

Leeds United: Gary Sprake, Paul Madeley, Trevor Cherry, Terry Yorath, Gordon McQueen, Frank Gray, Gary Liddell, Allan Clarke, Mick Jones, Mick Bates, Eddie Gray
Goal: Clarke 15
Manager: Don Revie

Referee: Sven Jonsson (Sweden) **Att:** 16,276

It was an opportunity to give a taste of Europe to some of United's fringe players under the captaincy, for the first time, of Paul Madeley.

Young Scottish striker Gary Liddell was given his debut and at the other end of the scale, the vastly experienced Gary Sprake was back in goal for what was his last game in a European tie.

Despite the Norwegians' rigid man-marking plan, it took United just quarter of an hour to open the scoring, Allan Clarke chesting down Eddie Gray's centre and despatching a left-foot shot past Inge Thun.

But United, with the Gray brothers in midfield tandem, didn't find it so easy to break down a well organised Norwegian defence after that and Stromsgodset equalised ten minutes later when Eddie Gray headed out a free-kick aimed into the United box and Odd Amundsen smacked a low angled drive through a packed penalty area into the bottom corner.

The local fans then roared with delight when Steinar Petterson 'nutmegged' Gordon McQueen, but the cheers turned to groans as he shot straight at Sprake.

Liddell nearly marked his debut with a couple of goals but Thun saved one effort with his feet and when the young striker did get round the goalkeeper on another occasion, Johnny Pederson cleared off the line and Stromsgodset hung on to a famous draw.

Dons overcome plucky Harps at Pittodrie

Dundee 1 (Stewart), Twente Enschede 3 (Achterberg, Jeuring 2)
Dynamo Tbilisi 5 (G Nodia, Gavasheli, L Nodia, Manuchar, Machidze), Slavia Sofia 1 (Zheliazkov)
Eikisehirspor 0, Cologne 0
Espanol 0, Racing White 3 (Koens, Polleunis, Teugels)
Fenerbahce 5 (Turan 3, Arpacioglu, Kalpakaslan), Arges Pitesti 1 (Rosu)
Ferencvaros 0, Gwardia Warsaw 1 (Szymczak)
Fiorentina 0, Universitatea Craiova 0
Fortuna Dussledorf 1 (Hesse), Naestved 0
Frederikstad 0, Dynamo Kiev 1(Kondratov)
Grasshoppers 1 (Noventa pen), Tottenham Hotspur 5 (Chivers 2, Evans, Gilzean 2)
Hibernian 2 (Black, Higgins), Keflavik 0
Ipswich Town 1 (Rubonan og), Real Madrid 0
Kosice 1 (Pollak), Honved 0
Lazio 3 (Chinaglia 2 – 2 pens), Sion 0
Nice 3 (Van Dijk, Molitor 2), Barcelona 0
Oesters 1 (Svensson), Feyenoord 3 (Van Hanegem 2, Wery)
Patras 2 (Dandelis, Spentzopoulos), Graz 1 (Koleznik)
Panathinaikos 1 (Andoniadis), OFK Belgrade 2 (Lukic 2)
Ruch Chorzow 4 (Bula, Marx, Herisz, Masczyk), Wuppertal 1 (Kohle pen)
Stromsgodset 1 (Amundsen), Leeds United 1 (Clarke)
Sliema Wanderers 0, Locomotiv Plovdiv 2 (Vasillev, Camilleri og)
Stuttgart 9 (Ettmayer 2, Brenninger pen, Ohlicher, Mail, Entenmann 2, Weidmann), Olympiakos Nicosia 0
Tatran Presov 4 (Novak, Turcanyi, Sobota, Cabala), Velez Mostar 2 (Kvesic 2)
Torino 1 (Bul), Locomotiv Leipzig 2 (Lowe, Koditz)
Union Luxembourg 0, Marseille 5 (Hardt og, Kuszowski 3, Buigues)
Vitoria Setubal 2 (Jose Torres 2), Beerschot 0
Carl Zeiss Jena 3 (Bransch, Schlutter, Scheitler), Mikkelin 0

SNIFFER STRIKES: United striker Allan Clarke slots the ball past Inge Thun for the opening goal against battling Norwegian side Stromsgodset.

UEFA Cup
First round second leg
(at Elland Road, Leeds)
Wednesday, October 3, 1973

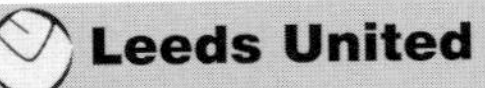

Leeds United		**6**
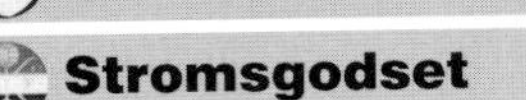 **Stromsgodset**		**1**

Leeds United win 7-2 on agg

Leeds United: David Harvey, Paul Reaney (Sean O'Neill 80), Trevor Cherry, Billy Bremner, Roy Ellam, Terry Yorath, Peter Lorimer, Allan Clarke (Billy McGinlay 76), Mick Jones, Mick Bates, Frank Gray
Goals: Clarke 11, 42, Jones 20, 84, F Gray 57, Bates 62
Manager: Don Revie

Stromsgodset: Inge Thun, Per Rune Wollner (Per Stale Aarseth 84), Johnny Vidar Pedersen, Tor Alskaer Nostdahl, Svein Dahl Andersen, Odd Amundsen, Finn Olsen, Bjorn Andersen, Thorodd Pressberg, Steinar Pettersen, Ingar Pettersen (Bjorn Erik Halvorsen 84)
Goal: S Pettersen 18
Manager: Erik Eriksen

Referee: Richard Casha (Malta) **Att:** 18,711

The joy of six

But United forced to work hard

DESPITE their surprise home draw, Stromsgodset knew they would be in for a long night in the return leg a fortnight later.

So it proved as Leeds won 6-1 at Elland Road for a comfortable 7-2 aggregate victory

However, the battling Norwegians gave a good acount of themselves and always tried to get forward whenever they had a bit of possession.

Stromsgodset had made a remarkable climb up the Norwegian League moving up from the Fourth Division to the First and European football in ten years.

Once again it was Allan Clarke who opened the scoring, snapping up Svein Anderson's back-pass to beat goalkeeper Inge Thun. But, as in the first leg, Stromsgodset hit back, Steinar Pettersen swapping passes with Bjorn Andersen before shooting past David Harvey.

Any hopes of a sensation dissolved three minutes later when Mick Jones regained United's lead and they went into the interval 3-1 up with Clarke's second goal, set up by Jones and Billy Bremner, after Stromsgodset failed to clear a corner.

Frank Gray registered his first European goal with a right-foot shot from Peter Lorimer's cross and Mick Bates took a leaf out of Lorimer's book with a blistering 20-yard drive to make it 5-1.

That was the signal for Revie to blood a couple more youngsters, sending on Billy McGinlay for his debut and introducing defender Sean O'Neill.

Three minutes from the end Jones completed the scoring after good work by Lorimer and to cap a satisfactory night's work reserve centre half Roy Ellam came through his first senior outing since breaking his arm the previous season without any problems.

FIRST BLOOD: Frank Gray, who scored his first European goal against Stromsgodset.

Hibs book another date with Leeds

UNITED were drawn to face Scottish side Hibernian in the second round.

It was a repeat of their Fairs Cup clash in 1967 when Don Revie's team were pushed hard by the Edinburgh side.

Hibs were unable to improve on their 2-0 home victory over Keflavik, but Pat Stanton's goal in Iceland gave them a 1-1 draw and a 3-1 aggregate victory.

Ipswich hung on to their slender advantage over Real Madrid with a courageous 0-0 draw in the Bernabeu Stadium, a result which confirmed Bobby Robson's status as one of England's top up-and-coming managers.

Goals by Peter Eastoe and Jim McCalliog, who had started his career as an amateur with Leeds, gave Wolves victory over Belenenses. McCalliog didn't make the first team at Leeds, but found fame at Sheffield Wednesday and Wolves and became a full Scottish international.

Tottenham thrashed Grasshoppers 4-1 with World Cup hero Martin Peters netting two of the goals.

Arthur Graham was on target again as Aberdeen won 3-1 at Finn Harps to seal a 7-2 aggregate win but fellow Scots Dundee were sunk 4-2 in Holland by an excellent Twente Enschede side who had won 3-1 at Dens Park.

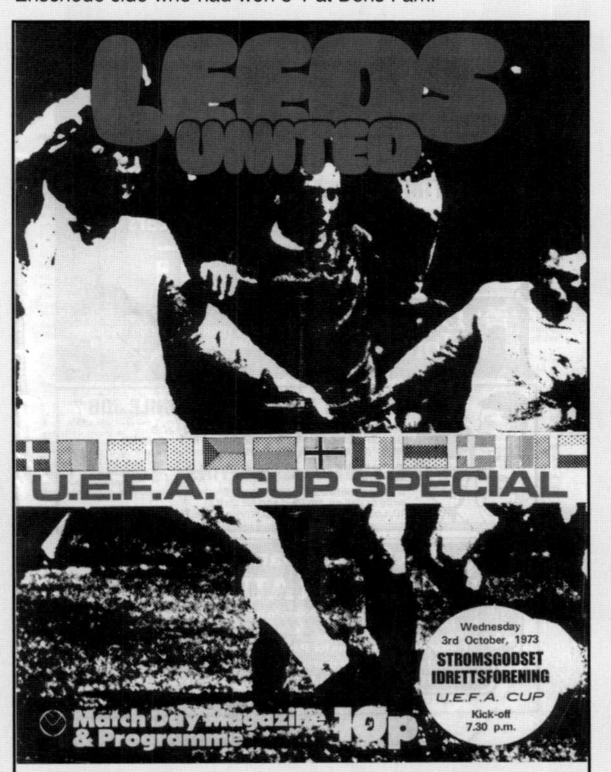

New look United

UNITED'S image was not only improving on the field.

The club had appointed its first public relations officer, Peter Fay, who introduced several new initiatives.

While United were producing a new brand of attacking football, the club programme was overhauled and named Programme of the Year.

More revolutionary were the pre-match warm-ups on the pitch and the wearing of stocking tabs which were handed over to eager fans at the final whistle.

First round, second leg

Arges Pitesti 1 (Dobrin), Fenerbache 1 (Turan)
Fenerbache win 6-2 on agg
Barcelona 2 (Soltil, Juanito), Nice 0
Nice win 3-2 on agg
Beerschot 0, Vitoria Setubal 2 (Jose Maria, Duda)
Vitoria Setubal win 4-0 on agg
Cologne 2 (Lauscher, Lohr), Eskisehirsport 0
Cologne win 2-0 on agg
Dynamo Kiev 4 (Troshkin, Kolotov, Buriak, Blokhin), Fredrikstad 0
Dynamo Kiev win 5-0 on agg
Feyenoord 2 (Kristensen, De Jong), Osters 1 (Cluft)
Feyenoord win 5-2 on agg
Finn Harps 1 (Harkin), Aberdeen 3 (Robb, Graham, Miller)
Aberdeen win 7-2 on agg
Graz 0, Patras 1 (Spentzopoulos)
Patras win 3-1 on agg
Gwardia Warsaw 2 (Wisniewski pen, Szymczak), Ferencvaros 1 (Mate)
Gwardia Warsaw win 3-1 on agg
Honved 5 (Pinter 2, Fule, Szucs, Bortak og), Kosice 2 (Pollak, Stafura)
Honved win 5-3 on agg
Inter Milan 2 (Moro, Boninsegna), Admira Vienna 1 (Kaltenbrunner)
aet 2-2 on agg. Admira Vienna win on away goals
Keflavik 1 (Zakariasson), Hibernian 1 (Stanton)
Hibernian win 3-1 on agg
Leeds United 6 (Clarke 2, Jones 2, F Gray, Bates), Stromsgodset 1 (Pettersen)
Leeds United win 7-2 on agg
Lokomotiv Leipzig 1 (Lisiewicz, Matoul), Torino 1 (Sala)
Lokomotiv Leipzig win 4-2 on agg
Lokomotiv Plovdiv 1 (Vasilliev), Sliema Wanderers 0
Lokomotiv Plovdiv win 3-0 on agg
Marseille 7 (Magnusson, Skoblar 3, Kuszowski, Bracci pen, Tresor), Union Luxembourg 1 (Ney)
Marseille win 12-1 on agg
Mikkeli 0,Carl Zeiss Jena 3 (Irnscher, Ducke 2)
Carl Zeiss Jena win 6-0 on agg
Molenbeek 1 (Polleunis), Espanyol 2 (Amiano, Salsona)
Molenbeek win 4-2 on agg
Naestved 2 (Olsen, Ottosen), Fortuna Dusseldorf 2 (Seel, Hertzog)
Fortuna Dusseldorf win 3-2 on agg
OFK Belgrade 0, Panathinaikos 1 (Demelo)
2-2 on agg. OFK Belgrade win on away goals
Olympiakos Nicosia 0, Stuttgart 4 (Ohlicher, Martin, Muller, Ettmayer)
Stuttgart win 13-0 on agg
Real Madrid 0, Ipswich Town 0
Ipswich Town win 1-0 on agg
Sion 3 (Isoz 2, Barberis), Lazio 1 (Garlaschelli)
Lazio win 4-3 on agg
Slavia Sofia 2 (Krastev, Grigorov), Dynamo Tbilisi 0
Dynamo Tbilisi win 4-3 on agg
Solna 1 (Aslund), BK Copenhagen 1 (Knutstensen)
BK Copenhagen win 3-2 on agg
Standard Liege 6 (Henrotay, Bukal 4, Govart), Ards 1 (Guy)
Standard Liege win 8-4 on agg
Tottenham Hotspur 4 (Lador og, Peters 2, England), Grasshoppers 1 (Eisener)
Tottenham Hotspur win 9-1 on agg
Twente Enschde 4 (Van Der Vall, Achterberg, Zuidema 2), Dundee (Johnston, Scott)
Twente Enschede win 7-3 on agg
Universitatea Craiova 1 (Oblemencho), Fiorentina 0
Universitatea Craiova win 1-0 on agg
Velez Mostar 1 (Golic), Tatran Presov 1 (Sobota)
Tatran Presov win 5-3 on agg
Wolverhampton Wanderers 2 (Eastoe, McCalliog), Belenenses 1 (Murca)
Wolverhampton Wanderers win 4-1 on agg
Wuppertal 5 (Stockl, Cremer 2, Propper, Reichert), Ruch Chorzow 4 (Benigier, Kopicera, Marx, Bula)
Ruch Chorzow win 8-6 on agg

UNITED 1973-74: Leeds United's international all stars line up for the new season. Back row, from left to right: Norman Hunter (England), Paul Madeley (England), Gordon McQueen (Scotland), Joe Jordan (Scotland), Paul Reaney (England). Middle row: Roy Ellam, Allan Clarke (England), Gary Sprake (Wales), David Harvey (Scotland), Mick Jones (England), Eddie Gray (Scotland). Front row: Peter Lorimer (Scotland), Mick Bates, Johnny Giles (Republic of Ireland), Billy Bremner (Scotland), Trevor Cherry (England), Frank Gray (Scotland), Terry Yorath (Wales).

International brigade

Leeds stars shine for club and country

OF the 18-man United squad pictured above at the start of the 1973-74 season only two failed to gain international recognition.

Mick Bates and Roy Ellam were the odd men out as Don Revie's glittering all stars were called up by their countries.

Skipper Billy Bremner had been part and parcel of the Scottish side for years and was the driving force behind their qualification for the 1974 World Cup when he was joined in Germany by Peter Lorimer, Joe Jordan and David Harvey. Jordan netted the winner against Czechoslovakia at Hampden in the week between the two Stromsgodset UEFA Cup ties which took the Tartan Army to their first World Cup finals for 16 years.

Gordon McQueen was capped just before the World Cup and went with the Scottish party to Germany but didn't figure in any of the games in the finals. Like Frank Gray, McQueen did not really establish himself in the national side until later in the 1970s. Eddie Gray won his first full honours in 1969 but injury restricted him to just a dozen Scottish appearances, the last coming in 1976.

England didn't make it to Germany to the disappointment of Allan Clarke, Norman Hunter and Paul Madeley. Terry Cooper, still battling back to full fitness after his broken leg, was no longer a regular part of the England set-up but Trevor Cherry went on to win 27 caps.

Gary Sprake, although ousted at Leeds as No1, was a permanent fixture in the Welsh side where he had been joined by Terry Yorath, while the experienced Johnny Giles was the captain of the Republic of Ireland.

FRONT- RUNNER: Joe Jordan, who came on as substitute for Scotland and scored the winner in the 2-1 victory over Czechoslovakia which booked Willie Ormond's side a place in the World Cup finals.

Below-par Leeds struggle to contain stylish Hibernian

United draw a blank

MR CONSISTENCY: United's versatile star Paul Madeley, who was one of the few Leeds men to live up to their reputation against Hibernian.

SCOTTISH club Hibernian were confident that they could nail the theory that football North of the border lacked quality other than Celtic and Rangers.

Hibs certainly proved that with their first leg display at Elland Road.

Even though United were without Norman Hunter, who was completing his three-match Euro-ban, Paul Reaney, Johnny Giles, Eddie Gray and up-and-coming central defender Gordon McQueen, Don Revie offered no excuses after his side were fortunate to escape with a 0-0 draw.

In Alex Cropley, Hibs had the best player on show, but fortunately for Leeds David Harvey and Paul Madeley kept cool heads on an uncomfortable night for a disjointed Leeds outfit.

Tony Higgins could have won it for the Scots but missed chances in the first and last minutes of the game, while Cropley's sublime ball skills ensured his side enjoyed the bulk of the chances.

United had an escape early on when Alan Gordon appeared to be pushed in the box, but referee Karoly Palotai waved aside appeals for a penalty.

Cropley then sent a 20-yard drive whistling over the top before Gordon intercepted a misplaced Mick Bates' pass and fed Higgins, whose low shot was saved by Harvey.

UEFA Cup
Second round first leg
(at Elland Road, Leeds)
Wednesday, October 21, 1973

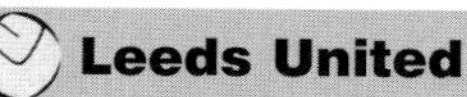 

Leeds United	**0**
Hibernian	**0**

Leeds United: David Harvey, Trevor Cherry, Paul Madeley, Billy Bremner, Roy Ellam, Terry Yorath, Peter Lorimer, Allan Clarke, Mick Jones (Joe Jordan HT), Mick Bates, Frank Gray (Sean O'Neill 55)
Manager: Don Revie

Hibernian: Jim McArthur, Des Bremner, Eric Shaedler, Pat Stanton, Jim Black, John Blackley, Bobby Seith (John Hazel 69), Tony Higgins, Alan Gordon, Alex Cropley, Arthur Duncan
Manager: Eddie Turnbull

Referee: Karoly Palotai (Hungary) **Att:** 27,145

United's only real chance of the first half came after 35 minutes when Clarke's back header was caught first time on the volley by Frank Gray but went just wide.

Revie, sensing the tie could be snatched away from Leeds' grasp, replaced knee injury victim Mick Jones with Joe Jordan, and United did improve, forcing goalkeeper Jim McArthur to make two fine saves to deny Peter Lorimer.

But there was no denying Hibs' superiority and manager Eddie Turnbull was justifiably upbeat – "I'm confident about the outcome at Easter Road."

Revie added: "We have no excuses tonight, even though we had so many players out. Hibernian are a great side and their chances tonight were a little better than ours.

"But remember, one goal for Leeds at Easter Road could be worth double. If we have our full side out I am certain it will be a great game up there."

Tottenham denied by Hermiston at Pittodrie

UNITED v Hibs was not the only Anglo-Scottish clash in the UEFA Cup second round.

Tottenham travelled north of the border to take on Aberdeen in the first leg, securing a 1-1 draw. Ralph Coates' early goal gave Spurs the lead which was wiped out three minutes from the end by Jim Hermiston's penalty.

Impressive Ipswich thumped Lazio 4-0 at Portman Road, Trevor Whymark scoring all the goals in the 17th, 43rd, 47th and 63rd minutes.

Second round, second leg

Admira Vienna 2 (Kaltenbruimer 2), Fortuna Dusseldorf 1 (Bude)
Aberdeen 1 (Hermiston pen), Tottenham Hotspur 1 (Coates)
Dynamo Kiev 1 (Buriak), BK Copenhagen 0
Dynamo Tbilisi 3 (Kipiani, G Nodia, L Nodia), OFK Belgrade 0
Feyenoord 3 (Schoenmaker 2, De Jong), Gwardia Warsaw 1 (Szymczak)
Ipswich Town 4 (Whymark 4), Lazio 0
Leeds United 0, Hibernian 0
Lokomotiv Plovdiv 3 (Bosakov, Iwanov, Bonev), Honved 4 (Kozma 2, Kocsis, Pal)
Lokomotiv Leipzig 3 (Matoul 2 – 1 pen, Koditz), Wolverhampton Wanderers 0
Marseille 2 (Lopez, Kuszowski), Cologne 0
Nice 4 (Molitor 4), Fenerbahce 0
Patras 1 (Davourlis pen), Twente Enschede 1 (Thijssen)
Ruch Chorzow 3 (Benigier, Kopicera, Bula), Carl Zeiss Jena 0
Standard Liege 2 (Bukal 2), Universitatea Craiova 0
Stuttgart 3 (Muller, Brenninger, Ohlicher), Tatran Presov 1 (Skorupa)
Vitoria Setubal 1 (Vicente), RWD Molenbeek 0

Jeepers, keepers!

Rookie duo the heroes for Leeds

SHAW THING: United goalkeeper, John Shaw, grasps the ball tightly as Hibs striker Alan Gordon prepares to pounce at Easter Road.

TEENAGE goalkeepers Glan Letheran and John Shaw became overnight sensations for United in a drama-drenched night in Edinburgh.

With Gary Sprake severing his long and distinguished association with Leeds by joining Birmingham in a £100,000 deal, Revie had bought Ayr United goalkeeper David Stewart as back-up to first choice David Harvey.

But Harvey was carrying a knee injury and was unable to play at Easter Road, while Stewart had not been a Leeds player long enough under UEFA rules to figure in the match.

Enter 19-year-old Shaw, United's third string goalkeeper, whose only other taste of European football had been the Lierse disaster in which he was substituted at half-time.

In addition to their goalkeeping crisis, Leeds were also without Gordon McQueen (groin), Norman Hunter (calf), Johnny Giles (calf), Paul Madeley (blisters) and Mick Jones (cold).

On the evidence of the first leg, United went into the game as rare underdogs but their dogged determination got them through an extraordinary night.

Anticipating a torrid evening, Revie played inspirational skipper Billy Bremner as sweeper ahead of his rookie goalkeeper and it proved a masterstroke.

Shaw's confidence soared after 10 minutes when he made a brilliant save from John Blackley, but Leeds, playing in all-yellow, almost broke the deadlock with their first corner. Frank Gray curled the ball in, Terry Yorath flicked it on and Roy Ellam smashed the ball against the underside of the bar before Hibs cleared.

Then it was United's turn to escape

Spurs march on but its the end of the line for Wolves

AS United laboured to get past Hibernian, Totteham had little difficulty with their Scottish opponents, Abderdeen.

Two late goals by substitute striker Chris McGrath capped a 4-1 home win for the north London side who eased through 5-2 on aggregate.

Wolves went out despite a 4-1 win at Molineux where Wolfram Lowe's second half goal gave Lokomotiv Leipzig overall victory on the away goals ruling.

Second round, second leg

BK Copenhagen 1 (Kristensen), Dynamo Kiev 2 (Kolotov, Troshkin)
Dynamo Kiev win 3-1 on agg
Carl Zeiss Jena 1 (Bransch), Ruch Chorzow 0
Ruch Chorzow win 3-1 on agg
Cologne 6 (Flohe, Muller 2, Overath pen, Lohr 2), Marseille 0
Cologne win 6-2 on agg
Fenerbachce 2 (Arpacioglu 2), Nice 0
Nice win 4-2 on agg
Fortuna Dusseldorf 3 (Brei 2, Geye), Admira Vienna 0
Fortuna Dusseldorf win 4-2 on agg
Gwardia Warsaw 1 (Szynczak pen), Feyenoord 0
Feyenoord win 3-2 on agg
Hibernian 0, Leeds United 0
0-0 on agg. Leeds United win 5-4 on penalties
Honved 3 (Kozma 2, Pinter), Lokomotiv Plovdiv 2 (Iwanov, Vasilev)
Honved win 7-4 on agg
Lazio 4 (Garlaschelli, Chinaglia 3 – 1 pen), Ipswich Town 2 (Viljoen, Johnson)
Ipswich win 6-4 on agg
OFK Belgrade 1 (Stojanovic), Dynamo Tbilisi 5 (Chelidze, G Nodia, Kipiani 2, Chereti)
Dynamo Tbilisi win 8-1 on agg
RWD Molenbeek 2 (Depireux, Veenstra), Vitoria Setubal 1 (Vicente)
2-2 on agg. Vitoria Setubal win on away goals
Tatran Presov 3 (Turcanyi 2 – 1 pen, Skorupa), Stuttgart 5 (Olicher 2, Handschuch 2, Turcanyo og) aet
Stuttgart win 8-4 on agg
Tottenham Hotspur 4 (Peters, Neighbour, McGrath 2), Aberdeen 1 (Jarvie)
Tottenham Hotspur win 5-2 on agg
Twente Enschede 7 (Pahlplatz 4, Zuideme, Van Der Vall pen, van Lerssel), Patras 0
Twente Enschede win 8-1 on agg
Universitatea Craiova 1 (Balan), Standard Liege 1 (Henrotay)
Standard Liege win 3-1 on agg
Wolverhampton Wanderers 4 (Kindon, Munro, Dougan, Hibbitt), Lokomotiv Leipzig 1 (Lowe)
4-4 on agg. Lokomotiv Leipzig win on away goals

United do it

How the penalty drama unfolded

Stanton (Hibs) misses 0-0
Lorimer (Leeds) scores 1-0
Cropley (Hibs) scores 1-1
Gray (Leeds) scores 2-1
Blackley (Hibs) scores 2-2
Bates (Leeds) scores 3-2
Bremner (Hibs) scores 3-3
Clarke (Leeds) scores 4-3
Hazel (Hibs) scores 4-4
Bremner (Leeds) scores 5-4

INSURANCE POLICY: United full-back Paul Reaney gets back to make sure this Hibs effort cleared the bar.

as Trevor Cherry chested an Alex Cropley shot off the line, Tony Higgins got to the rebound but the back-tracking Lorimer saved Leeds with another goal-line clearance.

It was all-action stuff and the drama moved up a notch when Shaw failed to reappear after the interval, having broken two fingers in his right hand. His replacement was 17-year-old Welsh youth international Letheran, a junior with hardly any reserve team experience never mind senior appearances.

But the superb Bremner marshalled his troops to such an effect that Letheran was rarely tested although it needed Bremner himself to head one effort off his own line.

Allan Clarke missed the chance to settle the issue when he shot wide after Black mistimed a clearance, but it was Hibs who finished the stronger and United held a collective intake of breath as a Cropley shot skimmed Letheran's bar late on.

The game went into extra-time, but two weary sides could not break the deadlock which had stretched to 210 minutes without a goal, so the issue was settled via penalties.

Hibs took the first one, but Pat Stanton, who had scored a hat-trick the previous weekend, missed the opening kick, smacking his shot against a post.

Both sides converted their next four kicks leaving Bremner to keep his head and lash the final match-winning penalty high into the net and send his team into ecstacy.

Neither of United's goalkeeping heroes were able to forge a career at Elland Road. Shaw didn't play for Leeds again but was a great servant at Bristol City while Letheran made one League appearance for the Whites before being released.

UEFA Cup
Second round second leg
(at Easter Road, Edinburgh)
Wednesday, November 3, 1973

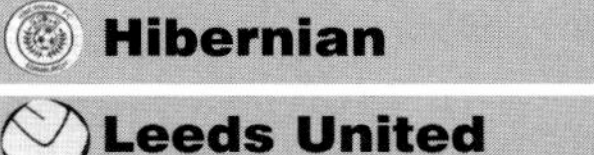

Hibernian 0
Leeds United 0

0-0 on agg after extra-time
Leeds United win 5-4 on penalties

Hibernian: Jim Arthur, Des Bremner, Eric Shaedler, Pat Stanton, Jim Black, John Blackley, Alex Edwards, Tony Higgins (John Hazel HT), Alan Gordon, Alex Cropley, Arthur Duncan
Manager: Eddie Turnbull

Leeds United: John Shaw (Glan Letheran HT), Paul Reaney, Trevor Cherry, Billy Bremner, Roy Ellam, Terry Yorath, Peter Lorimer, Allan Clarke, Mick Jones, Mick Bates, Eddie Gray
Manager: Don Revie

Referee: Paul Schiller (Austria) **Att:** 36,051

UEFA ban Revie for one match

HIBERNIAN protested to UEFA that Don Revie and trainer Les Cocker were on the pitch, passing on instructions during the penalty shoot-out.

Hibs held an impromtu board meeting within minutes of the match ending at Easter Road and seemed to have an ally in UEFA's representative at the game, Albert Gudmunsson, who said: "The referee was wrong to allow them to stay on the pitch."

Two of the Edinburgh club's directors flew to Switzerland the following day to lodge their protest which UEFA referred to their Control and Disciplinary Committee the following Thursday

In the meantime the draw took place, with Leeds in the hat and they were paired with Portuguese side Vitoria Setubal.

It was a tense week for United fans who feared they may be thrown out of the competition or be ordered to relay the game.

The matter was dealt with at a hearing in Berne, and decided that Revie should be suspended for one game and that Leeds should be fined £400 but UEFA ruled that Revie's presence on the pitch had no decisive influence to the outsome of the penalty shootout.

The decision meant Revie would not be permitted to enter the dressing rooms for the first leg against Setubal at Elland Road or approach the field of play.

The barred Revie said: "I'm sure Les will be able to motivate and prepare the team successfully. He knows all the right phrases. I have sat in snow, rain, burning sunshine, the lot, on touchlines in places as far apart as Oslo and Ankara, yet never sat in the directors' box."

Ten-man Setubal threaten to pull plug on United

Power failure

MANAGER-FOR-THE-NIGHT Les Cocker suffered a frustrating night as Portuguese League leaders Vitoria Setubal prevented United from building up a healthy first leg lead.

Apart from quality opposition, United also had to contend with the energy crisis prompted by rising oil prices and industrial action which was to lead to the three-day week. Power restrictions were imposed by Ted Heath's Conservative government so United called in a 10-ton generator to power the floodlights seperately from the National Grid. But with Revie watching from the stand in the lowest Euro crowd at Elland Road, United were unable to overpower a well drilled side which had nine successive seasons of European competition under their belt and had run Leeds close in the 1970-71 competition.

The game, played on a snow-covered surface, was not without incident, but United missed a great chance to settle the tie at Elland Road.

Setubal goalkeeper Joaquim Torres was outstanding, the pick of his saves denying Peter Lorimer from 25 yards.

The match then swung United's way in the 39th minute when Henrique Campora felled Terry Yorath and after consulting with one of his fellow Danish linesmen, referee Preben Christophersen sent off the Uruguayan midfielder. With a man advantage and over half the game to go United looked in control but they were continually frustrated by a well-drilled Setubal defence.

With just over an hour gone Cocker sent on young Frank Gray to add some creativity and stand-in manager Cocker was reward within seven minutes, Gray crossing for Trevor Cherry to smack home a left-footer for his first goal of the season.

Three minutes later Lorimer was brought down by Jose Mendes, and despite Setubal's protests, Christophersen pointed to the spot. Lorimer got up to take the penalty, but he underhit it, Joaquim Torres managed to parry the ball and was sharp enough to block Lorimer's follow up attempt. It was a priceless save and United were to suffer the consequences.

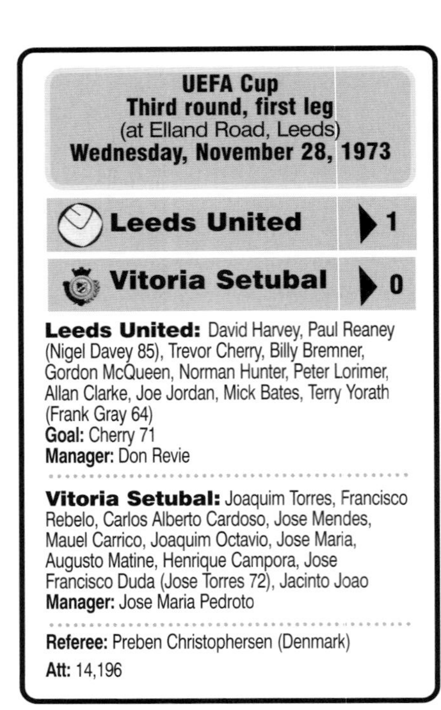

UEFA Cup
Third round, first leg
(at Elland Road, Leeds)
Wednesday, November 28, 1973

Leeds United 1

Vitoria Setubal 0

Leeds United: David Harvey, Paul Reaney (Nigel Davey 85), Trevor Cherry, Billy Bremner, Gordon McQueen, Norman Hunter, Peter Lorimer, Allan Clarke, Joe Jordan, Mick Bates, Terry Yorath (Frank Gray 64)
Goal: Cherry 71
Manager: Don Revie

Vitoria Setubal: Joaquim Torres, Francisco Rebelo, Carlos Alberto Cardoso, Jose Mendes, Mauel Carrico, Joaquim Octavio, Jose Maria, Augusto Matine, Henrique Campora, Jose Francisco Duda (Jose Torres 72), Jacinto Joao
Manager: Jose Maria Pedroto

Referee: Preben Christophersen (Denmark)
Att: 14,196

IN CHARGE: United trainer Les Cocker took control of the team against Vitoria Setubal while Don Revie served a one-match ban.

Whymark on the mark

TREVOR Whymark's late goal gave Ipswich a slender 1-0 home advantage over Twenre Enschede, whose midfielder Frans Thijssen was later to join the Portman Road club.

Tottenham returned from the long trek to the Soviet Union with a 1-1 draw in Tbilisi, where Ralph Coates first half goal put Spurs in control.

Third round, first leg

Dynamo Kiev 2 (Veremeev, Troshkin), Stuttgart 0
Dynamo Tbilisi 1 (Asatiani), Tottenham Hotspur 1 (Coates)
Fortuna Dussledorf 2 (Brei, Herzog), Lokomotiv Leipzig 1 (Matoul pen)
Honved 2 (Pusztai 2), Ruch Chorzow 0
Ipswich Town 1 (Whymark), Twente Enschede 0
Leeds United 1 (Cherry), Vitoria Setubal 0
Nice 1 (Enksson), Cologne 0
Standard Liege 3 (Piot pen, Lambrichts, Thissen), Feyenoord 1 (Kristensen)

Don's Euro finale

UEFA Cup
Third round, second leg
(at Bonfim Stadium, Setubal)
Wednesday, December 12, 1973

Vitoria Setubal 3

Leeds United 1

Vitoria Setubal win 3-2 on agg

Vitoria Setubal: Joaquim Torres, Francisco Rebelo, Carlos Alberto Cardoso, Jose Mendes, Manuel Carrico, Joaquim Octavio, Jose Maria, Augusto Matine (Joao Vicente HT), Jose Torres (Joaquim Arcanjo 80), Jose Francison 'Duda', Jacinto Joao
Goals: 'Duda' 52, 74, Jose Torres 62
Manager: Jose Maria Pedroto

Leeds United: David Harvey, Paul Reaney, Trevor Cherry, Terry Yorath, Gordon McQueen (Gary Liddell 80), Roy Ellam, Peter Lorimer, Jimmy Mann, Joe Jordan, Peter Hampton, Frank Gray
Goal: Liddell 82
Manager: Don Revie

Referee: Arie Van Gemert (Holland) **Att:** 25,000

United sunk in Portugal

WHAT proved to be Don Revie's last European game in charge ended in a disappointing defeat in Portugal.

Revie's top target at the start of the season had been the League Championship and United headed to Vitoria Setubal after a 3-0 win at Ipswich, stretching their unbeaten start in Division One to 19 games.

The UEFA Cup was not a high priority and Revie fielded an unfamiliar side in Portugal which included a first European start for 19-year-old Peter Hampton, who was given a man-marking role on Setubal play-maker Octavio. In attack, Jimmy Mann was making a rare appearance, while Frank Gray operated in an unusual position at sweeper.

United were on the back foot for most of the game but all was going well until the 52nd minute when Brazilian Duda squared the tie with a diving header after Gordon McQueen had only been able to partially clear a cross from the left. Ten minutes later and United were in deep trouble as the 6ft 5in Jose Torres flicked in Jose Mendes' cross with his head to put the Portuguese ahead overall. Lacking the likes of Billy Bremner, Allan Clarke, Paul Madeley and Mick Jones, United's young side were unable to turn the tide of attacking and Duda grabbed his second when he shot past David Harvey from 10 yards.

Setubal had rattled in three goals in a 22-minute spell – the first time in nine seasons in Europe that United had let in three goals in an away leg.

Revie made a late bold switch by withdrawing McQueen and sending on 18-year-old striker Gary Liddell who two minutes later drilled in a low shot past Joaquim Torres. But with only eight minutes left on the clock United were unabe to find that decisive second goal that would have put them through on the away goals ruling.

Revie was appointed England manager in July and had a magnificent record in Europe. Of the 78 matches played during his Elland Road reign, United had won 42 games, drawn 22 and lost just 14. In nine years, Revie had seen Leeds win Fairs Cup twice in three finals, reach the semi-finals once, and figure in a European Cup Winners' Cup final and a European Cup semi-final – a fantastic record of consistency.

FINAL LEGACY: Don Revie with the 1973-74 Championship trophy. United's relatively early exit from Europe left them to concentrate on securing their second-ever League title, leaving them to contest the European Cup the following season.

Spurs head in to quarter-finals

BOTH Tottenham and Ipswich moved relentlessly in to the quarter-finals as United fell by the wayside.

Free-scoring Spurs stuck five past Dynamo Tbilisi – all of them headers. Meanwhile, Ipswich completed the double over Dutch side Twente Enschede with goals by Colin Morris and Bryan Hamilton giving them a 2-1 victory in Holland.

Third round, second leg

Cologne 4 (Muller, Flohe 2, Lohr), Nice 0 *Cologne win 4-1 on agg*
Feyenoord 2 (Schienmaker, Van Hanegem), Standard Liege 0 *3-3 on agg. Feyenoord win on away goals*
Lokomotiv Leipzig 3 (Lisiewicz, Lowe, Frenzel), Fortuna Dussledorf 0 *Lokomotiv Leipzig win 3-2 on agg*
Ruch Chorzow 5 (Bon, Koipcera 2, Marx, Bula), Honved 0 *Ruch Chorzow win 5-2 on agg*
Stuttgart 3 (Ohlicher, Handschuch, Martin), Dynamo Kiev 0 *Stuttgart win 3-2 on agg*
Tottenham Hotspur 4 (McGrath, Chivers 2, Peters), Dynamo Tbilisi 1 (Ebreallze) *Tottenham Hotspur win 5-2 on agg*
Twente Enchede 1 (Streuer), Ipswich Town 2 (Morris, Hamilton) *Ipswich Town win 3-1 on agg*
Vitoria Setubal 3 (Duda 2 Jose Torres), Leeds United 1 (Liddell) *Vitoria Setubal win 3-2 on agg*

Tottenham crash at the final hurdle

TOTTENHAM Hotspur fell at the final hurdle amid disgraceful scenes in Rotterdam.

Billy Nicholson's team swept through the late stages of the competition by knocking out Cologne and Lokomotiv Leipzig.

That put the Londoners through to the final against Feyenoord, the Dutch side who had won the European Cup in 1971.

Spurs seemed on course for a 2-1 home win until Theo De Jong's late goal.

In the second leg Spurs fans rioted during the game which led to 70 arrests and 200 injured in the crush despite appeals for calm by Nicholson.

Feyenoord refused to be distracted by the off-the-field aggro and win 2-0 to lift the trophy.

Ipswich Town's tremendous run under the astute management of Bobby Robson ended in the quarter-finals when they went out on penalties to tough East German outfit Lokomotive Leipzig.

Quarter final, first leg

Cologne 1 (Muller), Tottenham Hotspur 2 (McGrath, Peters)

Ipswich Town 1 (Beattie), Lokomotiv Leipzig 0

Ruch Chorzow 1 (Schoenmaker), Feyenoord 1 (Maszczyk)

Stuttgart 1 (Stickel), Vitoria Setubal 0

Quarter final, second leg

Feyenoord 3 (Schoenmaker 2-1 pen, De Jong), Ruch Chorzow 1 (Marx) aet *Feyenoord win 4-2 on agg*

Lokomotiv Leipzig 1 (Giessner), Ipswich Town 0 *1-1 on agg after extra-time. Lokomotiv Leipzig win 4-3 on pens.*

Tottenham Hotspur 3 (Chivers, Coates, Peters), Cologne 0 *Tottenham Hotspur win 5-1 on agg*

Vitoria Setubal 2 (Jose Torres, Jose Maria), Stuttgart 2 (Ollicher, Stickel) *Stuttgart win 3-2 on agg*

Semi final, first leg

Feyenoord 2 (Schoenmaker 2), Stuttgart 1 (Brenninger)

Lokomotiv Leipzig 1 (Lowe), Tottenham Hotspur 2 (Peters, Coates)

Semi final, second leg

Stuttgart 2 (Brenninger 2), Feyenoord 2 (Ressel, Schoenmaker) *Feyenoord win 4-3 on agg*

Tottenham Hotspur 2 (McGrath, Chivers), Lokomotiv Leipzig 0 *Tottenham Hotspur win 4-1 on agg*

Final, first leg

(White Hart Lane, London)
May 21, 1974

Tottenham Hotspur 2, Feyenoord 2

Tottenham Hotspur: Jennings, Evans, Naylor, Pratt, England, Beal (Dillon 81), McGrath, Perryman, Chivers, Peters, Coates.

Goals: England 39, Van Daele og 62

Manager: Billy Nicholson

Feyenoord: Treijel, Rijsbergen, Van Daele, Israel, Vos, Schoenmaker, Jansen, Ressel, De Jong, Van Hanegem, Kristensen.

Goals: Van Hanegem 43, De Jong 84

Manager: Wiel Coerver

Referee: Rudolf Scheurer (Switzerland)

Attendance: 46,281

Final, second leg

(Feyenoord Stadium, Rotterdam)
May 29, 1974

Feyenoord 2, Tottenham Hotspur 0
Feyenoord win 4-2 on agg

Feyenoord: Treijel, Ramljak, Van Daele, Israel, Vos, Rijsbergen (Boskamp 78, – Wery 87), De Jong, Jansen, Ressel, Schoenmaker, Kristensen.

Goals: Rijsbergen 43, Ressel 84

Manager: Wiel Coerver

Tottenham Hotspur: Jennings, Evans, Naylor, Pratt (Holder 78), England, Beal, McGrath, Perryman,Chivers, Peters, Coates.

Manager: Billy Nicholson

Referee: Concetto Lo Bello (Italy)

Attendance: 68,000

Leading scorers:
9 – Schoenmaker (Feyenoord), 8 – Bukal (Standard Liege).

United storm to title

UNITED'S exit from the UEFA Cup cleared the path for Don Revie's squad to power their way to their second League title.

They didn't lose a game until they threw away a 2-0 lead at Stoke on February 23, 1974 and went down 3-2.

Despite a bit of a wobble towards the end of the season United sealed the title without kicking a ball when closest rivals Liverpool lost a midweek match at home to Arsenal. It was a deserved triumph for United who led from gun to tape and finished six points clear of the men from Anfield.

What is more, United stormed to the top despite a crop of nasty injuries to the likes of Johnny Giles, Mick Jones and Eddie Gray for long spells.

Division One 1973/74

	P	W	D	L	F	A	Pts
LEEDS UNITED	42	24	14	4	66	31	62
Liverpool	42	22	13	7	52	31	57
Derby County	42	17	14	11	52	42	48
Ipswich Town	42	18	11	13	67	58	47
Stoke City	42	15	16	11	54	42	46
Burnley	42	16	14	12	56	53	46
Everton	42	16	12	14	50	48	44
Queens Park Rgrs	42	13	17	12	56	52	43
Leicester City	42	13	16	13	51	41	42
Arsenal	42	14	14	14	49	51	42
Tottenham Hotspur	42	14	14	14	45	50	42
Wolverhampton W	42	13	15	14	49	49	41
Sheffield United	42	14	12	16	44	49	40
Manchester City	42	14	12	16	39	46	40
Newcastle United	42	13	12	17	49	48	38
Coventry City	42	14	10	18	43	54	38
Chelsea	42	12	13	17	56	60	37
West Ham United	42	11	15	16	55	60	37
Birmingham City	42	12	13	17	52	64	37
Southampton	42	11	14	17	47	68	36
Manchester United	42	10	12	20	38	48	32
Norwich City	42	7	15	20	37	62	29

United went in to the final game of the season at Queens Park Rangers with the championship in the bag and celebrates in style with Allan Clarke scoring the only goal of the game.

The week after United were crowned champions, Sir Alf Ramsey was sacked as England manager and was replaced by Revie in July. So while Revie and trainer Les Cocker prepared to take over the national team, Leeds fans could look forward to another crack at the European Cup.

CHAMPION CLARKE: Allan Clarke nets the winner at QPR as United celebrate the League Championship in style.

PLAYER POWER: United's 1973/74 Championship-winning squad. Back row, from left to right: David Harvey, Joe Jordan, Eddie Gray, Norman Hunter, Gordon McQueen, Allan Clarke, Paul Madeley, Paul Reaney, David Stewart. Front row: Frank Gray, Peter Lorimer, Johnny Giles, Billy Bremner, Terry Cooper, Mick Bates, Trevor Cherry, Terry Yorath.

Boss Clough out after just 44 days

ONE of football's biggest talking points in summer 1974 was who will replace Don Revie at Leeds?

Few would have guessed at the Leeds board's choice – Brian Clough.

The former Derby manager was a fierce critic of Revie and United's playing methods. It was not surprising that his move back into the big-time from Third Division Brighton was to provide one of the most bizarre chapters in Leeds United's history.

Clough's sidekick, Peter Taylor, remained at Brighton, leaving Clough to sweep through Elland Road like a whirlwind.

United's ageing squad, after years of Revie's methods, could not get to grips with Clough's abrasive style and tactics.

It was a marriage fashioned in hell and the divorce came after 44 turbulent days – Clough being sacked amid press reports of 'player-power'.

Clough later went on to build Nottingham Forest into a European superpower leaving Leeds supporters to contemplate what might have been had Clough stayed at Elland Road.

United's form under Clough had been poor, although it had not been helped by an 11-match ban imposed on skipper Billy Bremner. The Leeds skipper and Kevin Keegan were ordered off for fighting in the televised FA Charity Shield showpiece at Wembley – Clough's first game in charge as Leeds manager – and pulled off their shirts in disgust. Both vastly experienced internationals felt the full weight of football's authorities with crushing bans and a £500 fine each.

IN THE HOT SEAT (FOR THE TIME BEING): Leeds United's new boss Brian Clough with assistant Jimmy Gordon.

Under Clough United were a pale shadow of the side which had won the championship in dazzling style the previous season and needed to steady the ship.

They didn't look in great shape to tackle the cream of Europe, particularly as the talismanic Bremner would not be available until the second leg of the second round.

Maurice men's merry dance

IN CHARGE: Maurice Lindsay stepped in to the breach after Brian Clough's exit.

Zurich outclassed by United

MAURICE Lindley, who had been Don Revie's assistant manager, temporarily filled the void created by Brian Clough's departure.

He had just five days to prepare United for their opening European Cup tie against FC Zurich but his side rolled back the years with a brilliant performance, beating the champions, of Switzerland 4-1.

It took United just 14 minutes to get their European Cup band-wagon on the move. Joe Jordan headed a Paul Madeley cross into the path of Allan Clarke and he swept the ball through a ruck of players past goalkeeper Karl Grob.

By half-time Leeds were home and dry. Peter Lorimer scored from the penalty spot after Jordan was floored by Hilmar Zigerlig, who was also at fault for the third goal. The hapless defender was caught in possession by Clarke, who exchanged passes with Jordan before thumping home a shot from an acute angle.

United, showed no signs of letting up after the interval. Terry Cooper, playing his first Euroean tie for three years after recovering from a broken leg in a league game at Stoke, produced a classic moment straight after half-time.

Once regarded as England's greatest attacking full-back, Cooper bombed down the left, pushed the ball round Ernst Rutchmann one way, ran round the other, and whipped in a superb cross which Jordan, running in at full speed, sent flashing past Grob with his head.

Zurich grabbed a consolation in the final minute when United's markers failed to do their job and Jakob Kuhn broke away to centre for Ilija Katic to head past David Harvey at the near post. But that could not strip the gloss from another European night which left Lindsay a proud man.

"People were beginning to think it was not there any more, but it could have been six, seven or eight tonight. They went out and showed they could still play and just relieved themselves of all the pressures," he said.

European Cup Cup
First round, first leg
(at Elland Road, Leeds)
Wednesday, September 18, 1974

Leeds United 4

FC Zurich 1

Leeds United: David Harvey, Paul Reaney Terry Cooper, Terry Yorath, Gordon McQueen, Norman Hunter, Peter Lorimer, Allan Clarke, Joe Jordan, Johnny Giles, Paul Madeley
Goals: Clarke 15, 44, Lorimer 25 pen, Jordan 47
Manager: Maurice Lindsay

FC Zurich: Karl Grob, Max Heer, Ernst Rutschmann (Peter Marti 60), Hilmar Zigerlig, Renzo Bionda, Jakob Kuhn, Rosario Martinelli, Ilija Katic, Daniel Jeandupeaux, Pirmin Stierli, Rene Botteron
Goal: Katic 89
Manager: Friedhelm Konietzka

Referee: Jan Keizer (Holland) **Att:** 20,012

Celtic sweating

SCOTTISH champions Celtic were frustrated by Greek side Olympiakos at Parkhead.

Jock Stein's team trailed to a goal for much of the match and were only able to scramble an equaliser from Paul Wilson near the end.

First round, first leg

Celtic 1 (Wilson), Olympiakos 1 (Viera)
Feyenoord 7 (Schoenmaker, Kreuz 3, van Hanegem, Ressel), Coleraine 0
Hadjuk Split 7 (Zungul 2, Surjack, Jerkovic, Buljan), Keflavik 1 (Johannson)
Hvidovre 0, Ruch Chorzow 0
Jeunesse Esch 2 (Mond, Giuliani), Fenebache 3 (Osman, Cemil, Ender)
Leeds United 4 (Clarke 2, Lorimer pen, Jordan), FC Zurich 1 (Katic)
Levski Spartak 0, Ujpest Doza 3 (Horvath, Bene, A Dunai)
Omonia Nicosia conceded to Cork Celtic
Slovan Bratislava 4 (Novotny, Masny 2, Svehlik), Anderlecht 2 (Coeck, Van Himst)
St Etienne 2 (Revelli, Bereta), Sporting Lisbon 0
Universitatea Craiova 2 (Oblemenco 2 – 1 pen), Avitaberg 1 (Augustsson)
Valetta 1 (Magro), HJK Helsinki 0
Viking 0, Ararat Erevan 2 (Markarov 2)
Voest Linz 0, Barcelona 0

Byes: *Bayern Munich, Magdeburg*

No Greek gifts for Celtic as they crash out to Olympiakos

CELTIC tumbled out in Greece to Olympiakos on a bumpy pitch.

The Scots fell behind to Kritikopoulos' early diving header and conceded again after 24 minutes when Stavropoulos drove a free kick straight through the defensive wall. With Northern Ireland side Coleraine predictably thrashed by Feyenoord, Leeds were left to carry on Britain's hopes.

First round, second leg

Anderlecht 3 (Van Himst, Coeck, Thijssen), Slovan Bratislava 1 (Masny) *5-5 on agg. Anderlecht win on away goals.*
Ararat Erevan 4 (Markarov 3, Bondarenko), Viking 2 (Nilsen, Berland) *Ararat Erevan win 6-2 on agg*
Avitaberg 3 (Andersson, Almqvist 2), Universitatea Craiova 1 (Stefanescu) *Avitaberg win 4-3 on agg*
Barcelona 5 (Asensi, Clares 2, Juan Carlos, Rexach pen), Voest Linz 0 *Barcelona win 5-0 on agg*
Coleraine 1 (Simpson), Feyenoord 4 (Schoenmaker 3 – 1 pen, Kruez) *Feyenoord win 11-1 on agg*
FC Zurich 2 (Katic, Ruschmann pen), Leeds United 1 *Leeds United win 5-3 on agg*
Fenerbahce 2 (Cemil, Yilmaz), Jeunesse Esch 0 *Fenerbahce win 5-2 on agg*
HJK Helsinki 4 (Rahja, Peltonen, Hammalainen, Forssell), Valetta 1 (Giglio) *HJK Helsinki win 4-2 on agg*
Keflavik 0, Hadjuk Split 2 (Dloni, Majac) *Hadjuk Split win 9-1 on agg*
Olympiakos 2 (Kritikopoulos, Stavropoulos), Celtic 0 *Olympiakos win 3-1 on agg*
Ruch Chorzow 2 (Bula 2), Hvidovre 1 (Pedersen) *Ruch Chorzow win 2-1 on agg*
Sporting Lisbon 1 (Yazalde), St Etienne 1 (Revelli) *St Etienne win 3-1 on agg*
Ujpest Doza 4 (Bene 2, A Dunai 2), Leveski Spartak 1 (Voinov) *Ujpest Doza win 7-1 on agg*

WAITING IN THE WINGS: Jimmy Armfield was poised to takeover the Elland Road hot seat as United flew to Switzerland.

European Cup
First round, second leg
(at Letzigrund Stadium, Zurich)
Wednesday, October 2, 1974

FC Zurich 2

Leeds United 1

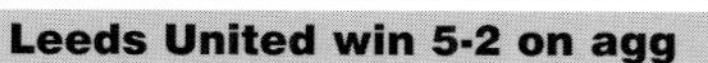

Leeds United win 5-2 on agg

FC Zurich: Karl Grob, Max Heer, Ernst Rutschmann, Hilmar Zigerlig (Peter Marti 70), Renzo Bionda, Jakob Kuhn, Rosario Martinelli, Ilija Katic, Daniel Jeandupeaux, Pirmin Stierli, Rene Botteron.
Goals: Katic 38, Rutschmann 42 pen
Manager: Freidhelm Konietzka

Leeds United: David Harvey, Paul Reaney, Trevor Cherry, Terry Yorath, Paul Madeley, Norman Hunter, Peter Lorimer, Allan Clarke, Joe Jordan, Mick Bates, Frank Gray (Peter Hampton 65)
Goal: Clarke 37
Manager: Maurice Lindley

Referee: Sergio Gonella (Italy) **Att:** 16,500

Leeds lose their Swiss timing but...

Jim'll fix it for United

MAURICE Lindsay was still in charge a fortnight later when United played in Zurich although the Leeds board were on the brink of naming Bolton manager Jimmy Armfield as Brian Clough's successor.

Contract talks with Armfield, the former England full-back, and a respected safe pair of managerial hands, were continuing as Leeds flew to Switzerland.

With a 4-1 lead, United were conservative in their approach to the game, particularly as they were without Billy Bremner, Terry Cooper, Johnny Giles and Gordon McQueen.

Zurich set the pace in the first half and David Harvey needed to be at his sharpest to deal with an effort from Daniel Jeandupeaux but chances for the home side were scarce.

On 37 minutes United strengthened their grip on the tie still further when Harvey launched a kick deep into Zurich territory, Allan Clarke read the ball perfectly, went past two defenders and clipped home a left-foot shot for his 10th goal in 11 games.

Rather than cave in, Zurich hit back from the kick-off. Hilmar Zigerlig and Rosario Martinelli opening up the Leeds defence for Ilija Katic to fire in the equaliser. Leeds seemed to panic at that stage and Harvey was forced to make a brave save at the feet of Jeandupeaux and then the Leeds goalkeeper received a bump on the head in that incident but still managed to pluck a dangerous Katic cross out of the air moments later.

Just before half-time United found themselves behind when Paul Reaney brought down Jeandupeaux in the box and Ernst Rutschmann thumped in the penalty via the bar.

Leeds regrouped and were able to kill the game off in the second period as the tie petered out, United going through 5-3 on aggregate.

European Cup
Second round, first leg
(at Nep Stadium, Budapest)
Wednesday, October 23, 1974

Ujpest Doza	1
Leeds United	2

Ujpest Doza: Adam Rothermel, Jeno Kellner, Laszlo Harsanyi, Jezsef Horvath, Laszlo Nagy, Ede Dunai, Andras Toth, Laszlo Fazekas, Laszlo Fekete, Ferenc Bene, Sandor Zambo (Antal Dunai 59)
Goal: Fazekas 20 pen
Manager: Pal Varhidi

Leeds United: David Harvey, Paul Reaney, Terry Cooper, Terry Yorath, Gordon McQueen, Norman Hunter, Peter Lorimer, Duncan McKenzie, Joe Jordan, Johnny Giles, Paul Madeley
Goals: Lorimer 8, McQueen 22
Manager: Jimmy Armfield

Referee: Kurt Tschenscher (West Germany)
Att: 20,000

CLOSE SHAVE: Trevor Cherry sends a header wide of the Ujpest post.

Jimmy's a winner

JIMMY Armfield marked his first European game in charge at Leeds with a famous victory.

United had been paired with old Hungarian rivals Ujpest Doza, whom they had met twice before in the old Fairs Cup competition, winning the first tie but losing the second when they were beaten in both legs.

Armfield knew his men faced a big job in Budapest against a side which had won the Hungarian League six years on the bounce and had only dropped two points from ten games in the current campaign.

Just eight minutes had gone when Terry Cooper, in a familiar advanced position of the left, crossed towards goal, forcing Ujpest 'keeper Adam Rothermel to palm the ball out, Duncan McKenzie collected the loose ball and played it to Peter Lorimer who lashed the ball in to the net.

McKenzie, a £250,000 Brian Clough summer signing from Nottingham Forest, was, like Armfield, making his European debut. He was playing for Allan Clarke, who was suffering from a bruised instep, and early on it looked as though McKenzie would be joining Clarke on the treatment table.

The striker was being battered from one side of the pitch to the other by the Hungarian defence and when he was hacked down from behind by Josef Horvath in the 15th minute, McKenzie snapped. He retaliated and was ordered off by German referee Kurt Tschenscher, who had given McKenzie little protection early on.

Advantage to Bayern

TWO goals by World Cup star Gerd Muller gave Bayern Munich the edge over Cup Winners Cup holders Magdeburg in the all German clash.

The big game between Feyenoord and Barcelona in Rotterdam ended goalless, the Dutch twice hitting the woodwork.

Second round, first leg

Anderlecht 5 (Rensenbrink 3 – 2 pens, Van Der Elst, Ladinsky), Olympiakos 1 (Persidis pen)
Bayern Munich 3 (Muller 2 – 1 pen, Wunder), Magdeburg 2 (Hansen og, Sparwasser)
Cork Celtic 1 (Tambling), Ararat Erevan 2 (Zanazansian, Kazarian)
Feyenoord 0, Barcelona 0
Hadjuk Split 4 (Jerkovic 2, Zungul, Mijac), St Etienne 1 (H Reveilli)
HJK Helsinki 0, Atvitaberg 3 (Almqvist 2, Hasselberg)
Ruch Chorzow 2 (Kopicera, Benigier), Fenebahce 1 (Niazi)
Ujpest Doza 1 (Fazeakas pen), Leeds United 2 (Lorimer, McQueen)

Tschenscher did little to enamour himself to United's players minutes later when Laszlo Fekete went steaming into the Leeds area and Terry Cooper clearly pulled out of a tackle. Fekete tumbled anyway and the referee gave a penalty which Laszlo Fazekas converted, despite a great attempt by David Harvey to save the kick.

Despite being down to ten men United stuck to their attacking gameplan and regained the lead on 22 minutes when Gordon McQueen headed in his first European goal from Johnny Giles' free-kick. McQueen went close with another header, Giles saw a 30-yard shot scrambled off the Ujpest line as United continued to attack when ever posible.

Harvey produced three excellent saves to deny Fekete, Fazekas and Ferenc Bene but there was still time for a sting in the tail of a remarkable match.

On 81 minutes Joe Jordan was brought down in the area but Lorimer smashed the ball against a post and seconds later it became a 10-a-side game as Laszlo Harsanyi brought down Terry Yorath and was ordered off for a second bookable offence.

Glorious return by Bremner

RETURN OF THE PRODIGAL SON: Leeds skipper Billy Bremner, who found the back of the net on his return to Euro action.

European Cup
Second round, second leg
(at Elland Road, Leeds)
Wednesday, November 6, 1974

Leeds United	**3**
Ujpest Doza	**0**

Leeds United win 5-1 on agg

Leeds United: David Harvey, Paul Reaney, Terry Cooper, Terry Yorath, Gordon McQueen, Norman Hunter (Trevor Cherry 42), Peter Lorimer (Carl Harris 70), Allan Clarke, Billy Bremner, Johnny Giles, Paul Madeley
Goals: McQueen 29, Bremner 46, Yorath 65
Manager: Jimmy Armfield

Ujpest Doza: Karoly Szigeti, Endre Kolar, Edie Dunai, Jeno Kellner, Sandor Zambo, Andras Sarlos, Laszlo Fekete (Antal Dunai 70), Andras Toth, Ferenc Bene, Laszlo Fazekas, Laszlo Nagy (Andras Torokcsik HT)
Manager: Pal Varhidi

Referee: Alfred Delacourt (Belgium) **Att:** 28,091

BILLY Bremner made a fairytale return against Ujpest Doza at Elland Road.

Because of the long ban imposed for his Charity Shield Wembley bust-up with Kevin Keegan, the Leeds skipper had barely an hour's first team action under his belt since the opening day of the season.

Typically he announced his return to the big-time with a goal in an easy 3-0 win over the Hungarians.

Leeds were already a goal up when Terry Cooper joined United's first attack after half-time and powered in a shot which was cleared at the expense of a corner. As the flag-kick was speared into the area, Terry Yorath, playing as a makeshift striker, headed the ball against the bar and Bremner headed in the rebound.

Crosses in the box had caused the Hungarians problems all night and they were found wanting again on 65 minutes when Paul Madeley's high centre was headed across goal by Allan Clarke and Yorath applied the finishing touch.

The game in the bag, manager Jimmy Armfield, introduced Carl Harris, 18 the previous Sunday, and United free-wheeled into the third round 5-1 on aggregate.

United had been set on their way by centre half Gordon McQueen, who got on the end of a well-flighted 29th minute flighted Johnny Giles free-kick to head in United's 150th goal in Europe.

After the game McQueen received the man of the match trophy made by Hungarian-born Barnsley sculptor Jim Badics, who had acted as Ujpest's interpreter during their stay in Yorkshire. United had chiselled out their own passage to the quarter-finals and could put the competition to bed until March.

Rexach treble sends Barcelona through

CARLOS Rexach hammered in a hat-trick as Barcelona outclassed Feyenoord in the Nou Camp 3-0 with goals after 34, 38 and 78 minutes.

French champions St Etienne produced a stunning comback to go through to the quarter-finals. Trailing 4-1 to Hadjuk Split they went through at home after extra-time.

Second round, second leg

Ararat Erevan 5 (Pogosjan 2, Zanazanian, Ishtoian, Andreasian), Cork Celtic 0
Ararat Erevan win 7-1 on agg
Atvitaberg 1 (Almqvist), HJK Helsiniki 0
Atvitaberg win 4-0 on agg
Barcelona 3 (Rexach 3), Feyenoord 0
Barcelona win 3-0 on agg
Fenerbahce 0, Ruch Chorzow 2 (Kopicera, Benigier)
Ruch Chorzow win 4-1 on agg
Leeds United 3 (McQueen, Bremner, Yorath), Ujpest Doza 0
Leeds United win 5-1 on agg
Magdeburg 1 (Sparwasser), Bayern Munich 2 (Muller 2)
Bayern Munich win 5-3 on agg
Olympiakos 3 (Galakos 3), Anderlecht 0
Anderlecht win 5-4 on agg
St Etienne 5 (Larque, Bathenay, Bereta pen, Triantafilos 2), Hadjuk Split 1 (Jovanovic) aet
St Etienne won 6-5 on agg

Out of sight

Belgians left in a fog by slick United

SAFE SCOT: David Stewart grabbed his European Cup chance with both hands against Anderlecht.

WHEN United resumed their European Cup the campaign in early March, they ghosted past Belgian champions Anderlecht in thick, swirling, fog at Elland Road.

Manager Jimmy Armfield gave a European debut to goalkeeper David Stewart as regular No 1 David Harvey had been injured in a car crash the previous month.

It was touch and go whether the game should have gone ahead but German referee Rudi Glockner started the match on time and the Belgians were soon chasing shadows.

Joe Jordan gave United an early lead when he collected Norman Hunter's superb through ball and smashed a low shot past startled goalkeeper Jan Ruiter.

Fans, who were able to see across the pitch but not each end, chanted "Tell us who scored!", the PA announcer duly obliging.

From what people could see United appeared to be in the ascendancy, so the crowd held its breath as the fog grew thicker and Glockner took the teams off to see if it would lift.

After 18 agonising minutes, play was resumed and two minutes before half-time Jordan headed on Johnny Giles' free-kick and Gordon McQueen's downward header defeated Ruiter.

With Leeds in command, Armfield made the surprising move of substituting Billy Bremner for the first time in his career quarter of an hour from the end as Terry Yorath joined the murky fray.

Anderlect continued to adopt a defensive posture, making good use of the offside trap, but Ludo Coeck missed a great chance to score near the end after being set up by Robbie Rensenbrink in a rare attack,

United, though were showing no signs of taking their foot off the gas and immediately took the game back to the Belgians. Eddie Gray had a shot blocked and Peter Lorimer, who had only been declared fit shortly before the kick-off, picked up the pieces to make it 3-0 a minute from time to virtually guarantee United's place in the semi-finals.

"It was one of the must crucial goals we have scored this season," said Armfield. "Anderlecht didn't score at Elland Road but they could still cause us plenty of trouble next week."

European Cup
Quarter-final, first leg
(at Elland Road, Leeds)
Wednesday, March 5, 1975

Leeds United 3

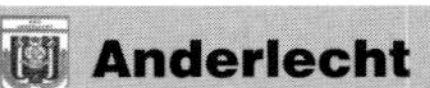

Anderlecht 0

Leeds United: David Stewart, Paul Madeley, Frank Gray, Billy Bremner (Terry Yorath 75), Gordon McQueen, Norman Hunter, Peter Lorimer, Allan Clarke, Joe Jordan, Johnny Giles, Eddie Gray
Goals: Jordan 9, McQueen 42, Lorimer 89
Manager: Jimmy Armfield

Anderlecht: Jan Ruiter, Gilbert Van Binst, Hugo Broos, Erwin Van Den Daele, Jean Thissen, Jean Dockx, Jan Verheyen, Francois Van Der Elst, Ludo Coeck, Paul Van Himst, Robbie Rensenbrink
Manager: Urbain Braems

Referee: Rudi Glockner (East Germany)
Att: 43,195

Advantage to Barcelona

FAVOURITES Barcelona were gifted a huge advantage when Swedish side Atvitaberg controversially agreed to play both quarter-final legs in the Nou Camp.

The wintry weather meant they could not play on their home ground and opted to switch the match to Barcelona where the climate was milder.

Barca won the 'home' leg 2-0, while St Etienne came back from 3-0 down in Poland to restrict Ruch Chorzow to a one-goal advantage. Holders Bayern Munich beat the Armenians, Ararat Erevan with two late goals.

Quarter-final, first leg

Barcelona 2 (Marinho, Clares), Atvitaberg 0
Bayern Munich 2 (Hoeness, Torstensson), Ararat Erevan 0
Leeds United 3 (Jordan, McQueen, Lorimer), Anderlecht 0
Ruch Chorzow 3 (Maszczyk, Benigier, Bula pen), St Etienne 2 (Larque, Triantafilos)

Holders Bayern find their second wind

AGAINST all expectations holders Bayern Munich made it through to the semi-finals.

The Germans' squad had looked weary after their exploits in winning the World Cup and their League form suffered to such an extend that manager Udo Lattek was sacked at the turn of the year and Dettmar Cramer brought back from the United States to take over again.

Bayern had also lost star defender Paul Brietner to Real Madrid, but despite low-key performances in the Bundeslegia, managed, like Leeds, to raise their game in Europe.

Although they lost in Armenia, the Germans went through 2-1 on aggregate, while Barcelona cruised past Atvitaberg.

St Etienne emerged as dark horses after completing a marvellous recovery against Ruch Chorzow, Henri Revelli's 81st minute penalty sending them through to the semi-finals.

Quarter-final, second leg

Anderlecht 0, Leeds United 1 (Bremner)
Leeds United win 4-0 on agg
Ararat Erevan 1 (Andreasian), Bayern Munich 0
Bayern Munich win 2-1 on agg
Atvitaberg 0, Barcelona 3 (Gallego, Asensi, Marinho) – played in Barcelona
Barcelona win 5-0 on agg
St Etienne 2 (Janvion, H Revelli pen), Ruch Chorzow 0
St Etienne win 4-3 on agg

There's no substitute for class

European Cup
Quarter-final, second leg
(at Parc Astrid Stadium, Brussels)
Wednesday, March 19, 1975

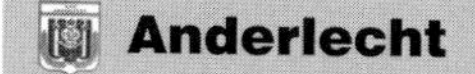 **Anderlecht**  **0**

Leeds United  **1**

Leeds United win 5-1 on agg

Anderlect: Leen Barth, Jean Dockx, Hugo Broos, Erwin Van Den Daele, Jean Thissen, Frankie van Der Elst, Ludo Coeck, Guido Nicolaes (Andrew Denul 65), Attila Ladynzinski, Paul Van Himst, Robbie Rensenbrink
Manager: Urbain Braems

Leeds United: David Stewart, Paul Reaney, Frank Gray, Billy Bremner, Gordon McQueen, Norman Hunter, Peter Lorimer, Allan Clarke, Joe Jordan, Terry Yorath, Paul Madeley
Goal: Bremner 75
Manager: Jimmy Armfield

Referee: Alfred Delacourt (Belgium) **Att:** 29,091

BILLY Bremner's response to being subbed in the first leg was to put on a magnificent display in rain-lashed Brussels, crowned by the only goal of the game.

And what a masterful goal it was. Just 15 minutes remained when Bremner timed an advanced run to perfection from the right, taking the pass on his chest to whip past left-back Hugi Broos in an instant.

The little Scot went steaming in towards goal, looked up as goalkeeper Leen Barth advanced and produced the perfect chip to send the ball looping over the Belgian's head. It was such a stunning strike that Barth turned round to Bremner and shook his hand.

Jimmy Armfield had got his tactics spot-on, leaving out Johnny Giles and Eddie Gray on a heavy pitch lashed by rain, sleet and snow and opted for the greater defensive qualities of Terry Yorath.

It was like a charm as Anderlecht were unable to make much progress against a superb Leeds defence although David Stewart made excellent saves in each half.

Confident Armfield said: "After this display, we do not fear any of the remaining sides."

MUD, GLORIOUS MUD: Mud-splattered Allan Clarke leaves the Anderlecht bog with manager Jimmy Armfield.

Advantage to

CHEERS: United players celebrate Allan Clarke's winner against Barcelona.

ELLAND Road was rocking as United beat mighty Barcelona to inch ever closer to their first European Cup final.

They deservedly beat the big-spending Catalan outfit 2-1 thanks to Allan Clarke's late winner.

The victory vindicated Jimmy Armfield's surprise team selection. He left out Norman Hunter, Trevor Cherry, Peter Lorimer and didn't recall the mercurial Duncan McKenzie although the former Nottingham Forest striker was now available after serving suspension.

Barcelona were built around Dutch superstar Johan Cruyff who had already inspired Ajax Amsterdam to three successive European crowns from 1971.

Three times European Footballer of the Year, the midfield genius moved to Barcelona for a world record £922,000 in 1973, the year after captaining Holland in the World Cup Final defeat against Germany.

It was the biggest game in United's

GOLDEN SHOT: United skipper Billy Bremner, the little man for the big occasion, drills the ball past Salvador Sadurni to get the Whites of

United

Clarke sniffs out semi-final winner

history and there was little wonder the club banked record receipts of £90,000 from the game.

United were given a dream start after only ten minutes when Johnny Giles flighted in a free kick from the left, Joe Jordan rose to flick it on to find the unmarked Billy Bremner, who kept his head to shoot unerringly high past Salvador Sadurni's right hand.

Despite falling a goal behind so early, the Catalan side continued to concentrate on defence with Cruyff helping out when needed at the back.

Yet despite all the left wing promptings of Eddie Gray, who gave Jesus Antonio De la Cruz an uncomfortable evening, United found chances hard to come by against a defence in which Brazilian star Mario Marinho excelled.

But it needed a super one-handed save by Sadurni to keep out a fierce Jordan shot just before half-time. Cryuff, on the occasions he did get into advanced positions, was always a threat and was at the heart of the move which brought Barca their surprise equaliser.

He slid through a brilliant pass to Juan Carlos Heredia and although Paul Reaney got in a tackle outside the box, referee Vital Loraux deemed it a foul. Up stepped Cruyff to roll the free-kick to Juan Manuel Asensi who drove it low past United's defensive wall and goalkeeper David Stewart.

United, who had looked like winners for much of the match, were now losing their grip of the game and in danger of actually losing. But they regained their composure and steeled themselves for a grandstand finish.

With 12 minutes remaining, Paul Madeley's pass released Reaney down the right where his pin-point centre found the head of Jordan. The Scot knocked the ball down into a small parcel of space where Allan Clarke, goal poacher extraordinaire, whipped the ball past Sadurni in an instant.

Elland Road was a cockpit of noise and it was hard to imagine such scenes were possible given the disastrous start to the season.

European Cup Cup
Semi-final, first leg
(at Elland Road, Leeds)
Wednesday, April 9, 1975

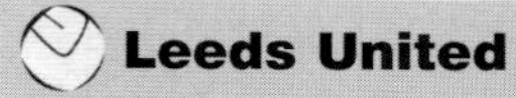
Leeds United 2

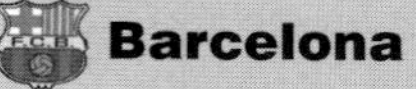
Barcelona  1

Leeds United: David Stewart, Paul Madeley, Frank Gray, Billy Bremner, Gordon McQueen, Paul Madeley, Terry Yorath, Allan Clarke, Joe Jordan, Johnny Giles, Eddie Gray
Goals: Bremner 10, Clarke 78
Manager: Jimmy Armfield

Barcelona: Salvador Sadurni, Enrique Costas (Joaquin Rife 65), Mario Marinho, Francisco Gallego, Jesus Antonio De La Cruz, Johan Neeskens (Juan Carlos Lopez 78), Carlos Rexach, Miguel Bianqueti, Johan Cruyff, Jan Manuel Asensi, Juan Carlos Heredia **Goal:** Asensi 65
Manager: Rinus Michels

Referee: Vital Loraux (Belgium) **Att:** 50,393

ying start against Barcelona at Elland Road.

Rising to the occasion

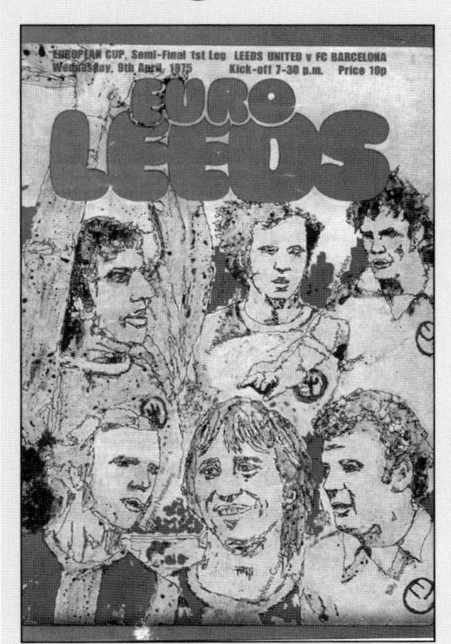

WHAT great timing. United's victory over Barcelona was their first win in seven matches.

The goals were also the first conceded that season by Barcelona in the European Cup.

The exciting match at Elland Road was a far greater spectacle than the 0-0 draw in France where holders Bayern Munich soaked up plenty of pressure from St Etienne and could have snatched victory late on.

Semi-final, first leg
Leeds United 2 (Bremner, Clarke), Barcelona 1 (Asensi)
St Etienne 0, Bayern Munich 0

European Cup
Semi-final, second leg
(at Nou Camp Stadium, Barcelona)
Wednesday, April 23, 1975

Barcelona	1
Leeds United	1

Leeds United win 3-2 on agg

Barcelona: Salvador Sadurni, Mario Marinho, Francisco Gallego, Miguel Bianqueti, Jesus Antonio De La Cruz, Johan Neeskens, Carlos Rexach, Juan Carlos Heredia, Johan Cruyff, Jan Miguel Asensi (Joaquim Rife HT), Manuel Clares
Goal: Clares 69
Manager: Rinus Michels

Leeds United: David Stewart, Trevor Cherry, Frank Gray, Billy Bremner, Gordon McQueen, Norman Hunter, Paul Madeley, Allan Clarke, Joe Jordan, Terry Yorath, Peter Lorimer
Goal: Lorimer 8
Manager: Jimmy Armfield

Referee: Erich Linemayer (Austria) **Att:** 110,000

WE'VE DONE IT: Billy Bremner (centre), Paul Madeley (left) and Allan Clarke celebrate reaching the European Cup final after the nerve-racking draw in Barcelona.

United survive Spanish Inquisition

Programa Oficial del F.C. BARCELONA

AFTER a night of unremitting tension and drama in the immense Nou Camp Stadium, United reached the European Cup final.

Even the boost of an early goal in Spain could not soothe the shredded nerves of the Whites' supporters.

Once again Joe Jordan's head unlocked Barcelona's defensive door, flicking on David Stewart's lengthy clearance to Peter Lorimer who despatched a trademark right-foot shot past Salvador Sadurni. It was his 30th goal in Europe – a British record – but few were so precious.

Barcelona would now have to score three times to prevent Leeds from becoming only the second English team to reach the European Cup final after Manchester United seven years earlier.

Barcelona had started at breakneck speed with a Juan Carlos Heredia header flashing just wide but Lorimer's thumping goal knocked the stuffing out of Rinus Michels' team and United defended with admirable poise for the rest of the first half with Frank Gray, at left back, giving Carlos Rexach little room for manouvre while Gordon McQueen repelled all Barca's high balls into the box.

But United's authority vanished after half-time as Michels introduced Joaquin Rife and pushed talented sweeper Mario Marinho further forward. As well as tactical changes, Barcelona added much more aggression to their game and Jordan required four stitches in a cheek after clashing with a defender.

Dutch ace Johan Neeskens made some big hits in midfield and Francisco Gallego was cautioned for a nasty foul on Billy Bremner as United were under the cosh.

The baying 110,000 crowd sensed United were wilting as Cruyff and Co seized control of the midfield, but time was running out for the home fans.

All United had to do was keep a cool head and see out the last half hour or so. But pressure was mounting on United by the minute and their splendid defence finally cracked with about 20 minutes left when Manuel Clares headed in Francisco Gallego's right-wing free kick.

Minutes later United suffered another devastating blow when scorer Clares pulled McQueen's shirt as they tangled for possession and the Leeds man retaliated by felling Clares and was sent off. The home fans pumped more voltage into the electric night air as chants of "Barca. Barca" boomed around the cavernous Nou Camp United's survival odds instantly lengthened but on a night of heroes one man emerged from their ranks to defy the rampant Barcelona attack – goalkeeper David Stewart, who was simply unbeatable in the dying stages.

He superbly kept out a Heredia header before somehow saved one-handed a deflected Johan Cruyff shot. Seconds remained when Neeskens headed the ball down to Cruyff close to goal but before he could get in a shot Stewart bravely smothered the ball at his feet. It was the final act on possibly the greatest night in United's history.

Manager Armfield said: "This must be the high spot of my football life and I include in that some great experiences as a player."

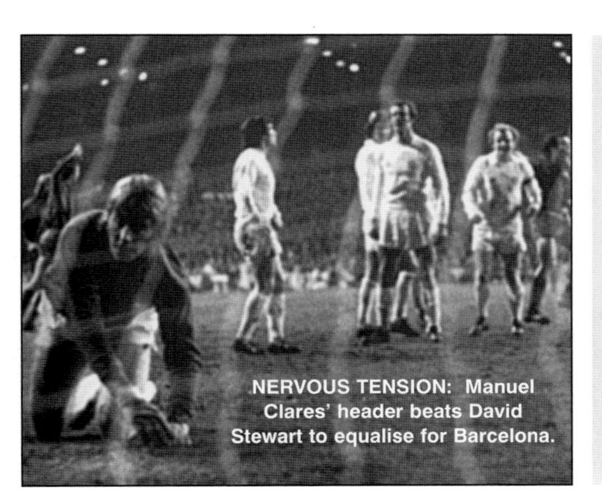

NERVOUS TENSION: Manuel Clares' header beats David Stewart to equalise for Barcelona.

Bring on Bayern

UNITED'S final opponents in Paris would be Bayern Munich, who won the trophy the previous year by thrashing Atletico Madrid 4-0.

The beat St Etienne 2-0 in a poor semi-final in Germany.

Semi-final, second leg

Bayern Munich 2 (Beckenbauer, Durnberger), St Etienne 0 *Bayern Munich win 2-0 on agg*

Barcelona 1 (Clares), Leeds United 1 (Lorimer) *Leeds United win 3-2 on agg*

Leeds and Bayern

CALM BEFORE THE STORM: United skipper Billy Bremner (l

CHALLENGERS: Leeds United 1974/75. Back row, left to right: Paul Madeley, Norman Hunter, Joe Jordan, Gordon McQueen, David Stewart, David Harvey, Eddie Gray, Allan Clarke, Paul Reaney. Front row: Peter Lorimer, Johnny Giles, Billy Bremner, Terry Cooper, Mick Bates, Frank Gray, Terry Yorath.

ready to rumble

changes pennants with Bayern counterpart Franz Beckenbauer.

20ème FINALE

COUPE DES CLUBS CHAMPIONS EUROPEENS

horaire de la rencontre

18 h 15	Ouverture des portes du Stade.
de 19 h 15 à 19 h 55	Programme musical par la Batterie Fanfare de la Garde Républicaine de Paris Exhibition par les Gymnastes de la Garde Républicaine.
20 h 00	Présentation d'anciens joueurs ayant illustré la Coupe des Clubs Champions Européens.
20 h 05	Entrée des équipes finalistes sur le terrain : **F.C. BAYERN de MUNICH** – Maillot Rouge, Culotte Rouge, Bas Rouge **LEEDS UNITED** – Maillot Blanc, Culotte Blanche, Bas blanc
20 h 10	Remise aux capitaines du F.C. BAYERN de MUNICH et de LEEDS UNITED d'un trophée offert par «L'EQUIPE» pour commémorer la 20ème Finale.
20 h 15	Coup d'envoi du match comptant pour la 20 ème Finale de la Coupe des Clubs Champions Européens. Arbitre : M. Michel KITABDJIAN Juges de touche : M.M. Robert HELIES et René VIGLIANI de la Fédération Française de Football
21 h 00	Mi-temps - Programme musical.
21 h 15	Reprise de la 2ème période de jeu.
22 h 00	Fin du match. Si à l'issue du temps réglementaire le résultat était nul il sera procédé à une prolongation de deux périodes de 15 minutes à partir de 22 h 15. Si au terme de la prolongation l'égalité subsistait entre les deux clubs la Finale serait rejouée le vendredi 30 mai à 20 h 15 au Stade du Parc des Princes. Dans ce cas le même horaire qu'indiqué ci-dessus serait appliqué.

ATTENTION - Les différentes cartes (Presse, Radio, Télévision, Cinéma, Service...) délivrées pour la Finale du 28 mai demeureront valables (mêmes places) pour l'éventuel match du 30 mai.

28 MAI 1975

Parc des Princes

PARIS

PROGRAMME OFFICIEL

5 F

CHAMPIONS: Bayern Munich's squad proudly display the European Cup they were defending against United. The Germans won the trophy by beating Atletico Madrid in Brussels in 1974. After a 1-1 draw at the Heysel Stadium, the teams met at the same venue two days later with Bayern winning 4-0, Gerd Muller and Uli Hoeness scoring two goals each.

Heartbreak in Paris

Final curse strikes again

European Cup Final
(at Parc des Princes Stadium, Paris)
Wednesday, May 285, 1975

Leeds United	**0**
Bayern Munich	**2**

Leeds United: David Stewart, Paul Reaney Frank Gray, Billy Bremner, Paul Madeley, Norman Hunter, Peter Lorimer, Allan Clarke, Joe Jordan, Johnny Giles, Terry Yorath (Eddie Gray 79)
Manager: Jimmy Armfield

Bayern Munich: Sepp Maier, Bernd Durnberger, Bjorn Andersson (Josef Weiss 5), George Schwarzenbeck, Franz Beckenbauer, Franz Roth, Conny Torstensson, Rainer Zobel, Gerd Muller, Uli Hoeness (Klaus Wunder 42), Hans-Josef Kappellmann
Goals: Roth 71, Muller 81
Manager: Dettmar Cramer

Referee: Michel Kitabdjian (France) **Att:** 48,374

WHAT was to have been the greatest night in Leeds United's history turned into a nightmare in Paris.

Despite dominating against a negative Bayern Munich, United's dreams of taking club football's greatest prize were blown apart by two late goals.

Off the field things were even worse as a portion of United's 8,000 following battled with security forces and police inside the ground and the riot spilled on to the Parisien boulevards late into the night.

Little went right for Leeds in the match as they claimed, with some justification, that they had suffered at the hands of poor referring. Just two years after the shambolic display by Greek referee Christos Michas in the Cup Winners' Cup final against AC Milan, Leeds found themselves on the receiving end of more bad decisions.

Bayern would probably not have agreed with that synopsis after coming off worst in some brutal early exchanges. Terry Yorath, whom Armfield had picked ahead of the more creative Eddie Gray, clattered into Bjorn Andersson, just as French referee Michael Kitabdjian blew for a foul against Frankie Gray. The challenge forced the Swedish international to limp off after only a few minutes but eventually toe-to-toe combat did give way to some football with United the more progressive of the teams.

The holders, who had beaten Atletico Madrid in the previous year's final, seemed content to let United come on to them. That simply invited trouble and they were lucky to survive two strong first half penalty appeals.

Both revolved around skipper Franz Beckenbauer, who had led his country to World Cup glory in Munich the previous summer.

First he seemed to thrust out an arm and handle the ball as he was on his knees with Peter Lorimer taking the ball around him in the area, then he clearly scythed down Allan Clarke as he bore down on goal.

Both appeals were rejected by Kitabdjian, but despite their frustration United continued to call the tune while Bayern lost inspirational midfielder Uli Hoeness just before half-time when he hurt himself when tackling Frankie Gray.

United's main attacking ploy was to deliver the ball accurately to the head of Joe Jordan who dominated the aerial challenges.

United continued to make chances but when they did get a sniff at goal they found World Cup winner Sepp Maier in stupendous form.

As Jordan skipped away from the Bayern defence and whipped in a right foot shot, the big German 'keeper made a spectacular leaping catch. United, with Billy Bremner and Johnny Giles running midfield, continued to press and were frustrated again just after an hour when Maier spread himself to deny Bremner from point-blank range after Paul Madeley headed on Peter Lorimer's free-kick.

It seemed the breakthrough had arrived on 67 minutes when United won a free-kick. Giles flighted the ball into the area where Madeley headed it on. A Bayern defender struggled to head the ball out cleanly and the ball fell to Lorimer who instantaneously thumped home a tremendous volley.

FLOODLIT ROBBERY: Allan Clarke is brought down in the area by Franz Beckenbauer, but no penalty is given. It was one of two loud United appeals for spot kicks rejected by referee Michel Kitabdjian.

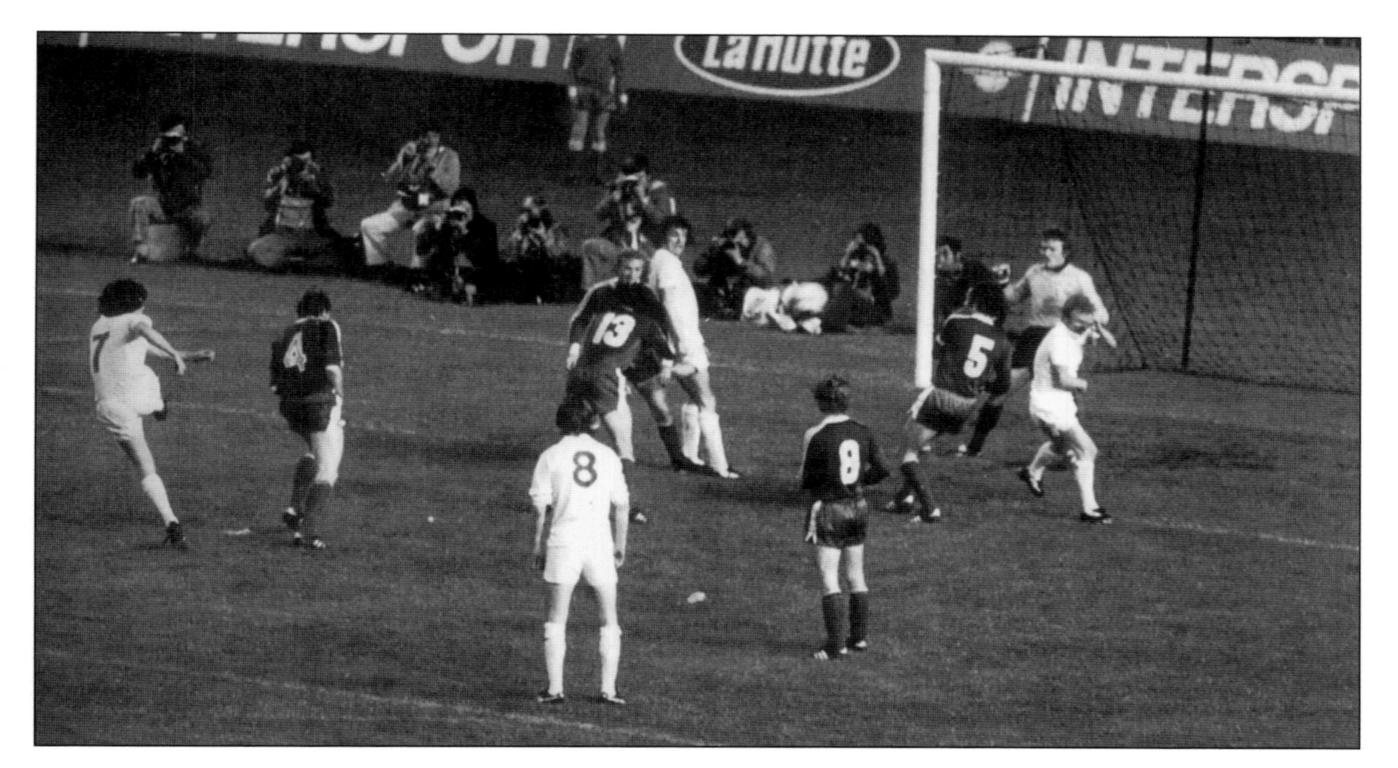

JOY TURNS TO DESPAIR: Peter Lorimer crashes a volley past Sepp Maier (above) as United's players wheel away in delight while goalkeeper Maier offers no protest (below) only for the goal to be controversially ruled out to the horror of Billy Bremner (right).

But to United's despair Kitabdjian, having already rejected two penalty claims, hesitated to give the goal and consulted with his linesman.

As the players, supporters and a 500 million television audience held its breath, the 'goal' was ruled out for offside.

Bremner was coming back from an offside position, but hardly interferring with play, and the Leeds skipper claimed that Lorimer's shot had hit an opponent anyway and Maier would not have saved it in any case.

It was a shattering blow and the turning point in the match. All hell had broken loose at the Leeds end of the all-seater Parc des Prince Stadium behind Maier's goal.

The mood grew darker when just minutes after the disallowed goal Bayern took the lead totally against the run of play.

Franz Roth swapped passes with Conny Torstensson down the left, raced past Paul Madeley and planted a left foot shot into David Stewart's left hand corner. It was a class goal, but totally out of keeping with Bayern's approach to the game.

United were broken. Eddie Gray was sent on to replace Yorath but the Scottish star had barely had a touch of the ball before Bayern doubled their advantage when Hans-Josef Kappellmann broke past Norman Hunter and Frank Gray on the right and delivered a superb cross into the box where master poacher Gerd Muller, who had barely had a kick all night, swept the ball home.

The smash and grab had been completed, leaving United empty handed from a controversial final for the second time in three years.

United ban cut

Armfield appeal sees punishment reduced

FURTHER agony was piled on United after their defeat in Paris.

The club was banned from European competition for four years for the shocking behaviour of some of its followers.

When referee Michel Kitabjian controversially disallowed Peter Lorimer's second half goal, trouble flared in the stands.

It transpired a Leeds fan had tried to scale the 10-foot fence surrounding the pitch but had been hurled back by one of the 200 track-suited judo experts from the Paris Police Sports Club.

The supporter was then beaten by about half a dozen police with truncheons. Some fans, already furious by events on the pitch, went to the aid of their colleague and inevitably became embroiled in a battle with police.

Violent Leeds fans began breaking up seats and throwing them over the fencing and beyond the 12-foot wide moat on to the field, flooring a ball boy, hitting a policeman and blinding a photographer in one eye. Bottles and cans were hurled at the electronic scoreboard as supporters fought with police.

With United trailing, the game was halted twice in the closing stages as the barrage continued and goalkeeper Sepp Maier said later: "The Leeds fans were a bigger danger to me than the Leeds forwards."

After lifting the cup Bayern went on an ill-advised lap of honour and had to beat a hasty retreat when they approached the Leeds end as they were bombarded by missiles.

Equally ill-advised in UEFA's view was the applause given to their supporters by the Leeds players.

It was a ghastly end to a depressing night and United's top brass knew they would be hit hard by UEFA's disciplinarians after seeing a showpiece final so badly tarnished.

Paris was a watershed for Leeds United.

FLOORED: Another view of the incident in which Allan Clarke was brought down by Franz Beckenbauer, only for referee Michel Kitabjian to turn down United's penalty claims.

Having failed to win and not qualified for Europe via the League it was the end of an era.

The ageing team was to be broken up and the challenge of conquering Europe was never to be taken by again by the likes of warriors Billy Bremner, Johnny Giles and Norman Hunter.

United chairman Manny Cussins said: "My deepest sorrow is that ten great years in Europe should end on such a sour and tragic note."

But he knew no words were going to spare his club from punishment.

UEFA secretary Hans Bangerter, said: "It is totally inexcusable for the Leeds players to go to their supporters and applaud them as they did at the end of the game. This will have to be taken into consideration by the Control and Disciplinary Committee at its meeting in mid-June."

Trouble had actually flared long before the kick-off with windscreens of cars parked near the stadium smashed and a supermarket trashed. Damage was also done to boat trains between Victoria Station in London and Dover.

The journey home for United's beaten army of fans was a long one with delays at Calais because of striking French seamen.

On June 13 the UEFA Disciplinary Commission slapped a four-year ban on United but it was reduced to two after a well-argued appeal by manager Jimmy Armfield.

Writing in the first home programme of the following season he said: "We simply had to appeal over that sentence. I felt – and still do feel – that to hold a football club responsible for the behaviour of its 'supporters' outside the jurisdiction of its own ground is morally and legally wrong."

Referee Kitabjian's display was apparently marked two out of 20 by UEFA, but that was no consolation to United, now frozen out of Europe

Leading scorers: 5 – Almqvist (Atvitaberg), Markarov (Ararat Erevan), Muller (Bayern Munich)

EUROPEAN RETURN: United's squad for 1979/80 which competed in the UEFA Cup. Back row, from left to right: Alan Curtis, Gary Hamson, Paul Madeley, John Hawley, Eddie Gray. Middle row: Dave Merrington (assistant manager), Keith Parkinson, Paul Hart, David Harvey, John Lukic, Ray Hankin, Byron Stevenson, Syd Farrimond (coach). Front row: Carl Harris, Kevin Hird, Peter Hampton, Jimmy Adamson (manager), Trevor Cherry, Arthur Graham, Brian Flynn.

Back in business

Adamson's United regain place in Europe

JIMMY Armfield steered his new-look United to fifth place in 1975/76 and the following season they slipped to tenth spot as the break up of Don Revie's master side continued.

Johnny Giles' last game for United had been in Paris, Billy Bremner was to move on to Hull City, Norman Hunter to Bristol City, Paul Reaney to Bradford City, Allan Clarke to Barnsley as player-manager while Scottish duo Joe Jordan and Gordon McQueen crossed the Pennines to link up with arch rivals Manchester United.

In summer 1978 the Leeds board moved Armfield aside after four years in charge. After a brief spell under former Celtic supremo Jock Stein, who had been in charge when the Hoops became the first British club to win the European Cup in 1967, United eventually recruited Sunderland manager Jimmy Adamson. The former Burnley defender had once turned down managing England during the later stages of his playing career at Burnley because he felt he lacked the neccessary experience.

The Leeds side was virtally unrecognisable to the one which had contested the European Cup final but, despite a decline in Elland Road attendances, they finished fifth in 1978/79 to recapture a place in Europe.

The draw was kind to United, handing them a first round tie with Maltese minnows Valetta, but Leeds had won only one of their opening eight games which included a 7-0 League Cup thrashing at Arsenal.

No joy for Kidd as Toffees come unstuck

ALL four English teams launched their UEFA Cup campaigns abroad.

While United and Ipswich cantered to easy wins against mediocre opposition, both Everton and West Brom lost.

The Toffees, who included future Leeds coach Brian Kidd in their attack, went down 1-0 to Feyenoord, while the Baggies, under the management of Ron Atkinson, lost 2-0 at Carl Zeiss Jena.

First round, first leg

Aberdeen 1 (Harper), Eintracht Frankfurt 1 (Cha)
Arhus 1 (Oben), Stal Mielec 1 (Karas)
Aris Salonika 3 (Kouris, Pallas pen, Zintros), Benfica 1 (Reinaldo)
Atletico Madrid 1 (Cano), Dynamo Dresden 2 (Hafner, Weber)
Bohemians Prague 0, Bayern Munich 2 (Kraus, Rummenigge)
Borussia Moenchengladbach 3 (Lienen, Nickel pen, Kulik), Viking 0
Carl Zeiss Jena 2 (Schnuphase, Lindemann), West Bromwich Albion 0
Dundee United 0, Anderlecht 0
Dynamo Bucharest 3 (Multescu, Georgescu, Vrinceanu), Alki Larnaca 0
Dynamo Kiev 2 (Bessanov, Demianenko), CSKA Sofia 1 (Metodiev)
FC Zurich 1 (Zwickker), Kaiserslautern 3 (Neues pen, Bongartz, Wolf)
Feyenoord 1 (Notten), Everton 0
Galatasaray 0, Red Star Belgrade 0
Glenavon 0, Standard Liege 1 (Edstroem)
Inter Milan 3 (Muraro, Baresi, Marini), San Sebastian 0
Kalmar 2 (Sunesson, Sandberg), Keflavik 1 (Margeirsson)
Kuopio 1 (Pirinen), Malmo 2 (Andersson, Prytz pen)
Lokomotive Sofia 3 (Dangov, Velichkov, Sokolov), Ferencvaros 0
Napoli 2 (Damian pen, Agostmelli), Olympiakis 0
Ordu 2 (Cihan, Anf), Banik Ostrava 0
Perugia 1 (Vujadinovic og), Dynamo Zagreb 0
Progress Neidercorn 0, Grasshoppers 2 (Hermann, Egli)
Rapid Vienna 0, Miskolc 1 (Fuko)
Shakhtjor Donetsk 2 (Sokolovski 2), Monaco 1 (Petit)
SK Vienna 0, Universitatea Craiova 0
Skied Oslo 1 (Rein), Ipswich Town 3 (Mills, Turner, Mariner)
Sporting Gijon 0, PSV Eindhoven 0
Sporting Lisbon 2 (Fernandos 2), Bohemians 0
Stuttgart 1 (Danova og), Torino 0
Valetta 0, Leeds United 4 (Graham 3, Hart)
Widzew Lodz 2 (Boniek, Kowenicki), St Etienne (Platini)
Zbrojovka Brno 6 (Janecka 2, Jarusek 2, Mazura, Kroupa), Esbjerg 0

Mediterranean cruise

Plain sailing on United's Euro return

KING ARTHUR: Arthur Graham, hits the white sand-based pitch as he nets one of his goals in Gzira.

UNITED'S re-introduction to European football was a gentle affair – a 4-0 stroll against Maltese minnows Valetta.

Of the United starting line-up only Paul Madeley and Eddie Gray were survivors of the Paris disaster.

Madeley was now exclusively a central defender and his partnership with Paul Hart was one of the main reasons United had fought their way back into Europe.

David Harvey, who also had considerable European experience, was in goal while full-backs Kevin Hird and Peter Hampton, completed the back-line.

Midfield was patrolled by diminutive Welsh international Brian Flynn and Trevor Cherry with Eddie Gray and fellow Scot Arthur Graham on the flanks while powerful Ray Hankin teamed up in attack at the National Stadium in Gzira with new signing Alan Curtis.

Ordinarily it was a low-key fixture which Leeds expected to win but given it was their return to Europe the match attracted plenty of attention.

Jimmy Adamson banned his players from sunbathing because the heat was so intense.

But it was not just the sauna heat of the Mediterranean sun which United had to contend with. Most of the players had never come across such a pitch as the one they encountered in Malta.

UEFA Cup
First round, first leg
(at National Stadium, Gzira)
Wednesday, September 19, 1979

Valetta	0
Leeds United	4

Valetta: Frank Grima, Raymond Gauci, Emanuel Farrugia, Joe Addilla, Charles Spitieri, Dennis Fenech, Vincent Magro, Leonard Farrugia, Charles Agius, Emanual Seychell (Paul Curmi 81), Cario Seychell
Manager: John Calleja

Leeds United: David Harvey, Kevin Hird, Peter Hampton, Brian Flynn, Paul Hart, Paul Madeley, Eddie Gray, Trevor Cherry, Ray Hankin, Alan Curtis, Arthur Graham (Carl Harris 78)
Goals: Graham 12, 46, 52, Hart 33
Manager: Jimmy Adamson

Referee: Rudolf Renggli (Switzerland) **Att:** 18,000

There was hardly a blade of grass to be seen. It was made of layers of cinder with sawdust and sand on top while sea water was sprinkled on it before kick off to make it a bit softer. The glare from the pitch's near-white surface was intense.

The locals also tried to make life as difficult as possible by exploding fire-crackers behind the seven-foot fencing surrounding the pitch.

How United would have prayed for the heavy rain which fell on the nearby-town of Mosta on the same day – but instead had to sweat it out in the blazing sun.

Prospects of a major upset melted after 12 minutes when Gray swung in a corner which was headed on by Hart for Graham to sweep the ball home.

Gray struck a post with a 25-yard shot midway through the half but United eased towards the interval with a second goal, Hart heading in Hird's cross from the right from six yards.

The third goal came straight after half-time when Leeds swept down the middle and Curtis teed up Graham who clipped home a 20-yard shot.

The same combination made it 4-0 when Curtis made ground down the right and centred for Graham to lob in his hat-trick goal to seal United's 50th victory in Europe.

With United in complete control Graham went off with blisters on his feet after pounding round the rock-hard pitch. But it was the part-timers of Valletta who had been run off their feet.

After seeing Valetta crash to their heaviest home defeat in seven years of European competition, their coach John Calleja, who had once spent 10 months on a physical education course at Carnegie College in Leeds, said of United's performance, "It was one of the best displays I've seen by any foreign side here. It was so complete."

RAPID FIRE: Just 20 seconds have gone and Gary Hamson jumps in the air to get out of the way of Alan Curtis' shot which put United ahead.

Fans go AWOL

...and miss out as hot shot Curtis nets in 20 seconds

UNITED'S European return at Elland Road was given a miss by thousands of fans.

Only 13,682 bothered to watch the second leg mis-match against Valetta – but United had closed down part of the ground.

Once again Leeds had been blighted by crowd trouble with a hail of missiles being thrown on the pitch at the home game against Manchester City four days earlier.

The United board chose to close half of the South Stand preventing access to 2,745 seats in the section where the troubled had flared.

Leeds had not made a good start to the season with supporters unhappy with the standard of football and opted to vote with their feet in a European tie which had virtually been decided. Any doubt about the issue was settled after just 20 seconds.

From United's first attack, Brian Flynn sent Arthur Graham scampering down the right and his cross was slid into the net by Alan Curtis. It was United's fastest-ever European goal, beating Mike O'Grady's effort against Lyn Oslo in 1969 by 15 seconds.

After that it was one-way traffic

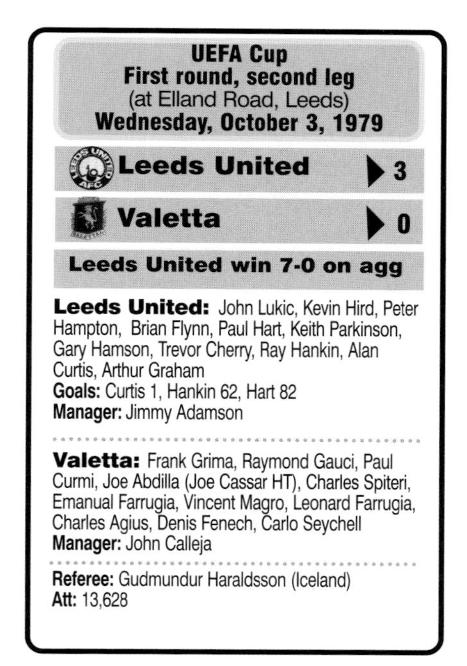

UEFA Cup
First round, second leg
(at Elland Road, Leeds)
Wednesday, October 3, 1979

Leeds United	**3**
Valetta	**0**

Leeds United win 7-0 on agg

Leeds United: John Lukic, Kevin Hird, Peter Hampton, Brian Flynn, Paul Hart, Keith Parkinson, Gary Hamson, Trevor Cherry, Ray Hankin, Alan Curtis, Arthur Graham
Goals: Curtis 1, Hankin 62, Hart 82
Manager: Jimmy Adamson

Valetta: Frank Grima, Raymond Gauci, Paul Curmi, Joe Abdilla (Joe Cassar HT), Charles Spiteri, Emanual Farrugia, Vincent Magro, Leonard Farrugia, Charles Agius, Denis Fenech, Carlo Seychell
Manager: John Calleja

Referee: Gudmundur Haraldsson (Iceland)
Att: 13,628

towards the Maltese goal in which high-flying airline courier Frank Grima gave an inspired display.

Even playing at half-pace Leeds carved open the Valetta defence time and time again but the 23-year-old 'keeper tipped a stream of headers over the bar and shots round his posts with Curtis being the main sufferer.

He even pushed a 26th minute penalty from Kevin Hird over the bar after Peter Hampton had been brought down by Vincent Magro.

United's frustration continued for over an hour until Ray Hankin, who announced he wanted to leave the club, headed in from just three yards.

Paul Hart nodded in Flynn's free-kick eight minutes from the end to wrap up a tame game which had seen Gary Hamson, a £140,000 signing from Sheffield United make his debut. It had certainly been a quiet first outing for United's other debutant, teenage goalkeeper John Lukic, who hardly got a touch of the ball.

With Hankin seemingly on his way out, manager Jimmy Adamson had signed muscular striker Wayne Entwistle from his old club, Sunderland, on the day of the Valetta game.

Cocker's death overshadows United victory

JUST 24 hours after United's win over Valetta at Elland Road, former trainer Les Cocker collapsed and died when overseeing a Doncaster Rovers' training session. He was aged 55.

He was assistant manager at Belle Vue to Billy Bremner, having linked up with the old Leeds skipper after Don Revie sensationally quit the England job to take a lucrative post with the United Arab Emirates in the Middle East.

Les Cocker.

Revie was bitterly criticised by the Football Association, who suspended him until he was willing to face a charge of bringing the game in to disrepute.

Revie later won a High Court case against the FA and was granted an injunction quashing the ban.

United's two-leg victory over Valetta could not have been much easier and provided some welcome relief after a torrid start to the season.

However, it was not a great night for two other English clubs in the UEFA Cup.

Alistair Brown was sent off at half-time at The Hawthorns after a scuffle with a Carl Zeiss Jena player. The Baggies, already 2-0 down from the first leg, went out 4-1 on aggregate.

Everton lost 1-0 in each leg to Feyenoord, but Ipswich demolished amateurs Skied Oslo 7-0 at Portman Road.

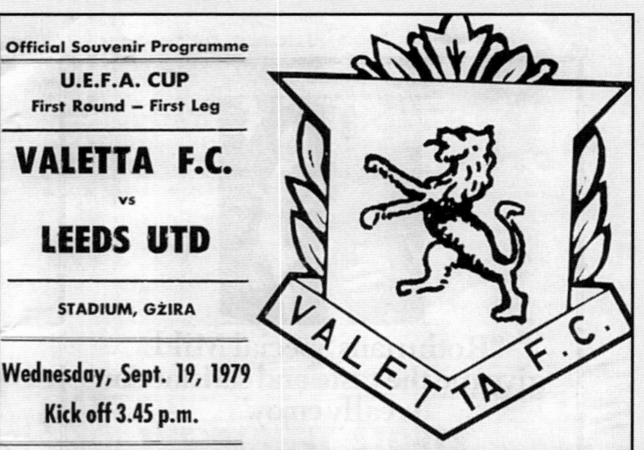

LEEDS UNITED (England), playing staff for season 1978/79 (Back Row): Paul Madeley, John Hawley, Paul Hart, David Stewart, Ray Hankin, David Harvey, Keith Parkinson, Tony Currie, Byron Stevenson; (Front Row): Frank Gray, Eddie Gray, Peter Lorimer, Brian Flyn, Trevor Cherry, Arthur Graham, Carl Harris, Peter Hampton.

First round, second leg

Alki Larnaca 0, Dynamo Bucharest 9 (Georgescu 3 – 1 pen, Vrinceanu 2, Augustin, Talanar, Multescu, Moldovan)
Dynamo Bucharest win 12 -0 on agg

Anderlecht 1 (Nielsen), Dundee United 1 (Kopel)
1-1 on agg. Dundee United win on away goals

Banik Ostrava 6 (Knapp, Vojacek, Nemec, Lica 2, Danek). Ordu 0
Banik Ostrava win 6-2 on agg

Bayern Munich 2 (Rummenigge, Breitner pen), Bohemians Prague 2 (Ondra, Prokea)
Bayern Munich win 4-2 on agg

Benfica 2 (Reinaldo, Jorge Gomes), Aris Salonika 1(Semertzidis)
Aris Salonika win 4-3 on agg

Bohemians 0, Sporting Lisbon 0
Sporting Lisbon win 2-0 on agg

Viking 1 (Bjornsen), Borussia Moenchengladbach 1 (Kulik)
Borussia Moenchengladbach win 4-1 on agg

CSKA Sofia 1 (Metodiev), Dynamo Kiev 1 (Burjak)
Dynamo Kiev win 3-2 on agg

Dynamo Dresden 3 (Riedel, Ruiz og, Weber), Atletico Madrid 0
Dynamo Dresden win 5-1 on agg

Dynamo Zagreb 0, Perugia 0
Perugia win 1-0 on agg

Eintracht Frankfurt 1 (Holzenbein), Aberdeen 0
Eintracht Frankfurt win 2-1 on agg

Esjberg 1 (Bach), Zbrojovka Brno 1 (Jarusek)
Zbrojovka Brno win 7-1 on agg

Everton 0, Feyenoord 1 (Budding)
Feyenoord win 2-0 on agg

Ferencvaros 2 (Pusztal, Pogany og), Lokomotiv Leipzig 0
Lokomotiv Leipzig win 3-2 on agg

Grasshoppers 4 (Ponte, Pfister, Egli, Hermann), Progres Niedercorn 0
Grasshoppers win 6-0 on agg

Ipswich Town 7 (Wark, Muhren 2, Thijssen, Mariner, McCall 2), Skied Oslo 0
Ipswich Town win 10-1 on agg

Kaiserslautern 5 (Melzer 2, Kaminke, Wendt, Geye), FC Zurich 1 (Zappa)
Kaiserslautern win 8-2 on agg

Keflavik 1 (Andreasson og), Kalmar 0
2-2 on agg. Keflavik win on away goals

Leeds United 3 (Curtis, Hankin, Hart), Valetta 0
Leeds United win 7-0 on agg

Malmo 2 (Ardvisson 2), Kuopio 0
Malmo win 4-1 on agg

Monaco 2 (Onnis, Dalger), Shakhtar Donetsk 0
Monaco win 3-2 on agg

Miskolc 3 (Szalai, Fekete, Tatar), Rapid Vienna 2 (Keglevits, Sallmayer)
Miskolc win 4-2 on agg

Olympiakos 1 (Karavitis), Napoli 0
Napoli win 2-1 on agg

PSV Eindhoven 1 (van der Kerkhof), Sporting Gijon 0
PSV Eindhoven win 1-0 on agg

Red Star Belgrade 3 (Savic 2, Milovanovic), Galatasaray 1 (Gungor)
Red Star Belgrade win 3-1 on agg

San Sebastian 2 (Satrustegui 2), Inter Milan 0
Inter Milan win 3-2 on agg

Stal Mielec 0, Aarhus 1 (Jensen)
Aahus win 2-1 on agg

Standard Liege 1 (Edstrom), Glenavon 0
Standard Liege win 2-0 on agg

St Etienne 3 (Rep 3), Widzew Lodz 0
St Etienne win 4-2 on agg

Torino 2 (Sala, Graziani), VfB Stuttgart 1 (Ohlicher) aet
2-2 on agg. VfB Stuttgart win on away goals

Universitatea Craiova 3 (Camataru 2, Geolgau), SK Weiner 1 (Drabits)
Universitatea Craiova win 3-1 on agg

West Bromwich Albion 1 (Wile), Carl Zeiss Jena 2 (Raab 2 – 1 pen)
Carl Zeiss Jena win 4-1 on agg

Students hand out lesson

RUMBLINGS of discontent continued at Elland Road and the uneasy mood was not helped by a comprehensive 2-0 defeat in Romania by Universitatea Craiova.

Relatively unknown outside their own country, Craiova's team were all students at the town's university but were far from an amateur set-up. They had won the Romanian Cup in 1977 and 1978 and had collected the League Championship in 1974.

The current batch boasted six Romanian internationals so their progress was of special interest to England who had been paired with them, Hungary and Norway in the qualifying group of the 1982 World Cup.

The supremely fit students certainly showed their class in a blistering opening in which they threatened to sweep United away with their lightning raids engineered by midfielder Illie Balaci.

United should have been behind after just four minutes when Paul Hart miskicked in defence but Aurel Beldaneau missed an open goal.

The pressure was intense with eight corners coming in the opening 12 minutes and 18-year-old goalkeeper John Lukic finally cracked when he failed to gather at the near post and Balaci thumped home a header.

Struggling United were chasing shadows and when right winger Zoltan Crisan motored past Byron Stevenson and Eddie Gray he was blocked by a desperate Ray Hankin. Young Lukic wasn't tested from the resulting penalty as Beldeanu lifted his kick over the bar with 29 minutes left.

Under the circumstances United would have settled for a one goal deficit and 18 minutes from the end Adamson confirmed that thinking by taking off winger Carl Harris and sending on Gary Hamson to shore up midfield.

Just when hard-pressed Leeds looked as though they were going to escape with a narrow defeat, key man Balaci's diamond of a 35-yard pass found Rodion Camataru whose flick was powered home by substitute Mirea Irimescu with seven minutes remaining.

There was still time for Leeds to gain a flicker of hope from the game when defender Nicholae Tilhoi fouled Brian Flynn in the dying stages and was sent off for a second bookable offence meaning he would miss the return leg.

UEFA Cup
Second round, first leg
(at Central Stadium, Craiova)
Wednesday, October 24, 1979

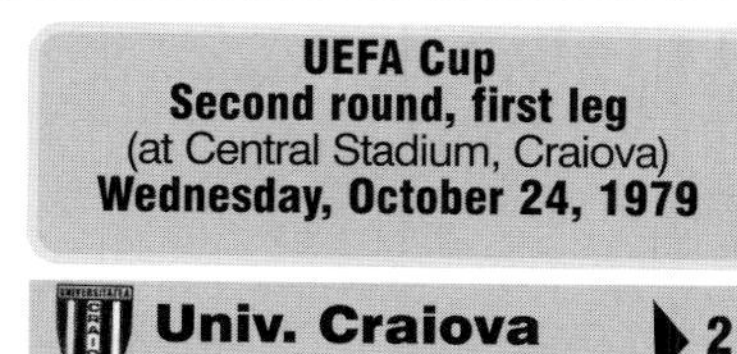

Univ. Craiova 2

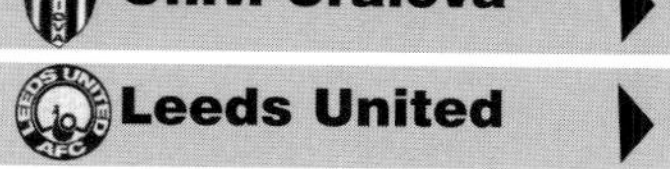

Leeds United 0

Universitatea Craiova: Gabriel Boldici, Nicolae Negrila, Nicolae Tilihoi, Nicolae Ungureanu, Ion Geolgau (Constantin Donose 77), Costica Stefanescu, Zoltan Crisan, Illie Balacai, Rodion Camataru, Aurel Beldeanu, Sorin Cirtu (Mircea Irimescu 68)
Goals: Balaci 12, Irimsescu 83
Manager: Valentin Staenscu

Leeds United: John Lukic, Kevin Hird, Byron Stevenson, Brian Flynn, Paul Hart, Paul Madeley, Eddie Gray, Trevor Cherry, Ray Hankin, Alan Curtis, Carl Harris (Gary Hamson 70)
Manager: Jimmy Adamson

Referee: Gianfranco Menegali (Italy) **Att:** 25,000

Struggling British clubs fail to register

BRITAIN'S three remaining clubs in the UEFA Cup failed to score a goal between then in the third round.

As United crashed in Romania, Ipswich drew 0-0 with Grasshoppers in Zurich and Dundee United were surprisingly beaten 1-0 at home by unfancied Czech side Miskolc.

Second round, first leg

Aarhus 1 (Sander), Bayern Munich 2 (Rummenigge 2)
Aris Salonika 1 (Semertzidis), Perugia 1 (Rossi)
Banik Ostrava 1 (Nemec), Dynamo Kiev 0
Borussia Moenchengladbach 1 (Hannes), Inter Milan 1 (Altobelli)
Dundee United 0, Miskolc 1 (Fekete)
Dynamo Bucharest 2 (Multescu pen, Augustin), Eintracht Frankfurt 0
Dynamo Dresden 1 (Weber pen), VfB Stuttgart 1 (Forster)
Feyenoord 4 (Petursson 3 – 1 pen, van Demsen), Malmo 0
Grasshoppers 0, Ipswich Town 0
Lokomotiv Sofia 4 (Mikhailov 4 – 1 pen), Monaco 2 (Onnis 2 – 1 pen)
PSV Eindhoven 2 (Van Der Kerkof, Koster), St Etienne 0
Red Star Belgrade 3 (Savic pen, Muslin, Sestic), Carl Zeiss Jena 2 (Rabb 2 – 1 pen)
Sporting Lisbon 1 (Pernandes), Kaiserslautern 1 (Bongartz)
Standard Liege 2 (Riedl, Sigurdvinsson pen), Napoli 1 (Capone)
Universitatea Craiova 2 (Balaci, Irimoscu), Leeds United 0
Zbrojovka Brno 3 (Kolasek 2, Janecka), Keflavik 1 (Georgsson)

Another demo as dispirited United crash out

Storm clouds gathering

UNDER FIRE: United boss Jimmy Adamson.

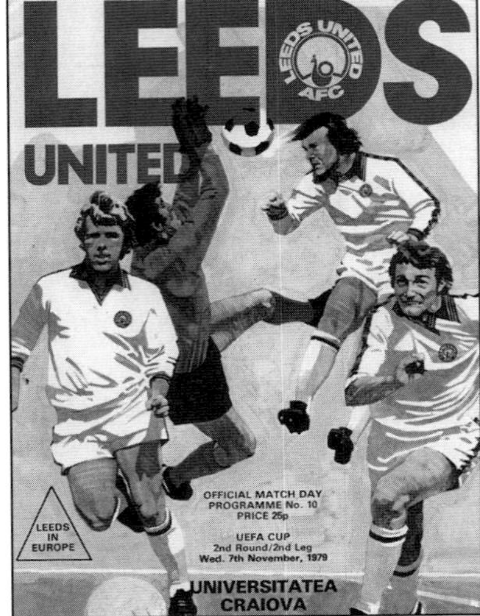

UEFA Cup
Second round, second leg
(at Elland Road, Leeds)
Wednesday, November 7, 1979

Leeds United	**0**
Univ. Craiova	**2**

Universitatea Craiova win 4-0 on agg

Leeds United: John Lukic, Trevor Cherry, Byron Stvenson, Brian Flynn, Paul Hart, Paul Madeley, Eddie Gray, Keith Parkinson (Carl Harris 62), Ray Hankin, Alan Curtis, Arthur Graham
Manager: Jimmy Adamson

Universitatea Craiova: Gabriel Boldici, Nicolae Negrila, Adrian Bumbescu, Nicolae Ungureanu, Aurel Ticleanu (Constantin Donose 89), Costica Stefanescu, Ion Geolgau (Petre Purima 89), Illie Balaci, Rodion Camataru, Aurel Beldeanu, Sorin Cirtu
Goals: Cirtu 68, Beldeanu 85
Manager: Valentin Stanesc

Referee: Antonin Wencl (Czechoslovakia)
Att: 14,438

TENSION continued to mount as Jimmy Adamson's team failed to convince his increasingly critical fans.

United's form going into the return leg against Craiova could not have been much worse.

The previous Saturday they crashed 3-1 at home to Bristol City in front of a mere 17,376 – the lowest weekend United gate since the club's old Second Division days.

After that debacle there was a 1,000 strong demonstration by angry fans demanding that Adamson should go.

It was hardly the right atmosphere to prepare for a European tie in which Leeds would have to recover from a two-goal first leg deficit.

Not surprisingly, United were found lacking in front of another meagre crowd as the sprightly Romanians repeated their first leg victory to cruise through 4-0 on aggregate.

United need an early goal to give themselves a chance of staging a fightback but they blew the opportunity in the early stages.

Just 30 seconds were on the clock when Welsh international Bryon Stevenson, fed by Arthur Graham, scooted down the left and put in a fine cross, but Paul Hart, who had been pushed into midfield, headed badly wide.

Minutes later Graham, back in the side after missing four games with an ankle injury, was denied by a point-blank save by goalkeeper Gabriel Boldici.

Gradually Craiova adjusted to the pace of the game and started to look dangerous on the break and it needed a great save by John Lukic from Rodion Camataru to keep United in business.

But the longer the game went on the more United's desparation increased while the Romanians' confidence grew.

On 68 minutes United cruelly fell behind as Sorin Cirtu's pot shot seemed to be going wide until it took a wild deflection off Stevenson and lobbed into the opposite corner.

Both Graham, who had proved a bargain £100,000 buy from Aberdeen, and Eddie Gray went close to a United equaliser before the visitors rubber-stamped their place in the third round with a stunning goal by Aurel Beldeanu.

lllie Balaci clipped in a corner from the right deep outside the Leeds box and Beldeau hit an unstoppable 30-yard piledriver past a helpless Lukic.

With just five minutes left many United fans were already making for the exits, some to stage another anti-Adamson demonstration with chants demanding the return of Don Revie. Mounted police were called in to break up the demonstrators who had just witnessed United's third successive home loss.

A defiant Adamson said: "I select the side and dictate the policies of the team. The fans are entitled to have a go. As far as I am concerned it was a disaster as Europe is important."

German domination

ALL British clubs were wiped out of the UEFA Cup after the second round, Ipswich and Dundee United joining Leeds in the ditch of defeat – one of the worst domestic showings in the competition.

In stark contrast, clubs from the Bundeslegia were utterly dominant.

Five German clubs reached the last eight – and they provided all four of the semi-finalists.

A great comeback against Bayern Munich earned Eintracht Frankfurt a place in the final where they beat Borussia Moenchengladbach on away goals.

Trailing 3-2 after the first leg, Fred Schaub scored the only goal in Frankfurt nine minutes from the end – just four minutes after coming on as a substitute.

Sadly Schaub was to died in a car crash some years later at the age of 42.

Second round, second leg

Bayern Munich 3 (Hoeness 2, Breitner), Aarhus 1 (Mikkelsen) *Bayern Munich win 5-2 on agg*

Carl Zeiss Jena 2 (Trocha, Topfer), Red Star Belgrade 3 (Kurbjeweit, Filipovic, Blagojevic) *Crvena Zevedza win 6-4 on agg*

Dynamo Kiev 2 (Demianenko, Khapsalis), Banik Ostrava 0 *Dynamo Kiev win 2-1 on agg*

Eintracht Frankfurt 3 (Cha, Holzenbeim, Nickel), Dynamo Bucharest 0 aet *Eintracht Frankfurt win 3-2 on agg*

Inter Milan 2 (Altobelli 2), Borussia Moenchengladbach 3 (Nickel 2 – 1 pen, Ringels) aet *Borussia Moenchengladbach win 4-3 on agg*

Ipswich Town 1 (Beattie), Grasshoppers 1 (Sulser) *1-1 on agg. Grasshoppers win on away goal*

Kaiserslautern 2 (Geye, Nueues pen), Sporting Lison 0 *Kaiserslautern win 3-1 on agg*

Keflavik 1 (Olafsson), Zbrojovka Brno (Kroupa, Vojacek) *Zbrojovka Brno win 5-1 on agg*

Leeds United 0, Universitatea Craiova 2 (Cirtu, Beldeanu) *Universitatea Craiova win 4-0 on agg*

Malmo 1 (Arvidsson), Feyenoord 1 (Petursson) *Feyenoord win 5-1 on agg*

Miskolc 3 (Borostyan, Tatar 2 – 1 pen), Dundee United 1 (Kopel) *Miskolc win 4-1 on agg*

Monaco 2 (Christophe, Onnis), Lokomotiv Sofia 1 (Mikhailov) *Lokomotiv Sofia win 5-4 on agg*

Napoli 1 (Damiam), Standard Liege 1 (Riedl) *Standard Liege win 3-2 on agg*

Perugia 0, Aris Salonika 3 (Kouis, Semertzidis, Zindros) *Aris Salonika win 4-1 on agg*

St Etienne 6 (Lanos, Santini, Platini 2, Roassey, Rep pen), PSV Eindhoven 0 *St Etienne win 6-2 on agg*

VfB Stuttgart 0, Dynammo Dresden 0 *1-1 on agg. VfB Stuttart win on away goal*

Third round, first leg

Bayern Munich 2 (Rummenigge, Janzon), Red Star Belgrade 0

Borussia Moenchengladbach 2 (Nickel 2), Universitatea Craiova 0

Eintracht Frankfurt 4 (Cha, Nickel, Muller, Lottermann), Feyenoord 1 (Stafleu)

Grasshoppers 0, VfB Stuttgart 2 (Klotz, Hadewicz)

Lokomotiv Sofia 1 (Mikhailov), Dynamo Kiev 0

Miskolc 0, Kaiserslautern 2 (Weildt, Bongartz)

St Etienne 4 (Platini, Larios, Lopez, Rousseu), Aris Salonika 1 (Semertzidis)

Standard Liege 1 (Voordeckers), Zbrojovka 2 (Svoboda, Doeak)

Third round, second leg

Aris Salonika 3 (Zindros, Pallas pen, Janvion og), Monaco 3 (Larios, Zimako, Rep) *St Etienne win 7-4 on agg*

Dynamo Kiev 2 (Blokin, Khapsalis), Lokomotiv Sofia 1 (Spasov) *2-2 on agg. Lokomotiv Sofia win on away goals*

Feyenoord 1 (Peters), Eintracht Frankfurt 0 *Eintracht Frankfurt win 4-2 on agg*

Kaiserslautern 6 (Neues pen, Meltzer, Brummer, Kanuke, Bongartz, Stabel pen), Miskolc 1 (Borostyan) *Kaiserslautern win 8-1 on agg*

Red Star Belgrade 3 (Savic, Petrovic, Repcic), Bayern Munich 2 (Hoeness 2) *Bayern Munich win 4-3 on agg*

Universitatea Craiova 1 (Imescu), Borussia Moenchengladbach 0 *Borussia Moenchengladbach win 2-1 on agg*

VfB Stuttgart 3 (H Muller, Martin, Kelsch), Grasshoppers 0 *VfB Stuttgart win 5-0 on agg*

Zbrojovka Brno 3 (Jaruaek, Kroupa 2), Standard Liege 2 (Edstrom, Dematos) *Zbrojovka Brno win 5-3 on agg*

Quarter-final, first leg

Eintracht Frankfurt 4 (Nachtwih, Lorant pen, Nickel, Karger), Zbrojovka 1 (Horny)

Kaiserslautern 1 (Brummer), Bayern Munich 0

St Etienne 1 (Platini pen), Borussia Moenchengladbach 4 (Nielsen 2, Nickel, Lienen)

VfB Stuttgart 3 (Muller, Volkert 2 – 1 pen), Lokomotiv Sofia 1 (Kolev)

Quarter-final, second leg

Bayern Munich 4 (Hoeness 2, Janzon, Breitner pen), Kaiserslautern 1 (Wendt) *Bayern Munich win 4-2 on agg*

Borussia Moenchengladbach 2 (Thychosen, Hannes), St Etienne 0 *Borussia Moenchengladbach win 6-1 on agg*

Lokomotiv Sofia 0, VfB Stuttgart 1 (Ohlicher) *VfB Stuttgart win 4-2 on agg*

Zbrojovka Brno 3 (Horny, Kotasek, Kopenec), Eintracht Frankfurt 2 (Karger, Neuberger) *Eintracht Frankfurt win 6-4 on agg*

Semi-final, first leg

Bayern Munich 2 (Hoeness, Breitner pen), Eintracht Frankfurt 0

VfB Stuttgart 2 (Olicher, Volkert pen), Borussia Moenchengladbach 1 (Nickel)

Semi-final, second leg

Borussia Moenchengladbach 2 (Matthause, Schafer), VfB Stuttgart 0 *Borussia Moenchengladbach win 3-2 on agg*

Eintract Frankfurt 5 (Pezzey 2, Karger 2, Lorant pen), Bayern Munich 1 (Dremmler) aet *Eintracht Frankfurt win 5-3 on agg*

Final, first leg

(Bokelberg Stadium, Moenchengladbach)
May 7, 1980
Borussia Moenchengladbach 3,
Eintracht Frankfurt 2

Borussia Moenchengladbach: Kneib, Schafer, Hannes, Schaffer, Ringels, Matthaus, Nielsen (Thychosen 86), Kulik, Del'Haye (Bodaker 72), Nickel, Lienen
Goals: Kulik 45, Matthaus 77, Kulik 88
Manager: Jupp Heynckes
Eintracht Frankfurt: Pahl, Neuberger, Pezzey, Korbel, Ermanntraut, Lorant, Holzenbein (Nachtweih 79), Nickel, Borchers, Karger (Trapp 81), Cha
Goals: Karger 37, Holzenbein 71
Manager: Friedel Rausch
Referee: Emilio Carlos Guruceta Muro (Spain)
Attendance: 25,000

Final, second leg

(Wald Stadium, Frankfurt)
May 21, 1980
Eintracht Frankfurt 1
Borussia Moenchengladbach 0
3-3 on aggregate
Eintracht Frankfurt win on away goals.

Eintracht Frankfurt: Pahl, Neuberger, Pezzey, Korbel, Ermanntraut, Lorant, Holzenbein, Nickel, Borchers, Nachtweih (Schaub 77), Cha
Goal: Schaub 81
Manager: Friedel Rausch
Borussia Moenchengladbach: Kneib, Schafer, Hannes, Fleer, Ringels, Bodeker, Matthaus (Thychosen 86), Kulik, Nielsen (Del'Haye 68), Nickel, Lienen
Manager: Jupp Heynckes
Referee: Alexis Ponnet (Belgium)
Attendance: 59,000

Leading scorers: 7 Hoeness (Bayern Munich), Nickel (Borussia Moenchengladbach), 6 – Mikhailov (Lokomotiv Sofia), 5 – Platini (St Etienne), Rep (St Etienne)

Sgt Wilko's barmy army

JIMMY Adamson hung on until October 1980 before bowing to the inevitable and was replaced by old Leeds hero Allan Clarke, who had done well in his first managerial appointment at Barnsley.

But Clarke could not arrest United's decline and they plunged into the Second Division after 18 years in the top flight.

He paid the price with his job and Eddie Gray was handed the task of rebuilding the squad at the club who reportedly £1.5 million in debt.

Although he nurtured some talented young players player-manager Gray could not mould United into promotion contenders and was sacked in October 1985.

As one legend from the Revie era departed another, Billy Bremner, returned.

The Doncaster Rovers boss did take United to the play-offs and an FA Cup semi-final but, the following season was one of anti-climax and despite an upsurge in attendances, Bremner was axed.

United were second to bottom of the Second Division when Howard Wilkinson was appointed manager in October 1988.

He recognised the vast potential at Elland Road and needed little persuading to move from First Division Sheffield Wednesday to sign a four-year deal.

Backed by major investment by the Leeds board, he rapidly assembled a new-look team under the leadership of former Scotland star Gordon Strachan and United won the Second Division title in 1990.

The big-spending gamble had paid off and United took the First Division by surprise in their first season back by finishing fourth – just outside a European slot.

Champions for the third time

HOWARD Wilkinson's squad, bolstered by more signings simply got better in 1991/92.

They out-lasted bitter rivals Manchester United in the title run-in to take the League Championship – something no Leeds fan would have felt possible just three years earlier.

A 3-2 victory at Sheffield United in the penultimate game of the season, coupled with a Manchester United defeat at Liverpool saw Wilko's men crowned champions for the third time in the club's proud history.

With the honour came entry to the highly lucrative European Cup.

Division One 1991/92

	P	W	D	L	F	A	Pts
LEEDS UNITED	42	22	16	4	74	37	82
Manchester United	42	21	15	6	63	33	78
Sheffield Wed	42	21	12	9	62	49	75
Arsenal	42	20	15	8	81	46	72
Manchester City	42	20	10	12	54	42	70
Liverpool	42	16	16	10	47	40	64
Aston Villa	42	17	9	22	59	44	60
Nottingham Forest	42	16	11	15	60	58	59
Sheffield United	42	16	9	17	65	63	57
Crystal Palace	42	14	15	13	53	61	57
Queens Park Rgrs	42	12	18	12	48	47	54
Everton	42	13	14	15	52	51	53
Wimbledon	42	13	14	15	53	53	53
Chelsea	42	13	14	15	50	60	53
Tottenham Hotspur	42	15	7	20	58	63	52
Southampton	42	14	10	18	50	68	52
Oldham Athletic	42	14	9	19	63	68	51
Norwich City	42	11	12	19	47	63	45
Coventry City	42	11	11	20	35	44	44
Luton Town	42	10	12	20	38	71	42
Notts County	42	10	10	22	40	62	40
West Ham United	42	9	11	22	37	59	38

WILKINSON'S WONDERS: The 1991/92 squad celebrate their Championship success. Back row, from left to right: Dylan Kerr, Mick Hennigan (assistant manager), Jon Newsome, Lee Chapman, Sean Hardy (kit man), Chris Fairclough, John Lukic, Mel Sterland, Carl Shutt, Eric Cantona, John McClelland, Alan Sutton (physio), Peter Haddock. Front row: Howard Wilkinson (manager), Rod Wallace, Tony Dorigo, Gordon Strachan, David Batty, Gary Speed, Gary McAllister, Steve Hodge.

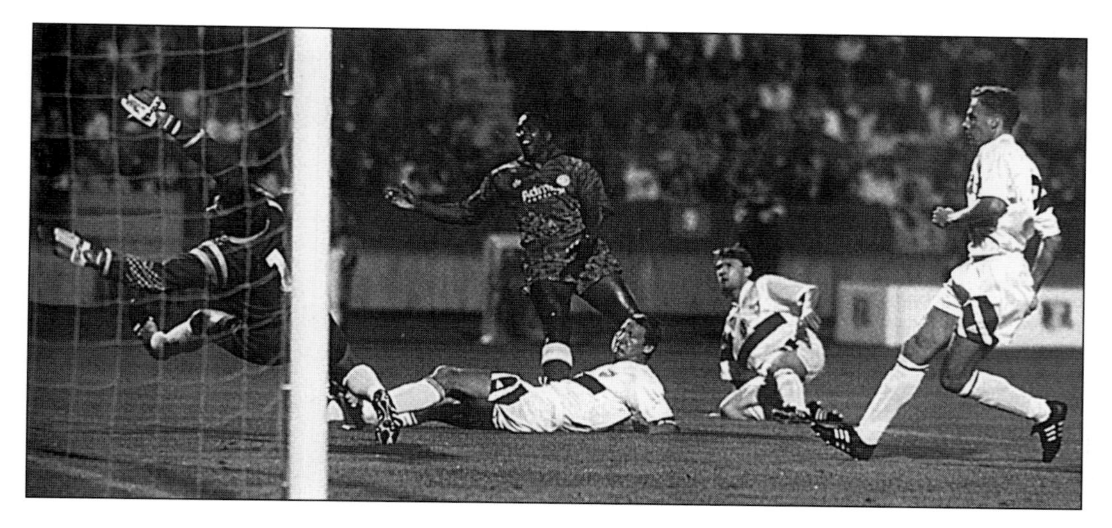

ROCKY THWARTED: United's new £2m signing from Arsenal David Rocastle goes close to breaking the deadlock in Stuttgart.

A pain in the Necker

European Cup
First round, first leg
(at Neckar Stadium, Stuttgart)
Wednesday, September 16, 1992

VfB Stuttgart	**3**
Leeds United	**0**

VfB Stuttgart: Ike Immel, Uwe Schneider, Michael Frontzeck, Slobodan Dubajic, Thomas Struntz (Gunther Schafer 89), Guido Buchwald, Andreas Buck, Eyjolfur Sverrisson, Fritz Walter (Adrian Knup 83), Mauritzio Gaudino, Ludwig Kogel
Goals: Walter 62, 68, Buck 82
Manager: Christophe Daum

Leeds United: John Lukic, David Rocastle (Steve Hodge HT), Tony Dorigo, David Batty, Chris Fairclough, Chris Whyte, Eric Cantona (Carl Shutt 63), Gordon Strachan, Lee Chapman, Gary McAllister, Gary Speed
Manager: Howard Wilkinson

Referee: Rune Larsson (Sweden) **Att:** 38,000

EUROPEAN CUP football returned to Leeds for the first time in 17 years but few could have imagined such a dramatic re-introduction.

Having failed to start in any of United's opening eight competitive games of the 1992/93 season, new £2 million signing David Rocastle did begin United's first round game in Germany at Stuttgart.

The former Arsenal and England midfielder had been the big purchase of the summer but didn't feature in the FA Charity Shield side which beat Liverpool 4-3 at Wembley when Eric Cantona netted a hat-trick.

However, he did figure in the high-profile Makita Tournament at Elland Road which, ironically paired United with Stuttgart, with whom they had been drawn against in Europe, in the opening match.

United won 2-1 with Rocastle scoring but lost in the Makita final to Italian side Sampdoria.

When United met the Germans again in the European Cup, Wilkinson was adamant that the earlier meeting at Elland Road was irrelevent. He opted for Rocastle's experience in the Neckar Stadium but withdrew him at half-time with the score goalless and replaced him with another former England international, Steve Hodge.

United had gone closest to breaking the deadlock in a low-key first 45 minutes when Cantona's chip stretched Ike Immel and then the Frenchman's header hit an upright.

Apart from an away goal, everything was going according to plan up to the hour mark with neither side able to create many chances but United's team, many of whom had no previous European experience, seemed to lose concentration and the Germans took full advantage.

The nature of the German opener was cruel on United. Cantona, in pulling a hamstring, miscued a pass to give Stuttgart possession. There still seemed little danger until Chris Whyte slipped as he attempted to block Ludwig Kogel's cross and Fritz Walter, the Bundesliga's leading scorer was left free to impudently lob the ball past the exposed John Lukic, who had been enjoying good form since his return to Elland Road from Arsenal where he had won a stack of honours.

Striker Walter snatched another four minutes later as United failed to properly clear a corner. Lukic was able to parry Eyloful Sverrisson's drive but Walter snapped in the rebound.

When Andreas Buck added the third by cutting in from the flank where David Batty was operating at right back and sent a fine diagonal shot past Lukic eight minutes from time it seemed as though United were as good as out.

Disappointed Leeds boss Wilkinson said: "It was an absolutely crazy result. We were comfortable for 60 minutes."

Stuttgart stutter

Heroic United close to comeback glory

EVEN United's ardent fans gave their favourites little hope of overturning the 3-0 deficit they brought back from Germany.

UEFA told United to cut their capacity by 6,000 for the return leg because of security reasons, but only 20,000-plus fans turned up at Elland Road for the live televised return. Despite the lack of numbers inside the stadium United produced a memorable comeback in one of the famous old ground's great European nights.

The task facing United was enormous. They would have to become the first British side in the competition's 37-year history to overturn a three-goal deficit if they were to progress into the second round.

Howard Wilkinson went for broke with an attacking line-up which included progressive midfielder Scott Sellars, in his second spell at the club, at right back. Needing an early goal, United duly got it with Gary Speed's left-foot volley as Wilkinson's attacking line-up flooded forward in waves and came close to a second goal several times.

They threw caution to the wind but were caught out when Andreas Buck equalised on the night after a rare German raid down the right after 34 minutes. It meant that United would have to score five times if they were going to topple their German visitors.

But within four minutes of Buck's goal Gary McAllister made it 2-1 with a penalty and Eric Cantona cranked up the pressure with United's third on 66 minutes.

Roared on by the crowd, Leeds were playing inspired high-octane football and the Germans simply could not cope. Lee Chapman headed in with 10 minutes left to make it 4-1 on the night and 4-4 overall. There was no let-up as Leeds piled on the pressure, knowing another goal would put them through. Creaking Stuttgart sent on Swiss international Adrian Knup and Jovo Simakic in the dying minutes for

European Champions Cup
First round, second leg
(at Elland Road, Leeds)
Wednesday, September 30, 1992

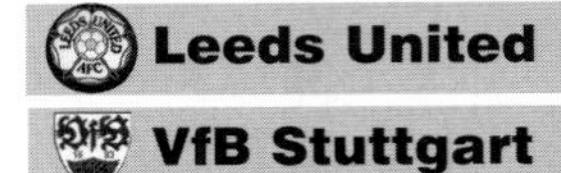

Leeds United 4
VfB Stuttgart 1

4-4 on agg.
Match awarded 3-0 to Leeds United as Stuttgart fielded an ineligible player

Leeds United: John Lukic, Scott Sellars, Tony Dorigo, David Batty, Chris Fairclough, Chris Whyte, Gordon Strachan, Eric Cantona, Lee Chapman, Gary McAllister, Gary Speed
Goals: Speed 18, McAllister 38 pen, Cantona 66, Chapman 80
Manager: Howard Wilkinson

VfB Stuttgart: Ike Immel, Gunther Schafer, Michael Frontzeck, Slobodan Dubajic, Thomas Strunz, Guido Buchwald, Andreas Buck, Eyjolfur Sverrisson, Fritz Walter (Adrian Knup 80), Mauritzio Gaudino (Jovica Simanic 83), Ludwig Kogel
Goal: Buck 33
Manager: Christophe Daum

Referee: Kim Milton Nielsen (Denmark)
Att: 20,457

Impressive Rangers slice open Danish

SCOTTISH champions Rangers put on an assured display in both legs against Lyngby, the Danish side.

Goals by English forward Mark Hateley, son of Liverpool's Tony Hateley, and Pieter Huistra gave them a 2-0 lead to take away where they won 1-0 with an Ian Durrant goal.

A key figure in those double shut-outs was left-back David Robertson, who went on to join Leeds in summer 1997. Hateley, too was to have a brief spell on loan at Elland Road.

The first round pitched most of the big boys against smaller clubs, with Barcelona struggling to dispose of Norway's Viking Stavanger by a single goal.

Preliminary round, first leg

Klakisvar 1 (Danielsen), Skoto Riga 3 (Astafiev 2, Semenov)
Olympija Ljubljana 3 (Ubavic, Topic, Vrabec), Norma Tallin 0
Shelbourne 0, Tavria Simferopol 0
Valetta 1 (Zerafa), Maccabi Tel Aviv 2 (Cohen, Mimni)

Preliminary round, second leg

Maccabi Tel Aviv 1 (Melika), Valetta 0
Maccabi Tel Aviv win 3-1 on agg
Norma Tallin 0, Olympija Ljubliana 2 (Zulic, Djuramovic)
Olympija Ljubliana win 5-0 on agg
Skonto Riga 3 (Yeliseyev, Semenov, Astafiev), Klakisvar 0
Skonto Riga win 6-1 on agg
Tavria Simferopol 2 (Shevchenko, Skeikhametov), Shelbourne 1 (Dally)
Tavria Simferopol win 2-1 on agg

First round, first leg

AC Milan 4 (Van Basten 2, Albertini, Papin), Olimpija Ljubljana 0
AEK Athens 1 (Alexandris), Apoel Nicosia 1 (Hadjilukas)
Barcelona 1 (Amor), Viking Stavanger 0
FK Austria 3 (Hasenhuttl, Fridrikas, Kogler), CSKA Sofia 1 (Shiskov)
Glentoran 0, Marseille 5 (Voller, Martin Vasquez 2, Sauzee, Ferreri)
Gothenburg 2 (Eskeleinen, Ekstrom), Besiktas 0
Kuusyi 1 (Rinne), Dynamo Bucharest 0
Lech Poznan 2 (Trzeciak, Podbrozny), Skonto Riga 0
Maccabi Tel Aviv 0, Brugge 1 (Staelens)
PSV Eindhoven 6 (Koeman, Ellerman 3, Kieft, Numan), Zalgiris Vilnius 0
Rangers 2 (Hateley, Huistra), Lyngby 0
Sion 4 (Hottinger, Tulio 2, Assis), Tavria Simferopol 1 (Shevchenko pen)

through

LEAPY LEE: United striker Lee Chapman wins this header despite the combined efforts of Eyjolfur Sverrisson (centre) and Guido Buchwald.

striker Fritz Walter and midfield creator Maurizio Gaudino to hold on to their fragile lead and somehow the visitors survived United's late barrage.

The tie finished 4-4 with Buck's away goal proving decisive leaving brave United to take the plaudits for a magnificent display.

While Stuttgart celebrated, United were given a standing ovation by their supporters, unaware that their heroes were about to be handed a dramatic stay of execution.

Foreign exchange sees Germans break the rules

IT transpired that in their panic to get on their substitutes, Stuttgart coach Christophe Daum had finished up with more than the permitted four foreign players on the field by using Adrian Knup late in the game.

The rules governing 'foreign players' were quite complicated. Only three such players were allowed among the starting line-up and substitutes.

However, UEFA regulations allowed a player to drop his foreign tag if he had played for an interrupted period of five years in the country of his national association, three years of which must have been spent in playing youth football.

Hence Leeds were able to register Welsh international Gary Speed as a non-foreign player as he had been at Elland Road since leaving school while Gary McAllister, Gordon Strachan and Eric Cantona, who played in both legs against Stuttgart, were regarded as foreign players.

defence to cruise in to second round

Slovan Bratislava 4 (Gostic, Dubovsky 2, Morvec), Ferencvaros 1 (Lipcsei)
Union Luxembourg 1 (Deville), FC Porto 4 (Semedo, Couro, Toni, Domingos)
VfB Stuttgart 3 (Walter 2, Buck), Leeds United 0
Vikingur 0, CSKA Moscow 1 (Korsakov)

First round, second leg

Apoel Nicosia 2 (Gogic, Sasulitis), AEK Athens 2 (Sabanadzovic, Alexandris)
3-3 on agg. AEK Athens win on away goals
Besiktas 2 (Metin, Feyyaz), Gothenburg 1 (Eskeleinen)
Gothenburg win 3-2 on agg
Brugges 3 (Staelens, Verheyen 2), Maccabi Tel Aviv 0 in Liege
Brugges win 4-0 on agg
CSKA Moscow 4 (Sergeyev, Korsakov, Grishin, Kolesnikov), Vikingur 0
CSKA Mosow win 5-0 on agg
CSKA Sofia 3 (Metkov, Andonov 2 – 1 pen), FK Austria 2 (Flogel, Ivanauskas)
FK Austria win 5-4 on agg
Dynamo Bucharest 2 (Gerstenmajer, Demollari), Kuusysi 0 aet
Dynamo Bucharest win 2-1 on agg
Ferencvaros 0, Slovan Bratislava 0
Slovan Bratislava win 4-1 on agg
Leeds United 4 (Speed, McAllister, Cantona, Chapman), VfB Stuttgart 1 (Buck)
Leeds United awarded match 3-0 on forfeit as Stuttgart included a fourth foreign player.
Lyngby 0, Rangers 1 (Durrant)
Rangers win 3-0 on agg
Marseille 3 (Oman-Biyik, Pele, Boli), Glentoran 0
Marseille win 8-0 on agg
Olimpija Ljubljana 0, AC Milan 3 (Massaro, Rijkaard, Tassotti)
AC Milan win 7-0 on agg
FC Porto 5 (Kostadinov 2, Toni 2, Jose Carlos), Union Luxembourg 0
FC Porto win 9-1 on agg
Skonto Riga 0, Lech Poznan 0
Lech Poznan win 2-0 on agg
Tavria Simferopol 1 (Shevchenko pen), Sion 3 (Tulio, Carlos Luis, Domingos)
Sion win 7-2 on agg
Viking Stavanger 0, Barcelona 0
Barcelona win 1-0 on agg
Zalgiris Vilnius 0, PSV Eindhoven 2 (Numan, Romario)
PSV Eindhoven win 8-0 on agg

Numbers up for Daum as UEFA order replay

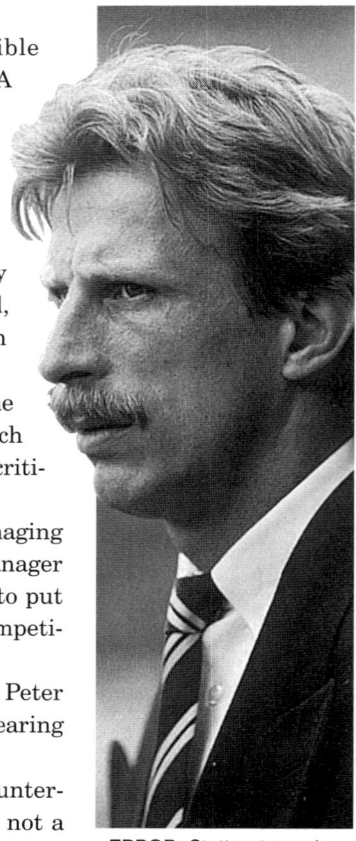

ERROR: Stuttgart coach Christophe Daum's miscalculation offered United a European Cup lifeline

AFTER hearing of Stuttgart's possible breach of the rules, United faxed the FA for clarification the day after their heroic exit.

UEFA immediately launched an inquiry and ruled that Leeds should be reinstated in the draw until a decision was made. The stakes immediately increased as the draw paired United, should they be reinstated, with Scottish giants Glasgow Rangers.

It had been an amazing blunder by the normally efficient Germans and their coach Christophe Daum came in for plenty of criticism at home.

United secretary Nigel Pleasants, managing director Bill Fotherby and general manager Alan Roberts headed out to Switzerland to put United's case for re-admission to the competition.

They were later joined by club solicitor Peter McCormack in Zurich where the UEFA hearing was convened.

After United were able to rubbish counterclaims by Stuttgart that Gary Speed was not a bone-fide assimilated player, United put their case to have the Germans thrown out of the competition.

There were fears that Stuttgart, backed by the influential German FA, would escape with a fine, but at 9pm on Saturday, October 9, UEFA announced that United would be awarded the home match 3-0 and that the teams should play-off in a third game.

United were given 48 hours to appeal against the ruling and although the general feeling was that Stuttgart had got away with bending the rules, a Leeds board meeting accepted the decision but sought to have the play-off at Elland Road.

But the wheels had already been set in motion by UEFA's Match and Grounds Committee and no appeal could be made against the decision to have the match replayed at a neutral venue.

Rotterdam was widely tipped as the likely venue but it emerged on Tuesday, October 6, that the massive Nou Camp Stadium in Barcelona would host the tie just three days later at 8.15pm on a Friday night.

No League fixtures were being played on Saturday because of internationals the following week and Wilkinson was able to get permission from various international managers to field England duo David Batty and Tony Dorigo, Gary McAllister (Scotland), Gary Speed (Wales) and Eric Cantona (France).

The 'Great Escape' which the team almost pulled off on the field had been achieved off it. Now the ball was back at the players' feet to ensure justice was done.

COOL CARL: United substitute Carl S

Hero

JUMP FOR JOY: Gordon Strachan leaps in to the arms of Gary Speed after netting his opener against Stuttgart.

es the ball past Stuttgart goalkeeper Ike Immel to clinch the 2-1 play-off victory in a near deserted Nou Camp Stadium in Barcelona.

of the Nou Camp

It's an open and Shutt case for United battlers

SUPER-SUB Carl Shutt fired himself into Leeds United folklore with the winning goal against Stuttgart.

Extra-time in the play-off was looming when Shutt, 31 the previous Saturday, came off the bench to earn United a birthday bonus.

Only 7,400 were in Barcelona's vast Nou Camp bowl to see United triumph 2-1. Most were curious local schoolchildren who had been let in free, but an estimated 2,500 Leeds fans paid homage to Catalonia – a remarkable turnout considering that the match was arranged at such short notice.

As UEFA had ruled that the tie was a category A match – the reason they had trimmed the capacity at Elland Road – thousands of Spanish police and Barcelona officials were on duty to oversee just a handful of fans.

It was a predictably tense and tight match with United spurred on by their fans and a sense of injustice which even stretched right up to the kick-off when United were kept waiting for the Stuttgart team-sheet and had to plead for match-balls to warm up.

United broke through on 33 minutes when skipper supreme Gordon Strachan unleashed a rising drive from 25 yards past Ike Immel.

European Champions Cup
First round, play-off
(at Nou Camp Stadium, Barcelona)
Friday, October 9, 1992

Leeds United	2
VfB Stuttgart	1

Leeds win play-off 2-1

Leeds United: John Lukic, Jon Newsome, Tony Dorigo, David Batty, Chris Fairclough, Chris Whyte, Gordon Strachan, Eric Cantona (Carl Shutt 76), Lee Chapman, Gary McAllister, Gary Speed
Goals: Strachan 33, Shutt 77
Manager: Howard Wilkinson

VfB Stuttgart: Ike Immel, Gunther Schafer, Michael Frontzeck, Slobodan Dubajic, Thomas Strunz (Alexandrer Strehmel 24), Guido Buchwald, Andreas Buck, Eyjolfur Sverrisson (Adrian Knup 80), Fritz Walter, Andre Golke, Ludwig Kogel
Goal: Golke 38
Manager: Christophe Daum

Referee: Fabio Baldas (Italy) **Att:** 7,400

But the dogged Germans were level six minutes later when Andre Golke headed in to put the tie right back in the melting pot.

With 15 minutes left Shutt went on to replace Eric Cantona up front and his first task was to help defend a Stuttgart corner. It was Shutt who headed the ball away and it arrived at the feet of Tony Dorigo, United's £1.3 million signing from Chelsea.

By the time Dorigo looked up the energetic Shutt was already racing towards the German goal. The Australian-born defender delivered the pass into space, Shutt collected it, muscled his way past the last defender and calmly despatched the ball past Immel.

The stunning victory set up 'The Battle of Britain' against Glasgow Rangers, who were hailed as one of the best-ever sides to come out of Scotland.

Lukic punches United's lights out

GOLDEN GLOVES: United goalkeeper John Lukic, under pressure from Richard Gough, miscues his punch and the ball ended up in the back of the net.

AN estimated £4m was riding on "The Battle of Britain". That was the estimated value of progress to the group stages of the European Cup.

The victors would go into the money-dripping final last eight in which two groups of four would play in a league format – in the forerunner of today's Champions League – with the winners playing in the final.

Either United or Rangers were expected to bank £915,00 for simply winning the tie and would pick up an estimated £210,000 per point thereafter in the league stage from their six matches. The Glasgow club upped the stakes even higher when they were prepared to pay £20,000 a man to get through.

United faced a wall of noise at Ibrox in the first leg, but within 69 seconds the stadium sat in stunned silence.

With no tickets being sold to Leeds fans because of fears of potential crowd trouble Gary McAllister's blockbusting volley didn't get the verbal acknowledgement it deserved.

Leeds won an early corner and it was only partially cleared to McAllister, twice rejected after trials at Ibrox as a youngster, and he despatched a superb shot past Andy Goram.

But the volume was back on full blast when John Lukic lost the flight of the ball in the glare of the floodlights at a corner and punched it into his own net.

Rangers were uplifted by the goal but United came close to getting back in front when Jon Newsome's header from a corner struck a post.

Just as it seemed as though United had ridden the storm, Ally McCoist grabbed Rangers' second as United were undone at another corner. Lukic parried Dave McPherson's header and the razor-sharp McCoist swept in his 25th goal in 21 matches.

Leeds though, with Gordon Strachan outstanding on his return to Scotland, controlled large parts of the game and the tie was very much in the balance at the final whistle.

European Cup
Second round, first leg
(at Ibrox Stadium, Glasgow)
Wednesday, October 21, 1992

Rangers 2

Leeds United 1

Rangers: Andy Goram, Stuart McCall, David Robertson, Richard Gough, David McPherson, John Brown, Trevor Steven (Pieter Huistra 74), Ian Ferguson, Ally McCoist, Mark Hateley, Ian Durrant
Goals: Lukic og 21, McCoist 37
Manager: Walter Smith

Leeds United: John Lukic, Jon Newsome, Tony Dorigo, David Batty, Chris Fairclough, Chris Whyte, Gordon Strachan (David Rocastle 87), Eric Cantona (Rod Wallace 78), Lee Chapman, Gary McAllister, Gary Speed
Goal: McAllister 1
Manager: Howard Wilkinson

Referee: Alphonse Constantin (Belgium) **Att:** 43,251

Maldini on the mark

PAOLO Maldini netted AC Milan's winner in Slovan Bratislava while holders Barcelona forced a 1-1 draw at CSKA Moscow.

FC Porto scored twice in the last ten minutes to draw 2-2 in Sion.

First round play-off

Leeds United 2 (Strachan, Shutt), VfB Stuttgart 1 (Golke) *Leeds United qualify for second round*

Second round, first leg

AEK Athens 1 (Dimitriadis), PSV Eindhoven 0
Brugges 2 (Verheyen, Booy), FK Austria 0
CSKA Moscow 1 (Grishin), Barcelona 1 (Beguiristain)
Dynamo Bucharest 0, Marseille 0
Gothenburg 1 (Bengtsson), Lech Poznan 0
Rangers 2 (Lukic og, McCoist), Leeds United 1 (McAllister)
Sion 2 (Orlando, Assis), FC Porto 2 (Semedo, Couto)
Slovan Bratislava 0, AC Milan 1 (Maldini)

Power Rangers

Inspired Goram shatters United

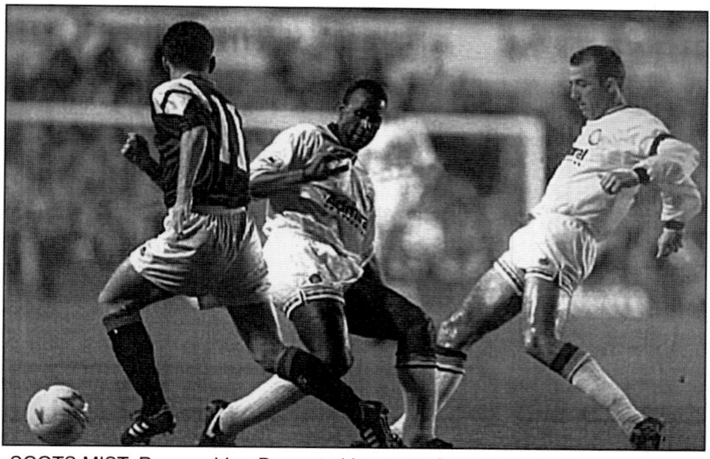
SCOTS MIST: Rangers' Ian Durrant skips away from United's David Rocastle and Gary McAllister.

ALL those English jokes about Scottish goalkeepers didn't raise much of a laugh when United were sent tumbling out of the European Cup by Rangers.

An inspired performance by Andy Goram broke United's hearts as the Scottish champions pulled off a superb 2-1 smash-and-grab victory at Elland Road to seal a 4-2 aggregate victory.

While United had been partially derailed at Ibrox by John Lukic's error, Rangers' No 1 Goram, pulled off a catalogue of outstanding saves.

As at Ibrox there was a brilliant early goal for the away side.

Goram had a magnificent second-minute save to deny Eric Cantona and seconds later United found themselves trailing.

Ally McCoist headed a clearance towards the corner of the Leeds area where the swivelling Mark Hateley acrobatically sent a stunning volley whizzing past Lukic from 25 yards.

It was a hammer blow for United who were getting little exchange out of Lee Chapman's aerial duels with Richard Gough and John Brown.

Leeds, who drafted in David Rocastle for the injured David Batty in only his second start for the club, gradually worked a way round the back of the Rangers' defence but twice the outstanding Goram, a £1 million signing from Hibernian, denied Eric Cantona, and Leeds-born Stuart McCall kicked off the line from Chris Whyte at a corner.

Howard Wilkinson said: "Once that first goal goes in there is a whole different projection on the game. It made us do everything we didn't want to do. It was like trying to carry a ton weight up the down escalator."

His men had to be more gung-ho that they anticipated and had to take risks to get back in the tie. That left them open to the counter and Rangers took advantage with brilliant effect. Hateley created space down the left with a smart dummy and took Ian Durrant's pass in his stride. He delivered the perfect cross for the predatory Ally McCoist to angle a fine header back beyond Lukic.

United substitute Rod Wallace saw Goram push his shot against a post and although Cantona's 85th minute goal was deserved, Goram still had time to save from Cantona, Wallace and Speed to guarantee victory.

European Champions Cup
Second round, second leg
(at Elland Road, Leeds)
Wednesday, November 4, 1992

Leeds United 1

Rangers 2

Rangers win 4-2 on agg

Leeds United: John Lukic, Jon Newsome, Tony Dorigo, David Rocastle (Steve Hodge 62), Chris Fairclough (Rod Wallace 62), Chris Whyte, Gordon Strachan, Eric Cantona, Lee Chapman, Gary McAllister, Gary Speed
Goal: Cantona 85
Manager: Howard Wilkinson

Rangers: Andy Goram, Stuart McCall, David Robertson, Richard Gough, David McPherson, John Brown, Dale Gordon (Alexei Mikhailichenko 71), Ian Ferguson, Ally McCoist, Mark Hateley, Ian Durrant
Goals: Hateley 3, McCoist 59
Manager: Walter Smith

Referee: Alexei Spirin (Russia)
Att: 25,118

Barcelona crash out

BIGGEST shock of the night was Barcelona's home defeat at the hands of CSKA Moscow.

Barca, who had beaten Sampdoria at Wembley to win the trophy the previous season, threw away a 2-0 lead in the Nou Camp as the Russians stormed home in the second half.

Brazilian striker Romario scored a hat-trick as PSV Eindhoven overhauled AEK Athens and AC Milan looked strong, winning both legs against Slovan Bratislava. Another of the favourites, Marseille, got past Dynamo Bucharest with a double from Croatian striker Alein Boksic.

Second round, second leg

AC Milan 4 (Boban, Rijkaard, Simone, Papin), Slovan Bratislava 0 *AC Milan win 5-0 on agg*
Barcelona 2 (Nadal, Beguiristain), CSKA Moscow (Bukhamanov, Mashkarin, Korsakov) *CSKA Moscow win 4-3 on agg*
FK Austria 3 (Zsak, Fridrikas, Ivanauskas), Brugges 1 (Van Der Heyden) *3-3 on agg. Brugges win on away goals*
Lech Poznan 0, Gothenburg 3 (Ekstroem, Nilsson, Mild) *Gothenburg win 4-0 on agg*
Leeds United 1 (Cantona), Rangers 2 (Hateley, McCoist) *Rangers win 4-2 on agg*
Marseille 2 (Boksic 2), Dynamo Bucharest 0 *Marseille win 2-0 on agg*
Porto 4 (Costa, Domingos, Kostadinov, Magalhaes), Sion 0 *Porto win 6-2 on agg*
PSV Eindhoven 3 (Romario 3), AEK Athen 0 *PSV Eindhoven win 3-1 on agg*

Eric's exit from Leeds

WITHIN days of the defeat by Rangers, Eric Cantona, the catalyst of United's title success the previous season was surprisingly transferred to arch rivals Manchester United for a bargain £1.2 million.

The enigmatic French star went on to win a stack of honours with the Red Devils and his move caused a lot of resentment at Elland Road.

While Alex Ferguson's team went from strength to strength across the Pennines, the wheels fell off Leeds' season in dramatic fashion.

Their form away from home collapsed and they struggled to 17th place in the Premiership.

After the poor defence of their Premiership title, Howard Wilkinson went about reconstructing his squad and steered them to fifth place in 1993-94. They finished in the same position the following campaign, but this time it was good enough to capture a place in the UEFA Cup.

By then the likes of David Batty, Chris Whyte and free-scoring Lee Chapman had moved on but United were relishing another crack at Europe.

CONTROVERSIAL MOVE: Eric Cantona, who switched to Manchester United.

Gers' glorious failure

RANGERS made a bold bid for European glory after eliminating United.

They went in to Group A along with Marseille, Brugges and CSKA Moscow.

Confidence in the Gers camp was sky-high following their two-leg triumph over Leeds and the proceeded to show it was no fluke.

Despite being unbeaten in the group they were just pipped by big-spending Marseille for a place in the final against AC Milan, runaway victors in Group B.

Rangers fought back from being 2-0 down in their opening game against Marseille at Ibrox to draw 2-2, but failure to beat the French side was to cost Walter Smith's team in the long run.

CSKA Moscow's home tie against Rangers was played in Berlin because of the Russian winter and Ian Ferguson's goal gave the Scots a valuable win.

It was soon clear Rangers and Marseille would fight it out at the top of Group A and Smith's squad continued to keep the French outfit within their sights.

Despite having Mark Hateley sent off they squeezed past Brugges 2-1 at home on the same night that Marseille thrashed CSKA 6-0.

Ian Durrant's spectacular equaliser in Marseille meant the teams went in to the final game with all to play for.

Rangers were frustratingly held 0-0 at home by CSKA, but Alen Boksic's early goal in Brugges was enough to put Marseille through.

Italian champions AC Milan were hot favourites to win the final in Munich but Marseille became the first French side to win the trophy thanks to centre-back Basile Boli's header from a corner just before half-time.

Champions League
Group A

Brugges 1 (Amokachi), CSKA Moscow 0
Rangers 2 (McSwegan, Hateley), Marseille 2 (Boksic, Voller)
CSKA Moscow 0, Rangers 1 (Ferguson)
Marseille 3 (Sauzee pen, Boksic 2), Brugges 0
Brugges 1 (Dziubinski), Rangers 1 (Huistra)
CSKA Moscow 1 (Fayzulin), Marseille 1 (Abedi Pele) in Berlin
Marseille 6 (Sauzee 3 – 1 pen, Abedi Pele, Ferreri, Desailly), CSKA Moscow 0
Rangers 2 (Durrant, Nisbet), Brugges 1 (Staelens)
Marseille 1 (Sauzee), Rangers 1 (Durrant)
CSKA Moscow 1 (Sergeev), Brugges 2 (Schaessens, Verheyen) in Berlin
Brugges 0, Marseille 1 (Boksic)
Rangers 0, CSKA Moscow 0

Group A

	P	W	D	L	F	A	Pts
Marseille	6	3	3	0	14	4	9
Rangers	6	2	4	0	7	5	8
Brugges	6	2	1	3	5	8	5
CSKA Moscow	6	0	2	4	2	11	2

Group B

AC Milan 4 (Van Basten 4 – 1 pen), Gothenburg 0
Porto 2 (Magalhaes, Jose Carlos), PSV Eindhoven 2 (Romario 2)
Gothenburg 1 (Eriksson), Porto 0
PSV Eindhoven 1 (Romario), AC Milan 2 (Rijkaard, Simone)
PSV Eindhoven 1 (Numan), Gothenburg 3 (Nilsson, Ekstroem 2)
Porto 0, AC Milan 1 (Papin)
Gothenburg 3 (Nilsson, Ekstroem, Martinsson), PSV Eindhoven 0
AC Milan 1 (Eranio), Porto 0
Gothenburg 0, AC Milan 1 (Massaro)
PSV Eindhoven 0, Porto 1 (Jose Carlos pen)
AC Milan 2 (Simone 2), PSV Eindhoven 0
Porto 2 (Ze Carlos, Timofte), Gothenburg 0

Group B

	P	W	D	L	F	A	Pts
AC Milan	6	6	0	0	11	1	12
Gothenburg	6	3	0	3	7	8	6
Porto	6	2	1	3	5	5	5
PSV Eindhoven	6	0	1	5	4	13	1

Final
(Olympic Stadium, Munich)
May 26, 1993
AC Milan 0
Marseille 1

AC Milan: Rossi, Tassotti, Costacurta, Baresi, Maldini, Donadoni (Papin 54), Albertini, Rijkaard, Lentini, Massaro, Van Basten (Eranio 85)
Manager: Fabio Capello
Marseille: Barthez, Angloma (Durand 61), Desailly, Boli, Di Meco, Eydelie, Sauzee, Deschamps, Abedi Pele, Boksic, Voller (Thomas 78)
Goal: Boli 44
Manager: Raymond Goethals
Referee: Kurt Rothlisberger (Switzerland)
Attendance: 64,000

Leading scorers: 7 – Romario (PSV Eindhoven), 6 – Boksic (Marseille), Sauzee (Marseille), Van Basten (AC Milan), 4 – Simone (AC Milan), Verheyen (Brugges)

English clubs avoid preliminary pitfalls

THE collapse of the Soviet Union and the fall of the Berlin Wall saw the formation of several new countries which were welcomed with open arms by UEFA.

It meant that the UEFA Cup was now a huge competition, but United, along with other clubs from England, Italy, Spain, Germany, Holland, France, Belgium and the Soviet Union did not have to go through the preliminary round.

Joining United as the Premier League representatives were Manchester United, Liverpool and Nottingham Forest.

Blackburn Rovers, featuring former Leeds hero David Batty, flew the flag in the Champions League, while the English representatives in the European Cup Winners' Cup were Everton.

An added complication was the Inter-Toto Cup, a competition which had been introduced in 1995. The winners of that competition, played in June and July, would gain entry to the preliminary rounds of the UEFA Cup.

British clubs were invited to join it, but most looked upon it as an unwanted extension to the season.

Tottenham Hotspur, Wimbledon, Sheffield Wednesday, Partick Thistle and Ton Pentre, from the Welsh League, all took part in the group stages. The English clubs fielded a combination of youngsters and loan players and none of the British sides qualified.

Qualifying round, first leg

Afan Lido 1 (Moore), Yelgava Riga 2 (Zujevs, Bogdans)
Apollon Athens 1 (Kola), Olympia Lubijana 0
Bangor City 0, Widez Lodz 4 (Czerwiec 2, Koniarek 2)
Botev Plovdiv 1 (Gerov), Dynamo Tbilisi 0
Brondby 3 (Hansen, Bjur, Sand), Inkaras Kaunas 0
Crusaders 1 (Hunter), Silkeborg 2 (Fernandez, Larsen pen)
Dundalk 0, Malmo 2 (Pettersson, Andersson)
Dynamo Bucharest 0, Levski Sofia 1 (Iwanov)
Fenerbahce 2 (Bulent, Bolic), Partizan Tirana 0
Glenavon 0, Hamarfjordur 0
Hibernians Paolola 2 (Lawrence, Sultana), Chornomorets 5 (Guiseinov, Gashkin, Musolitin 2, Kardash)
Jeunesse Esch 0, Lugano 0
Kapaz 0, FK Austria 4 (Mjelder, Belajic, Flogel, Pacult)
Kosice 0, Ujpest Budapest 1 (Tiefenbach)
KS Tirana 0, Hapoel Beer Sheva 1 (Ziberlins)
Lillestroem 4 (Inglestad, Ingebrigsten, Guldrandsen 2), Flora Tallin 0
Motherwell 1 (McSkimming), MyPa 3 (Gronholm, Tiainen, Manlio)
Omonia Nicosia 3 (Valentin 2 – 1 pen, Malekos), Sliema Wanderers 0
Orebro 0, Avenir Beggen 0
Raith Rovers 4 (Dair, Rougier, McAnespie, Cameron), Gotu 0
Red Star Belgrade 0, Neuchatel Xamax 1 (Wittl)
Shelbourne 0, Akranes 3 (Gunnlaugsson 2, Reynisson)
Skonto Riga 1 (Babicevs), Maribor Branik 0
Slavia Sofia 0, Olympiakos 2 (Ivic, Juskowiak)
Slovan Bratislava 4 (Tittel, Rusnak 2, Faktor), Osijek 0
Sparta Prague 3 (Nedved 2, Lokvenc), Galatasaray 1 (Saunders)
Sturm Graz 0, Slavia Prague 1 (Bejbl pen)
Tampere 0, Viking Stavanger 4 (Lehtinen og, Ostenstad, Medalen, Sorloth)
Universitatea Craiova 0, Dynamo Minsk 0
Vardar Skopje 1 (Nikolovski), Samtredia 0
Zaglebie Lubin 0, Shirak Gumri 0
Zimbru Chisinau 2 (Gavriliuc, Rebeja), Hapoel Tel Aviv 0

Qualifying round, second leg

Akranes 3 (Jonsson, Thordasson, Petursson), Shelbourne 0 *Akranes win 6-0 on agg*
Avenir Beggen 1 (Holtz), Orebro 1 (Birgirsson) *Second leg ruled 3-0 to Avenir Beggen as Orebro fielded an ineligible player.*
Chornomorets 2 (Kozakevich, Musolitin), Hibernians Paola 0 *Chornomorets win 7-2 on agg*
Dynamo Minsk 0, Universitatea Craiova 0 *0-0 on agg. Dynamo Minsk win 3-1 on penalties*
Dynamo Tbilisi 0, Botev Plovdiv 1 (Vidolov) *Botev Plovdiv win 2-0 on agg*
FK Austria 5 (Mjelde 2, Ogris 2, Glatzer), Kjapaz 1 (Suleimaov) *FK Austria win 9-1 on agg*
Flora Tallin 1 (Korgalidze), Lillestroem 0 *Lillestroem win 4-1 on agg*
Galatasaray 1 (Saunders), Sparta Prague 1 (Nedved) *Sparta Prague win 4-2 on agg*
Gotu 2 (H Jarnskor, M Jarnskor), Raith Rovers 2 (McInally, Crawford) *Raith Rovers win 6-2 on agg*
Hamarfjordur 0, Glenavon 1 (Johnston) *Glenavon win 1-0 on agg*
Hapoel Beer Sheva 2 (Gusev, Avigdror), KS Tirana 0 *Hapoel Beer Sheva win 3-0 on agg*
Hapoel Tel Aviv 0, Zimbru Chsinau 0 *Zimbri Chisinau win 2-0 on agg*
Inkaras Kaunas 0, Brondby 3 (Moller 2, Risager) *Brondby win 6-0 on agg*
Levski Sofia 1 (Vasiliev), Dynamo Bucharest 1 (Lupu) aet *Dynamo Bucharest win 2-1 on agg*
Lugano 4 (Erceg 3, Esposito), Jeunesse Esch 0 *Lugano win 4-0 on agg*
Malmo 2 (Andersson, Fjellstrom), Dundalk 0 *Malmo win 4-0 on agg*
Maribor Branik 2 (Strebal, Frecelj), Skonto Riga 0 *Maribor Branik win 2-1 on agg*
MyPa 0, Motherwell 2 (Burns, Arnott) *3-3 on agg.MyPa Anjalankoski win on away goals*
Neuchatel Xamax 0, Red Star Belgrade 0 *Neuchatel Xamax win 1-0 on agg*
Olympiakos 1 (Ivic), Slavia Sofia 0 *Olympiakos win 3-0 on agg*
Olympia Lubjiana 3 (Bozgo 2, Zulic), Apollon Athens (Kola) 1 *Olympia Lubjiana win 3-2 on agg*
Osijek 0, Slovan Bratlislava 2 (Rusnak, Luis Gomes) in Zagreb *Slovan Bratislava win 6-0 on agg*
Partizan Tirana 0, Fenerbahce 4 (Bulent, Kamalettin, Bolicm Aykut) *Fenerbahce win 6-0 on agg*
Shirak Gumri 0, Zaglebie Lubin 1 (Machaj) in Erevan *Zaglebie Lubin win 1-0 on agg*
Silkeborg 4 (Larsen, Fernandez, Sommer 2), Crusaders 0 *Silkeborg win 6-1 on agg*
Slavia Prague 1 (Hysky), Sturm Graz 1 (Haas) *Slavia Prague win 2-1 on agg*
Sliema Wanderers 1 (Suda), Omonia Nicosia 2 (Valentin, Panayiotou) *Omonia Nicosia win 5-1 on agg*
Viking Stavanger 3 (Bergersen 2, Sorloth), Tampere 1 (Wiss pen) *Viking Stavanger win 7-1 on agg*
Widez Lodz 1 (Pikuta), Bangor City 0 *Widez Lodz win 5-0 on agg*
Ujpest Budapest 2 (Berczy, Szanyo), Kosice 1 (Weiss) *Ujpest Budapest win 3-1 on agg*
Samtredia 0, Vardar Skopje 2 (Serafimovski, Petrevski) *Vardar Skopje win 3-0 on agg*
Yelgava Riga 0, Afan Lido 0 *Yelgava Riga win 2-1 on agg*

Byes: ***Aalst, AC Milan, Auxerre, Barcelona, Bayern Munich, Benfica, Farense, Freiburg, Inter Milan, Kaiserslautern, Lazio, Leeds United, Lens, Lierse, Liverpool, Locomotiv Moscow, Lyon, Manchester United, Monaco, Nottingham Forest, PSV Eindhoven, Real Betis, Roda, Rotor Volgograd, Roma, Seville, Spartak Vladikavkaz, Standard Liege, Vitoria Guimares, Werder Bremen.***

Intertoto Cup winners Strasbourg and Bordeaux also qualified for the first round.

Yeboah: Prince

Wilko's gamble breaks the bank at Monte Carlo

HOWARD Wilkinson took a major risk when he recruited African hotshot Tony Yeboah to fill the scoring boots of Lee Chapman.

But the gamble paid off in spectacular fashion as the Ghana international's goals had been one of the springboard's for United's charge into Europe.

Despite initial doubts about his fitness, Yeboah proved a clinical finisher with a powerful shot who looked worth every penny of the £3.4 million United had paid German club Eintracht Frankfurt to add firepower to a wilting attack.

United were hoping for a gentle reintroduction to European football but were paired with star-studded Monaco, the champions of France, who were European Cup semi-finalists in 1994, losing to AC Milan.

But Jean Tigana's side could not tame the peerless Yeboah, who scored a remarkable hat-trick as United stormed to a stunning 3-0 victory in the high-tech Louis II Stadium.

Just three minutes had ticked by when Yeboah made his first incision. The ball was played into the Monaco box and goalkeeper Fabien Piveteau collided with central defender Lillian Thuram, dropped the ball and the alert Yeboah skilfully hooked the ball over the French pair into the net.

United were forced back by some skilful midfield play by Belgian international Enzo Schifo but United's central defenders, David Wetherall and John Pemberton, were in determined mood, while Brian Deane, Yeboah's strike partner, put in an enormous amount of work in attack.

United grew in confidence as the game went on and doubled their lead with a fantastic strike from Yeboah. Receiving a Gary McAllister throw, he turned sharply to lose his marker and curled a magnificent shot beyond the reach of Marc Delaroche, who had come on for the injured Piveteau at half-time.

It simply went from bad to worse for Monaco as Delaroche and Basile Boli were involved in a shuddering collision ten minutes from time, leaving Yeboah to lob in his hat-trick goal.

After lengthy medical assistance, both the substitute goalkeeper and defender Boli were stretchered off and Tigana brought on an outfield player, Claude Puel in goal for the remainder of the game.

United had all the luck that was going but Wilkinson was not complaining and saluted Yeboah, who scored another amazing hat-trick in a 4-2 win at Wimbledon 11 days later.

WILKO'S WONDERS: United's 1995/96 squad face the camera ahead of their UEFA Cup campaign. Back row, from left to right: David White, Brian Deane, Carlton Palmer, John Lukic, David Wetherall, Mark Beeney, Phil Masinga, Lucas Radebe, Paul Beesley. Middle row: Mick Hennigan (assistant manager), Matthew Smithard, Mark Ford, Noel Whelan, Rob Bowman, Mark Tinkler, Andy Couzens, Kevin Sharp, Tony Dorigo, Nigel Worthington, David O'Leary, David Williams (coach), Geoff Ladley (physio). Front row: Rod Wallace, Tony Yeboah, Gary McAllister, Howard Wilkinson (manager), John Pemberton, Gary Speed, Gary Kelly.

# of Monaco

THE PREDATOR: Noel Whelan looks on in amazement as striker supreme Tony Yeboah hooks in United's opener against Monaco.

UEFA Cup
First round, first leg
(at Louis II Stadium, Monte Carlo)
Wednesday, September 12, 1995

 **Monaco**  **0**

 **Leeds United**  **3**

Monaco: Fabien Piveteau (Marc Delroche HT, – Claude Puel 81), Patrick Valery, Eric Di Meco, Lilian Thuram, Basile Boli, Franck Dumas, Manuel Dos Santos, Sylvain Legwinski (Thierry Henry 69), Enzo Schifo, Christopher Wreh, Anderson da Silva
Manager: Jean Tigana

Leeds United: John Lukic, Gary Kelly, Tony Dorigo (Paul Beesley HT), John Pemberton, David Wetherall, Noel Whelan, Carlton Palmer, Gary McAllister, Gary Speed, Brian Deane, Tony Yeboah
Goals: Yeboah 2, 65, 81
Manager: Howard Wilkinson

Referee: Jose Maria Encinar (Spain) **Att:** 15,000

"Words can't describe Tony Yeboah nor his importance to the team. he's always been able to score straightforward goals, but increasingly he is scoring more difficult ones."

Championship-winning midfielders Gary McAllister and Gary Speed, now supplemented by the arrival of £2.6 million Carlton Palmer from Sheffield Wednesday, were the men responsible for supplying Yeboah the ammuntion – and he certainly pulled the trigger.

Monaco coach Jean Tigana said: "It was a horrible night for us. Not only did we lose the match but we also lost two players. I have no hope for the return match."

Reds hit back at double to impale Vladi

LIVERPOOL joined United as winners, coming from a goal down to win 2-1 at Spartak Vladikavkaze with strikes by Steve McManaman and Jamie Redknapp.

Manchester United, featuring former Leeds player Denis Irwin, were held 0-0 by Rotor Volgograd but Nottingham Forest, managed by former European Cup winner Frank Clark, lost 2-1 in Sweden to Malmo after leading through Ian Woan's first half strike.

First round, first leg

AC Milan 4 (Savicevic, Machaj og, Weah, Boban), Zaglebie Lubin 0
Hapoel Beer Sheva 0, Barcelona 7 (De La Pena, Roger 3, Oscar Garcia, Figo 2)
Bayern Munich 0, Lokomotiv Moscow 1 (Kharlachiov)
Brondby 3 (Hansen, Eggen, Bjur pen), Lillestroem 0
Chornomorets 1 (Kozakevich), Widez Lodz 0
Farense 0, Lyon 1 (Giuly)
Fenerbahce 1 (Aykut), Real Betis 2 (Pier, Sabas)
FK Austria 1 (Kogler), Dynamo Minsk 2 (Zhuraviel, Shukanov)
Freiburg 1 (Todt), Slavia Prague 2 (Novotny, Penicka)
Glenavon 0, Werder Bremen 2 (Cardoso, Vier)
Lazio 5 (Casiraghi 3 – 1 pen, Rambaudi, Signori pen), Omonia Nicosia 0
Lens 6 (Camara 2, Meyrieu, Tieni 2, Boli), Avenir Beggen 0
Levski Sofia 1 (Vasilev), Aalst 2 (Markov og, Paas)
Lierse 1 (Huysmans pen), Benfica 3 (Valdo pen, Marcelo, Benfo)
Lugano 1 (Carrasco), Inter Milan 1 (Roberto Carlos)
Malmo 2 (Persson, Andersson), Nottingham Forest 1 (Woan)
Monaco 0, Leeds United 3 (Yeboah 3)
MyPa 1 (Mahlio), PSC Eindhoven 1 (Ronaldo) in Lahti
Neuchatel Xamax 1 (Jeanneret), Roma 1 (Moriero)
Olympiakos 2 (Juskowiak, Skartados pen), Maribor Branik 0
Raith Rovers 3 (Lennon 2, Wilson), Akranes 1 (Thordarsson)
Roda 5 (Van Galen, Roselofsen, Babangida, Graef, de Kock pen), Olympia Lubjiana 0
Rotor Volvograd 0, Manchester United 0
Seville 2 (Suker 2), Botev Plovdiv 0
Slovan Bratislava 2 (Tittel, Sobona), Kaiserslautern 1 (Hollerbach)
Sparta Prague 0, Silkeborg 1 (Fernandez)
Spartak Vladikavkaz 1(Kasimov), Liverpool 2 (McManaman, Redknapp)
Strasbourg 3 (Zitelli, Leboeuf pen, Batiole), Ujpest Budapest 0
Viking 1 (Ulfstein), Auxerre 1 (West)
Zimbru Chisinau 1 (Testimitanu), Jelgava Riga 0
Vardar Skopje 0, Bordeaux 2 (Bancarel 2)
Vitoria Guimaraes 3 (Estevan 2, Edinho), Standard Liege 1 (Schepens)

Cool hand Lukic

King John exorcises ghost of Ibrox

SUPERB goalkeeping by John Lukic prevented French aristocrats Monaco from pulling off a sensational comeback at Elland Road.

Howard Wilkinson's team, holding a 3-0 first leg lead, didn't know whether to stick or bust against the casino kings from Monte Carlo – and almost paid the price.

A 1-0 victory was scant reward for the French side whose free-flowing football was in stark contrast to spluttering United whose failure to keep the ball for any great length of time meant they were chasing shadows for most of the evening. Jean Tigana's side had no option to attack and did so with great style, while United were on a hiding to nothing after their spectatcular first leg triumph.

Belgian international Enzo Schifo pulled the strings for Monaco in midfield and the home goal had come under threat several times before Schifo nudged a 22nd minute free-kick to his right and £4.3 million Brazilian forward Sonny Anderson's 20-yard shot was deflected past Lukic.

A deflected goal was the only way past an inspired Lukic who three times made outstanding saves from Schifo, Manuel Dos Santos and Michael Madar as United's night threatened to develop into French farce.

The pick of the trio was a remarkable twisting save to edge a Madar header round a post midway through the second half.

SUPER SAVER: United goalkeeper John Lukic kept Monaco at bay with a string of fine saves.

Lukic's display also helped wipe out the memories of Ibrox – a nightmare he had to live with for three years. On that occasion he punched a corner in to his own net after being blinded by the floodlights, but against Monaco, the 34-year-old played an absolute blinder.

The modest Lukic, on the brink of making his 400th appearance for Leeds said: "That's what I'm paid for. It is a team game. It is not about individuals. The team gained the right outcome over the two legs. If people want to say nice things about me that's fine, but I am paid to do a job."

His display earned him a standing ovation from the Leeds fans and manager Howard Wilkinson, who rewarded Lukic with a new two-year contract in the summer, believed the 'keeper was playing as well as at any time in his career.

With Basile Boli keeping a tight rein on hat-trick hero Tony Yeboah, United struggled to make much headway with a couple of long-range pot shots by Gary McAllister and a clearance by Franck Dumas under pressure from Brian Deane the closest they came to scoring. But as time drifted away Wilkinson was able to give youngsters Mark Tinkler and Andy Couzens their first sample of European action.

Monaco were seeds in United's section F of the draw and Leeds fully expected to take over their seeding and play one of Brondby, Slavia Prague or Raith Rovers from the same group.

But by the time United company secretary Nigel Pleasants and general manager Alan Roberts flew to Geneva for the second round draw, UEFA had moved the goalposts.

Because four of the seeded teams had been knocked out in the eight groups, UEFA promoted everyone up the listings and it was decided that the next four clubs down their list who had not been seeded would now be seeded. As a result the groupings were changed to four of eight teams.

The outcome was that United were paired with class Dutch outfit PSV Eindhoven – a tie that would not be possible under the original UEFA listings.

ends nightmare

MAC ATTACK: United's Gary McAllister flips the ball past Emmauel Petit.

UEFFA Cup
First round, second leg
(at Elland Road, Leeds)
Wednesday, September 26, 1995

Leeds United 0
Monaco 1

Leeds United win 3-1 on agg

Leeds United: John Lukic, Gary Kelly, Paul Beesley, David Wetherall, John Pemberton (Andy Couzens 80), Carlton Palmer, David White (Mark Tinkler 54), Gary McAllister, Gary Speed, Brian Deane, Tony Yeboah
Manager: Howard Wilkinson

Monaco: Fabien Barthez, Lilian Thuram, Claude Puel, Basile Boli, Franck Dumas, Emmanuel Petit, Manuel Dos Santos (Christopher Wreh 82), Laurent Viaud (Dan Petersen 62), Enzo Schifo, Anderson Da Silva, Michael Madar
Goal: Anderson da Silva 23
Manager: Jean Tigana

Referee: Serge Muhmenthaler (Switzerland)
Att: 24,501

Man United cut down by Rotor's blades

MANCHESTER United crashed out of the UEFA Cup in sensational style to little known Rotor Volgograd at Old Trafford.

Without former Leeds striker Eric Cantona, who was serving an eight month ban for attacking a fan, the Red Devils went 2-0 down inside 24 minutes.

Paul Scholes pulled one back on the hour and in a dramatic finale goalkeeper Peter Schmeichel headed an equaliser from a corner but Alex Ferguson's team could not find a winner.

Second round, second leg

Aalst 1 (Lamberg), Levski Sofia 0 *Aalst win 3-1 on agg*

Akranes 1 (Gunnlaugsson), Raith Rovers 0 *Raith Rovers win 3-2 on agg*

Auxerre 1 (Silvestre), Viking 0 *Auxerre win 2-1 on agg*

Avenir Beggen 0, Lens 7 (Camara, Meyrieu, Boli, Delmotte 2, Tieni 2) *Lens win 13-0 on agg*

Barcelona 5 (Guardiola, Hagi, Velamazan, Carreras, Amor), Hapoel Beer Sheva *Barcelona win 12-0 on agg*

Benfica 2 (Joao Pinton, Kennedy), Lierse 1 (Van Kerckhoven) *Benfica win 5-2 on agg*

Bordeaux 1 (Lizarazu pen), Vardar Skopjie 1 (Serafimovski) *Bordeaux win 3-1 on agg*

Botev Plovdiv 1 (Iwanov), Seville 1 (Monchu) *Seville win 3-1 on agg*

Dynamo Minsk 1 (Belkevich), FK Austria 0 *Dynamo Minsk win 3-1 on agg*

Inter Milan 0, Lugano 1 (Carrasco) *Lugano win 2-1 on agg*

Jelgava Riga 1 (Zujevs), Zimbru Chisinau 2 (Gavriliuc 2) *Zimbru Chisinau win 3-1 on agg*

Kaiserslautern 3 (Wegmann 2, Wollitz), Slovan Bratislava 0 *Kaiserslautern win 4-2 on agg*

Leeds United 0, Monaco 1 (Anderson Silva) *Leeds United win 3-1 on agg*

Lillestroem 0, Brondby 0 *Brondby win 3-0 on agg*

Liverpool 0, Spartak Vladikavkaz 0 *Liverpool win 2-1 on agg*

Lokomotiv Moscow 0, Bayern Munich 5 (Klinsmann 2, Herzog, Scholl, Strunz) *Bayern Munich win 5-1 on agg*

Lyon 1 (Sassus), Farense 0 *Lyon win 2-0 on agg*

Manchester United 2 (Scholes, Schmeichel), Rotor Volgograd 2 (Nidergaus, Veretvennikov) *2-2 on agg. Rotor Volograd win on away goals*

Maribor Branik 1 (Karic pen), Olympiakos 3 (Ivic, Skartados pen, Chantzidis) *Olympiakos win 5-1 on agg*

Nottingham Forest 1 (Roy), Malmo 0 *2-2 on agg. Nottingham Forest win on away goals*

Olympia Lubjiana 2 (Bozgo pen, Zulic pen), Roda 0 *Roda win 5-2 on agg*

Omonia Nicosia 1 (Xiourouppas), Lazio 2 (Casiraghi, Di Vaio) *Lazio win 7-1 on agg*

PSV Eindhoven 7 (Ronaldo 4, Jonk 2, Hoekstra), MyPa 1 (Keskitalo) *PSV Eindhoven win 8-2 on agg*

Real Betis 2 (Alexis pen, Canas), Fenerbahce 0 *Real Betis win 4-1 on agg*

Roma 4 (Balbo 2, Fonseca, Rueda og), Neuchatel Xamax 0 *Roma win 5-1 on agg*

Slavia Prague 0, Freiburg 0 *Slavia Prague win 2-1 on agg*

Silkeborg 1 (Duus), Sparta Prague 2 (Lokvenc, Nemec) *2-2 on agg. Sparta Prague win on away goals*

Ujpest Budapest 0, Strasbourg 2 (Mostovoi, Zitelli) *Strasbourg win 5-0 on agg*

Werder Bremen 5 (Hobsch 3, Basler pen, Borowka), Glenavon 0 *Werder Bremen win 7-0 on agg*

Widez Lodz 1 (Mikhalchuk), Chornomorets 0 aet *1-1 on agg. Chornomorets win 6-5 on penalties*

Zaglebie Lubin 1 (Krzyzanowski), AC Milan 4 (Eranio, Simone, Boban 2) *AC Milan win 8-1 on agg*

UEFA Cup
Second round, first leg
(at Elland Road, Leeds)
Wednesday, October 17, 1995

 **Leeds United**  **3**

 **PSV Eindhoven**  **5**

Leeds United: John Lukic, Gary Kelly, Tony Dorigo (Paul Beesley 77), John Pemberton, David Wetherall, Noel Whelan (Rod Wallace 79), Carlton Palmer, Gary McAllister, Gary Speed (Andy Couzens 26), Brian Deane, Tony Yeboah
Goals: Speed 6, Palmer 48, McAllister 72
Manager: Howard Wilkinson

PSV Eindhoven: Ronald Waterreus, Chris van Der Weerden, Ernest Faber, Stan Valckx, Arthur Numan, Edward Linskens, Marciano Vink (Boudewijn Pahlplatz 71), Wim Jonk, Rene Eilkelkamp, Philip Cocu, Luc Nilis
Goals: Eijkelkamp 11, Vink 35, Jonk 39, Nilis 83, 88
Manager: Dick Advocaat

Referee: Antonio Lopez Nieto (Spain) **Att:** 24,846

Leeds put by artistic

MAJESTIC PSV Eindhoven left United's Euro future hanging by a thread with a blistering display at Elland Road. The Dutch stars made the most of the vast amount of space afforded by the Leeds defence to sweep to a 5-3 victory leaving Howard Wilkinson and his team needing a mathematical miracle in Holland.

It was United's 100th competitive game in Europe but turned into a night to forget after they fought back from being 3-1 down to 3-3 only to fall to two late goals by Belgian striker Luc Nilis.

Defiant Wilkinson, who just hours before the tie, rejected the chance to become the Football Association's

GREAT START: Gary Speed's header gives United an early, but short-lived, lead against PSV at Elland Road.

Forest star Stone rolls over classy Auxerre

STEVE Stone kept the home fires burning for England as Nottingham Forest won 1-0 in Auxerre.

His 23rd minute goal was enough to give Forest victory over the highly-rated French side, but Liverpool were held to a 0-0 stalemate in Denmark by Brondby.

Jurgen Klinsmann netted twice as Bayern Munich, one of the competition favourites, earned a 2-0 win in Kirkaldy against Raith.

Second round, first leg

Auxerre 0, Nottingham Forest 1 (Stone)
Barcelona 3 (Kodro 2, Celades), Vitoria Guimaraes 0
Bordeaux 2 (Histolloles, Witsche pen), Rotor Volgograd 1 (Huard og)
Benfica 1 (Panduru), Roda 0
Brondby 0, Liverpool 0
Chornomorets 0, Lens 0
Kaiserslautern 1 (Koch), Real Betis 3 (Alfonso 2, Alexis)
Leeds United 3 (Speed, Palmer, McAllister), PSV Eindhoven 5 (Eijkelamp, Vink, Jonk, Nilis 2)
Lugano 1 (Shalimov), Slavia Prague 2 (Vagner, Penicka)
Lyon 2 (Devaux, Deplace), Lazio 1 (Winter)
Raith Rovers 0, Bayern Munich 2 (Klinsmann 2)
Roma 4 (Vanderhaeghe og, Van der Hoorn og, Balbo, Totti), Aalst 0
Seville 1 (Juanito), Olympiakos 0
Sparta Prague 4 (Friedek, Nedved 2 – 1 pen, Buda), Zimbru Chisinau 3 (Sucharev, Testimitaunu 2 -1 pen)
Strasbourg 0, AC Milan 1 (Simone)
Werder Bremen 5 (Schtaniuk og, Basler 2, Hobsch, Bode), Dynamo Minsk 0

flat on canvas Dutch masters

technical director in favour of staying at Elland Road, remained upbeat.

"It is not impossible. We have got to go there and score three goals. Of course I believe we can do it. That's why I'm in this job."

It was a crazy game which, on another night, could have been 7-6 to Leeds. PSV had the rub of the green but their better range of passing at greater speed gave them a deserved victory.

Influential midfielder Gary Speed headed United in front after just six minutes but PSV's close range equaliser fell kindly to Rene Eijkelkamp after a rebound from a Tony Dorigo tackle was deflected into his path. United were rocked by two goals inside four minutes shortly after the injured Speed's departure.

Both goals stemmed from Wim Jonk whose initial shot was deflected in off Marciano Vink and Leeds protested at the award of the free-kick from which Jonk slammed in Eindhoven's third.

Attack was United's only option and both Brian Deane and Tony Yeboah missed easy chances as Leeds mounted a spirited response.

Three minutes after the interval Carlton Palmer was left free to drive the ball home and the match seemed to be swinging United's way when Gary McAllister curled in the equaliser with 18 minutes left.

But PSV had always looked dangerous and counter-attacked with venom to steal United's thunder in an astonishing finale

Again Leeds were unhappy about the award of a free-kick seven minutes from time. Jonk coolly lifted the ball over the defence and Nilis calmly drove in an angled drive.

United had barely time to get up from that hammer blow when Nilis sliced through United defence, gathered Philip Cocu's flick, and shot past Lukic.

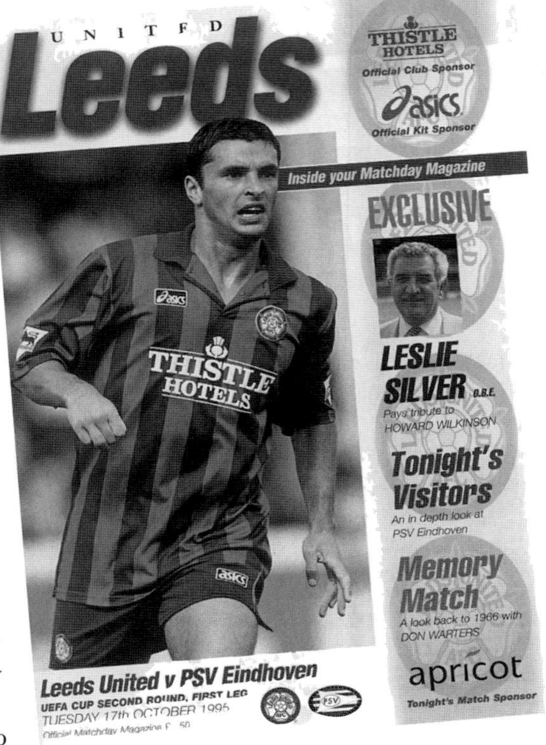

DANGER MAN: PSV's two-goal Luc Nilis skips past Tony Dorigo and John Pemberton.

Outplayed United can't match PSV

Whites suffer their heaviest aggregate defeat in Europe

GO, GARY GO: United's Gary Kelly pulls away from PSV's Dutch international Philip Cocu.

BRAZILIAN superstar Ronaldo had missed PSV Eindhoven's five-star showing at Leeds but was back in the firing line at the Phillips Stadium.

Having shaken off an ankle injury he returned to help the Dutch side cruise to a 3-0 win.

In truth, they didn't need him as the 8-3 aggregate added up to United's worst European defeat.

United were never in the game once Philip Cocu scored the first of his two goals after just 13 minutes and the slick home team won at a canter.

United needed to do something drastic to repair the damage at Elland Road and boss Howard Wilkinson sprang a huge surprise by naming the inexperienced 19-year-old defender Rob Bowman in his line-up. He was detailed to man-mark Luc Nilis, the man whose late double had killed off Leeds in the first leg.

But Bowman, making his first senior appearance in three seasons, struggled to contain the wily Nilis who slipped the ball through for Cocu's opener.

United battled bravely and both Carlton Palmer and Tony Yeboah missed a couple of half chances to get United back in the match, if not the tie.

But two minutes before half-time United were on the back foot again when John Pemberton, under pressure from the ever-alert Nilis, lobbed the ball over John Lukic for an own-goal.

It was one-way traffic in the second half as Wilkinson sent on youngsters Kevin Sharp and Mark Ford to gain vital experience while the Dutch remained in total command.

Ronaldo showed some neat skills to trick the United defence but Cocu crowned a fine display with the third when Wim Jonk's pass beat United's rickety offside trap and Cocu slipped the ball past the advancing Lukic.

After the glory in Monaco, United had gone crashing out of Europe on the back of three successive heavy defeats.

It was a sad end to what had been United's 100th competitive match in Europe – excluding the 1971 Fairs Cup play-off with Barcelona.

UEFFA Cup
Second round, second leg
(at Phillips Stadium, Eindhoven)
Wednesday, October 31, 1995

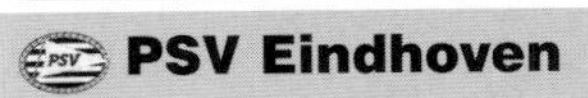
PSV Eindhoven 3

Leeds United 0

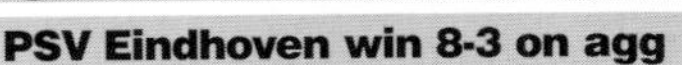
PSV Eindhoven win 8-3 on agg

PSV Eindhoven: Ronald Waterreus, Geoffrey Prommayon, Ernest Faber, Stan Valckx, Arthur Numan, Edward Linskens (Peter Hoekstra 70), Marciano Vink (Boudewijn Pahlplatz 75), Wim Jonk, Philip Cocu (Tom Van Der Leegte 81), Ronaldo, Luc Nilis
Goals: Cocu 13, 74, Pemberton og 43
Manager: Dick Advocaat

Leeds United: John Lukic, Gary Kelly, Paul Beesley (Mark Ford 75), David Wetherall, John Pemberton, Rob Bowman, Carlton Palmer, Gary McAllister, Gary Speed (Kevin Sharp 55), Noel Whelan (David White 59), Tony Yeboah
Manager: Howard Wilkinson

Referee: Marc Batt (France) **Att:** 25,750

Unstoppable goal-machine Klinsmann Bayern's inspiration

UNITED'S deadly German rivals, Bayern Munich, hoisted the UEFA Cup in fine style. With striker Jurgen Klinsmann virtually unstoppable, Bayern, once renowned for their defensive posture, scored goals at will.

He ended the competition with 15 goals, including four in the third round demoiltion of Benfica and the last goal of the two-legged final against French side Bordeaux.

Liverpool stumbled out at home when they failed to break down Brondby at Anfield, and were shattered when Dan Eggen scored the only goal of the contest in the 78th minute at Anfield.

That left Notingham Forest, battling to regain the glory days they had enjoyed under ex-Leeds boss Brian Clough, to fight England's corner.

They had a fine run to the quarter-finals but were thrashed 5-1 at the City Ground by Bayern, the irrepressible Klinsmann scoring twice.

Young Norwegian Alf-Inge Haaland featured in Forest's exciting campaign which saw them knock out Malmo and two top French sides, Auxerre and Lyon, before coming up against Franz Beckenbauer's free-scoring German side in the last eight.

Haaland moved to Elland Road from Forest in June 1997 for £1.6 million.

Surprise package were Slavia Prague, who pulled off a major shock in the quarter-finals by beating Roma.

They won the first leg 2-0 but the Italians levelled the tie in the Olympic Stadium, only for the brave Czechs to snatch a winner seven minutes from the end of extra-time.

Both clubs were to meet United in the near future.

Second round, second leg

Aalst 0, Roma 0 *Roma win 4-0 on agg*
AC Milan 2 (Baggio 2 – 1 pen), Strasbourg 1 (Sauzee) *AC Milan win 3-1 on agg*
Bayern Munich 2 (Klinsmann, Babbel), Raith Rovers 1 (Herzog og) *Bayern Munich win 4-1 on agg*
Dynamo Minsk 2 (Khatskevich pen, Shukanov), Werder Bremen 1 (Bode) *Werder Bremen win 6-2 on agg*
Lazio 0, Lyon 2 (Maurice, Assadourian) *Lyon win 4-1 on agg*
Lens 4 (Meyrieu, Vairelles, Dehu, Foe), Chornomorets 0 *Lens win 4-0 on agg*
Liverpool 0, Brondby 1 (Eggen) *Brondby win 1-0 on agg*
Nottingham Forest 0, Auxerre 0 *Nottingham Forest win 1-0 on agg*
Olympiakos 2 (Sapanis, Juskowiak pen), Seville 1 (Suker) aet *2-2 on agg. Seville win on away goals*
PSV Eindhoven 3 (Cocu 2, Pemberton og), Leeds United 0 *PSV Eindhoven win 8-3 on agg*
Real Betis 1 (Jarni), Kaiserslautern 0 *Real Betis win 4-1 on agg*
Roda 2 (Hesp, Trost), Benfica 2 (Hassan 2) *Benfica win 3-2 on agg*
Rotor Volgograd 0, Bordeaux 1 (Bancarel) *Bordeaux win 3-1 on agg*
Slavia Prague 1 (Smicer), Lugano 0 *Slavia Prague win 3-1 on agg*
Vitoria Guimaraes 0, Barcelona 4 (Kodro, Oscar Garcia, Celades, Sergi) *Barcelona win 7-0 on agg*
Zimbru Chisineau 0, Sparta Prague 2 (Koller, Vonasek) *Sparta Prague win 6-3 on agg*

Third round, first leg

AC Milan 2 (Weah 2), Sparta Prague 0
Bayern Munich 4 (Klinsmann 4), Benfica 1 (Dimas)
Bordeaux 2 (Dutuel, Croci), Real Betis 0
Brondby 2 (Moller, Bjur), Roma 1 (Fonseca)
Nottingham Forest 1 (McGregor), Lyon 0
PSV Eindhoven 2 (Ronaldo pen, Nilis), Werder Bremen 1 (Bode)
Seville 1 (Suker), Barcelona 1 (Hagi)
Slavia Prague 0, Lens 0

Third round, second leg

Barcelona 3 (Bakero, Popescu, Roger), Seville 1 (Moya)
Barcelona win 4-2 on agg
Benfica 1 (Valdo), Bayern Munich 3 (Klinsmann 2, Herzog)
Bayern Munich win 7-2 on agg
Lens 0, Slavia Prague 1 (Poborsky) aet *Slavia Prague win 1-0 on agg*
Lyon 0, Nottingham Forest 0 *Nottingham Forest win 1-0 on agg*
Real Betis 2 (Alexis, Stostic), Bordeaux 1 (Zidane) *Bordeaux win 3-2 on agg*
Roma 3 (Totti, Balbo, Garbom), Brondby 1 (Moller) *Roma win 4-3 on agg*
Sparta Prague 0, AC Milan 0 *AC Milan win 2-0 on agg*
Werder Bremen 0, PSV Eindhoven 0 *PSV Eindhoven win 2-1 on agg*

Quarter-final, first leg

AC Milan 2 (Eranio, Baggio), Bordeaux 0
Barcelona 2 (Bakero, Abelardo), PSV Eindhoven 2 (Nilis 2)
Bayern Munich 2 (Klinsmann, Scholl), Nottingham Forest 1 (Chettle)
Slavia Prague 2 (Poborsky, Vagner), Roma 0

Quarter-final, second leg

Bordeaux 3 (Tholot, Dugarry 2), AC Milan 0 *Bordeaux win 3-2 on agg*
Nottingham Forest 1 (Stone), Bayern Munich 5 (Klinsmann 2, Ziege, Strunz, Papin) *Bayern Munich win 7-2 on agg*
PSV Eindhoven 2 (Zenden, Eykelkamp), Barcelona 3 (Bakero, Figo, Sergi) *Barcelona win 5-4 on agg*
Roma 3 (Moriero 2, Giannini), Slavia Prague 1 (Vavra) aet *3-3 on agg. Slavia Prague win on away goals*

Semi-finals, first leg

Bayern Munich 2 (Witeczek, Scholl), Barcelona 2 (Oscar Garcia, Hagi)
Slavia Prague 0, Bordeaux 1 (Dugarry)

Semi-finals, second leg

Barcelona 1 (de la Pena), Bayern Munich 2 (Babbel, Witeczek) *Bayern Munich win 4-3 on agg*
Bordeaux 1 (Tholot), Slavia Prague 0 *Bordeaux win 2-0 on agg*

Final, first leg

(Olympic Stadium, Munich)
May 1, 1996
Bayern Munich 2
Bordeaux 0

Bayern Munich: Khan, Babbel, Matthaus (Frey 54), Helmer, Ziege, Kreuzer, Hamann, Sforza, Scholl, Papin (Witeczek 70), Klinsmann
Goals: Helmer 34, Scholl 60
Manager: Franz Beckenbauer
Bordeaux: Huard, Grenet, Dogon, Friis-Hansen, Lizarazu, Croci, Lucas, Dutuel, Witschge, Bancarel, Tholot (Anselin 90)
Manager: Gernot Rohr
Referee: Serge Muhmenthaler (Switzerland)
Attendance: 63,000

Final, second leg

(Parc Lescure Stadium, Bordeaux)
May 15, 1996
Bordeaux 1
Bayern Munich 3
(Bayern Munich win 5-1 on agg)

Bordeaux: Huard, Bancarel, Dogon, Friis-Hansen, Lizarazu (Anselin 32), Croci (Dutuel 58), Lucas (Grenet 80), Zidane, Witschge, Tholot, Dugarry
Goal: Dutuel 75
Manager: Gernot Rohr
Bayern Munich: Khan, Babbel, Matthaus, Helmer, Ziege, Strunz (Zieckler 60), Frey, Sforza, Scholl, Klinsmann, Kostadinov (Witeczek 75)
Goals: Scholl 53, Kostadinov 65, Klinsmann 77
Manager: Franz Beckenbauer
Referee: Vadim Zhuk (Belarus)
Attendance: 36,000

Leading scorers: 15 – Klinsmann (Bayern Munich), 6 – Ronaldo (PSV Eindhoven), 5 – Nedved (Sparta Prague), Nilis (PSV Eindhoven)

United's change of direction

UNITED continued to struggle in the Premiership after their exit from the UEFA Cup.

They did reach the sixth round of the FA Cup, losing to Liverpool after a replay at Anfield, and made it to the League Cup final.

At Wembley they were turned over 3-0 by Aston Villa a result that signalled the beginning of the end of Wilkinson's reign.

With United struggling in the League and the door to Europe closed by the failure to win either of the domestic cups it meant that there would be no European football at Elland Road in 1996/97.

Wilkinson held on until September 1996 when Leeds lost 4-0 at home to Manchester United – Eric Cantona among the scorers. It was the final straw for Wilko. He was sacked after eight years in charge – less than 11 months after United's undignified exit at the hands of PSV Eindhoven.

It was a time of great change for United. Chairman Leslie Silver, 71, had resigned towards the end of the previous season because of ill health and Bill Fotherby took over the chairmanship.

The summer also saw the departure of three of United's Championship-winning team. Scottish international midfielder Gary McAllister opted to link up with former Leeds hero Gordon Strachan at Coventry, while fellow midfielder Gary Speed moved on to Everton for £3,5millon. The third move saw goalkeeper John Lukic, 35, return to Arsenal for the second time in his career.

Before he left, Wilkinson recruited young midfielder Lee Bowyer (Charlton), goalkeeper Nigel Martyn (Crystal Palace), Lee Sharpe (Manchester United) and Liverpool's veteran goalscoring legend Ian Rush.

They hardly had time to get to know their new boss before ex-Arsenal boss George Graham, who won a stack of honours at Highbury, was brought in.

Graham initially opted for a back to basics approach in which the emphasis was on defence, but he did unearth a genuine goalscorer in Jimmy-Floyd Hasselbaink from Portuguese football. Goals eventually began to flow and United finished the 1997/98 campaign in fifth place – high enough to recapture a UEFA Cup place the following season.

WHOLE NEW BAWL GAME: New United boss George Graham, who replaced Howard Wilkinson (top) barks out his orders from the Leeds dug-out.

UEFA Cup entries climb above 100 mark

A STAGGERING 101 teams competed in the 1998/99 UEFA Cup.

Sorting the wheat from the chaff started with a preliminary round, followed by a qualification round.

Clubs from England (including United), Italy, Germany, Spain, France, Holland, Portugal, the three Intertoto Cup winners and 16 clubs eliminated from the Champions League qualifying round came in at the first round stage.

Preliminary round, first leg

Akranes 3 (Adolfsson, Eyjolfsson, Ivisic), Zalgiris Vilnius 2 (Skinderis, Vasiliauskas)
Arges Pitesti 5 (Emirbakan og, Barbu 2, Bardes, Jelaveanu), Dynamo Baku 1 (Alijew pen)
Belshina Bobruisk 0, CSKA Sofia 0
Ekeren 4 (Van Ankeren, Morhaye 2, Kovacs), Sarajevo 1 (Feratovic)
Ferencvaros 6 (Fulop, Selimi, Schultz 2, Vamosi, Matyus), Principal 0
Hapoel Tel Aviv 3 (Simerotic pen, Tubi, Tikva), FinnPa 1 (Hautala)
Inter Bratislava 2 (Suchancok, Miklos), Tirana 0
Kolkheti Poti 0, Red Star Belgrade 4 (Ognjenovic, Acimovic 2, Pantelic)
Mura 6 (Citer 2, Lukic 2, Cipot, Galie), Daugava 1 (Ridnyj)
Newtown 0, Wisla Krakow 0
Omonia Nicosia 5 (Kitanov 2, Rauffman pen, Panayiotou, Kontolefteros), Linfield 1 (Ferguson)
Otelul Galati 3 (Stefan, Mihalache, Male pen), Sloga 0
Sadam 0, Polonia 2 (Olisadebe, Bak)
Shelbourne 3 (Porrini og, Rutherford, Morley), Rangers 5 (Albertz 2 pens, Amato 2, Van Bronckhorst) in Tranmere
Shaktjor Donetsk 2 (Seleznev, Kriventsov pen), Birkirkara 1 (Zammit)
Shirak 0, Malmor 2 (Pavlovic, Olsson)
Tiligul Tiraspol 0, Anderlecht 1 (Staelens)
Torshavn 2 (Johannesen 2), Vaasa 0
Union Luxembourg 0, Gothenburg 3 (Ekstrom, Nusson pen, Hermansson)
Zeljeznicar 1 (Vazda), Kilmarnock 1 (McGowne)

Preliminary round, second leg

Anderlecht 5 (Stoica, de Boeck, Dheedene, Taument, Aarst), Tiligul Tiraspol 0 *Anderlecht win 6-0 on agg*
Birkikara 0, Shaktjor Donetsk 4 (Seleznev, Krivencov, Kovales 2 -1 pen) *Shaktjor Donetsk win 6-1 on agg*
CSKA Sofia 3 (Petrov, Naidenov, Stanchev), Belshina Bobruisk 1 (Balashov) 1 *CSKA Sofia win 3-1 on agg*
Daugava 1 (Szarando), Mura 2 (Vugrincic, Ristic) *Mura win 8-2 on agg*
Dynamo Baku 0, Arges Pitesti 2 (Mutu, Jelaveanu) *Arges Pitesti win 7-1 on agg*
FinnPa 1 (Geagea), Hapoel Tel Aviv 3 (Tikva 2, Tubi) *Hapoel Tel Aviv win 6-2 on agg*
Gothenburg 4 (Ekstroem 3, Henriksson), Union Luxembourg 0 *Gothenburg win 7-0 on agg*
Kilmarnock 1 (Mahood), Zeljeznicar 0 *Kilmarnock win 2-1 on agg*
Linfield 5 (Feeney, Gorman 2, McDonald, Ferguson), Omonia Nicosia 3 (Marantos, Kitanov, Ioaldou) *Omonia Nicosia win 8-6 on agg*
Malmo 5 (Thylander, Kindvall 3, Gudmundsson), Shirak 0 *Malmo win 7-0 on agg*
Polonia 3 (Moskal, Wedzynski, Bak), Sadam 1 (Krolov) *Polonia win 5-1 on agg*
Principal 1 (Pasqui), Ferencvaros 8 (Selimi 2, Kovas 2, Kriston, Nagy, Schultz, Jagodies) *Ferencvaros win 14-1 on agg*
Rangers 2 (Johansson 2), Shelbourne 0 *Rangers win 7-3 on agg*
Red Star Belgrade 7 (Pantelic, Ognjenovic 2 – 1 pen, Gojkovic, Micic 3), Kolkheti Poti 0 *Red Star Belgrade win 11-0 on agg*
Sarajevo 0, Ekeren 0 *Ekeren win 4-1 on agg*
Sloga 1 (Stankovski), Otelul Galati 1 (Mihalache) *Otelul Galati win 4-1 on agg*
Tirana 0, Inter Bratislava 2 (Balonie, Miklos) *Inter Bratislava win 4-0 on agg*
Vaasa 4 (Souste 2, Tarkkio, Nygaard), Torshavn 0 *Vaasa win 4-2 on agg*
Wisla Krakow 7 (Kulawik 2, Sunday, Kaliciak, Dubicki, Pater 2), Newtown 0 *Wisla Krakow win 7-0 on agg*
Zalgiris Vilnius 1 (Stesko), Akranes 0 *3-3 on agg. Zalgiris Vilnius win on away goals*

Byes: ***AEK Athens, Brann, Dynamo Moscow, FC Zurich, Fenerbahce, Grazer, Hadjuk Split, Istanbulspor, Molde, Osijek, PAOK Salonika, Rapid Vienna, Rotor Volgograd, Servette, Sigma Olomouc, Silkeborg, Slavia Prague, Stromsgodset, Trabzonspor, Vejle***

Qualifying round, first leg

Arges Pitesti 2 (Muti, Barbu), Istanbulspor 0
Brann 1 (Kvisvik), Zalgiris Vilnius 0
Ekeren 1 (Morhaye), Servette 4 (Rey 2 – 1pen, Wolf, Durix)
FC Zurich 4 (Sant'ana, Djordjevic, Chassot, Tanone), Shaktjor Donetsk 0
Fenerbahce 1 (Kamalettin)
Ferencvaros 4 (Selinu, Lendvai, Nyilas, Vmcze), AEK Athens 2 (Nikolaidis, Sebwe)
Gothenburg 2 (Hermansson, Persson), Hadjuk Split 1 (Brajkovic), Malmo 1 (Bjamasson)
Hapoel Tel Aviv 1 (Tubi), Stromsgodset 0
Molde 0, CSKA Sofia 0
Mura 0, Silkeborg 0
Omonia Nicosia 3 (Raunmann 2, Malekos), Rapid Vienna 0
Osijek 3 (Krpan, Prsic, Vranjes), Anderlecht 1 (Claeys)
Polonia 0, Dynamo Moscow 1 (Gusev)
Rangers 2 (Kanchelskis, Wallace), PAOK Salonika 0
Red Star Belgrade 2 (Skoric pen, Ognjenovic pen), Rotor Volvograd 1 (Abramov)
Sigma Olomouc 2 (Krohmer, Koenig), Kilmarnock 0
Slavia Prague 4 (Vagner 2, Kozel, Skala 0, Inter Bratislava 0
Vaasa 0, Graz 0
Vejle 3 (Wael 2, Soggard), Otelul 0
Wisla Krakow 5 (Dubicld, Kulawik 3, Zaja), Trabzonspor 1 (Vugrinec)

Qualifying round, second leg

Anderlecht 2 (Aarst, Stolca), Osijek 0 *3-3 on agg. Anderlecht win on away goals*
AEK Athens 4 (Nikolaidis 3 – 2 pens, Donis), Ferencvaros 0 *AEK Athens win 6-4 on agg*
CSKA Sofia 2 (Petkov, Stanchev), Molde 0 *CSKA Sofia win 2-0 on agg*
Dynamo Moscow 1 (Terechin), Polonia 0 *Dynamo Moscow win 2-0 on agg*
Fenerbahce 1 (Balic), Gothenburg 0 *2-2 on agg Fenerbahce win on away goals*
Graz 3 (Luhovy, Grimm, Drechsler), Vaasa 0 *Graz win 3-0 on agg*
Inter Bratislava 2 (Babnic, Ovad), Slavia Prague 0 *Slavia Prague win 4-2 on agg*
Istanbulspor 4 (Akyuz, Yalcin, Yozgatli. Kocaman), Arges Pirtesti 2 (Mutu, Barbu) *4-4 on agg. Arges Pitesti win on away goals*
Kilmarnock 0, Sigma Olomouc 2 (Heinz, Mucha) *Sigma Olomouc win 4-0 on agg*
Malmo 1 (Ohlsson), Hadjuk Split 2 (Vucko 2) *Hadjuk Split win 3-2 on agg*
Otelul 0, Vejle 3 (Jung, Graulund, Wael)
Vejle win 6-0 on agg
PAOK Salonika 0, Rangers 0 *Rangers win 2-0 on agg*
Rapid Vienna 2 (Herat, Wagner), Omonia Nicosia 0 *3-3 on agg. Rapid Vienna win on away goals*
Rotor Volgograd 1 (Zemov), Red Star Belgrade 2 (Ognjenovic, Dudic) *Red Star Belgrade win 4-2 on agg*
Servette 1 (Rey pen), Ekeren 2 (Karlen og, Karagiannis) *Servette win 5-3 on agg*
Shaktar Donetsk 3 (Orbu 2, Shtoltsers), FC Zurich 2 (Bartlett 2) *FC Zurich win 6-3 on agg*
Silkeborg 2 (Sorensen, Larsen), Mura 0 *Silkeborg win 2-0 on agg*
Stromsgodset 1 (Michaelsen), Hapoel Tel Aviv 0 aet *1-1 on agg. Stromsgodset win 4-2 on penalties*
Trabozonspor 1 (Huseyn), Wisla Krakow 2 (Sunday, Kulawik) *Wisla Kracow win 7-2 on agg*
Zalgiris Vilnius 0, Brann 0 *Brann win 1-0 on agg*

Byes: *Aston Villa, Atletico Madrid, Blackburn Rovers, Bordeaux, Celta Vigo, Feyenoord, Gelsenkirchen, Leeds United, Liverpool, Lyon, Maritimo, Marseille, Monaco, Real Betis, Real Sociedad, San Sebastian, Schalke, Sporting Lisbon, Stuttgart, Vitesse Arnhem, Vitoria Setubal, Willem II Intertoto Cup winners Bologna, Werder Bremen and Valencia and teams eliminated from Champions League – Anorthsis, Bayer Leverkusen, Beitar Jerusalem, Branic Maribor, Brugges, Celtic, Dynamo Tbilisi, Fiorentina, Grasshoppers, Kosice, Litets Lovech, Lodz, Metz, Obilic, Parma, Skonto Riga, Roma, Sparta Prague, Steaua Budapest, Udinese, Ujpest Doza – also qualified for the first round.*

GRAHAM'S UNITED: The 1997/98 Leeds squad which brought European football back to Elland Road. Back row, from left to right: Bruno Ribeiro, Richard Jobson, David Wetherall, Mark Beeney, Nigel Martyn, Robert Molenaar, Gunnar Halle, Lee Bowyer. Middle row: David O'Leary (assistant manager), David Swift (senior physio), Pierre Laurent, Jimmy-Floyd Hasselbaink, Lee Sharpe, David Hopkin, Harry Kewell, Andy Gray, Rod Wallace, David Williams (coach). Front row: Ian Harte, Alf-Inge Haarland, Lucas Radebe, George Graham (Manager), David Robertson, Derek Lilley, Gary Kelly.

Graham's rebuilding job

GRADUALLY George Graham was rebuilding Leeds United.

One of his main aims was to lower the age of the squad and they went into the 1998/99 UEFA Cup campaign with a group of players whose average age was 24.

A major plus had been the winning of the FA Youth Cup which saw several young players like Jonathan Woodgate and Stephen McPhail knocking on the first team door, which had already been battered down by the likes of talented Aussie Harry Kewell and Irish left-back Ian Harte, the nephew of Gary Kelly, who had made the right-back slot his own.

In goal, Nigel Martyn was rock-solid, while Lee Bowyer was proving a real dynamo in midfield where he was joiined by David Hopkin, a £3.25 million purchase from Crystal Palace in summer 1997.

Graham's other recruits included £2m utility player Alf-Inge Haaland, who had European experience with Nottingham Forest, and left-back David Robertson, who had played in the Champions League for Rangers, against Leeds in the Howard Wilkinson era. Another Norwegian, Gunnar Halle, was a useful utility player.

In an effort to support Jimmy-Floyd Hasselbaink, Dutch striker Clyde Wijnhard was brought in from Willem II.

There was certainly a continental air to Graham's squad. His ability to spot a central defender saw him pick up another Dutch player, Robert Molenaar from Volendam for a bargain £1m and a fee of £1.3 million was paid to Rapid Vienna for Austrian utility defender Martin Hiden.

When Graham and his assistant David O'Leary went to watch Hasselbaink playing for Boavista against Vitoria Setubal, midfielder Bruno Ribeiro caught their eye and Leeds snapped the Portuguese Under-21 player up for £500,000.

First round, first leg

Anderlecht 0, Grasshoppers 2 (Comisetti, Tikva)
Arges Pitesti 0, Celta Vigo 1 (Sanchez)
Aston Villa 3 (Charles, Vassell 2), Stromsgodset 2 (Michelsen, George)
Atletico Madrid 2 (Juninho, Jose Mari), Obilic 0
Beitar Jerusalem 1 (Abuksis pen), Rangers 1 (Albertz)
Blackburn Rovers 0, Lyon 1 (Bak)
Bordeaux 1 (Hatz og), Rapid Vienna 1 (Freund)
Branic Maribor 0, Wisla Cracow 2 (Frankowsi, Pater)
Brann 2 (Moen, Loweik), Werder Bremen 0
Dynamo Moscow 2 (Golovskoi, Ostrovski), Skonto Riga 2 (Micholaps, Pakhar)
FC Zurich 4 (Nixon, Hodel, Bartlett, Chassot), Anorthosis 0
Fenerbahce 1 (Moldovan), Parma 0
Fiorentina 2 (Edmundo 2), Hadjuk Split 1 (Vucko)
Kosice 0, Liverpool 3 (Berger, Riedle, Owen)
Leeds United 1 (Hasselbaink), Maritimo 0
Litech Lovech 1 (Stoilov), Graz 1 (Lipa)
LKS Lodz 1 (Matys), Monaco 3 (Bendkowski og, Trezeguet pen, Spehar)
Red Star Belgrade 2 (Ognjenovic, Drulic), Metz 1 (Rodriguez)
Schalke1 (Wilmots), Slavia Prague 0
Servette 2 (Pizzinat, Melunovic), CSKA Sofia 1 (Stanchev)
Sigma Olomouc 2 (Heinz 2), Marseille 2 (Ravanelli, Roy)
Silkebourg 0, Roma 2 (Toni, Alenichev)
Sparta Prague 2 (Cilek, Lokvenc), Real Sociedad 4 (Kovacevic 2, Aldeondo, de Pedro)
Sporting Lisbon 0, Bologna 2 (Nervo, Conceicao)
Steaua Bucharest 3 (Linear, Rosu, Dumitrescu), Valencia 4 (Illie 2, Angulo 2)
Udinese 1 (Walem), Bayer Leverkusen 1 (Kirsten)
Ujpest Budapest 0, Brugges 5 (Jankauskas, Dic, Vermant, Anie, Ekakia)
Vejle 1 (Graulund), Real Betis 0
Vitesse Arnhem 3 (Laros, Perovic, Machlas), AEK Athens 0
Vitoria Guimaraes 1 (Geraldo), Celtic 2 (Larsson, Donnelly)
VfB Stuttgart 1 (Bobic), Feyenoord 3 (Van Gastel, Tomasson 2)
Willem II 3 (Ramzy, Arts, Schenning), Dynamo Tbilisi 0

Jimmy grabs last-gasp advantage

HARD task-master George Graham preached patience after seeing United hit a brick wall on their return to Europe after a three-year absence.

Graham had skilfully steered the Whites into the UEFA Cup where they discovered stubborn opponents in unknown Portuguese side Maritimo, from the island of Madeira.

The only goal of the game came in the 82nd minute from time when United's Dutch striker Jimmy-Floyd Hasselbaink was brought down on the edge of the box.

Hasselbaink, signed to fill the goalscoring boots of Tony Yeboah, clipped the resulting free-kick wide of goalkeeper Yves Van Der Straeten's left hand to give United a priceless victory.

Van Der Straeten had held firm throughout the game behind a strong Portuguese defence and pulled off a great diving stop to prevent substitute Lee Sharpe's volley from making it 2-0.

A second goal could well have wrapped up the tie but ex-Arsenal boss Graham was just relieved United had won the game without conceding.

His last European tie had been the 1995 European Cup Winners Cup final when Nayim's last-gasp goal from the half-way line saw Real Zaragoza beat Arsenal so was happy enough with victory over Maritimo."I was despairing the goal would never come. We expected them to defend and I thought they did it well but this is something the players and the fans are going to have to live with.

"European games can be frustrating and your patience can wear a bit thin. But I think we got what we deserved by winning the game."

Leeds went hunting for an early goal but didn't get it when Hasselbaink's fellow Dutch striker Clyde Wijinhard saw a good chance blocked by Belgian 'keeper Van Straeten. Leeds then looked to their exciting Australian-born winger Harry Kewell to break the deadlock and he sent a volley whistling over.

Just before the hour, Hasselbaink, who netted a hat-trick against Maritimo the last time he played against them in the Portuguese League when he was a Boavista player, thumped a shot against an upright.

But just as it looked as though Hasselbaink, whose goals had propelled Leeds to fifth position in the Premiership and UEFA qualification the previous season, ended the agony with his late free-kick.

The goal stopped a sequence of three successive home defeats in Europe – PSV Eindhoven, Monaco and Rangers – and ensured a big crowd of 38,033 attracted by cut-price tickets, went home happy. It was United's biggest attendance for a Euro night since 50,393 squeezed in to see the 1975 European Cup semi-final against Barcelona.

United now knew the strength of Maritimo's defence but their attack remained an unknown quantity as, apart from some wild speculative long-range shots, they failed to test Nigel Martyn in the Leeds goal.

RIDING HIGH: Jimmy Floyd Hasselbaink celebrates his winner against Maritimo by giving Robert Molenaar a lift.

UEFA Cup
First round, first leg
(at Elland Road, Leeds)
Tuesday, September 15, 1998

Leeds United	**1**
Maritimo	**0**

Leeds United: Nigel Martyn, Martin Hiden, Ian Harte, Robert Molenaar, Lucas Radebe, David Hopkin (Lee Sharpe 75), Alf-Inge Haaland (Bruno Ribeiro), Lee Bowyer, Harry Kewell, Jimmy-Floyd Hasselbaink, Clyde Wijnhard (Derek Lilley 61)
Goal: Hasselbaink 82
Manager: George Graham

Maritimo: Yves Van Der Straeten, Rui Oscar, Carlos Jorge, Jorge Soares, Jose D Silva, Eusebio Sousa, Marcio Antonio (Nelson Antonio da Gama 87), Adelino Lopes (Manuel De Silva Cruz 66), Paulo Sergio Da Silva, Johann Deveau (Herivelto Da Silva Moreira 65), Alex Bunbury
Manager: Augusto Soares Inacio

Referee: Alain Sars (France) **Att:** 38,033

Late night for United after penalty shoot-out

SMART MART: United's Austrian defender Martin Hiden clears in spectacular fashion in Funchal as Robert Molenaar (right) roars his approval.

Madeira is no piece of cake

SOMEHOW Leeds United's players managed to stage a drama in Madeira to match their managerial merry-go-round.

In what was to be George Graham's last match in charge as Leeds manager before his defection to Tottenham Hotspur, United won a nerve-jangling penalty shoot-out to defeat Maritimo.

There had been enormous speculation that Graham wanted to return to London for personal reasons and the White Hart Lane club were on the lookout for a replacement for Christian Gross as manager. The media were quick to put the pieces together and the build-up to United's rematch against Maritimo was dominated by 'Graham for Spurs' stories.

United lost 1-0 the second leg in regulation time and with neither side able to conjure up a winner the game was decided by spot-kicks deep into the steamy night in the foothills of Funchal, the Madeiran capital.

The match kicked off late to accommodate Portuguese television coverage and Lee Sharpe's tie-breaking penalty didn't hit the back of the Maritimo net until 11.45pm.

Maritimo had been quickly into their stride with a three-man attack led by Canadian international Alex Bunbury and it needed a super save from Nigel Martyn to keep the Portuguese at bay.

United looked to be edging to half-time with a 0-0 scoreline in their back pocket when defender Jorge Soares headed home a free-kick.

The odds had swung in Maritimo's favour but Graham sent on striker Clyde Wijnhard for midfielder Lee Bowyer in an effort to get a crucial away goal.

But it didn't come and United needed to show all their resiliance in extra-time and were let off the hook when Manuel Cruz blazed a good chance over the bar from 12 yards.

Tension was mounting and Leeds suffered a further blow when assistant manager David O'Leary was ordered from the bench by Austrian referee Fritz Stuchlich for vigorously protesting against substitute Pedro Antonio's theatrical diving.

But it was United who kept their calm in the Atlantic air as Alf-Inge Haaland converted the opening penalty. Bunbury responded, Ian Harte made it 2-1 before Paulo da Silva missed. Danny Granville, who had only come on for his debut seconds before the end of extra-time, scored with his first kick to give United a 3-1 cushion. Soares couldn't handle the pressure and missed his effort, leaving Sharpe to complete the job with his left foot.

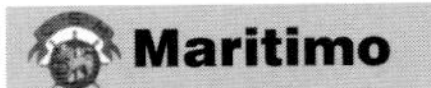

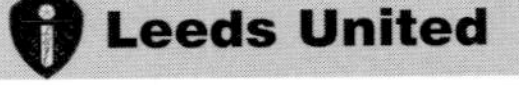

1-1 on agg after extra-time
Leeds United win 4-1 on penalties

Maritimo: Yves Van Der Straeten, Rui Oscar, Carlos Jorge, Jorge Soares, Eusebio Sousa, Marcio Antonio, Jose de Silva, Adelino Lopes (Pedro Paulo Antonio 85), Nelson Antonio da Gama (Manuel de Silva Cruz 65), Pedrag Jokanovic (Paulo Sergio da Silva 64), Alex Bunbury
Goal: Suarez 45
Manager: Augusto Suares Inacio

Leeds United: Nigel Martyn, Martin Hiden, Ian Harte, Robert Molenaar, Lucas Radebe, David Hopkin (Danny Granville 120), Alf-Inge Haaland, Lee Bowyer (Clyde Wijnhard 75), Gunnar Halle, Harry Kewell (Lee Sharpe 76), Jimmy-Floyd Hasselbaink
Manager: George Graham

Referee: Fritz Stuchlich (Austria) **Att:** 7,400

O'Leary moves to top of the list

UNITED'S fears that George Graham's future lay in London proved true.

Despite initially fending off Tottenham's approach for Graham, it was clear that the Whites would be unable to hang on to a man whose heart was on a move to the capital.

On October 1, after several weeks speculation, Graham took over at White Hart Lane on a four-year contract reputedly worth £6 million.

Ironically, his last Premiership game in charge was a 3-3 draw against Spurs at White Hart Lane and his departure after the Maritimo game was a huge blow to the Leeds board who were seeing the canny Scot's well-laid plans come to fruition.

The day after Graham's departure, United were paired with Italian giants Roma with the first leg scheduled for October 20 in the Olympic Stadium in Rome.

BOSS IN WAITING: David O'Leary.

It was a tasty prospect, but chairman Peter Ridsdale knew his priority was getting the right manager.

Former Elland Road favourite Gordon Strachan, manager at Coventry City, was a popular tip for the job but the big early front runner was Leicester City's Martin O'Neill. Leeds's first overtures to the Foxes were rejected but O'Neill himself said he would like to talk to United but his hands were tied by his contract. At the height of the speculation O'Neill's Leicester won 1-0 at Elland Road with assistant manager David O'Leary in temporary charge of Leeds.

O'Leary had not, as some thought, followed Graham to Spurs to be his second in command, but remained at Leeds and the crowd backed O'Leary at the Leicester game despite him saying that he was not in for the job.

Ridsdale announced that O'Leary and Eddie Gray would be in total control of first team matters for the Premiership game at Nottingham Forest and the trip to Rome. Sweeping changes were made by O'Leary for a 1-1 draw at the City Ground and handed a debut to England Under- 18 centre-half Jonathan Woodgate.

From being the outsider O'Leary had moved to the top of the queue on a groundswell of popular support.

Stan's the man for Villa

ASTON Villa overcame a potential slip in snowy Norway when Stan Collymore's hat-trick earned a 3-0 win at Stromsgodset.

In the first leg Villa trailed 2-0 at home with seven minutes left before young two-goal substitute Darius Vassell inspired an amazing comeback.

He came on in the 80th minute, three minutes later Gary Charles pulled a goal back and Vassell, future England material, scored a minute from the end and in injury time.

First round, second leg

AEK Athens 3 (Nikolaidis 2, Kopitsis), Vitesse Arnhem 3 (Machlas 2, Reuser) *Vitesse Arnhem win 6-3 on agg*

Anorthosis 2 (Fischer og, Krcmarevic), FC Zurich 3 (Sant'Anna, Bartlett 2) *FC Zurich win 7-2 on agg*

Bayer Leverkusen 1 (Beinlich), Udinese 0 *Bayer Leverkusen win 2-1 on agg*

Bologna 2 (Nervo, Signori pen), Sporting Lisbon 1 (Leandro) *Bologna win 4-1 on agg*

Brugges 2 (Borklemans, Vermant), Ujpest Budapest 2 (Kopunovic, Szanyo pen) *Brugges win 7-2 on agg*

Celtic 2 (Stubbs, Larsson), Vitoria Guimaraes 1 (Soderstroem) *Celtic win 4-2 on agg*

CSKA Sofia 1 (Stanchev), Servette 0 *2-2 on agg. CSKA Sofia win on away goals*

Celta Vigo 7 (Penev 3, Mazinho, Sanchez, Alberto 2), Arges Pitesti 0 *Celta Vigo win 8-0 on agg*

Dynamo Tbilisi 0, Willem 3 (Valk, Ceesay, Ramzy) *Willem II win 6-0 on agg*

Feyenoord 0, VfB Stuttgart 3 (Balakov, Djordjevic, Bobic) *VfB Stuttgart win 4-3 on agg*

Grasshoppers 0, Anderlecht 0 *Grasshoppers win 2-0 on agg*

Graz 2 (Golombek, Akwuegbu), Litech Lovech 0 *Graz win 3-1 on agg*

Hadjuk Split 0, Fiorentina 0 *Fiorentina win 2-1 on agg*

Liverpool 5 (Redknapp 2, Ince, Fowler 2), Kosice 0 *Liverpool win 8-0 on agg*

Lyon 2 (Caveglis, Grassi pen), Blackburn Rovers 2 (Perez, Flitcroft) *Lyon win 3-2 on agg*

Marseille 4 (Dugarry 2, Pires 2), Sigma Olomouc 0 *Marseille win 6-2 on agg*

Martitimo 1 (Jorge Soares), Leeds United 0 aet *1-1 on agg. Leeds United win 4-1 on pens*

Metz 2 (Kastendeuch, Meyrieu pen), Red Star Belgrade 1 (Marinovic) aet *3-3 on agg. Red Star Belgrade win 4-3 on pens*

Monaco 0, LKS Lodz 0 *Monaco win 3-1 on agg*

Obilic 0, Atletico Madrid 1 (Kiko) *Atletico Madrid win 3-0 on agg*

Parma 3 (Saffet og, Crespo, Boghossian), Fenerbahce 1 (Baljic) *Parma win 3-2 on agg*

Real Betis 5 (Perez 3, George, Galvez), Vejke 0 *Real Betis win 5-1 on agg*

Real Sociedad 1 (Kovacevic), Sparta Prague 0 *Real Sociedad win 5-2 on agg*

Roma 1 (Delvecchio), Silkeborg 0 *Roma win 3-0 on agg*

Skonto Riga 2 (Pachars 2), Dynamo Moscow 3 (Gusev, Golovski, Terechin) *Dynamo Moscow win 5-4 on agg*

Slavia Prague 1 (Dostalek), Schalke 0 aet *Slavia Prague win 5-4 on pens*

Stromsgodset 0, Aston Villa 3 (Collymore 3) *Aston Villa win 6-2 on agg*

Valencia 3 (Roch, Lopez, Lucarelli), Steaua Bucharest 0 *Valencia win 7-3 on agg*

Werder Bremen 4 (Wicky, Wiedener, Maksimov, Flo), Brann 0 *Werder Bremen win 4-2 on agg*

Wisla Kracow 3 (Zajac 2, Kulawik), Branic Maribor 0 *Wisla Kracow win 5-0 on agg*

United's

UEFA Cup
Second round, first leg
(at Olympic Stadium, Rome)
Tuesday, October 20, 1998

Roma	1
Leeds United	0

Roma: Antonio Chimenti, Cafu, Aldair Dos Santos, Antonio Zago, Vicent Candela, Damiano Tommasi, Luigi Di Baggio, Eusebio Di Francesco (Dmitri Alenichev HT), Alessandro Frau (Gustavo Bartlet 57), Marco Delvecchio, Francesco Totti
Goal: Delvecchio 18
Manager: Zdenek Zeman

Leeds United: Nigel Martyn, Martin Hiden, Gunnar Halle, Robert Molenaar, Lucas Radebe, Lee Bowyer, Stephen McPhail, David Hopkin, Bruno Ribeiro, Harry Kewell (Alf Inge-Haaland 67), Jimmy-Floyd Hasselbaink (Clyde Wijnhard 78)
Manager: David O'Leary

Referee: Nieto Lopez (Spain) **Att:** 43,003

FALL GUY: Down goes Roma's Alessandru Frau – and

James keep Reds in hunt

DAVID James put up an inspired display for Liverpool to keep out Valencia in a 0-0 draw at Anfield.

Robbie Fowler, to join Leeds in 2001, had scored twice in the previous round, but didn't get a look in this time and was substituted by Michael Owen.

Another Spanish side Celta Vigo also drew a blank against Premiership opposition, Aston Villa winning away with a Julian Joachim goal.

Celtic had skipper Tom Boyd sent off in their 1-1 draw with FC Zurich in Glasgow, while Glasgow rivals Rangers enjoyed a great win at Bayer Leverkusen.

Second round, first leg

Bayer Leverkusen 1 (Reichenberger), Rangers 2 (Van Bronckhorst, Johansson)
Bologna 2 (Signori, Ingesson), Slavia Prague 1 (Dostalek 67)
Celta Vigo 0, Aston Villa 1 (Joachim)
Celtic 1 (Brattbakk), FC Zurich 1 (Fischer)
CSKA Sofia 2 (Genchev, Naidenov), Atletico Madrid 4 (Torrisi, Roberto Fresnedoso, Kiko 2)
Dynamo Moscow 2 (Nekrasov 2), Real Sociedad 3 (Kovacevic 2, De Pedro)
Grasshoppers 0, Fiorentina 2 (Batistuta, Robbiati)
Graz 3 (Akwuegbu 2, Ehmarm), Monaco 3 (Spehar 2, Giuly)
Liverpool 0, Valencia 0
Red Star Belgrade 1 (Skoric pen), Lyon 2 (Grassi, Kanoute) in Bucharest
Roma 1 (Delvecchio), Leeds United 0
Stuttgart 1 (Akpoborie), Brugges 1 (Vennant)
Vitesse Arnhem 0, Bordeaux 1 (Wiltord)
Werder Bremen 1 (Herzog), Marseille 1 (Maurice)
Willem II (Bombarda), Real Betis 1 (Alexis)
Wislaw Kracow 1 (Kulawik), Parma 1 (Chiesa)

Roman soldiers

es United's Bruno Ribeiro.

Olympian display clinches it for fans' hero O'Leary

MANAGERLESS United took lire-rich Italian giants Roma down to the wire in the Olympic Stadium to virtually seal David O'Leary's appointment as the new chief.

Against a backcloth of uncertainty following George Graham's exit, few pundits gave United's young side much hope in the Italian capital.

Despite having Portuguese midfielder Bruno Ribeiro sent off ten minutes into the second half for a second bookable offence, Leeds put on a vibrant display to restrict the club second in Serie A to a 1-0 first leg lead.

The only goal came after 18 minutes when United's defence backed off and Francesco Totti played a fine ball in for Marco Delvecchio to stride into the Leeds box and clip past Nigel Martyn.

But the expected avalanche didn't occur with United, who included 18-year-old Stephen McPhail in midfield in his first European game, going desperately close to an equaliser.

Five minutes after Delvecchio's strike McPhail slipped the ball through for Ribeiro but his effort came back off the woodwork and Gunnar Halle was to suffer a similar fate when he cut in from the wing and shot against the foot of a post.

When Spanish referee Nieto Lopez sent off Ribeiro after a foul on Allessandro Frau, Lucas Radebe expertly regrouped his side and Roma, seeking their 12th straight home win in Europe, rarely looked like adding to their lead.

It was clear that United had been well prepared for the match – even though caretaker boss O'Leary had to watch from the back of the presidential box in the Olympic Stadium. He had received a one-match ban from the bench following his 'dismissal' in Madeira in the previous round. Instructions were relayed to the players from the dug out by Eddie Gray, who had stepped up from a coaching role to act as O'Leary's assistant.

It was a tremendous battling performance by United and went a long way to cementing O'Leary's appointment after days of speculation about who would become Graham's successor. The travelling army of 1,500 fans certainly roared their approval.

The spirit and togetherness United showed in Rome which made O'Leary's appointment a formality.

He said: "Overall I thought it was a very creditable performance by the whole team, but we have to have that kind of standard week in, week out."

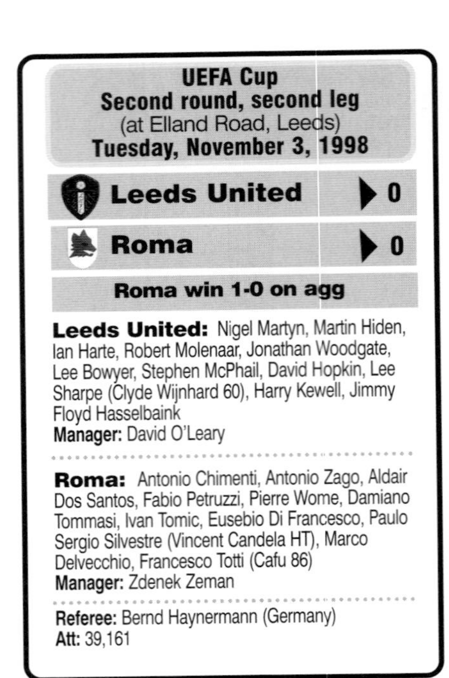
UEFA Cup
Second round, second leg
(at Elland Road, Leeds)
Tuesday, November 3, 1998

Leeds United	**0**
Roma	**0**

Roma win 1-0 on agg

Leeds United: Nigel Martyn, Martin Hiden, Ian Harte, Robert Molenaar, Jonathan Woodgate, Lee Bowyer, Stephen McPhail, David Hopkin, Lee Sharpe (Clyde Wijnhard 60), Harry Kewell, Jimmy Floyd Hasselbaink
Manager: David O'Leary

Roma: Antonio Chimenti, Antonio Zago, Aldair Dos Santos, Fabio Petruzzi, Pierre Wome, Damiano Tommasi, Ivan Tomic, Eusebio Di Francesco, Paulo Sergio Silvestre (Vincent Candela HT), Marco Delvecchio, Francesco Totti (Cafu 86)
Manager: Zdenek Zeman

Referee: Bernd Haynermann (Germany)
Att: 39,161

WOME WOE: Roma's Pierre Wome (second from right) is shown the red card. Lee Bowyer, Stephen McPhail and David Hopkin wait to take the resulting fee-kick.

Ten-man Roma hold off United

ROME was not built in a day but David O'Leary was quickly getting his foundations in place to construct a new-look Leeds United.

Italian giants Roma drew 0-0 at Elland Road to ensure that Marco Delvecchio's first leg goal was sufficient to see them through to the third round.

Even the dismissal of Pierre Wome before half-time could not give United the momentum they needed to stave off the Roman invasion – but O'Leary's troops looked capable of being a force in the future.

Leeds, lacking injured skipper Lucas Radebe, were able to welcome back Nigel Martyn in goal after missing the previous three games with a rib injury. The big Cornishman was soon tested as he plunged at the feet of the ever-dangerous Delvecchio as expensively-assembled Roma dominated first-half possession but Leeds created the better chances.

Lee Sharpe miscued a shot after Jimmy Floyd Hasselbaink's good work down the right created a good opening. All-action midfielder Lee Bowyer then took centre stage, bursting through on 41 minutes but shot straight at 'keeper Antonio Chimeti.

But Bowyer presented Leeds with an opportunity of a different kind just before the interval when he went down under a challenge by Wome and the Cameroon international, who had

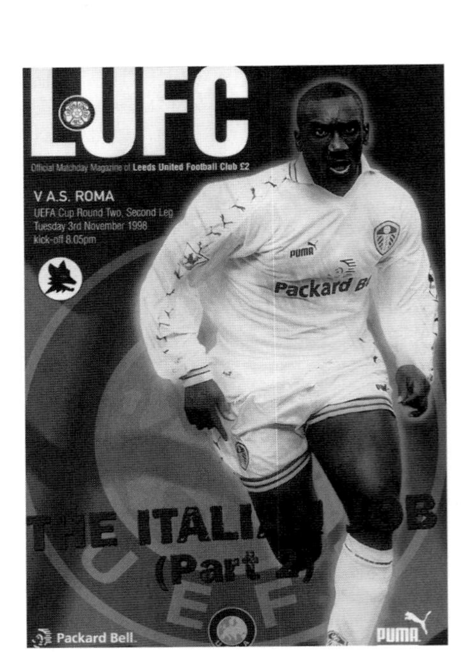

already been booked, was ordered off,

But United could not make their numerical advantage tell despite Bowyer's energy and a mature performance by teenager Jonathan Woodgate at the back alongside the solid Robert Molenaar.

As in Rome, United had failed to take their chances and paid a high price against top quality opposition who were able to keep United at arm's length fairly comfortably.

Roma's defence was unrelenting and their midfield men worked doubly hard to make up for the loss of one of their key players.

Roma's strength in depth was reflected in the closing stages when they were able to bring on Brazilian star full-back Cafu to rampage down the right and send in a fierce shot which Martyn did well to beat away.

O'Leary said: "I'm disappointed that we lost against Roma because we made enough scoring opportunities to have beaten them but I was also proud of the showing we put up."

Brits crash out as Parma sweep to glory

BRITISH progress ground to a halt before the UEFA Cup reached the quarter-final stage.

Joining United in a second round exit were Aston Villa, outclassed at home by Celta Vigo, and Celtic, who had a disastrous night in Zurich, conceeding four goals in 24 second half minutes.

Liverpool got through on away goals in an extraordinary finale in Valencia.

After a goalless first leg, they trailed to a Claudio Lopez goal with nine minutes remaining when Steve McManaman levelled and Patrik Berger netted five minutes later. Chaos followed as McManaman and Paul Ince were sent off and David James conceded another Lopez goal – but Liverpool hung on.

They had less luck on their next visit to Spain, losing 3-1 to Villa's conqurers, Celta Vigo, then losing 1-0 at Anfield.

Rangers, who beat Bayer Leverkusen in the second round, battled to a 1-1 draw at Ibrox against highly-fancied Parma, ex-Leeds Championship winner Rod Wallace scoring.

They looked on course for a famous victory in Italy thanks to a Jorge Albertz goal but Sergio Porrini's red card just before the interval undid all the good work and Parma won 3-1.

The Italians, winners in 1995, went on to win the competition again thanks to some outstanding attacking displays and proved too strong for Marseille in the final, which was now no longer a two-legged affair.

There was some British interest as the final in Moscow as the referee was Scotland's Hugh Dallas, who had been injured by an explosive device launched by fans in the Fiorentina v Grasshoppers second round tie. The match was abandoned and Fiorentina thrown out of the competition.

Second round, second leg

Aston Villa 1 (Collymore pen), Celta Vigo 3 (Sanchez Moreno, Mostovoi, Penev)
Celta Vigo win 3-2 on agg
Atletico Madrid 1 (Juninho pen), CSKA Sofia 0
Atletico Madrid win 5-2 on agg
Bordeaux 2 (Micoud, Wiltord), Vitesse Arnhem 1 (Jochemsen)
Bordeaux won 3-1 on agg
Brugges 3 (De Cock, Claessens, Illic), Stuttgart 2 (Verlaat, Bobic) aet
Brugges win 4-3 on agg
Fiorentina 2 (Oliveira 2), Grasshoppers 1 (Gren) in Salerno. Match abandoned at half-time because of crowd trouble.
Match awarded 3-0 to Grasshoppers. Fiorentina expelled from competition.
Leeds United 0, Roma 0
Roma win 1-0 on agg
Lyon 3 (Caveglia 2, Cocard), Red Star Belgrade 2 (Bunjevcevic, Ognjenovic)
Lyon win 5-3 on agg
Marseille 3 (Maurice, Issa, Dugarry), Werder Bremen 2 (Eilts, Herzog)
Marseille win 4-3 on agg
Real Betis 3 (Finidi, Benjamin, Sanchez), Willem II 0
Real Betis in 4-1 on agg
Real Sociedad 3 (Kovacevis 2, De Paula), Dynamo Moscow 0
Real Sociedad win 6-2 on agg
Slavia Prague 0, Bologna 2 (Signori, Cappiolli)
Bologna win 4-1 on agg
Monaco 4 (Gava 2, Spehar, Diawara), Graz 0
Monaco win 7-3 on agg
Parma 2 (Fiore, Zajac og), Wislaw Kracow 1 (Zajac)
Parma win 3-2 on agg
Rangers 1 (Johansson) Bayer Leverkusen 1 (Kirsten)
Rangers win 3-2 on agg
Valencia 2 (Lopez 2), Liverpool 2 (McManaman, Berger)
2-2 on agg. Liverpool win on away goals
FC Zurich 4 (Del Signore, Chassot, Bartlett, Sant'Anna), Celtic 2 (O'Donnell, Larsson)
FC Zurich win 5-3 on agg

Third round, first leg

Bologna 4 (Fontolan 2, Kolyvanov, Eriberto), Real Betis 1 (Zarandona)
Celta Vigo 3 (Mostovoi, Karpine, Gudelj), Liverpool 1 (Owen)
Grasshoppers 3 (Kavelashvili, Turkyilmaz, Comisetti), Bordeaux 3 (Wiltord 2, Micoud)
Lyon 1 (Bak), Brugges 0
Monaco 2 (Trezeguet pen, Guily), Marseille 2 (Pires, Camara)
Rangers 1 (Wallace), Parma 1 (Balboa)
Real Sociedad 2 (Kovacevic, Fresnedoso), Atletico Madrid 1 (Juninho)
Roma 1 (Toni), FC Zurich 0

Third round, second leg

Atletico Madrid 4 (Jugovic 2 – 1pen, Sann, Jose Mari), Real Sociedad 1 (Javier Garcia) aet
Atletico Madrid win 5-3 on agg
Bordeaux 0, Grasshoppers 0
3-3 on agg. Bordeaux win on away goals
Brugges 3 (De Brul, De Cock, Anic), Lyon 4 (Caveglia 3, Dhorasso)
Lyon win 5-3 on agg
Liverpool 0, Celta Vigo 1 (Revivo)
Celta Vigo win 4-1 on agg
Marseille 1 (Camara), Monaco 0
Marseille win 3-2 on agg
Parma 3 (Balbo, Fiore, Chiesa pen), Rangers 1 (Albertz pen)
Real Betis 1 (Oli), Bologna 0
Bologna win 4-2 on agg
FC Zurich 2 (Bartlett 2), Roma 2 (Delvecchio, Toni)
Roma win 3-2 on agg

Quarter-final, first leg

Atletico Madrid 2 (Jose Mari, Fresnedoso), Roma 1 (Di Biagio)
Bologna 3 (Signori 2, Binotto), Lyon 0
Bordeaux 2 (Micoud, Wiltord), Parma 1 (Crespo)
Marseille 2 (Maurice 2), Celta Vigo 1 (Mostovoi)

Quarter-final, second leg

Celta Vigo 0, Marseille 0
Marseille win 2-1 on agg
Lyon 2 (Caveglia 2), Bologna 0
Lyon win 3-2 on agg
Parma 6 (Crespo 2, Chiesa 2, Veron, Balbo pen), Bordeaux 0
Parma win 7-2 on agg
Roma 1 (Delvecchio), Atletico Madrid 2 (Aguilera, Fresnedoso)
Atletico Madrid win 4-2 on agg

Semi-final, first leg

Atletico Madrid 1 (Juninho pen), Parma 3 (Chiesa 2, Crespo)
Marseille 0, Bologna 0

Semi-final, second leg

Bologna 1 (Paramatti), Marseille 1 (Blanc pen)
1-1 on agg. Marseille win on away goals
Parma 2 (Balbo, Chiesa), Atletico Madrid 1 (Fresnedoso)
Parma win 5-1 on agg

Final

(Luzhniki Stadium, Moscow)
May 12, 1999
Parma 3
Marseille 0

Parma: Buffon, Thuram, Sensini, Cannavaro, Fuser, Baggio, Veron (Fiore 77), Boghossian, Vanoli, Crespo (Asprilla 84), Chiesa (Balbo 73)
Goals: Crespo 26, Vanoli 36, Chiesa 55
Manager: Alberto Malesani
Marseille: Porato, Blondeau, Blanc, Domoraud, Edson da Suva (Camara HT), Issa, Bravo, Brando, Gourveimec, Pires, Maurice
Manager: Rolland Gourbis
Referee: Hugh Dallas (Scotland)
Attendance: 61,000

Leading scorers: 8 – Chiesa (Parma), Kulawik (Wisla Kracow), 7 – Caveglia (Lyon), Ognjenovi (Red Star Belgrade), 6 – Bartlett (FC Zurich), Crespo (Parma), Nikolaides (AEK Athens)

O'LEARY'S BABES: Leeds United 1999/2000, bidding for UEFA Cup glory. Back row, from left to right: Robert Molenaar, Michael Bridges, Jonathan Woodgate, Nigel Martyn, Michael Duberry, Paul Robinson, Eirik Bakke, Alf-Inge Haaland, David Hopkin. Middle row: Sean Hardy (kit man), Bruno Ribeiro, Ian Harte, David Batty, Gary Kelly, Danny Mills, Darren Huckerby, Eddie Gray (assistant manager), David Swift (physio) Front row: Stephen McPhail, Alan Smith, Harry Kewell, Peter Ridsdale (chairman), Lucas Radebe, David O'Leary (manager), Lee Bowyer, Matthew Jones, Martin Hiden.

Young squad earn their Euro chance

MANAGER David O'Leary was not afraid to give youth a chance as he moulded a more attacking squad than the one left by George Graham.

There had been signs in the latter part of Graham's reign that United had the capability of throwing off their defensive shackles.

In addition to the introduction of centre back Jonathan Woodgate, who won an England cap at the end of the 1998/99 season, O'Leary bloodied exciting teenage striker Alan Smith, who netted with his first kick in the Premiership after coming on as substitute in a 3-1 win at Liverpool.

That victory lifted United in to fifth place in November 1998 and they kept up among the front runners all season, finishing fifth to gain a UEFA Cup place for the second year running.

In addition to the young talent already at the club, O'Leary brought back Leeds-born David Batty for a second spell at Elland Road in a £4.4 million deal with Newcastle United.

O'Leary's rebuilding went on through the summer with the departure of forward Clyde Winjhard to neighbours Huddersfield Town, while ex-England winger Lee Sharpe, David Wetherall and Gunnar Halle all went to Bradford City while Danny Granville moved on to Manchester City after a loan spell.

In came Charlton full-back Danny Mills, Norwegian midfielder Eirik Bakke from Sogndal, Chelsea defender Michael Duberry and Sunderland striker Michael Bridges.

The total cost of the quartet was £15 million, but United's plans were disrupted on the eve of the season when Jimmy-Floyd Hasselbaink, the leading scorer for the last two seasons, asked for a transfer.

Atletico Madrid, who, like United, were earmarked for the UEFA Cup, had bid for the Dutch international, but Peter Ridsdale rejected the offer.

Hasselbaink, who had two years to run on his contract, was offered a deal by United which would have made him the best paid player at the club.

However, Hasselbaink threatened to go on strike so Leeds finally accepted a £12 million bid from Atletico three days before the start of the new season.

The Premiership campaign opened with a disappointing 0-0 home draw with Derby County, but the highlight of the day was the unveiling of a bronze statue at Elland Road of Billy Bremner, hero of so many European campaigns in the Don Revie era. Bremner, one of the all-time greats, had died in December 1997 but a new breed of stars were on the verge of making their own piece of United history with their bid for Euro glory.

Cup winners added to UEFA Cup mix

THE UEFA Cup continued to grow to mammoth proportions after the scrapping of the European Cup Winners Cup.

The last ECWC final was held at Villa Park in 1999, Lazio beating Mallorca 2-1.

The winners of national cups now went in to the UEFA Cup which had 142 teams contesting the 1999/2000 competition.

Apart from clubs, like United, who qualified via their league position, 16 losers from the Champions League third qualifying round would enter the UEFA Cup at the first round stage along with the three Intertoto Cup winners.

Clubs from smaller nations, like Andorra and Liechtenstein, plus three clubs who had qualified via their country's fair-play ranking were obliged to play in the qualifying round.

Qualifying round, first leg

Anderlecht 6 (Goor 2, Gunnarsson og, Zetterberg, Bassegio, Radzinski), Leitftur 1 (De Boeck og)
Ankaragucu 1 (Unal), Torshvn 0
Apoel Nicosia 0, Levski Sofia 0
BATE Borisov 1 (Lisovski), Lokomotiv Moscow 7 (Janashia 3, Loskov, Sarkisian, Bulykin 2)
Belshina 1 (Khyrpack), Omonia Nicosia 5 (Kalotheou, Michalovic, Rauffmann, Kaiafas, Konstantinidis)
Bodo Glimt 1 (Staurvik), Vaduz 0
Cwmbran Town 0, Celtic 6 (Berkovic, Tebily, Larsson 2, Viduka, Brattbakk) at Cardiff
Erevan 0, Hapoel Tel Aviv 2 (Harazi 2)
Ferencvaros 3 (Horvath, Fuzi, Kovacs), Constructorul 1 (Comlionoc)
Gorica 2 (Mitrakovic pen, Zlogar), Inter Cardiff 0
Gothenburg 3 (Andersson, Karlsson 2), Cork City 0
Grasshoppers 4 (Chapiusat 2, Isabella 2), Bray Wanderers 0
Hadjuk Split 5 (Bulat, Baturina, Grdic, Leko, Dranja), Dudelange 0
HJK Hesinki 2 (Rafael, Ylola), Shirak 0
Inter Bratislava 3 (Gwerich, Kratochvil, Pernis), Bylis 1 (Jakupi)
Klaksvik 0, Graz 5 (Radovic 2, Standfest 3)
Krivbas 3 (Ponomanenko, Paljaritsis, Moroz), Shamkir 0
KR Reykjavik 1 (Hinriksson), Kilmarnock 0
Lantana 0, Torpedo Kutaisi 5 (Gwadachiani, Janashia, Ioanidze, Chkhetiani, Megreladze)
Lokomotiv Tbilisi 1 (Kebadze), Linfield 0
Lyngby 7 (Hermansen 2, M Jensen, C Jensen, Magleby, Luthje, Havlykke), Birkikara 0
Maccabi Tel Aviv 3 (Kubicka 2 – 1 pen, Basis), Kaunas 2 (Papecko)
Metalurg Zaphorizia 3 (Boulders, Verpakosvsky, Dragun), Lech Poznan 2 (Zijuravski, Kajewski)
Mondercange 2 (Christophe, Neves), Dynamo Bucharest 6 (Lupescu pen, Petre, Mihalcea, Mutu 2, Niculae)
Neftchi 1 (Vasiliev 2), Red Star Belgrade 3 (Boskovic, Pjanovic, Pantelic)
Olimpija 1 (Moro), Kareda 1 (Fomenka)
Portadown 0, CSKA Sofia 3 (Mantchev, Kovacevic, Boukarev)
Riga 0, Helsingborg 0
Serif 1 (Mujiri), Sigma Olomouc 1 (Kovac)
Shaktjor Donetsk 3 (Seleznev, Shtolcers 2), Sileks 1 (Gogic)
Sliema Wanderers 0, FC Zurich 3 (Kavelashvili, Bartlett, Kebe)
Steaua Bucharest 3 (Ilie 2, Ciocoiu), Levadia 0
Tulevik 0, Brugges 3 (Defkandre pen, Jankauskas 2)
Vardar 0, Legia Warsaw 5 (Mieciel, Czereszewski, Srutna 2, Wroblenski)
Viking 7 (Aarsheim, Svensson 2, Dadson 3, Nygaard), Principat 0
Vllaznia 1 (Sinani), Spartak Trnava 1 (Leitner)
Vojvodina 4 (Suskavcevic, Jankovic 2 – 1 pen, Jovic), Ujpest Budapest 0
Vaasa 1 (Pohja), St Johnstone 1 (Lowndes)

Qualifying round, second leg

Birkikara 0, Lyngby 0 *Lyngby win 7-0 on agg*
Bray Wanderers 0, Grasshoppers 4 (Tikva 2, De Napoli, Muff) *Grasshoppers win 8-0 on agg*
Bylis 0, Inter Bratislava 2 (Nemeth 2) *Inter Bratislava win 5-1 on agg*
Brugge 2 (Jankauskas, De Brul), Tulevik 0 *Brugges win 5-0 on agg*
Celtic 4 (Brattbakk, Smith, Mjallby, Johnson), Cwmbran Town 0 *Celtic win 10-0 on agg*
Constructorul 1 (Zabolotny), Ferencvaros 1 (Horvath) *Ferencvaros win 4-2 on agg*
Cork City 1 (Morley), Gothenburg 0 *Gothenburg win 3-1 on agg*
CSKA Sofia 5 (Petkov pen, Litera 2, Hristov pen, Simeonov), Portadown 0 *CSKA Sofia win 8-0 on agg*
Dynamo Bucharest 7 (Mutu 2 – 1 pen, Niculae 3, Fogel og, Petre), Mondercange 0 *Dynamo Bucharest win 13-2 on agg*
Dudelange 1 (Kabongo), Hadjuk Split 1 (Jazic) *Hadjuk Split win 6-1 on agg*
Graz 4 (Ramusch, Akwuegbo, Dimitrovic, Adu Tutu), Klaksvik 0 *Graz win 9-0 on agg*
Hapoel Tel Aviv 2 (Pisont, Antebe), Erevan 1 (Gogoladze) *Hapoel Tel Aviv win 4-1 on agg*
Helsingborg 5 (Andersson, Jonsson, Powell, Prica, Bakkerund), Riga 0 *Helingborg win 5-0 on agg*
Inter Cardiff 1 (Mainwaring), Gorica 0 *Gorica win 2-1 on agg*
Kareda 2 (Fomenka 2), Olimpija 2 (Moro, Kmetech) *3-3 on agg. Olimpija win on away goals*
Kaunas 2 (Pacevicius 2), Maccabi Tel Aviv 1 (Basis) *Maccabi Tel Aviv win 4-3 on agg*
Kilmarnock 2 (Wright, Bagan), KR Reykjavik 0 aet *Kilmarnock win 2-1 on agg*
Lech Poznan 3 (Golinski, Kubicki, Mackiewicz), Metalurg Zaphorizia 1 (Boulders) *Lech Poznan win 5-4 on agg*
Legia Warsaw 4 (Czeresewski, Karwan, Sokolowski, Mieciel), Vardar 0 *Legia Warsaw win 9-0 on agg*
Leiftur 0, Anderlecht 3 (Van Diemen, Zetterberg 2 pens) *Anderlecht win 9-1 on agg*
Levadia 1 (Olumets), Steaua Bucharest 4 (Reghecampf og, Rosu, Ilie 2) *Steaua Bucharest win 7-0 on agg*
Levski Sofia 2 (Sirakov, Pazin), Apoel Nicosia 0 *Levski Sofia win 2-0 on agg*
Linfield 1 (Larmour), Lokomotiv Tbilisi 1 (Kebadze) *Lokomotiv Tbilisi win 2-1 on agg*
Lokomotiv Moscow 5 (Chugainov, Loskov, Smertin, Kharlachyov 2), Borisov 0 *Lokomotiv Moscow win 12-1 on agg*
Omonia Nicosia 3 (Rauffmann 3), Belshina 0 *Omonia Nicosia win 8-1 on agg*
Principat 0, Viking Stavanger 11 (Dadason 2, Berre 3, Berland 2, Sanne 3, Mathiasen) *Viking win 18-0 on agg*
Red Star Belgrade 1 (Pantelic), Neftchi 0 *Red Star Belgrade win 4-2 on agg*
Shamkir 0, Krivbas 2 (Simakov 2) *Krivbas win 5-0 on agg*
Sigma Olomouc 0, Serif 0 *1-1 on agg. Sigma Olomouc win on away goals*
Sileks 2 (Ignatov pen, Simovski), Shaktjor Donetsk 1 (Matvejev) *Shaktjor Donetsk win 4-3 on agg*
Spartak Trnava 2 (Uljaky 2), Vllaznia 0 *Spartak Trnava win 3-1 on agg*
St Johnstone 2 (Simao 2), Vaasa 0 *St Johnstone win 3-1 on agg*
Torpedo Kutaisi 4 (Ioanidze, Megreladze 3), Lantana 2 (Leitan, Dolinin) *Torpedo Kutaisi win 9-2 on agg*
Torshvn 0, Ankaragucu 1 (Mkhalele) *Ankaragucu win 2-0 on agg*
Ujpest Budapest 1 (Kovacs), Vojvodina 1 (Bratis) *Vojovidina win 5-1 on agg*
Vaduz 1 (Wegmann), Bodo Glimt 2 (Saeternes 2) *Bodo Glimt win 3-1 on agg*
FC Zurich 1 (Kebe), Sliema Wanderers 0 *FC Zurich win 4-0 on agg*

Byes: *AB Copenhagen, Ajax, Amica, Aris Salonica, Atletico Madrid, Beira Mar, Benfica, Bologna, Brugge, Bystrica, Celta Vigo, Debrecen, Deportivo La Coruna, Fenerbahce, Juventus, Ionikos, Kaiserslautern, Karpaty, LASK Linz, Lausanne, Leeds United, Legia Warsaw, Lens, Lierse, Monaco, Montpellier, Nantes, Newcastle United, Osijek, Panathinikos, PAOK Salonika, Roda, Roma, Slavia Prague, Sporting Lisbon, Stabaek, Tottenham Hotspur, Udinese, Vitoria Setubal, Vitesse Arnhem, Werder Bremen, Wolfsburg, Zenit, Intertoto Cup winners: Montpellier, Juventus, West Ham United and teams eliminated from the Champions League third qualifying round – Aalborg, AEK Athens, Anorthosis, Brondby, Hapoel Haifa, Lyon, Mallorca, MTK Budapest, Parma, Partizan Belgrade, Rapid Vienna, Servette, Skonto Riga, Teplice, Widzew Lodz, Zimbru Chisinau*

Tie switched from Belgrade to Holland

THE draw for the first round of the UEFA Cup for 1999-2000 threw up a massive headache for United.

They were paired with Partizan Belgrade which would involve a journey to the war-torn capital of Yugoslavia.

It was a logistical nightmare with the conflict in the powderkeg of the Balkans putting the safety of United's players in jeopardy it was soon clear that UEFA would have to consider moving the first match away from Belgrade.

Clearly the Yugoslavs didn't want to lose ground advantage, but after weighing up all the options UEFA ruled that the first leg should be played at a neutral venue – but not after coming in for criticism for allowing teams from the two countries be be drawn against each other in the first place.

Partizan, the Yugoslav champions, were knocked out of the Champions League by Spartak Moscow at the qualification stage and moved into the UEFA Cup. Despite the NATO operations in the Balkans, United, who had finished fourth in the Premiership and were seeded in the UEFA Cup, found themselves facing a trip to shell-shattered Belgrade.

With no commercial airlines flying over Yugoslavian air space it would be near impossible for United to reach Belgrade.

UEFA bought more time by ruling that the first leg would now be played at Elland Road with the return in Belgrade on September 28.

United made plans to charter three private aircraft to go to Belgrade but it was becoming ever clearer that they would not be allowed to go.

United chairman Peter Ridsdale said: "The Foreign Office position is very clear, they will not recommend that any English citizen goes to Belgrade."

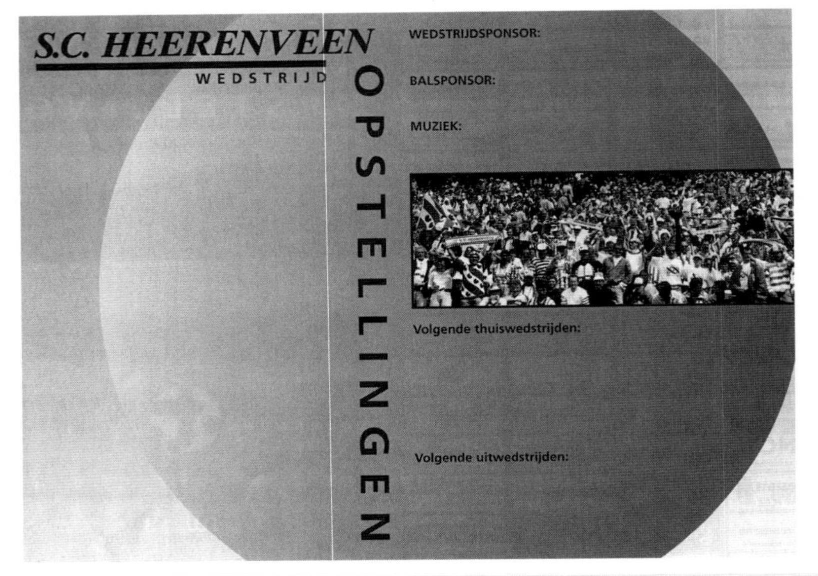

Commercial flights to the Yugoslavian capital had not been restored so UEFA ruled that the second leg would switch back to Leeds as originally planned with the first leg being staged at a neutral venue in Holland.

Vitesse Arnhem's ground was the first choice, but that was deemed unsuitable and just days before the first leg was to be played it was agreed that the Abe Lenstra Stadium in Heerenveen would host the controversial tie on Tuesday, September 14, with a 5.30pm kick-off.

Although Partizan had lost ground advantage at least they had been able to see United playing three times, while Leeds boss David O'Leary had to rely of video tapes of Partizan to work out his tactics.

Impressive Premiership quartet looking good fo

ENGLISH clubs enjoyed a fine start to the UEFA Cup with all four winning their first round first leg matches.

Two days after Leeds won in Heerenveen, Tottenham and West Ham won 3-0 at home to Osijek and Zimbru Chisinau, respectively while big-spending Newcastle eased to a 2-0 win at CSKA Sofia.

First round, first leg

AB Copenhagen 0, Grasshoppers 2 (Yakin, Ekoku)
Ajax 6 (Verlaat pen, Reuser, Knopper, Mahlas 2, Wamberto), Bystricia 1 (Verlaat og)
Amica 2 (Dawidovski, Bosacki), Brondby 0
Anderlecht 3 (Bajrektarevic og, Radzinski 2), Olimpija 1 (Ekmecic)
Anorthosis 1 (Engomitis), Legia Warsaw 0
Aris Salonika 1 (Matzios pen), Servette 0
Atletico Madrid 3 (Gammarra, Hasselbaink, Paunovic), Ankaragucu 0
Beira Mar 1 (Fary), Vitesse Arnhem 2 (Van Hooijdonk, Grozidic)
Benfica 0, Dynamo Bucharest 1 (Nastase)
Bodo Glimt 0, Werder Bremen 5 (Pizarro 2, Bogdanovic 2, Maximov)
Celtic 2 (Larsson 2 – 1 pen), Hapoel Tel Aviv 0
CSKA Sofia 0, Newcastle United 2 (Solano, Ketsbaia)
Gorica 0, Panathinikos 1 (Limperopoulos)
Graz 3 (Akwuegbo 2, Tuto), Spartak Trnava 0
Hadjuk Split 0, Levski Sofia 0
Hapoel Haifa 3 (Tourgeman 2, Sivilia), Brugge 1 (Jankauskas)
Helsingborg 1 (Jonsson), Karpaty 1 (Getsko)
HJK Helsinki 0, Lyon 1 (Vairelles)
Inter Bratislava 1 (Lalik), Rapid Vienna 0
Ionikos 1 (Dimitriadis), Nantes 3 (Lievres, Monterrubio 2)
Kaiserslautern 3 (Kock, Djorkaeff, Marschall), Kilmanock 0
Lausanne 3 (Kuzba, Mazzone 2), Celta Vigo 2 (Rapo og, Karpin)
Lech Poznan 1 (Zurawski pen), Gothenburg 2 (Andersson, Mild)
Lokomotiv Tbilisi 0, PAOK Salonika 7 (Georgiadis 2, Sabri, Froussos 2, Marangos, Frantzeskos)
Lyngby 1 (Bidstrup), Lokomotiv Moscow 2 (Chugainov, Bulyakin)
Maccabi Tel Aviv 2 (Kubickia, Ben Dayan), Lens 2 (Sakho, Job)
Monaco 3 (Simeone 2, Trezeguet), St Johnstone 0
MTK Budapest 0, Fenerbahce 0
Omonia Nicosia 2 (Kondolefteros 2), Juventus 5 (Inzaghi 2, Kovacevic, Esnaider, Del Piero)
Parma 3 (Di Vaio 2, Baggio), Krivbas 2 (Palynianitsa, Monarov)
Partizan Belgrade 1 (Tomic), Leeds United 3 (Bowyer 2, Radebe) in Heerenveen
Red Star Belgrade 0, Montpellier 1 (Loko) in Sofia
Roda 2 (Doomernik, Zafarin), Shaktjor Donetsk 0
Roma 7 (Aldair, Monetlla, Alenichev 3, Assuncao, Delvecchio), Vitoria Setubal 0

Double Dutch for Lee

UEFA Cup
First round, first leg
(at Abe Lenstra Stadium, Heerenveen)
Tuesday, September 14, 1999

 **Partizan Belgrade**  **1**

 **Leeds United** **3**

Partizan Belgrade: Nikola Damjanac, Vuk Rasovic, Aleksandar Stanojevic, Branko Savic, Dorde Tomic, Mladen Krstajic, Vladimir Ivic (Nenad Stojakovic 88), Goran Trobok, Ivica Iliev (Mirorad Pekovic 70), Mateja Kezman, Sasa Ilic (Marjan Gersimovski 81)
Goal: Tomic 20
Manager: Miodrag Jesic

Leeds United: Nigel Martyn, Danny Mills, Ian Harte, Jonathan Woodgate, Lucas Radebe, Gary Kelly, David Batty, David Hopkin, Lee Bowyer, Harry Kewell, Michael Bridges (Alan Smith 70)
Goals: Bowyer 26, 82, Radebe 39
Manager: David O'Leary

Referee: Herbert Fandel (Germany) **Att:** 4,950

SHOOTING STAR: Lee Bowyer celebrates his opener against Partizan Belgrade.

TWO-GOAL Lee Bowyer shook off a hamstring strain to put United within touching distance of a place in the UEFA Cup second round.

The midfielder, who only passed a fitness test on the morning of the match, crowned a tireless display as United took a 3-1 first leg advantage after a roller-coaster match in the Dutch town of Heerenveen.

There was also joy for skipper Lucas Radebe, who scored a rare goal – his second in five years – and Gary Kelly, making his first Leeds appearance for 18 months after an operation on his shins.

United should have had a penalty after just seven minutes when Scottish midfielder David Hopkin was floored in the box but the appeal fell on deaf ears.

United continued to dominate with Bowyer and Kelly both going close. But after 20 minutes Partizan took the lead against the run of play when goalkeeper Nigel Martyn uncharacteristically fumbled Mateja Kezman's shot and Dorde Tomic punished the error.

But six minutes later another goalkeeping mistake enabled United to draw level when Nikola Damjanac totally missed Ian Harte's corner and Bowyer coolly fired in the equaliser from just inside the 18-yard box.

Partizan responded with a raid down United's right which ended with Radebe tripping the skilful Kezman but United keeper Martyn made a tremendous save, diving low to his right, to keep out Vuk Rasovic's penalty.

Partizan seemed deflated by the miss and their heads dropped still further after 39 minutes when Radebe scored a bizarre goal. Harte curled in a free-kick, Jonathan Woodgate headed it on, and Radebe, who had slipped and was lying on the turf hooked home a volley.

It was a real collectors' item for the South African and United's 1,500 travelling fans, who dominated the rival support with their singing, they knew they were home and dry when the Whites went 3-1 up in the closing stages when Bowyer's speculative effort from outside the box slipped past the miserable Damjanac and in to the net.

second round

Sigma Olomouc 1 (Kobylik), Mallorca 3 (Engonga, Tristran, Stankovic)
Skonto Riga 1 (Astafyev), Widzew Lodz 0
Stabaek 1 (Finstad), Deportivo La Coruna 0
Steaua Bucharest 2 (Ciocoiu, Danciulescu), LASK Linz 0
Teplice 3 (Frydek, Kolomazni, Rizek), Ferencvaros 1 (Kovacs)
Torpedo Kutaisi 0, AEK Athens 1 (Zikos)
Tottenham Hotspur 3 (Leonhardsen, Perry, Sherwood), Zimbru Chisinau 0
Udinese 1 (Sottil), Aalborg 0
Viking 3 (Svensson, Berre, Espevoll), Sporting Lisbon 0
Vojvodina 0, Slavia Prague 0 in Skopje
West Ham United 3 (Wanchope, Di Canio, Lampard), Osijek 0
Wolfsburg 2 (Akonner, Juskowiak), Debrecen 0
Zenit 0, Bologna 3 (Ventola, Signori 2 – 1 pen)
FC Zurich 1 (Jamarauli), Lierse 0

Partizan only offer token resistance

New man Huckerby gets off the mark in Europe

MATCH WINNER: Darren Huckerby.

DARREN Huckerby emerged from the shadows to rubber stamp United's passage into the second round of the UEFA Cup.

The jet-heeled £4 million striker, signed from Coventry City just after the start of the season with money from the sale of Jimmy-Floyd Hasselbaink, had yet to nail down a regular first team place in his first few weeks with United.

But he got the only goal of the game against Partizan Belgrade at Elland Road to seal a comfortable 4-1 aggregate win.

His maiden European goal came in the 55th minute when Harry Kewell popped a ball through to the speedy Huckerby who forced the ball home from an acute angle.

United were never in any danger of losing a tie they had effectively won in Holland 17 days earlier.

They allowed Partizan to fiddle about with the ball in midfield where the visitors' showed plenty of skill but little penetration and United goalkeeper Nigel Martyn was a virtual spectator, such was the dominance of United's backline of Lucas Radebe, Jonathan Woodgate, Gary Kelly and Ian Harte.

United were content to hit their opponents on the break and missed three good chances inside the six-yard area in the first half to extend their overall lead.

A Lee Bowyer volley from a Harte cross, a David Hopkin shot over the bar and a Kewell shot which was blocked by Nikola Damjanac should all have found the target.

It was left to Huckerby to end the home fans' frustration after more good work from Kewell, who was rapidly earning many admirers on the continent.

CREATOR: Harry Kewell, who set up Darren Huckerby's goal, skips past a Partizan Belgrade defender.

UEFA Cup
First round, second leg
(at Elland Road, Leeds)
Thursday, September 30, 1999

Leeds United ▶ 1

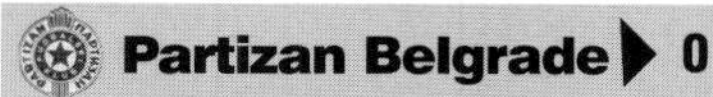

Partizan Belgrade ▶ 0

Leeds United win 4-1 on agg

Leeds United: Nigel Martyn, Gary Kelly, Ian Harte, Jonathan Woodgate, Lucas Radebe, David Batty, David Hopkin (Eririk Bakke 80), Lee Bowyer, Harry Kewell (Matthew Jones 85), Darren Huckerby, Michael Bridges (Alan Smith 67)
Goal: Huckerby 55
Manager: David O'Leary

Partizan Belgrade: Nikola Damjanac, Zoltan Sabo, Aleksandar Stanojevic, Marjan Gerasimovski, Branko Savic, Dorde Tomic, Vladimir Ivic (Nenad Stojakovic 87), Goran Trobok (Igor Duljaj 66), Miroad Pekovic, Dragan Stojisavljevic, Goran Obradovic (Srdan Baljak 63)
Manager: Miidrag Jesic

Referee: Fritz Stuchlik (Austria) **Att:** 39,806

O'Leary plays down chances

DESPITE the professional manner in which United had despatched tricky opponents Partizan Belgrade, manager David O'Leary felt his young side were still not ready to win the competition.

"The UEFA Cup is a great experience for us and I am confident that even the young players have the right temperament to do well in it. But, to be honest, I don't believe it's a competition we can win this season," said the Leeds boss.

"I don't think at the moment we have a squad who can play regularly on a Thursday night and then again on Sunday in the League. Our main priority this season remains trying to get into the top three in the top three in the Premier League and winning a place in next season's Champions League."

The following day United faced a trip into the unknown when the UEFA Cup third round draw paired them with Lokomotiv Moscow.

It was the first time that United would meet Russian opposition since they first played in Europe in 1966.

English clubs through, but Celtic are sole Scots' survivors

ENGLAND'S four representatives, all holding first leg leads, advanced to the second round, West Ham's 3-1 win in Osijek being the most impressive second leg display.

Newcastle, now featuring ex-Leeds midfield star Gary Speed in midfield, were denied victory at St James' Park by a late CSKA Sofia equaliser.

St Johnstone and Kilmarnock went out, leaving Celtic as Scotland's remaining club.

First round, second leg

Aalborg 1 (Matova), Udinese 2 (Muzzi, Locatelli) *Udinese win 3-1 on agg*

AEK Athens 6 (Ciric pen, Bjekovic, Maladenis, Kopitsis 2, Nikolaidis), Torpedo Kutaisi 0 *AEK Athens win 7-0 on agg*

Ankaragucu 1 (Birol), Atletico Madrid 0 *Atletico Madrid win 3-1 on agg*

Bologna 2 (Fontolan, Cipriani), Zenit 2 (Pavov, Kondrasjov) *Bologna win 5-2 on agg*

Brondby 4 (Madsen 2, Da Silva, Christensen), Amica 3 (Kryszalowicz 2, Kukielka) *Amica win 5-4 on agg*

Brugges 4 (Verheyen, Borklemans, Jansen 2), Hapoel Haifa 2 (Rosso) *5-5 on agg. Hapoel Haifa win on away goals*

Bystrica 1 (Malatinsky), Ajax 3 (Arveladze, Bobsun, Laudrup) *Ajax win 9-2 on agg*

Celta Vigo 4 (McCarthy 3, Mostovoi), Lausanne 0 *Celta Vigo win 6-3 on agg*

Debrecen 2 (Sabo 2), Wolfsburg 1 (Akpoborie) *Wolfsburg win 3-2 on agg*

Dynamo Bucharest 0, Benfica 2 (Maniche, Chano) *Benfica win 2-1 on agg*

Deportivo La Coruna 2 (Jokanovic, Conceicao), Stabaek 0 *Deportivo La Coruna win 2-1 on agg*

Fenerbahce 0, MTK Budapest 2 (Kenesei 2) *MTK Budapest win 2-0 on agg*

Ferencvaros 1 (Matyus), Templice 1 (Rade) *Templice win 4-2 on agg*

Gothenburg 0, Lech Poznan 0 *Gothenburg win 2-1 on agg*

Grasshoppers 1 (Magro), AB Copenhagen 1 (Hansen) *Grasshoppers win 3-1 on agg*

Hapoel Tel Aviv 0, Celtic 1 (Larsson) *Celtic win 3-0 on agg*

Juventus 5 (Kovacevis 3, Tacchinardi, Conte), Omonia Nicosia 0 *Juventus win 10-2 on agg*

Karpaty 1 (Getsko), Helsingborg 1 (Jonsson) *aet 2-2 on agg. Helsingborg win 4-2 on pens*

Kilmarnock 0, Kaiserslautern 2 (Djorkaeff, Ranzy) *Kaiserslautern win 5-0 on agg*

Krivbas 0, Parma 3 (Boghossian, Crespo, Di Vaio) *Parma win 6-2 on agg*

LASK Linz 2 (Stumpf, Sane), Steaua Bucharest 3 (Ciociou, Sabrin, Duro) *Steaua Bucharest win 5-2 on agg*

Leeds United 1 (Huckerby), Partizan Belgrade 0 *Leeds United win 4-1 on agg*

Legia Warsaw 2 (Mieciel, Czereszewski), Anorthosis 0 *Legia Warsaw win 2-1 on agg*

Lens 2 (Nouma, Delporte), Maccabi Tel Aviv 1 (Basis) *Lens win 4-3 on agg*

Levski Sofia 3 (Ivanko pen, Banchev, Dimitrov), Hadjuk Split 0 *Levski Sofia win 3-0 on agg*

Lierse 3 (Van Meir, Huysegems, Zdebel), FC Zurich 4 (Jamarauli, Frick, Eydelie, Daems pen) *FC Zurich win 5-3 on agg*

Lokomotiv Moscow 3 (Kharlachyov, Drozdov, Janashia), Lyngby 0 *Lokomotiv Moscow win 5-1 on agg*

Lyon 5 (Anderson, Blanc, Linares, Vairelles 2), HJK Helsinki 1 (Lehkosuo) *Lyon win 6-1 on agg*

Mallorca 0, Sigma Olomouc 0 *Mallorca win 3-1 on agg*

Montpellier 2 (Oudec, Loko), Red Star Belgrade 2 (Jelic, Boskovic pen) *Montpellier win 3-2 on agg*

Nantes 1 (Da Rocha), Ionikos 0 *Nantes win 4-1 on agg*

Newcastle United 2 (Shearer, Robinson), CSKA Sofia 2 (Litera, Simeonov) *Newcastle United win 4-2 on agg*

Olimpia 0, Anderlecht 3 (Koller, Radzinski 2) *Anderlecht win 6-1 on agg*

Osijek 1 (Bulbalo), West Ham United 3 (Kitson, Ruddock, Foe) *West Ham United win 6-1 on agg*

Panathinaikos 2 (Sigurdssin, Nassiopoulos), Gorica 0 *Panathiniakos win 3-0 on agg*

PAOK Salonika 2 (Valencia pen, Salpigidid), Lokomotiv Tbilisi 0 *PAOK Salonika win 9-0 on agg*

Rapid Vienna 1 (Zingler), Inter Bratislava 2 (Suchanok, Babnic) *Inter Bratislava win 3-1 on agg*

St Johnstone 3 (Leonard og, Dasovic, O'Neil), Monaco 3 (Prso, Riise, Legwinski) *Monaco win 6-3 on agg*

Servette 1 (Lonfat), Aris Salonika 2 (Andriolo, Kyzeridis) *Aris Salonika win 3-1 on agg*

Shaktjor Donetsk 1 (Benjo), Roda 3 (Tchoutan, Van Der Luer, Van Dessel) *Roda win 5-1 on agg*

Slavia Prague 3 (Petrous, Dosek, Zelenka), Vojvodina 2 (Belic, Bogdanovic) *Slavia Prague win 3-2 on agg*

Spartak Trnava 2 (Muzlay 2), Graz 1 (Stadfest) *Graz win 4-2 on agg*

Sporting Lisbon 1 (Ayew pen), Viking 0 *Viking win 3-1 on agg*

Vitesse Arnhem 0, Beira Mar 0 *Vitesse Arnhem win 2-1 on agg*

Vitoria Setubal 1 (Maki), Roma 0 *Roma win 7-1 on agg*

Werder Bremen 1 (Ailton), Bodo Glimt 1 (Staurvik) *Werder Bremen win 6-1 on agg*

Widzew Lodz 2 (Wichniarek, Gesior), Skonto Riga 0 *Widzew Lodz win 2-1 on agg*

Zimbru Chisinau 0, Tottenham Hotspur 0 *Tottenham Hotspur win 3-0 on agg*

Full steam ahead

United derail Loco challenge

HEAD OVER HEELS: Alan Smith acrobatically nets United's third goal.

HARRY Kewell's brilliant late goal gave United a three-goal cushion to take to Russia in their bid to make it through to the third round of the UEFA Cup.

United had turned on the style to power into a 3-0 lead but feared the worst nine minutes from the end when free-kick specialist Dmitri Loskov curled the ball past Nigel Martyn and suddenly – with away goals counting double – the complexion of the tie had changed dramatically.

Lokomotiv's attacking play had deserved a goal but their defence had looked shaky and fatally conceded just two minutes after being thrown a lifeline by Loskov. But it was more down to Kewell's brilliance than a defensive howler. The maurading Australian, took the ball on his chest on the left flank and smacked a low-angled drive into the bottom left-hand corner of goalkeeper Rusian Nigmatullin's net.

It was a classy goal which encapsulated a quality display by United against a top class side in one of the most entertaining European games seen at Elland Road.

Any angled ball into the Russian box spread panic in to the red ranks and it was no surprise when United surged ahead after 27 minutes, Lee Bowyer lashing home.

Just before the interval Bowyer, hotly tipped for full England honours, headed his second from Michael Bridges' teasing cross from the left.

Lokomotiov almost got back on track when Alexei Arifoullin hit the United bar with a 35-yard dipping shot which fooled Martyn, who then twice saved brilliantly to keep out a power-packed shots from the excellent Loskov.

But the Muscovites' vunerability at the back was exposed again when they failed to deal with crosses by Kewell and Gary Kelly, leaving Alan Smith to score with an overhead kick for United's third goal.

Kewell's late strike after Loskov's goal put United in command of the tie.

UEFA Cup
Second round, first leg
(at Elland Road, Leeds)
Thursday, October 21, 1999

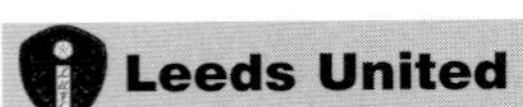

Leeds United 4

Lokomotiv Moscow 1

Leeds United: Nigel Martyn, Gary Kelly, Ian Harte, Jonathan Woodgate, Lucas Radebe, David Batty, Lee Bowyer, Stephen McPhail, Harry Kewell, Michael Bridges (Darren Huckerby 62), Alan Smith
Goals: Bowyer 27, 45, Smith 56, Kewell 83
Manager: David O'Leary

Lokomotiv Moscow: Rusian Nigmatullin, Alexei Arifullin, Igor Chugainov, Oleg Pashinin (Sarkis Oganesyan 61), Albert Sarkisian (Vladimir Maminov 75), Andrei Lavrik, Alexei Smertin, Yuri Drozdov, Yevgeni Kharlachev, Dmitri Loskov, Zaza Dzanashia (Dmitri Bulykin 38)
Goal: Loskov 81
Manager: Yuri Syomin

Referee: Wolfgang Stark (Germany) **Att:** 37,814

Buoys shattered by Larsson's double fracture

CELTIC'S star striker Henrik Larsson suffered a double fracture of a leg as his side went down 1-0 in Lyon.

Newcastle returned from Zurich with a 2-1 win, ex-England captain Alan Shearer getting what turned out to be the winning goal.

Tottenham, under the guidance of former Leeds boss George Graham, beat Kaiserslautern with a Steffan Iversen penalty, but West Ham lost 2-0 in Romania to Steaua Bucharest.

Second round, first leg

Anderlecht 2 (Koller 2), Bologna 1 (Signori)
Aris Salonika 2 (Andrioli, Kyzeridis), Celta Vigo 2 (Karpin 2)
Atletico Madrid 1 (Baraja), Amica 0
Deportivo La Coruna 3 (Pauleta, Djalminha pen, Maakay), Montpellier 1 (Romero og)
Gothenberg 0, Roma 2 (Montella 2)
Graz 2 (Lipa, Pamic), Panathinikos 1 (Sypniewski)
Hapoel Haifa 0, Ajax 3 (Mahlas, Knopper, Laudrup)
Inter Bratislava 0, Nantes 3 (Sibierski pen, Da Rocha, Carriere)
Leeds United 4 (Bowyer 2, Smith, Kewell), Lokomotiv Moscow 1 (Loskov)
Lens 4 (Brunel, Nouma, Nyarko, Blanchard), Vitesse Arnhem 1 (Van Hooijdonk)
Levski Sofia 1 (Youffou), Juventus 3 (Oliseh, Kovacevic 2)
Lyon 1 (Blanc), Celtic 0
MTK Budapest 2 (Egressy, Eros), AEK Athens 1 (Ciric)
PAOK Salonika 1 (Frantzeskos), Benfica 2 (Nuno Gomes, Ronaldo)
Parma 1 (Cannavarro), Helsingborg 0
Roda 0, Wolfsburg 0
Slavia Prague 3 (Ulich 2, Kuchar), Grasshoppers 1 (Yakin)
Steaua Bucharest 2 (Rosu, Ilie), West Ham United 0
Teplice 1 (Verbir), Mallorca 2 (Tristan 2)
Tottenham Hotspur 1 (Iversen pen), Kaiserslautern 0
Udinese 1 (Sosa), Legia Warsaw 0
Werder Bremen 0, Viking 0
Widzew Lodz 1 (Wichniarek pen), Monaco 1 (Guily)
FC Zurich 1 (Castillo), Newcastle United 2 (Maric, Shearer)

HARRY COOL: United's Harry Kewell skips bast Lokomotiv's Igor Chugainov.

UEFA Cup
Second round, second leg
(at Lokomotiv Stadium, Moscow)
Thursday, November 4, 1999

Lokomotiv Moscow	**0**
Leeds United	**3**

Leeds United win 7-1 on agg

Lokomotiv Moscow: Rusian Nigmatullin, Alexei Arifullin, Igor Chugainov (Semin Semenko 77), Sarkis Oganesyan, Oleg Pashin (Yevgeni Kharlachev HT), Andrei Solomatin, Albert Sarkisian, Andrei Lavrik, Alexei Smertin, Dmitri Loskov, Dmitri Bulykin (Rousian Piminov 73)
Manager: Yuri Syomin

Leeds United: Nigel Martyn, Gary Kelly, Ian Harte, Jonathan Woodgate, Lucas Radebe, David Batty, Lee Bowyer (Alf-Inge Haaland HT), Stephen McPhail (David Hopkin 80), Eirik Bakke, Harry Kewell (Darren Huckerby 66), Michael Bridges
Goals: Harte pen 16, Bridges 28, 45
Manager: David O'Leary

Referee: Alain Sars (France) **Att:** 8,000

Brilliant Bridges

Two-goal striker cashes in as United romp home

MICHAEL Bridges turned on a majestic performance in Russia to put the brakes on Lokomotiv Moscow.

The £5.6 million summer signing from Sunderland had not looked back since netting a hat-trick at Southampton in only his second appearance in a Leeds shirt.

Now he was starting to make his mark in Europe with a couple of goals as United won 3-0 to cruise into the draw for the fourth round.

All the goals came in the first-half as United extended their unbeaten run to 13 matches.

United set their stall out to defend early on as the slick Russians came powering out of the blocks like an Olympic sprinter.

But despite a few narrow squeaks in and around Nigel Martyn's goal, United weathered the storm and counter-attacked to devastating effect.

Harry Kewell was a particularly dangerous outlet for United and it was no surprise that he won a penalty in the 16th minute when defender Alexei Arifullin brought him down with a clumsy challenge. Ian Harte rammed in the spot kick to put United 1-0 ahead and 5-1 up on aggregate The home side seemed to lose heart after that – many of their fans had already given up hope with only 8,000 supporters in the Lokomotiv Stadium – and United took complete control.

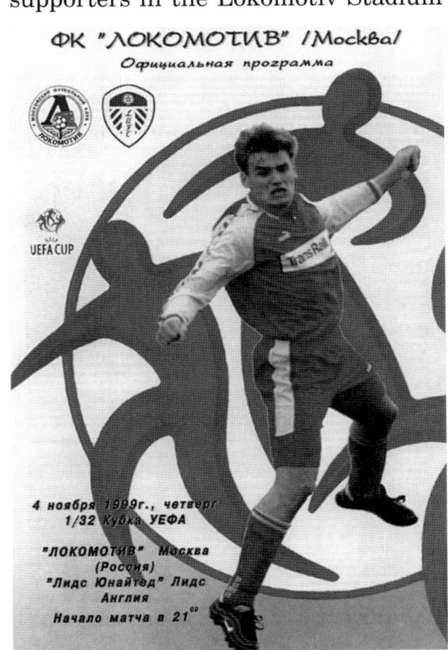

Bridges ran unchallenged into the box to get on the end of Lee Bowyer's header down and lifted the ball over the exposed Rusian Nigmatullin.

On the stroke of half-time, Erik Bakke took a quick free-kick while the Lokomotiv players had switched off and picked out Bridges with a 40-yard pass. The Leeds striker made it 3-0 with an exquisite finish.

United were in such command that manager David O'Leary was able to rest midfielder Bowyer, who had been nursing a groin strain, at half-time, while Kewell was given a well-earned break just after an hour.

The only disappointing note for United from another excellent night's European work was a booking for inspirational skipper Lucas Radebe – his third of the tournament – which would rule him out of the first leg of the next round.

The bitter Cold War

Clubs' icy relations as Moscow tie is frozen off

UNITED made a 3,000-mile round trip to Russia without kicking a ball in anger.

The third round draw had handed them a return trip to the Russian capital – this time to face Spartak Moscow, a stronger outfit than Lokomotiv.

But there were bitter exchanges between hosts Spartak Moscow and the Leeds party after the first leg tie was postponed in sub-zero temperatures.

Spartak manager and chief executive Oleg Romantsev was furious that the game did not take place and believed United had used dirty tricks to get their way.

The Russian propaganda was to rumble on to such an extent that Leeds chairman Peter Ridsdale wrote a letter of complaint to UEFA.

Swedish referee Anders Frisk called the game off at 1pm on the day of the game who said the surface of the Dynamo Stadium pitch was too dangerous to play on.

That came as little surprise to Leeds boss David O'Leary, who aborted the United training session on the pitch after just ten minutes the previous night when the mercury plunged to -17°C.

"The surface was like concrete," said O'Leary. "It was a disgrace."

It was a view shared by referee Frisk, but not Spartak, who suggested that United were afraid to play. The Russians, who said the undersoil heating at the ground had been switched on for a week, said the cold snap was unprecedented.

Spartak had suggested switching their home leg to Vladikavkaz because the weather would be warmer there. However, that plan was vetoed because the southern city was close to war-torn Chechnya.

Frisk, whose decision to call the game off was backed to the hilt by United, said: "The match will not be played tonight. Regulations then stipulate that the game should be played tomorrow. But the Russians cannot guarantee the weather and the pitch for tomorrow either, so we have postponed the game.

"Both clubs are in negotiations to fix a new date and venue. It must be in a place that can be 100 per cent guaranteed. It is quite obvious that the pitch was too hard and there is also a question about the weather, which was also a consideration for tomorrow. It's also due to be very cold."

Graham's agony

GEORGE Graham's Tottenham were just seconds away from progressing to the third round in Germany when Kaiserslautern scored twice in the final minute to turn the tie on its head.

Spurs, holding a single goal first leg advantage. looked like securing a trademark Graham 0-0 away draw when they were shattered by a goal from Andreas Buck and an own-goal by Republic of Ireland full back Stephen Carr at the death.

Second round, second leg

AEK Athens 1 (Ciric pen), MTK Budapest 0 2-2 *on agg. AEK Athens win on away goals*

Ajax 0, Hapoel Haifa 1 (Rosso pen) *Ajax win 3-1 on agg*

Amica 1 (Jackiewicz), Atletico Madrid 4 (Hasselbaink, Capdevila, Baraja, Correa) *Atletico Madrid win 5-1 on agg*

Benfica 1 (Kandourov), PAOK Salonika 2 (Marangos, Sabry) *3-3 on agg. Benfica won 4-1 on pens*

Bologna 3 (Eribeto, Ze Elias, Nervo), Anderlecht 0 *Bologna win 4-2 on agg*

Celta Vigo 2 (Djorovic, Turdo), Aris Salonika 0 *Celta Vigo win 4-2 on agg*

Celtic 0, Lyon 1 (Vairelles) *Lyon win 2-0 on agg*

Grasshoppers 1 (Yakin), Slavia Prague 0 *Slavia Prague win 3-2 on agg*

Helsingborg 1 (Stavrum), Parma 3 (Di Vaio 3) *Parma win 4-1 on agg*

Juventus 1 (Kovacevic), Levski Sofia 1 (Atanassov)

Kaiserslautern 2 (Buck, Carr og), Tottenham Hotspur 0 *Kaiserslautern win 2-1 on agg*

Legia Warsaw 1 (Czereszewski), Udinese 1 (Sosa) *Udinese win 2-1 on agg*

Lokomotiv Moscow 0, Leeds United 3 (Harte pen, Bridges 2) *Leeds United win 7-1 on agg*

Mallorca 3 (Nadal, Stankovic, Nino), Templice 0 *Mallorca win 5-1 on agg*

Monaco 2 (Lamouchi, Tezeguet), Widzew Lodz 0 *Monaco win 4-1 on agg*

Montpellier 0, Deportivo La Coruna 2 (Maakay, Pauleta) *Deportivo La Coruna win 5-1 on agg*

Nantes 4 (Sibierski, Monterrubio, Devineau, Da Rocha), Inter Bratislava 0 *Nantes win 7-0 on agg*

Newcastle United 3 (Maric, Ferguson, Speed), FC Zurich 1 (Jamarauli) *Newcastle United win 5-2 on agg*

Panathinikos 1 (Pflipsen pen), Graz 0 *2-2 on agg. Panathinikos win on away goals*

Roma 1 (Fabio Junior), Gothenberg 0 *Roma win 3-0 on agg*

Viking 2 (Berland, Dadson), Werder Bremen 2 (Wiedener, Herzog) *2-2 on agg. Werder Bremen win on away goals*

Vitesse Arnhem 1 (Kreek), Lens 1 (Blanchard) *Lens win 5-2 on agg*

West Ham United 0, Steaua Bucharest 0 *Steaua Bucharest win 2-0 on agg*

Wolfsburg 1 (Akonner), Roda 0 *Wolfsburg win 1-0 on agg*

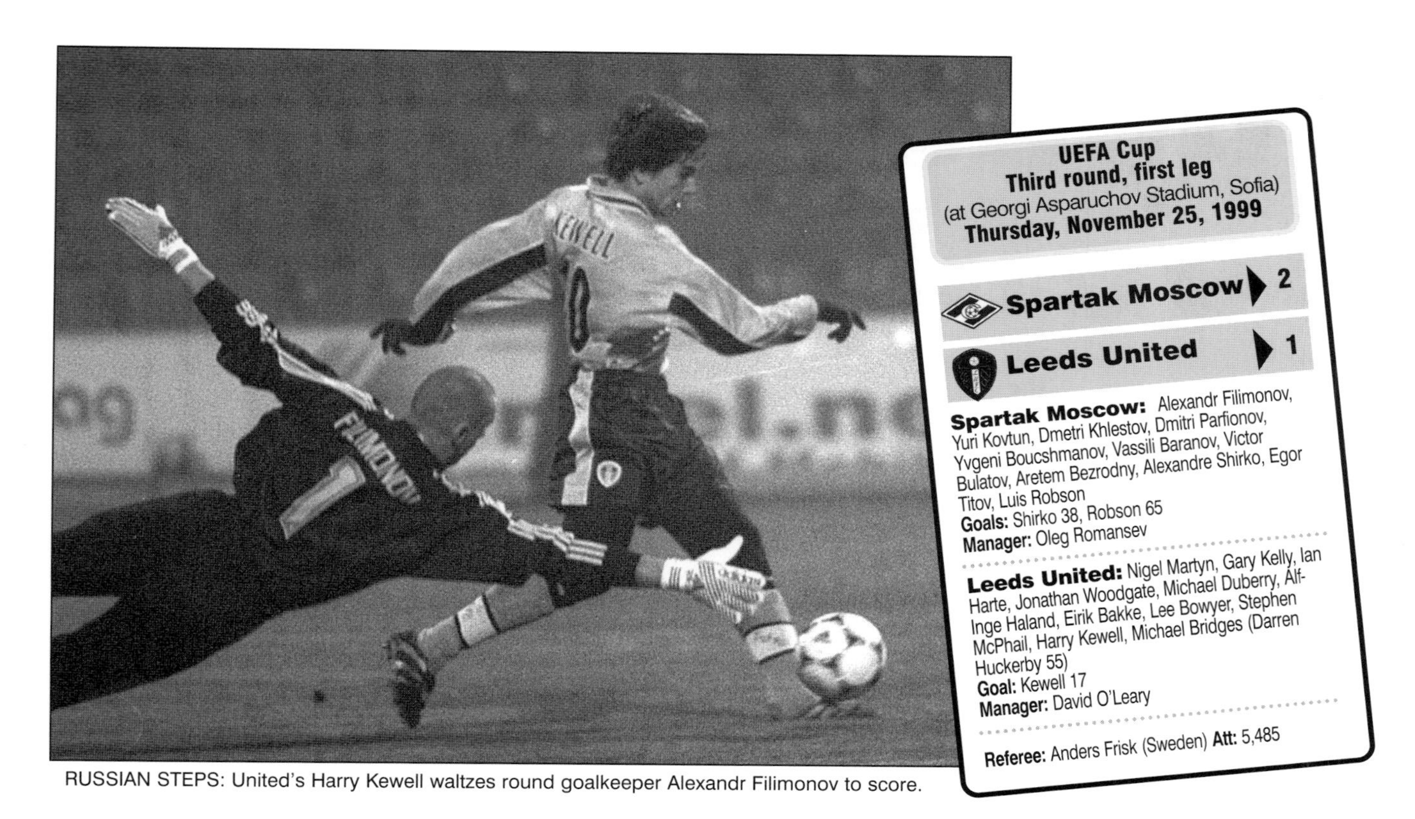

RUSSIAN STEPS: United's Harry Kewell waltzes round goalkeeper Alexandr Filimonov to score.

Sofia, so good

HARRY Kewell's priceless goal kept United firmly in the tie against the vastly experienced Spartak Moscow in Bulgaria.

The reluctant Russians, who were in a mid-season break from their league because of the cold weather, eventually agreed to their home leg being staged in the Bulgarian capital of Sofia on Thursday, December 2 – a week after the original game should have been played.

United, stripped of the services of midfielder David Batty through injury and skipper Lucas Radebe because of suspension were perhaps fortunate to escape with just a 2-1 defeat.

The calming influence of England man Batty was sorely missed when the Russians finally got their act together in the second half and threatened to overrun a United side which contained eight players aged under 22.

With 14 wins from their last 16 matches, United were brimming full of confidence at the start and played some sparkling stuff, capped by Kewell's 17th minute goal.

Kewell nets priceless goal

The quick-thinking Australian shone through the smog which hung over the Georgi Asparuchov Stadium in those early stages.

He saw a fine near-post header come back off the bar and minutes later got his reward by latching on to a back pass and steering the ball home from an acute angle.

It was one-way traffic as David O'Leary's Premiership leaders showed little fear against a club which had won the Russian League seven times in the previous eight years.

But the tide turned after Michael Bridges damaged a shin after a collision with goalkeeper Alexandr Fillimonov. Although Kewell continually posed a threat, Spartak gradually got a foothold in the game and Nigel Martyn had to look sharp to tip a bending shot from Victor Bulatov over the bar.

From the half-hour mark United were being rolled back by the slick-passing Russians who drew level through Alexander Schirko.

No matter how hard they tried United could not get hold of the ball in midfield and showed little as attacking force in the second half.

However, Spartak's domination brought them only one goal, a neat bout of inter-passing leaving Brazilian Luis Robson a simple tap-in.

As the temperatures dipped, so did United's performance level, but Alf-Inge Haaland and Michael Duberry, making fairly rare first team appearances did well to keep Spartak at bay.

O'Leary knew a 2-1 defeat was not the end of the world but was worried that the long-distance travelling and high number of fixtures were threatening to burn out his young stars.

"They are learning all the time," he said, "but I'm worried because we have such a hectic schedule over the next few weeks and we have not got a big enough squad to cope with all those demands."

Lucas aid a real boost

Skipper Radebe's gamble pays off with late winnner

GOAL HERO: United skipper Lucas Radebe.

UEFA Cup
Third round, second leg
(at Elland Road, Leeds)
Thursday, December 9, 1999

Leeds United 1

Spartak Moscow 0

2-2 on agg Leeds United win on away goals

Leeds United: Nigel Martyn, Gary Kelly, Ian Harte, Jonathan Woodgate, Lucas Radebe, Eirik Bakke, Lee Bowyer, Stephen McPhail, Harry Kewell, Michael Bridges, Alan Smith (Darren Huckerby 72)
Goal: Radebe 84
Manager: David O'Leary

Spartak Moscow: Alexandr Filimonov (Andrei Smetanin 37), Vadim Evseev, Dmetri Khlestov, Dmitri Parfionov, Yvgeni Boucschmanov, Vassil Baranov, Victor Bulatov, Andrei Tikhonov, Alexandr Schirko, Egor Titov, Luis Robson
Manager: Oleg Romansev

Referee: Alain Sars (France) **Att:** 39,732

A LATE split-second decision by United skipper Lucas Radebe turned the tie against Spartak Moscow on its head.

Leeds were just six minutes away from going out of the UEFA Cup when they won a corner. Captain Radebe was originally going to stay back but, having seen Spartak struggle with the high ball in their defence all night, changed his mind.

What a decision it turned out to be as he headed in Stephen McPhail's corner-kick to send Elland Road wild.

United had the edge at 2-2 on aggregate thanks to Harry Kewell's away goal but had to endure a nerve-jangling finish as the classy Russian side poured forward in search of the goal which would have eliminated David O'Leary's young battlers.

It was edge-of-your-seat stuff but goalkeeper Nigel Martyn and his troops stood firm to win through to the last sixteen.

It was a classic encounter. Spartak were all guile, movement and touch but lacked that killer punch and were blunted by a defence in which Radebe and Jonathan Woodgate were outstanding. In contrast, Leeds were fast and direct, feeding a stream of crosses in to the Spartak box which unnerved the visiting defence.

PASS MASTER: Lee Bowyer strokes the ball past Spartak skipper Andrei Tikhonov.

Spartak began the brighter with Luis Robson denied by a Martyn block as United were opened up by some smart one-touch football.

Gradually, United got the measure of Spartak's game and Ian Harte's left-foot crosses in the box always promised to provide an opening. Michael Bridges stabbed one Harte delivery against a post, then headed another over the bar.

Goalkeeper Alexandr Filimonov had looked very shaky against the high ball and in the 35th minute fell awkwardly when struggling to deal with another centre. His replacement, Andrei Smetanin was quickly called in to action, getting down to hold a Lee Bowyer drive.

Spartak went close when Egor Titov crashed a shot just beyond Martyn's right-hand post while Smetanin covered himself in glory with a brave block to deny Bowyer then flew to his left to push out a fierce 25-yard free-kick from Bridges.

But for all his shot-stopping heroics, Smetanin and his defenders looked vulnerable to the high ball and paid the price when Radebe stole up for only his third goal for the club.

O'Leary on the offensive

VICTORY over Spartak Moscow had been doubly sweet for United boss David O'Leary.

He was delighted to knock out a club with whom relations had become strained after the row over the Moscow pitch.

Not only that, but Spartak had not even started in the UEFA Cup.

They were a Champions League side but UEFA, in their wisdom, deemed that some clubs who failed to make the grade in the Champions League could drop in to the UEFA Cup.

It was a system which drew strong criticism from O'Leary, who wrote in programme notes, "To me the UEFA Cup is a big adventure and let's see how far we can go.

"I don't believe we have the squad to win it. But then I don't think UEFA want us to.

"They just want us to keep the competition warm until the teams from the Champions League have decided who is going to join us. I find that farcical."

Spartak Moscow were one of eight teams entered the UEFA Cup at the third round stage after finishing third in the first phase of the Champions League.

There were 12 groups in the Champions League first phase, but four with the worst records did not move in to the UEFA Cup and were eliminated.

The successful eight were O'Leary's old team Arsenal, German duo Bayer Leverkusen and Borussia Dortmund, Galatasaray, Graz from Austria, Greek side Olympiakos, Scottish champions Rangers, and Spartak Moscow.

Arsenal made the most of their reprieve with late goals by Nigel Winterburn and Denis Bergkamp sealing a 3-0 home win against French side Nantes. The Gunners drew the second leg 3-3 to progress. But there was agony for Rangers. Former Leeds striker Rod Wallace netted the second goal as they beat highly-rated Germans Borussia Dortmund 2-0 at Ibrox. The Gers looked set to hold on in Germany but Freddie Bobic levelled in the 90th minute. Extra-time didn't produce any more goals and the Scots went out 3-1 on penalties after being just seconds from going through.

Of the other original entrants from the Premiership, Newcastle United, featuring ex-Elland Road favourite Gary Speed, failed to break down Roma, the side which had knocked Leeds out the previous year.

Leeds had lost to Roma by a lone goal and this time it was the Magpies who suffered the same fate as Francesco Totti's first leg penalty proved decisive.

When the fourth road draw was made O'Leary learned that his team were to make a return trip to the Italian capital to have another crack at Roma when the UEFA Cup competition resumed in March.

EURO CASULATIES: Former Leeds stars Rod Wallace (left) and Gary Speed went out of the UEFA Cup at the third round stage with their respective clubs, Rangers and Newcastle.

Meanwhile, United, going well in the Premiership, were looking to book a Champions League slot for 2000/01

Third round, first leg

AEK Athens 2 (Nikolaides 2), Monaco 2 (Guily, Simeone)
Ajax 0, Mallorca 1 (Tristran)
Arsenal 3 (Overmars pen, Winterburn Bergkamp), Nantes 0
Bologna 1 (Signori), Galatasaray 1 (Hakan Sukur)
Celta Vigo 7 (Karpin 2 – 1 pen, Makelele, Turdo 2, Juanfran, Mostovoi), Benfica 0
Deportivo La Coruna 4 (Olivares og, Pauleta, Djalminha, Donato), Panathinikos 2 (Warzycha, Galetto)
Lens 1 (Schojonberg og), Kaiserslautern 2 (Sikora og, Wagner)
Lyon 3 (Anderson 2, Vairelles), Werder Bremen 0
Olympiakos 1 (Yannakopoulos), Juventus 3 (Tudor, Kovacevic, Inzaghi)
Parma 2 (Di Vaio, Stanic), Sturm Graz 1 (Schopp)
Rangers 2 (Kohler og, Wallace), Borussia Dortmund 0
Roma 1 (Totti pen), Newcastle United 0
Slavia Prague 4 (Dostalek, Horvath 2, Dosek), Steaua Bucharest 1 (Lutu)
Udinese 0, Bayer Leverkusen 1 (Ballack)
Wolfsburg 2 (Juskowiak, Akonner pen), Atletico Madrid 3 (Aguilera 2, Hasselbaink)

Third round, first leg

Atletico Madrid 2 (Hasselbaink, Correa), Wolfsburg 1 (Akonnor pen) *Atletico Madrid win 5-3 on agg*
Bayer Leverkusen 1 (Ballack), Udinese 2 (Margiotta 2) *2-2 on agg. Udinese win on away goals*
Benfica 1 (Caceres og), Celta Vigo 1 (McCarthy) *Celta Vigo win 8-1 on agg*
Borussia Dortmund 2 (Ikpeba, Bobic), Rangers 0 *2-2 agg. Borussia Dortmund win 3-1 on pens*
Galatasaray 2 (Sas, Umit), Bologna 1 (Ventola) *Galatasaray win 3-2 on agg*
Graz 3 (Reinmayr 2, Vastic), Parma 3 (Stanic 2, Crespo) aet *Parma win 5-4 on agg*
Juventus 1 (Kovacevic), Olympiakos 2 (Djordjevic 2 – 1 pen) *Juventus win 4-3 on agg*
Kaiserslautern 1 (Hristov), Lens 4 (Job 2, Strasser og, Nyarko) *Lens win 5-3 on agg*
Leeds United 1 (Radebe), Spartak Moscow 0 *2-2 on agg. Leeds United win on away goals*
Mallorca 2 (Soler pen, Biagini), Ajax 0 *Mallorca win 3-0 on agg*
Monaco 1 (Simeone), AEK Athens 0 *Monaco win 3-2 on agg*
Nantes 3 (Sibierski 2, Vahirua), Arsenal 3 (Grimandi, Henry, Overmars) *Arsenal win 6-3 on agg*
Newcastle United 0, Roma 0 *Roma win 1-0 on agg*
Panathinikos 1 (Asanovic pen), Deportivo La Coruna 1 (Makaay) *Deportivo La Coruna win 5-3 on agg*
Steaua Bucharest 1 (Ciocoiu), Slavia Prague 1 (Dostalek) *Slavia Prague win 5-2 on agg*
Werder Bremen 4 (Bode, Herzog pen, Baumann, Pizarro), Lyon 0 *Werder Bremen win 4-3 on agg*

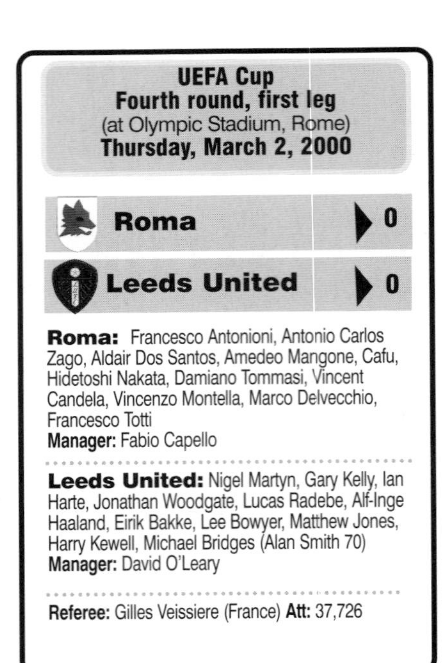

UEFA Cup
Fourth round, first leg
(at Olympic Stadium, Rome)
Thursday, March 2, 2000

Roma	**0**
Leeds United	**0**

Roma: Francesco Antonioni, Antonio Carlos Zago, Aldair Dos Santos, Amedeo Mangone, Cafu, Hidetoshi Nakata, Damiano Tommasi, Vincent Candela, Vincenzo Montella, Marco Delvecchio, Francesco Totti
Manager: Fabio Capello

Leeds United: Nigel Martyn, Gary Kelly, Ian Harte, Jonathan Woodgate, Lucas Radebe, Alf-Inge Haaland, Eirik Bakke, Lee Bowyer, Matthew Jones, Harry Kewell, Michael Bridges (Alan Smith 70)
Manager: David O'Leary

Referee: Gilles Veissiere (France) **Att:** 37,726

TOWER OF STRENGTH: United defender Jonathan Woodgate rises to the occasion in Rome.

Magical Martyn

HOPE sprang eternal for United after a tremendous defensive display in the Eternal City against Roma.

Goalkeeper Nigel Martyn put on a fantastic performance to hold the big-spending Italians to a 0-0 draw and gave United a real chance of avenging the previous season's defeat in the same competition.

Fabio Capello's Roman legions were held at bay by David O'Leary's young gladiators in the Olympic Stadium against all the odds.

Roma had won 16 of their previous 17 European encounters, with their only defeat coming against Atletico Madrid in the quarter-final of the UEFA Cup the previous season. Those statistics became even more intimidating as Roma had won five and drawn two of their previous meetings with English sides on their home soil.

They had also beaten United 1-0 17 months earlier just before O'Leary had taken charge so there were few people that gave United much chance of making further progress.

But O'Leary got his tactics spot-on, using three centre-backs and bringing in young Welsh international Matthew Jones to man-mark striker Francesco Totti.

'Keeper is England's No 1, claims Ridsdale

Inevitably the Italians had the bulk of possession but United went close early on through Eirik Bakke and Harry Kewell kept the home side on their toes with a couple of shots which were not too wide of the mark.

But it was 33-year-old Martyn's performance in goal which rightly earned the plaudits as he made a string of super saves to deny Totti and his co-striker Marco Delvecchio.

The modest Martyn played down his role in a classic away performance.

"Fortunately a lot of the shots were straight at me. I had to make sure I kept a clean sheet. That was the important thing if we weren't going to score, so I was very pleased."

Chairman Peter Ridsdale, who hailed Martyn as England's best, said: "The defence was magnificent. To come out of a game like that without conceding a goal was a magnificent achievement and the tie is now nicely set up for next week.

"But we know how hard they are to break down, although the difference this time as opposed to when we played them last is that we don't have to win by two clear goals."

Rampant Gunners run riot

CHAMPIONS League drop-outs Arsenal virtually booked their UEFA Cup quarter-final place by thumping Deportivo La Coruna 5-1 at Highbury.

The Spaniards were well in the tie until the dismissal of scorer Djalminha and collapsed in the second half.

Leeds players past and future netted twice in Madrid with Jimmy-Floyd Hasselbaink scoring for Atletico and Olivier Dacourt responding for Lens in a 2-2 draw.

Fourth round, first leg

Atletico Madrid 2 (Hasselbaink 2), Lens 2 (Dacourt 2)
Arsenal 5 (Dixon, Henry 2, Kanu, Bergkamp), Deportivo La Coruna 1 (Djalminha pen)
Borussia Dortmund 0, Galatasaray 2 (Hakan Sukur, Hagi)
Juventus 1 (Kovacevic), Celta Vigo 0
Mallorca 4 (Stankovic 3 – 2 pens, Tristan), Monaco 1 (Simeone)
Parma 1 (Crespo), Werder Bremen 0
Roma 0, Leeds United 0
Slavia Prague 1 (Zanchie og), Udinese 0

Kewell's jewel

UNITED'S Aussie star Harry Kewell, coveted by a string of Italian clubs, slapped a few more million lira on his head with a spectacular winner against Roma.

Serie A giants AC Milan, Inter Milan and Lazio had all shown an interest in the 21-year-old, who had hinted that he may like to play in Italy sometime in the future.

No wonder United chairman Peter Ridsdale was prepared to hike up Kewell's pay, even though the Australian star was only eight months into his four-year contract.

Kewell's 67th minute strike sent United into the quarter-finals of the UEFA Cup on an Elland Road night of glory.

Roma had not conceded a goal in Europe for more than nine hours, so it was always going to need something special for United to break the dead-lock.

It came midway through the second half as Lee Bowyer, attacking the Don Revie Stand end, switched the ball in-field to Kewell who shifted the ball to his left before unleashing a 20-yard angled drive. Goalkeeper Francesco Antonioli, at full stretch to his left, got a hand to the ball but was beaten by sheer power and accuracy.

Although Kewell was the match-winner and was at the heart of all United's best attacking moments, the home heroes were Alf-Inge Haaland and Lucas Radebe in defence. The Norwegian-South African combination ensured that Marco Delvecchio and Vincenzo Montella were blotted out despite the promptings of the classy Francesco Totti.

Nigel Martyn, hero of the first leg was well protected, particularly by Haaland, who was only in the side because of injury to Jonathan Woodgate.

On limited possession, Leeds made the better chances with Eirik Bakke, developing well in midfield, bringing Antonioli to his knees, while Kewell also employed the Italian 'keeper with a hard 30-yard drive. Supreme skill by Kewell just after the hour created the chance of the night for Bowyer, but the midfielder screwed a good chance wide. Minutes later, though, Kewell struck his golden goal and United's defence remained cool, calm and collected in the final heated moments of an intense battle.

Roma, unable to make any meaningful progress, reached boiling point at the end.

Deep into injury-time Antonio-Carlos Zago clashed with United substitute Alan Smith and the pair were booked. It was Zago's second caution, but he was unwilling to go and in the jostling that followed Vincent Candela also saw red for butting another sub, Darren Huckerby, who had only been on the pitch a couple of minutes.

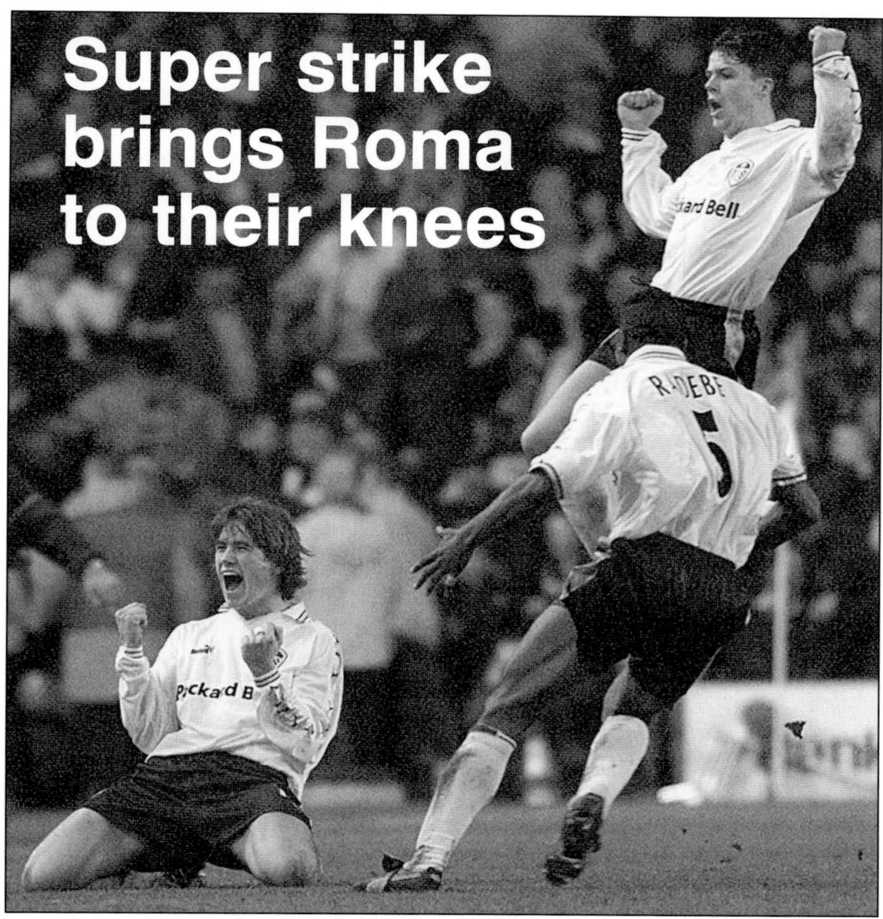

HARRY COOL: Harry Kewell celebrates his match-winner against Roma with a bit of help from Ian Harte (right) and Lucas Radebe.

UEFA Cup
Fourth round, second leg
(at Elland Road, Leeds)
Thursday, March 9, 2000

Leeds United	**1**
Roma	**0**

Leeds United win 1-0 on agg

Leeds United: Nigel Martyn, Gary Kelly, Ian Harte, Lucas Radebe, Alf-Inge Haaland, Eirik Bakke (Matthew Jones 84), Lee Bowyer, Stephen McPhail (Darren Huckerby 89), Jason Wilcox, Harry Kewell, Michael Bridges (Alan Smith 82)
Goal: Kewell 67
Manager: David O'Leary

Roma: Francesco Antonioni, Antonio Carlos Zago, Aldair Dos Santos, Alessandro Rinaldi, Amedeo Mangone, Hidetoshi Nakata (Eusebio Di Francesco 77), Damiano Tommasi, Vincent Candela, Vincenzo Montella, Marco Delvecchio, Francesco Totti
Manager: Fabio Capello

Referee: Jose-Maria Garcia-Aranda Encinar (Spain)
Att: 39,149

No quarter

Italians wiped out

UNITED'S conquest of Roma put the tin lid on a disastrous night for Italian football as both Juventus and holders Parma also went out of the competiton.
That left Italy with no representation in the last eight of the UEFA Cup for the first time since 1984.

Juventus were thrashed 4-0 in Spain by Celta Vigo while Parma were undone by a second half own-goal by Fabio Cannavaro which enabled Werder Bremen to win 3-1 and over turn a 1-0 first leg deficit.

Italy's fourth representatives Udinese went out on away goals to Slavia Prague, who were United's quarter-final opponents.

Arsenal slipped to a last-minute 2-1 defeat in Coruna, but were already ahead from the first leg at Highbury.

While United took on Czech Republic outfit Slavia Prague, the Gunners were paired with tough German squad Werder Bremen, who had beaten Parma, Lyon, Viking Stavanger and Bodo Glimt on their way to the last eight.

The Germans were negative in the extreme in the first leg at Highbury, but Arsenal still managed to win 2-0 with goals from Freddie Ljungberg and Thierry Henry.

Also impressive were Turkish side Galatasaray who won 4-1 at Mallorca.

Fourth round, second leg

Celta Vigo 4 (Makelele, Birindelli og, McCarthy 2), Juventus 0 *Celta Vigo win 4-1 on agg*

Deportivo La Coruna 2 (Victor, Ivan), Arsenal 1 (Henry) *Arsenal win 6-3 on agg*

Galatasaray 0, Borussia Dortmund 0 *Galatasaray win 2-0 on agg*

Leeds United 1 (Kewell), Roma 0 *Leeds United win 1-0 on agg*

Lens 4 (Nouma 2, Sahko, Brunel), Atletico Madrid 2 (Hasselbaink, Kiko) *Lens win 6-4 on agg*

Monaco 1 (Simeone), Mallorca 0 *Mallorca win 4-2 on agg*

Udinese 2 (Fiore, Sosa), Slavia Prague 1 (Koller) *2-2 on agg. Slavia Prague win on away goals*

Werder Bremen 3 (Dabrovski, Bode, Cannavaro og), Parma 1 (Stanic) *Werder Bremen win 3-2 on agg*

Quarter-final, first leg

Arsenal 2 (Henry, Ljungberg), Werder Bremen 0

Celta Vigo 0, Lens 0

Leeds United 3 (Wilcox, Kewell, Bowyer), Slavia Prague 0

Mallorca 1 (Lauren), Galatasaray 4 (Arif, Emre, Hakan Sukur, Okan)

UNITED put themselves within touching distance of their first UEFA Cup semi-final for 29 years with a 3-0 demolition of Slavia Prague at Elland Road.

Only an amazing about-turn in the Czech Republic would deny David O'Leary's young guns a place in the last four of the competition for the first time since 1971.

United would have undoubtably accepted a three-goal margin before the kick-off but at the final whistle knew they should have already booked that semi-final spot. Three goals was a moderate return for a game they dominated from start to finish as Slavia were swept aside by United power and passion.

It took United just two minutes to open up the Czech defence but Harry Kewell shot tamely at goalkeeper Radek Cerny, who later produced a fine diving save to his right to deny the young Australian at the expense of a corner.

Patience had been a splendid virtue in United's European campaign and it

given by United

took them just over half an hour to get the reward their enterprising play deserved.

Lee Bowyer picked off a poor Prague free-kick, ran past a midfield challenge before sliding the ball into the path of Jason Wilcox on the left. The winger gleefully smashed in his first European goal since his £3 million transfer from Blackburn Rovers three months earlier.

Bowyer, always in the thick of the action, fluffed a close range chance just before the break, but nine

Semi-final within sight after Slavia demolition

minutes after half-time United took complete control when Kewell tapped in Eirik Bakke's perfect far-post cross.

Better was to come from United just before the hour when Michael Bridges' marvellous pass sent Bowyer bursting through and he arrowed a low shot past Cerny.

Bridges, at the hub of much of United's good work, marred an excellent performance by failing with a one-on-one opportunity with Cerny and Leeds seemed to lose their way a bit after that.

When Slavia skipper Karel Rada was ordered off for his second bookable offence with 15 minutes remaining, the opportunity presented itself for United to rub home their advantage. Instead they appeared to opt to keep a crucial clean sheet to take to Prague where they would be without Bowyer, whose needless booking – when United were 3-0 up – ruled him out of the return leg under the totting up procedure.

But that was a minor blemish on another great European night for United. O'Leary beamed: "It was a wonderful performance and I was delighted with the players. The football was excellent. The way we played and the tempo we played at, I don't think they could cope with it."

GOLDEN GOALS:
Lee Bowyer (left) hammers in United's third goal.

Jason Wilcox (above), United's recent recruit from Blackburn, celebrates United's opener against Slavia Prague.

UEFA Cup
Quarter-final, first leg
(at Elland Road, Leeds)
Thursday, March 16, 2000

Leeds United	3
Slavia Prague	0

Leeds United: Nigel Martyn, Gary Kelly, Ian Harte, Lucas Radebe, Alf-Inge Haaland, Eirik Bakke, Lee Bowyer, Stephen McPhail (Darren Huckerby 76), Jason Wilcox, Harry Kewell, Michael Bridges (Alan Smith 86)
Goals: Wilcox 39, Kewell 54, Bowyer 59
Manager: David O'Leary

Slavia Prague: Radek Cerny, Petr Vicek (Rober Vagner 55), Karel Rada, Tibor Koller, Lukas Dosek, Adam Petrous, Tomas Kuchard, Richard Dostalek (Martin Hysky 64), Pavel Horvath, Ivo Ulich, Tomas Dosek
Manager: Frantisek Cipro

Referee: Markus Merk (Germany) **Att:** 39,519

Slavia Czech-mate

.. but it's United who move into semi-finals

COMMANDER IN CHIEF: United's Lucas Radebe moves in to block a shot by Slavia's Lukas Dosek.

EVEN if they were some way off their best there was no denying United's right to a place in the UEFA Cup semi-finals.

They lost 2-1 to Slavia in the Strahov Stadium but were never in any danger of being on the wrong end of a Czech aggregate upset.

Stephen McPhail and Michael Bridges squandered early opportunities to put the tie beyond doubt as United appeared the have the midfield guile to open up the home side at will on a surface which quickly cut up. The same two players, and Harry Kewell, missed further first-half chances, while Slavia shoud have made United pay for their profligacy.

Goalkeeper Nigel Martyn fly-kicked a couple of clearances straight to striker Ludek Zelenka, but he failed to take his opportunities.

Much of United's play was slack, despite a hard night's graft in midfield by Matthew Jones, in for the suspended Lee Bowyer.

Just as United looked as though they were happy to amble through the match, they struck a minute after the interval.

The influential McPhail released a perfect pass for Kewell to smash in a left-foot shot between goalkeeper Radek Cerny and the near post. It meant Prague needed to score five goals to deny United, who retreated into their defensive shell after Kewell's goal, knowing that the job had been done.

Those tactics gave something for the home fans to cheer as Slavia belatedly pushed forward and drew level on the night when the ball was threaded right across United's box and Czech Republic midfield international Ivo Ulich applied a smart finish.

Later Zelenka went down theatrically in the box in a challenge with Ian Harte and got up to net the penalty which gave Slavia a 2-1 consolation victory.

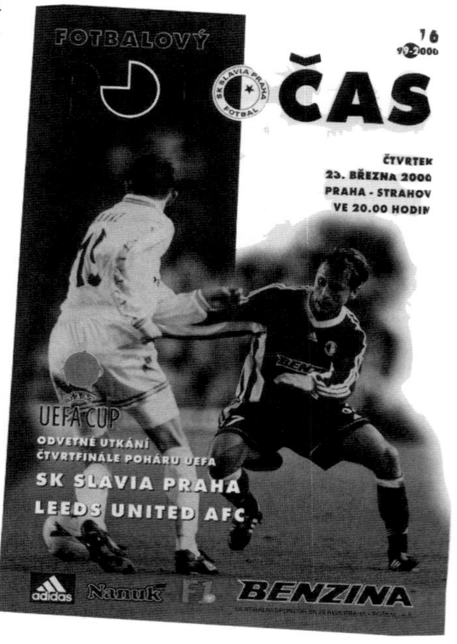

UEFA Cup
Quarter-final, second leg
(at Strahov Stadium, Prague)
Thursday, March 23, 2000

Slavia Prague 2

Leeds United 1

Leeds United win 4-1 on agg

Slavia Prague: Radnek Cerny, Lubos Kozel, Libor Koller, Martin Hysky, Lukas Dosek, Richard Dostalek (Jiri Lerch 53), Tomas Kuchard (Martin Vozabal 84), Jiri Skala, Ivo Ulich, Tomas Dosek (Robert Vagner 53), Ludek Zelenka
Goals: Ulich 52, 79 pen
Manager: Frantisek Cipro

Leeds United: Nigel Martyn, Gary Kelly, Ian Harte, Lucas Radebe, Jonathan Woodgate, Alf-Inge Haaland, Eirik Bakke, Matthew Jones, Stephen McPhail, Michael Bridges (Alan Smith 48), Harry Kewell
Goal: Kewell 47
Manager: David O'Leary

Referee: Marcus Merk (Germany) **Att:** 13,460

O'Leary's delight at young team's achievement

MANAGER David O'Leary branded United's overall display in Prague as a "disgrace" but could not hide his delight at reaching the last four.

"It is absolutely fantastic. I don't like being beaten and I had a few things to say after the game but it is all part of the learning process because they are young players. We deserve to be where we are because we have taken every-body on."

The semi-final draw handed United a fearsome task – a trip to Turkey to face Galatasaray, whose fans were known to generate a hostile atmosphere at the Ali Sami Yen Stadium in Istanbul.

The other semi pitted Arsenal against French side Lens, so the hope of an all-English final in Copenhagen was still on the cards.

Ray Parlour scored a hat-trick as Arsenal marched in to the last four. He scored in the 8th, 25th and 70th minutes in a 4-2 win at Werder Bremen to complete a 6-2 aggregate romp.

Arsenal's other goalscorer in Germany, Thierry Henry, was sent off five minutes after scoring Arsenal's fourth goal and would be ruled out of the semi-final.

But football was to take a back seat to the horrifying events that were about to unfold on the streets of Istanbul.

Quarter-final, second leg

Galatasaray 2 (Capone, Hakan Sukur), Mallorca 1 (Carlos) *Galatasaray win 6-2 on agg*

Lens 2 (Ismael pen, Nouma), Celta Vigo 1 (Revivo) *Lens win 2-1 on agg*

Slavia Prague 2 (Ulich 2 – 1 pen), Leeds United 1 (Kewell) *Leeds United win 4-2 on agg*

Werder Bremen 2 (Bode, Bogdanovic), Arsenal 3 (Parlour 3, Henry) *Arsenal win 6-2 on agg*

Hell on earth

Two Leeds fans killed in Turkey

DEATH cast a dark shadow over United's UEFA Cup semi-final in Istanbul.

The fatal stabbings of fans Christopher Loftus, 35, and Kevin Speight, 40, on the streets of the Turkish capital rendered the first leg match in the Ali Sami Yen Stadium virtually irrelevent.

United's fans had been warned to expect a welcome to 'Hell' and duly received it when violence broke out in Taksim Square in the heart of the Turkish city. Horrifying pictures were beamed around the world within hours of the deaths of the two Leeds supporters, leaving the football world numb.

There were calls for the match against Galatasaray to be called off but European football's governing body, along with the Football Association, both expressed their desire for the match to go ahead despite the deaths.

Leeds chairman Peter Ridsdale, who visited other injured stab victims in hospital, diplomatically accepted the decision to play but there was outrage among many United fans that the authorities should allow the game to take place.

As the dreadful news of the murders filtered back to Yorkshire, Elland Road became a shrine to the two supporters bonded together after the killings in Istanbul.

The newly-unveiled Billy Bremner statue, gates and rail-ings to the entrance of the ground were bedecked with flowers and tributes to the murdered men

While moving tributes were made and supporters united in grief, a war of words was being fought behind the scenes between United and Galatasaray.

UNITED IN GRIEF: A fan surveys the tributes left at Elland Road in memory of the two dead United supporters.

Stunned United's nightmare in Istanbul

WALL OF DEATH: United players Ian Ha
riot shields thrust in the night

THE murder of the two Leeds fans did little to cool the fanatical passion in the stadium the following night.

There was little diplomacy and decency in the air – except from the visitors who wore black armbands as a mark of respect for the dead, while Galatasaray chose not to. Several hundred United supporters who had made the journey to Istanbul to follow their team orchestrated their own version of a minute's silence.

With the game ready to start, arms raised, they turned their backs in unison on the pitch – a clear message of how deeply they felt about the match taking place.

United's players, arms linked together in a huddle before the kick-off appeared to be emotionally-drained by the events of the last 24 hours.

Although the stadium was only small, it was ram-jam full with the home fans making a cacophony of noise.

With Romanian star Gheorghe Hagi pulling the strings in midfield, Galatasaray made most of the running in the first half with United, not surprisingly, subdued.

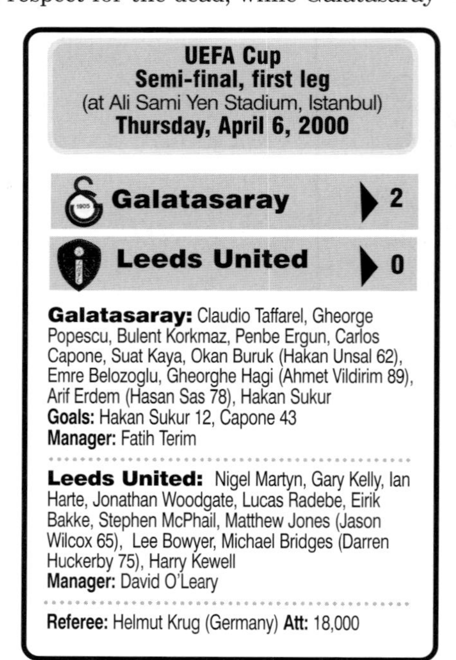

UEFA Cup
Semi-final, first leg
(at Ali Sami Yen Stadium, Istanbul)
Thursday, April 6, 2000

Galatasaray	2
Leeds United	0

Galatasaray: Claudio Taffarel, Gheorge Popescu, Bulent Korkmaz, Penbe Ergun, Carlos Capone, Suat Kaya, Okan Buruk (Hakan Unsal 62), Emre Belozoglu, Gheorghe Hagi (Ahmet Vildirim 89), Arif Erdem (Hasan Sas 78), Hakan Sukur
Goals: Hakan Sukur 12, Capone 43
Manager: Fatih Terim

Leeds United: Nigel Martyn, Gary Kelly, Ian Harte, Jonathan Woodgate, Lucas Radebe, Eirik Bakke, Stephen McPhail, Matthew Jones (Jason Wilcox 65), Lee Bowyer, Michael Bridges (Darren Huckerby 75), Harry Kewell
Manager: David O'Leary

Referee: Helmut Krug (Germany) **Att:** 18,000

After 13 minutes Arif Erdem swung in a dangerous centre from the left and striker Hakan Suker escaped his marker to headed past Nigel Martyn powerfully.

United had half-chances through Harry Kewell and Michael Bridges but were rocked a couple of minutes from the interval when the defence failed to clear a dangerous free-kick and Brazilian defender Carlos Capone scrambled the ball home.

But as the influence of the veteran Hagi waned in the second half, United came more into the match and should have had an away goal to take back to Elland Road.

United's pace in attack opened up the Galatasaray defence and Bridges saw his intial shot blocked by Claudio Taffarel. The ball came back to the young Leeds striker but he shot into the side netting with the goal gaping.

But the match was largely irrelevant given the mayhem which had occured the night before.

United and their fans simply wanted to get back home to their families.

Chairman Peter Ridsdale said: "No-one should ever have to set off to a football match with any doubt whatsoever about the likelihood of being able to return home safely. I sincerely hope that in the depths of despair at the totally unnecessary loss of life, we all ensure that football can never again become a reason to justify anyone being injured or killed."

en Huckerby and Jason Wilcox look drained as they leave the field protected by
revent them being struck by missiles from the frenzied Turkish crowd.

BONDING TOGETHER: United players link their arms in a pre-match huddle

Right: A programme from the ill-fated UEFA Cup semi-final against Galatasaray in Istanbul

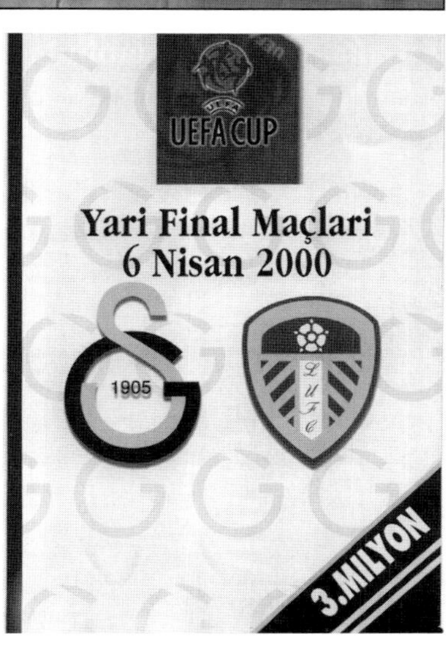

Game on after UEFA's inquiry

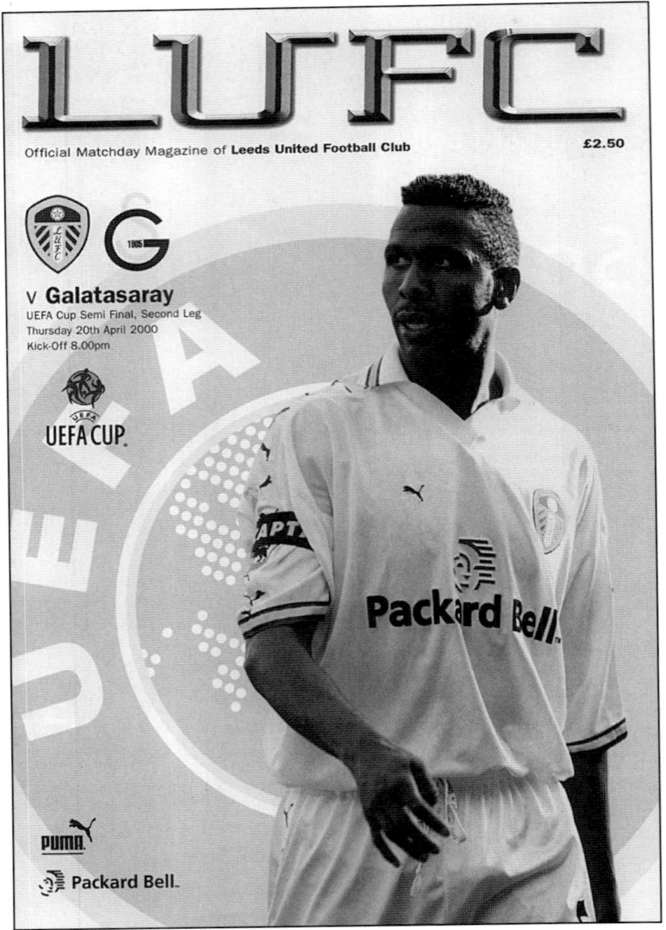

GRUDGE MATCH: The semi-final second leg against Galatasary was the subject of much arguement, but went ahead as scheduled.

INEVITABLY there was a huge public debate about whether the Istanbul game should have ever been staged.

Peter Ridsdale, who won plenty of plaudits about the way he and his club handled themselves during the traumatic trip, said the deaths of Christopher Loftus and Kevin Speight would live with everyone forever at Elland Road.

"Much has been written in the Press about our decision to play the game in Istanbul. Although the decision had to be made quickly and in the immediate aftermath of the murders, I still believe it was the only decision that could be taken," he said.

"I never wanted to give anyone, no matter what nationality, or whoever they supported, an excuse to believe that by causing injury to others their team could gain an advantage or pass through to the next round of any competition.

"Had we not played in Istanbul on April 6 it is my sincere belief that Galatasaray would have progressed to the UEFA Cup final without playing football, and that could not be right."

Ridsdale revealed that the United squad had received death threats at their hotel on the night of the killings.

He also felt that the Galatasaray had tried to take advantage of the killings in the first leg and showed a lack of sympathy towards Leeds.

As the focus switched to the return leg, tensions mounted still further with the Turkish FA demanding that the match be played at a neutral ground should United not be able to guarantee the safety of the Galatasaray supporters and officials.

Leeds responded that they would withdraw from the competition if the match was not played at Elland Road. They also slammed Turkish suggestions that if the match is played at Leeds then it should be behind closed doors.

UEFA stepped in and held an inquiry into the events at Istanbul and how to tackle the second leg.

No Turkish side had ever won a European trophy and the semi-final with United was viewed as one of the biggest games in that club's country and their government became embroiled in the row before Turkish Sports Minister Firet Unlu tried to take the sting out of the situation by going on television to say: "I'd like to apologise to the people of the world for the double killing." UEFA also ruled that United would be charged for failing to control their players in the first leg as four of them – Harry Kewell, Matthew Jones, Lee Bowyer and Ian Harte, were booked by German referee Helmut Krug.

The announcement did little to allay fears in Yorkshire that UEFA were to cave in to Galatasaray's demands to play at a neutral venue.

But UEFA sided with United on that issue. The second leg would be played at Elland Road and the Turkish fans would not be allowed to travel in the interests of safety.

All 1,750 tickets allocated to the Turkish fans were to be returned to UEFA who would only permit the Turkish club 80 tickets for officials and guests.

Police and media seemed to outnumber fans at a hostile Elland Road as a massive security cordon encircled the ground as they eyes of the world were focussed on Leeds.

The atmosphere was extremely tense as the teams arrived with one of the three coaches bearing the Turkish club's officials having a window smashed.

Such was the fevered interest that a tented village for television and radio crews was set up on Fullerton Park opposite the ground with one television crew allegedly attacked when filming by a small pocket of fans.

It was a ghoulish spectacle and the tension spilled over into the match which kicked-off ten minutes late in a downpour after mounted police clashed with fans.

UEFA Cup
Semi-final, second leg
(at Elland Road, Leeds)
Thursday, April 20, 2000

Leeds United	**2**
Galatasaray	**2**

Galatasaray win 4-2 on agg

Leeds United: Nigel Martyn, Danny Mills, Ian Harte, Lucas Radebe, Jonathan Woodgate, (Darren Huckerby HT), Lee Bowyer, Eirik Bakke, Stephen McPhail, Jason Wilcox, Michael Bridges, Harry Kewell
Goal: Bakke 16, 68
Manager: David O'Leary

Galatasaray: Claudio Taffarel, Carlos Capone, Gheorghe Popescu, Bulent Korkmaz, Penbe Ergun, Okan Buruk (Hasan Sas 87), Suat Kaya (Ahmet Yildirim 81), Emre Belozoglu, Gheorghe Hagi, Arif Erdem (Hakan Unsal HT), Hakan Sukur
Goals: Hagi 5 pen, Hakan Sukur 42
Manager: Fatih Terim

Referee: Lubos Michel (Slovakia) **Att:** 38,406

ON YOUR WAY: Referee Lubos Michel points to the tunnel as Harry Kewell is red-carded for his inoccuous challenge on Gheorghe Popescu.

Night of tears

Kewell sent off at hostile Elland Road

UNITED'S hopes of a semi-final comeback were effectively over by the fifth minute when Galatasaray extended their overall advantage to 3-0.

Gheorghe Hagi slipped the ball through for Hakan Sukur, who was upended by Jonathan Woodgate's sliding challenge on the wet turf and Romanian master Hagi tucked away the penalty. United now had to score at least four goals to reach their first European final since 1975.

The penalty, though, could not damped the bristling atmosphere inside the stadium and United responded well, equalising after 16 minutes when Eirik Bakke rose unchallenged to head past Claudio Taffarel from Jason Wilcox's right wing cross.

The former Brazilian international goalkeeper then pawed away an Ian Harte header from another well-delivered Wilcox flag-kick. Leeds, roared on by their fans, had recovered from that early penalty shock and pushed hard for a second goal.

But they were caught just before half-time when the ever-dangerous Sukur took a through-ball in his stride, drifted inside a couple of defenders and curled the ball past goalkeeper Nigel Martyn.

The tension in the stands had spilled on to the pitch with the clash of footballing styles bringing a flurry of bookings – and immediately after Galatasary's second goal United's task became increasingly hopeless.

The ball was pumped forward from the kick-off for Harry Kewell to contest possession with Gheorghe Popescu. As the pair collided Popescu went down holding his head – even though television replays suggested there was no contact with the former Tottenham player's head.

Kewell was red-carded and Popescu was branded a 'cheat' by Leeds boss David O'Leary in an emotional post-match press conference.

However, Slovakian referee Lubos Michel appeared to balance matters up moments after Kewell's dismissal when Lee Bowyer was sent spinning to the sodden turf by Emre Belozoglu's challenge and the Turk was ordered off although he had to be physically hauled off the pitch by his coach, Fatih Terim.

The second-half, although fraught, didn't have the nasty edge of the first 45 minutes as Leeds, led by Wilcox's forays down the left, played neat football without really breaking down the Galatasaray rearguard.

United, whose form had been rocked by events in Turkey, did spare themselves the ignomy of losing a seventh successive match when Bakke repeated his first-half trick of heading in a Wilcox corner. There were 23 minutes left but the miracle simply didn't happen and Galatasaray became the first Turkish club to reach a European final.

Battling Turks spike Arsenal's big guns

IRONICALLY, the 2000 UEFA Cup would be contested by two sides that were not originally in the competition – Galatasaray and Arsenal – both clubs having come in via the backdoor as Champions League rejects.

All Leeds fans were rooting for Arsenal in the final after the impressive Gunners won home and away in their semi-final against French side Lens.

But it all went wrong in the final as the Highbury side came up against an inspired goalkeeper in Claudio Taffarel and also missed several good chances.

Even when the talismanic and volatile Gheorghe Hagi was sent off early in extra-time, Arsenal could not score and the match went to penalties after extra-time. Patrick Vieira and Davor Suker both hit the woodwork with their kicks, leaving Gheorghe Popescu – the man United fans believed got Harry Kewell dismissed in the Elland Road semi-final, to net the winner.

Semi-final, first leg

Arsenal 2 (Bergkamp 2), Lens 0
Galatasaray 2 (Hakan Sukur, Capone), Leeds United 0

Semi-final, second leg

Leeds United 2 (Bakke 2), Galatasaray 2 (Hagi pen, Hakan Sukur) *Galatasaray win 4-2 on agg*
Lens 1 (Nouma), Arsenal 2 (Henry, Kanu) *Arsenal win 2-1 on agg*

Final

(Idreatspark Stadium, Copenhagen)
May 17, 2000
Galatasaray 0
Arsenal 0
(after extra-time, Galatasaray win 4-1 on penalties

Arsenal: Seaman, Dixon, Keown, Adams, Silvinho, Parlour, Petit, Vieira, Overmars (Suker 114), Bergkamp (Kanu 74), Henry
Manager: Arsene Wenger
Galatasaray: Taffarel, Capone, Popescu, Korkmaz, Ergun, Okan (Hakan Unsal 83), Umit, Suat (Ahmet 94), Arif (Hasan Sas 94), Hagi, Hakan Sukur
Manager: Fatih Terim
Referee: Nieto Lopez (Spain)
Attendance: 38,919

Leading scorers: 10 – Kovacevic (Juventus), 7 – Henry (Arsenal), Hasselbaink (Atletico Madrid), Di Vaio (Parma)

CHAMPIONS LEAGUE CHALLENGERS: United's 2000/01 squad prepare to take on the cream of the continent. Back row, from left to right: Michael Bridges, Michael Duberry, Robert Molenaar, Danny Milosevic, Nigel Martyn, Paul Robinson, Jonathan Woodgate, Eirik Bakke, Mark Viduka, Matthew Jones. Middle row: David Hancock (physio), Sean Hardy (kit man), Steve Sutton (goalkeeping coach), Gary Kelly, David Batty, Ian Harte, Danny Mills, Lee Bowyer, Eddie Gray (assistant manager), Roy Aitken (first team coach). Front row: Alan Smith, Darren Huckerby, Harry Kewell, Peter Ridsdale (chairman), Lucas Radebe, David O'Leary (manager), Jason Wilcox, Olivier Dacourt, Stephen McPhail.

Champions League here we come

THE tragic events in Turkey came in the middle of a terrible run of results for United who went eight games without a win, including six successive defeats.

But they were able to regain some form after the UEFA Cup semi-final and were unbeaten in their final five Premiership matches.

On the final day of the season United drew 0-0 at West Ham while Liverpool, United's main rivals for third place and a Champions League spot, Liverpool, lost 1-0 at Bradford.

The only goal at Valley Parade, netted by Leeds old boy David Wetherall, not only preserved the Bantams' Premiership status but earned neighbours Leeds a place in Europe's elite competition.

Charting the path to the Champions League final

THE UEFA Champions League is the most prestigious competition in world club football.

Originally it was fought for on a knockout basis by Europe's most powerful football nations (United reaching the 1975 final) – but it had expanded in to a virtual Euro league.

United last qualified for the competition in 1992/93 – the first season group stages were introduced.

But more countries and clubs became involved but clubs of the major footballing nations no longer needed to top their league to qualify.

Manchester United won the trophy outright in 1999, having qualified as Premiership runners-up to Arsenal. Leeds qualified for the 2000/01 competition by finishing third. They came in at the third qualifying round.

The qualifying rounds were designed to come up with 16 teams to join those 16 clubs who had automatically qualified for the group stages. The top two in each group then moved in to the knockout stages and eventually on to the final itself.

Qualifying round, first leg

Birkikara 1 (Nwoko), KR Reykjavik 2 (Sigthorsson, Juliussin)
Dudelange 0, Leveski Sofia 4 (Ivanov 2, Ivankov pen, Isykhmeistruk)
Haka 1 (Wilson), Linfield 0
Klaksvik 0, Red Star Belgrade 3 (Ilic, Stevanovic, Mirkovic)
Shirak 1 (Takmadyan), BATE Borisov 1 (Kutuzov)
Skonto Riga 2 (Kolesnicenko 2 – 1 pen), Shamkir 1 (Kulikov)
Sloga 0, Shelbourne 1 (Baker)
SK Tirana 2 (Dede, Fortuzi), Zimbru Chisinau 3 (Berco 2, Boret)
TNS 2 (Wright, Toner), Levadia 2 (Bragin, Krasnopjorov)
Zalgiris Kaunas 4 (Ksanavicius 2, Zuta, Tuotkalis), Brontnjo 0

Qualifying round, second leg

BATE Borisov 2 (Rogozhkin, Loshenkov), Shirak 1 (Takmadyan) *BATE Boriov win 3-2 on agg*
Brotnojo 3 (Katic 2 – 1 pen, Juricic), Zalgiris Kaunas 0 *Zalgiris Kaunas win 4-3 on agg*
KR Reykjavik 4 (Winnie, Benediktsson, Sigurdsson, Marteisson), Birkikara 1 (Spiteri) *KR Reykjavik win 6-2 on agg*
Levadia 4 (Krom, Fenin, Tselnokov, Edwards og), TNS 0 *Levadia win 6-2 on agg*
Levski Sofia 2 (Ivanov, Ivankov pen), Dudelange 0 *Levski Sofia win 6-0 on agg*
Linfield 2 (Ferguson 2 – 1 pen), Haka 1 (Kovacs pen) *2-2 on agg. Haka win on away goals*
Red Star Belgrade 2 (Boskovic, Drulic), Klaksvik 0 *Red Star Belgrade win 5-0 on agg*
Shamkir 4 (Kvaratskhelia 3, Kulikov), Skonto Riga 1 (Samisevas) aet *Shamkir win 5-3 on agg*
Shelbourne 1 (Haylock), Sloga 1 (Nuhiji pen) *Shelbourne win 2-1 on agg*
Zimbru Chisinau 3 (Oprea 2, Boret), SK Tirana 2 (Rrezart, Kenesei)

Byes: *Anderlecht, Anorthosis, Besikitas, Brondby, Dunaferr, Dynamo Bucharest, Graz, Hadjuk Split, Hapoel Tel Aviv, Inter Bratislava, Helsingborg, Mariobor, Polonia Warsaw, Rangers, Rosenborg, Shakthtor Donetsk, Slavia Prague, Torpedo Kutaisi*

Second qualifying round, first leg

Anderlecht 4 (Baseggio, Koller 3), Anorthosis 2 (Pavlovits, Papavasiliou)
Beskitas 1 (Nouma), Levski Sofia 0
Brondby 3 (Bagger, Lindrup, Madsen), KR Reykjavik 1 (Danielsson)
Dynamo Bucharest 3 (Lupu pen, Mihalcea, Niculae), Polonia Warsaw 4 (Wyeszcycki 2, Olisadebe, Golaszewski)
Hadjuk Split 0, Dunaferr 2 (Tokoli, Lengyel)
Haka 0, Inter Bratislava 0
Helsingborg 0, BATE Borisov 0
Rangers 4 (Johnston, Albertz pen, Dodds 2), Zalgiris Kaunas 1 (Kuta)
Red Star Belgrade 4 (Drulic 2, Boskovic, Pjanovic), Torpedo Kutaisi 0
Shakhtjor Donetsk 4 (Atelkin 3, Belik), Levadia 1 (Rychkov)
Shelbourne 1 (Foran), Rosenborg 3 (Berg, Winsnes, Belsvik)
Slavia Prague 1 (Zelenka), Shamkir 0
Sturm Graz 3 (Vastic, Reinmayr, Neukirchner), Hapoel Tel Aviv 0
Zimbru Chisinau 2 (Kulik pen, Epureanu), Maribor 0

Second qualifying round, first leg

Anorthosis 0, Anderlecht 0 *Anderlecht win 4-2 on agg*
BATE Borisov 0, Helsingborg 3 (Santos, Andersson, Wahlstedt) *Helsingborg win 3-0 on agg*
Dunaferr 2 (Zavadsskzi, Tekely), Hadjuk Split 2 (Bilic 2) *Dunaferr win 4-2 on agg*
Hapoel Tel Aviv 1 (Balili), Graz 2 (Korsos, Kocian) *Graz win 5-1 on agg*
Inter Bratislava 1 (Nemeth), Haka 0 aet *Inter Bratislava win 1-0 on agg*
KR Reykjavik 0, Brondby 0 *Brondby win 3-1 on agg*
Levadia 1 (Bragin), Shakhtjor Donetsk 5 (Vorobei 3 – 1 pen, Atekin, Zubov) *Shakhtjor Donetsk win 9-2 on agg*
Levski Sofia 1 (Markov), Besiktas 1 (Tayfur) *Besiktas win 2-1 on agg*
Maribor 1 (Ceh), Zimbrau Chisinau 0 *Zimbru Chisinau win 2-1 on agg*
Polonia Warsaw 3 (Olisadebe 2, Golaszweski), Dynamo Bucharest 1 (Tames) *Polonia Warsaw win 7-4 on agg*
Rosenborg 1 (Berg), Shelbourne 1 (Foran) *Rosenborg win 4-2 on agg*
Shamkir 1 (Kvaratshkelia), Slavia Prague 4 (Dostalek, Dosek 2, Svakera) *Slavia Prague win 5-1 on agg*
Torpedo Kutaisi 2 (Imedadze, Janashia), Red Star Belgrade 0 *Red Star Belgrade win 4-2 on agg*
Zalgiris Kaunas 0, Rangers 0 *Rangers win 4-1 on agg*

Byes: *AC Milan, Dynamo Kiev, Dynamo Zagreb, Feyenoord, Galatasaray, Hamburg, Herfolge, Inter Milan, Leeds United, Lokomotiv Moscow, Lyon, Panathinikos, Porto, Sparta Prague, St Gallen, Tirol Innsbruck, 1860 Munich, Valencia*

Third qualifying round, first leg

AC Milan 3 (Shevchenko 2, Comandini), Dynamo Zagreb 1 (Pilipovic)
Anderlecht 1 (Koller), Porto 0
Besiktas 3 (Nihat, Nouma, Karhan), Lokomotiv Moscow 0
Brondby 0, Hamburg 2 (Barbarez, Mahdavikia)
Dunaferr 2 (Legyel, Tokoli), Rosenborg 0
Dynamo Kiev 0, Red Star Belgrade 0
Graz 2 (Schopp 2 pen), Feyenoord 1 (Korneev)
Helsingborg 1 (Hansson), Inter Milan 0
Herfolge 0, Rangers 3 (Albertz, Wallace, Amoruso)
Inter Bratislava 1 (Nemeth), Lyon 2 (Anderson, Delmotte)
Leeds United 2 (Smith, Harte pen), 1860 Munich 1 (Agostino)
Polonia Warsaw 2 (Klebowicz, Kaliszan), Panathinikos 2 (Warzycha, Fissas)
St Gallen 1 (Amopah), Galatasaray 2 (Jardel 2)
Shakhtjor Donesk 0, Slavia Prague 1 (Dosek)
Tirol Innsbruck 0, Valencia 0
Zimbru Chisinau 0, Sparta Prague 1 (Obajdin)

Third qualifying round, second leg

Dynamo Zagreb 0, AC Milan 3 (Shevchenko 2, Jose Mari) *AC Milan win 6-1 on agg*
Feyenoord 1 (Jochemsen), Graz 1 *Graz win 3-2 on agg*
Galatasary 2 (Zellweger og, Jardel pen), St Gallen 2 (Gane, Amoah) *Galatasaray win 4-3 on agg*
Hamburg 0, Brondby 0 *Hamburg win 2-0 on agg*
Inter Milan 0, Helsingborg 0 *Helsingborg win 1-0 on agg*
Lokomotiv Moscow 1 (Cherevchenko), Besiktas 3 (Nouma, Nihat, Tayfur) *Beskitas win 6-1 on agg*
Lyon 2 (Marlet, Malbranque), Inter Bratislava 1 (Pinte) *Lyon win 4-2 on agg*
1860 Munich 0, Leeds United 1 (Smith) *Leeds United win 3-1 on agg*
Panathinikos 2 (Limberopoulos, Pflipsen pen), Polonia Warsaw 1 (Bak) *Panathinikos win 4-3 on agg*
Porto 0, Anderlecht 0 *Anderlecht win 1-0 on agg*
Rangers 3 (Wallace, Johnston, Kanchelskis), Herfolge 0 *Rangers win 6-0 on agg*
Red Star Belgrade 1 (Boskovic), Dynamo Kiev 1 (Bialkevich) *1-1 on agg Dynamo Kiev win on away goals*
Rosenberg 2 (Berg, Belsvik), Dunaferr 1 (Tokoli) *Rosenberg win 4-3 on agg*
Slavia Prague 0, Shakhtjor Donetsk 2 (Vorobiev, Atklkin) *Shakhtjor Donetsk win 2-1 on agg*
Sparta Prague 1 (Obadjin), Zimbru Chisinau 0 *Sparta Prague win 2-0 on agg*
Valencia 4 (Mendieta 2 – 1 pen, Alonso 2), Tirol Innsbruck 1 (Gilewicz) *Valencia win 4-1 on agg*

Red cards prove costly

Kapitanis calamity

UEFA Champions League
Third qualifiing round, first leg
(at Elland Road, Leeds)
Wednesday, August 9, 2000

Leeds United: Nigel Martyn, Gary Kelly, Ian Harte, Michael Duberry, Lucas Radebe, Lee Bowyer, Olivier Dacourt, Eirik Bakke, Michael Bridges (Danny Mills 78), Alan Smith, Mark Viduka
Goals: Smith 39, Harte 71 pen
Manager: David O'Leary

1860 Munich: Michael Hofmann, Ned Zelic, Marco Kurz, Martin Stranzel (Bernhard Winkler 81), Harald Cerny, Tomas Votava, Erik Mykland, Daniel Bierofka (Stephan Passlack HT), Thomas Hassler, Martin Max, Paul Agostino
Goal: Agostino 90
Manager: Werner Lorant

Referee: Costas Kapitanis (Cyprus) **Att:** 33,769

BIZARRE refereeing and a late German goal took the shine off United's victory over TSV Munich 1860.

Thanks to their performances in the UEFA Cup the previous season, United didn't enter the preliminary stages of the Champions League until the third qualifying round and were paired with the club that had finished fourth in the Bundeslegia. The winners would go into the money-spinning Champions League first group stage.

United went into the first leg at Elland Road without Harry Kewell, Jason Wilcox, Jonathan Woodgate, David Batty, Stephen McPhail and Matthew Jones – all through injury.

Patched-up United won 2-1 but all the talk was about the shambolic performance of Cypriot referee Costas Kapitanis who dismissed three players and baffled everyone with a series of mysterious decisions.

United seemed to be cruising as they led 2-0 with 15 minutes remaining against ten men, Munich's Australian star Ned Zelic having been ordered off for a second late tackle just before half-time.

Then it all turned sour as United's new £7.2 million record signing from French club Lens, Olivier Dacourt, was harshly dismissed for a second yellow card offence, Kapitanis insisting his stumble was a deliberate dive.

United were then stunned when Dacourt's midfield partner Eirik Bakke was shown the red card for handball with just six minutes left. With an extra four minutes added on, United had to endure a nervy finish and just as they looked like holding out conceded a goal right at the end of the match, Paul Agostino heading in a priceless away goal.

It took the shine off an encouraging display by United 10 days ahead of their Premiership opener against Everton.

Up front Alan Smith was a constant menace and put United ahead when newcomer Mark Viduka pressurised defender Martin Stranzl into a poor header back towards goal and Smith cashed in on a hesitant 1860 defence to fire United ahead.

The hapless Kapitanis then handed David O'Leary's boys a penalty which was hotly contested by the visitors and struck firmly past goalkeeper Michael Hofmann in the 71st minutes by Ian Harte.

The 36-year-old referee then seemed to totally lose the plot as United slipped from a position of relative comfort to a match which hung in the balance.

UEFA's delegate at the match later revealed that there would be an investigation into the referee's performance. But for United the damage had been done. Both Dacourt and Bakke would miss the return leg leaving O'Leary with a major midfield selection headache.

LIFT OFF: Alan Smith, arms outstretched, and Michael Bridges, wheel away in glee after Smithy netted United's opening goal of their Champions League campaign against 1860 Munich.

HEAD TO HEAD: United defender Jonathan Woodgate, a key figure in shutting out the 1860 Munich attack, wins this aerial duel with Paul Agostino in the Olympic Stadium.

UEFA Champions League
Third qualifying round, second leg
(at Olympic Stadium, Munich)
Wednesday, August 23, 2000

1860 Munich	**0**
Leeds United	**1**

Leeds United win 3-1 on agg

1860 Munich: Michael Hofmann, Stephan Passlack (Bernhard Winkler 63), Marco Kurz, Martin Stranzl, Harald Cerny, Daniel Borimov (Markus Beirele 76), Erik Mykland, Daniel Bierofka (Roman Tyce 73), Thomas Hassler, Martin Max, Paul Agostino
Manager: Werner Lorant

Leeds United: Nigel Martyn, Gary Kelly, Ian Harte, Jonathan Woodgate, Michael Duberry, Lucas Radebe, Danny Mills, Lee Bowyer, Matthew Jones (Gareth Evans 73), Alan Smith, Mark Viduka
Goal: Smith 46
Manager: David O'Leary

Referee: Claus Larsen (Denmark) **Att:** 45,000

Alan strikes Olympic gold

BATTLING United turned in an Olympian display in the Olympic Stadium to open the door to Champions League riches.

In-form Alan Smith's winner was valued at £10 million – the sum United could expect to bank from the first group stages of the competition.

The Rothwell-born striker's goal immediately after half-time gave United a 1-0 victory in Bavaria as progressed 3-1 on aggregate.

But it was hard work as David O'Leary had to reshuffle his limited resources, particularly in midfield. Lee Bowyer was his only recognised regular first-teamer in that department. Young Matthew Jones, although nowhere near fully fit, was forced into action and defenders Gary Kelly and Lucas Radebe moved in to the middle of the park.

Predictably Leeds were on the backfoot early on as former German midfieldmeister Thomas Hassler ran the match in a frantic opening and just before half-time he curled a free-kick around United's defensive wall but it came back off a post.

Goal-line clearances by Jonathan Woodgate, Danny Mills and Michael Duberry kept United in the hunt while goalkeeper Nigel Martyn was cool, calm and collected behind them, a splendid one-handed save from Daniel Borimov being the pick of his stops.

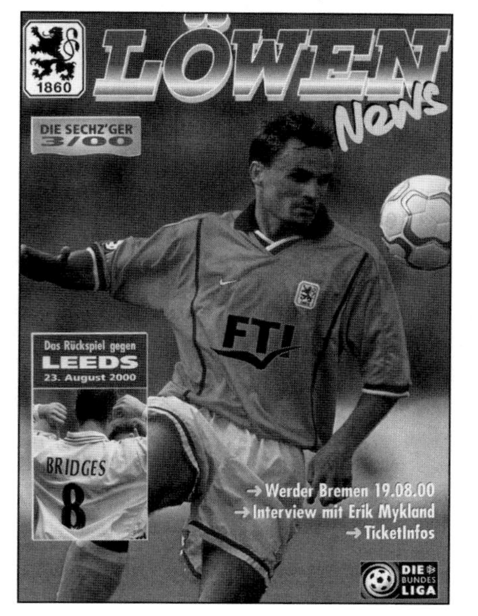

United crafted their winner with some smart work by Aussie striker Mark Viduka, a £6 million summer recruit from Celtic. He beat two defenders and Smith was able to finish stylishly from 10 yards out and the youngsters's stock was to rise still further when he soon earned his first call-up for the full England squad.

The draw for the group stages of the Champions League put United in dreamland as they were pitted with mighty Barcelona, Italian giants AC Milan and Besiktas, which meant a harrowing return to the Turkish capital of Istanbul just six months after the deaths of supporters Christopher Loftus and Kevin Speight.

Catatalan catastrophe

Weakened United crash in Barca

UEFA Champions League
First phase, Group H, Match 1
(at Nou Camp Stadium, Barcelona)
Wednesday, September 13, 2000

Barcelona 4

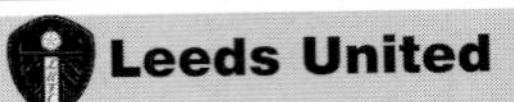 

Leeds United 0

Barcelona: Richard Detruel, Frank De Boer, Fernandez Aberlardo, Barjuan Escusa 'Sergi' Lopez, Segu 'Gerard'. Philip Cocu (Emmanuel Petit 54), 'Simao' Sabrosa, Vitor Borba Ferreria 'Rivaldo' (Perez Munoz 'Alfonso' 77), Marc Overmars, Patrick Kluivert, Garcia Lara 'Dani' (Ivan de la Pena 65
Goal: Rivaldo 9, De Boer 20, Kluivert 75, 83
Manager: Lorenzo Serra Ferrer

Leeds United: Nigel Martyn, Gary Kelly, Ian Harte, Lucas Radebe (Danny Hay 85), Michael Duberry, Danny Mills, Lee Bowyer, Olivier Dacourt, Lee Bowyer, Stephen McPhail (Tony Hackworth 75), Alan Smith, Michael Bridges
Manager: David O'Leary

Referee: Markus Merk (Germany) **Att:** 85,000

UNDER-STRENGTH United were blown away in Barcelona in their opening game in Group H of the first phase of the Champions League

Affording the Catalan kings too much respect, and too much room in midfield, David O'Leary's side were swamped in front of 85,000 in the vast Nou Camp Stadium.

To take on a club like Barcelona United needed their full squad available but O'Leary simply didn't have it at his disposal. At the end of a 4-0 beating by the slick Spaniards United had rookies like central defender Danny Hay and reserve team striker Tony Hackworth on the pitch.

United simply could not paper over the loss of quality players like Harry Kewell, Jonathan Woodgate, David Batty, Eirik Bakke, Jason Wilcox and Mark Viduka, the latter on duty with Australia in the Olympic Games.

On their last visit to play Barcelona, United had won through to the 1975 European Cup final but the current crop of young stars could not match that mature vintage.

Brazilian midfielder Rivaldo, the World Footballer of the Year, prised Michael Duberry and fired a crisp shot past Nigel Martyn.

Ten minutes later the lead was doubled when Dutch international Frank De Boer smashed a stunning free-kick past Martyn from 30 yards.

Injury-hit United were struggling but did improve after half-time and may have reduced the arrears when Ian Harte got behind the Barca defence to collect Michael Bridges' centre but his shot was blocked.

It seemed as though United were going to keep the defeat within the bounds of respectability but endured a nightmare final 15 minutes when Patrick Kluivert gobbled up two chances after smooth approach work opened up United's tiring team.

To compound a bad night, skipper Lucas Radebe was stretchered off with his neck in a brace after a collision with team-mate Duberry, paving the way for New Zealand defender Hay to come on for his debut.

Radebe was taken to hospital for a scan and X-rays but fortunately the injury was not too serious and the South African star was only to miss the next two games.

A frank O'Leary admitted: "We came up against some of the best players in the world and we were well and truly beaten. You need your quality players. We missed too many of them. We came to do our best, but our best was not good enough."

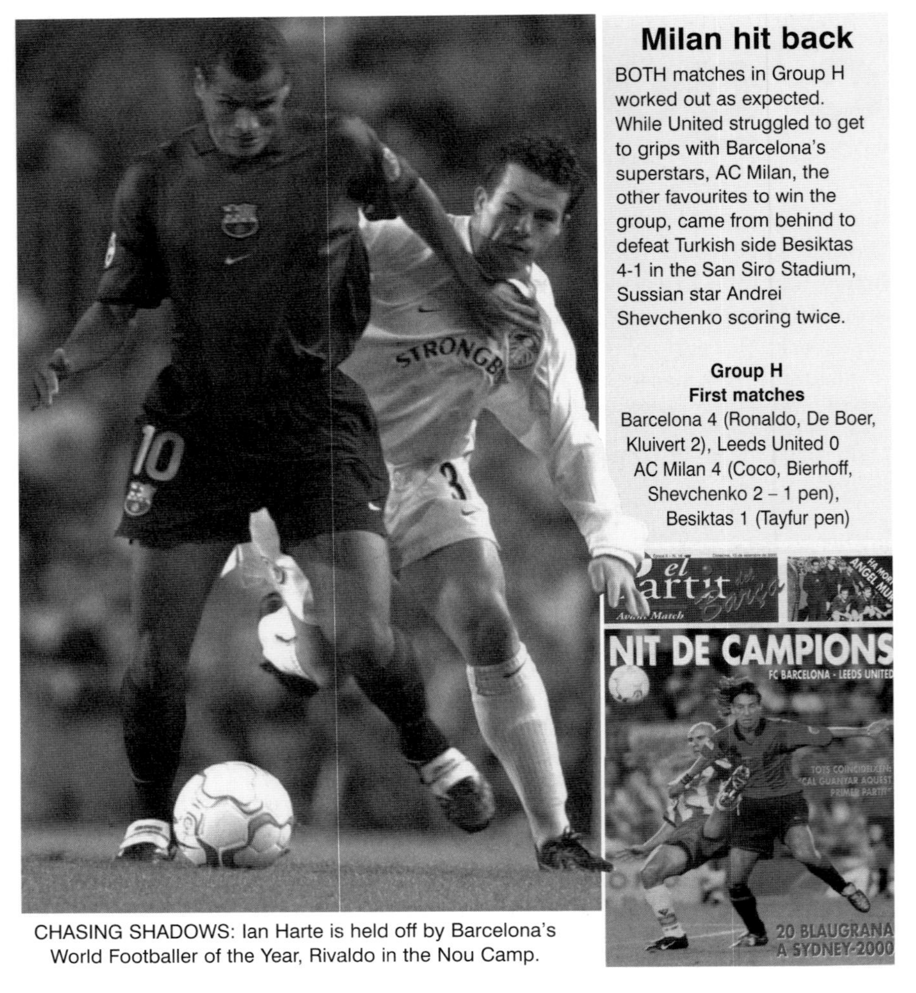

CHASING SHADOWS: Ian Harte is held off by Barcelona's World Footballer of the Year, Rivaldo in the Nou Camp.

Milan hit back

BOTH matches in Group H worked out as expected. While United struggled to get to grips with Barcelona's superstars, AC Milan, the other favourites to win the group, came from behind to defeat Turkish side Besiktas 4-1 in the San Siro Stadium, Sussian star Andrei Shevchenko scoring twice.

Group H
First matches
Barcelona 4 (Ronaldo, De Boer, Kluivert 2), Leeds United 0
AC Milan 4 (Coco, Bierhoff, Shevchenko 2 – 1 pen), Besiktas 1 (Tayfur pen)

Handed a lifeline

Last gasp Dida blunder gives United famous win

UNITED were literally handed a Champions League lifeline by AC Milan goalkeeper Dida.

The Brazilian international let a Lee Bowyer shot slip from his grasp and over the line to give United a priceless late victory at rain-lashed Elland Road.

Bowyer's 25-yard shot a minute from the end appeared to have been covered by Dida near his left-hand post in front of the Don Revie Stand. But the greasy ball was like a bar of soap and Dida saw it escape his clutches and pop into the net to turn the formbook upside down.

It was a courageous and memorable victory for United, who were once again shorn of key players.

Mark Viduka didn't arrive back from the Olympic Games in time to play and a posse of other star names were still ruled out through injury.

UEFA Champions League
First phase, Group F, Match 2
(at Elland Road, Leeds)
Tuesday, September 19, 2000

Leeds United	**1**
AC Milan	**0**

Leeds United: Nigel Martyn, Gary Kelly, Ian Harte, Michael Duberry, Danny Mills, Lee Bowyer, Olivier Dacourt, Eirik Bakke, Dominic Matteo, Michael Bridges, Alan Smith,
Goal: Bowyer 89
Manager: David O'Leary

AC Milan: Nelson De Jesus Silva 'Dida', Thomas Helveg, Alessandro Costacurta, Federico Giunti (Luca Savdati 90), Jose Antonio Chamot, Paolo Maldini, Demetrio Albertini, Francesco Coco, Andres Guglilmpietro 'Guly' (Diego De Ascentis 59), Andrei Shevchenko, Oliver Bierhoff
Manager: Alberto Zaccheroni

Referee: Gunter Benko (Austria) **Att:** 35,398

SINGING IN THE RAIN: Lee Bowyer salutes his late, late winning goal and prepares to be mobbed by Alan Smith, Dominic Matteo and Olivier Dacourt.

But United did have new signing Dominic Matteo from Liverpool featuring on the left side of midfield. Leeds had paid the Anfield club £4.75 million for Matteo several weeks early but had to wait for a troublesome knee injury to clear up before giving him his first start.

Milan boasted the likes of Andrei Shevchenco and Olivier Bierhoff in attack, but United's defence blotted out the Ukranian-German combination with the unlikely centre-back partnership of Danny Mills and Michael Duberry performing heroics in the pouring rain. United made most of the running in the first half and almost broke the deadlock when an Eirik Bakke header from a Bowyer cross skimmed the bar while Alan Smith and Michael Bridges worked tirelessly in attack.

Gradually Shevchenko came into the picture but was denied by a brilliant tackle by Mills.

Chances were few and far between and the best came 13 minutes from the end when Shevchenko collected a miscue from Mills and seemed certain to stride forward and score but inexplicably passed to Bierhoff, who was yards offside.

Milan paid for that miscalucation as Bowyer's sheer drive and will-to-win gave United a welcome victory with his dramatic winner.

With Besiktas next up at Elland Road, while the two favourites Barcelona and AC Milan clashed in the Nou Camp, United knew they had the chance to seize control of the 'Group of Death'.

It's all square

GROUP H, dubbed the 'Group of Death' was split wide open by victories for United and Besiktas.

In Turkey, Barcelona were thumped 3-0 by Besiktas, leaving all four clubs with a win each after a couple of games.

Group H
Second matches

Besiktas 3 (Ahmet 2, Nouma), Barcelona 0
Leeds United 1 (Bowyer), AC Milan 0

THUMP: Eirik Bakke puts his right foot behind the ball to send United 4-0 up with a 25-yard shot.

UEFA Champions League
First phase, Group F, Match 3
(at Elland Road, Leeds)
Tuesday, September 26, 2000

Leeds United	**6**
Besiktas	**0**

Leeds United: Nigel Martyn, Gary Kelly, Ian Harte, Lucas Radebe, Danny Mills, Eirik Bakke, Olivier Dacourt (Stephen McPhail 75), Lee Bowyer, Dominic Matteo, Alan Smith (Darren Huckerby 80), Mark Viduka
Goal: Bowyer 7, 90, Viduka 12, Matteo 22, Bakke 65, Huckerby 90
Manager: David O'Leary

Besiktas: Ike Shorunmu, Miroslav Kahran, Havutcu Tayfur, Ahmet Dursan, Kahveci Nihat, Markus Munch, Bozkurt Umit, Dmitry Khlestov, Guracar Erman (Zafer Rahim 82), Uzulmez Ibrahim (Ozdilek Mehmet 72), Pascal Nouma (Ulusal Fazli 72)
Manager: Nevio Scala

Referee: Melo Pereira Vitor Manuel (Portugal)
Att: 34,485

Six of the best

United storm to top of the group

RAMPANT United stormed to the top of the Champions League Group H with a 6-0 demolition of Beskitas.

David O'Leary's young lions roared to United's biggest win at Elland Road for 16 years with an electrifying attacking display.

With Barcelona losing 2-0 at home to AC Milan, United found themselves at the head of the pack at the halfway stage with a great chance of going through to the next round.

"These nights don't come round very often and I thought we were marvellous," said O'Leary.

In the wake of the murder of two Leeds supporters in Istanbul in April, a massive security operation ensured the game against the Turks went ahead without incident. There had been genuine efforts by Leeds chairman Peter Ridsdale and his Besiktas counterpart Sedar Bilgili to build bridges between the clubs in the light of the horrors of Istanbul.

Besiktas players handed bouquets of flowers to fans and to chairman Ridsdale just before the kick-off as a mark of respect to the two dead fans and were warmly applauded by the Elland Road crowd. But Besiktas looked nervous from the start and United were quick to cash in. Only eight minutes had gone when Ian Harte's left-wing cross was forced home by Lee Bowyer.

Mark Viduka then saw his shot cannon off goalkeeper Ike Shorunmu and on to the bar, but the big Australian, back from national duty in the Olympic Games, didn't have to wait long before getting his first United goal since his £6 million switch from Celtic as he was left unmarked to head in Gary Kelly's right-wing centre.

Besiktas simply could not cope with United's skill, power and movement, with Alan Smith at the hub of everything.

United who went 3-0 up when Olivier Dacourt's low cross created more defensive panic and Dominic Matteo pounced for his first goal since his move from Liverpool. Only the bar prevented Matteo from making it 4-0 but United fans saw their side finish with a flourish.

After a brief spell of Besiktas pressure United moved back into goalscoring mode when Eirik Bakke extended the lead with a 25-yard drive after being superbly set-up by Viduka.

The tiring Turks were then tormented by the pace of substitute Darren Huckerby who rattled in the fifth goal from close range then zipped down the left and crossed for Bowyer to make it 6-0 in injury-time – United's biggest home win since they beat Oldham by the same score on September 29, 1984. But this goal glut was on a bigger stage and the whole of Europe was taking notice.

TWO GOAL HERO: Lee Bowyer scored his second in the final moments.

canes Turks

TURKISH DELIGHT: Lee Bowyer (pictured above) gets in before Dominic Matteo to give United an early lead against Besiktas.

Mark Viduka (right) gets his United scoring career up and running with the second goal.

Barca in bother

WHILE United were hammering Besiktas, Barcelona crashed 2-0 in the Nou Camp to AC Milan.

Goals by Francesco Coco on the stroke of half time and German striker Oliver Bierhoff on 71 minutes gave the Italians victory.

Group H
Third Matches

Barcelona 0, AC Milan 2 (Coco, Bierhoff)
Leeds United 6 (Bowyer 2, Viduka, Matteo, Bakke, Huckerby)

Nouma ban increased

DEMORALISED Besiktas were at odds with themselves long before the end of their 6-0 humiliation at Elland Road.

Players were arguing among themselves and striker Pascal Nouma lost his cool and was cautioned for throwing his shirt at his club's bench as he was substituted.

Things got worse for Nouma, who was suspended for three games by UEFA's Control and Disciplinary Board for striking Danny Mills while the ball was out of play. Besiktas appealed and UEFA duly increased his suspension to four games.

Rivaldo saves Barca

THEIR 0-0 draw at Besiktas, coupled with Barcelona's 3-3 draw at AC Milan, where Rivaldo scored a hat-trick, meant that victory over the Catalans the following week at Elland Road would put David O'Leary's team into the money-spinning second phase.

Group H
Match 4

Besiktas 0, Leeds United 0
AC Milan 3 (Albertini 2, Jose Mari), Barcelona (Rivaldo 3)

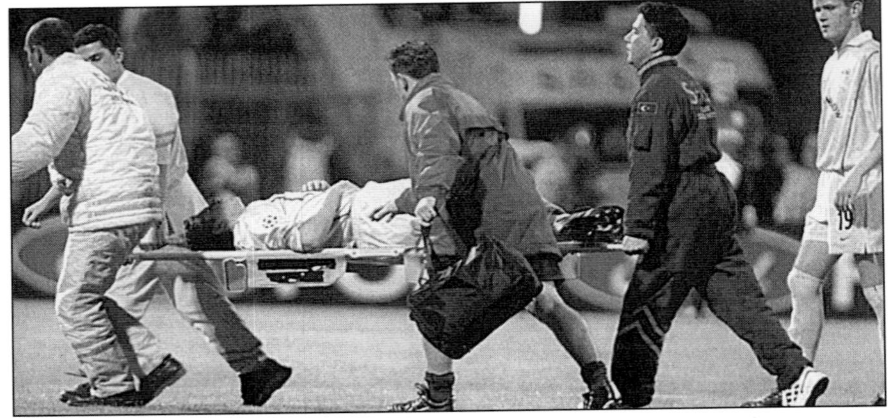

END OF THE LINE: Michael Bridges is stretchered off in Turkey and out for nearly two years.

Making a point

Quiet Euro debut for 'keeper Robinson

MATURING United remained on course for a place in the second phase of the Champions League with a precious point in Turkey.

United kept their heads in the intimidating atmosphere of the Inonu Stadium on an emotional return to Turkey where two of their fans had been killed in April.

There was also plenty of intimidation on the pitch as they came up against some strongarm tactics of a side hell-bent on avenging their humiliating defeat at Elland Road.

United remained calm, but one player who lost his cool paid a high price. Reacting to yet another foul, Michael Bridges stumbled and twisted his ankle, causing ligament damage which was to force him out of the game for the best part of two years.

He was in good company in the treatment room as Harry Kewell, Lucas Radebe, Nigel Martyn, Olivier Dacourt, David Batty and Jason Wilcox all missed the Turkish trip.

"The way we are going we are not going to have anyone left," moaned O'Leary.

Goalkeeper Martyn had pulled a groin in a 3-1 Premiership home victory over Charlton, so that paved the way for England Under-21 goalkeeper Paul Robinson to make his Champions League debut.

The match was in stark contrast to the fluent football United had served up in that attacking Elland Road feast. They did create early chances and Eirik Bakke should have done better in the fourth minute when he fired straight at goalkeeper Ike Shorunmu from close range. A goal then would have silenced the fervent Besiktas fans who were pouring out several inflammatory chants from the terraces.

Robinson was well protected by United's solid back-four and was hardly called in to action in his first Leeds start for 16 months.

Given the number of absent stars – and the loss of the suspended Alan Smith – it was a precious point against a side who had thumped Barcelona 3-0 on the same pitch. But despite the efforts by the clubs to prevent trouble there were still a number of disgraceful scenes with the visiting press coach stoned on its journey to the stadium and a bottle hurled at the stricken Bridges as he was stretchered off to the dressing room.

Thankfully, the small number of Leeds fans who had made the trip, did not get caught up in any aggro and in an effort to avoid confrontation with local hot-heads were ferried to the Inonu Stadium by boat after a two-hour ride along the Bosphorus River.

It may not have all been plain sailing in Istanbul but United were still at the helm in Group H.

UEFA Champions League
First phase, Group H, Match 4
(at Inonu Stadium, Istanbul)
Wednesday, October 18, 2000

Besiktas 0

Leeds United 0

Besiktas: Ike Shorunmu, Miroslav Kahran, Havutcu Tayfur, Ali Eren (Alacayir Murat 63), Ahmet Dursan (Akman Ayhan 81), Kahveci Nihat, Ozdilek Mehmet (Uzulmez Ibrahim 81), Markus Munch, Bozkurt Umit, Dmitry Khlestov, Sulun Yasin
Manager: Nevio Scala

Leeds United: Paul Robinson, Gary Kelly, Ian Harte, Jonathan Woodgate, Danny Mills, Eirik Bakke, Jacob Burns, Lee Bowyer, Dominic Matteo, Michael Bridges (Darren Huckerby 28 – Stephen McPhail 86), Mark Viduka
Manager: David O'Leary

Referee: Jan Wegereet (Holland) **Att:** 20,000

Seconds from glory

Last-gasp Rivaldo denies United win

UEFA Champions League
First phase, Group F, Match 5
(at Elland Road, Leeds)
Tuesday, October 24, 2000

 **Leeds United**  1

 **Barcelona**  1

Leeds United: Paul Robinson, Gary Kelly, Ian Harte, Jonathan Woodgate, Danny Mills, Lee Bowyer, Olivier Dacourt (Jacob Burns 75), Eirik Bakke, Dominic Matteo, Alan Smith, Mark Viduka
Goal: Bowyer 4
Manager: David O'Leary

Barcelona: Richard Dutruel, Carles Puyol, Fernandez Aberlardo, Barjuan Esclusa 'Sergi', Michael Reiziger (Lopez Segu 'Gerard 67), 'Xavi Hernandez Creus, Phillip Cocu, Luis Enrique (Garcia Lara 'Dani' 67), Perez Munoz 'Alfonso', 'Simao' Sabrosa, Vitor Borba Ferreria 'Rivaldo'
Goal: Rivaldo 90
Manager: Lorenzo Serra Ferrer

Referee: Terje Hauge (Norway) **Att:** 34,485

GUTTED United came within 25 seconds of qualifying for the second phase of the Champions League and eliminating mighty Barcelona.

Elland Road was stunned when Brazilian superstar Rivaldo fired home in the fourth minute of injury-time to break United's hearts.

There were howls of derision when the fourth official held up the board showing the amount of additional time to be played.

Having withstood a virtual Spanish siege in the second half, United were within touching distance of a famous victory and qualification when Philip Cocu swung in a cross from the left, substitute Gerard rose to head the ball against the base of a post and the rebound was drilled home by Rivaldo.

Despite the lateness of Barcelona's equaliser there was little doubt they merited it as United were kept in the match by a brilliant display by Paul Robinson. The young goalkeeper produced five world class saves, four from Rivaldo and one from Alphonso, as Leeds came under tremendous pressure.

United's preparations for a game of such magnitude had hardly gone to plan. They went into the game on the back of a 3-0 defeat at Manchester United where they had been forced to play a string of reserve players because of the depth of the injury list.

David O'Leary had been able to get some of his stars partly fit for the Barcelona battle and early on United more than matched the Catalan giants and were boosted by Lee Bowyer's fifth minute goal.

After Mark Viduka was fouled on the left, Bowyer bent in a direct free-kick from 20 yards which found the top right of Richard Dutruel's corner.

The French goalkeeper then made a fine sprawling save to keep out an Alan Smith drive before Robinson's athleticism denied the outstanding Rivaldo as Barcelona rolled United back. Despite enormous presure, Jonathan Woodgate and Danny Mills were heroic in the heart of the defence in the pouring rain while behind them, Robinson looked simply unbeatable. When he was defeated after 76 minutes by Rivaldo it was disallowed for offside.

But with Leeds fans screaming for the final whistle their team simply ran out of time and cracked at the death with the goal coming in the fourth minute of added on time.

CATCH ME IF YOU CAN: Alan Smith's skill leaves Barcelona's Michael Reiziger on the deck.

Rivaldo saves Barca

RIVALDO'S late Elland Road equaliser had massive implications.

Not only did it deny United instant progress to the second phase but also kept Barcelona in the competition.

United knew they would travel to Italy needing a point against AC Milan, who had already sealed their qualification with a 2-0 in Beskitas.

Group H
Match 5

Besiktas 0, AC Milan 2 (Shevchenko, Jose Mari)
Leeds United 1 (Bowyer), Barcelona 1 (Rivaldo)

Night of heroes

United kings of cool in style capital of Milan

MATT FINISH: United's Dominic Matteo launches himself at Lee Bowye

UNITED strode like a colossus on another big European stage to tear up the formbook.

This time their 1-1 draw in the magnificent San Siro Stadium with AC Milan was enough to stamp their passport into the second phase of the Champions League.

United and their fans could look forward to at least £10 million and six more big matches against the cream of the continent – not bad for a side who were given little progress from the "Group of Death".

But United's young side had learned rapidly from that opening 4-0 beating in Barcelona when they afforded the opposition too much respect.

Against AC Milan, another of Europe's elite, they richly deserved their point to open the door to the last sixteen – although Barcolona took their exit with a touch of bitterness.

There had been pre-match talk that Barcelona had offered the Italian club a £1.6 million sweetener to beat Leeds, whose own players were on £25,000 a man bonus should they achieve second phase qualification. The claims of finanicial inducements were denied by both clubs.

Milan were already through but were surprised by the positive fashion by which Leeds went about their business.

United had their hearts in their mouths midway through the first-half when Gary Kelly was adjudged to handled in the box. Andrei Shevchenko stepped up to take the penalty, sent Paul Robinson the wrong way but saw the ball hit the outside of the left-hand post.

United made the most of that let-off and after a series of promising raids won a corner on the left just before half-time.

Lee Bowyer's delivery was perfect and Dominic Matteo's header sent United's 6,000 travelling fans wild with delight.

United were firmly in charge of the group and although Brazilian star Serginho equalised after a surging run and fine shot to set up a tense final 22 minutes.

United held firm on a pitch that cut up badly with Lucas Radebe making a welcome return to European action for the first time since his head injury in Barcelona, while Robinson again underlined his potential with several top drawer saves.

After the final whistle the Leeds party went back out on the San Siro pitch to celebrate with their army of fans with a good old-fashioned half-hour sing-song on United's biggest night out in 25 years.

The only downside was a stabbing incident in which 31-year-old Leeds fan Lee Dyson was wounded 13 times, requiring two operations in a Milanese hospital.

in the San Siro

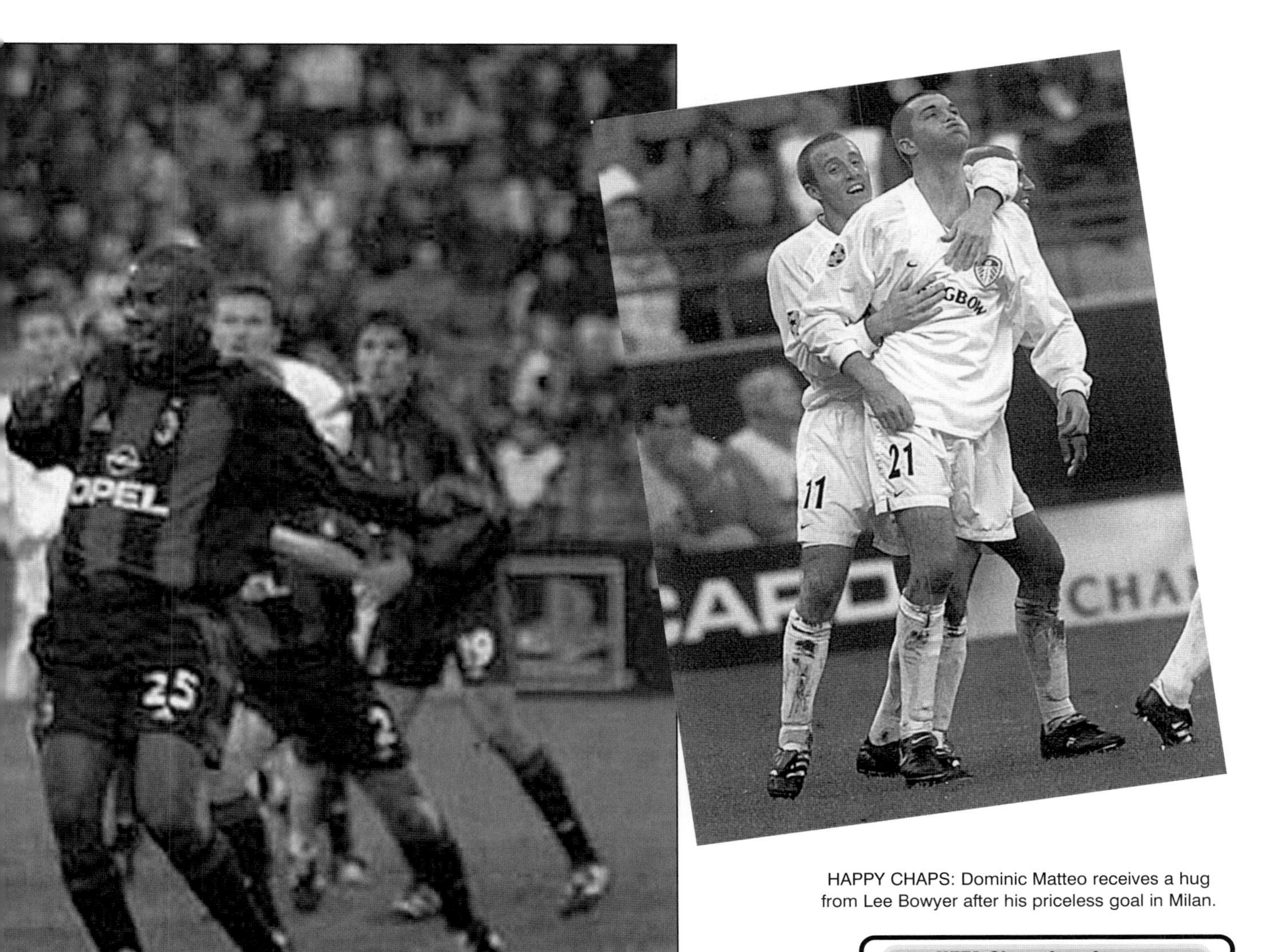

…rner to head United in the the lead against AC Milan.

HAPPY CHAPS: Dominic Matteo receives a hug from Lee Bowyer after his priceless goal in Milan.

UEFA Champions League
First phase, Group F, Match 6
(at San Siro Stadium, Milan)
Wednesday, November 9, 2000

 **AC Milan**  1

 **Leeds United**  1

AC Milan: Nelson De Jesus Silva 'Dida', Thomas Helveg, Paolo Maldini, Jose Vitor Roque Junior, Jose Antonio Chamot, Gennaro Ivan Gattuso, Demetrio Albertini, 'Leonardo' Nascimento De Araujo (Zvonimir Boban 54), Sergio Claudio Dos Santos 'Serginho', Andreiy Shevchenko, Oliver Bierhoff
Goal: Serginho 68
Manager: Alberto Zaccheroni

Leeds United: Paul Robinson, Gary Kelly, Ian Harte, Lucas Radebe, Danny Mills, Lee Bowyer, Olivier Dacourt, Eirik Bakke, Dominic Matteo, Alan Smith, Mark Viduka
Goal: Matteo 44
Manager: David O'Leary

Referee: Kim Milton Nielsen (Denmark) **Att:** 52,289

Barca's wild conspiracy theory

UNITED'S priceless point meant that Barcelona's 5-0 demolition of Besiktas was immaterial.

While David O'Leary's boys marched on in to the cash-rich second phase of the Champions League, Barca dropped into the UEFA Cup.

Barcelona president Joan Gaspart was an unhappy man, believing that Milan had not done enough to beat Leeds.

"I am very disappointed in the Italians. They went round saying they would beat Leeds, that their honour was at stake – and then they can only draw."

His words did Leeds a great disservice but no one in the Elland Road camp could give a fig about the fantastical conspiracy theory which held not a drop of water.

Group H
Match 5

AC Milan 1 (Serginho), Leeds United 1 (Matteo)
Barcelona 5 (Cocu, Luis Enrique 2, Rivaldo pen, Gabri), Besiktas 0

Group H

	P	W	D	L	F	A	Pts
AC Milan	6	3	2	1	12	6	11
Leeds United	6	2	3	1	9	6	9
Barcelona	6	2	2	2	13	9	8
Besiktas	6	1	1	4	4	17	4

AC Milan and Leeds United qualify for second phase. Barcelona drop in to UEFA Cup. Besiktas eliminated

Gunners and Red Devils join United in second phase

UNITED were part of a three-pronged English assault on the top club prize in Europe.

Impressive Arsenal finished at the top of Group B with the same number of points as Lazio. However, despite having an inferior goal difference than the Italians, the Gunners headed the group on the basis that they had better results in the two meetings with the Roman cub.

Manchester United progressed in Group G behind Anderlecht – but only just.

Needing victory at Old Trafford against Dynamo Kiev, they led with a Teddy Sheringham goal, but Kiev substitute Demetradze missed a tap-in near the end which would have knocked out Sir Alex Ferguson's side.

The top two in each group went in to Phase Two, the third team dropped in to the UEFA Cup and the bottom club were eliminated.

Group A

Spartak Moscow 2 (Titov, Bezrodny), Bayer Leverkusen 0
Sporting Lisbon 2 (Sa Pinto, Cruz), Real Madrid 2 (Roberto Carlos, Rui Jorge)
Bayer Leverkusen 3 (Ramelow, Brdaric, Neuville), Sporting Lisbon 2 (Cruz, Sa Pinto pen)
Real Madrid 1 (Helguera), Spartak Moscow 0
Spartak Moscow 3 (Robson, Marcao 2), Sporting Lisbon 1 (Sa Pinto)
Bayer Leverkusen 2 (Schneider, Ballack), Real Madrid 3 (Roberto Carlos 2, Guti)
Real Madrid 5 (Guti 2, Helguera, Raul, Figo pen), Bayer Leverkusen 3 (Brdaric, Kirsten, Rink)
Sporting Lisbon 0, Spartak Moscow 3 (Dimas og, Titov 2)
Bayer Leverkusen 1 (Ballack), Spartak Moscow 0
Real Madrid 4 (Guti, Savio, Morientes 2), Sporting Lisbon 0
Sporting Lisbon 0, Bayer Leverkusen 0

Group A

	P	W	D	L	F	A	Pts
Real Madrid	6	4	1	1	15	8	13
Spartak Moscow	6	4	0	2	9	3	12
Bayer Leverkusen	6	2	1	3	9	12	7
Sporting Lisbon	6	0	2	4	5	15	2

Group B

Shakhtjor Donetsk 0, Lazio 3 (Lopez, Nedved, Inzaghi)
Sparta Prague 0, Arsenal 1(Silvinho)
Arsenal 3 (Wiltord, Keown 2), Shakhtjor Donetsk 2 (Bakharev, Vorobei)
Lazio 3 (Inzaghi 2, Simeone), Sparta Prague 0
Arsenal 2 (Ljungberg 2), Lazio 0
Sparta Prague 3 (Rosicky, Hornak, Jarosik), Shakhtjor Donetsk 2 (Zubov, Abramov)
Lazio 1 (Nedved), Arsenal 1 (Pires)
Shakhtjor Donetsk 2 (Gleveckas, Zubov pen), Sparta Prague 1 (Jarosik)
Arsenal 4 (Parlour, Lauren, Dixon, Kanu), Sparta Prague 2 (Labant pen, Rosicky)
Lazio 5 (Lopez 3, Favalli, Veron), Shakhtjor Donetsk 1 (Vorebei),
Shakhtjor Donetsk 3 (Atelkin, Vorobei, Bielik), Arsenal 0
Sparta Prague 0, Lazio 1 (Ravanelli)

Group B

	P	W	D	L	F	A	Pts
Arsenal	6	4	1	1	11	8	13
Lazio	6	4	1	1	13	4	13
Shakhtjor Donetsk	6	2	0	4	10	15	6
Sparta Prague	6	1	0	5	6	13	3

Group C

Lyon 3 (Anderson, Houttuin, Marlet), Heerenveen 1 (Talan)
Valencia 2 (Baraja, Alosnso), Olympiakos 1 (Djordjevic)
Heerenveen 0, Valencia 1 (Kily Gonzalez)
Olympiakos 2 (Ofori-Quaye, Giovanni), Lyon 1 (Foe)
Olympiakos 2 (Giovanni 2), Heerenveen 0
Valencia 1 (Zahovic), Lyon 0
Heerenveen 1 (Jensen), Olympiakos 0
Lyon 1 (Marlet), Valencia 2 (Sanchez, Baraja)
Heerenveen 0, Lyon 2 (Malbranque, Marlet)
Olympiakos 1 (Djordjevic pen), Valencia 0
Lyon 1 (Laigle), Olympiakos 0
Valencia 1 (Alonso), Heerenveen 1 (Venema)

Group C

	P	W	D	L	F	A	Pts
Valencia	6	4	1	1	7	4	13
Lyon	6	3	0	3	8	6	9
Olympiakos	6	3	0	3	6	5	9
Heerenveen	6	1	1	5	3	9	4

Group D

Galatasaray 3 (Jardel, Hagi, Capone), Monaco 2 (Nonda, Simone pen)
Rangers 5 (Mols, De Boer, Albertz, Van Bronckhorst, Dodds), Sturm Graz 0
Monaco 0, Rangers 1 (Van Bronckhorst)
Sturm Graz 3 (Yuran, Schopp, Schupp), Galatasaray 0
Galatasaray 3 (Bulent, Hakan Unsal, Jardel), Rangers 2 (Kancheslskis, Van Bronckhorst)
Monaco 5 (Simone 3, Farnerud, Nonda), Sturm Graz 0
Rangers 0, Galatasary 0
Sturm Graz 2 (Schopp 2) Monaco 0
Monaco 4 (Contreras, Bonnal, Simone, Nonda), Galatasaray 2 (Hakan Unsal, Korkmaz)
Sturm Graz 2 (Yuran, Prilasnig), Rangers 0
Galatasaray 2 (Ergun pen, Jardel), Graz 2 (Yuran, Hakan Unsal og)
Rangers 2 (Miller, Mols), Monaco 2 (Costinha, Simone)

Group D

	P	W	D	L	F	A	Pts
Sturm Graz	6	3	1	2	9	12	10
Galatasaray	6	2	2	2	10	13	8
Rangers	6	2	2	2	10	7	8
Monaco	6	2	1	3	13	10	7

Group E

Hamburg 4 (Yeboah, Mahdavikia, Butt pen, Kovac), Juventus 4 (Tudor, Inzaghi 3 – 1 pen)
Panathinikos 1 (Warzycha), Deportivo La Coruna 1 (Naybet)
Deportivo La Coruna 2 (Pandiani, Scaloni), Hamburg 1 (Barbarez)
Juventus 2 (Tacchinardi, Trezeguet), Panathinikos 1 (Goumas)
Hamburg 0, Panathinikos 1 (Nassiopoulos)
Juventus 0, Deportivo La Coruna 0
Deportivo La Coruna 1 (Victor), Juventus 1 (Inzaghi)
Panathinikos 0, Hamburg 0
Deportivo La Coruna 1 (Pandiani), Panathinikos 0
Juventus 1 (Kovacevic), Hamburg 3 (Prager, Yeboah, Panadic)
Hamburg 1 (Mahdavika), Deportivo La Coruna 1 (Makaay)
Panathinikos 3 (Paulo Sousa, Basinas pen, Warzycha), Juventus 1 (Inzaghi)

Group E

	P	W	D	L	F	A	Pts
D'tivo La Coruna	6	2	4	0	6	4	10
Panathinikos	6	2	2	2	6	5	8
Hamburg	6	1	3	2	9	9	6
Juventus	6	1	3	2	9	12	6

Group F

Helsingborg 1 (B Johansen), Bayern Munich 3 (Scholl, Salihamidic, Jancker)
Rosenborg 3 (Berg, F Johnsen, Skammelsrud pen), Paris St Germain 1 (Christian)
Bayern Munich 3 (Jancker, Elber, Linke), Rosenborg 1 (Sorensen)
Paris St Germain 4 (Anelka, Robert, Christian, El Karkouri), Helsingborg 1 (B Johansen)
Paris St Germain 1 (Leroy), Bayern Munich 0
Rosenborg 6 (Johnsen 3, Strand 2, S Johansen og), Helsingborg 1 (Prica)
Bayern Munich 2 (Salihamidizic, Sergio), Paris St Germain 0
Helsingborg 2 (Jansson, Santos), Rosenborg 0
Bayern Munich 0, Helsingborg 0
Paris St Germain 7 (Dehu, Charistian, Anelka 2, Luccin, Leyroy, Robert pen), Rosenborg 2 (George 2)
Helsingborg 1 (Persson), Paris St Germain 1 (Anelka)
Rosenborg 1 (Johnsen), Bayern Munich 1 (Jeremies)

Group F

	P	W	D	L	F	A	Pts
Bayern Munich	6	3	2	1	9	4	11
Paris St Germain	6	3	1	2	14	9	10
Rosenborg	6	2	1	3	13	15	7
Helsingborg	6	1	2	3	6	14	5

Group G

Manchester United 5 (Cole 3, Irwin pen, Sheringham), Anderlecht 1 (Koller)
PSV Eindhoven 2 (Lucius, Bruggink), Dynamo Kiev 1 (Shatskikh)
Anderlecht 1 (Dheedene), PSV Eindhoven 0
Dynamo Kiev 0, Manchester United 0
Dynamo Kiev 4 (Gusin, Shatskih, Demetradze 2), Anderlecht 0
PSV Eindhoven 3 (Bouma, Van Bommel, Kezman), Manchester United 1 (Scholes pen)
Anderlecht 4 (Vaschuk og, Radzinski 2, Stoica), Dynamo Kiev 2 (Kaladze, Bialkevich)
Manchester United 3 (Sheringham, Scholes, Yorke), PSV Eindhoven 1 (Van Bommel)
Anderlecht 2 (Radzinski 2), Manchester United 1 (Irwin pen)
Dynamo Kiev 0, PSV Eindhoven 1 (Ooijer)
Manchester United 1 (Sheringham), Dynamo Kiev 0
PSV Eindhoven 2 (Ramzi 2), Anderlecht 3 (Crasson, Koller, Youla)

Group G

	P	W	D	L	F	A	Pts
Anderlecht	6	4	0	2	11	14	12
Manchester United	6	3	1	2	11	7	10
PSV Eindhoven	6	3	0	3	9	9	9
Dynamo Kiev	6	1	1	4	7	8	4

The Real deal

Mesmerised by Madrid's magic

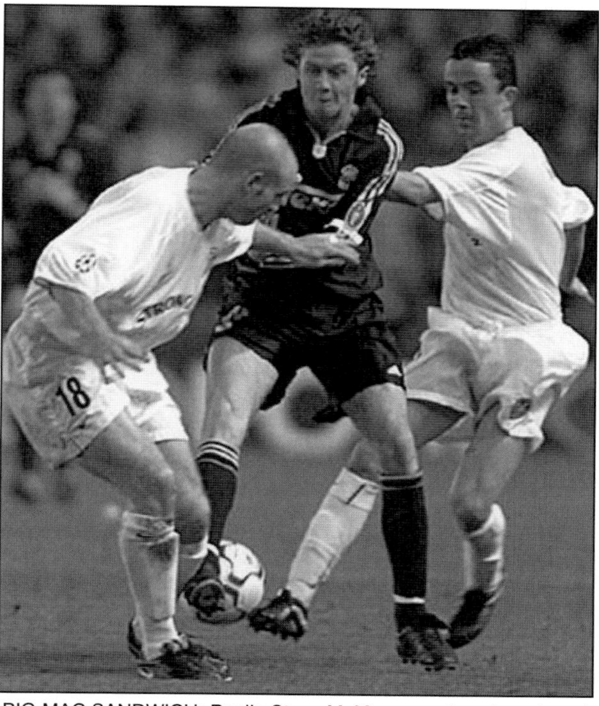

BIG MAC SANDWICH: Real's Steve McManaman is outnumbered by United's Danny Mills and Gary Kelly.

IF United thought the Champions League was going to get any easier after emerging from a tough first phase then they were wrong.

Once again the draw threw up mouth-watering prospects – going head-to-head with Real Madrid, Lazio and Anderlecht in Group D of the second phase.

David O'Leary's team would have to re-double their efforts if their exciting European campaign was going to stretch into the quarter-finals.

First up were Spanish masters Real Madrid, the European champions, at Elland Road.

In Don Revie's early days at Leeds he changed the blue and old gold kit to all-white because one day he wanted United to be on a par with mighty Madrid, whose all white strip was famous throughout the world.

Real had dominated the European Cup in the 1960s with men like Alfredo di Stefano, Ferenc Puskas and Francisco Gento true giants of the game. The modern-day idols like Roberto Carlos, the explosive attacking Brazilian left-back, Portuguese maestro Luis Figo and red-hot raider Raul made Madrid everyone's favourites to retain their crown.

At Leeds, Madrid showed their true colours with a comfortable 2-0 victory, orchestrated by a fine midfield display by Steve McManaman, the former Liverpool midfielder.

Stripped of leading midfielders like David Batty, Olivier Dacourt and Eirik Bakke, and the wing play of Harry Kewell, Leeds simply didn't have the men to deny Real a wealth of possession. Had Jonathan Woodgate converted a close range chance early on or 19-year-old goalkeeper Iker Casillas not made an outstanding save to keep out a Dominic Matteo header then United may have had a lead to protect.

Instead the makeshift midfield of Matteo, Lee Bowyer, Gary Kelly and young Aussie Jacob Burns ran tirelessly to stem fluent Madrid. Chances came and went for the visitors and just as though it looked as though determination would get United a point, Madrid struck at the double.

Midway through the second half Real skipper Fernando Hierro rose above Woodgate to head the opener past Paul Robinson, who picked the ball out of his net again two minutes later after a crisp finish by Raul following a splendid sweeping move down United's right flank.

It was game, set and match to Real and there were no complaints from the United camp about being beaten by such a great side.

Rio on his way

THE day before the Real Madrid match, United announced they had reached an agreement with West Ham to sign England defender Rio Ferdinand for £18 million – a world record for a defender.

Meanwhile, Canadian striker Tomasz Radzinski's goal earned Anderlecht a 1-0 home win over fancied Italians Lazio, who were next on United's European tour.

However, Ferdinand would not be eligible to play in Rome. The first Champions League match he would be available to play in would be the third game of the second phase, at home to Anderlecht.

Group D
Match 1

Anderlecht 1 (Radzinski), Lazio 0
Leeds United 0, Real Madrid 2 (Hierro, Raul)

UEFA Champions League
Second phase, Group D, Match 1
(at Elland Road, Leeds)
Wednesday, November 22, 2000

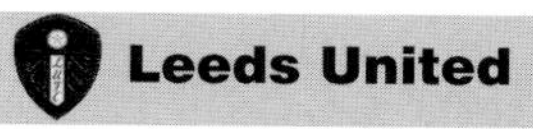

Leeds United 0

Real Madrid 2

Leeds United: Paul Robinson, Danny Mills, Ian Harte, Lucas Radebe, Jonathan Woodgate, Gary Kelly, Lee Bowyer, Jacob Burns (Jason Wilcox 60), Dominic Matteo, Alan Smith, Mark Viduka
Manager: David O'Leary

Real Madrid: Iker Casillas, Claude Makelele, Fernando Hierro, Ivan Campo, Roberto Carlos, Ivan Helguera, Jose Maria Gutierrez Hernandez 'Guti', (Pedro Munitis 89), Sorele Geremi, Steve McManaman, Luis Figo ('Savio' Bortolini Pimenetel 84), Gonzalez Blanco Raul
Goal: Hierro 66, Raul 68
Manager: Vicente Del Bosque

Referee: Dick Jol (Holland) **Att::** 36,794

Rome falls to

DAVID O'Leary's young gladiators came of age in Rome's Olympic Stadium.

Their shock 1-0 victory against big-spending Lazio put them back in contention for a place in the Champions League quarter-finals.

United had become a team to be feared throughout the continent and their latest upset was fully merited.

Two young England prospects gave England's new national coach Sven-Goran Eriksson plenty to think about, as Alan Smith grabbed a brilliant winning goal and Jonathan Woodgate was a tower of strength at the back.

The moment which sent United's travelling fans into ecstacy came ten minutes from the end of a fascinating encounter when co-striker Mark Viduka backheeled the ball in to the path of Smith and the Rothwell raider angled a superb shot past Angelo Peruzzi.

GOLDEN GOAL: United's young rising star Alan Smith salutes his winner which came ten minutes from time when he slid the ball under the despairing body of Lazio goalkeeper Angelo Peruzzi.

Leeds legions

Young guns send message to Sven

Leeds made a positive start, going close early on when Eirik Bakke's downward header from a corner which was cleared off the line by Attillo Lombardo.

Lazio responded with a Hernan Crespo volley which went just wide of a post with Paul Robinson beaten and United had a let off when Giuseppe Pancaro headed a Juan-Sebastian Veron corner against an upright from just four yards out.

Woodgate then denied Marcelo Salas with a glancing header from Pavel Nedved's dangerous ball into the area and then headed off the line when Salas got a header in on goal. Despite Lazio pressure, United went close to taking the lead before half-time when Lee Bowyer was only a fraction away from getting to Mark Viduka's perfectly-flighted cross to the far post.

Nedved's shooting continued to be a source of concern for United, but the Serie A side appeared to be running out of ideas and United took control.

Smith sent a shot over the bar and that was the cue for David O'Leary to send on injury-hit Harry Kewell for his first taste of the Champions League.

Kewell played his part in the build-up to the goal, slipping the ball to fellow Aussie Viduka whose backheel enabled Smith to roll the ball under Peruzzi into the right corner of the net.

It was probably United's best result of the Champions League campaign and O'Leary, whose own stock was rising in the managerial world, could not hide his delight.

"It gets better and better for us. You think what we did in Milan and now we've been to another famous stadium and come away with a teriffic result."

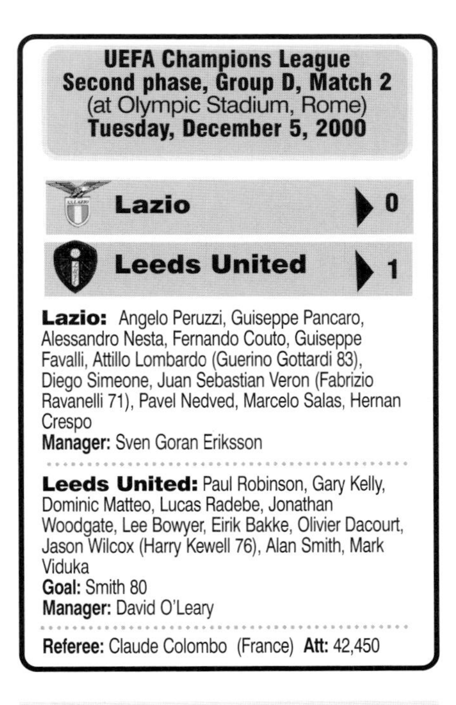

UEFA Champions League
Second phase, Group D, Match 2
(at Olympic Stadium, Rome)
Tuesday, December 5, 2000

Lazio	**0**
Leeds United	**1**

Lazio: Angelo Peruzzi, Guiseppe Pancaro, Alessandro Nesta, Fernando Couto, Guiseppe Favalli, Attillo Lombardo (Guerino Gottardi 83), Diego Simeone, Juan Sebastian Veron (Fabrizio Ravanelli 71), Pavel Nedved, Marcelo Salas, Hernan Crespo
Manager: Sven Goran Eriksson

Leeds United: Paul Robinson, Gary Kelly, Dominic Matteo, Lucas Radebe, Jonathan Woodgate, Lee Bowyer, Eirik Bakke, Olivier Dacourt, Jason Wilcox (Harry Kewell 76), Alan Smith, Mark Viduka
Goal: Smith 80
Manager: David O'Leary

Referee: Claude Colombo (France) **Att:** 42,450

United's double target

UNITED'S stunning victory in Rome meant that back-to-back victories over Belgian champs Anderlecht would seal a quarter-final. Real Madrid continued to live up to their top billing by demolishing Anderlecht 4-1 in the Bernabeau

Group D
Match 2

Lazio 0, Leeds United 1 (Smith)
Real Madrid 4 (Morientes, Figo pen, Helgurera, Roberto Carlos), Anderlecht 1 (Stoica)

Bow's golden arrow

HEADLINE MAKER: Lee Bowyer celebrates his late winner against Anderlecht.

THERE was no keeping Lee Bowyer out of the headlines.

The all-action midfielder put his off-the-field troubles behind him to fire United a step closer to the European Champions League quarter-finals.

His brilliantly-taken 87th minute winner saw Leeds snatch a dramatic 2-1 comeback victory over Anderlecht at Elland Road.

United were staring defeat squarely in the face when the Belgians opened the scoring midway through the second-half.

But Bowyer, who made the 70-mile motorway dash from Hull Crown Court just in time to be named in the Leeds team, turned the game around for United after Ian Harte's free-kick equaliser.

The win left Leeds with a firm grip on second spot in Group D behind Real Madrid although they were staring defeat in the face when Romanian international Alin Stoica shot Anderlect ahead after 65 minutes when Bart Goor's backheel opened up United's defence.

The goal had come against the run of play, but within ten minutes Harte got Leeds back on track by bending a free-kick around the Anderlecht wall from 25 yards to beat goalkeeper Zvonko Milojevic at his near post.

United pressed hard for a winner while the Belgians, cheered on by a sizeable following, hit back on the counter-attack.

From one swift break giant 6ft 8in striker Czech international Jan Koller missed a great chance and Leeds made the most of their escape. Anderlecht skipper Glen De Boeck let the ball slip under his foot 25 yards from his own-goal and Alan Smith was able to slide a pass through to the energetic Bowyer, who drilled a 12-yard angled shot under Milojevic for the winner.

Even then Leeds still required Nigel Martyn to make a splendid save to deny Tomasz Radzinski in injury-time as United hung on for a priceless win.

Rio Ferdinand and Lucas Radebe had blotted out the Belgian attack and there was another bonus for United fans as Harry Kewell, absent through injury for most of the season, came off the bench for a slice of the action.

UEFA Champions League
Second phase, Group D, Match 3
(at Elland Road, Leeds)
Tuesday, February 13, 2001

Leeds United 2

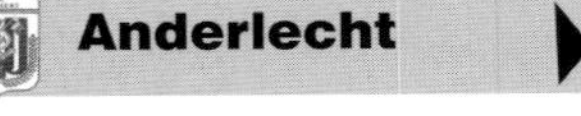
Anderlecht 1

Leeds United: Nigel Martyn, Danny Mills, Ian Harte, Lucas Radebe, Rio Ferdinand, Lee Bowyer, David Batty, Olivier Dacourt (Eirik Bakke 72), Dominic Matteo (Harry Kewell 53), Alan Smith, Mark Viduka
Goals: Harte 77, Bowyer 86
Manager: David O'Leary

Anderlecht: Zvonko Milojevic, Bertrand Crasson, Glen De Boeck, Aleksander Illic, Didier Dheedene, Yves Vanderhaeghe, Walter Bassegio, Alin Stoica, Bart Goor, Tomasz Radzinski, Jan Koller
Goal: Stoica 64
Manager: Aime Antheunis

Referee: Karl-Erik Nilsson (Sweden) **Att:** 36,064

Courting trouble

DAVID O'Leary's preparations for the match had been disrupted by a high-profile Crown Court case at Hull where Lee Bowyer and Jonathan Woodgate had denied charges of causing actual bodily harm to a student following an incident in Leeds city centre.

Despite not training for a couple of weeks, Bowyer was not going to miss the Anderlecht match, but Woodgate did not play for the duration of the case.

Woodgate's replacement was £18 million Rio Ferdinand, who was making his Champions League debut.

Woodgate was not the only absentee. A month after Ferdinand's arrival, United took Republic of Ireland sharpshooter Robbie Keane on a sixth-month loan from Italian club Inter Milan for six months with a view to a £12 million deal going through. The former Wolves and Coventry player's previous taste of European action with Inter meant that he was not eligible to play for the rest of United's Champions League campaign.

Lazio crashed to their third successive defeat against maximum men Madrid.

Group D
Third matches

Leeds United 2 (Harte, Bowyer), Anderlecht 1 (Stoica)
Real Madrid 3 (Morientes, Helguera, Figo pen), Lazio 2 (Crespo, Gottardi)

Brilliant United cruise in to last eight

Muscles in Brussels

UEFA Champions League
Second phase, Group D, Match 4
(at Vanden Stock Stadium, Brussels)
Wednesday, February 21, 2001

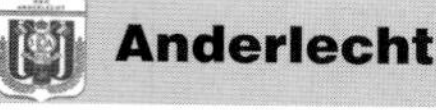

Anderlecht	**1**
Leeds United	**4**

Anderlecht: Zvonko Milojevic, Bertrand Crasson, Glen De Boeck, Aleksander Illic (Aruna Dindane 39), Didier Dheedene, Yves Vanderhaeghe, Walter Bassegio, Alin Stoica, Bart Goor, Tomasz Radzinski, Jan Koller
Goal: Koller 76
Manager: Aime Antheunis

Leeds United: Nigel Martyn, Danny Mills, Ian Harte, Rio Ferdinand, Lucas Radebe, Olivier Dacourt, David Batty, Eirik Bakke, Dominc Matteo, Alan Smith, Mark Viduka (Harry Kewell 83)
Goals: Smith 13, 38, Viduka 34, Harte pen 81
Manager: David O'Leary

Referee: Rune Pedersen (Norway) **Att:** 28,000

TWO-GOAL Alan Smith made a fool of Anderlecht coach Aime Antheunis as United turned on a sparkling display in Brussels.

The Belgians' coach branded Leeds "lucky" after the first leg, claiming "I did not see Leeds as a strong side".

Those words were rammed down his throat as United put together a superb display to win 4-1 at Anderlecht's Constant Vanden Stock fortress.

Anderlecht had won 21 successive games there, beating some of Europe's finest sides in the process, but were dismantled by a Leeds side bristling with skill, power and confidence.

The rout started after 13 minutes when Smith ended his 11-week goal drought by blasting home a Mark Viduka cross. The big Australian striker then ended his own nine-match barren run by heading in United's second.

Leeds were sweeping forward with some wonderful flowing football and went 3-0 up before half-time with a picturebook goal, Smith chipping the ball over goalkeeper Zvonko Milojevic after Anderlecht were opened up by another spell of crisp, first-time Leeds passing.

Anderlecht improved after the break and pulled a goal back when giant centre-forward Jan Koller got his head on the end of a 75th minute free-kick.

But fittingly Leeds had the final word when Viduka was brought down in the area and Ian Harte stepped up to round off a night to remember with his penalty kick. It meant that Leeds had the luxury of qualifying for the Champions League quarter-finals with two Group matches still to play.

David O'Leary, who was unable to field first leg hero Lee Bowyer because of his appearance at Hull Crown Court, said: "It's a great feeling to be in the quarter-finals already and I am delighted for English football."

The Leeds boss added: "I am immensely proud of my players because a lot was said after the game in Leeds."

Antheunis, who later claimed his first leg comments had been taken out of context, discovered that his utterings had provided the perfect motivation for a fired-up United.

KNEES UP: United's David Batty and Anderlecht's Water Baseggio hold nothing back as they contest possession.

Real Madrid ease through

REIGNING champions Real Madrid dropped their first point in the group in a 2-2 draw at Lazio, but like United qualified for the quarter-finals with two matches to spare.

Group D
Fourth Matches

Anderlecht 1 (Koller), Leeds United 4 (Smith 2, Viduka, Harte pen)
Lazio 2 (Nedved, Crespo), Real Madrid 2 (Solari, Raul)

Madrid finish top of group

REAL Madrid's victory over United ensured that the Spanish side won Group D with United as runners-up.

In the battle of the also-rans, Lazio, watched by only 10,000 fans, beat Anderlecht 2-1 in Rome.

Sven-Goran Eriksson had resigned as Lazio's coach in January to take over as England's first foreign coach. The Swede signed a five-and-a-half year deal reputedly worth £12.5m. Dino Zoff was installed as Eriksson's replacement at Lazio.

Group D
Fifth matches

Lazio 2 (Lopez, Baronio), Anderlecht 1 (Stoica)
Real Madrid 3 (Raul 2, Figo), Leeds United 2 (Smith, Viduka)

GET IN THERE: Mark Viduka's header draws United level against Real Madrid.

Leeds dealt Real bad hand

ONLY a controversial goal dented United's hopes of a share of the spoils against Euro-stars Real Madrid.

Polish referee Riszard Woljic apologised to the Leeds camp for failing to see striker Raul use his hand to slap the ball past an astonished Nigel Martyn for Real's eighth-minute equaliser.

Luckily there was nothing at stake apart from who would finish top of the group as both sides had already qualified for the quarter-finals.

At least Woljic had the bottle to admit he made a mistake. "He asked to come in to the dressing room," said Leeds boss David O'Leary, "He did so and apologised. I think that took a big man and a brave man to come in and fair play to him, particularly as we did not deserve to lose the game."

Raul, criticised by the Spanish press for his action, first admitted to the referee that he used his hand. He then changed his mind and said he hadn't.

He was not the only one to have a change of heart. UEFA fined him £7,500 and banned him for one match, only to change their mind later.

It was a bizarre incident in a strange game which began with Alan Smith's sixth minute opener. The young forward looked offside as he received Mark Viduka's right-wing pass before sliding the ball past Cesar.

Real responded with Raul's 'Hand of God' goal and took the lead four minutes from the break when Luis Figo's speculative low cross from the edge of the area hit a mound created by Martyn for his goalkicks on the edge of the six-yard box and the ball was deflected over the stranded Cornishman.

Leeds were always in contention in an open match and equalised on 54 minutes when Viduka headed in Ian Harte's corner. But the match ended in anti-climax for United as Real clinched the winner on the hour, Raul heading in £37 million Portuguese star Figo's cross.

United suffered more pain five minutes later when skipper Lucas Radebe twisted his right knee and hobbled out of the Bernabeu Stadium on crutches unable to play any further part in United's European Champions League adventure.

UEFA Champions League
Second phase, Group D, Match 5
(at Bernabeu Stadium, Madrid)
Tuesday, March 6, 2001

Real Madrid 3

Leeds United 2

Real Madrid: Cesar Sanchez Dominguez, Claude Makelele (Bortolini Pimental Savio 87), Santiago Solari, Fernando Ruiz Hierro, Aitor Karanka, Albert Celades, Sorele Geremi, Fernando Morientes (Pedro Munitis 76), Steve McManaman, Luis Figo (Alberto Rivera 90), Gonzalez Blanco Raul
Goals: Raul 7, 60, Figo 41
Manager: Vicente del Bosque

Leeds United: Nigel Martyn, Dominic Matteo, Ian Harte, Lucas Radebe (Gary Kelly 65), Rio Ferdinand, Eirik Bakke (Jason Wilcox 86), David Batty, Olivier Dacourt, Harry Kewell, Alan Smith, Mark Viduka
Goals: Smith 6, Viduka 54
Manager: David O'Leary

Referee: Ryszard Woljic (Poland) **Att:** 39,460

Floodlit robbery

Free-kick blunder denies United win

WIZARD OF OZ: Mark Viduka's header gives United the lead against Lazio.

UNITED found themselves at the heart of another controversial refereeing decision which cost their shadow side a famous Champions League double over Italian giants Lazio.

David O'Leary's battlers were hanging on to a 3-2 lead in injury-time at Elland Road when Austrian official Konrad Plautz missed a dreadful lunge by Pavel Nedved on young Irish full-back Alan Maybury, giving the free-kick to the Italians.

As the stricken Maybury, making his first start since March 1998, was carried off on a stretcher, Sinisa Mihajlovic stepped up and smashed the ball past Paul Robinson for an unmerited equaliser.

It was a sour end to an entertaining game in which both sides fielded weakened line-ups with qualification already determined.

Several Leeds stars were able to take a well-earned rest but their stand-ins put on a fine show despite falling behind to Fabrizio Ravanelli's 21st minute header.

It was the first time an Italian side had scored at Elland Road since Juventus drew 1-1 in the old Fairs Cup final 30 years ago.

Lee Bowyer knocked home a lofted shot from the edge of the area for his sixth goal of the European campaign six minutes later to put Leeds level.

But, from the restart Ravanelli, the former Middlesbrough man, stumbled dramatically after a Dominic Matteo challenge to buy Lazio a penalty on the half-hour which Mihajlovic lashed past Robinson.

But United's industry was rewarded when Jason Wilcox, enjoying a rare start, scored with his first goal of the season – volleying home in style from Ian Harte's free-kick.

Harte was the provider again just after an hour when he delivered a free-kick into the box for Mark Viduka to head in his 18th goal of the season. Immediately the Aussie hit-man was replaced by young Tony Hackworth, making his home debut, while Chilean World Cup star Marcelo Salas came on for Claudio Lopez as Lazio stepped up the pressure.

Just as it seemed United were going to earn victory they were denied by Mihajlovic's hammer blow.

Despite their disappointment, United maintained their record of never having lost at home to Italian opposition in eight meetings.

UEFA Champions League
Second phase, Group D, Match 6
(at Elland Road, Leeds)
Wednesday, March 14, 2001

Leeds United: Paul Robinson, Gary Kelly, Ian Harte, Danny Mills. Dominic Matteo, Alan Maybury (David Batty 90), Jacob Burns, Jason Wilcox, Lee Bowyer, Harry Kewell, Mark Viduka (Tony Hackworth 63)
Goals: Bowyer 28, Wilcox 43, Viduka 62
Manager: David O'Leary

Lazio: Luca Marchegiani, Franceso Colonnese, Fernando Couto, Sinisa Mihajlovic, Emanuele Pesaresi, Lucas Castroman (Daneile Ruggiu 88), Roberto Baronio, Dejan Stankovic, Pavel Nedved, Claudio Lopez (Marcelo Salas 64), Fabrizio Ravanelli
Goals: Ravanelli 21, Mihajlovic pen 29, 90
Manager: Dino Zoff

Referee: Konrad Plautz (Austria) **Att:** 36,741

Anderlecht consolation

LAZIO finished bottom of Group D because Anderlecht pulled off a surprise 2-0 win over leaders Real Madrid in Brussels.
Goals in the last five minutes by Aruna Dinane and Bart Goor ensured the Belgians finished their campaign on a high note in front of their own fans.

Group D
Sixth Matches
Anderlecht 2 (Dindane, Goor), Real Madrid 0
Leeds United 3 (Bowyer, Wilcox, Viduka), Lazio 3 (Ravanelli, Mihajlovic 2 – 1pen)

Group D

	P	W	D	L	F	A	Pts
Real Madrid	6	4	1	1	14	9	13
Leeds United	6	3	1	2	12	10	10
Anderlecht	6	2	0	4	7	12	6
Lazio	6	1	2	3	9	11	5

Premiership's power

FELLOW Premiership clubs Arsenal and Manchester United joined David O'Leary's young guns in the last eight of the Champions League.

Manchester United, for whom former Leeds defender Denis Irwin was a key member of the squad, made a flying start to Group A with victories over Panathinikos and Sturm Graz.

A point was gained in Spain against Valencia who then visited Old Trafford.

The Red Devils were on course for qualification thanks to Andy Cole's early goal, but a Wes Brown own-goal enabled Valencia to escape with a draw.

Paul Scholes, who was in fine goal-scoring form in the Champions League, then snatched a last-gasp equaliser in Greece against Panathinikos before qualification to the quarter-finals was secured for the fifth successive season with an easy 3-0 win over Sturm Graz.

Sir Alex Ferguson's squad finished with 12 points but Valencia topped the group.

Arsenal recovered from their heaviest away defeat in Europe – a 4-1 spanking at Spartak Moscow – to finish second in Group C behind Bayern Munich.

Arsene Wenger's squad threw away a 2-0 lead over the Germans at Highbury in the second match and were held 2-2.

However, when the matches resumed in February, Thierry Henry's header gave them a 1-0 win at Lyon, but in the return match the following week they conceded a last-minute equaliser to the French team to put a big question mark over qualification.

Another late Henry goal gave Arsenal a priceless victory over Spartak in their fifth game, and although they lost in Munich, the Gunners qualified.

They finished with the same number of points as Lyon, but went through as they had a better head-to-head record against the French team.

Group B was won by Spanish side Deportivo La Coruna, who just pipped Galatasaray, who had added the Super Cup to the UEFA Cup they had won the previous season.

Group A

Manchester United 3 (Sheringham, Scholes 2), Panathinikos 1 (Karagounis)
Valencia 2 (Carew, Sanchez), Sturm Graz 0
Panathinikos 0, Valencia 0
Sturm Graz 0, Manchester United 2 (Scholes, Giggs)
Sturm Graz 2 (Haas, Kocijan), Panathinikos 0
Valencia 0, Manchester United 0
Manchester United 1 (Cole), Valencia 1 (Brown og)
Panathinikos 1 (Goumas), Sturm Graz 2 (Schopp, Haas)
Panathinkos 1 (Seitaridis), Manchester United 1 (Scholes)
Sturm Graz 0, Valencia 5 (Ayala, Carew, Gonzalez, Alonso 2)
Manchester United 3 (Butt, Sheringham, Keane), Sturm Graz 0
Valencia 2 (Sanchez, Angloma), Panathinikos 1 (Basinas pen)

Group A

	P	W	D	L	F	A	Pts
Valencia	6	3	3	0	10	2	12
Manchester United	6	3	3	0	10	3	12
Sturm Graz	6	2	0	4	4	13	6
Panathinikos	6	0	2	4	4	10	2

Group B

AC Milan 2 (Jose Mari, Shevchenko pen), Galatasaray 2 (Jardel, Hasan Sas)
Paris St Germain 1 (Algerino), Deportivo La Coruna 3 (Naybet, Flores, Makaay)
Deportivo La Coruna 0, AC Milan 1 (Helveg)
Galatasaray 1 (Umit pen), Paris St Germain 0
Galatasaray 1 (Suat), Deportivo La Coruna 0
AC Milan 1 (Leonardo), Paris St Germain 1 (Anelka)
Deportivo La Coruna 2 (Victor, Djalminha pen), Galatasaray 0
Paris St Germain 1 (Robert), AC Milan 1 (Jose Mari)
Galatasaray 2 (Hagi, Jardel), AC Milan 0
AC Milan 1 (Shevchenko pen), Deportivo La Coruna 1 (Djalminha pen)
Paris St Germain 2 (Christian 2), Galatasaray 0

Group B

	P	W	D	L	F	A	Pts
D'tivo La Coruna	6	3	1	2	10	7	10
Galatasaray	6	3	1	2	6	6	10
AC Milan	6	1	4	1	6	7	7
Paris St Germain	6	1	2	3	9	11	5

Group C

Bayern Munich 1 (Jeremies), Lyon 0
Spartak Moscow 4 (Marcao 2, Titov, Robson), Arsenal 1 (Silvinho)
Arsenal 2 (Henry, Kanu), Bayern Munich 2 (Tarnat, Scholl)
Lyon 3 (Marlet, Anderson 2), Spartak Moscow 0
Bayern Munich 1 (Elber), Spartak Moscow 0
Lyon 0, Arsenal 1 (Henry)
Arsenal 1 (Bergkamp), Lyon 1 (Edmilson)
Spartak Moscow 0, Bayern Munich 3 (Scholl 2 – 1 pen, Sergio)
Arsenal 1 (Henry), Spartak Moscow 0
Lyon 3 (Gouvou 2, Laigle), Bayern Munich 0
Bayern Munich 1 (Elber), Arsenal 0
Spartak Moscow 1 (Parfenov pen), Lyon 1 (Anderson pen)

Group C

	P	W	D	L	F	A	Pts
Bayern Munich	6	4	1	1	8	5	13
Arsenal	6	2	2	2	6	8	8
Lyon	6	2	2	2	8	4	8
Spartak Moscow	6	1	1	4	5	10	4

THEATRES OF DREAMS: The cavernous Nou Camp Stadium (left) home of Barcelona, and, right, Real Madrid's Bernabeu Stadium.

Simply fan-tastic

Supporters turn out in huge numbers

THOUSANDS of United fans followed their heroes around the continent on a thrilling Champions League odyssey.

The journey took them to some of the greatest stadia in the world, including the Olympic Stadiums of both Munich and Rome, the awesome Nou Camp, home of Barcelona, Real Madrid's Bernabeu Stadium and the unforgettable San Siro in Milan.

An estimated 8,000 Leeds fans went to Milan, where qualification to the second stage was celebrated with a good old fashioned sing-song with the team, and 6,000 to Madrid.

The draw for the quarter-finals pitted United with Spanish la Liga champions Deportivo La Coruna, while Arsenal were paired with Valencia, Manchester United with Bayern Munich and Galatasaray would take on Real Madrid. Leeds would have home advantage first against Deportivo before going to Spain on April 17.

But there would be no mass presence of Leeds fans at the Riazor Stadium, as Deportivo originally handed United just 850 tickets. That figure was increased to 1,700 (the five per cent of Coruna's stadium's capacity) after talks with the Spanish club.

But first United wanted to build up a healthy lead to take to a country where they had already lost twice in the earlier stages of the competition.

WHERE IT ALL BEGAN: The Olympic Stadium, Munich, where United kicked off their Champions League campaign with a 1-0 win against 1860 Munich.

OUT IN FORCE: United fans show their true colours in the imposing San Siro (right), where a 1-1 draw with AC Milan took Leeds in to the second phase of the Champions League.

'Three-nil to the

ECSTATIC United fans roared with delight as once again their side made a mockery of their European detractors.

Deportivo midfielder Victor had dubbed Leeds "the weakest team left in the competition" when the quarter-final draw was made.

But just like Anderlecht's coach earlier in the tournament, he was forced to eat his words as United's dazzling display earned them a 3-0 first leg cushion to take to Coruna in northern Spain.

"Three-nil to the weakest team" boomed the delighted Leeds fans which could hardly have been music to the ears of Victor, who was left squirming on the bench as his team-mates were overpowered by a rampant Leeds.

Deportivo arrived with a reputation for being one of the most attack-minded sides in La Liga, but coach Javier Irureta opted for a more defensive approach at Elland Road – tactics which backfired badly.

The Spaniards simply didn't have the defensive strength to hold out against United's raw power on a wet and windy Yorkshire night.

UEFA Champions League
Quarter-final, first leg
(at Elland Road, Leeds)
Wednesday, April 4, 2001

Leeds United	3
Deportivo	0

Leeds United: Nigel Martyn, Danny Mills, Ian Harte, Dominic Matteo, Rio Ferdinand, Lee Bowyer, David Batty, Olivier Dacourt, Harry Kewell (Jason Wilcox 84), Alan Smith, Mark Viduka
Goals: Harte 26, Smith 51, Ferdinand 66
Manager: David O'Leary

Deportivo La Coruna: Jose Francisco Molina, Manuel Pablo, Enrique Fernandez Romero, Nourredine Naybet, Lionel Sebastian Scaloni (Diego Tristran 71), 'Cessar' Martin Villar, Aldo Pedro Duscher (Juan Carlos Valeron 54), 'Emerson' Moises Costa, Djalma Feitosa Dias 'Djalminha' Francisco Gozalez Perez 'Fran' (Walter Pandiani 71), Roy Makaay
Manager: Javier Irureta

Referee: Gilles Veissiere (France) **Att:** 35,508

RIO GRAND: Captaining United for the first time, Rio Ferdinand (above) receives congratulations of his team-mates after his first goal for the club put United 3-0 ahead against Deportivo.

TAKE HARTE: Free-kick specialist Ian Harte (left) fires United into the lead.

weakest team'

Fans taunt Victor as United sink Deportivo

Deadball specialist Ian Harte put United on their way by lashing home a 26th minute free-kick after Cesar Villar fouled the ever-dangerous Alan Smith on the edge of the penalty area.

Manager David O'Leary had emphasised the need to keep a clean sheet, but with Deportivo making little headway in midfield United were always able to counter attack swiftly.

Just six minutes in to the second-half United doubled their lead when Harte was sent scampering forward by Olivier Dacourt's fine pass and the Irishman delivered the ball in to the box where Smith darted between two defenders to head home the cross – his 15th goal of a thrilling season.

United continued to probe and went 3-0 up with just under a third of the match to play when Harte, once again in the thick of the action, delivered a dangerous corner in to the Deportivo area.

Substitute Juan Valeron made a mess of an attempted clearance and the ball fell for Rio Ferdinand to crash in a header for his first goal in United's colours.

It crowned a fantastic night for Ferdinand, skipper for the first time in the absence of the injured Lucas Radebe. It was his first goal for four years and capped a magnificent individual display.

The goal prompted United's delighted followers to chant their mocking song and soon forced Irureta in to making a switch to a more attacking formation.

Substitute Diego Tristan gave the Spaniards more craft and guile in attack, but Ferdinand and Dominic Matteo held firm in the heart of United's defence to keep that vital clean sheet.

Irureta conceded that his team were left with an awesome task to turn the tie round. "It will be difficult to reach the semi-final, but once we get back to the Riazor Stadium there is always hope. Miracles do happen in football, but Leeds are a strong team."

O'Leary mixed his delight with words of caution, knowing that Deportivo, unbeaten in their last 24 league games, would be a different proposition in their own backyard.

"The main thing was not to concede a goal and take whatever we got after that – so 3-0 is tremendous, but we've got to finish the job off," he said "It is only half-time and I've seen these results turned round before."

He had also seen a video tape of Deportivo's penultimate match in the group stage when they were 3-0 down to Paris St Germain after 55 minutes, yet hit back to win 4-3.

Bayern gain their revenge

BITTER Premiership rivals Manchester United crashed 1-0 at Old Trafford to a late goal by Sergio as Bayern Munich grabbed a sweet victory.

The Germans had been beaten by the Red Devils in the 1999 final in Barcelona when they led through Mario Basler until injury time before goals by Teddy Sheringham and Ole-Gunnar Solskjaer completed a European Cup, Premiership title and FA Cup treble for the men from Manchester.

This time it was the Bayern sub who turned the tables with an 86th minute winner which stunned most of the 66,584 crowd.

Arsenal had to come from behind to beat Valencia at Highbury – the first time the clubs had met since the Spanish team beat the Gunners in the Cup Winners Cup final in 1980.

Roberto Ayala netted for Hector Cupar's team four minutes before the interval, but the Gunners hit back in the second-half with two goals in three minutes from Thierry Henry and Ray Parlour.

Leeds would face the winners of the Arsenal-Valencia match if they got past Deportivo.

In the only tie not featuring an English club, Galatasaray produced a storming comeback to defeat favourites and holders Real Madrid in Istanbul.

Goals by Helguera and Claude Makelele put Madrid 2-0 up by half-time, but spurred on by a Umit Davala penalty just after the interval, the Turks went on to win with strikes from Hasan Sas and Mario Jardel, their Portuguese international forward.

It completed a fine double for Galatasaray, who had beaten Real 2-1 in the Super Cup final in Monaco at the beginning of the season.

Galatasaray's victory had not gone unnoticed and there were genuine fears that they could come face-to-face with United in the final just over 12 months after the dreadful scenes in Istbanbul in which fans Christopher Speight and Kevin Loftus died.

In the week building up to the Deportivo quarter-final at Elland Road, United also learned that former player David Rocastle, who played in the European Cup in the Howard Wilkinson era, had died of cancer at the age of 33. Rocastle had been a team-mate of David O'Leary at Arsenal.

Quarter-final first leg

Arsenal 2 (Henry, Parlour), Valencia 1 (Ayala)
Galatasaray 3 (Davala pen, Sas, Jardel), Real Madrid 2 (Helguera, Makelele)
Leeds United 3 (Harte, Smith, Ferdinand), Deportivo La Coruna 0
Manchester United 0, Bayern Munich 1 (Sergio)

English hopes are pinned on United

HOPES that David O'Leary would pitch his managerial skills against his old club, Arsenal, in the semi-final were dashed.

The Gunners were knocked out on the away-goals ruling by another big Spanish outfit, Valencia, who were guaranteed to provide United with another tough examination.

Arsene Wenger's side held out until 15 minutes from the end when big Norwegian striker John Carew scored the only goal of the game.

Valencia had been beaten by Real Madrid in the previous year's Champions League final by Real Madrid and now stood between United and a place in the 2001 final at the San Siro in Milan.

Hopes of an all-English final vanished as Manchester United crashed out in Germany. Already trailing 1-0 from the first leg, the Red Devils' task became even more difficult after Giovanni Elber scored inside five minutes.

Mehmet Scholl added a second before half-time and although Ryan Giggs pulled one back on 49 minutes, Bayern eased through 3-1 on aggregate to avenge their 1999 final defeat.

Before the kick-off a trickster sneaked on to the pitch in Manchester United kit and stood next to Andy Cole for the team photograph without anyone noticing.

Although hopes of an all-English final were sunk, the prospect of an all-Spanish were afloat.

Real Madrid marched in to the last four with a breathtaking first half display which wiped out Galatasary's first leg advantage. Raul (twice) and Ivan Helguera scored inside 37 minutes to blow away the shell-shocked Turks.

Quarter-final first leg

Bayern Munich 2 (Elber, Scholl), Manchester United 1 (Giggs)
Bayern Munich win 3-1 on agg
Deportivo La Coruna 2 (Djalminha pen, Tristan), Leeds United 0 *Leeds United win 3-2 on agg*
Real Madrid 3 (Raul 2, Helguera), Galatasaray 0
Real Madrid win 5-3 on agg
Valencia 1 (Carew), Arsenal 0 *2-2 on agg. Valencia win on away goals.*

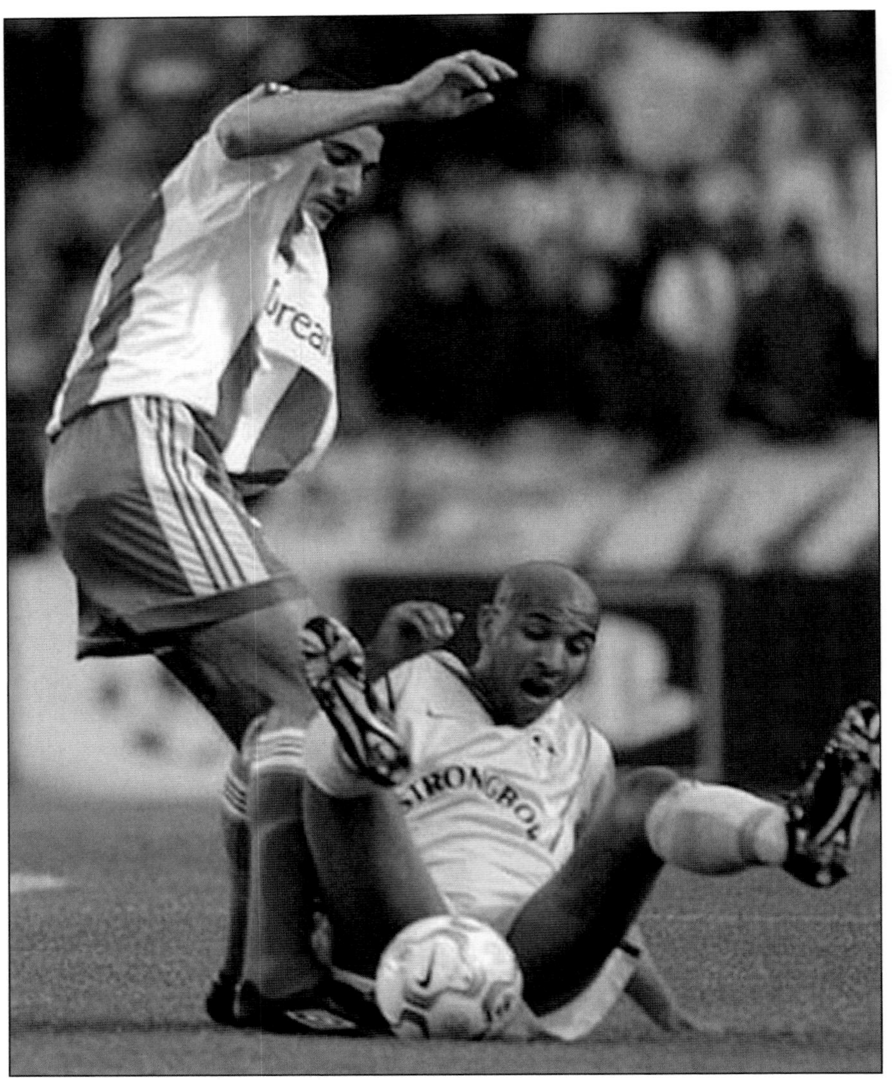

HOLDING COURT: United midfielder Olivier Dacourt endures an uncomfortable moment in Deportivo's Riazor Stadium.

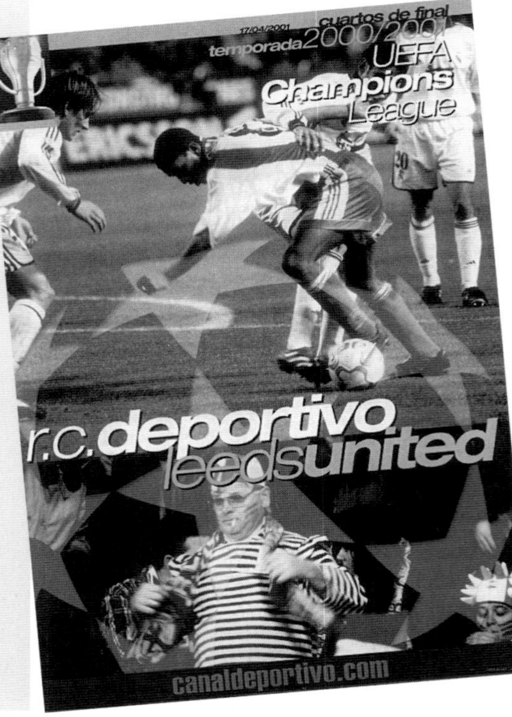

UEFA Champions League
Quarter-final, second leg
(at Riazor Stadium, Coruna)
Wednesday, April 17, 2001

Deportivo La Coruna 2

Leeds United 0

Leeds United win 3-2 on agg

Deportivo La Coruna: Jose Francisco Molina, Manuel Pablo, Nourredine Naybet, 'Donato' Gama da Silva, Enrique Fernandez Romero, 'Victor' Sanchez Del Amo (Diego Tristan 63), Mauro Silva, Francisco Gonzalez Perez 'Fran', Djalma Feitosa Dias 'Djalminha' (Juan Carlos Valeron 69), Roy Makaay, Walter Pandiani (Jose Oscar Turi Flores 79)
Goals: Djalminha pen 9, Tristan 73
Manager: Javier Irureta

Leeds United: Nigel Martyn, Danny Mills, Ian Harte, Dominic Matteo, Rio Ferdinand, Lee Bowyer, David Batty, Olivier Dacourt, Harry Kewell (Eirik Bakke 77), Alan Smith, Mark Viduka
Manager: David O'Leary

Referee: Stefano Braschi (Italy) **Att:** 36,500

United on the Riazor's edge

UNDER PRESSURE: Deportivo defender Nourredine Naybet hoofs the ball clear as United striker Alan Smith moves in for the kill.

UNITED rode their luck to survive a nerve-wracking ordeal in the Riazor Stadium before clinching a Champions League semi-final showdown with Valencia.

The three-goal cushion United had built up on home soil was just enough to see them through the sternest of Spanish inquisitions.

The final 17 minutes were torture for the pocket of 1,700 Leeds fans who had made the journey to the North-West corner of Spain as Deportivo pounded United seeking the goal that would take the tie in to extra-time.

It was a great effort by Deportivo, who took United apart at times, but they were made to pay for their cautious tactics at Elland Road.

O'Leary's boys cling on to claim place in semi-finals

It was tense stuff for the entire 90 minutes and United were pulled this way and that by the Spaniards slick passing and movement.

United's game plan of keeping it tight in the opening period was thrown in the Bay of Biscay when the home side grabbed the early goal they needed to get back in the tie.

The ball was curled into the box after just eight minutes and Harry Kewell pushed Victor to present Deportivo with a penalty which Brazilian midfielder Djalminha despatched past Nigel Martyn.

As the home support grew even more passionate, United were subjected to wave after wave of Coruna attacks but Rio Ferdinand and Dominic Matteo were heroic in the eye of the storm, while Martyn made crucial saves to deny Enrique Romero and Dutch international striker Roy Makaay.

Martyn had missed most of the first two phases of the competition with a serious groin injury which sidelined him for four months and Paul Robinson had played superbly as his deputy. But Martyn returned for the quarter-finals in tip-top form to keep Coruna at bay.

United knew that if they could score it would ease the pressure but, despite the efforts of Alan Smith, simply could not turn the tide towards the home goal.

United defended as though their lives depended on it and as the clock ticked beyond the hour mark, Deportivo went for broke by putting on striker Diego Tristan and attacking midfielder Juan Valeron for Victor and Djalminha.

Coach Javier Irureta's gamble paid off within minutes as Tristan fired home Valeron's low 73rd minute pass to the near post.

The tension went up a few more notches but battling Deportivo were unable to find that equaliser and referee Stephano Braschi's final whistle was greeted with relief and joy in equal measure by the United squad and their followers.

A relieved David O'Leary said: "I'm delighted for the players. What an adventure for this side at their first attempt in the Champions League, especially given the groups we've come through, the difficult circumstances we've faced and everything else which has been thrown at us.

"But to be in the last four of one of the greatest competitions in the world is all down to the players. It's an unbelieveable achievement and I'm amazed."

DOM ON THE SPOT: All eyes look for the officials after Dominic Matteo went close to breaking the deadlock for United against Valencia at Elland Road.

United draw

No birthday present

UNITED could not quite deliver the 43rd birthday present manager David O'Leary craved.

They were held 0-0 by a vastly experienced Valencia at Elland Road and knew they faced an uphill task in Spain where they had already come to grief in Barcelona and Coruna in their thrilling Champions League campaign.

Tickets for United's biggest game in 25 years sold out within hours.

Fans were clamouring to see United's youngsters take on a Valencia team which had been moulded by Hector Cupar in to one of the best on the continent.

Valencia did not possess world stars but they proved physically strong and mentally tough in a cut-and-thrust encounter.

It was a massive match, with 54 television channels giving live coverage to the game.

After Ian Harte tested Santiago Canizares' fingertips with a trademark free-kick, Nigel Martyn needed to be alert to keep out a spectatcular overhead kick by Norwegian international John Carew after Juan Sanchez's surge down United's left flank.

United were having their hands full containing the Spaniards, who also came close when the impressive Gazizka Mendieta looped a header against the bar.

United should have taken the lead just after the half-hour was up but Alan Smith glanced a close-range header wide of Canizares' left-hand post from just five yards.

United increased the tempo after the break as they attacked the Don Revie Stand and came within a whisker of breaking the deadlock when Lee Bowyer flicked on Harte's corner from the left and Dominic Matteo soared in at the back post only to see the bleach-haired Canizares claw the ball away on his goal-line.

The ever-willing Smith smacked in a volley as Leeds turned up the heat which led to yellow cards for Ruben Baraja and Amedeo Carboni which ruled them out of the return leg in the Mestalla Stadium.

United were forcing the issue and the woodwork came to Valencia's rescue as Smith chipped the ball over Canizares and Lee Bowyer headed against ther bar.

Having survived long spells of pressure Valencia came out of their trenches towards the end and Carew miscued a good opportunity wide after Mendieta's header picked him out in the box.

CENTRE OF ATTENTION: Lee Bowyer fends off Zlatko Zahovic (left) and an airborne Kily Gonzalez to get in a shot at Valencia's goal.

a blank

or boss O'Leary

Then, in injury time, substitute Vicente Rodriguez sent in a dipping shot which £18 million Rio Ferdinand headed off the line to keep United's dreams alive.

Valencia's defence may have lacked pace, but it was packed with experience and craft. Like fellow Spanish side Real Madrid they had managed to keep United's eager attack at arm's length.

"We would have liked to have scored a couple of goals but we were up against a very good side. Valencia have good players and an excellent system, was O'Leary's verdict.

He added: "I don't think this tie is over," believing his men had the firepower to find the net in the return leg so a score draw would be good enough to send Leeds through.

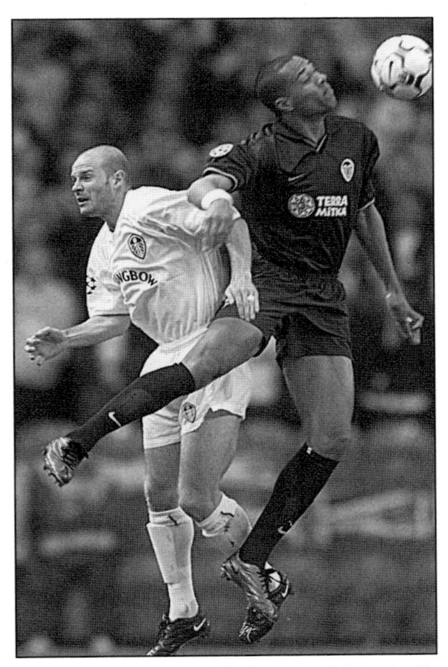

DANNY BOY: Danny Mills in an aerial dual with big striker John Carew.

Advantage to Bayern

BRAZILIAN striker Gionanni Elber netted the only goal of the semi-finals as Bayern Munich pulled off a superb 1-0 win at Real Madrid.

The Germans were on hot a hot streak of form, having topped both groups in the early phases and defeated Manchester United twice in the quarter-finals.

Defensively they were very strong, with national goalkeeper Oliver Kahn proving an inspiration in goal and Mehmet Scholl sparkling in midfield.

Semi-finals, first leg

Leeds United 0, Valencia 0

Real Madrid 0, Bayern Munich 1 (Elber)

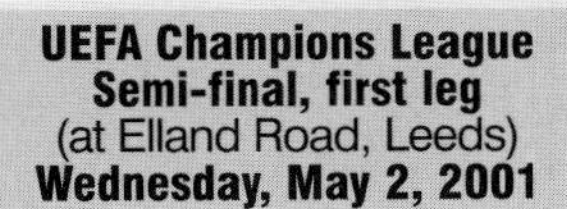

UEFA Champions League
Semi-final, first leg
(at Elland Road, Leeds)
Wednesday, May 2, 2001

Leeds United 0

Valencia 0

Leeds United: Nigel Martyn, Danny Mills, Ian Harte, Dominic Matteo, Rio Ferdinand, Lee Bowyer, David Batty, Olivier Dacourt, Harry Kewell, Alan Smith, Mark Viduka
Manager: David O'Leary

Valencia: Jose Santiago Canizares, Jocelyn Angloma, Roberto Fabian Ayala, Mauricio Pellegrino, Amedeo Carboni, Gaizka Mendieta, Kily Gonzalez (Rodriguez Guillen Vicente 89), David Albeda, Ruben Baraja, Juan Sanchez (Zlatko Zahovic 66), John Carew
Manager: Hector Raul Cupar

Referee: Pierluigi Collina (Italy) **Att:** 36,437

Pain in Spain

Smith off as run ended

UNITED'S European dream finally ended as it had begun with a comprehensive defeat in Spain.

The adventure had started with a 4-0 thumping in Barcelona and 15 matches later ground to a halt in Valencia at the end of a 3-0 defeat.

O'Leary's team could have little complaint as they finished in a mess in the Mestalla Stadium where Valencia maintained their decade-long unbeaten record in Europe.

United's pre-match preparations were rocked by UEFA on the eve of the game. They ruled that Lee Bowyer would receive a three-match ban – starting in Valencia – for an alleged stamp on Juan Sanchez in the first leg.

Leading referee Pierluigi Collina, whose handing of the first leg had drawn high praise, had seen nothing wrong with the incident and Bowyer said he had merely tried to step over his opponent.

That did not wash with UEFA, who had spotted the incident on video and to rub salt in to Bowyer's wounds said he would not be able to appeal against the ban until three days after the Valencia return leg.

United's sense of injustice grew after just 16 minutes when Sanchez stooped to meet Gaizka Mendieta's curling cross from the left and the ball appeared to hit him on the forearm and cannon in to the net.

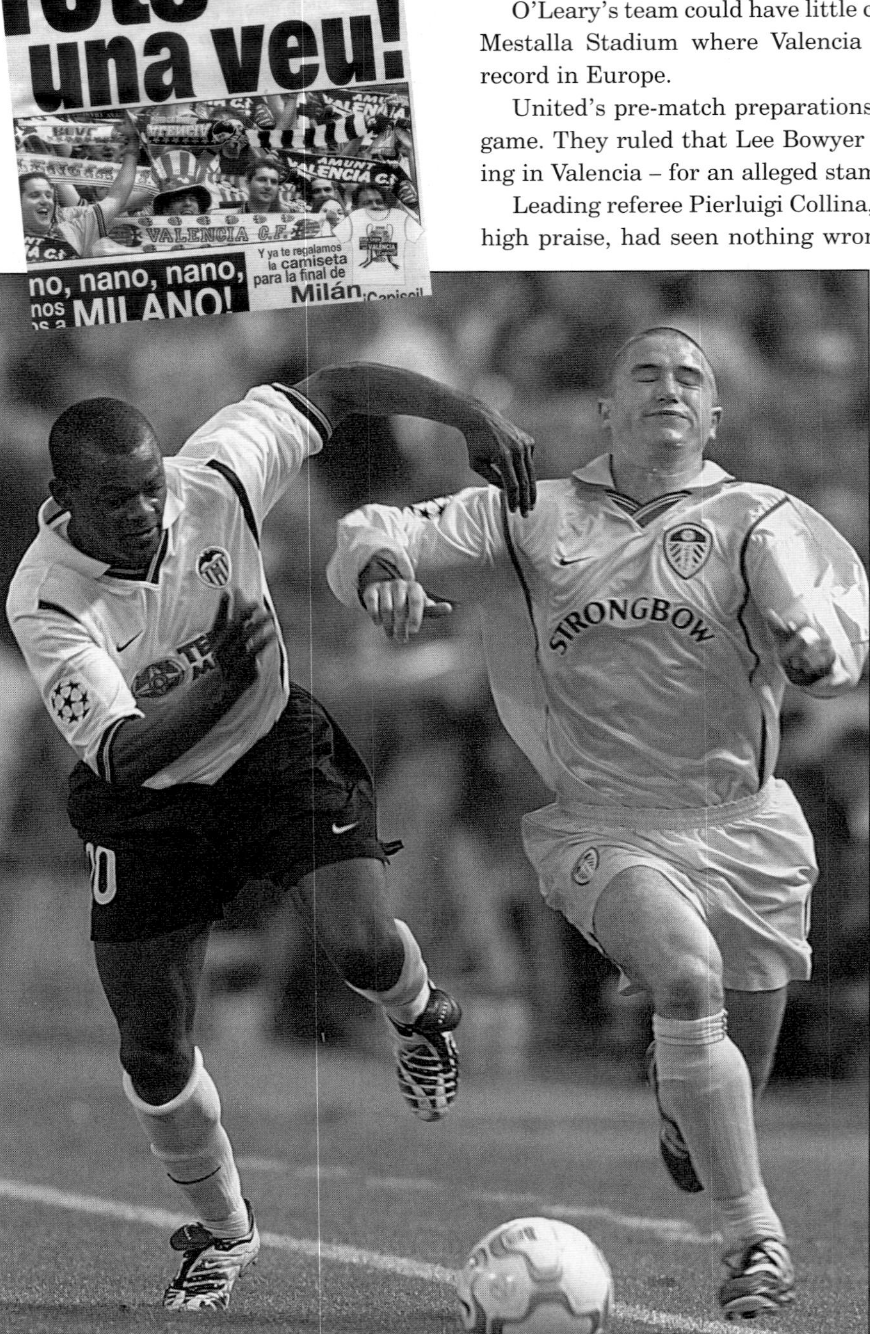

CLOSE SHAVE: Harry Kewell, sporting one of the crew-cuts which the United squad had prior to the match in Valencia, sprints past Jocelyn Angloma.

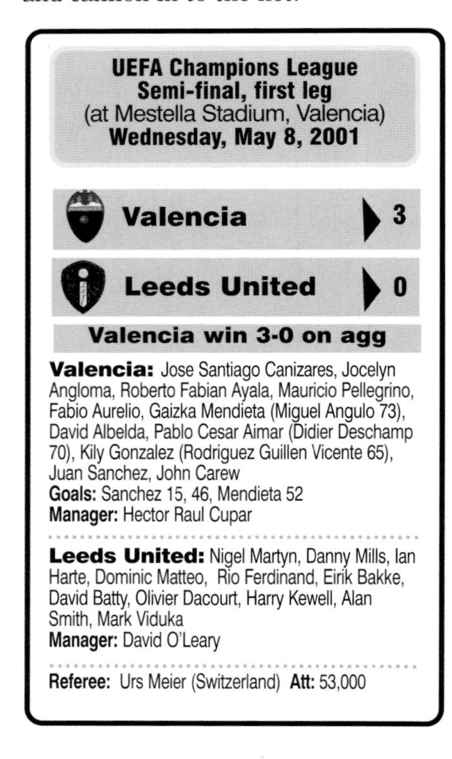

UEFA Champions League
Semi-final, first leg
(at Mestella Stadium, Valencia)
Wednesday, May 8, 2001

Valencia	**3**
Leeds United	**0**

Valencia win 3-0 on agg

Valencia: Jose Santiago Canizares, Jocelyn Angloma, Roberto Fabian Ayala, Mauricio Pellegrino, Fabio Aurelio, Gaizka Mendieta (Miguel Angulo 73), David Albelda, Pablo Cesar Aimar (Didier Deschamp 70), Kily Gonzalez (Rodriguez Guillen Vicente 65), Juan Sanchez, John Carew
Goals: Sanchez 15, 46, Mendieta 52
Manager: Hector Raul Cupar

Leeds United: Nigel Martyn, Danny Mills, Ian Harte, Dominic Matteo, Rio Ferdinand, Eirik Bakke, David Batty, Olivier Dacourt, Harry Kewell, Alan Smith, Mark Viduka
Manager: David O'Leary

Referee: Urs Meier (Switzerland) **Att:** 53,000

for United

by Valencia

Despite appeals to Swiss referee Urs Meier the goal stood. "It was a disgraceful decision," railed O'Leary.

His team managed to regain their composure and although they had come under a huge amount of pressure reached half-time still only 1-0 down.

The Irishman knew that if they could keep it tight and pinch a goal United would be gaining the upper hand. But those plans were torn up just 100 seconds after the restart when Sanchez took advantage of space in front of United's defence to fire past Martyn from 25 yards.

A tie which was gradually slipping from United's grasp vanished six minutes later when the outstanding Mendieta drove in another long range effort.

United were down and out, and a bad night became even worse in the dying seconds of injury time when a frustrated Alan Smith was red-carded for a lunge at substitute Vicente Rodriguez.

It was a sour note on which to end a magnificent Champions League campaign in which United had continually upset the odds.

O'Leary had no complaints about the result in Valencia. "The best team won", was his blunt assessment.

Munich on the march

BAYERN Munich completed the double over Real Madrid to book their final spot against Valencia in Milan.

An early Munich goal by Giovanni Elber was wiped out by Luis Figo to give Real Madrid hope but Jens Jermies netted a 35th minute winner for the Germans.

Semi-final, second leg

Valencia 3 (Sanchez 2, Mendieta), Leeds United 0
Valencia win 3-0 on agg
Bayern Munich 2 (Elber, Jermies), Real Madrid 1 (Figo)
Bayern Munich win 3-1 on agg

END OF THE LINE: Leeds skipper Rio Ferdinand crouches in misery at the final whistle in Valencia ending United's exciting Champions League adventure.

Munich's king Kahn

PENALTIES were the name of the game as Bayern Munich held their nerve to beat Valencia in a nerve-jangling final in the San Siro Stadium in Milan.

The Spaniards were given the perfect start when Gaizka Mendieta netted a third minute penalty. Bayern, who had won their 17th Bundeslegia title three days earlier, levelled with a spot-kick of their own by Steffan Effenberg.

Extra-time failed to split the teams and the match was decided by penalties, Oliver Kahn saving Valencia's fifth penalty to give Bayern their first European Cup since 1976.

British interest in the final was confined to Munich's 19-year-old midfielder, Owen Hargreaves, whose energetic performance earned him an England call-up from Sven-Goran Eriksson.

Final
(San Siro Stadium, Milan)
May 23, 2001
Bayern Munich 1
Valencia 1
(after extra-time, Bayern Munich win 5-4 on penalties)

Bayern Munich: Kahn, Sagnol, Lizarazu, Kuffour, Andersson, Linke, Scholl (Sergio 108), Salihamidzic (Jancker HT), Elber (Zickler 102), Hargreaves, Effenberg
Goal: Effenberg 51 pen
Manager: Ottmar Hitzfeld
Valencia: Canizares, Angloma, Carboni, Ayala (Djukic 89), Pellegrino, Baraja, Aimar (Albelda HT), Kily Gonzalez, Sanchez (Zahovic 65), Mendieta, Carew
Goal: Mendieta 3 pen
Manager: Hector Raul Cupar
Referee: Dick Jol (Holland)
Attendance: 71,500

Leading scorers: 9 – Jardel (Galatasaray), Shevchenko (AC Milan), 7 – Koller (Anderlecht), Raul (Real Madrid), Smith (Leeds United), Vorobei (Shaktjhor Donetsk)

Return to UEFA Cup

FOUR games – four defeats. That was United's Champions League record in Spain.

They were beaten by La Liga sides Barcelona, Real Madrid, Deportivo La Coruna and Valencia – but could still cut the mustard in the Premiership. Despite their punishing schedule, David O'Leary's team were able to finish strongly to book a return ticket to Europe.

United resumed domestic duty five days after their Valencia defeat to wrap up the Premiership campaign by beating Bradford City 6-1 and Leicester 3-1 at Elland Road.

United had won eight of their last nine league matches but Liverpool's 4-0 thumping of Charlton on the last day of the season at Anfield earned the Merseyside club third place by a point and a passport to the Champions League behind winners Manchester United and runners-up Arsenal.

That left United back in the UEFA Cup knowing they still had some work to do to break into the elite in English football.

United were joined in the first round of the 2001/02 UEFA Cup by Chelsea, Ipswich Town and Aston Villa, one of three Intertoto Cup winners, as England's representatives.

Maritimo, United's first round opponents, came through their qualifying round with home and away victories over Sarajevo.

A total of 82 clubs were involved in the qualifying round. Teams eliminated from the qualifying stages of the Champions League also dropped into the UEFA Cup.

Clubs who finished third in their group in the first phase of the Champions League switched to the UEFA Cup third round.

READY FOR THE OFF: United's 2001/02 squad which set off in pursuit of UEFA Cup glory. Back row, from left to right: Danny Hay, Mark Viduka, Michael Duberry, Dominic Matteo, Danny Milosevic, Nigel Martyn, Paul Robinson, Jonathan Woodgate, Lucas Radebe, Eirik Bakke. Middle row: Dave Hancock (physiotherapist), Sean Hardy (kit man), Steve Sutton (goalkeeping coach), Steve McGregor, Gary Kelly, David Batty, Ian Harte, Danny Mills, Lee Bowyer, Robbie Keane, Brian Kidd (coach), Eddie Gray (assistant manager), Roy Aitken (second team coach). Front row: Alan Maybury, Jason Wilcox, Michael Bridges, Harry Kewell, Peter Ridsdale (chairman), Rio Ferdinand, David O'Leary (manager). Olivier Dacourt, Alan Smith, Stephen McPhail, Jacob Burns.

Clubs in the UEFA Cup qualification shake-up

Qualifying Round, first leg

AEK Athens 6 (Tsartas, Zagorakis, Lakis, Nikolaidis 2, Konstantinidis), Grevenmacher 0
Ararat Erevan 0, Hapoel Tel Aviv 2 (Toema, Osterc)
Atlantas 0, Rapid Bucharest 4 (Schumacher, Pancu, Nita, Sumudica)
Birkirkara 0, Lokomotiv Tbilisi 0
Brasov 5 (Buga, Sandor, Isaila, Badea), Mika 1 (Nazaryan)
Brondby 2 (Jonson, Bagger), Shelbourne 0.
Brugge 4 (Lange 2, Lembi, Medoza), Akranes 0
Cosmos 0, Rapid Vienna 1 (Wallner)
CSKA Kiev 2 (Kostyshyn, Maltsey), Jokerit 0
Cwmbran Town 0, Slovan Bratislava 4 (Mojic, Obzera, Vittek, Sobona)
Debrecen 3 (Bajzat, Ulveczki, Tiber), Otaci 0
Dinaburg 2 (Sorosh, Pucinskas), Osijek 1 (Vuka)
Dynamo Bucharest 1 (Niculescu), Dynamo Tirana 0
Dynamo Tbilisi 2 (Daraselia, Mikuchadze), BATE Borisov 1 (Hanchryk)
Dynamo Zagreb 1 (Gondzic), Flora 0
Etzella 0, Legia 4 (Magiera, Kucharski, Wrobleswki, Mierzejewski)
Fylkir 2 (McFarlane, Stigsson), Pogon 1 (Dzwigala).
Glenavon 0, Kilmarnock 1 (Innes)
HB Torshavn 2 (Mortansson 2), Graz 2 (Akwuegbu 2)
HJK Helsinki 2 (Kallio, Jensen), Ventspils 1 (Rimkus)
Longford Town 1 (O'Connor), Litech Lovech 1 (Yurukov)
Maccabi Tel Aviv 6 (Ben Dayan, Dago 3, Banin, Biton), Zalgiris Vilnius 0
Maritimo 1 (Dinda), Sarajevo 0
Matador Puchev 3 (Breska, Pernis, Belak), Sliema Wanderers 0
Midtjylland 1 (Pimpong), Glentoran 1 (Glendinning)
MyPa 1 (Lindberg), Helsingborg 3 (Eklund, Prica, Linstrom)
Neftchi 0, Gorica 0
Obilic 4 (Simonovic, Zoric, Mladenovic, Filipovic), Gl Gotu 0
Olimpija 4 (Komac, Tiganj, Tigank, Calleja), Shafa 0
Olympiakos 2 (Themistocleous, Kozlej), Dunaferr 2 (Sowunmi, Tokoli)
Pelister 0, St Gallen 2 (Pereira, Dal Santo)
Polonia 4 (Tarachulski 2, Moskal 2), TNS Llansantffraid 0
Ruzomberok 3 (Fabula 2, Oravec), Belshina 1 (Rak)
Shakhtjor Soligorsk 1 (Padrez), CSKA Sofia 2 (Mantchev, Giglio)
SK Tirana 3 (Foruzi 2, Helezei), Apollon 2 (Zoumparis)
Santa Coloma 0, Partizan Belgrade 1 (Cakar)
Trans 1 (Gruznov), Elfsborg 3 (Luncstrom, Andreasson 2)
Vaduz 3 (Niederhauser, Merenda 2), Varteks 3 (Bjelanovic 3)
Vardar 0, Standard Liege 3 (Meyssen, Blay, Walem)
Viking 1 (Fuglestad), Brotnjo 0
Zimbru Chisinau 0, Gaziantep 0

Qualifying round, second leg

Akranes 1 (Karvelsson), Brugges 6 (Lembi 2, Englebert, Van Der Hayden, Mendoza, Martens) *Brugges win 10-0 on agg*
Apollon 3 (Miserdovski, Kavazis, Spoljaric), SK Tirana 1 (Fortuzi) *Apollon win 5-4 on agg*
BATE Borisov 4 (Lisovsky, Kutuzov pen, Loshankov, Grigoriv), Dynamo Tbilisi 0 *BATE Borisov win 5-2 on agg*
Belshina 0, Ruzomberok 0 *Ruzomberok win 3-1 on agg*
Brotnjo 1 (Jerkovic), Viking 1 (Tihinen) *Viking win 2-1 on agg*
CSKA Sofia 3 (Mantchev 2, Gglio), Shaktjor Soligorsk 1 (Bezborodov) *CSKA Sofia win 5-2 on agg*
Dynamo Tirana 1 (Dhembi), Dynamo Bucharest 3 (Niculescu, Mihalcea, Dragan) *Dynamo Bucharest win 4-1 on agg*
Dunaferr 2 (Sowunmi, Tokoli), Olympiakos 4 (Kozlej, Radosavljevic, Themistocleous, Aristocleous) *Olympiakos win 6-4 on agg*
Elfsborg 5 (Andreasson 3, Klarstrom 2), Trans 0 *Elfsborg win 8-1 on agg*
Flora 0, Dynamo Zagreb 1 (Allas og) *Dynamo Zagreb win 2-0 on agg*
Gaziantep 4 (Fatih, Romashenko, Ozer, Mustafa), Zimbri Chisinau 1 (Cebotariu) *Gaziantep win 4-1 on agg*
Gl Gotu 1 (Jarnskor pen), Obilic 1 (Simonovic) *Obilic win 5-1 on agg*
Glentoran 0, Midtylland 4 (Skoubo 2, From, Pimpong) *Midtylland win 5-1 on agg*
Gorica 1 (Tezacki), Neftchi 0 *Gorica win 1-0 on agg*
Graz 4 (Brunmayr 2, Tokic, Milinkovic), Torshavn 0 *Graz win 4-2 on agg*
Grevenmacher 0, AEK Athens 2 (Lakis, Konstantinidis) *AEK Athens win 8-0 on agg*
Hapoel Tel Aviv 3 (Psterc, Domb, Udi), Ararat Erevan 0 *Hapoel Tel Aviv win 5-0 on agg*
Helsingborg 2 (Prica, Eklund), MyPa 1 (Puhakainen) *Hesingborg win 5-2 on agg*
Jokerit 0, CSKA Kiev 2 (Zakarlyuka, Kossyrin) *CSKA Kiev win 4-0 on agg*
Kilmarnock 1 (Mitchell), Glenavon 0 *Kilmarnock win 2-0 on agg*
Legia Warsaw 2 (Mierzejewski, Karwan), Etzella 1 (Leweck) *Legia Warsaw win 6-1 on agg*
Litech Lovech 2 (Jancovic 2 – 1 pen), Longford Town 0 *Litech Lovech win 3-1 on agg*
Lokomotiv Tbilisi 1 (Anchabadze), Birkikara 1 (Zahra) *1-1 on agg. Birkikara win on away goals*
Mika 0, Brasov 2 (Sandor, Buga) *Brasov win 7-1 on agg*
Osijek 1 (Balatinec pen), Dinaburg 0 *2-2 on agg. Osijek win on away goals*
Otaci 1 (Samkov pen), Debrecen 0 *Debrecen win 2-1 on agg*
Partizan Belgrade 7 (Ivic 2, Delibasic, Cakar 2-1 pen, Vukic, Iliev), Santa Coloma 1 (Ariaz pen) *Partizan Belgrade win 8-1 on agg*
Pogon 1 (Dzwigala), Fylkir 1 (Johnsson) *Fylkir win 3-2 on agg*
Rapid Bucharest 8 (Nita 2, Sumudica 2 – 1 pen, Schumacher, Bogdanovic 2, Bratu), Atlantas 0 *Rapid Bucharest win 12-0 on agg*
Rapid Vienna 2 (Lagonikakis 2), Cosmos 0 *Rapid Vienna win 3-0 on agg*
Sarajevo 0, Maritimo 1 (Bruno) *Maritimo win 2-0 on agg*
Shafa 0, Olimpija 3 (Kosic, Komac, Jolic) *Olympjia win 7-0 on agg*
Shelbourne 0, Brondby 3 (Bagger, Jorgensen, Madsen) *Brondby win 5-0 on agg*
Sliema Wanderers 2 (Busuttil, Said), Matador 1 (Pernis pen) *Matador win 4-2 on agg*
Slovan Bratislava 1 (Meszaros), Cwmbran Town 0 *Slovan Bratislava win 5-0 on agg*
St Gallen 2 (Gane 2), Pelister 3 (Dal Santo og), Deliovski, Stojmenovski) *St Gallen win 4-3 on agg*
Standard Liege 3 (Lukunku 2, Walem), Vardar 1 (Abazi) *Standard Liege win 6-1 on agg*
TNS Llanantffraid 0, Polonia Warzaw 2 (Bak, Bartczak) at Wrexham *Polonia Warsaw win 6-0 on agg*
Varteks 6 (Mumiek pen, Bjelanovic, Andricevic, Drobne 2, Rezic), Vaduz 1 (Merenda) *Varteks win 9-4 on agg*
Ventspils 0, HJK Helsinki 1 (Roiha) *HJK Helsinki win 3-1 on agg*
Zalgiris Vilnius 0, Maccabi Tel Aviv 1 (Goldberg) *Maccabi Tel Aviv win 7-0 on agg*

***Byes:** AC Milan, Anzhi, Bordeaux, Chelsea, Chernomorets, Dnepr, Dynamo Moscow, Fiorentina, Freiburg, Genclerbirligi, Hertha Berlin, Hibernian, Inter Milan, Ipswich Town, Karnten, Leeds United, Liberec, Odd Grenland, Olomouc, PAOK Salonika, Pribram,Real Zaragoza, Roda, Sedan, Servette, Silkeborg, Sporting Lisbon, Strasbourg, Torpedo Moscow, Twente Enschede, Union Berlin, Utrecht, Viktoria Zizkov, Valencia, Westerlo.*

Intertoto Cup winners: Aston Villa, Troyes, Paris St Germain and teams eliminated from the Champions League third qualifying round – Ajax, FC Copenhagen, Grasshoppers, Hadjuk Split, Haka, Halmstad, Inter Bratislava, Levski Sofia, Parma, Rangers, Red Star Belgrade, Shakhtjor Donetsk, Slavia Prague, Steaua Bucharest, Tirol Innsbruck, Wisla Krakow.

No fun in Funchal

DAVID O'Leary made it plain that United's new target for 2001-02 would be the Premiership.

They certainly began well enough and were top of the Premiership – including a 2-1 victory at Arsenal – as they headed to Madeira to take on Maritimo.

United had come a long way in the three years since they last scraped past the Portuguese League side under George Graham and were expected to win at a canter.

With a heroic Champions League campaign behind them, United were regarded as a big fish in the UEFA Cup sea.

But they made a spluttering start to their campaign in more ways than one.

Just ten minutes after take off to Madeira the United plane turned round and returned to Leeds/Bradford airport upon hearing of UEFA's decision to postpone all European games in the wake of the September 11 Twin Towers terrorist attack in New York.

The Maritimo game was put back a week and when it did start United may well have been still buckled up on the plane.

Despite missing Alan Smith, Lee Bowyer, Olivier Dacourt and Eirik Bakke, United still had enough big name players to put Maritimo to the sword.

Instead they gave a shoddy display which was summed up by the nature of the goal they conceded to give the islanders a shock 1-0 victory.

United had fashioned next to nothing in the opening half-hour and seemed to have little appetite for the game. As the match wore on the home side grew in confidence while Leeds' discomfort grew. On 34 minutes 'Bruno ' Fernandes punted a 35-yard free-kick into the box where it was missed by everybody and ended up in the back of Nigel Martyn's net.

While Maritimo threatened to add to their lead, United struggled to get their passing game together and the nearest they came was an Ian Harte free-kick on the stroke of half-time and a last-minute opportunity for former Inter Milan striker Robbie Keane, who was making his United European debut having been ineligble for the Champions League the previous season.

The heady evenings against the likes of Barcelona, AC Milan, Lazio and Anderlecht seemed a million miles away from the 10,000 capacity Barreiros Stadium on a small Atlantic island.

An unhappy O'Leary dismissed any thoughts of his team being complacent, but believed his side had the quality to turn the tie round.

"I hope it is a kick up the backside for the players. If it isn't then we're going to go out of this competition early doors," he said.

ME AND MY SHADOW: Ian Harte is in hot pursuit of Maritimo's 'Andre' Neles.

It's any Port in a storm for United

UEFA Cup
First round, first leg
(at Barreiros Stadium, Funchal)
Thursday, September 20, 2001

Maritimo 1

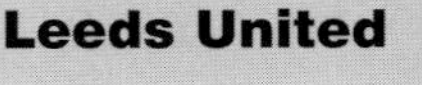

Leeds United 0

Maritimo: Nelson Vasco, Eloii Da Jesus Vieire Alves 'Albertino', Paulo Sergio Da Silva, Mitchel van Der Gaag, Nuno Miguel Pedro De Sousa 'Briguel', Jailton Santos ''Dinda' (Joel Dos Santos 85), Jose Antonio Zeca, Marcelo Pereira Fernandes 'Bruno', Daniel Kenedy, 'Andre' Moreira Neles (Alan Da Costa Silva 75), Joaquim Manuel Lima Ferraz 'Quim' (Eire Freire Gomes 'Gaucho' 61)
Goal: Bruno 32
Manager: Nelo Vingada

Leeds United: Nigel Martyn, Danny Mills, Ian Harte, Rio Ferdinand, Dominic Matteo, Gary Kelly, David Batty, Stephen McPhail (Jason Wilcox 58), Harry Kewell, Robbie Keane, Mark Viduka
Manager: David O'Leary

Referee: Jack Van Hulten (Holland) **Att:** 10,500

UEFA Cup
First round, first leg
(at Elland Road, Leeds)
Thurssday, September 27, 2001

Leeds United	**3**
Maritimo	**0**

Leeds United win 3-0 on agg

Leeds United: Nigel Martyn, Danny Mills, Ian Harte, Dominic Matteo, Rio Ferdinand, Eirik Bakke, David Batty, Olivier Dacourt, Harry Kewell, Robbie Keane, Mark Viduka
Goals: Keane 20, Kewell 37, Bakke 82
Manager: David O'Leary

Maritimo: Nelson Vasco, Eloi Da Jesus Vieire Alves 'Albertino', Paulo Sergio Da Silva, Mitchel Van Der Gaag, Nuno Miguel Pedro De Sousa 'Briguel', Adelino Augusto Lopes 'Lino", Jailton Santos 'Dinda' (Joel Dos Santos 16 - Eirc Freire Gomes 'Gaucho HT), Jose Antonio Zeca, Marcelo Perira Fernandes 'Bruno' (Andre' Moreira Neles 59), Daniel Kenedy, Joquim Manuel Lima Ferraz 'Quim'
Manager: Nelo Vingada

Referee: Stefano Farina (Italy) **Att:** 38,125

KEEN AS MUSTARD: Striker Robbie Keane shakes off three Maritimo defenders to blast United ahead at Elland Road with his first European goal for the club.

It's plain sailing against Maritimo

NORMAL service was resumed as a night of potential disaster turned in to one of relative comfort for United.

Goals by Robbie Keane, Harry Kewell and Eirik Bakke saw them cruise to a 3-0 win over Maritimo who were brave, but outclassed.

Unlike the first game, United looked as though they meant business and took just 20 minutes to get on level terms when David Batty hoisted a long ball over the top of a square defence and Robbie Keane wriggled away from his minders to despatch an angled drive past goalkeeper Nelson Vasco.

United were up and running and the Portuguese were undone by another long pass on 37 minutes when Rio Ferdinand slid the ball down Maritimo's right flank, Mark Viduka took the ball on to the byeline and crossed firmly to the back post where fellow Australian Harry Kewell tucked away a header.

With Olivier Dacourt running the midfield with Batty, United were in firm control and Maritimo were reduced to taking long range pot shots at Nigel Martyn, but only the Brazilian Dinda was able to call the United keeper in to action.

With half an hour left to find a goal to get his team back in business Maritimo manager Nelo Vingada went for broke by reshaping his side to include two strikers and a couple of wingers.

But no sooner had Maritimo settled in to their new pattern then the issue was settled when Kewell broke free down the left. His shot crashed against the goalkeeper and the energetic Bakke drove in the loose ball.

Maritimo's heads dropped to their chins and Leeds should have added to their goal tally but missed several chances, most falling to the left foot of Robbie Keane.

HARRY ON HIGH: An airborne Harry Kewell heads United 2-0 up against Maritimo.

But United did not need the insurance of an extra goal and a big crowd, drawn to Elland Road by cut-price tickets, managed to revive memories of the previous season's great European nights with bags of appreciative vocal support.

Tractor Boys sink Torpedo in Russia

UNFANCIED Ipswich Town turned on the style in Moscow to sink Torpedo 2-1 (3-2 on agg) with second half goals by Finidi George and Marcus Stewart (penalty).

Aston Villa paid for a sloppy home performance and went out against Varteks.

First round, first leg

AEK Athens 2 (Tsartas pen, Nikolaidis), Hibernian 0
Ajax 2 (Ibrahimovic, Machlas), Apollon 0
Aston Villa 2 (Angel 2), Varteks 3 (Bjelanovic 2, Karic)
BATE Borisov 0, AC Milan 2 (Shevchenko, Moreno)
Bordeaux 5 (Pauleta 2, Christian, Dugarry 2), Debrecen 1 (Tiber)
Celta Vigo 4 (Karpin 2, Edu, Katanha pen), Sigma Olomouc 0
Chelsea 3 (Gudjohnsen 2, Lampard), Leveski Sofia 0
Chernomrets 0, Valencia 1 (Mista)
CSKA Sofia 3 (Mantchev 2, Panev), Shakhtjor Donetsk 0
Dynamo Bucharest 1 (Mihalcea pen), Grasshoppers 3 (Chapuisat, Nunez, Mwaruwaru)
Dnepr 0, Fiorentina 0 in Kryvyi Rih
Dynamo Moscow 1 (Khazov), Birkikara 0
Dynamo Zagreb 2 (Agic, Sedlovski), Maccabi Tel Aviv 2 (Goldberg, Dago)
FC Copenhagen 2 (Fernandez 2), Obilic 0
Genclerbirligi 1 (Zdebel), Halmstad 1 (Selakovic)
Gorica 1 (Tezacki), Osijek 2 (Turkovic, Besirevic)
Hadjuk Split 2 (Deranja, Srna), Wisla Kracow 2 (Zurawski, Moskalewicz)
Haka 1 (Vaisanen pen), Union Berlin 1 (Ristic)
Hapoel Tel Aviv 1 (Ryndziuk og), Gaziantep 0
Inter Bratislava 1 (Kratchochvil), Litechs Lovech 0
Inter Milan 3 (Dalmmat, Kallon, Di Baggio), Brasov 0 in Trieste
Ipswich Town 1 (Bramble), Torpedo Moscow 1 (Vyazmikin)
Karnten 0, PAOK Salonika 0 in Graz
Kilmarnock 1 (Dargo), Viking 1 (Sanne)
Legia Warsaw 4 (Karwan, Vukovic, Kucharski 2), Elfsborg 1 (Lundstrom)
Liberec 2 (Baffour, Nezmar), Slovan Bratislava 0
Maritimo 1 (Bruno), Leeds United 0
Matador Ouchev 0, Freiberg 0
Midtylland 0, Sporting Lisbon 3 (Babb, Beto, Jardel)
Odd Greland 2 (Fevang, Van Ankeren), Helsingborg 2 (Hansson, Dos Santos)
Olimpija 2 (Zioncar 2), Brondby 4 (Bagger, Johansen pen, Niznik 2 – 1 pen)
Olympiakos 2 (Aristocleous, Radosavljevic), Brugges 2 (Verheyen, Clement)
Paris St Germain 0, Rapid Bucharest 0
Parma 1 (Milosevic pen), HJK Helsinki 0
Partizan Belgrade 1 (Bajic), Rapid Vienna 0
Polonia 1 (Bak), Twente Enschede 2 (Kollman, Van Der Laan) in Lodz
Pribram 4 (Kulic 3, Otepka), Sedan 0
Real Zaragoza 3 (Yordi, Juanele, Jose Ignacio), Silkeborg 0
Roda 3 (Nygaard, Anastasiou 2), Fylkir 0
Servette 1 (Oruma), Slavia Prague 0
St Gallen 2 (Jefferson, Mokoena), Steaua Bucharest 1 (Neagu)
Standard Liege 2 (Moriera 2), Strasbourg 0
Troyes 6 (Loko 2, Boutal 3, Meniri), Ruzomberok 1 (Kurty)
Utrecht 3 (Van Den Bergh, Tanghe, Glusevic), Graz 0
Viktoria Zizkov 0, Tirol Innsbruck 0
Westerlo 0, Hertha Berlin 2 (Schmidt, Beinlich)

First round, second leg

AC Milan 4 (Rui Costa, Moreno, Sarr, Inzaghi pen), BATE Borisov 0 *AC Milan win 6-0 on agg*
Apollon 0, Ajax 3 (Van Der Vaart, Ibrahimovic, Wamberto) in Nicosia *Ajaz win 5-0 on agg*
Birkikara 0, Dynamo Moscow 0 *Dynamo Moscow win 1-0 on agg*
Brasov 0, Inter Milan 3 (Ventola 2, Guglielminpietro) *Inter Milan win 6-0 on agg*
Brondby 0, Olimpija 0 *Brondby win 4-2 on agg*
Brugges 7 (Lange 2, Sillah, Martens, Englebert, Simons, Ceh), Olympiakos 1 (Themistocleous) *Brugge win 9-3 on agg*
Debrecen 3 (Plokai, Kerekes 2 – 1 pen), Bordeaux 1 (Pauleta) *Bordeaux win 6-4 on agg*
Elsborg 1 (Karlsson), Legia Warsaw 6 (Yahaya, Sokokowski 2, Skaw, Kucharski, Kielbowicz) *Legia Warsaw win 10-2*
Fiorentina 2 (Adani, Chiesa), Dnepr 1 (Slabishev) *Fiorentina win 2-1 on agg*
Freiburg 2 (Coulibaly, Tanko), Matador Puchev 1 (Pernis) *Freiburg win 2-1 on agg*
Fylkir 1 (Johannesson), Roda 3 (Zafarin, Berglund, Anastasiou) *Roda win 6-1 on agg*
Gaziantep 1 (Ryndziuk), Hapoel Tel Aviv 1 (Osterc) *Hapoel Tel Aviv win 2-1 on agg*
Grasshoppers 3 (Baturina, Chapuisat, Morales), Dynamo Bucharest 1 (Mihalcea pen) *Grasshoppers win 6-2 on agg*
Graz 3 (Bazina, Brunmayr, Akwuegbu), Utrecht 3 (Kuijt, Zwaanswijk, Jochemsen) *Utrecht win 6-3 on agg*
Halmstad 1 (Arvidsson), Genclerbirligi 0 *Halmstad win 2-1 on agg*
Helsingborg 1 (Alvaro), Odd Grenland 1 (Fevang) *3-3 on agg. Helsingborg win on away goals*
Hertha Berlin 1 (Marcelinho), Westerlo 0 *Hertha Berlin win 3-0 on agg*
Hibernian 3 (Luna 2, Zitelli), AEK Athens 2 (Tsartas 2) aet. *AEK Athens win 4-3 on agg*
HJK Helsinki 0, Parma 2 (Marchionni, Bonazzoli) *Parma win 3-0 on agg*
Leeds United 3 (Keane, Kewell, Bakke), Maritimo 0 *Leeds United win 3-1 on agg*
Levski Sofia 0, Chelsea 2 (Terry, Gudjohnsen) *Chelsea win 5-0 on agg*
Litechs Lovech 3 (Jankovic 2, Petrov), Inter Bratislava 0 *Litechs Lovech win 3-1 on agg*
Maccabi Tel Aviv 1 (Nimni pen), Dynamo Zagreb 1 (Agic) *3-3 on agg. Maccabi Tel Aviv win on away goals.*
Obilic 2 (Vujosevic 2), FC Copenhagen 2 (Fernandez 2) *FC Copenhagen win 4-2 on agg*
Sigma Olomouc 4 (Siegl, Kotrys, Mucha 2), Celta Vigo 3 (McCarthy, Caceres, Coira) *Celta Vigo win 7-4 on agg*
Osijek 1 (Fuka), Gorica 0 *2-2 on agg. Osijek win on away goals*
PAOK Salonika 4 (Kostantinidis 2, Kafes, Luciano), Karnten 0 *PAOK Salonika win 4-0 on agg*
Rapid Bucharest 0, Paris St Germain 1 (Alosio) aet. Abandoned after 113 minutes because of floodlight failure. Game awarded 3-0 to Paris St Germain as Rapid Bucharest failed to have back-up generator. *Paris St Germain win 3-0 on agg*
Rapid Vienna 5 (Wallner 2, Taument, Wagner 2), Partizan Belgrade 1 (Cakar) *Rapid Vienna win 5-1 on agg*
Red Star Belgrade 0, CSKA Kiev 0 *CSKA Kiev win 3-2 on agg*
Ruzomberok 1 (Oravec), Troyes 0 *Troyes win 6-2 on agg*
Sedan 3 (N'Diefi, Brogno 2 – 1 pen), Pribram 1 (Siegl) *Pribram win 5-3 on agg*
Shakhtjor Donetsk 2 (Zubov, Vorobei), CSKA Sofia 1 (Okoronkwo og) *CSKA Sofia win 4-2 on agg*
Silkeborg 1 (Larsen), Real Zaragoza 2 (Yodi, Jamelli) *Real Zaragoza win 5-1 on agg*
Slavia Prague 1 (Petros), Servette1 (Oruma) *Servette win 2-1 on agg*
Slovan Bratislava 1 (Mojic), Liberec 0 *Liberec win 2-1 on agg*
Sporting Lisbon 3 (Jardel 2, Skriver og), Midtjylland 2 (Lindqvist, Souko) *Sporting Lisbon win 6-2 on agg*
Steaua Bucharest 1 (Raducanu), St Gallen 1 (Guido) *St Gallen win 3-2 on agg*
Strasbourg 2 (Ljuboja 2), Standard Liege 2 (Goosssens, Vandooren) *Standard Liege win 4-2 on agg*
Tirol Innsbruck 1 (Glider), Viktoria Zizkov 0 *Tirol Innsbruck win 1-0 on agg*
Torpedo Moscow 1 (Viazmikin), Ipswich Town 2 (George, Stewart pen) *Ipswich Town win 3-2 on agg*
Twente Enschede 2 (Kollmann, Booth), Polonia 0
Twente Enschede win 4-1 on agg
Union Berlin 3 (Djurkovic, Chifon, Koilov), Haka 0 *Union Berlin win 4-1 on agg*
Valencia 5 (Sanchez 2, Illie, Salva, Rufete), Chernomorets 0 *Valencia win 6-0 on agg*
Varteks 0, Aston Villa 1 (Hadji) *3-3 on agg. Varteks win on away goals*
Viking 2 (Sanne, Nevland), Kilmarnock 0 *Viking win 3-1 on agg*
Wisla Kracow 1 (Frankowski), Hadjuk Split 0 *Wisla Kracow win 3-2 on agg*
Anzhi 0, Rangers 1 (Konterman). Tie decided over one match played in Warsaw

Just plain Loko

Fans frustrated by crazy United finale

FITTINGLY a player named Loko had the final say in one of the craziest European games seen at Elland Road in years.

Former French international Patrice Loko's double strike for Troyes dented United's hopes of rubber-stamping their passage through to the third round of the UEFA Cup.

United's 4-2 victory was expected to be enough to survive in the second leg but knew the tie should already have been secured.

United were guilty of missing a sack-load of chances against a weak Troyes defence and were finally punished for their own slackness.

When Lee Bowyer drilled in his second goal to make it 4-1 46 seconds after the interval United seemed in complete control.

Three minutes later Algerian international Medhi Menhiri was red-carded for elbowing two-goal Mark Viduka in the face and United were handed a golden opportunity to extend their advantage.

But instead of going for the jugular, too many United players tried too many fancy tricks too early and the French team were able to regroup and regain their confidence. United gradually lost the plot and Troyes, whose boss Alain Perrin bravely opted to stay with a three-man attack despite his side's numerical disadvantage, gained their reward eight minutes from the end when 31-year-old Loko got on the end of Jerome Rothen's cross from the right to jab the ball in and keep the tie very much alive.

Frustrated Leeds manager David O'Leary said: "When they went down to ten men we stopped playing. I feel when you have teams by the throat then you have to finish them off and we had a chance to do that tonight."

It had taken Viduka just five minutes to put United ahead, skipping through three feeble challenges before drilling a low shot past goalkeeper Tony Heurtebis.

Viduka was constantly involved and set up United's second, swept home in style from just inside the box by Bowyer.

But Troyes, slick in possession, hit back minutes later when Loko gathered Nicolas Gousse's pass and rounded Martyn for a vital away goal.

United continued to make, and waste, more good chances but their anxiety eased in the 43rd minute when Viduka nodded in Bowyer's headed flick from Keane's right-wing cross.

During the interval £7 million Seth Johnson, signed from Derby County, appeared on the Elland Road pitch and Leeds fans soon had more to cheer when Bowyer gave United a three-goal cushion.

It looked plain sailing against ten men, but after frittering away more opportunities United were caught cold at the end by veteran Loko as Leeds made what should have been a simple job a rather tricky one.

STATELY DUKE : Mark Viduka slams in the opening goal against French side Troyes after just six minutes at Elland Road.

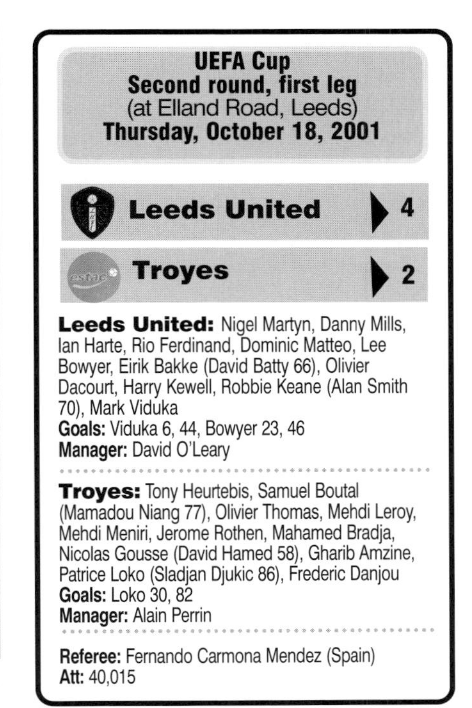

UEFA Cup
Second round, first leg
(at Elland Road, Leeds)
Thursday, October 18, 2001

Leeds United	4
Troyes	2

Leeds United: Nigel Martyn, Danny Mills, Ian Harte, Rio Ferdinand, Dominic Matteo, Lee Bowyer, Eirik Bakke (David Batty 66), Olivier Dacourt, Harry Kewell, Robbie Keane (Alan Smith 70), Mark Viduka
Goals: Viduka 6, 44, Bowyer 23, 46
Manager: David O'Leary

Troyes: Tony Heurtebis, Samuel Boutal (Mamadou Niang 77), Olivier Thomas, Mehdi Leroy, Mehdi Meniri, Jerome Rothen, Mahamed Bradja, Nicolas Gousse (David Hamed 58), Gharib Amzine, Patrice Loko (Sladjan Djukic 86), Frederic Danjou
Goals: Loko 30, 82
Manager: Alain Perrin

Referee: Fernando Carmona Mendez (Spain)
Att: 40,015

United survive hell of Troyes

IRISH sharpshooter Robbie Keane spared United's blushes with a goal he didn't realise his team urgently needed.

Leeds, trailing 3-1 were facing an embarrasing UEFA Cup second round exit at the hands of Troyes when Keane struck with 14 minutes to go.

Just minutes before his priceless strike he had asked midfielder Eirik Bakke – "Do we need another one?"

Fortunately the Norwegian's maths were up to scratch and 21-year-old Keane obliged when he timed his movement to perfection to nip behind the Troyes defence to head home.

"I looked at the linesman straight away to make sure I wasn't offside, and luckily the flag stayed down," said Keane, of his most important goal since his high-profile arrival from Inter Milan.

The 3-2 defeat was United's fifth in succession on the continent and Troyes coach Alain Perrin described United as 'lucky' after seeing his side outplay the Whites in the second half.

Troyes, sat in the heart of the champagne region of France, were certainly bubbly after Gharib Amzine smashed in an eight-minute opener from distance that swerved past Martyn.

United knew they had a game on their hands but levelled soon afterwards through Mark Viduka.

But United's two-goal lead was trimmed again before half-time when David Hamed scored with a well-struck deflected free-kick.

United, who had Michael Duberry making his first start for over a year because of injury to Rio Ferdinand, were struggling to come to terms with the speed and sharpness of the Troyes attacks and the home side deservedly made it 3-1 through Jerome Rothen's neat finish just before the hour.

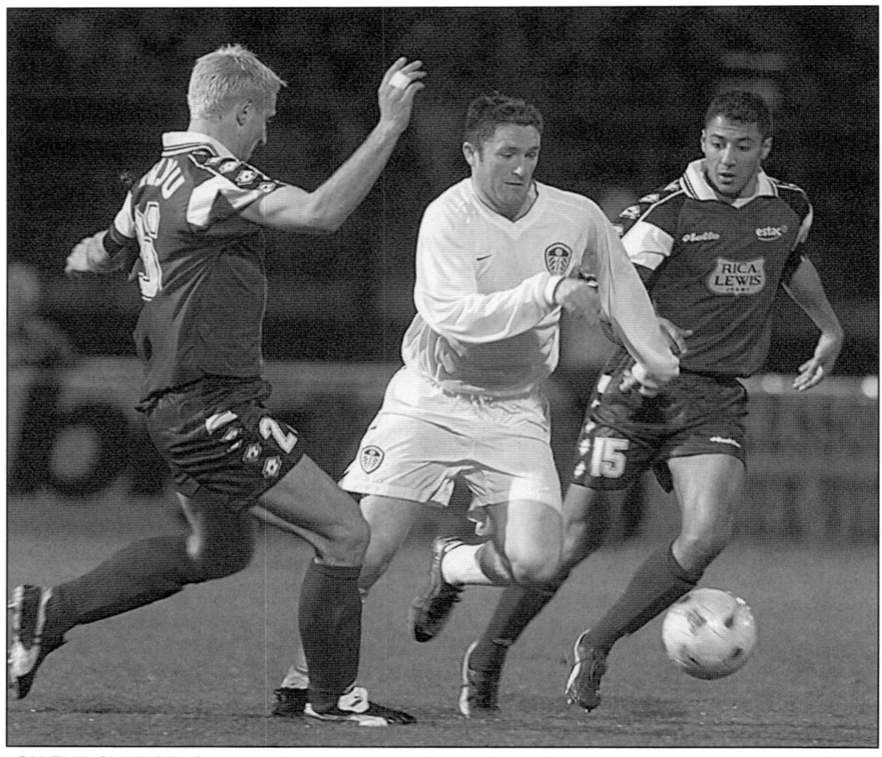

ON THE CHARGE: Goal hero Robbie Keane darts between Frederique Danjou (left) and Gharib Amzine as United threaten in Troyes.

At 3-1 down United were in deep trouble but it could have been worse as the French side's first leg hero Patrice Loko missed a simple opportunity with just Nigel Martyn to beat.

Had it gone in than United were staring at elimination but the let-off proved to be a tie-turning moment as United gradually edged their way back and were saved by Keane's priceless goal.

Troyes, who had beaten Newcastle United in the final of the Intertoto Cup to qualify for the more senior UEFA Cup had proved a real handful on their own pitch.

United's form in the four matches so far in the competition had been mixed, with flashes of brilliance mixed with dollops of lethargy.

UEFA Cup
Second round, second leg
(at de l'Aube Stadium, Troyes)
Thursday, November 1, 2001

Troyes 3
Leeds United 2
Leeds United win 6-5 on agg

Troyes: Tony Heurtebis, Mohamed Bradja (Frederic Adam 80), Frederic Danjou, Olivier Thomas, David Hamed, Rafik Saifi (Nicolas Gousse 75), Gharib Amzine, Jerome Rothen, Carl Tourenne, Patrice Loko, Samuel Boutal
Goals: Amzine 7, Hamed 38, Rothen 58
Manager: Alain Perrin

Leeds United: Nigel Martyn, Danny Mills, Ian Harte,Dominic Matteo, Michael Duberry, Eirik Bakke, David Batty, Olivier Dacourt, Harry Kewell (Jason Wilcox HT), Robbie Keane, Mark Viduka
Goals: Viduka 14, Keane 77
Manager: David O'Leary

Referee: Massimo de Santis (Italy) **Att:** 14,500

Stuttering Chelsea suffer humilating exit

CHELSEA were the biggest casualties in the second round – crashing out to Israeli side Hapoel Tel Aviv.

After steamrollering past Levski Sofia, the expensively assembled collection of continental Blues were, like United, touted as possible UEFA Cup winners.

They were drawn with Hapoel Tel Aviv and there was talk of switching the away leg after a plane from Israel mysteriously exploded and crashed in to the Black Sea with the loss of 77 lives.

It emerged that several players at the Stamford Bridge club were unwilling to travel and six senior players, including skipper Marcel Desailly, didn't fly out.

Two late goals gave Hapoel a 2-0 first leg lead, while Chelsea had Mario Melchiot sent off.

Despite having their key players back for the return, Chelsea could only draw and stumbled out of the competition.

At least they got further than Aston Villa who had been embarassingly eliminated by Croatian minnows Varteks.

Ipswich were enjoying their return to European football.

George Burley's team may have been struggling in the Premiership but followed their opening round victory against Torpedo Moscow with a 3-1 win at Helsingborg, Marcus Stewart sealing an impressive overall display by the Suffolk side with two goals in the last ten minutes.

Rangers, who beat Anzhi in a one-off match in the first round as it was too dangerous to travel to Macedonia, looked a force to be reckoned with as they cruised past Dynamo Moscow. Fellow Scots Kilmarnock and Hibernian had gone out in the first round.

Second round, first leg

AC Milan 2 (Rui Costa, Shevchenko), CSKA Sofia 0
Bordeaux 2 (Pauleta, Christian), Standard Liege 0
Celta Vigo 3 (Mostovoi 3), Liberec 1 (Edu og)
FC Copenhagen 0, Ajax 0
CSKA Kiev 0, Brugge 2 (Verheyen 2)
Fiorentina 2 (Morfeo, Nuno Gomes), Tirol Innsbruck 0
Freiburg 0, St Gallen 1 (Mokoena)
Grasshoppers 4 (Nunez 3, Petric), Twente Enschede 1 (Polak)
Halstad 0, Sporting Lisbon 1 (Niculae)
Hapoel Tel Aviv 2 (Gershon pen, Klecschenco), Chelsea 0
Inter Milan 2 (Kallon 2), Wisla Kracow 0
Ipswich Town 0, Helsingborg 0
Leeds United 4 (Viduka 2, Bowyer 2), Troyes 2 (Loko 2)
Legia Warsaw 1 (Karwan), Valencia 1 (Ilie pen)
Osijek 1 (Mijatovic), AEK Athens 2 (Zagorakis, Nikolaides)
PAOK Salonika 6 (Yasemakis 2, Okkas 2, Konstantinidis, De Souza), Pribram 1 (Siegl)
Paris St Germain 4 (Ronaldinho 2, Mendy, Anelka), Rapid Vienna 0
Rangers 3 (Amoruso, Ball, De Boer), Dynamo Moscow 1 (Gusev)
Real Zaragoza 0, Servette 0
Roda 4 (Soetaers 2, Berglund, Sonkaya), Maccabi Tel Aviv 1 (Horvath)
Union Berlin 0, Litechs Lovech 2 (Boumsosusov, Petrov)
Utrecht 1 (Jochemsen), Parma 3 (Di Vaio 2, Bonazzoli)
Varteks 3 (Bjelanovic, Murniek, Karic pen), Brondby 1 (Niznik)
Viking 0, Hertha Berlin 1 (Preetz)

Second round, second leg

AEK Athens 3 (Lakis, Tsartas, Konstantinidis), Osijek 2 (Feruzem og, Mitu) *AEK Athens win 5-3 on agg*
Ajax 0, FC Copenhagen 1
FC Copenhagen win 1-0 on agg
Brondby 5 (Borovic og, Bagger, Jonson 3), Varteks 0 *Brondby win 6-3 on agg*
Brugges 5 (Martens 3, Verheyen, Mendoza), CSKA Kiev 0 *Brugges win 7-0 on agg*
Chelsea 1 (Zola), Hapoel Tel Aviv 1 (Osterc) *Hapoel Tel Aviv won 3-1 on agg*
CSKA Sofia 0, AC Milan 1 (Inzaghi) *AC Milan win 3-0 on agg*
Dynamo Moscow 1 (Gusev), Rangers 4 (De Boer, Khomutosky og, Flo, Lovenkrands) *Rangers win 7-2 on agg*
Helsingborg 1 (Eklund), Ipswich Town 3 (Hreidarsson, Stewart 2) *Ipswich Town win 3-1 on agg*
Hertha Berlin 2 (Alves, Sverrisson), Viking 0 *Hertha Berlin win 3-0 on agg*
Liberec 3 (Stajner, Nezmar 2), Celta Vigo 0 *Liberec win 4-3 on agg*
Litechs Lovech 0, Union Berlin 0 *Litechs Lovech win 2-0 on agg*
Maccabi Tel Aviv 2 (Biton 2), Roda 1 (Lawal) *Roda win 5-3 on agg*
Parma 0, Utrecht 0 *Parma win 3-1 on agg*
Pribram 2 (Cizek, Kucera), PAOK Salonika 2 (De Souza, Yasemakis) *PAOK Salonika win 8-3 on agg*
Rapid Vienna 2 (Wallner 2), Paris St Germain 2 (Potillon, Leal) *Paris St Germain win 6-2 on agg*
Sevette 1 (Oruma), Real Zaragoza 0 *Servette win 1-0 on agg*
Sporting Lisbon 6 (Jardel 3 – 1 pen, Jao Pinto, Niculae, Paulo Bento), Halstad 1 (Nordstrand) *Sporting Lisbon win 7-1 on agg*
Standard Liege 0, Bordeaux 2 (Dugarry, Pauleta) *Bordeaux win 4-0 on agg*
Tirol Innsbruck 2 (Gilewicz 2), Fiorentina 2 (Nuno Gomez, Morefeo) *Fiorentina win 4-2 on agg*
Troyes 3 (Anzine, Hamed, Rothen), Leeds United 2 (Viduka, Keane) *Leeds United win 6-5 on agg*
Twente Enschede 4 (Van Der Laan 2, Cairo, El Brazi), Grasshoppers 2 (Chapuisat, Mwaruwari) *Grasshoppers win 6-5 on agg*
Valencia 6 (Albelda, Illie, Djukic, Aimar pen, Sanchez, Angulo), Legia Warsaw 1 (Svitlica) *Valencia win 7-2 on agg*
Wisla Kracow 1 (Zurawski), Inter Milan 0 *Inter Milan win 2-1 on agg*

PHEW: Joy and relief are etched on the faces of Robbie Keane, Rio Ferdinand, Alan Smith and Olivier Dacourt after Smith's winner.

UEFA Cup
Third round, first leg
(at Hardturm Stadiu,m, Zurich)
Thursday, November 22, 2001

Grasshoppers	**1**
Leeds United	**2**

Grasshoppers: Peter Jehle, Bouba Diop Papa, Marc Hodel, Boris Smiljanic, Roland Schwegler, Richard Nunez, Ricardo Cabanas (Mate Baturina 74), Mihai Tararache (Mladen Petric 88), Pascal Castillo, Benjamin Mwaruwari (Andres Gerber 90), Stephane Chapuisat
Goal: Chapuisat 18
Manager: Hans-Peter Zaugg

Leeds United: Nigel Martyn, Danny Mills, Ian Harte, Rio Ferdinand, Dominic Matteo, Eirik Bakke, David Batty, Olivier Dacourt, Jason Wilcox, Alan Smith, Robbie Keane
Goals: Harte 73, Smith 79
Manager: David O'Leary

Referee: Lucilio Cardoso Cortez Batista (Portugal)
Att: 15,000

Back to Grass roots football

Martyn's penalty save turns tide

ENGLAND'S number one Nigel Martyn produced a heroic display in rain-lashed Zurich to pull United out of the mire.

Trailing 1-0, Leeds were kept in the game early in the second-half by the 35-year-old goalkeeper who showed the watching Sven-Goran Eriksson just why he was deserved his run in the national team

After United dominated the early stages United were rocked after 18 minutes when the Swiss side scored.

It was going to take something special to beat Martyn and Stephane Chapuisat produced it with a superb 22-yard strike which gave the Cornishman no chance.

Now Grasshoppers were buzzing on a sodden surface which cut up badly as United were given a hard time in the Hardturm Stadium and it needed all of Martyn's experience and skill to get them through.

Three excellent saves shortly after the interval kept United's heads above water, but he topped that with a brilliant penalty save. United were unhappy with the award as Rio Ferdinand's shirt tug on Richard Nunez appeared to be outside the box – but at least the referee opted to keep his red card in his pocket and only caution the Leeds skipper.

Martyn then beat out the spot-kick from Nunez and made a a point-blank block to deny Ricardo Cabanas on the follow up to ensure some kind of justice was done.

United, who had Jason Wilcox making a rare appearance on the left of midfield, were quick to build on Martyn's good work and six minutes later equalised with a curling free-kick from Ian Harte.

The comeback was completed seven minutes after that with Alan Smith scoring his first goal since the start of the season to silence the noisy home fans.

A relieved David O'Leary said: "We could have been badly punished, but we weren't.

"The penalty incident then woke us up a little bit. I didn't think it was a penalty and Rio couldn't believe the decision was given, but we got out of jail with a good save by Nigel."

Brilliant Harry goes solo

GUESSING GAME: More Harry Kewell brilliance gets Grasshoppers defender Boris Smiljanic in a spin.

HARRY Kewell answered David O'Leary's prayers with an Elland Road wonder goal to light United's path to the last 16 of the UEFA Cup.

The Australian whizz-kid had only shown glimpses of his outstanding ability during the season and prompted the Leeds boss to have a heart-to-heart with the player.

Whatever was said seemed to do the trick as he scored a stunning goal in a 2-2 draw which saw United progress 4-3 on aggregate.

The scoreline suggests it was close, but United were never really in any danger of throwing away the advantage they had gained in Zurich.

An attacking Leeds line-up saw Alan Smith on the right, Robbie Keane on the left and Kewell floating behind Mark Viduka. Just for good measure new £11million striker Robbie Fowler was watching in the stands following his switch from Liverpool.

England forward Fowler was cup-tied but like the rest of the Leeds fans was purring at Kewell's explosive contribution in the 19th minute.

United cleared a corner at the South Stand end to the edge of their own box where Olivier Dacourt cleverly switched the ball to Kewell on the right.

Although he was 75 yards from goal there was only one thing on his mind as he shot like a bolt of white-lightning past two hapless Grasshoppers defenders before lifting a perfect shot over advancing goalkeeper Peter Jehle.

Kewell almost made it 2-0 but saw a thumping 25-yard drive cannon back off the bar.

United were looking comfortable but the half ended in bizarre fashion when defensive trio Nigel Martyn, Rio Ferdinand and Danny Mills got in a mess and Richard Nunez lobbed in a soft goal in injury-time.

But Swiss celebrations were short lived as Mills played in Keane who tucked away a right-foot shot from 20 yards to make it 2-1 on the night.

Leeds were distinctly low-key in the second-half and were never quite able to put enough daylight between themselves and the battling Grasshoppers outfit.

Martyn made a fine leaping save to his right to tip away a fierce shot from substitute Luca Ippoliti to spare United an anxious last seven minutes, but Grasshoppers did make Leeds pay for more slackness in the dying seconds when Nunez popped the ball in to Martyn's bottom right-hand corner.

But by that time United were safely through to the next round in February when Dutch side PSV Eindhoven lay in wait.

UEFA Cup
Third round, second leg
(at Elland Road, Leeds)
Thursday, December 6, 2001

 **Leeds United**  2

 **Grasshoppers**  2

Leeds United win 4-3 on agg

Leeds United: Nigel Martyn, Gary Kelly, Ian Harte, Rio Ferdinand, Danny Mills, Alan Smith, David Batty, Olivier Dacourt, Harry Kewell, Robbie Keane, Mark Viduka
Goals: Kewell 19, Keane 45
Manager: David O'Leary

Grasshoppers: Peter Jehle, Marc Hodel, Mihail Tararache, Bouba Diop Papa, Roland Schwegler, Boris Smiljanic (Ariel Morales 74), Ricardo Cabanas (Luca Ippoliti 66), Pascal Castillo, Andres Gerber (Benjamin Mwaruwari 59), Richard Nunez, Stephane Chapuisat
Goals: Nunez 45, 90
Manager: Hans-Peter Zaugg

Referee: Frank De Bleeckere (Belgium) **Att:** 40,014

Vieri treble spells trouble for Ipswich

CHRISTIAN Vieri's hat-trick in Milan ended Ipswich's UEFA Cup run. Alan Armstrong's late goal at Portman Road had given the East Anglians a slender advantage to defend in the San Siro.

But Inter's Italian international Vieri swept in goals after 18, 34 and 70 minutes in a 4-1 win.

Scottish clubs Celtic and Rangers had their fate settled by penalties.

The Hoops finished 1-1 on aggregate with Valencia, only to lose the penalty shoot-out 5-4 at Parkhead.

The blue half of Glasgow had more luck after Rangers and Paris St Germain failed to produce a goal between them over both legs, the men from Ibrox winning 4-3 on penalties in the French capital.

Third round, first leg

AC Milan 2 (Shevchenko, Inzaghi), Sporting Lisbon 0
AEK Athens 3 (Tsartas pen, Zagorakis, Konstaninidis), Litechs Lovech 2 (Yankovic, Rakita)
Bordeaux 1 (Miranda), Roda 0
Brugges 4 (Englebert, Van Der Heyden, Mendoza, De Brul), Lyon 1 (Luyindaula)
FC Copenhagen 0, Borussia Dortmund 1 (Herrlich)
Feyenord 1 (Ono), Freiburg 0
Fiorentina 0, Lille 1 (Bakari)
Grasshoppers 1 (Chapuisat), Leeds United 2 (Harte, Smith)
Hapoel Tel Aviv (Osterc, Domb), Lokomotiv Moscow 1 (Izmailov)
Ipswich Town 1 (Armstrong), Inter Milan 0
Liberec 3 (Lukas, Johana, Jun), Mallorca 1 (Biagini)
PAOK Salonika 3 (Yasemakis 2, Udeze), PSV Eindhoven 2 (De Jong, Bruggink)
Parma 1 (Johansen og), Brondby 0
Rangers 0, Paris St Germain 0
Servette 0, Hertha Berlin 0
Valencia 1 (Vicente), Celtic 0

Third round, second leg

Borussia Dortmund 1 (Sorensen), FC Copenhagen 0
Borussia Dortmund win 2-0 on agg
Brondby 0, Parma 3 (Mboma, Nakata, Lamouchi)
Parma win 4-1 on agg
Celtic 1 (Larsson), Valencia 0 aet
1-1 on agg. Valencia win 5-4 on penalties
Freiberg 2 (Kehl, Kobiashvilli pen), Feyenoord 2 (Van Hooijdonk, Leonardo)
Feyenoord win 3-2 on agg
Hertha Berlin 0, Servette 3 (Hilton, Frei, Obradovic)
Servette win 3-0 on agg
Inter Milan 4 (Vieri 3, Kallon), Ipswich Town 1 (Armstrong pen)
Leeds United 2 (Kewell, Keane), Grasshoppers 2 (Nunez 2)
Leeds United win 4-3 on agg
Lille 2 (Cheryrou, Sterjovski), Fiorentina 0
Lille win 3-0 on agg
Litechs Lovech 1 (Yurukov), AEK Athens 1 (Gamarra)
AEK Athens win 4-3 on agg
Lokomotiv Moscow 0, Hapoel Tel Aviv 1 (Osterc)
Hapoel Tel Aviv win 3-1 on agg
Lyon 3 (Anderson 3), Brugges 0
4-4 on agg. Lyon win on away goals
Mallorca 1 (Eto'o pen), Liberec 2 (Baffour, Stajner)
Liberec win 5-2 on agg
Paris St Germain 0, Rangers 0 aet
0-0 on agg. Rangers win 4-3 on agg
PSV Eindhoven 4 (Vennegoor of Hesselink 2, Gakhokidze, Van Bommel pen), PAOK Salonika 1 (De Souza)
PSV Eindhoven win 6-4 on agg
Roda 2 (Anastasiou pen, Lawal), Bordeaux 0
Roda win 2-1 on agg
Sporting Lisbon 1 (Niculae), AC Milan 1 (Moreno)
AC Milan win 3-1 on agg

Disciplined United

Dutch draw a welcome return to form

UNITED shook off their lethargy to rekindle hopes of European glory with a crucial 0-0 draw against Dutch masters PSV Eindhoven.

Few gave out-of-touch Leeds a prayer in the impressive Philips Stadium but United, without a win in seven matches rose to the occasion to give themselves a great chance of reaching the UEFA Cup quarter-finals.

The Dutch champions, who had lost only one of their previous 36 League games at home, were, in the final analysis, fortunate that David O'Leary's team of battlers didn't return to Yorkshire with a victory.

Key for United was the return of Danny Mills, Lee Bowyer and Alan Smith, who had all been on the side-lines for various spells because of domestic suspensions. United's indiscipline throughout the season – on and off the field – had been a source of concern for O'Leary but he had no complaints in Holland in a booking-free performance.

Indeed it was the frustrated Dutch who were handing out most of the punishment with Marc Van Bommel, whose name had been linked with a move to Elland Road, fortunate not to incur the displeasure of Italian referee Stefano Branchi.

PSV began brightly and Nigel Martyn was forced to make two smart saves in the opening five minutes and there was relief when Dominic Matteo escaped from being punished for hand-ball in his own area just before the interval.

But United had seized control after the early Dutch pressure and Alan Smith, who must have impressed the watching England coach Sven-Goran Eriksson, came close to turning the ball in after good work by co-striker Mark Viduka.

The Leeds duo linked up again midway through the first half as a one-two ended with Smith bringing a good save from Patrick Lodewijks, who was only able to parry the ball and Viduka's looping header on the follow-up seemed destined for the net only for a defender to hook it clear from under the bar with Viduka wheeling away to celebrate a goal.

UEFA Cup
Fourth round, first leg
(at Phillips Stadium, Eindhoven)
Thursday, February 21, 2002

PSV Eindhoven	**0**
Leeds United	**0**

PSV Eindhoven: Patrik Lodewijks, Kasper Bogelund, Kevin Hofland (Yuri Nikiforov 67), Andre Ooijer, Wilfred Bouma, Dennis Rommeddahl, Marc Van Bommel, Johann Vogel, Giorgi Gakhokidze, Arnold Bruggink (John De Jong 35), Jan Vennegor of Hesselink (Mateji Kezman 59)
Manager: Eric Gerets

Leeds United: Nigel Martyn, Danny Mills, Ian Harte, Rio Ferdinand, Dominic Matteo, Lee Bowyer, Eirik Bakke, Olivier Dacourt, Harry Kewell, Alan Smith, Mark Viduka
Manager: David O'Leary

Referee: Stefano Branchi (Italy) **Att:** 32,000

United continued to carry the greater threat after the break with the PSV goalkeeper saving well to deny Harry Kewell while Ian Harte went close with a 25-yard free-kick.

Leeds kept driving forward and Smith almost broke the deadlock late on but United had given themselves a good platform on which to progress to a quarter-final against either Rangers or another Dutch club, Feyenoord.

Pleased O'Leary said: "The team I put out was one I've been wanting to field for a while, and it's been a long time since I have been able to do that."

The only down-side for Leeds was their failure to score an away goal which meant they would not be able to go on all-out attack against a PSV side containing several lightning-quick players, notably Danish right-winger Denis Rommedahl.

SUPER SAVER: United keeper Nigel Martyn is at full stretch to keep out this effort from PSV's Andre Ooijer.

Bitter taste of Vennegor is hard to swallow

Leeds out to late goal

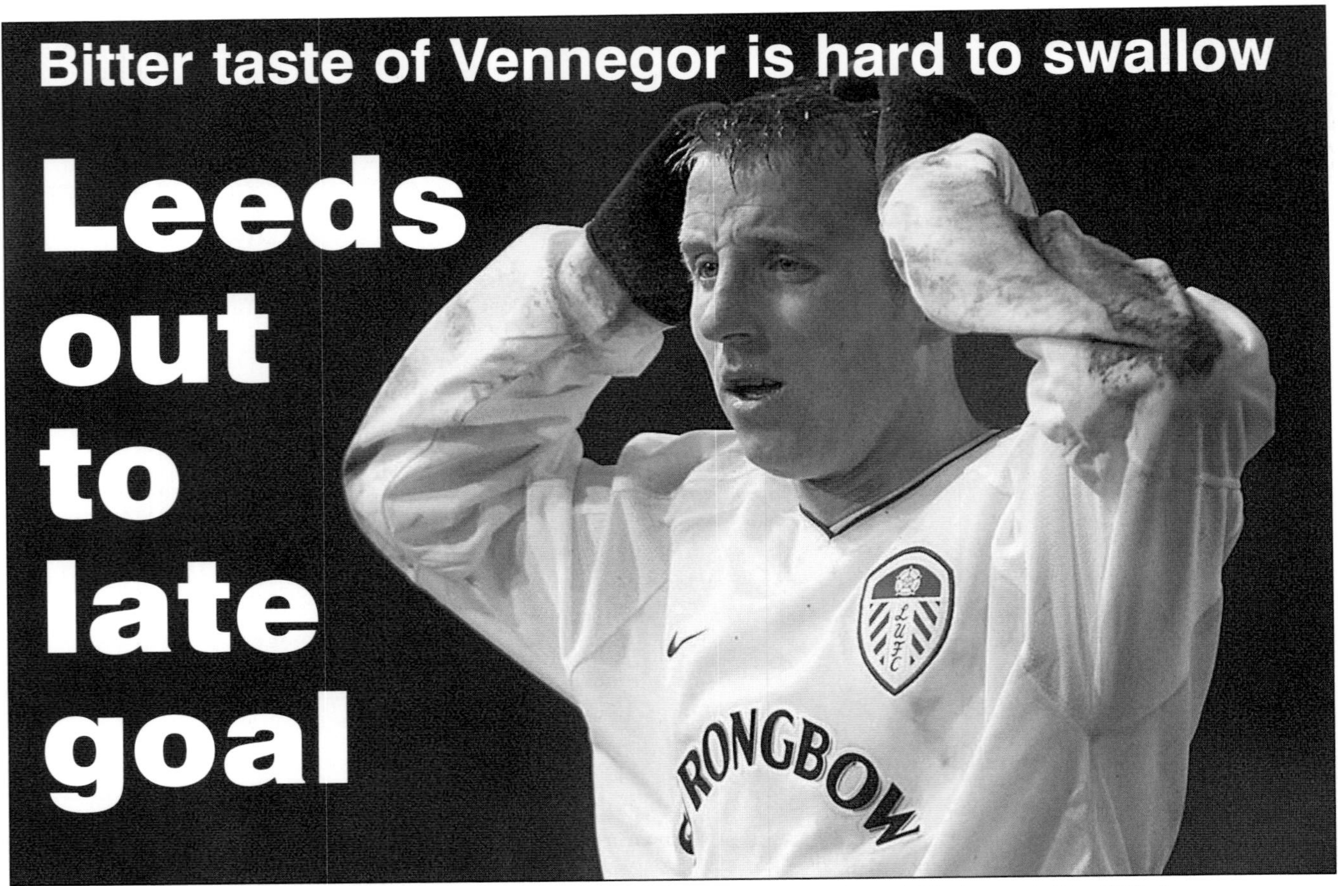

STUNNED: United midfielder Lee Bowyer can't believe it as the final whistle blows – United are out of the UEFA Cup.

ALL the hard work United had done in Holland was undone by a man sporting the craziest name in football.

Jan Vennegor of Hesselink netted a dramatic last-minute winner to give PSV Eindhoven a 1-0 victory which stunned Elland Road.

Just as extra-time was beckoning, Theo Lucius found himself in space in the Leeds penalty area. His shot looped off Nigel Martyn on to the bar but before United's defence could get its bearings Hesselink dived in bravely to head a dramatic winner to set up an all-Dutch quarter-final against Feyenoord, conquerers of Rangers.

The result left Leeds without a win in nine games and without a goal in five of their previous six matches.

Yet they started full of confidence with Mark Viduka and Eirik Bakke both testing goalkeeper Patrick Lodewijks in the early stages.

United were putting together some controlled attacking football and another super passing move down the left involving Bakke, Harry Kewell and Viduka, ended with Kewell coming close.

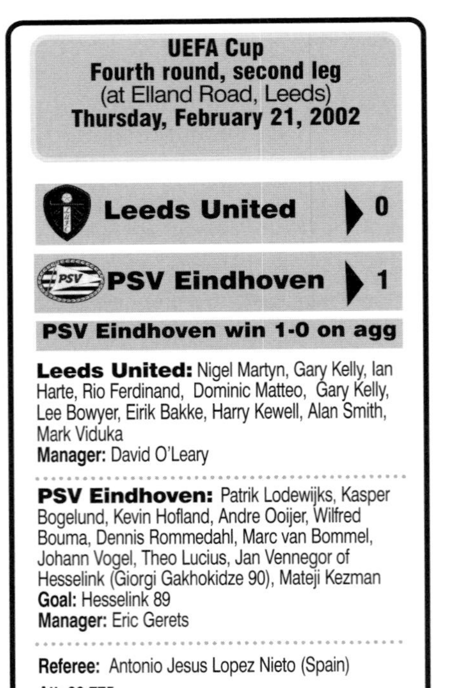

UEFA Cup
Fourth round, second leg
(at Elland Road, Leeds)
Thursday, February 21, 2002

Leeds United	**0**
PSV Eindhoven	**1**

PSV Eindhoven win 1-0 on agg

Leeds United: Nigel Martyn, Gary Kelly, Ian Harte, Rio Ferdinand, Dominic Matteo, Gary Kelly, Lee Bowyer, Eirik Bakke, Harry Kewell, Alan Smith, Mark Viduka
Manager: David O'Leary

PSV Eindhoven: Patrik Lodewijks, Kasper Bogelund, Kevin Hofland, Andre Ooijer, Wilfred Bouma, Dennis Rommedahl, Marc van Bommel, Johann Vogel, Theo Lucius, Jan Vennegor of Hesselink (Giorgi Gakhokidze 90), Mateji Kezman
Goal: Hesselink 89
Manager: Eric Gerets

Referee: Antonio Jesus Lopez Nieto (Spain)
Att: 39,775

Kewell should have given United the lead when United attacked again, this time down the right. Viduka cleverly cut the ball back and although Alan Smith could not quite reach the ball it ran to Kewell who thumped it over the top. United were setting the tempo and PSV, who had not won a European away tie in the course of their season, were restricted to some half-hearted counter attacks.

But all that changed after half-time when Van Bommel took total control of the midfield.

As Leeds got bogged down on a heavy pitch, Van Bommel ran the show and United were gradually pushed back.

Martyn was forced to make a brilliant full-length save to push away Mateji Kezman's angled drive, while Rio Ferdinand and Dominic Matteo had to be at their best to prevent PSV turning their increasing pressure in to goals.

But United were punished for not scoring earlier in the match when they were dominant as Hesselink's late goal gave O'Leary's men simply no time to get back in the match.

With United slipping down the League table and out of both domestic cups they had a real fight on their hands to qualify for Europe again.

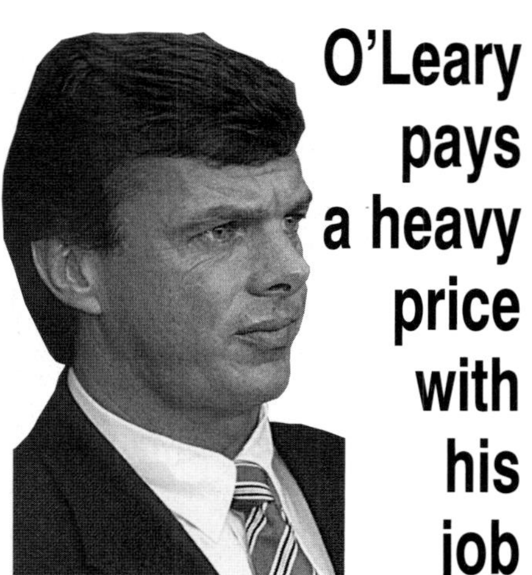

OUT: David O'Leary.

O'Leary pays a heavy price with his job

THAT sickening late home defeat against PSV Eindhoven was to be David O'Leary's swansong at Elland Road.

Although United did scrape in to the UEFA Cup again, he was sacked before the start of the 2002/03 campaign just 15 months after leading United to the European Cup semi-finals.

There had been rumours of a split between O'Leary and chairman Peter Ridsdale and matters came to a head with the £30m summer sale of skipper Rio Ferdinand to arch rivals from over the Pennines, Manchester United.

Ferdinand had been a member of the England World Cup squad which included Danny Mills, Nigel Martyn and Robbie Fowler, while Robbie Keane, Ian Harte and Gary Kelly were in the Republic of Ireland side.

Failure to reach the Champions League had hit United's finances hard and it was known that they needed to sell players with Lee Bowyer seemingly heading to Liverpool – only for the deal to fall through.

He had been cleared of affray and causing greivous bodily harm with intent in the infamous court case. Jonathan Woodgate, who hardly played for the duration of the proceedings, was aquitted of GBH but found guilty of affray.

Both men's England careers were put on hold with Woodgate, who was sentenced to 100 hours community service, being told that he would not be considered until after the World Cup.

Pierre's Dutch double

FORMER Premiership stars Pierre Van Hooijdonk and Jon-Dahl Tomasson were the goal heroes as Feyenoord won the UEFA Cup in their own backyard.

Former Celtic and Nottingham Forest striker Van Hooijdonk scored twice and Danish international Tomasson, who had an unsuccessful spell at Newcastle, also found the net as the side from Holland beat Borussia Dortmund 3-2 in their own stadium in Rotterdam.

Van Hooijdonk was the competition's leading scorer and was Feyenoord's hero in the all-Dutch quarter-final against PSV Eindhoven, conquerors of United.

His last-minute goal in the home tie ensured the match went to penalties which Feyenoord won 5-4. Feyenoord also knocked out Rangers in the fourth round.

Fourth round, first leg

Hapoel Tel Aviv 0, Parma 0
Inter Milan 3 (Zanetti, Kallon, Ventola), AEK Athens (Zagorakis)
Lille 1 (Bassir), Borussia Dortmund 1 (Ewerthon)
Lyon 1 (Govou), Liberec 1 (Stajner pen)
PSV Eindhoven 0, Leeds United 0
Rangers 1 (Ferguson pen), Feyenoord 1 (Ono)
Roda 0, AC Milan 1 (Jose Mari)
Valencia 3 (Hilton og, Aimar, Salva), Servette 0

Fourth round, second leg

AC Milan 0, Roda 1 (Luypers) aet *1-1 on agg. AC Milan win 3-2 on penalties*
AEK Athens 2 (Konstantinidis, Nikolaidis), Inter Milan 2 (Gresko, Ventola) *Inter Milan win 5-3 on agg*
Borussia Dortmund 0, Lille 0 *1-1 on agg. Borussia Dortmund win on away goals*
Feyenoord 3 (Van Hooijdonk 2, Kalou), Rangers 2 (McCann, Ferguson pen) *Feyenoord win 4-3 on agg*
Leeds United 0, PSV Eindhoven 1 (Vennegor of Hesselink) *PSV Eindhoven win 1-0 on agg*
Liberec 4 (Nezmar 2, Stajner, Neumann), Lyon 1 (Muller) *Liberec win 5-2 on agg*
Parma 1 (Bonazzoli), Hapoel Tel Aviv 2 (Osterc, Pison) *Hapoel Tel Aviv win 2-1 on agg*
Servette 2 (Robert, Frei), Valencia 2 (Sanchez, Angiulo) *Valencia win 5-2 on agg*

Quarter-final, first leg

Hapoel Tel Aviv 1 (Clescenko), AC Milan 0 in Nicosia
Inter Milan 1 (Materazzi), Valencia 1 (Rufete)
Liberec 0, Borussia Dortmund 0 in Prague
PSV Eindhoven 1 (Kezman), Feyenoord 1 (Van Hooijdonk)

Quarter-final, second leg

Borussia Dortmund 4 (Amoruso, Koller, Ricken, Ewerthon), Liberec 0 *Borussia Dortmund win 4-0 on agg*
Feyenoord 1 (Van Hooijdonk), PSV Eindhoven 1 (Van Bommel) aet *2-2 on agg. Feyenoord win 5-4 on penalties*
AC Milan 2 (Rui Costa, Gershon og), Hapoel Tel Aviv 0 *AC Milan win 2-1 on agg*
Valencia 0, Inter Milan 1 (Ventola) *Inter Milan win 2-1 on agg*

Semi-final, second leg

Borussia Dortmund 4 (Amoruso 3 – 1 pen, Heinrich), AC Milan 0
Inter Milan 0, Feyenoord 1 (Cordoba og)

Semi-final, second leg

Feyenoord 2 (Van Hooijdonk, Tomasson), Inter Milan 2 (Zanetti, Kallon pen) *Feyenoord win 3-2 on agg*
AC Milan 3 (Inzaghi, Chamot, Serginho pen), Borussia Dortmund 1 (Ricken) *Borussia Dortmund win 5-3 on agg*

Final

(Feyenoord Stadium, Rotterdam)
May 8, 2002
Borussia Dortmund 2
Feyenoord 3

Borussia Dortmund: Lehmann, Evanilson, Dede, Ricken (Heinrich 69), Worns, Reuter, Ewerthon (Addo 61), Koller, Amoruso, Rosicky.
Goals: Amoruso pen, Koller
Manager: Mattias Sammer
Feyenoord: Zoetebier, Gyan, Rzasa, Ono (De Haan 75), Van Wonderen, Paauwe, Bosvelt, Kalou (Elmander 75), Van Hooijdonk, Van Persie (Leonardo 62), Tomasson
Goals: Van Hooijdonk 2 – 1 pen, Tomasson
Manager: Bert van Marwijk
Referee: Vitor Manuel Melo Pereira (Portugal)
Attendance: 48,500

Leading scorers: 8 – Van Hooijdonk, 7 – Bjelanovic (Varteks), Osterc (Hapoel Tel Aviv), 6 – Jardel (Sporting Lisbon), Nunez (Grasshoppers), Tsartas (AEK Salonika).

It's Ell-Tel in the United hot-seat

UNITED'S choice for David O'Leary's successor was Terry Venables, the former England coach.

The 59-year-old Londoner had taken the national side to the Euro 96 semi-final and had considerable managerial experience with Tottenham Crystal Palace and QPR, but possibly his greatest achievement was steering Barcelona to the Spanish title in 1985 and to the European Cup final the following year when they lost on penalties to Steaua Bucharest.

United enter the UEFA Cup at the first round stage in 2002/03.

Qualifying round, first leg

Aberdeen 1 (Mackie), Nistru 0
AIK Solna 2 (Hock, Nordin), Vestmannaejar 0
Amica 5 (Bieniuk, Dembinski, Krol, Dawidowski 2), TNS Llasantffraid 0
Anorthosis 3 (Piekarski, Kowwalczyk, Xiourouppas pen), Grevenacher 0
Arats 0, Servette 2 (Toure 2)
Atgrau 0, Matador Puchov 0
Avenir Beggen 0, Ipswich Town 1 (Stewart)
Bangor City 1 (Roberts), Sartid 0
Brann 2 (Knudsen, F Olsen), Suduva 3 (Zitinskas 2, Radzinevicius)
Encamp 0, Zenit 5 (Arshavin 2, Spivak pen, Makarov, Ossipou)
FC Copenhagen 3 (Johnsson 2, R Larsen), Lokomotiv Tbilisi 1 (Janashia)
Domagnanu 0, Viktoria Zizkov 2 (Sabou, Straceny)
Dynamo Minsk 1 (Tsyhalka), CSKA Sofia 4 (Mukasi, Dimitrov 2, Brito)
Dynamo Tbilisi 4 (Da Rosha, Sashiashvilli 2, Daraselia), TVMK Tallin 1 (Leetman)
Ferencvaros 4 (Tokoli 2, Gera, Szkukalek), AEL Limassol 0
Fylkir 1 (Sverrison pen), Mouscron 1 (Gregoire)
Hadjuk Split 3 (Dolonga, Pletikosa pen, Derenja), Gotu 0
Glentoran 0, Wisla 2 (Zurawski pen, Dubicki)
Gomel 1 (Borel), HJK Helsinki 0
Hapoel Tel Aviv 1 (Abukasis), Partizani 0
Kairat 0, Red Star Belgrade 2 (Bogdanovic, Mrda)
Klaksvik 2 (Morkore 2), Ujpest Budapest 2 (Juhar, Farkas)
Levadia Tallin 0, Maccabi Tel Aviv 2 (Prohorekous, Strool)
Lexioes 2 (Antchovets, Brito), Belasica 2 (Ahmetovic 2)
Litechs Lovech 5 (Nikolov, Stoilov, Yuvov 2, Rousev), Atlanta 0
Metalurg Zaphorizhya 3 (Akipyan, Ivanov, Brdanin), Birkikara 0
Metalurgs 0, Karnten 2 (Maric, Bubalo)
MyPa 1 (Manso), Odense 0
Pobeda 2 (Nielsen og, Krstev), Midtjylland 0
Primorje 6 (Zlatkovic 4, Gregoric, Ranic), Zvartnots 1 (Davityan)
Rapid Bucharest 2 (Schumacher 2), Gorica 0
Senec 1 (Juska), Siroki Brijeg 2 (Katic 2)
Shamrock Rovers 1 (McGuinness), Djurgaarden 3 (Wowoak, Stefanidis, Kallstrom)
Sigma Olomouc 2 (Putik, Ekwueme), Sarajevo 1 (Osmanhodiz)
SK Tirana 0, National 1 (Radu pen)
Sliema Wanderers 1 (Da Nascimento), Polonia 3 (Bartczak, Bak, Volenkwor)
Staebaek 4 (Finstad, T Gudmundsson, Baldvindson 2), Linfield 0
Vaduz 1 (Burgmeir), Livingston 1 (Rubio)
Varteks 5 (Huljev, Hrman, Mumlak pen, Karic, Skeplic), Dundalk 0
Ventspils 3 (Landregrev 2, Rimkus), Lugano 0
Zimbru Chisinau 3 (Frunza 2, Gvazava), Gothenburg 1 (Henriksson)

Qualifying round, second leg

AEL Limassol 2 (Kyriakou, Sebok), Ferencvaros 1 (Licsei) *Ferencvaros win 5-2 on agg*
Atlantas 1 (Tamosaukas), Litechs Lovech 3 (Roussev, Hidiouad pen, Jelebkovic) *Litechs Lovech win 8-1 on agg*
Belascia 1 (Baldovaliev), Lexioes 2 (Brito, Nene) *Lexioes win 4-3 on agg*
Birkikara 0, Metalurg Zaphorizhya 0 *Metalurg Zaphorizhya win 3-0 on agg*
CSKA Sofia 1 (Sakiri pen), Dynamo Minsk 0
Djurgaarden 2 (Wowoah, Chanko), Shamrock Rovers 0 *Djurgaarden win 5-1 on agg*
Dundalk 0, Varteks 4 (Kristic, Haliloviv, Huljev, Fumic) *Varteks win 9-0 on agg*
Dynamo Minsk win 5-1 on agg
HJK Helsinki 0, Gomel 4 (Nazarov, Blizniuk 2, Razumau) *Gomel win 5-0 on agg*
Gorica 1 (Perja og), Rapid Bucharest 3 (Godfroid, Schumacher 2) *Rapid Bucharest win 5-1 on agg*
Gotu 0, Hadjuk Split 8 (Erceg 3, Andric 2, Pletikosa pen, Carevic 2) *Hadjuk Split win 11-0 on agg*
Gothenburg 2 (Rosenkvist 2), Zimbru Chisinau 2 (Gvazava, Cebotari) *Zimbru Chisinau win 5-3 on agg*
Grevenmacher 2 (Kandu, Albrecht), Anorthosis 0 *Anorthosis win 3-2 on agg*
Ipswich Town 8 (Miller 2, Counago 3, Brown, McGreal, Ambrose), Avenir Beggen 1 (Molitor) *Ipswich Town win 9-1 on agg*
Karnten 4 (Ambrosius 3, Bubalo), Metalurgs 2 (Katasonov, Ivanov) *Karnten win 6-2 on agg*
Linfield 1 (Ferguson), Staebaek 1 (Gudmunsson) *Staebaek win 5-1 on agg*
Livingston 0, Vaduz 0 *1-1 on agg. Livingston win on away goals*
Lokomotiv Tbilisi 1 (Janashia), FC Copenhagen 4 (Zuma, Petersson 2, Jonsson) *FC Copenhagen win 7-2 on agg*
Lugano 1 (Andreoli), Ventspils 0 *Ventspils win 3-1 on agg*
Maccabi Tel Aviv 2 (Pasins og, Prohorekous), Levadia Tallin 0 *Maccabi Tel Aviv win 4-0 on agg*
Matador Puchov 2 (Breska, Strba), Atyrau 0 *Matador Puchov win 2-0 on agg*
Midtylland 3 (Pimpong, Kristensen, Jessen), Pobeda 0 aet *Midtylland win 3-2 on agg*
Mouscron 3 (Dugardein, Bakadal, Gregoire), Fylkir 1 (Asbjornsson) *Mouscron win 4-1 on agg*
Nistru 0, Aberdeen 0 *Aberdeen win 1-0 on agg*
National Bucharest 2 (Illie, Rdu), SK Tirana 2 (Merkoci, Zaccanti) *National Bucharest win 3-2 on agg*
Odense 2 (Miti 2), MyPa 0 *Odense win 2-1 on agg*
Partizani 1 (Brachini), Hapoel Tel Aviv 4 (Afek, Balilni 2, Udi) *Hapoel Tel Aviv win 5-1 on agg*
Polonia 2 (Bak, Bartczak), Sliema Wanderers 0 *Polonia win 5-1 on agg*
Red Star Belgrade 3 (Gvozdenovic, Pjanovic, Krivokapic), Kairat 0 *Red Star Belgrade win 5-0 on agg*
Sarajevo 2 (Obuca, Osmanhodzic), Sigma (Putik) *3-3 on agg. Sarajevo win 5-3 on penalties*
Sartid 2 (Zecevic, Mirosavljevic), Bangor 0 *Sartid win 2-1 on agg*
Servette 3 (Cruz 2, Frei), Araks 0 *Servette win 5-0 on agg*
Siroki Brijeg (Erceg, Hrgovic 2), Senec 0 *Siroki Brijeg win 5-1 on agg*
Sudova 3 (Razinevicius 3), Brann 2 (Dhleko 2) *Sudova win 6-4 on agg*
TNS Llansantffraid 2 (Anthrobus, Toner), Amica 7 (Krol 3, Burkhadt 2, Sobocinski, Ludzinski) at Newtown *Amica win 12-2 on agg*
TVMK Tallin 0, Dynamo Tbilisi 1 (Akhalaia) *Dynamo Tbilisi win 5-1 on agg*
Ujpest Budapest 1 (Horvath), Klaksvik 0 *Ujpest Budapest win 3-2 on agg*
Vestmannaejar 1 (Thorvaldsson), AIK Solna 3 (Rubarth, Hock 2) *AIK Solna win 5-1 on agg*
Wisla Krakow 4 (Kuzba 2, Uche 2), Glentoran 0 *Wislaw Krakow win 6-0 on agg*
Viktoria Zizkov 3 (Chihuri, Janousek, Kruty), Domagnano 0 *Viktoria Zizkov win 5-0 on agg*
Zenit 8 (Ossipov 2, Randjelovic 3, Spivak 2, Miceika), Encamp 0 *Zenit win 13-0 on agg*
Zvartnots 2 (Nazaryan pen, Avanesyan), Primorje 0 *Zvartnots win 6-3 on agg*

Byes: *Anderlecht, Ankaragucu, Austria Vienna, Besiktas, Blackburn Rovers, Bordeaux, Chelsea, Chievo Verona, CSKA Moscow, Denzilspor, Dynamo Zagreb, Grasshoppers, Heerenveen, Hertha Berlin, Iraklis, Kocaelispor, Lazio, Leeds United Lorient, PAOK Salonika, Panathinikos, Paris St Germain, Parma, Porto, Rangers, Schalke, Slavia Prague, Utrecht, Viking, Vitesse Arnhem, Werder Bremen,*
Intertoto Cup winners: Fulham, Malaga, VfB Stuttgart and teams eliminated from the Champions League third qualifying round – Apoel Nicosia, Boavista, Brondby, Celtic, Fenerbahce, Graz, Legia Warsaw, Levski Sofia, Liverec, Partizan Belgrade, Shakhtjor Dontesk, Sparta Prague, Sporting Lisbon, Sturm Graz, Zalaegersegi, Zeljeznicar.

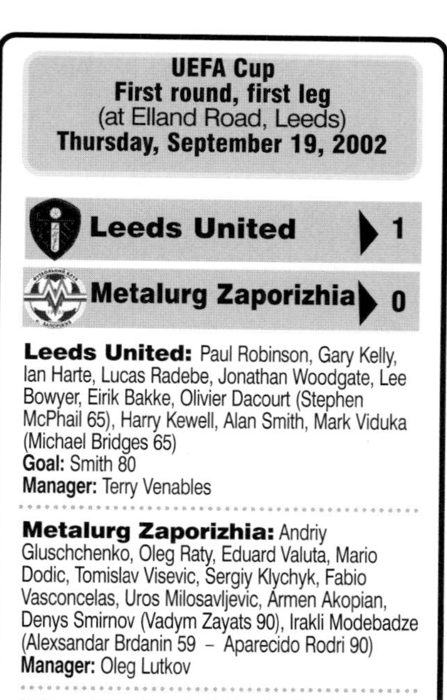
UEFA Cup
First round, first leg
(at Elland Road, Leeds)
Thursday, September 19, 2002

Leeds United 1

Metalurg Zaporizhia 0

Leeds United: Paul Robinson, Gary Kelly, Ian Harte, Lucas Radebe, Jonathan Woodgate, Lee Bowyer, Eirik Bakke, Olivier Dacourt (Stephen McPhail 65), Harry Kewell, Alan Smith, Mark Viduka (Michael Bridges 65)
Goal: Smith 80
Manager: Terry Venables

Metalurg Zaporizhia: Andriy Gluschchenko, Oleg Raty, Eduard Valuta, Mario Dodic, Tomislav Visevic, Sergiy Klychyk, Fabio Vasconcelas, Uros Milosavljevic, Armen Akopian, Denys Smirnov (Vadym Zayats 90), Irakli Modebadze (Alexsandar Brdanin 59 - Aparecido Rodri 90)
Manager: Oleg Lutkov

Referee: Mikko Vuorela (Finland) **Att:** 30,000

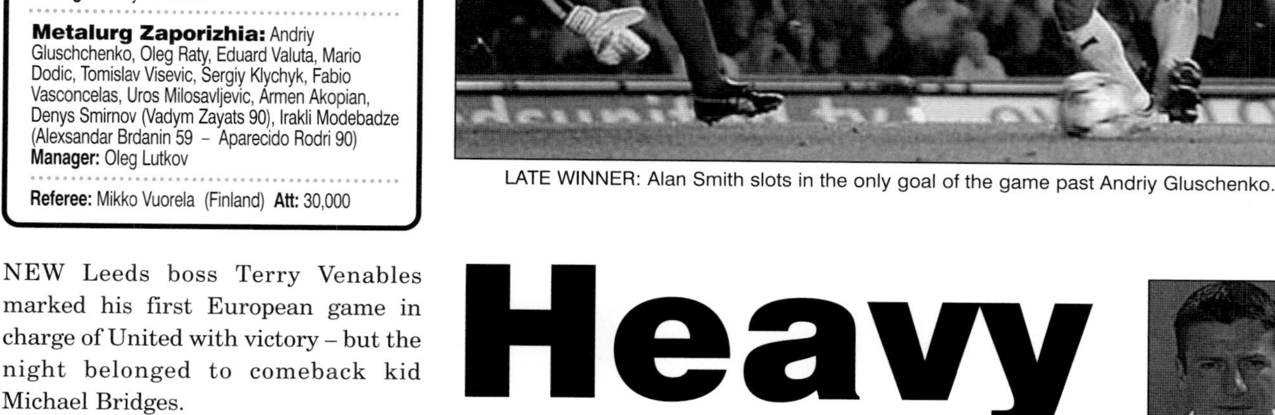
LATE WINNER: Alan Smith slots in the only goal of the game past Andriy Gluschenko.

Heavy Metal

Michael Bridges.

Stubborn Ukrainians rock United

NEW Leeds boss Terry Venables marked his first European game in charge of United with victory – but the night belonged to comeback kid Michael Bridges.

The popular striker put a near two-year nightmare behind him to set up United's slender 1-0 victory over Ukrainian minnows Metalurg Zaporizhia.

The 24-year-old forward sprang from the bench for his first competitive game for 23 months to lay on Alan Smith's precious 80th minute goal.

Leeds had endured a frustrating night as Metalurg virtually pulled all their men behind the ball, but substitute Bridges' arrival for the ineffective Mark Viduka came as Leeds were getting up a full head of steam.

With time drifting away, he chased a rather aimless ball down the inside-right channel and muscled a defender off the ball and cut it back for Smith to roll in a simple goal.

"It was a big game for him tonight," said Venables of Bridges, who had not played since being injured in the 0-0 Champions League draw against Besiktas in Turkey in 2000.

"I thought he did really well. There must have been times when he was very, very low in the last few years. I am pleased for him," added Venables.

Despite the victory it was far from a vintage Leeds performance against the time-wasting Ukrainians' ultra-defensive tactics which looked like paying off as they battled stoutly, particularly in the second half when Leeds began to move the ball about much quicker then they had in a sterile opening 45 minutes.

United wanted too many touches on the ball in the first half and Zaphorizia were able to shut down the spaces fairly comfortably. The visitors always looked suspect to crosses, but the problem for Leeds was that their delivery into the box was simply not good enough.

Although they were hardly flowing, Leeds at least were attacking with more fire after half-time and goalkeeper Andriy Gluschenko thrust out his left hand to prevent a Smith header from arrowing in to the top corner.

Some of skipper Gluschenko's saves were unorthodox but mightly effective as he denied Ian Harte and Harry Kewell in quick succession, then Harte went close with a trademark free-kick and substitute Stephen McPhail teased the best cross of the night on to the head of Eirik Bakke but the Norweigian's effort was blocked.

The pressure and the chances mounted and Metalurg's armour was finally dented with ten minutes left.

United continued to force the pace after the goal and it needed a spectacular save by Gluschenko to tip over a blistering volley from Lucas Radebe from United's 16th – and final – corner of the night in injury time.

As he looked ahead to a long journey to the Ukraine, Venables admitted: "We have a bit to do."

Just in the Nick of time

UP FOR IT: Danny Mills and a Zaphorizia player in aerial combat, while the watchiing Nicky Barmby awaits the outcome.

ONE of Terry Venables' pre-season signings, Nick Barmby, got United off the hook in Ukraine.

Barmby, a £2.75million August signing from Liverpool, had worked with Venables at one of his previous clubs, Tottenham.

The 77th minute goal he scored against Metalurg Zaporizhia may not have been the best of the attacking midfielder's career but it was priceless for Leeds. It earned them a 1-1 draw to enable them to scrape through 2-1 on aggregate against extremely modest opposition.

After their ultra-cautious approach in the first game, United were promised by caretaker-manager Oleg Lutkov that they would face a different attack-minded outfit in the second leg which was played in the city of Dnepropetrovsk because the stadium at Zaporizhia, 50 miles further south, was deemed unfit to stage European football. The Dneproperovsk pitch wasn't the greatest and it took United some time to get adjusted to it, while Metalurg were hardly progressive.

But United were stunned on 24 minutes when Brazilian Fabio Vasconcelos crashed a shot against the bar and before any defenders could react, Irakili Modebadze headed the rebound in an arc over the despairing Paul Robinson.

United were denied an equaliser when Dominic Matteo's close range shot was brilliantly stopped by goalkeeper Andry Glushchenko and United continued to struggle to break down the Ukranian defence.

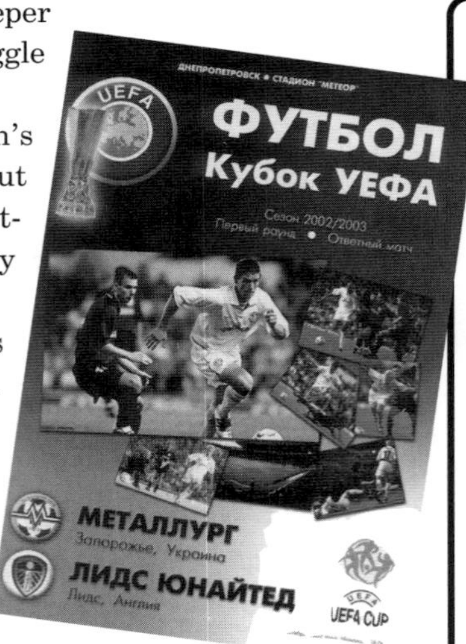

It could have been worse when Armen Akopyan's curling free-kick hit a post with Robinson beaten, but by then there were signs that Zaporizhia were starting to tire and Leeds stepped up the pace with Harry Kewell posing an increasing threat down the left.

It was the Australian's surging run 13 minutes from the end which took him past Eduard Valuta and crossed dangerously in to the box. Goalkeeper Gluschenko deflected the ball away to Alan Smith whose header was going wide but Barmby stole in unmarked to shoot in to an unguarded net from close range.

With an away goal in the bank, United were in control and any hope Metalurg had of getting back in the tie vanished when Uros Milosavljevic was sent off for a second bookable offence after lashing out at Barmby.

An extremely relieved Venables said: "It was a dramatic game. The goal was against the run of play, but it made us seriously worry. I am happy we could equalise in normal time. I think the class of my players told in the end."

UEFA Cup
First round, second leg
(at Meteor Stadium, Dnepropetrovsk)
Thursday, October 3, 2002

Metalurg Zaporizhia 1

Leeds United 1

Leeds United win 2-1 on agg

Metalurg Zaporizhia: Andriy Glushchenko, Oleg Raty, Eduard Valuta, Mario Dodic, Tomislav Visevic, Sergiy Klyuchyk, Mykola Lapko, Uros Milosavljevic, Armen Akopian, Fabio Vasconcelas, Irakli Modebadze
Goal: Modebadze 24
Manager: Oleg Lutkov

Leeds United: Paul Robinson, Gary Kelly, Ian Harte, Danny Mills, Dominic Matteo (Michael Duberry 90), Lee Bowyer, Eirik Bakke, Stephen McPhail, Nick Barmby, Harry Kewell, Alan Smith
Goal: Barmby 77
Manager: David O'Leary

Referee: Muhittin Bosat (Turkey) **Att:** 6,500

French connection see Fulham home

FULHAM'S French foreign legion ensured a winning start to the Cottagers first-ever European campaign.

They went in to the UEFA Cup as one of the three Intertoto Cup winners and were rewarded with a 1-0 away win in the first round, first leg against Hadjuk Split, with a Steed Malbranque goal. Malbranque and fellow Frenchman Steve Marlet netted in the 2-2 return at Loftus Road.

Ipswich and Celtic also got through, but Chelsea, for the third year running, and Rangers were surprise big-name casualties.

First round, first leg

Aberdeen 0, Hertha Berlin 0
AIK Solna 3 (Nordin, A Andersson, Rubarth), Fenerbahce 3 (Revivo, Johnson, Stevic)
Anderlecht 0, Stabaek 1 (Michelsen)
Ankaragucu 1 (Niculescu), Alaves 2 (Astudillo, Navarro)
Apoel Nicosia 2 (Sztipanovics, Khachatryan), Graz 0
Austria Vienna 5 (Janocko 2, Feitoza pen, Helstad 2), Shakthjor Donetsk 1 (Bielik)
Besiktas 2 (Pancu, Ahmet Dursun), Sarajevo 2 (Obuca, Osmanhodzic)
Blackburn Rovers 1 (Grabbi), CSKA Sofia 1 (Dimitrov)
Bordeaux 6 (Sommeil, Dugarry, Feindouno, Pauleta pen, Vavrik, Darcheville), Matador Puchov 0
Celta Vigo 2 (Cataha, McCarthy), Odense 0
Celtic 8 (Larsson 3, Petrov, Sutton, Lambert, Hartson, Valgaeren), Sudova 1 (Radzineviciius)
Chelsea 2 (Hasselbaink, De Lucas), Viking Stavanger 1 (Wright)
CSKA Moscow 1 (Popov), Parma 1 (Mutu)
Denzilspor 2 (Ozkan 2), Lorient 0
Dynamo Zagreb 6 (Maric, Mitu, Olic, Polovancec, Petrovic 2), Zalaegersegi 0
FC Copenhagen 0, Djurgaarden 0
Ferencvaros 4 (Tokolic 2, Lipscei, Dragoner), Kocaelispor 0
Gomel 1 (Icvanov), Schalke 4 (Sand, Varela, Matella, Rodriguez)
Grasshoppers 3 (Baurina, Barijho, Nunez), Zenit 1 (Filatov)
Hadjuk Split 0, Fulham 1 (Malbranque)
Ipswich Town 1 (Armstrong), Sartid 1 (Mirosavljevic)
Iraklis 4 (Mieciel, Stoltidis, Gonias 2), Anorthosis 2 (Neophytou 2)
Karnten 0, Hapoel Tel Aviv 4 (Halmai, Welton, Gershon, Udi)
Lazio 4 (Manfredini, Lopez, Inzaghi, Cesar), Xanthi 0
Leeds United 1 (Smith), Metalurg Zaporiziya 0
Legia Warsaw 4 (Zielinski, Vukovic, Svitlica 2), Utrecht 1 (Van Mol)
Leixoes 2 (Brito, Detinho), PAOK Salonika 1 (Kukielka)
Levski Sofia 4 (Simonovic 2, Telkiyski 2), Brondby 1 (Madsen)
Liberec 3 (Nezmar, Zboncuk, Gyan), Dynamo Tbilisi 2 (Daraselia, Anchabadze)
Litechs Lovech 0, Panathinikos 1 (Jelenkovic og)
Maccabi Tel Aviv 1 (Dago), Boavista 0
Midtylland 1 (Laursen), Varteks 0
Metalurgs Donetsk 2 (Tchoutang 2), Werder Bremen 2 (Lisztes, Verlaat)
Mouscron 2 (Mpenza 2), Slavia Prague 2 (Vachousek, Petrous)
National Bucharest 3 (Curt, Illie pen, Olah), Heerenveen 0
Paris St Germain 3 (Ronaldinho, Pochettino, Cardetti), Ujpest Budapest 0
Porto 6 (Jankauskas 2, Darlei, Riberiro, Postiga 2), Polonia 0
Primorje 0, Wisla Kracow 2 (Uche, Kuzba)
Red Star Belgrade 0, Chievo Verona 0
Servette 2 (Obradovic, Frei), Amica Wronki 3 (Krol, Zienczuk)
Sparta Prague 3 (Pospisil, Baranek, Poborsky), Siroki Brijego 0
Sporting Lisbon 1 (Tonito), Partizan Belgrade 3 (Hugo og, Delibasic, Iliev)
Sturm Graz 5 (Wetl, Szabics, Dag, Mujiriz 2), Livingston 2 (Zarate, Lovell)
Viktoria Zizkov 2 (Piki, Straceny), Rangers 0
Vitesse Arnhem 1 (Peeters), Rapid Bucharest 1 (Lensci)
VfB Stuttgart 4 (Amanatidis, Kuranyi 2, Gleb), Ventspils 1 (Rimkus)
Zeljeznicar 0, Malaga 0
Zimbru Chisinau 0, Real Betis 2 (Perez, Dinu og)

First round, second leg

Alaves 3 (Dursun og, Turiel 2), Ankaragucu 0 *Alaves win 5-1 on agg*
Amica Wronki 1 (Burkhadt), Servette 2 (Frei 2) *4-4 on agg. Amica Wronki win on away goals*
Anorthoosis 3 (Ketsbaia, Majak, Xiourouppas), Iraklis 1 (Fofonka) *5-5 on agg Anorthosis win on away goals*
Boavista 4 (Strool og, Jocivalter 2, Serginho), Maccabi Tel Aviv 1 (Torjmau) *Boavista win 4-2 on agg*
Brondby 1 (Jonson), Levski Sofia 1 (Ivankov pen) *Levski Sofia win 5-2 on agg*
Chievo Verona 0, Red Star Belgrade 2 (Guozdenonic, Milovanoic) *Red Star Belgrade win 2-0 on agg*
CSKA Sofia 3 (Gargorov 2, Agnaldo), Blackburn Rovers 3 (Thompson, Ostenstad, Duff) *4-4 on agg. Blackburn Rovers win on away goals*
Djugaarden 3 (Albechtsen og, Elmander, Kallstrom pen), FC Copenhagen 1 (Zizkovic) *Djurgaarden win 3-1 on agg*
Dynamo Tbilisi 0, Liberec 1 (Zboncak) *Liberec win 4-2 on agg*
Fenerbachce 3 (Gunes, Johnson, Serhat), AIK Solna 1 (Hoch) *Fenerbahce win 6-4 on agg*
Fulham 2 (Marlet, Malbranque pen), Hadjuk Split 2 (Dolonga, Vejic) *Fulham win 3-2 on agg*
Graz 1 (Ehmann), Apoel Nicosia 1 (Daskalakis) *Apoel Nicosia win 3-1 on agg*
Hapoel Tel Aviv 0, Karnten 1 (Oberleitner) *Hapoel Tel Aviv win 4-1 on agg*
Heerenveen 2 (Hansson, Denneboom), National 0 *National win 3-2 on agg*
Hertha Berlin 1 (Preetz), Aberdeen 0 *Hertha Berlin win 1-0 on agg*
Kocaelispor 0, Ferencvaros 1 (Lipcsei) *Ferencvaros win 5-0 on agg*
Livingston 4 (Wilson 2 – 1 pen, Xausa, Andrews), Sturm Graz 3 (Sbabics 2, Mujiri) *Sturm Graz win 8-6 on agg*
Lorient 3 (Kroupi, Guel, Gauvin), Denizlispor 1 (Martini og) *Lorient win 7-3 on agg*
Matador Puchov 1 (Muzlag), Bordeaux 4 (Savio, Darchville 2, Feindouno) *Bordeaux win 10-1 on agg*
Metalurg Zaphoriziya 1 (Modebadze), Leeds United 1 (Barmby) *Leeds United win 2-1 on agg*
Odense 1 (Derveld), Celta Vigo 0 *Celta Vigo win 2-1 on agg*
PAOK Salonika 4 (Salpingidis, Okhas 2, Koutsopoulos), Leixoes 1 (Pedras) *PAOK Salonika win 5-3 on agg*
Panathinikos 2 (Warzcha 2), Litechs Lovech 1 (Graf) *Panathinikos win 3-1 on agg*
Parma 3 (Adriano, Mutu 2), CSKA Moscow 2 (Semak 2) *Parma win 4-3 on agg*
Partizan Belgrade 3 (Delibasic, Zivkovic, Cakar), Sporting Lisbon 3 (Tonito, Kutuzov, Contraras) *Partizan Belgrade 6-4 on agg*
Polonia 2 (Lukasiewicz, Kus), Porto 0 *Porto win 6-2 on agg*
Rangers 3 (de Boer 2, Arveladze), Viktoria Zizkov 1 (Licka) aet *3-3 on agg. Viktoria Zizkov win on away goals*
Rapid Bucharest 0, Vitesse Arnhem 1 (Peeters) *Vitesse Arnhem win 2-1 on agg*
Sarajevo 0, Besiktas 5 (Pancu, Uzulmez, Dursun pen, Sulun, Begecarslau) *Besiktas win 7-2 on agg*
Sartid 0, Ipswich Town 1 (M Bent pen) *Ipswich Town win 2-1 on agg*
Shakhtjor Donetsk 1 (Lewandowski), Austria Vienna 0 *Shaktjor Donetsk win 5-2 on agg*
Schalke '04 4 (Wilmots, Hanke 2, Kmetsch), Gomel 0 *Schalke win 8-1 on agg*
Siroki Brijeg 0, Sparta Prague 1 (Jarosik) *Sparta Prague win 4-0 on agg*
Staebaek 1 (Wilhelmsson), Anderlecht 2 (De Bilde, MacDonald) *2-2 on agg. Anderlcht win on away goals*
Sudova 0, Celtic 2 (Fernandez, Thompson) *Celtic win 10-1 on agg*
Ujpest Budapest 0, Paris St Germain 1 (Benachour) *Paris St Germain win 4-0 on agg*
Utrecht 1 (Kuijt), Legia Warsaw 3 (Kucharski, Svitlica 2) *Legia Warsaw win 7-2 on agg*
Varteks 1 (Mumlek), Midtjlland 1 (Pingpong) *Midtjlland win 2-1 on agg*
Ventspils 1 (Landgrev), VfB Stuttgart 4 (Tiffert 2, Ganea, Amanatidis) *VfB Stuttgart win 8-2 on agg*
Viking 4 (Berre, Kopteff, Nevland 2), Chelsea 2 (Lampard, Terry) *Viking win 5-4 on agg*
Werder Bremen 8 (Verlaat, Micoud 2, Borowski 2, Charisteas, Klasnic 2) Metalurgs Donetsk 0 *Werder Bremen win 10-2 on agg*
Wisla Crakow 6 (Zurawski 2 – 1 pen, Uche, Jop, P Brozek, Stolarczyk), Primorje 1 (Zatkovic)
Xanthi 0, Lazio 0 *Lazio win 4-0 on agg*
Zalaegersegi 1 (Sabo), Dynamo Zagreb 3 (Mitu, Olic pen, Mujdn) *Dynamo Zagreb win 9-1 on agg*
Zenit 2 (Kerzhakov 2), Grasshoppers 1 (Baturina) *Grasshoppers win 4-3 on agg*

Kewell spares United blushes

Victory better late than never

Harry Kewell.

UEFA Cup
Second round, first leg
(at Elland Road, Leeds)
Thursday, October 31, 2002

Leeds United 1

Hapoel Tel Aviv 0

Leeds United: Paul Robinson, Gary Kelly, Ian Harte, Lucas Radebe, Jonathan Woodgate, Eirik Bakke, Olivier Dacourt (Stephen McPhail 65), Nick Barmby (Michael Bridges 69), Alan Smith, Harry Kewell, Mark Viduka (Danny Mills 90)
Goal: Kewell 83
Manager: Terry Venables

Hapoel Tel Aviv: Shavit Elimelech, Rahamin Halic, Ygal Antebi, Shimon Gershon, Asaf Domb, Afek Omri, Gabor Halmai (Shay Abutbul 65), Josef Abukasis, Salim Toama, Pini Balili (Kfir Udi 84), Carlos Welton (Seghy Clescenko 59)
Manager: Dror Kashtan

Referee: Jack Van Hulton (Holland) **Att:** 31,867

HARRY Kewell snatched victory for below-par Leeds United as they struggled to a 1-0 victory over Hapoel Tel Aviv at Elland Road.

Terry Venables' side looked as though they were going to be denied by the Israeli outfit until the Aussie seized on to Alan Smith's hooked overhead pass and crashed in a deflected shot from 12 yards with just seven minutes remaining.

Of equal importance was a stunning late save by goalkeeper Paul Robinson to tip away a ferocious free-kick by Salim Toama. That ensured that Leeds kept a clean sheet which meant an away goal would leave Hapoel with a difficult job to progress to the third round.

Hapoel were already handicapped because UEFA had ruled that they could not play in Tel Aviv because of fears over security – a decision their chief Dror Kashtan branded "unfair".

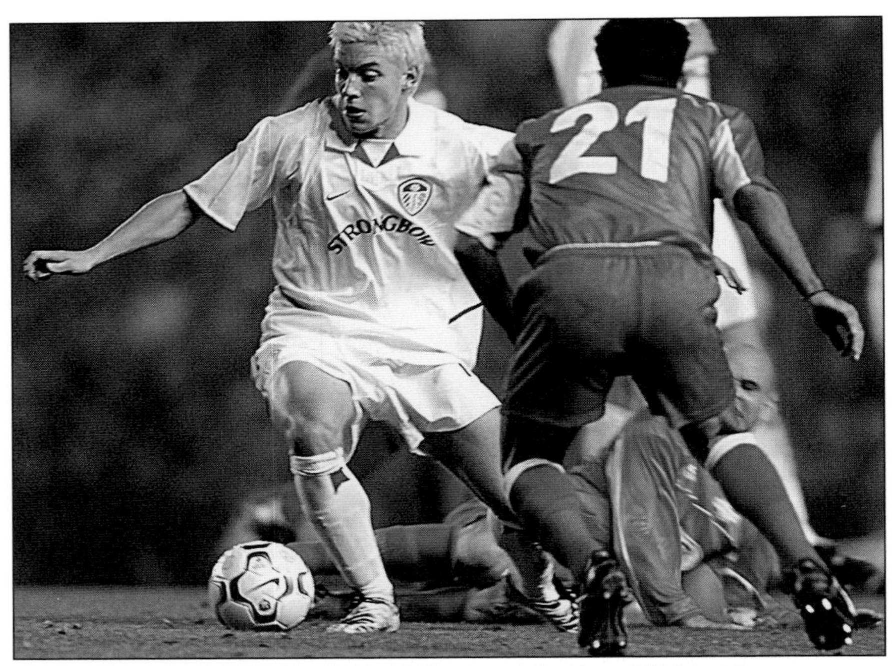

TWINKLING FEET: Alan Smith dribbles through the Hapoel Tel Aviv defence.

His team certainly caused Leeds some problems, particularly in the first half, when Robinson made two superb saves, clutching a goal-bound lob from speedy Pini Balili and pushing away a thumping free-kick from the dangerous Toama.

Following Maccabi Haifa's 3-0 defeat of Manchester United earlier in the week, it was clear that football in Israel was on a high and Hapoel, who beat Chelsea, Lokomotiv Moscow and Parma on their way to a UEFA Cup quarter-final last season, showed their pedigree.

They were willing to take the game to Leeds and defended stoically, particularly in the second-half as Leeds gained attacking momentum. United didn't really get going in the first period but still posed a threat. Nick Barmby's overhead kick struck the inside of a post and bounced along the line to safety. Minutes later Mark Viduka saw a free-kick hit the bar with goalkeeper Shavit Elimelech beaten.

When Ian Harte's free-kick suffered a similar fate – curling against the woodwork junction – on the hour, Venables admitted he thought it was going to be one of those nights.

But led by the indefatigable Alan Smith, Leeds kept hammering away and gained their reward with Kewell's strike to give Leeds their first win in six matches.

Venables said: "I do not think you are going to get many big leads in this competition because the teams are very, very close – and there are still the ones to come in from the Champions League."

Super Smith to the fore

UEFA Cup
Second round, second leg
(at Artemio Franchi Stadium, Florence)
Thursday, November 14, 2002

 **Hapoel Tel Aviv**  **1**

Leeds United  **4**

Leeds United win 5-1 on agg

Hapoel Tel Aviv: Shavit Elimelech, Rahamin Halic, Shimon Gershon, Asaf Domb, Yakov Hillel, Josef Abukasis, Gabor Halmai Salim Toama, Afek Omri (Ben Zion Luz HT), Albert Knafo (Pini Balili 62), Serghy Cleschenko (Kfir Udi HT)
Goals: Abukasis 2
Manager: Dror Kashtan

Leeds United: Paul Robinson, Gary Kelly, Ian Harte, (Frazer Richardson 66) Michael Duberry, Lucas Radebe (Matthew Kilgallon 61), Lee Bowyer, Eirik Bakke (Stephen McPhail 55), Nick Barmby, Jason Wilcox, Harry Kewell, Alan Smith
Goals: Smith 30, 53, 61, 82
Manager: Terry Venables

Referee: Fritz Stuchlik (Austria) **Att:** 4,000

ALAN Smith's rapid progress was confirmed with a four-goal demolition of Hapoel Tel Aviv.

The 22-year-old England striker had a field day in front of goal as Leeds cruised through after an earlier scare.

He netted all the goals in a 4-1 win – equalling the best-ever haul in a European match by a Leeds player set by Peter Lorimer, whose four-timer came in the 9-0 rout of Spora Luxembourg in 1967.

With UEFA switching the game from Israel to the Italian city of Florence, Leeds followers made up the large majority of the sparse 4,000 crowd spread out in the Artemio Franchi Stadium.

But the Yorkshire following were stunned as Hapoel levelled the tie within 80 seconds of the start. Eirik Bakke was harshly penalised for a tackle on Salim Toama on the edge of the box and Josef Abukasis, whose shooting had been a feature of the first leg, curled a 25-yard free-kick past Paul Robinson off an upright.

It took time for United to recover but with Harry Kewell threatening, United looked more than capable of regaining overall control and on the half-hour Bakke slipped in Smith whose left-footed angled drive nestled in the corner of Shavit Elimelech's goal.

Almost immediately, Ian Harte's error presented Hapoel with an opening and Omri Afek clipped the bar with a shot from the ege of the area.

Harte almost made amends soon afterwards with a free-kick that thumped against the bar but the tie was effectively settled in the period just after half-time.

Hapoel pressurised a Leeds defence which had several shaky moments until Smith's harrying paid off in the 54th minute to put United 2-1 up. He squeezed between defender Asaf Domb and the advancing Elimelech to hook the ball towards goal from a tight angle and it span over the line.

After that it was easy for United with Smith completing his hat-trick just after the hour when he followed up his own blocked header to drive the ball home.

United were in such control that rookie defenders Matthew Kilgallon and Frazer Richardson were sent on for their senior debuts.

Hapoel's bad night got worse when goalscorer Abukasis received his second yellow card and was ordered off with 12 minutes left and Smith wrapped up a memorable evening as he had time and space to plant Kewell's perfect cross past the stranded Elimelech.

STRIKE ONE: Alan Smith fires in United's equaliser, the first of four goals for the Rothwell raider.

Owen double sparks efficient Liverpool

UEFA Cup holders Liverpool remained on course to retain the trophy they had won in the dramatic 2002 final against Spanish side Alaves.

The Reds dropped in to the competition from the Champions League at the third round stage and promptly beat Dutch side Vitesse Arnhem 1-0 home and away in their usual efficient style with both goals coming from Michael Owen.

Fulham lost their second round first leg 2-1 at Hertha Berlin, the Germans winning the match with an own-goal by Argentinian striker Facundo Sava, who sliced in a free-kick by Brazilian Marcelinho.

The Cottagers were held 0-0 in the second leg and tumbled out. They were joined by Ipswich whose exit at the same stage came in agonising fashion.

They took a 1-0 advantage to Liberec where they were beaten by a Bafour Gyan goal and went on to lose 4-2 on penalties.

The other Premiership outfit, Blackburn Rovers, lost 1-0 in the all-British tie at Celtic, Henrik Larsson netting the goal.

The Scottish side then put on a brilliant performance at Ewood Park and deservedly won with goals by star Swedish striker Larsson and former Rovers player Chris Sutton.

Celtic's reward was a tough double-header against Spanish side Celta Vigo in the third round. Once again the prolific Larsson scored the only goal in Glasgow – his 24th of the season – which gave the Hoops their eighth successive home victory in Europe.

Celtic manager Martin O'Neill, whom United had wanted to replace George Graham and David O'Leary at Elland Road, was dismissed from the dugout in the 87th minute for arguing with officials.

Second round, first leg

Alaves 1 (Fernandez), Besiktas 1 (Karmona og)
Anderlecht 3 (Jestrovic 2, Dindane), Midtylland 1 (Kristensen)
Apoel Nicosia 0, Hertha Berlin 1 (Karwan)
Boavista 2 (Silva, Eder), Anorthosis 1 (Michaelski)
Celta Vigo 3 (Jose Ignacio, Edu, McCarthy), Viking 0
Celtic 1 (Larsson), Blackburn Rovers 0
Durgaarden 0, Bordeaux 1 (Feindouno)
Dynamo Zagreb 0, Fulham 3 (Boa Morte, Marlet, Hayles)
Fenerbahce 1 (Washington), Panathinikos 1 (Basinas)
Ferencvaros 0, VfB Stuttgart 0
FK Austria 0, Porta 1 (Derlei)
Ipswich Town 1 (D Bent), Liberec 0
Lazio 1 (Fiore), Red Star Belgrade 0
Leeds United 1 (Kewell), Hapoel Tel Aviv 0
Legia Warsw 2 (Dudek, Svitlica pen), Schalke 3 (Varela 2, Sand)
Malaga 2 (Romero, Dely Valdes), Amica Wronki 1 (Jikia)
National Bucharest 0, Paris St Germain 2 (Leroy, Luiz)
PAOK Salonika 2 (Chasiotis, Yiasoumi), Grasshoppers 1 (Nunez pen)
Parma 2 (Donati, Mutu), Wisla Kracow 1 (Zurawski)
Partizan Belgrade 3 (Lazovic, Sillic, Vukic), Slavia Prague 1 (Dostalek)
Sparta Prague 1 (Jarosik), Denzilspor 0
Sturm Graz 1 (Szabics), Levski Sofia 0
Viktoria Zizkov 0, Real Betis 1 (Denilson)
Vitesse Arnhem 2 (Amoah, Verlaat og), Werder Bremen 1 (Verlaat)

Second round, second leg

Amica Wronki 1 (Gesior), Malaga 2 (Silva, Musampa) *Malaga win 4-2 on agg*
Anorthosis 0, Boavista 1 (Silva pen) *Boavista win 3-1 on agg*
Blackburn Rovers 0, Celtic 2 (Larsson, Sutton) *Celtic win 3-0 on agg*
Besiktas 1 (Ilhan), Alves 0 *Besiktas win 2-1 on agg*
Bordeaux 2 (Feindouno 2), Djurgaarden 1 (Elmander) *Bordeaux win 3-1 on agg*
Denzilspor 2 (Ozkan 2), Sparta Prague 0 *Denzilspor win 2-1 on agg*
Fulham 2 (Malbranque, Boa Morte), Dynamo Zagreb 1 (Olic) *Fulham win 5-1 on agg*
Grasshoppers 1 (Cabanas), PAOK Salonika 1 (Markos) *PAOK Salonika win 3-2 on agg*
Hapoel Tel Aviv 1 (Abukasis), Leeds United 4 (Smith 4) *Leeds United win 5-1 on agg*
Hertha Berlin 4 (Preetz, Marcelinho, Beinlich, Luizao), Apoel Nicosia 0 *Hertha Berlin win 5-0 on agg*
Levski Sofia 1 (Simonovic), Sturm Graz 0 *1-1 on agg. Sturm Graz win 8-7 on penalties*
Midtylland 0, Anderlecht 3 (Seol, Jestrovic, Dindane) *Anderlecht win 6-1 on agg*
Liberec 1 (Gyan), Ipswich Town 0 *1-1 on agg. Liberec win 4-2 on penalties*
Panathinikos 4 (Lyberopoulos, Goumas, Michelsen, Warzcha), Fenerbahce 1 (Sanli) *Panathinikos win 5-2 on agg*
Porto 2 (Postiga, Derlei), FK Austria 0 *Porto win 3-0 on agg*
Paris St Germain 1 (Leroy), National Bucharest 0 *Paris St Germain win 3-0 on agg*
Real Betis 3 (Casas, Sanchez pen, Tomas), Viktoria Zizkov 0 *Real Betis win 4-0 on agg*
Red Star Belgrade 1 (Boskovic), Lazio 1 (Chiesa) *Lazio win 2-1 on agg*
Schalke 0, Legia Warsaw 0 *Schalke win 3-2 on agg*
Slavia Prague 5 (Vachovsek 2, Petrous pen, Gedeon, Adauto), Partizan Belgrade 1 (Ivic) aet *Slavia Prague win 6-4 on agg*
VfB Stuttgart 2 (Amanatidis, Fernando Meira), Ferecvaros 0 *VfB Stuttgart win 2-0 on agg*
Viking 1 (Sigurdsson), Celta Vigo 1 (Mostovoi) *Celta Vigo win 4-1 on agg*
Werder Bremen 3 (Baumann, Krstajic, Chariteas), Vitesse Arnhem 3 (Levchenko pen, Claessens, Mbamba) *Vitesse Arnhem win 5-4 on agg*
Wisla Kracow 4 (Kosowski, Zurawski 2, Dubicki), Parma 1 (Adriano) *Wisla Kracow win 5-3 on agg*

Third round, first leg

AEK Athens 4 (Georgatos, Niolaidis, Petkov,Zagorakis), Maccabi Haifa 0
Besiktas 3 (Pancu, Yildirim, Nouma), Dynamo Kiev 1 (Husin)
Bordeaux 0, Anderlecht 2 (Jestrovic, Hasi)
Brugge 1 (Van der Heyden), VfB Stuttgart 2 (Balakov, Kuranyi)
Celtic 1 (Larsson), Celta Vigo 0
DIspor 0, Lyon 0
Hertha Berlin 2 (Beinlich, Sava og), Fulham 1 (Marlet)
Liberec 2 (Zboncak, Slovak pen), Panathinikos 2 (Basinas pen, Olisadebe)
Malaga 0, Leeds United 0
PAOK Salonika 1 (Georgiadis), Slavia Prague 0
Paris St Germain 2 (Nyarko, Fiorese), Boavista 1 (Claudio)
Porto 3 (Postiga, Derlei, Jankaukas), Lens 0
Real Betis 1 (Perez), Auxerre 0
Sturm Graz 1 (Amoah), Lazio 3 (Chiesa, Inzaghi 2)
Vitesse Arnhem 0, Liverpool 1 (Owen)
Wislaw Krakow 1 (Poulsen og), Schalke 1 (E Mpenza)

Third round, second leg

Anderlecht 2 (Dindane, Jestrovic), Bordeaux 2 (Darchville 2) *Anderlecht win 4-2 on agg*
Auxerre 2 (Tanio, Lachuer), Real Betis 0 *Auxerre win 2-1 on agg*
Boavista 1 (Silva pen), Paris St Germain 0 *2-2 on agg. Boavista win on away goals*
Celta Vigo 2 (Jesuli, McCarthy), Celtic 1 (Hartson) *2-2 on agg. Celtic win on away goals*
Dynamo Kiev 0, Besiktas 0 *Besiktas win 3-1 on agg*
Fulham 0, Hertha Berlin 0 *Hertha Berlin win 2-1 on agg*
Lazio 0, Sturm Graz 1 (Szebics) *Lazio win 2-1 on agg*
Leeds United 1 (Bakke), Malaga 2 (Dely Valdes 2) *Malaga win 2-1 on agg*
Lens 1 (Song), Porto 0 *Porto win 3-1 on agg*
Liverpool 1 (Owen), Vitesse Arnhem 0 *Liverpool win 2-0 on agg*
Lyon 0, Denzilspor 1 (Ozhan) *Denzilspor win 1-0 on agg*
Hacabi Haifa 1 (Badir pen), AEK Athens 4 (Katsouranis, Lakis 2, Nalitzis) *AEK Athens win 8-1 on agg*
Panathinikos 1 (Fyssas), Liberec 0 *Panathinikos win 3-2 on agg*
Schalke 1 (Hajto), Wisla Kracow 4 (Zurawski 2, Uche, Koswowski) *Wisla Kracow win 5-2 on agg*
Slavia Prague 4 (Skacel, Vachousek, Kuka 2), PAOK Salonika 0 *Slavia Prague win 4-1 on agg*
VfB Stuttgart 1 (Gleb), Brugges 0 *VfB Stuttgart win 3-1 on agg*

Gritty draw eases pressure on Terry

UEFA Cup
Third round, first leg
(at La Roseleda Stadium, Malaga)
Thursday, November 28, 2002

 **Malaga**  **0**

 **Leeds United** **0**

Malaga: Pedro Contreras, 'Josemi' Gonzalez Rey, Fernando Sanz, Mikel Roteta, Vicente Valcarce, Antonio 'Manu' ('Edgar' Patricio De Carvalho Pacheco 67), Carlos 'Sandro' Sierra, Marcelo Romero, Raul Iznata (Sergio 'Koke' Contreras Pardo 67), Kiki Musampa, Julio Cesar Dely Valdes
Manager: Joaquin Peiro Lucas

Leeds United: Paul Robinson, Gary Kelly, Ian Harte, Michael Duberry, Jonathan Woodgate, Lee Bowyer, Stephen McPhail, Eirik Bakke, Jason Wilcox, Hary Kewell, Alan Smith
Manager: Terry Venables

Referee: Alfredo Trentalonge (Italy) **Att:** 35,000

EYES ON THE BALL: Michael Duberry clears his lines in United's dull 0-0 draw in Malaga.

UNITED'S season – and Terry Venables' job – hung in the balance as United headed to the Spanish coastal resort of Malaga.

Life at Elland Road had been no holiday for Venables as United's form had dipped alarmingly in the Premiership, leaving them hovering above the relegation zone. They went to Spain on the back of two successive defeats – a 4-2 thumping at home by Bolton and and 2-0 loss at Tottenham where one of the goals was scored by former Leeds favourite Robbie Keane.

Terry Venables.

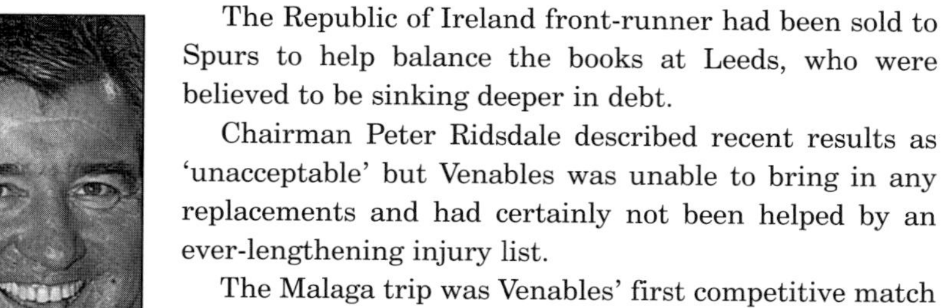

The Republic of Ireland front-runner had been sold to Spurs to help balance the books at Leeds, who were believed to be sinking deeper in debt.

Chairman Peter Ridsdale described recent results as 'unacceptable' but Venables was unable to bring in any replacements and had certainly not been helped by an ever-lengthening injury list.

The Malaga trip was Venables' first competitive match in Spain since his halcyon days at Barcelona but he had to prepare his side without nine first team squad members – including strikers Mark Viduka and Robbie Fowler, the latter still waiting to make his European debut for Leeds because of injury.

The UEFA Cup was providing some relief for United's domestic difficulties, but all was not right in the Leeds camp with Venables fining Olivier Dacourt for critical comments he made in a French magazine about the United boss.

But Leeds showed plenty of commitment in the La Roseleda Stadium where a superb defensive display by Jonathan Woodgate was able to muffle the drumbeats of the Spanish club's supporters.

United posed little threat in a poor game with Harry Kewell's early testing shot being one of the few times the visitors showed much of a cutting edge.

United had plenty of possession in the first half, while Woodgate was able to keep the toothless Malaga attack at bay. Only once in the first half did the Spaniards get behind the Leeds defence but Kiki Musampa shot over the bar after working himself in to a good position.

United seemed content to contain and Malaga came closest to breaking the deadlock when substitute Edgar dragged a shot wide from a good position and Mikel Roteta had a header well saved after a Musampa cross.

Paul Robinson then had to look sharp to save an 80th minute Dely Valdes header after the home striker had beaten Woodgate in the air for the first time in the match.

There was some late pressure on the Leeds goal, but United hung on for their first clean sheet in six games.

The result stopped the rot and gave United the edge going to Elland Road two weeks later, but the lack of creativity was an increasing worry for supporters.

BODY BLOW: United's Jonathan Woodgate and Gary Kelly can't believe it as Manu and Marcelo Romero celebrate Dely Valdes' winner.

End of the Euro

UEFA Cup
Third round, second leg
(at Elland Road, Leeds)
Thursday, December 12, 2002

 **Leeds United**  1

 **Malaga**  2

Malaga win 2-1 on agg

Leeds United: Paul Robinson, Danny Mills, Jason Wilcox, Michael Duberry, Jonathan Woodgate, Gary Kelly, Paul Okon, Eirik Bakke, Lee Bowyer, Michael Bridges (Robbie Fowler 9), Alan Smith
Goals: Bakke 22
Manager: Terry Venables

Malaga: Pedro Contrearas, Mikel Roteta, Fernando Sanz, Vicente Valcarce, Antonio 'Manu', Sanchez Gomez (Carlos Sandro 57), Marcelo Romero, 'Gerado' Garcia Leon, Kiki Musampa (Miguel Angel 78), Dely Valdes, Dario Silva (Carlos Oliveira Litos 90)
Goals: Dely Valdes 13, 79
Manager: Joaquin Peiro

Referee: Massimo Busacca (Switzerland) **Att:** 34,754

UNITED'S miserable season plumbed new depths as they crashed out of the UEFA Cup, casting immediate doubt over the future of manager Terry Venables.

Having done all the hard work in Spain, United blew it against European first-timers Malaga.

The 2-1 defeat was Leeds' seventh loss of the season on home soil and left them with just a relegation battle to fight.

By the end fans were chanting for Venables to go as his team disintegrated in the second half.

United, up to their eyeballs in debt, made a nightmare start when Michael Bridges, who had only fought his way back to something near match fitness after two years out with injury, snapped his left Achilles less than ten minutes in to the game. The injury was to rule him out for the rest of the season and cast a shadow of his future.

United barely had time to digest poor Bridges' departure when Kiki Musampa sped past Danny Mills down the left and his cross was steered home by Panamanian striker Dely Valdes.

For a side which had yet to come back from a goal down to win a game during the season it was the worst possible start.

United, though did show fighting spirit and drew level when substitute Robbie Fowler, making his United Euro debut, lofted a pass to the far post where Eirik Bakke crashed in the equaliser.

Despite the scoreline, United were being pulled about by some clever midfield play and only a fistful of saves by in-form Paul Robinson kept United afloat.

ine

Although Lee Bowyer went close with a diving header just after half-time, United were generally second best in a match with Musampa and Mikel Roteta forcing good saves from Robinson, who had been one of the few bright lights in a poor campaign.

United were clinging on rather than looking likely to score the goal they needed and were shattered when the tricky Dely Valdes forced his way past Jonathan Woodgate and hit a left-foot shot in to the far corner of Robinson's net.

A minute later Bowyer was lucky to stay on the field when he stamped on Gerado – an incident which had the Malaga substitutes leaping out of their dug-out in rage.

It was a sour note on which to end five successive years of European football.

It's all change at the top

UNITED'S UEFA Cup defeat – and the team's crippling debts – had massive implications.

Days after the Malaga debacle Lee Bowyer was handed a six-match ban by UEFA who reviewed his stamp on Gerado on video.

That had no effect on United as a club as the controversial Bowyer didn't play for Leeds again and weeks later left on a cut-price fee for West Ham.

With cash-strapped United desperate to cut the wage bill and bring in funds, Robbie Fowler was sold to Manchester City. He was followed by Jonathan Woodgate's departure to Newcastle a move bitterly opposed by manager Terry Venables and the fans who were shocked that the club's future had been mortgaged on the expectancy of continued Champions League success.

Chairman Peter Ridsdale, once the darling of the fans, was coming in for increasing criticism from supporters.

With United still hovering just above the relegation zone, Venables was axed and former Sunderland and Manchester City boss Peter Reid installed on a temporary basis towards the end of March.

Reid did what was required and was given the job on a full-time basis – but not by Ridsdale.

The chairman who had 'lived the dream' by helping to build a young, predominantly British, team to compete in Europe at the highest level stepped down and soon left the club.

He was replaced by Professor John McKenzie, an economics specialist, who rewarded Reid with a three-year contract shortly after United won 3-2 at Arsenal. That result guaranteed United's Premiership safety and also handed the title to Manchester United.

Reid's task, on a limited budget, was to steady the ship and get United challenging for a place in Europe again. But the high-profile departures continued with Harry Kewell's cut-price move to Liverpool and Olivier Dacourt's transfer to Roma.

The 2003 UEFA Cup almost came back to Britain.

Celtic enjoyed a thrilling run to the final, knocking out Liverpool on the way, but lost in extra-time in the final against Porto despite two more Henrik Larsson goals.

Fourth round, first leg

Auxerre 0, Liverpool 1 (Hyppia)
Celtic 3 (Lambert, Maloney, Petrov), VfB Stuttgart 1 (Kuranyi)
Hertha Berlin 3 (Alves 2, Van Burik), Boavista 2 (Rui Oscar, Goulant)
Lazio 3 (Lazetic, Jop og, Chiesa), Wisla Kracow 3 (Uche, Zurawski 2 – 1 pen)
Malaga 0, AEK Athens 0
Panathinikos 3 (Olisadebe 2, Lyberopoulos), Anderlecht 0
Porto 6 (Capucho, Derlei, Ricardo Costa, Jankauskas, Deco, Alenichev), Denzilspor 1 (Kratochvil)
Slavia Prague 1 (T Dosek), Besiktas 0

Fourth round, second leg

AEK Athens 0, Malaga 1 (Sanchez) *Malaga win 1-0 on agg*
Anderlecht 2 (Jestrovic 2), Panathinikos 0 *Panathinikos win 3-2 on agg*
Besiktas 4 (Pancu, Ronaldo, Guiaro, Dursan), Slavia Prague 2 (Dostalek, Hrdlicka) *Besiktas win 4-2 on agg*
Boavista 1 (Avalos), Hertha Berlin 0 *3-3 on agg. Boavista win on away goals*
Denzilspor 2 (Martin, Ozkan), Porto 2 (Derlei, Clayton) *Porto win 8-3 on agg*
Liverpool 2 (Owen, Murphy), Auxerre 0 *Liverpool win 3-0 on agg*
Wisla Kracow 1 (Kuzba), Lazio 2 (Fernando Couto, Chiesa) *Lazio win 5-4 on agg)*
VfB Stuttgart 3 (Tiffert, Gleb, Mutzel), Celtic 2 (Thompson, Sutton) *Celtic win 5-4 on agg*

Quarter-final, first leg

Celtic 1 (Larsson), Liverpool 1 (Heskey)
Lazio 1 (Inzaghi), Besiktas 0
Malaga 1 (Dely Valdes), Boavista 0
Porto 0, Panathinikos 1 (Olisadebe)

Quarter-final, second leg

Besiktas 1 (Yalcin), Lazio 2 (Fiore, Castroman) *Lazio win 3-1 on agg*
Boavista 1 (Luiz Claudio), Malaga 1 *1-1 on agg. Boavista win 4-1 on penalties*
Liverpool 0, Celtic 2 (Thompson, Hartson) *Celtic win 3-1 on agg*
Panathinikos 0, Porto 2 (Derlei 2) *Porto win 2-1 on agg*

Semi-final, second leg

Celtic 1 (Larsson), Boavista 1 (Valgaeren og)
Porto 4 (Maniche, Derlei 2, Helder Postiga), Lazio 1 (Lopez)

Semi-final, first leg

Boavista 0, Celtic 1 (Larsson) *Celtic win 2-1 on agg*
Lazio 0, Porto 0 *Porto win 4-1 on agg*

Final

(Olypico Stadium, Seville)
May 21, 2003
Celtic 2
Porto 3
(after extra-time)

Celtic: Douglas, Valgaeren (Laursen 64), Balde, Mjallby, Agathe, Lennon, Lambert (McNamara 76), Petrov (Maloney 104), Thompson, Sutton, Larsson
Goals: Larsson 45, 57
Manager: Martin O'Neill
Porto: Vitor Baia, Paulo Ferreira, Jorge Costa (Emanuel 71), Carvalho, Valente, Costinha (Ricardo Costa 9), Alenichev, Deco, Maniche, Capucho (Ferrerira 98), Derlei
Goals: Derlei 45, 115, Alenichev 54
Manager: Jose Mourinho
Referee: Michel Lubos (Slovakia)
Attendance: 52,972

Leading scorers: 11 – Larsson (Celtic), 10 – Derlei (Porto), Zurawski (Wisla Kracow)

United Euro statistics

UNITED'S record in the European Cup/Champions league is:

P40 W22 D6 L12 F77 A42

UNITED'S rcord in the European Cup Winners Cup is:

P9 W5 D3 L1 F13 A3

UNITED'S record in the Inter-Cities Fairs Cup/UEFA Cup is:

P99 W48 D27 L24 F158 A87

UNITED'S total record in Europe is:

P148 W75 D36 L37 F248 A132

Not included in the playing records above is the home game v VfB Stuttgart (4-1 but awarded 3-0 to Leeds by UEFA).

UNITED have met teams representing the following countries, number of different teams in brackets: Belgium (3), Czechoslovakia (2), England (1), France (2), Germany (1), Germany, East (3), Germany, West (3), Holland (2), Hungary (2), Israel (1), Italy (7), Luxemburg (1), Malta (1), Norway (3), Portugal (2), Rumania (2), Russia (2), Scotland (5), Spain (6), Switzerland (2), Turkey (3), Yugoslavia (3), Ukraine (1), Total 58.

TEAMS drawn against more than once: Ujpest Dosza (Hungary) 3, Valencia (Spain 3), Anderlecht (Belgium) 2, Barcelona (Spain) 2, Ferencvaros (Hungary) 2, Hibernian (Scotland (2), Maritimo (Portugal) 2, PSV Eindhoven (Holland) 2, Rangers (Scotland) 2, AS Roma (Italy) 2, Standard Liege (Belgium) 2, Vitoria Setubal (Portugal) 2, Partizan Belgrade (Yugoslavia) 2.

In addition Barcelona played Leeds a third time in the Inter-Cities Fairs Cup Play-Off in 1971.

Miscellany

●Dino Zoff played in goals for Napoli in 1968 and managed Lazio against Leeds in 2001.

●Brothers Bill and Bob Shankly have managed teams v United, Bill (Liverpool) in 1971 and Bob (Dundee) in 1968.

●In 1996 Monaco used no less than four goalkeepers v United with Fabien Barthez being the fourth and most successful in the tie but Tony Yeboah's away hat-trick saw his team through.

●United used three keepers v Hibernian in 1973. David Harvey played in the home tie and Glan Letheran came on at half-time for John Shaw in the away leg.

●Robbie Rensenbrinck (DWS Amsterdam/Anderlecht) and Helmut Haller (Bologna/Juventus) have played for two teams v United.

●Jock Stein managed Celtic against Leeds in 1970 and managed United for 44 days later in the decade before accepting the Scotland manager's job.

●United have never lost in a toss or penalty shootout and only the home play-off v Real Zaragoza in 1965/66 was lost.

●United have played in the final of all three European competitions.

●When United lifted the then Fairs Cup after a 0-0 away draw at Ferencvaros they were watched by 76,000 spectators. Two years later only 5,400 turned up at the same venue for the second leg of a European Cup tie between the same sides.

●On 6 December 2001 the attendance at Elland Road for Grasshoppers of Zurich was exactly one supporter down from the previous round game versus Troyes.

●United have never won an away tie in Scotland despite playing there seven times.

●Jimmy Greenhoff was transferred during a cup final. He played in the first game of an Inter-Cities Fairs Cup Final then was transferred to Birmingham City before the return leg.

●Both Dominic Matteo and Lucas Radebe had scored two European goals apiece by the end of the 2002-03 season without either scoring a League goal for Leeds.

●Duncan McKenzie was sent off in his only European appearance for United – at Ujpest Doza in 1974. Mick Bates is the only United player to be sent off twice in Europe.

Attendances

Gross Attendances: Home – 2,336,314
Gross Attendance: Away – 2,231,200
Largest home: 50,498 v Rangers 1967/68
Smallest home: 13,682 v Valletta 1978/79
Average home: 32,449 Average away: 30,989
Largest away: 136,505 at Hampden Park v Celtic 1969/70
Smallest away: 2,500 at Luxembourg v Spora 1966/67

Best and worst scores

Biggest home win: 10-0 v Lyn Oslo (European Cup) 1969/70
Biggest away win: 9-0 v Spora Luxembourg (Inter-Cities Fairs Cup) 1967/68
Biggest aggregate win: 16-0 v Lyn Oslo and Spora Luxembourg as above
Biggest home defeat: 3-5 v PSV Eindhoven (UEFA Cup) 1995/96 and 0-4 v SK Lierse (Inter-Cities Fairs Cup) 1971/72
Biggest away defeat: 0-4 v Barcelona (Champions League) 2000/01
Biggest aggregate defeat: 3-8 v PSV Eindhoven (UEFA Cup) 1995/96

Getting a result

No. of ties determined by toss of disc: 2 – both won
No. of ties determined by penalty shootouts: 2 – both won
No. of ties in which away goal rule applied: 3 – all won
No. of play-offs to determine the team going through: 2 – lost to Real Zaragoza and beat VfB Stuttgart (not including play-off for the retention of the Inter-Cities Fairs Cup which Barcelona won 2-1 in Barcelona).
No. of away legs played on neutral grounds as home grounds were unavailable: 4 (Heerenveen, Sofia, Dnepropetovsk and Florence).

Red cards

(United players)

Charlton v Valencia (h) 1965, Giles v Real Zaragoza (a) 1966, Bates v Partizan Belgrade (a) 1967, Cooper v Hannover 96 (a) 1969, Bates v Dresden (a) 1970, Clarke v Hadjuk Split (h) 1973, Hunter v AC Milan (a) 1973, McKenzie v Ujpest Doza (a) 1974, McQueen v Barcelona (a) 1975, Ribeiro v Roma (a) 1998, Kewell v Galatasaray (h) 2000, Smith v Valencia (a) 2001.
Total: 12 (3 at home, 9 away)

(Opposition players)

Videgany (Valencia) h 1966, Sanchez-Lage (Valencia) h 1966, Violetta (Real Zaragoza) h 1966, Geyger (Dynamo Dresden) a 1970, Campora (Vitoria Setubal) h 1973, Wome (Roma) h 1998, Zago (Roma) h 2000, Candela (Roma) h 2000, Rada (Slavia Prague) h 2000, Belozoglu (Galatasaray) h 2000, Meniri (Troyes) h 2001, Milosavljevic (Metalurg Zaporiziya) a 2002, Abukasis (Hapoel Tel Aviv) a 2002.
Total: 13 (10 at home, 3 away)

Appearances and scorers

European Cup and Champions League
(40 games)

Appearances

Harte 17, Madeley 17, Smith 16, Viduka 16, Mills 15/1, Bowyer 15, Lorimer 15, Matteo 15, Bremner 14, Dacourt 14, Hunter 14, Reaney 14, Clarke 13, Giles 13, Martyn 12, Batty11/1, Kelly 11/1, Bakke 10/2, Cooper 10, Radebe 10, Yorath 8/1, M.D. Jones 8, Jordan 8, Sprake 8, E.Gray 7/1, Charlton 7, Ferdinand 7, McQueen 7, Kewell 6/3, F.T. Gray 6, Robinson 6, Cantona 5, Chapman 5, Dorigo 5, Fairclough 5, Lukic 5, McAllister 5, Speed 5, Stewart 5, Strachan 5, Whyte 5, Woodgate 5, Harvey 4/1, Bridges 4, Duberry 4, Bates 3/3, Burns 3/1, Newsome 3, Wilcox 2/3, Cherry 2/1, Rocastle 2/1, McPhail 1/2, Belfitt 1, Hibbitt 1, M. Jones 1, McKenzie 1, Maybury 1, O'Grady 1, Sellars 1, Hackworth 0/2, Hodge 0/2, Huckerby 0/2, Shutt 0/2, Rod Wallace 0/2, Evans 0/1, Galvin 0/1, Hampton 0/1, Harris 0/1, Hay 0/1.
Total 440/37

Scorers

M.D.Jones 8, Lorimer 7, Smith 7, Bowyer 6, Bremner 6, Clarke 6, Giles 4, Harte 4, Viduka 4, McQueen 3, Belfitt 2, Cantona 2, Hibbitt 2, Jordan 2, McAllister 2, Matteo 2, Bakke 1, Chapman 1, Ferdinand 1, Huckerby 1, O'Grady 1, Shutt 1, Speed 1, Strachan 1, Yorath 1, Wilcox 1.
Total 77

European Cup Winners Cup
(9 games)

Appearances

Harvey 9, Hunter 9, Lorimer 9, Cherry 8, Reaney 8, Bremner 7, Giles 6/1, Jordan 6/1, Bates 6, M.D. Jones 6, Madeley 6, Clarke 5, Yorath 4/3, McQueen 2/1, Charlton 2, Ellam 2, E.Gray 2, F.T.Gray 1/1, Galvin 1.
Total 99/7

Scorers

M.D. Jones 3, Jordan 3, Clarke 2, Lorimer 2, Bates 1, Cherry 1, Giles 1.
Total 13

UEFA Cup and Inter-Cities Fairs Cup
(99 games excluding 1971 play-off)

Appearances

Bremner 55, Hunter 54/1, Reaney 51/3, Lorimer 49/1, Sprake 48/2, Madeley 47/1, Charlton 46, Giles 41, Cooper 38, E.Gray 30/1, Harte 28, M.D. Jones 28, Kewell 28, Kelly 24, Martyn 24, Bowyer 23, Belfitt 22/3, Bakke 21/1, O'Grady 19, J.Greenhoff 18/1, Bates 17/6, Bell 17, Radebe 17, Clarke 15, Woodgate 15, McPhail 14/2, Bridges 13/2, Smith 12/7, Harvey 12/2, Mills 12/1, Cherry 10, Storrie 10, Batty 9/1, Viduka 9, Yorath 8/3, Dacourt 8, Matteo 8, Wilcox 7/3, Haaland 7/2, Hibbitt 7/2, Ferdinand 7, Lukic 7, Hopkin 6/1, Keane 6, Robinson 6, Duberry 5/1, F.T.Gray 5/1, Johanneson 5/1, Curtis 4, Ellam 4, Flynn 4, Hankin 4, Hart 4, Hasselbaink 4, Hiden 4, McAllister 4, Molenaar 4, Palmer 4, Pemberton 4, Speed 4, Wetherall 4, Yeboah 4, Jordan 3/3, Davey 3/2, M. Jones 3/2, Barmby 3, Collins 3, Deane 3, Graham 3, Hampton 3, Hird 3, McQueen 3, Peacock 3, Whelan 3, Beesley 2/2, Galvin 2/1, Dorigo 2, Faulkner 2, Halle 2, Mann 2, Parkinson 2, Shaw 2, Stevenson 2, Huckerby 1/8, Wijnhard 1/3, Harris 1/2, Sharpe 1/2, Hamson 1/1, Liddell 1/1, Ribeiro 1/1, White 1/1, Bowman 1, Kennedy 1, Okon 1, Couzens 0/2, O'Neill 0/2, Ford 0/1, Fowler 0/1, Granville 0/1, Letheran 0/1, Lilley 0/1, Kilgallon 0/1, McGinley 0/1, Richardson 0/1, Sharp 0/1, Tinkler 0/1, Rod Wallace 0/1.
Total 1,089/93

Scorers

Lorimer 21, Bremner 10, Charlton 10, Johanneson 8, Kewell 8, Bowyer 7, Smith 7, Belfitt 6, Clarke 6, Giles 6, J.Greenhoff 6, M.D, Jones 6, E. Gray 5, Bakke 4, Madeley 4, Graham 3, Keane 3, Viduka 3, Yeboah 3, Bates 2, Bridges 2, Cooper 2, Hart 2, Harte 2, O'Grady 2, Radebe 2, Barmby 1, Bell 1, Cherry 1, Curtis 1, Galvin 1, F.T. Gray 1, Hankin 1, Hasselbaink 1, Huckerby 1, Hunter 1, Liddell 1, McAllister 1, Palmer 1, Peacock 1, Speed 1, Storrie 1, Wilcox 1, Own-Goal 1.
Total 158

Leading appearance makers (all European competitions)

Hunter 77/1, Bremner 76, Lorimer 73/1, Reaney 73/1, Madeley 70/1, Giles 60/1, Sprake 56/2, Charlton 55, Cooper 48, Harte 45.

Leading goalscorers (all European competitions)

Lorimer 30, Jones 17, Bremner 16, Clarke 14, Smith 14, Bowyer 13, Giles 11, Charlton 10, Belfitt 8, Johannesson 8, Kewell 8.
Lorimer's total is an English club record shared with Ian Rush of Liverpool.

Goal records

Fastest goals for: Alan Curtis, 15 seconds v Valletta 1979/80 (h), Mike O'Grady, 35 seconds v Lyn Oslo 1969-70 (h), Mick Bates, 60 seconds v Rapid Bucharest 1972-73 (a), Rod Belfitt, 63 seconds v Kilmarnock 1966-67 (h), Gary McAllister, 69 seconds v Rangers 1992-93 (a)
Fastest goal against: Marcelino Martinez Cao (Real Zaragoza) 54 seconds 1965-66 (play-off at Elland Road)
Most European goals in a season: Mick Jones 8 (1969-70)
Most European goals in a career: Peter Lorimer 30 (1965-75)

Hat-tricks

No opposing player has ever scored a hat-trick against United while eight have been recorded for the Elland Road side.

Albert Johanneson	3	H	v DWS Amsterdam, October 26, 1966
Rod Belfitt	3	H	v Kilmarnock, April 19 1967
Peter Lorimer	4	A	v Spora Luxembourg, October 3, 1967
Albert Johanneson	3	H	v Spora Luxembourg, October 17, 1967
Mick Jones	3	H	v Lyn Oslo, September 17, 1969
Arthur Graham	3	A	v Valletta, September 19, 1979
Tony Yeboah	3	A	v Monaco, September 26, 1995
Alan Smith	4	A	v Hapoel Tel Aviv, November 14, 2002

Penalties scored

Johnny Giles	H	v DWS Amsterdam, October 26, 1966
Johnny Giles	H	v Bologna, April 19, 1967
Peter Lorimer	A	v Spora Luxembourg, October 3, 1967
Johnny Giles	H	v Rangers, April 9, 1967
Johnny Giles	H	v Standard Liege, March 18, 1970
Peter Lorimer	A	v Dynamo Dresden, October 21, 1970
Johnny Giles	H	v Vitoria Setubal, March 10, 1971
Peter Lorimer	H	v FC Zurich, September 18, 1974
Gary McAllister	H	v VfB Stuttgart, September 30, 1972
Ian Harte	A	v Lokomotiv Moscow, November 4, 1999
Ian Harte	A	v 1860 Munich, August 9, 2000
Ian Harte	A	v Anderlecht, February 21, 2001

Total: 12

Ten penalties have been scored against United

Players' Euro career records

	Appearances	Goals
Nick Barmby (England)	3	1
Eirik Bakke (Norway)	31/3	5
Mick Bates (England)	26/9	3
David Batty (England)	20/2	0
Paul Beesley (England)	2/2	0
Rod Belfitt (England)	23/2	8
Willie Bell (Scotland)	17	1
Rob Bowman (England)	1	0
Lee Bowyer (England)	38	13
Billy Bremner (Scotland)	76	16
Michael Bridges (England)	17/2	2
Jacob Burns (Australia)	3/1	0
Eric Cantona (France)	5	2
Lee Chapman (England)	5	1
Jack Charlton (England)	55	10
Trevor Cherry (England)	20/1	2
Allan Clarke (England)	33	14
Bobby Collins (Scotland)	3	0
Terry Cooper (England)	48	2
Andy Couzens (England)	0/2	0
Alan Curtis (Wales)	4	1
Olivier Dacourt (France)	22	0
Nigel Davey (England)	3/2	0
Brian Deane (England)	3	0
Tony Dorigo (England)	7	0
Michael Duberry (England)	9/1	0
Roy Ellam (England)	6	0
Gareth Evans (England)	0/1	0
Chris Fairclough (England)	5	0
John Faulkner (England)	2	0
Rio Ferdinand (England)	14	1
Brian Flynn (Wales)	4	0
Mark Ford (England)	0/1	0
Robbie Fowler (England)	0/1	0
Arthur Graham (Scotland)	3	3
Chris Galvin (England)	3/2	1
Eddie Gray (Scotland)	39/2	5
Frank Gray (Scotland)	12/2	1
Johnny Giles (Eire)	60/1	11
Danny Granville (England)	0/1	0
Jimmy Greenhoff (England)	18/1	6
Alf Inge Haaland (Norway)	7/2	0
Tony Hackworth (England)	0/2	0
Gunnar Halle (Norway)	2	0
Peter Hampton (England)	3/1	0
Gary Hamson (England)	1/1	0
Ray Hankin (England)	4	1
Carl Harris (Wales)	1/3	0
Paul Hart (England)	4	2
Ian Harte (Eire)	45	6
David Harvey (Scotland)	25/3	0
Jimmy Floyd Hasselbaink (Holland)	4	1
Danny Hay (New Zealand)	0/1	0
Terry Hibbitt (England)	8/2	2
Martin Hiden (Austria)	4	0
Kevin Hird (England)	3	0
Steve Hodge (England)	0/2	0
David Hopkin (Scotland)	6/1	0
Darren Huckerby (England)	1/10	2
Norman Hunter (England)	77/1	1
Albert Johanneson (South Africa)	5/1	8
Matthew Jones (England)	4/2	0
Mick Jones (England)	42	17
Joe Jordan (Scotland)	17/4	5

	Appearances	Goals
Robbie Keane (Eire)	6	3
Gary Kelly (Eire)	35/1	0
David Kennedy (England)	1	0
Harry Kewell (Australia)	34/3	8
Matthew Kilgallon (England)	0/1	0
Glan Letheran (Wales)	0/1	0
Gary Liddell (Scotland)	1/1	1
Derek Lilley (Scotland)	0/1	0
Peter Lorimer (Scotland)	73/1	30
John Lukic (England)	12	0
Gary McAllister (Scotland)	9	3
Billy McGinley (Scotland)	0/1	0
Duncan McKenzie (England)	1	0
Steve McPhail (Eire)	15/4	0
Gordon McQueen (Scotland)	12/1	3
Paul Madeley (England)	70/1	4
Jimmy Mann (England)	2	0
Nigel Martyn (England)	36	0
Dominic Matteo (Scotland)	23	2
Alan Maybury (Eire)	1	0
Danny Mills (England)	27/2	0
Robert Molenaar (Holland)	4	0
Jon Newsome (England)	3	0
Mike O'Grady (England)	20	3
Paul Okon (Australia)	1	0
Sean O'Neill (England)	0/2	0
Carlton Palmer (England)	4	1
Keith Parkinson (England)	2	0
Alan Peacock (England)	3	1
John Pemberton (England)	4	0
Lucas Radebe (South Africa)	27	2
Paul Reaney (England)	73/3	0
Bruno Ribeiro (Portugal)	1/1	0
Frazer Richardson (England)	0/1	0
Paul Robinson (England)	12	0
David Rocastle (England)	2/1	0
Scott Sellars (England)	1	0
Kevin Sharp (England)	0/1	0
Lee Sharpe (England)	1/2	0
John Shaw (England)	2	0
Carl Shutt (England)	0/2	1
Alan Smith (England)	28/7	14
Gary Speed (Wales)	9	2
Gary Sprake (Wales)	56/2	0
Byron Stevenson (Wales)	2	0
Gordon Strachan (Scotland)	5	1
David Stewart (Scotland)	5	0
Jim Storrie (Scotland)	10	1
Mark Tinkler (England)	0/1	0
Mark Viduka (Australia)	25	7
Rod Wallace (England)	0/3	0
David Wetherall (England)	4	0
Noel Whelan (England)	3	0
David White (England)	1/1	0
Chris Whyte (England)	5	0
Clyde Wijnhard (Holland)	1/3	0
Jason Wilcox (England)	9/6	2
Jonathan Woodgate (England)	20	0
Tony Yeboah (Ghana)	4	3
Terry Yorath (Wales)	20/7	1
Own-Goal		1
Totals	1,628/135	248

The team v Barcelona in 1971 Fairs Cup Play-Off in 1971 is not included in the above. The line-up was: Sprake, Reaney, Davey, Bremner, Charlton, Hunter, Lorimer, Jordan, Belfitt, Giles, Galvin. Scorer: Jordan.